W9-CRK-651

SOEKARNO, FOUNDING FATHER OF INDONESIA

VERHANDELINGEN
VAN HET KONINKLIJK INSTITUUT
VOOR TAAL-, LAND- EN VOLKENKUNDE

192

BOB HERING

SOEKARNO

Founding father of Indonesia

1901-1945

KITLV Press
Leiden
2002

Published by:
KITLV Press
Koninklijk Instituut voor Taal-, Land- en Volkenkunde
(Royal Institute of Linguistics and Anthropology)
PO Box 9515
2300 RA Leiden
The Netherlands

Cover: Creja Ontwerpen, Leiderdorp

ISBN 90 6718 191 9

Printed in the Netherlands

Inhoud

CHAPTER I

The first two windu, 1901-1917

'He who desires to become a Soekarno must first pick the proper date of birth. June 1901 is not a bad choice at all,' wrote one of Soekarno's early biographers, Dutch writer Paul van 't Veer (1964:5).[1] Soekarno explained to his American biographer, Cindy Adams, that his own Balinese mother had told him:

> 'And you, my son, will be a man of glory, a great leader of his people, because your mother gave birth to you at dawn. We Javanese believe that one born at the moment of sunrise is predestined. Never, never forget you are a child of the dawn.'
>
> Soekarno added: 'With me, it wasn't only the dawn of a new day, but also the dawn of a new century.'[2]

And indeed it was a dawning, not only of a new century, but of a new era. The Dutch colonial government, characteristically autocratic, was then implementing a progressive Ethical Policy.[3] This new approach dragged ever increasing numbers of Indonesian subjects under the widening umbrella

---

1   As to the chapter title, in a Javanese magico-mystical perspective, a recurrent rhythmic development within the *cakra manggilingan* (wheel of history) oscillates between periods of disorder and order, with power ebbing and flowing and reflecting the ruler's own lack or plenty of *wahyu* (divine radiance). On the diminutive human scale, cyclical development takes place in *windu*, cycles of eight years. Here, too, passion and lust (*hawa nafsu*) or too much *pamrih* (self-interest) may negatively affect one's inner harmony and happiness, while *rila* (resignation), *narima* (acceptance) and *sabar* (patience) may have a positive effect. On the use of *windu* see Adams 1965:77 and Ganis Harsono 1977:5-6. Ganis (now deceased) and his wife Diati possess a large and truly unique collection of Soekarno memorabilia, data which we often scrutinized and copied when staying at their hospitable Jakarta home at Jl. Bendungan Hilir during 1976-1978 and later, among others, used for our monographs devoted to Soekarno.
2   Adams 1965:17. Cindy Adams, described by one of her journalist friends Bernie Kalb as a 'good-looking wise-guy babe', first met Soekarno in August 1961 when she interviewed him for the North American Newspaper Alliance. After this meeting a correspondence ensued for two years, until in August 1963 Adams received a letter from the then US Ambassador to Indonesia Howard Jones with the message that Soekarno wanted her to do a biography on him. Adams arrived in Jakarta in December 1963 to commence work on the collaborative autobiography. See Adams 1965:13-6.
3   A survey dealing with the Ethical Policy is in Poeze 1982:xi-xxv.

of westernization and modernization. Whatever was good in European Holland – be it education, welfare economics, or health care – was deemed beneficial for all those living and toiling in Holland's overseas island-empire. At that time a Javanese elementary schoolteacher, Soekemi Sosrodihardjo, was posted to Soerabaja with his Balinese wife and their one-year-old daughter, Soekarmini. She was born on 13 March 1899 when the Javanese/Balinese couple still resided in Singaradja. On 6 June 1901 Soekarmini's younger brother, Koesno, was born in the densely crowded but rather well-to-do new Peneleh ward in Lawang Seketeng alley (by one source referred to as Jalan Pahlawan 88). This ward on Soerabaja's eastern rim, just west of the Kerkhoflaan European cemetery and facing the eastern bank of the *kali* (river) Mas, was mainly inhabited by indigenous Indonesians.[4] Exactly two weeks before his birth the volcano Keloed on the border of Pasoeroean and Kediri residencies had one of its heaviest eruptions. Mudflows destroyed parts of the Blitar district and ashes covered an area of 115 square kilometres. This auspicious omen contributed to the myth surrounding the birth of Soekarno.[5] The same was the case with Tjokroaminoto, his first political mentor and father-in-law, whose birth in Bakoer on 16 August 1882 was connected with one of the greatest volcanic eruptions ever: that of Krakatau in the Soenda straits, west of Banten, on 26-28 August 1883.[6]

Soekarno's socio-cultural environment

In order to place Soekarno in a cultural context, we should first look more closely at the main ingredients of Javanese society. According to the Javanese conception of social classes, Javanese village communities are populated by *wong cilik*, or common people. There were also *wong cilik* inhabiting towns and cities such as Blitar, where Soekarno's father hailed from,[7] and Soerabaja, where he got his second posting as an elementary teacher. These *wong cilik* usually formed the lower strata of society, occupying a great range of jobs

---

[4]   Solichin Salam 1966:33, 277 and 30 March 1971 interview with Ibu Soekarmini Wardojo (formerly Ibu Soekarmini Poegoeh) in Blitar, 30 March 1971. Both list Koesno as his name by birth. Sastrawidjojo, however, in his mss 'Soekarno', p. 47 refers to Koesnososro. Kuijk and Van Veen 1967:55 lists Djalan Pahlawan 88, but during our visit to it on 2 April 1971 it was still called Lawang Seketeng. On the Peneleh ward see Broeshart 1995:24, 94, 131, and *Kaart van Soerabaja 1905*, in the area marked R.

[5]   The meteorological data are taken from *ENI* II:353; *Jaarboek Mijnwezen* 1907:185-6 with Hugo Cool's survey of the literature on the eruption; the 1911 *BOW Verslag* 1912:220. On the self-invoked myth, see Adams 1965:18.

[6]   On the connection Amelz 1952, I:50, on the eruption *ENI* II:443.

[7]   'Biografi singkat Bung Karno' in Rachmawati Soekarno 1984:123.

mostly as manual labourers (*tukang*). In these centres a relatively small but modern production sector evolved, which during the era of the Ethical Policy came to include hundreds of thousands of Indonesian wage earners. The unschooled were at the bottom of this social class, next to a layer of relatively skilled manual labourers, often only partially employed. In Soerabaja they usually lived in *kampung*, which can be thought of as shantytowns. Such *kampung* in many ways resembled rural Javanese villages: a cluster of *bambu* or cement dwellings, with residents participating in joint clean-ups, road repair and guard duty against robbers. They were governed by elected *kepala kampung* (headmen). Soerabaja *kampung* differed from rural Javanese villages in that they were urban. These Soerabaja urban *kampung* were found inside downtown city blocks like cavities in teeth, or on the edge of the city. So they were not surrounded by irrigated fields (*sawah*), and their inhabitants were not at all involved in tedious farming work as were inhabitants of the rural Javanese *kampung*. Some urban Soerabaja *kampong* households, though, still maintained small garden patches, growing *ubi* (sweet potatoes) and *jagung* (corn), or had small *ayam* (chicken) and *bebek* (ducks) coops or kept *perkutut* (turtledove, *Geopelia striata*) in elevated cages.

As to Soerabaja's remarkable economic growth, it was on the whole generated by the vast sugar-growing enterprises of its hinterland, starting early in the second half of the nineteenth century. Thus, earlier and stronger than in any other colonial city, Soerabaja's industrial production grew, fed by the demands of the mechanized factories of the sugar plantations, the vast harbour facilities and the naval establishment. So much so that in 1875 Soerabaja was labelled by some as 'the Liverpool of the Indies'. With this solid foundation, a layer of experienced and specialized *tukang* were thus employed predominantly in the metal industries of Soerabaja and then in Semarang, together with machinists and other technicians working in the expanding rail and tramway sector, as well as the specialists engaged in the public utility works of these cities. These constituted the core of a developing modern working class. In addition, manual labour sectors existed in the mainly non-mechanized Asian-run businesses such as *batik*, *kretek* (cigarette) and rice-polishing enterprises. Fragmentation among these many relatively small enterprises, along with the many cottage industries and the employment of much female labour, weakened the position of the labour force engaged in all these sectors. For 1905 the total of all these industrial labourers was estimated at 530,000. By the time Soekarno had almost reached his teens in 1912, there were some 10,518 Indonesians employed in the metal industry sector alone. Fourteen years later, when Soekarno was living in Bandoeng far from Soerabaja, the working force in that industry in Soerabaja amounted to 11,521, of whom 8,881 were schooled *tukang*. The state rail and tramway personnel amounted in 1917 to some 20,000, of whom 75% were

Indonesian.[8] In 1921 Soekarno, on leave from Bandoeng's Technical Faculty, served a brief stint with Soerabaja's railway system in order to financially support the family of his father-in-law, Tjokroaminoto, who was then in jail charged with perjury in connection with the so-called B section of the Sarekat Islam based in West Java's Preanger.[9]

In the western industry and transport sectors of Soerabaja and Semarang, where the slowly emancipating modern labourers' class stood directly in class opposition to their western employers, there were some other impeding factors. In the first place there was considerable social distance, often even distrust, between western employer and indigenous employee, causing employers to view any form of labour protest or agitation as intolerable subversion. On the other hand, a relatively high percentage of the specialized workforce in Soerabaja were Chinese, and it remained cumbersome to organize them harmoniously with Javanese, Madurese or Buginese labourers (with the latter already imbued with the defiant *arek Soeraboyo* image) in one workable trade union association, let alone to get them together to wage political action on specific issues. So when conflict situations arose, ethnic cultural and anti-western sentiments prevailed over any mobilizing of people along class lines. Even when socialist and anti-capitalist notions were introduced, they seemed to fit smoothly into the process of a national or nationalist consciousness prudently aimed at questioning alien rule.[10]

Javanese such as the Soekemi family considered themselves as belonging to a slightly higher social level than the *wong cilik* or *tukang* (described above) or even the *wong saudagar* (described below); they were part of the so-called *priyayi*. However, the Soekemi family can also be considered as part of the *kaum urban,* or neo-*priyayi* segment. Pramoedya Ananta Toer sees them as belonging to the *kaum urban,* the westernized urban or urbanized community which was able to pluck the fruits of whatever education the Dutch provided these *priyayi* under the aegis of the reforms then afoot inspired by the Ethical Policy. Neo-priyayization was, in fact, the development of a 'metropolitan superculture', a hybrid type of mestizo culture, found in many colonial and post-colonial cities, usually borne by western-educated members of the

---

[8]   Vreede 1926:8; Seegers 1987:17, 64-73; *ENI* IV, 33; Broeshart 1995:18, 28; Von Faber 1931: 176-7, 185-6.
[9]   On Tjokro's eight-month jail term (August 1921-May 1922) see Tichelman 1985:383; Vb. 2 May 1923 D 6, Vb. 14 February 1923 no. 48. For Soekarno's six-month stint with the state railways with a monthly wage of *f* 265, see Solichin Salam 1966:43 and Im Yang Tjoe 1933:12. However, the wage they record seems highly unlikely, and Soekarno himself mentions a more modest wage of *f* 165 in Adams 1965:56.
[10]   For defiant *arek Soeraboyo* images, see Frederick 1989:6-11; 'Si Doel, Arek Suroboyo', *Tempo* 10 July 1982:77-8 and Siauw Giok Thjan 1982:2, 29, 85, note 5.

burgeoning indigenous middle class.[11] This group included members of the administrative hierarchy in positions ranging from small-town government clerks and elementary school principals, such as Soekarno's father, to rather high-ranking officials in the larger cities. Such traditional administrative personnel, called the *pamong praja*, constituted the hard core of the *priyayi*. A rather limited, still higher, upper class or nobility, the *ndara*, was concentrated mainly in the two senior principalities, the Kesultanan of Yogyakarta and the Kesoesoehoenan in Soerakarta (or Solo), and the junior Paku Alaman and Mangkoenegaraan in these two cities, respectively. These were the four truncated court centres of south-central Java into which the once proud Javanese empire of Mataram split in the wake of successive alien (Dutch and also Anglo) intrusion, commencing as early as 1755. There are also Javanese solely engaged in trade. These petty traders and merchants, called *wong saudagar*, are located primarily in urban and semi-urban centres, where they often inhabit separate quarters of the city or town, called the *kauman*, a part often surrounding the local mosque.

Apart from these broadly horizontal groups there is a vertical division of Javanese society based largely upon the extent of participation in Islam. This mainly differentiates *wong abangan* from *santri*. *Abangan* (from the Javanese word 'red') are those who choose not to live according to the principal tenets of Islam as understood by the Javanese. For instance, they do not perform the *salat* (prayer) five times daily, nor do they fast during the month of *puasa* (Ramadan), or desire to make the *haj* (pilgrimage to Mecca). The *santri* or *putihan*, the white ones, sometimes referred to as *muslim fanatik,* though one should not interpret this label too literally, do follow Islamic principles seriously and hence differ sharply in these respects from the *abangan*, the red ones. Even the *wali songo*, the nine saints, who were instrumental in Java's Islamization with a majority among them still allowing a continuum between the pre-Islamic past and the new faith, were divided into red and white camps. Soenan Giri in particular adhered rigidly to a path banning everything not strictly in accordance with Islam, while red *wali* such as Soenan Kalidjaga, Soenan Koedoes and Soenan Moeria were more willing to compromise with Javanese culture so as to better disseminate the new religion.

Although the criterion of differentiation is basically the degree of participation in Islam, the groups can certainly be viewed as two sub-cultures with contrasting world views, values and orientations within Javanese culture. In this context it is worth noting that many people referred to by outsiders as *abangan* studiously avoid the term in describing themselves, since, outside the western-educated middle class, it is widely regarded as derogatory.

---

[11] For Pramoedya Ananta Toer see his 27 February 1988 letter to Bob Hering. For neo-priyayization turn to Hering 1996:16.

Therefore, many prefer to call themselves *kejawen*, practitioners of *Islam Jawa* (Javanese Islam), or, simply 'Muslim', with the understanding that they put greater emphasis on the mystical/cosmological features than the legalistic or ritualistic dimensions of Islam.[12] Nonetheless, the broader relationship of *kejawen* to Islam remains a complex matter. Thus, Clifford Geertz' labelling of *abangan* culture as highly Hindu-Buddhist in character has been challenged by, for instance, Marshall Hodgson, who wrote:

> Influenced by the polemics of a certain school of modern Shari'ah-minded Muslims, Geertz identifies 'Islam' only with what that school of modernists happens to approve, and ascribes everything else to an aboriginal or a Hindu-Buddhist background, gratuitously labelling much of the Muslim religious life in Java 'Hindu'. He identifies a long series of phenomena, virtually universal to Islam and sometimes found even in the Qur'an itself, as un-Islamic; and hence his interpretation of the Islamic past as well as of some recent anti-Islamic reactions is highly misleading.[13]

Mark Woodward (1989) extends this argument further, revealing strongly Islamic elements in many *kejawen* customs, while Robert Hefner (1993:2) posits:

> Though some authors commit the converse error of attributing too great a role to Islam in Javanese civilization, there is little doubt that Western (and even some Indonesian) characterizations of *abangan* tradition have underestimated Islamic influences, and overplayed 'Hindu' ones.

Be that as it may, like the *abangan*, *santri* are present at all social levels of Javanese society; there are *abangan* and *santri* among the *priyayi*, and even among the *ndara*. Geographically, however, many areas of Java have a predominantly *abangan* population, for instance in the *kejawen*, denoting here the inland area where Javanese under the sway of present or even past autonomous principalities are still catering to *kejawen* cultural traditions. The *santri*, on the other hand, predominate in areas along Java's northern coast, the so-called *pasisir*, where Islam, attracted by the coastal markets and trade centres, first struck root and where *santri* are still prominent as traders, moneylenders and merchants.

However, Javanese society may divide itself in other ways as well, while at the same time exhibiting the class divisions referred to earlier in this chapter. When this occurs, for instance among newly class-conscious *tukang* or other manual workers, it is necessary, if one is to understand that segment of society, to be clear which criterion of social stratification prevails.

---

12   For the material mentioned in this part of the text, see Hering 1986:6-8.
13   Hodgson 1974, II:551-2. For Clifford Geertz see his *The religion of Java* (1960:126-30).

Geertz has suggested that in Indonesia the fundamental social divisions
are according to *aliran*, not class. He does not deny the presence of class
awareness, but claims it is of markedly lower significance in influencing the
structure of society than is *aliran* affiliation.[14] In his view, an *aliran* sweeps
down through all levels of society, attracting adherents at all points. It is an
ideological movement pervading the whole of society. About its core many
reinforcing functional organizations cluster, such as women's clubs, youth
and student groups, labour unions, peasant cooperatives, charitable and
savings clubs, and religious or philosophical societies (C. Geertz 1970:15). It
is thus a comprehensive and complex pattern of social interaction, grouping
people together in large numbers under generalized categories via a set of
interrelated social reforms.

It would appear that one of the most important factors determining the
ideology of an *aliran* is religion (C. Geertz 1960:123). The first force toward
aliranization can be detected in the drive for pure orthodoxy and tradition-
alism in the practice of the Islamic religion, which took place around 1900.
The result was a widening estrangement of orthodox and syncretic interests
which split the community vertically down from high *priyayi* down to *abangan* into Islamic or *kejawen* (Jay 1963:104; Ricklefs 1981:112-9). The initial vertical stratification of society had occurred and it had done so along religious
lines. The Islamic side consisted of both reform and conservative Muslim
intellectuals, of *santri* traders and of *kampong santri*: *santri* village leaders and
santri villagers. The *kejawen* section of the community mostly included the
neo-*priyayi*, the old *priyayi* and the *kampong abangan*: *abangan* village leaders
and *abangan* villagers. Geertz also maintains that aliranization was initially
urban-centred. In fact, Geertz views urbanization as one of the contributing
factors to *aliran* emergence. The growth of towns forced the Javanese into
relationships which were more intimate and provided an environment con-
ducive to the evolution of locally based vertical, rather than regionally based
horizontal, forms of social integration – what Geertz has termed the filling
up of 'the hollow town' (C. Geertz 1965:77, 120).

Aliranization in the sense of politicization was apparently unknown in
Indonesia up until World War I. It emerged with the modern emancipatory
political party system and certainly had no place in the traditional micro/
macrocosmos view of society operating in Indonesia prior to Indianization
and Islamization. Up until World War I, community change was marked by
a continual absorption, adoption and accommodation of religious ideologies,
without great changes being wrought upon the majority of the population.
It is true that some religious/political integration did occur, but not at the
village level (Jay 1963:104). Two Dutch social scientists, Basuki Gunawan

---

[14]   Hering1986:7. For Geertz see his *Peddlers and princes* (1970:15).

and O.D. van den Muijzenberg, have added a useful note to the explanation of the Javanese *aliran* phenomenon. Following J.P. Kruijt and Walter Goddijn's study on the Dutch *'verzuiling'* (pillarization) phenomenon, they noticed a close historical resemblance between Dutch and Javanese forms of pillarization. Both forms came into being during the struggle for emancipation. For the Dutch that struggle was waged by the educationally and politically deprived nineteenth-century Roman Catholic minority and the equally deprived labour class of the early twentieth century against the prevailing Protestant socio-political culture. So the population of the Netherlands became divided ideologically between Protestant, Catholic and secular loyalties. Once extension of the Dutch franchise system enabled political articulation and mobilization of mass sentiment to emerge, concomitant tripartite ideological instability followed, only to be curbed by consensus arrangements occurring at the summit of the political pyramid and usually resulting in coalition governments being formed.[15] Ruth McVey, in an introduction to a Cornell Translation Series paper of Soekarno's 1926 *Indonesia Moeda* article 'Nationalisme, Islam dan Marxisme',[16] posits that with Holland being the only western 'democratic' model presented to educated Indonesians in colonial times, the latter were for a long time intrigued by Dutch consensus arrangements even as they reacted against colonial modes and European ways. In Soekarno's 1926 essay, where consensus among nationalists, Muslims and Marxists was being preached, the Dutch model certainly must have influenced Soekarno's thought patterns at that time. According to Ruth McVey, Soekarno, though otherwise borrowing heavily from Marx, was a member of an ambitious elite, linked by ties of family and cultural background to the middle layer of the *priyayi* class, immersed by education and ambition in Dutch colonial style modes.

Soekarno's early family surroundings and the fleeting impact of Sarinah

The lower and upper layers of this class were thus prone to intrusion by the petty-bourgeois element. So in a number of 1971 interviews with Ibu Soekarmini Wardoyo, Soekarno's elder sister, in the company of her fifty-one-year-

---

[15]   Kruijt and Goddijn 1962. For Indonesian *verzuiling* phenomena: Gunawan and Van den Muijzenberg 1967. For *verzuiling* phenomenon and its prominence in Dutch politics see Lijphart 1968.

[16]   Soekarno, *Nationalism, Islam and Marxism* (1970), but listing it as appearing in *Soeloeh Indonesia Moeda* instead of *Indonesia Moeda*, the organ of the Bandoeng Study Club started by Soekarno in 1926. *Soeloeh Indonesia Moeda*, also started by Soekarno, appeared for the first time in December 1927. See also Dahm 1969:63, 83. Giebels 1999:97 still lists it as appearing in the latter periodical.

old daughter Soekartini Saroyo, we were told that the initial little box-shaped cement house at Gang Lawang Seketeng, their slightly bigger home at the Residen Pamoedji Road in Modjokerto, and their later spacious homes at Blitar's Normaalschoolstraat – a dwelling provided by the government with father Soekemi then, in 1932, earning a monthly wage of *f* 300 – and at Blitar's Sultan Agoengweg 58 (which father Soekemi had bought after his retirement in 1934) increasingly bore some of the hallmarks of a Dutch home with heavy, though sparsely placed, baroque furniture. The walls were decorated with posters of cozy landscapes, while the living room was sprinkled with Dutch novels, theosophical and educational periodicals and magazines, and some pencil sketches made by the youngster Soekarno. Soekarno, thus, was drawn at a young age to the plastic arts, hardly a Javanese custom,[17] but clearly revealing his part-Balinese origins. Among themselves the family spoke Javanese, often mingled with Dutch, while reserving *ngoko* (Low Javanese) to address the two servants who attended them in Modjokerto. One of them was the elderly maiden Sarinah, whose bed Soekarno often shared when a youngster. Soekarno himself testifies in his 'autobiography':

> In my young days we shared the same narrow cot. When I had grown up a little, there was no Sarinah any more. I filled the void by sleeping with Soekarmini in the same bed.

And he continues, revealing the *kejawen* inclinations of his father rather than the legal or ritualistic dimensions of Islam, by stating:

> Later I slept with our dog Kiar, who was a mixture of fox terrier and something Indonesian – I don't know exactly what. Muslims supposedly don't like dogs, but I adored them.[18]

Roeslan Abdulgani, one of Soekarno's top advisers when Soekarno was president, commenting on Soekarno's obvious dependence on women throughout his life, states:

> Perhaps it's the maternal warmth he searches for over and over, I do not know. As a youngster, he was deeply attached to his mother and to the only other child in the family, an elder sister, with whom he shared a bed. The arms that comforted him when his mother wasn't around belonged to an elderly servant named Sarinah. [...] Since babyhood he had been attached to women. Even his great love was a woman twelve years older than he. Aside from his love for women physically, he is extremely drawn to them emotionally.[19]

---

[17] On the absence of a Javanese tradition of painting see McIntyre 1993:162.
[18] Adams 1965:25. Throughout his life Soekarno was fond of dogs: interviews with Ibu Inggit Garnasih, Ibu Fatmawati and Ibu Hartini, 30 March 1971, 8 May 1978, and 11 June 1983, respectively. See also Ramadhan 1981:394, 415, 418; Fatmawati Soekarno 1978:39; Abdul Karim 1982:74.
[19] Interview by Cindy Adams of Roeslan Abdulgani in Adams 1980:41-2. In a 15 June 1976

Louis Fischer, perhaps prompted by Marlene Dietrich's popular lyric 'Ich bin von Kopf bis Fuss auf Liebe eingestellt', puts it as follows:

> The best key to Sukarno is love. He is the great lover. He loves his country, he loves women, he loves to talk to women, he loves himself. The Dutch hated and hate him and therefore could establish no inner contact with him. The approach to Sukarno is through the heart. His approach is via the senses. (Fischer 1959:155.)

The only book-length study Soekarno devoted to Indonesian womanhood is dedicated to Sarinah, and in the preface he singles her out as the greatest single influence in his young life:

> I call this study Sarinah in order to show gratitude to the child servant of my early days [...]. She took care of me and helped my mother. It was from her that I got many tokens of love and affection. Also, it was from her that I learned to love the 'common people'. She was of the 'common people' herself, but of quite uncommon wisdom.[20]

Maternal and paternal influences

So Soekarno was surrounded by caring women from an early age, a pattern which repeated itself when he stayed for a while with his paternal grandparents in Toeloengagoeng. However, all this quite fits in with Javano-Balinese family life generally, where the wife or mother, often also active in petty trade outside the household (Soekarno's second wife Iboe Inggit Garnasih ran a *batik* fashion shop and sold *jamu*– a cosmetic she concocted having curative powers – while his paternal grandmother sold *batik* cloth as well[21]), focuses her activities mainly around the household of which she remains the pivot, the household being of a 'matrifocal' variety, whereas the father is extremely distant, keeping himself aloof from domestic matters. The father prefers to seek his place in the public political and religious realms outside the household; in the case of Soekarno's father, his public involvement was of a *kejawen*

---

interview with Abdulgani he confided to us that 'Soekarno loved women and his mother greatly; perhaps he searched for her and could never find the ideal'.

[20]   Soekarno 1986a:11. The ideas about women's emancipation and the role women should take in the revolution are also elaborated on in Soekarno's address to the Kursus Wanita in Koetaradja (Atjeh), 16 June 1948; see also an extract of it in ARA, CMI Document 5106, PG inv. 536. For an earlier 27 December 1928 lecture by Soekarno on 'The duties of Indonesian women to their country', see Pemoeda Indonesia Congress proceedings in ARA, Mr. 408/1929. For Sarinah being an 'ibu kedua' (second mother) to Soekarno see his sister's recollections in Saiful Rahim 1978:21.

[21]   For Inggit Garnasih's *jamu* and *batik* trade ventures and Soekarno's maternal grandmother's *batik* trading see respectively Ramadhan 1980:xi, 7; Hering 1991a:104 and Im Yang Tjoe 1933:4.

and theosophical bent (H. Geertz 1961:44-6, 107, 131; Koentjaraningrat 1957: 89). This spatial divergence between husband and wife is clearly symbolized in the organization of the Javanese traditional middle- and upper-class house. The front part of the house, the open *pendapa* and even the front garden, is oriented toward the world outside. It is the place, no matter how small, where visitors are received, where *wayang* and *slametan* performances or other religious or semi-religious practices are conducted and where professional meetings or talks are held. It is the realm of the husband or father, categorized as 'male'. The inner and back part of the house is the private, inner-oriented sphere of domestic duties where the mother reigns supreme. In traditional Javanese cosmology it is considered the 'female' part of the house (Rassers 1959:247). The distant father in Soekarno's case was further underscored by the son's use of *krama* (High Javanese) in addressing him. And while Soekemi's claim to respect was backed up by ancient supernatural sanction, his overall aloofness made him quite different in Soekarno's eyes from the far more approachable, loving and caring mother and other would-be mothers still to cross his path.

In the Adams autobiography Soekarno recalls his father as sometimes loving, being quite concerned about him when the only son fell ill, lying under his cot for weeks on end, even arranging a change of name for his son in order to forever ward off evil spirits considered responsible for Koesno's frequent bouts of illness when little.[22] While this may demonstrate the gentler side of Soekarno's father, it is also enmeshed in *utang budi* (moral debt), where the son needs to fit in with the outer-oriented realm of the father, who himself bears the ultimate responsibility for moulding the son for future and useful membership in that far more outer-directed public sphere. But Soekarno also recalls his father as a stern and far-too-demanding disciplinarian, taking recourse to caning him quite harshly when he, Soekarno, behaved in an uncaring manner toward aminals or was late coming home from a fishing expedition (Adams 1965:23-4; Solichin Salam 1966:40). Also, and obviously with the advantages of Dutch-oriented education in mind, Soekemi engaged an Indo-European female tutor, a Miss Maria Paula (de) la Rivière, to teach his son Dutch one hour each weekday. He later took to lying about his son's age in order to secure him a place at a western-oriented public school.[23] Soekemi's concern that Soekarno gain fluency in Dutch had naturally much to do with his own western-oriented upbringing. Soekemi's own

[22]   See for lying under Soekarno's cot, the change of names and the *Mahabharata* inspiration behind it, Solichin Salam 1966:35-6; Adams 1965:26-7.

[23]   Adams 1965:29, though the name is misspelled; for the proper name see Visker 1989:173. Dahm also refers to a female Dutch teacher being hired, Dahm 1969:28, and Solichin Salam 1966: 41 to a Miss Brunet[te] de la Roche Brune teaching him French at home during his Modjokerto ELS school years, a name also mentioned in Visker 1989:119.

subsequent promotions,[24] first to teacher and then to principal/supervisor of schools concerned with the education of indigenous children, his rather close association as an indispensable Kawi-language assistant to the well-known Eurasian scholar Herman Neubronner van der Tuuk while in Bali, as well as a life-long connection with the Theosophical Association of the Indies (TS), were all matters quite instrumental in moulding his son in predominantly western-oriented ways.

The impact of theosophy

That during the interbellum period many among the Javanese upper and middle classes and some Sumatran intellectuals were attracted to theosophy is owing primarily to the following factors. The TS's affinity with Javanese nobles (considered by theosophy to be of Aryan kin or descent),[25] its concepts of eclectic or syncretic positions, millennial cultism and the belief in mystic powers of life and matter, from the turn of the century, led to a rather broad following among the more educated Javanese, mostly aristocratic and active in Boedi Oetomo, and a score of Sumatran intellectuals (Agoes Salim, Amir Sjarifoeddin and Aboe Hanifah, for instance). TS also made inroads among some Javanese nobles (Soewardi Soerjaningrat, Soetamto Soeriokoesoema and Tjipto Mangoenkoesoemo) and Indo-Europeans and Chinese, politically active in Douwes Dekker's Indische Partij. Initially as a Netherlands chapter, the first theosophical branch was founded in Java in 1883,[26] followed by a separate Indies chapter in 1912. Molly Bondan née Warner (1912-1990), an Auckland-born British immigrant from a theosophical home, reports that between 1914 and 1929 (Molly and her family had settled in Sydney in 1919) a number of Indonesians frequented Australian Theosophical conferences.

[24]   Soekemi attended a *kweekschool* (teachers' college), one of five existing in the Indies at the time, in Probolinggo, where he received a stipend of 15 guilders a month. As a tutor in Soerabaya his monthly wage was *f* 27.50. After becoming a principal/supervisor his monthly salary was raised to *f* 50, with an annual increment of *f* 10 per month, see *Staatsblad* 1913, no. 270. He was also decorated twice by the Dutch government for his service record with the silver star. See for details on wages and the decorations respectively, *ENI* V:303, *ENI* III:89. For more intimate details, see Sastrawidjaja, p. 44; Solichin Salam 1966:33; Soebagijo 1978:22-3; Im Yang Tjoe 1933: 4, 6-7 and Kuijk and Van Veen 1967:55.
[25]   De Tollenaere 1996:121, 302-3, where Javanese nobles (the most notable TS member was Prince Mangkoe Negoro VII (pp. 318-9)) are contrasted with earlier Polynesian and Malay migrants, with the latter being inferior to the former. This seems to clash with Molly Bondan's view considering theosophists' rejection of racism as a strong drawing card for educated Indonesians to join it; see Hardjono and Warner 1995:205.
[26]   By Baron F. Tengnagel (1831-1893), a younger brother of Bob Hering's maternal great-grandfather, Daniël Cornelis Tengnagel (1829-1880). See for the former *ENI* VI:392, and for the latter Bloys van Treslong Prins 1934-39, II:172.

She also notes that by 1930 there were 2,100 members of the society in Indonesia, about 50% Dutch, 40% Indonesian and 10% Chinese.[27]

So, like Jawaharlal Nehru,[28] Soekarno owed part of his education to theosophists. Through his father's theosophical membership he gained early and constant access to the rich resources of Soerabaja's Theosophical Library then located at the Princesselaan, as well as to the Volksbibliotheek (People's Library) of the Vrijmetselaarsloge (Freemason's Lodge) on the Toendjoengan thoroughfare. By his own account and also by Bondan's,[29] Soekarno read widely on political and philosophical thought, including Jefferson, Burke, Paine, Beatrice and Sydney Webb, Hegel, Kant, Rousseau, Voltaire, Marx, Engels and Lenin. As to Marxist philosophy, Soekarno would later call himself a *plonco* (a novice), referring to the influence of Coos Hartogh, his teacher of German for four years at the Soerabaja Regentstraat HBS, who taught him about Marxist ideology and principles.[30] Years after his HBS schooling Soekarno, in a letter to yet another Dutch social democrat, J.E. Stokvis, would still refer to himself as a *plonco* when it came to interpreting Marxist economics at the time of the financial crisis in the Indies.[31] This debt and Soekarno's appropriate deference to his Dutch social-democratic friends and mentors remain barely touched upon by Soekarno's western biographers.

Returning to the TS, it seems that somewhat later than Soekarno, Hatta as well had close contacts with the society both in the Indies and in the Netherlands, and though he refused to actively join it, he still accepted a scholarship from some Dutch theosophists that enabled him to pursue his economics studies in Rotterdam (Hatta 1979:150-2). Other Sumatran intellectuals like Amir Sjarifoeddin and Aboe Hanifah attended lectures held by the Jakarta chapter of the society several times a week, covering the same western thinkers as Soekarno had before them (Hardjono and Warner 1995: 206; Abu Hanifah 1972:64).

[27]   Hardjono and Warner 1995:205. These 1930 figures are also cited in *ENI* VI:392.
[28]   De Tollenaere 1996:271 for Motilal and Jawaharlal Nehru's Theosophical Society membership.
[29]   For Soekarno see Adams 1965:39, for Molly Bondan's see Hardjono and Warner 1995:205-6.
[30]   Soekarno, 'Mendjadi pembantu Pemandangan' ('Becoming an assistant of *Pemandangan*', an Indonesian daily) in Soekarno 1959:510. For Hartogh see Solichin Salam 1966:41; Tichelman 1985:417-22, 445-50; Verbaal 12 December 1919, no. 73. From the latter one is able to conclude that Hartogh's Marxist-inspired credo was of a moderate kind resembling that of Karl Kautsky, a man he introduced to his pupil Soekarno when Soekarno was in his late teens; see Chapter III.
[31]   See Soekarno's letter to Stokvis, Soekamiskin, 28 October 1931 (IISG archives).

The impact of Van der Tuuk

Another early influence of Soekarno's father on his only son was inspired
by the impact Van der Tuuk (1824-1894) had upon Soekemi, while Soekemi
served as Van der Tuuk's language assistant in Bali.[32] Van der Tuuk, one of
the first westerners to completely adapt himself to local surroundings, took a
Balinese *nyai*, dressed in indigenous garb, lived in an *atap* hut in *desa* Baratan,
near Soekemi's own dwelling, and stayed aloof from Dutch officialdom as
often as he could (Nieuwenhuys 1988:130, 136, 150, 152-4). His lifestyle must
have struck a chord with his young Javanese assistant. Of mixed blood himself, Van der Tuuk often clouded his own descent in mystical or mythical
fashion. This is also evident in Soekemi's own *kejawen*-inspired philosophical
make-up, where such stories are often perceived not just as mere fabrications,
but far more as indications that behind historical facts a number of *kejawen*
elements such as *rasa*, *wahyu* and *karsa* play a significant role.[33] These were
influential in Soekarno's thinking throughout his life. As Vickers (1996:16)
has it:

> These school teachers were forerunners of the educationally borne modernity
> which was to link Bali to the educated elite of a nascent Indonesia. But that would
> not occur until the 1920s, when the son of one of these school teachers and a
> Balinese woman would emerge as part of a group of nationalist political leaders.
> This son, Sukarno, future president of the Republic of Indonesia, was caught up
> by the attempts to shape an Indonesian identity out of the inconsistent meeting
> of new ideas of freedom, self autonomy, and equality with colonial structures of
> domination, control, and social division.

Soekarno's immediate ancestry

During his first teaching post in Bali as a tutor at a government elementary
school at Singaradja, Soekarno's father Raden Soekemi Sosrodihardjo (1869-
1945),[34] who hailed from the east Javanese town of Blitar, and as we have

---

[32]   Vickers 1996:16; Solichin Salam 1966:32 and Sastrawidjaja's mss on Soekarno 1993:44, 46-7,
on Soekemi being Van der Tuuk's assistant and the influence the latter exerted upon the former.
This was also confirmed in an interview with retired district head I Ketut Loka, Soekarno's
maternal cousin at Banjar Bale Agung, Buleleng, on 15 July 1971.
[33]   Sastrawidjaja p. 47. For *kejawen* aspects of *rasa* (intuitive feeling), *wahju* (divine inspiration)
and *karsa* (wish fulfilment) see Stange 1984:119 and Mulder 1992:27-9. Soekarno's interpretation
of *wahyu* in Soekarno 1969:41.
[34]   Soekemi, also named Raden Sosrodihardjo, died 8 May 1945 at the age of seventy-six. See
Asia Raya, 8 May 2605 (1945), page 1, where a photograph of him is shown in the right column
of the page. Kuijk and Van Veen 1967:55, mistakenly list Soekemi as a teacher at a *kweekschool*

seen was a practising theosophist and *kejawen* by religion (Adams 1965:21), had met a young Balinese woman named Ni Njoman Rai Siremben. She stemmed from the old *pasek* family of *banjar* (ward) Balé Agoeng of the town of Boeleleng in northern Bali,[35] since 1854 under direct Dutch control. The *pasek* clans, more or less a kind of non-noble village gentry, had for ages been the primus inter pares in a number of north and northeast Balinese villages. As tradition records it, the *pasek* Gelgel of that village in Kloengkoeng had swarmed all over Bali, and in the wake of this exodus had been instrumental as core villagers (*krama desa*) in founding quite a number of villages.[36] This powerful movement of commoners (*sudra* or *jaba*, outsiders, not belonging to the *triwangsa* noble caste) challenged the dominance in Bali of the so-called Siwaite hierarchy, embodied by the Brahman priesthood. This hierarchy was carefully protected by the Dutch during their rather short-lived control of the island. The largest group to challenge Brahman interpretation was (and still is) the *pasek* movement, claiming as its ideological ancestor a Mpu Kuturan alias Mpu Rajakretha, a Javanese Buddhist priest who hailed from eastern Java and came to Bali in 1001, who is still seen as the founder of the present *pasek* temple order.[37]

In the case of Soekarno's mother, members of her *pasek* branch usually served as headmen of Balé Agoeng.[38] Claims made by the Indonesian publicist Soebagijo that a powerful *jaba* named Made Pasek, adviser to the king of Boeleleng, was in fact the father of Soekarno's mother (Soebagijo 1978: 13) are highly unlikely. Made Pasek and his brother Ketut Pasek had gained much renown as war leader and administrator, respectively, in the service of the king of Gianjar, until Gianjar was incorporated into the kingdom of Kloengkoeng in the mid-1880s to form a 'southern front' against the Dutch in North Bali.[39] Made Pasek thus had no connection whatsoever with the

---

(vocational school) for Indonesian teachers in Bali. At that time no such school existed in Bali. More plausible are the accounts of Sastrawidjaja, p. 45 and Soebandi 1991, II:107 listing him as a *guru* at the Sekolah Dasar no. 1 (indigenous public school) in the Paketan ward of Singaradja; this was also confirmed in an interview with I Ketut Loka, a *pasek* relative of Soekarno's mother, 15 July 1971 in Buleleng.

[35]   Soekarno's *pasek* descent has escaped the scrutiny of most of his western biographers in spite of the fact that a 30 August 1946 Dutch Nefis XG 5/5570 report 'De stamboom van Soekarno' (Soekarno's family tree) specifically refers to it, as well as most of the Bali-based *pasek* literature; see, for instance, Soebandi 1991:107-8.

[36]   For the traditional accounts, see Sugriwa 1957 and the *Babad Pasek Gelgel* n.d.

[37]   Soebandi 1991, III:37. On the *pasek* clan in general see Utrecht 1974:26 and Palm 1966:6, 17.

[38]   Interview with Ernst Utrecht, 1 March 1979, Amsterdam; interview with I Ketut Loka, 15 July 1971, Buleleng. I Ketut Loka shares with Soekarno the same Balinese great-grandfather.

[39]   Schulte Nordholt 1996:174-5. A more elaborate treatment of these two brothers is in Soebandi 1991, II:74-90.

puri (royal centre) of Boeleleng nor did he ever reside there, let alone beget a daughter in Dutch-occupied territory. Of greater interest are the reports of the courtship between Soekemi Sosrodihardjo and Ni Njoman Rai. The former served as a *guru* (teacher) at the Sekolah Dasar number 1 in the Peketan ward and used to frequent the *pura* (temple) of *desa* Balé Agoeng in order to familiarize himself with aspects of Balinese culture so closely akin to his own Javanese cultural background. There he often watched religious/ritual dances performed by two Balinese maidens: one his future wife and the other a close girlfriend of the former named Ni Made Latri. It seems that initially our young *guru* had some difficulty in deciding whom he would court in earnest. Finally he decided to woo Ni Njoman Rai, only to find out that her agreement to marry – she was impressed by her suitor's brightness and descent from a learned (*alim*) mystically inclined father[40] – could be obtained by the simple procedure of a *ngerorod* or *mrangkat* (Balinese terms for a *kawin lari*), that is, a runaway marriage, or elopement. And so they did, first seeking refuge in the home of a local policeman and then making their union legal by declaring before an indigenous judge that they had acted out of love, paying the registry fee of twenty-five guilders immediately afterwards.[41]

In his interviews with Cindy Adams and with Solichin Salam, Soekarno claimed that his mother belonged to the Brahman caste and was linked to the royal house of Singosari, while his father was of noble birth descended from yet another royal house, that of Kediri.[42] Ernst Utrecht, like Soekarno an *arek Suraboyo*,[43] and close to Soekarno during the period he served in Soekarno's 1959-1965 Dewan Pertimbangan Agung (Highest Advisory Council), considered Soekarno's descent claims as an obvious attempt to enhance (in 1964) his charisma in a country still fond of its feudal and heroic past.[44]

---

[40]   For Raden Hardjodikromo see Im Yang Tjoe 1933:3-4 and Solichin Salam 1966:31.

[41]   Solichin Salam 1966:107-8, see also Soebagijo 1978:21-8.

[42]   Adams 1965:19. The Brahman status of Soekarno's mother is also reported by Dahm 1969: 23, and by Solichin Salam 1966:31. Solichin Salam 1966:212 also reports the descent of Soekarno's mother and father from the royal houses of Singasari and Kediri respectively. Legge 1984:17 doubts the Brahman status and considers a Brahman/Javanese wedding at that time rather unlikely.

[43]   Literally meaning 'the indigenous or real Surabayan' who was usually characterized as strong-minded and quick to assert himself, see Solichin Salam 1966:33-4; Frederick 1989:1; Siauw Giok Tjhan 1982:85, note 5.

[44]   Utrecht 1969:5. Several indigenous accounts credit Soekarno with a royal genealogy (similar to 1974 accounts linking Soeharto with such lines: 'Disekitar "silsilah POP" itu', *Tempo*, 9 November 1974, pp. 45-6; Hellypradibyo and H. Pratikno, in *Bingkisan Trikora* 1964:62-3; Oemar Bey, 'Sukarno anak siapa?' in *Sketsmana*, no. 53, 1967, both claiming him to be the son of Pakubuwono X; Thojib Djumadi, 'Perjuangan Pangeran Serang', *Jaja Baya* no. 11, 15 November 1981; Poerwadihie-Atmodihardjo, 'Bung Karno tedhak turune Sunan Kalijaga?', *Jaja Baya* no. 12, 15 December 1981, link him with even more ancient Javanese courts. Absence of birth registration data and other verifiable evidence render confirmation of all these claims impossible.

Charisma, here understood as attributing supernatural qualities to a ruler or leader with whom one enjoys a diffuse and dependent relationship similar to that between parent and child, may seem reprehensible to westerners, but to Indonesians the notion of charismatic leadership stood central in the political ideologies of both the earlier Hinduized and Islamized realms, if not stemming from even more ancient indigenous traditions. Neither claim made by Soekarno about his royal ancestry seems very plausible, though there is an outside chance that in the distant past blood links with noble courtiers were formed through liaisons with female concubines belonging to Soekarno's maternal and paternal forebears. In such a case family oral tradition, whether true or fabricated, may have caused Soekarno to make these claims. However, no reliable written records have been traced so far to substantiate Soekarno's allegations. In spite of the absence of reliability, a host of Indonesian literary authorities still persist in spreading Soekarno's claims to royal ancestry.[45] However, in the more immediate recorded past, the *pasek* have obtained a status only a bit higher than the common people of Bali, the so-called *sudra* or *jaba* (Balinese for *rakyat*, or commoners). As to Raden Soekemi Sosrodihardjo's own status, he was certainly not a *ndoro* or a *ningrat* (persons of princely blood or persons with considerable influence at the Javanese courts). Soekarno's father and his immediate forebears clearly belonged to the lesser Javanese nobility, as indicated by the title *raden* and his profession as an elementary school principal in the Dutch-style educational system. To the myths Soekarno himself revealed about his own roots – be it at a time when his political prowess was clearly on the wane – one must add some others. First are those of a general character, followed by some of a personal and private nature.

Myth making: old and new

That Soekarno chose the royal house of Kediri was inspired by yet another myth associated with the eleventh-century king of Kediri, Djojobojo, the producer of the famous Djojobojo *pralambang* (prophecies). It is almost certain that the king of the Hindu-Javanese realm of Kediri did not utter these *pralambang* himself but that they were produced by the *guru* and court clerics, who in turn legitimized their predictions by linking them to the king of their realm, whom they perceived as possessing *wahyu*-like supernatural qualities. Later they formed the foundation of even more modern and topical prophecies which then found their way to the all-too-eager listeners in Java's

---

[45]   For instance by Andjar Any 1978:18-9, 1978b:7-20; Solichin Salam 1966:212; Soebagijo 1978: 13-5, 23; Erka 1978a:12; Saiful Rahim 1989:11-2.

overcrowded countryside. As the Dutch scholar J.A.B. Wiselius revealed in 1872, the historical ruler of Kediri, Jaya Bhaya (c. 1150 AD), 'made prophecies to the Javanese people of disasters and humilities they would have to suffer before they could have power and esteem'.[46] Such a final indigenous regeneration would occur under the auspices of a *ratu adil* – a just king – with natural disasters announcing his imminent arrival. But before such a just age would finally come about, several intermittent just rulers, mainly under priestly messianic guidance, having both Islamic Mahdi and Buddhist Eruçakra overtones, would pave the way. Thus, Diponegoro, the hero of the 1825-1830 Java War, was perceived as wearing both the Mahdi and Eruçakra mantles, while a generation before even a westerner like Thomas Stamford Raffles was seen as the envoy of the prince from Kling (Dahm 1969:7).

Soekarno's first political mentor, Tjokroaminoto, during the heyday of Sarekat Islam, was cloaked with that messianic garb for a while. However, Tjokro was quick to defuse the old myth, declaring that 'the eagerly awaited *ratu adil* was not to appear in the shape of an individual but in the shape of socialism' (Lind 1983:21). And when in the late 1920s and early 1930s Soekarno had picked up the fallen 'just king' mantle of his erstwhile political mentor, the Javanese among his following were also quick to identify him as a *ratu adil*. Soekarno was thus a late link in an age-old tradition. But like Tjokro before him, Soekarno did not view the *ratu adil* as an individual personality but as a social condition. He later elaborated his views more fully in his 1930 *Indonesia menggoegat* and his 1944 Pantja Sila addresses (Soekarno 1978:53-5, 1931:39-41, 1965:28).

At the time, the growing influence of Japan became a recognized link in the Djojobojo prophecy, since it included an interim rule of a yellow race to pave the way for indigenous power. As late as 1934, a 1 May 1912 version of the Djojobojo legend, recorded by a former Djokja-based *jaksa tinggi* (public prosecutor at the appellate level) Raden Nitipradja in *Het Tijdschrift*, was cited in the Volksraad by the nationalist leader Mohammad Hoesni Thamrin as follows:

> When Java has become so reduced politically, a yellow race will master it but only for the duration of one maize crop, then it will fall back into the hands of the Javanese, so with the white lotus flower [the Dutch] withered, a time of genuine bliss will arrive for Java.[47]

Two years earlier a certain Soenarto had widely circulated another prophecy, of which one passage reads as follows:

---

[46]   Wiselius 1872. About the Jangka Jayabaya (Jayabaya Prophecies) with its historical periodization and political symbology, see Florida 1995:273-5.
[47]   *Handelingen Volksraad* 1934-1935:173; also recorded in *De Pacific* 1937:55-6.

Ing wektu kang orah suwe maneh. Nagara Indonesia bakal mardika Madege
omah 13 tahun sawise Sabda iki. Dene dadine omah 50 tahun sawise Sabda

(In a time not far from now/ The state of Indonesia will be free/ That house will
be erected 13 years after this word/ And that house will be completed 50 years
after that) (Supomo Surjohudjojo n.d.:5).

My own father, F.Ch. Hering, a Javanese and Sundanese language expert,
showed me still another text just prior to the Pacific War, stating the following in *ngoko*:

Jen negoro djowo gedené woes sagadong kelor hingkono bakal di teken dening
wong tjino. Hananging lawasé moeng saoemoeré djagoeng, sawoesé hikoe bakal
balihono hing tangané wong djowo. Jen toendjoeng poetih woes sirno, hingkono
moektiné wong djowo.

(When the country of Java has become great it will be overwhelmed by the
Chinese – only to fall into Javanese hands again after the corn has ripened. When
the white lotus has withered, the Javanese will experience bliss again.)

At a more personal level and appearing when Soekarno's power had waxed
considerably, we must include some myths concerning his immediate ancestry. Like the *guru* of yesteryear, several learned or not so learned individuals,
both indigenous and foreign, were eager to reveal Soekarno's real ancestry. Entire genealogies were constructed suggesting that the people's idol
stemmed from or had blood links with such powerful royal houses as the
house of Mataram and with Soenan Kalijaga, the most renowned of the *wali*,
who brought Islam to Java's shores.[48] Foreigners such as the Indo-European
Karel Snijtsheuvel, and the unnamed Indonesia correspondent for the Dutch
weekly *Haagsche Post* (with the latter even claiming Soekarno as a former
fellow-student at the TH), mention a highly placed Dutch *totok* father, a '*gou-
verneur*' (governor, one rank below the governor-general residing in Bogor),
who begot Soekarno either by Sarinah or by another unnamed Indonesian
female. Soekemi and his Balinese wife here only functioned as foster parents,
receiving money drafts each three months from a shadowy 'real' and repent-
ant father mainly for covering the costs of Soekarno's secondary and tertiary
education.[49] In the context of these indigenous reports extolling Soekarno's

---

[48]   See for these Indonesian accounts notes 44 and 45. For descent of Kalijaga, see Florida 1995:
329, note 16 and Solichin Salam 1974:46, citing a 1958 address by Soekarno made in Demak (the
former centre of Kalijaga's power). Penders 1974:3, 205 note 3, claiming Professor G. Reesink
(sic) as his informant (interview Djakarta September 1970), refers to Soekarno's claims of descent
from the Sultans of Demak made during the Japanese occupation 'in order to gain support of
Indonesian Muslims for the Japanese cause'. In our own Jakarta, 3 July 1976 interview with G.J.
(Han) Resink we were told that such information was never imparted to Penders.
[49]   'De Westerse vlotheid van Indonesia's president; Ir. Soekarno is feitelijk een Indo-
European', *De Haagsche Post*, 3 November 1956:5 and Snijtsheuvel 1958:82-4.

royal ancestry, it may be significant to note that in a recent well-documented study by the American anthropologist John Pemberton, no mention at all is made of the royal forebears of Indonesia's first president. Pemberton, how-ever, chronicles the Soeharto family's claims, linking them with the royal house of Mangkunegara, and reports further that Soeharto, his wife, and one of his closest advisers personally indulged in seeking contact with legendary characters from Java's past by means of spirit mediums.[50]

As for the Dutch newspaper accounts, they seem to have upset Soekarno as well. In his 'autobiography' he cites them and clearly rejects their cred-ibility. For him, Soekemi and Ni Njoman Rai are his real parents and he also regrets that his father is no longer with him to confirm that simple fact.[51] Some official correspondence in the wake of the Dutch articles also indicates that the 'Indonesian government considered the allegations insulting to the [Indonesian] head of state', especially in view of the fact that 'Indonesian press organs during the Dutch "Royal House Question" [the so-called Greet Hofmans affair][52] were requested to deal with that issue quite delicately [...] which they did'.[53] Snijtsheuvel's account and that of *De Haagsche Post*, claim-ing an unnamed Dutch governor as Soekarno's 'real father', are even less plausible. At the time of Soekarno's birth in 1901 the position of governor (of West, Central or East Java) did not exist. The mere existence of such a repent-ant father having become a Dutch governor long after he begot Soekarno was rejected firmly by Ch.O. van der Plas, governor of East Java in 1936-1941, a frequent visitor to our home at Oranje Boulevard 4 in post-war Jakarta.[54] Therefore it is no wonder that more serious biographers such as Dahm and

50   Pemberton 1994:305-7. Pemberton's study also presents a brilliant ethnographic analysis of Orde Baru cultural ideology and practice.
51   Adams 1965:18-9. Legge 1984:25 and Dahm 1969:23, note 2 consider the accounts as hav-ing no foundation at all, though Penders 1974:5, citing an unnamed 'explanation', suggests 'that Raden Sukemi's selection of Karna was a reflection on Sukarno's illegitimacy', since in the 'Mahabharata story Karna was the illegitimate son of Bataru Surya, the Sun God, and Dewi Kunti Nalibrata'. Abu Hanifah 1972:18-21, with some relish compares the Dutch accounts with an unnamed Javanese account since they are so similar, and then blames Soekarno's vanity for bringing it all up again in his 'autobiography'. Soekarno, when interviewed by Kanzoo Tsoetsoemi about his life, also mentioned Soekemi and his paternal grandparents without mentioning a royal lineage at all. See 'Mengoendjoengi orang-orang Indonesia jang terkemoeka; Kesan tentang Ir. Soekarno', *Djawa Baroe* 1-1(1943):6.
52   See for this affair, splitting the Dutch royal palace into 'a Juliana and a Bernhard camp', Giebels 1995:407-19.
53   Letter R.C. Pekelharing to Ministerie van Buitenlandse Zaken VCZ 77853/GS 10633/5077, Djakarta 20 November 1965, p. 1.
54   Interview with Van der Plas, The Hague, 14 April 1974, where he ruled himself out as well as all the other gubernatorial colleagues at the time. Also, Van der Plas, familiar with the Dutch accounts, thought the idea of a highly placed repentant father paying for Soekarno's education while Soekarno was boarding at the home of 'a radical nationalist' (Tjokro) very unlikely. As to Snijtsheuvel, his credibility is further marred by allegations, of 2,000 Japanese being killed

Legge consider these indigenous and Dutch accounts of Soekarno's royal ancestry to be mere fabrications. Naturally, Soekarno is himself to blame for conjuring up stories about a royal lineage, even going so far as to involve his maternal grandfather in a so-called Singaradja *puputan*.[55] Utrecht maintains that by doing so during the 1964-1965 talks with the rather good-looking and shapely American ghostwriter, Soekarno was eagerly trying to prop up his waning charisma vis-à-vis his people on the one hand, as well as charming the all too impressionable Cindy Adams on the other. We feel, however, that far more was at stake at the time. Soekarno, in the wake of John Kennedy's assassination, was quite aware that any chance of a rapprochement with the only superpower in the Pacific had diminished if not evaporated altogether. Through Cindy Adams he thus tried to polish up once and for all an image he thought pleasing to a country still caught up in its own mystique of revolutionary and anti-colonial fervour.[56] The remarks made by Abu Hanifah in this context are not far off the mark:

> when Soekarno, the President, requested Cindy Adams to take down notes and write his autobiography, he was already 64 years old, and possibly he very much regretted that he had not made full use of the chances fate had given him during his lifetime. [...] Besides, he really had great charm [...]. Foreigners who hadn't known him before and had a prejudice against him changed overnight after talking with Soekarno [...]. It could be true that Soekarno found it necessary to build up a name, a glorious name, and like some people in Europe and America, he was frantically in search of a family tree, a famous one preferably. (Abu Hanifah 1972: 8, 21.)

Early upbringing: The first two windoe

In his recollections of his early upbringing, Soekarno told the Japanese journalist Kanzoo Tsoetsoemi that at an early age, after just being weaned ('setelah lepas dari soesoe iboe'), he left his parental home in Soerabaja to stay with

---

during the 6 March 1942 Tjiater Pass encounter with the Japanese vanguard then moving toward Bandoeng (Snijtsheuvel 1958:12). Such allegations are not supported at all by Nortier, Kuijt and Groen 1994:143-7.

[55] Adams 1965:19. No such Singaradja *puputan* ever took place. The only real *puputan*, on 20 September 1906 and 28 April 1908, occurred in Badoeng and Kloengkoeng respectively, far away from the dwelling grounds of Soekarno's Balinese forebears. For the 1906 and 1908 massacres see Schulte Nordholt 1996:213-6.

[56] Soekarno was also prompted by Howard Palfrey Jones, then US ambassador to Indonesia, who considered Soekarno's speaking talents to match those of William Jennings Bryan (see Jones 1971:218 and Adams 1965:20) and intimated to him that with his 'magnetic personality' he would have little difficulty convincing US audiences what the real Soekarno was all about, Adams 1965: 19-20.

his grandparents in the small East Javanese rural town of Toeloengagoeng. According to Im Yang Tjoe (1933:4, 6-7). Soekarno was sent there because his father's monthly wage of *f* 27,50 was far from adequate to care for the entire family of four, a situation that soon changed, however, when after short stints in Ploso and Sidoardjo Soekemi entered a higher wage scale. In Toeloeng-agoeng, Soekarno's paternal grandfather Raden Hardjodikromo taught him to be always righteous and fair, not to blame the servants for things he had done himself, or to harm weak and small animals he had captured, while his grandmother spoilt him terribly.[57] Other accounts reveal the impact made by the grandfather introducing Soekarno to the wondrous world of the *wayang*, allowing him to watch *wayang* performances until the early hours of the dawn.[58] His world was further embellished by his father when Soekarno at the age of six was reunited with his family in Soerabaja. In his own words Soekarno told Kanzoo Tsoetsoemi:

> When I turned six I returned to my father and mother in Soerabaja since I had to enter school there. My father particularly taught me to become a good human being [...]. He intended me to become a good fighter who would duly serve the fatherland. Father's desire remained so firm that somewhat later he changed my name, which at first was Koesno, to Soekarno. Soekarno comes from Karno; that is the name of a *ksatria* from the Mahabharata known to be honest and fear-less.[59]

Utrecht, a close top adviser to Soekarno during the Guided Democracy years, considers the Toeloengagoeng youthful *wayang* experiences as basic to an understanding of Soekarno's political drives at a riper age:

> the shadowplay performed by the *dalang* [puppeteer] on the screen usually showed a basic pattern: the ancient struggle between evil and good, between justice and injustice. Soekarno primarily saw it as a 'contradiction of forces'. He perceived the emergence of each such new force as a logical outcome to a contra-diction with an older power, which Soekarno while president often described as being purely a matter of dialectics. This dialectic appeared not in Marxist treatises alone, it formed the foundation as well for objective analyses of societies where sharp class contradictions were causing deep social tensions. So the *dalang* show-ing the Bharata Yuddha, depicting the long fraternal struggle between Pendawas and Korawas, could further be interpreted as a struggle of the submissive colonial

---

[57]   Kanzoo Tsoetsoemi, 'Mengoendjoengi orang-orang Indonesia jang terkemoeka; Kesan tentang Ir. Soekarno', *Djawa Baroe* 1-1 (1943):6.
[58]   Solichin Salam 1966:37-8; Legge 1984:22-3; Kuijk and Van Veen 1967:56-7; M.Y. Nasution 1951:13-4.
[59]   Kanzoo Tsoetsoemi, 'Mengoendjoengi orang-orang Indonesia jang terkemoeka; Kesan tentang Ir. Soekarno', *Djawa Baroe* 1-1 (1943):6. Dahm 1969:27, who cites the Japanese source, overlooks the first sentence of our quotation and places it in a Modjokerto context instead of a Soerabajan one.

people against enemies with the prime purpose to restore the illegally disturbed order so disrupted by foreign influence. (Utrecht 1969:10.)

As to Soekarno's further early educational experiences, the accounts by Dahm, Legge and Nasution are clearly in need of revision. Not merely because their accounts contradict each other, but also because they did not make use of information provided by Professor Mr Soenarjo and Drs Hermen Kartowisastro, both Modjokerto contemporaries of Soekarno. It seems that the young Soekarno, after his first *sekolah dasar* (a five-grade primary school established in 1893 as a First Class Indigenous School) years in the city of his birth, was then enrolled by his father at his father's own five-grade primary school in Modjokerto after Soekemi's posting to that town. His father's school was just around the corner from their house at Residen Pamoedji Road. Both the school and their former house are still to be seen in present-day Modjokerto. Soekarno's Modjokerto school recollections as told to Cindy Adams, revealing himself as a ringleader, a cock of the walk (*haantje-de-voorste* or *jago*), are substantiated by two Modjokerto contemporaries of Soekarno. Soenarjo, born in Madioen on 28 August 1902, a co-founder of PNI on 4 July 1927 in Bandoeng, during 1913 and 1914 on annual vacations from Madioen to Modjokerto relatives, recalls meeting Soekarno there on several occasions. Soekarno, a bit taller than Soenarjo, sporting a bicycle at the time, was considered by Soenarjo to be quite open in manner and a real leader of his school and soccer-club mates.[60] Another even closer Modjokerto mate, since they were neighbours, was Hermen Kartowisastro. A Volksraad member during 1937-1939 representing the rather conservative Vereeniging van Ambtenaren bij het Inlandsch Bestuur (VAIB, Association of Indigenous Civil Servants), Hermen Kartowisastro reveals that his own father befriended Raden Soekemi and that upon the former's advice Soekemi decided to enrol his son in the third grade of the seven-grade Europeesche Lagere School (ELS, European Higher Elementary School) in June 1911.[61] Thus not in the fourth grade – Soekarno had completed that grade at his father's school – since his proficiency in Dutch needed to be upgraded; which was accomplished by the already mentioned Mrs De la Rivière. Like Soenario, Hermen recalls his young neighbour as a *jago* and a good soccer-playing mate but also as a bad loser. On one such occasion Hermen cleaved Soekarno's spiked top with his own, a *gasing* (Indonesian for a spiked top or *heitol* – the Dutch name for such a toy), whereupon Soekarno grabbed Hermen's top and threw it away in a

[60]   Interview with Professor Mr Soenarjo 7 August 1976; see also Sunario 1981:52 and 1991: 38-9. For Soekarno's recollections, see Adams 1965:27-8.
[61]   Interview with Hermen Kartowisastro 7 August 1976; see also Hermen Kartowisastro 1978: 62 and Hermen's article 'Pemuda Soekarno kawan sekolah dan kawan mainku selama 1909-1919', *Simponi*, 25 June 1978:3-4.

nearby stream (Hermen Kartowisastro 1978:63-4).

After a period of four years (1911-1915) Soekarno left the Modjokerto ELS with a *klein-ambtenaars-diploma* (a civil service entry certificate) (M.Y. Nasution 1951:14), but instead of entering the Civil Service, he was, in June 1916, admitted to the Regentstraat Hogere Burger School (HBS, secondary high school) in Soerabaja. According to Hermen, Soekarno had been a brilliant ELS pupil and so had no difficulty whatsoever passing the rather tough entrance examination to the HBS.[62] During the entire HBS period Soekarno boarded with the Tjokroaminoto household, first at Gang Peneleh VII no. 29/31 and then from the second half of 1919 until mid-1921 at Plampitan, just a stone's throw south of Gang Peneleh.

There is still some doubt about the sources regarding Soekarno's educational and boarding expenses, particularly in view of Soekarno's own revelations to Cindy Adams about David Copperfield-like circumstances experienced during his early youth and teenage years (Adams 1965:22-3). Van der Plas and Anwar Tjokroaminoto, however, state that Soekarno's brother-in-law Mas Poegoeh (married to Soekarmini), Soekarno's father and Tjokroaminoto himself were all benefactors.[63] Mas Poegoeh, born 17 July 1898 in Sadon, Magetan, was a well-paid official in the colonial Public Works Department. After graduating in 1916 from Soerabaja's Koningin Emma School, he became an irrigation-works foreman and in 1920 a supervisor (Gunseikanbu 1944a:236). In supporting Soekarno, Poegoeh acted according to the Javanese code of *nggendong ngindit* (literally 'equalizing matters', by which wealthier relatives support their less prosperous kin). Van der Plas, a frequent visitor to the Bandoeng household of Soekarno and Inggit Garnasih, imparted to us that after Soekarno's separation from Siti Oetari, Inggit, who pawned part of her jewellery and ran a small *batik* shop and a *jamu* enterprise, also supported part of her lover's educational expenses as Poegoeh and Soekemi still did, Soekemi by that time being rather well off due to his promotion to educational supervisor.[64]

As for Tjokroaminato, who knew Soekarno's father quite well, he considered the young Soekarno as his *anak angkat* (adopted son), a bond further strengthened after Soekarno became engaged to Siti Oetari Tjokroaminotopoeteri in April 1920, just two months short of his nineteenth birthday. According to an *Inlandsche Persoverzichten* (IPO) report, Tjokroaminoto used Sarekat Islam funds to keep a 'boarding house' (referred to by some as the

---

[62]   Hermen Kartowisastro 1978:66. The Gunseikanbu data bank *Orang Indonesia* 1944a:465 lists the diplomas and degrees 'Ir Raden Soekarno' received: ELS (Modjokerto) 1915, Kleinambtenaars Examen 1915, HBS (Soerabaja) 1921, TH (Bandoeng) 1926.
[63]   Interview Van der Plas, 14 April 1974, The Hague and interview Anwar Tjokroaminoto, 15 June 1976, Jakarta.
[64]   Interview Van der Plas, 14 April 1974 and interview Inggit, 12 July 1976.

Soeharsikin boarding house, since it was his wife who instilled in her young boarders Indonesian nationalist sentiments) for some thirty needy young Indonesian pupils who paid modest fees for room and board.[65] In 1917, two *windu* from his year of birth, Soekarno and Ir Asser Baars, second-in-command of the Indische Sociaal-Democratische Vereeniging (ISDV) and teacher at a vocational school, the Koningin Emma School at Soerabaja's Prins Hendriklaan, met at Tjokro's home in Peneleh. Soekarno, already politically influenced in a moderate leftist direction by his German language HBS teacher Coos Hartogh (a member of the Soerabaja Municipal Council and like Baars a prominent member of the ISDV), was to swerve due to Baars in an even more radical direction (Utrecht 1969:11; Perthus 1976:154). Some four years before, when Soekarno was still a pupil at the Modjokerto ELS, Henk Sneevliet, then briefly employed by *Het Soerabajaasch Handelsblad*, had already made his way to Tjokro at Peneleh. More visits were to follow, but at the first one, Sneevliet recalls a Tjokro deeply enthralled by the contents of H.P.G. Quack's volume 5 of *De socialisten; Personen en stelsels*. This standard work Soekarno would later get hold of through his close friend and mentor Marcel Koch and also scrutinize often during his Bandoeng years.[66] However, before we pick up the story of Soekarno's further life, experienced by him as his formative years in Soerabaja, 'the cookshop of nationalism' (Adams 1931: 44), we must first describe more fully the dawn of a new politicized era and its impact on him in the next chapter.

---

[65]   *Overzicht Inlandsche pers* 1921-13:21. For the Internaat Soeharsikin: Tichelman 1985:58, 382, 668 and Amelz 1952, I:53.
[66]   Perthus 1976:91. For Koch introducing Quack to Soekarno: 5 January 1952 interview with Koch in Bandung at the Kenarilaan; Penbrook 1992. For later references to Quack by Soekarno see Soekarno 1931:61.

CHAPTER II

The dawn of a new politicized era

The situation of separate, though overlapping, cultural loyalties, driven by a common ethic of modernity and progress, existing in both the Soekemi and Tjokroaminoto households in Soerabaya at the turn of the century and into the first two decades of the twentieth, was in a sense reflected in the wider political arena. That period of roughly twenty-five years claimed by some as resembling an era of 'national awakening' or 'an age of motion', a *zaman ber-gerak,* bore the hallmarks of regional cultural identities and aspirations, thus rendering the label 'national' premature, if not irrelevant. Further, stressing the arrival of Boedi Oetomo (Noble Endeavour) as the sole initiator of such a 'national awakening' fails to take into account the significance of earlier movements seeking specific socio-political and cultural benefits. Moreover, it credits the upper crust of Javanese society with having blazed the trail toward 'national awakening', instead of viewing that endeavour where it should be: within the wider context of still ill-defined but nonetheless genuine quests for political maturity and social equity. This quest, a direct response to initial socio-political opportunities opened up by 'ethically' inspired associationism in vogue during the period, faced growing frustration when socio-political reform fell short of indigenous expectations (De Hoop 1984:134-5; Boeke 1923:165-7). The first response laid the foundations for a new solidarity to emerge among those literate indigenous and Indies-born (*peranakan*), both Indos and Chinese, who had received a Western-style education.[1] This possibility of receiving a Western-style education was created by a succession of crucially placed Dutch *ethici,* such as J.H. Abendanon, D. van Hinloopen Labberton, C. Snouck Hurgronje and G.A.J. Hazeu. Especially, the last three, after the prudent efforts of Abendanon, known for his sympathies for emancipation generated by that idol of Dutch *ethici* Kartini, caused something of a revolution in education and colonial administration in the early decades of the twentieth century.[2]

---

[1]   *Algemeen verslag Inlandsch onderwijs* 1900-1914; *Algemeen verslag onderwijs* 1915.
[2]   For Abendanon see Neys 1945:211-3; Van Miert 1991. For Abendanon and Kartini, see Soetomo 'Roch jang selaloe hidoep' in *Soeara Parindra* no. 3 (April 1938):128-9, and Soetomo's

Sensitive to *ningrat-priyayi* (high priyayi) aspirations, Snouck and Hazeu had conceived an associationist development model which aimed to attract highly educated westernized indigenous cadres, while simultaneously neutralizing inconvenient indigenous traditions. Ethnologists by profession, they were quite aware that the colonial community had developed only unilaterally and that it was governed in an authoritarian bureaucratic fashion, leaving no room for genuine popular representation. In such an environment, class distinctions were ill-defined and, moreover, overshadowed by colonial racial and caste discrepancies. Therefore, Snouck and Hazeu, in order to emancipate the indigenous populace, deemed it imperative that there be an undisturbed paternalistic education process buttressed through contact with members of the Western-educated Indonesian elite, ideas which also struck a chord with Van Hinloopen Labberton's theosophic ideology (De Hoop 1984: 25-8, note 60, 164). This, they hoped, would lead to a process of decentralization and detutelage (*decentralisatie en ontvoogding*).

Constitutional developments inspired by decentralization and detutelage

Among the representative structures set up by the ethically inspired colonial bureaucracy were the *gemeenteraden* (municipal councils) in some of the major cities. These narrowly franchised bodies were meant as a step on the road toward decentralization and detutelage which had started in the nineteenth century and gained momentum at the dawn of the twentieth. Decentralization in the sense of greater local autonomy was regulated by the Decentralisatiewet (Decentralization Act) of 23 July 1903 and the Locale Raden Ordonnantie (Local Councils Ordinance) of 8 March 1905 (Woesthoff 1915; Van der Zee 1928:1-18). So within the centralist bureaucratic structure, some administrative participation at municipal and regional levels was established. In 1908 the Kiesordonnantie (Electoral Ordinance) of that year enfranchised local male Europeans of a specific tax-paying category to vote for candidates for councillor of their local district. Indonesian councillors, on the whole senior civil servants, were still appointed by the governor-general. The installation ordinances of these councils also prescribed the ethnic composition of these bodies, following the tripartite (Europeans, Indonesians and Foreign Orientals) legislation and jurisdiction patterns of the time (Schrieke 1918:20). Thus a number of civil servants and local prominent citizens were

---

introduction to R.A.Kartini, *Mboekak pepeteng*, translated by R. Sasrasoegonda, Soerabaja, 1938. For Snouck Hurgronje's and Hazeu's 'evolutionary approach', which formed the foundation of the associationist education policies, turn to De Hoop 1984:24, 27-9, 41 and note 60 on p. 164. For Van Hinloopen Labberton, Tichelman 1985:212-3.

charged with carrying out the council's many tasks in addition to the often taxing demands of their own departments and vocations. This arrangement soon began to be questioned by a number of *ethici*, some of whom were councillors themselves. They perceived councils to be too elitist, marred by absenteeism due to members' other commitments, and prone to serving government rather than local interests, because of the lack of genuine democratic voting rights. Starting in 1908, these *ethici*, prompted by the electoral reforms of that year allowing council elections, began organizing *kiesvereenigingen* (electoral associations) locally, while regionally they established a Vereeniging voor Locale Belangen (Association to Promote Local Interests) (Schrieke 1918:69-73; Van der Zee 1928:52). The colonial government, in return, was prepared to relax article 111 of the Regeerings Reglement of 1854 somewhat. That article had prohibited the existence of political organizations in the Indies, but article 68c did permit the formation of societies and the holding of meetings for the purpose of recommending candidates for membership on local councils. All this doubtless aided in the formation of political parties in Indonesia, all of which, as described below, made their appearance at about that time. Nonetheless, regional and municipal councils could not be described as instruments of self-government for the local inhabitants. Composition of all the councils as originally established by specific *Instellingsordonnanties* (Acts of Incorporation) guaranteed absolute European majorities which were always far larger than proportional representation would have allowed (Schrieke 1918:12; Cobban 1970:117). Councils so composed thus did not approach the aims stated in the 1903 Decentralization Law, namely 'the achievement of self-government' (Cobban 1970:120).

The rise of urban Western-educated Indonesian elites

Within one generation the expansion of the educational sector produced a rather substantial group of graduates educated above the level of the vernacular *desa* schools and *volksscholen* (village schools), prompting one Javanese schoolteacher, Raden Soekemi Sosrodihardjo, to prepare his only son for Western-oriented secondary education. At the bottom of this educational pyramid were a few thousand who had completed Dutch-language junior and senior high school. At the apex of it, Soekarno somewhat later among them, were a few hundred more highly educated graduates at academic levels. This created a pool of indigenous graduates capable of carrying out many politically oriented organizational and journalistic activities, often utilizing the Malay (*Maleische*) language.[3] So, for graduates of the newly opened institu-

---

3   For priyayi and Western-schooled sons making these choices, see Gouda 1995:105; she also

tions of learning, fields like investigative journalism and political activism attracted the more ambitious among them. Soekarno's father fits the category of those less so inclined or motivated. He, instead, sought wider access to the lower tiers of the swiftly swelling indigenous colonial administration, since it agreed with his own concept of expedient, ethically inspired associationism. This is the course he clearly seems to have intended for his sole son Soekarno. Soekarno, however, saw things otherwise, as we will learn below.

The top layer of this educated group was rather homogeneous, being dominated by the lower *priyayi* of Soekemi's ilk and the neo-*priyayi*,[4] which included graduates and drop-outs from Dutch-language high schools, medical colleges, colleges for the civil service, and teachers' colleges. They usually harboured the highest of expectations from emancipation, but also absorbed some of the disappointment when no fitting professions or vocations were found to be available to them, and no accommodation with colonial hierarchical traditions was sought due to a newly acquired sense of self-consciousness. From this group a new, anti-traditional semi-intelligentsia would stem, mobile and active both journalistically and politically, the young Soekarno among them. The elderly would play important and often crucial roles in the *pergerakan* (movement) for political awakening until the mid-1920s. At that time the first generation of nationally conscious academics from universities and faculties in both Holland and Java would eclipse them, allowing one such graduate, *ingenieur* Soekarno, to erect a truly nationalist-inspired party.

The kaoem moeda jang madjoe dan modèrèn

In any case, this first-generation intelligentsia shared a common denominator, a feeling of belonging to a *kaoem moeda jang madjoe dan modèrèn*: a young generation at once progressive and modern.[5] Young groups of modern progressives, equipped with Dutch-language education (an experience earlier denied to their parents), had a set of new keys with which to unlock a 'progressive modernity'. A *zaman baru* (a new era) was very much on the move and equipped with a dynamic of its own. Saturated with norms, principles

---

reports (1995:79) that 3,339 Indonesian boys and 858 girls were enrolled at public Europeesche Lagere Scholen at the time of Soekarno's final year at the Modjokerto ELS (in 1915). See also Legge 1984:26.

[4]   Neo-priyayization was, in fact, the development of a 'metropolitan superculture', a hybrid type of mestizo culture, found in many colonial and post-colonial cities, borne by Western-educated members of the indigenous bourgeoisie, see Anderson 1973.

[5]   For the disappointment felt among the indigenous intelligentsia, turn to Archief Hazeu (H 1083), KITLV, Leiden, no. 4. For anti-traditional tendencies see Sastrasoeara, 'De inlandsche bestuursambtenaar' in *De Taak*, 16 March 1918. For the *kaum muda* see Shiraishi 1990:30-2.

and keywords, largely attuned to the then fashionable zeitgeist of colonial ethically minded policymakers and administrators, the mood seemed to affirm Dutch colonial aspirations and anticipations of more tranquil multi-ethnic relations to emerge under the aegis of mutually beneficient association-ism. So a *rust en orde* (tranquillity and order) climate, deemed imperative by Dutch colonial authorities now that their enforced 'pacification' schemes had come to seemingly fruitful ends, looked to enshrine what Clifford Geertz has so aptly called the 'spiritual balance of power',[6] a balance indispensable for alien power to retain respect and authority amidst cultural forces and streams (*aliran*) not of its own nor of its own making.

For the indigenous and *peranakan jeunesse dorée,* Dutch education together with Dutch language proficiency also facilitated their access to the Dutch 'world' in the colony, a 'world' much better suited to access the wider world outside its orbit than traditional or archaic modes had thus far been capable of. In Soekarno's case it caused father Soekemi to employ a female Dutch-lan-guage teacher for his son in order to prepare him for Dutch-language prim-ary and secondary schooling. At that stage Soekemi, very much wedded to the elitist/associationist principles of the Theosophic Society he belonged to, clearly envisaged for his only son a career very much like his own. Outside the Soekemi family circle a social and intellectual mobility thus emerged, which promised not only to transcend the rigidities and barriers surround-ing the racially stratified colonial state apparatus, but also those of the cul-tural environment closer to home – at least many of them thought, including Soekarno's parental mentor Soekemi, and Tjokroaminoto, Soekarno's first political mentor. However, it did not necessarily mean that all indigenous cultural baggage was to be abandoned altogether in the quest for Western-style modernity. Both Soekarno's *kejawen*-inspired father and paternal grand-parents are here in focus: they were ready to instil in the young Soekarno rather strong doses of the *kejawen* cosmological culture in the hope that entry into the world of the colonial bureaucracy would lead not only to a *modèrèn* way of thinking, which was also *maju,* but to *budi* (insight) as well. For them, *budi* formed the bridge between mystical ways of attaining self-esteem and spiritual integrity, on top of achieving new status by exposure to Western-style modern education. So, the grandparental and parental design sought input from both traditional and modern modes in the grooming of the young Soekarno, leaving a life-long impact upon their all-too-eager pupil. Here, it matched colonial associationism somewhat, where integrative educational patterns together with the detutelage sought in colonial administration pol-icies strove to accommodate indigenous customs and traditions, if not cater-

---

[6]   That zeitgeist is captured in De Hoop 1984:Ch. 1; for Geertz's 'spiritual balance of power' see C. Geertz 1972:64-5, a concept also discussed in C. Geertz 1968:Ch. 3.

ing to the traditional *ningrat-priyayi* bureaucracy (De Hoop 1984:100-9). These developments, however, generated dissent, causing conservative and more enlightened wings to emerge and plead their cause in both camps: within the Dutch colonial bureaucracy and among the indigenous intelligentsia.[7]

The pioneering role of Sang Pemula

It comes therefore as no surprise to see in the wake of the initial 'Ethical Policy' reforms a distinct proliferation of activities in 'modern' areas of intellectual and socio-political endeavour. Investigative journalism and printing and publishing ventures, as well as the entire realm of social activism and politics, were to undergo expansion and change. In publishing, the predominance of Indo enterprises was slowly taken over by mainly *peranakan* Chinese publishers, who, for instance, published one newspaper in Java in 1905 as against fifteen a mere six years later (*Koloniaal Verslag* 1911). Both Indo and Chinese newspaper and publishing houses engaged a growing number of *bumiputera* (native sons), first as *magang* (apprentice) journalists, and soon as editors and editors-in-chief. Some of these were to propel themselves into the realm of social activism and politics, such as the 'father of Indonesian journalism' Raden Mas Tirto Adhi Soerjo (1880-1918). A scion of a Bodjonegoro *regent* family, a STOVIA (School tot Opleiding van Inlandsche Artsen, School for training indigenous medical doctors) dropout, who after a one-year stint (April 1902 to April 1903) with the Indo (Overbeek Bloem)-led *Pemberita Betawi*[8] started his own publication: the weekly *Soenda Berita* (starting 17 August 1903). In 1906 he then pioneered the first *bumiputera* modern organization, the Sarekat Prijaji (Priyayi Association). This organization was designed to assist Javanese youth to enter Western-style schools and financially support and house them in Batavia. With a membership of 700 *priyayi*, according to Tirto, the Sarekat Prijaji, like the Chinese Tiong Hoa Hwee Koan (Chinese Association, THHK, founded in 1900) and the Boedi Oetomo (of 1908), had education as its main concern.[9] Two years later, on 1 January 1907, Tirto launched the first newspaper owned and run by *bumiputera*: *Medan*

---

[7]   For such polarization in the Dutch camp, the so-called gap between the Batavia-based bureaucrat/theorist ethically inspired clique and the 'practical men' of the BB, see Archief Hazeu (H 1083), KITLV, and also G.L. Gonggrijp 1944:79, 96.
[8]   For Tirto's background, his STOVIA years and early career see *Medan Prijaji* 3(1909):54, 667-9, 749 and Pramoedya Ananta Toer 1988a:22-9, 32-47.
[9]   For *Soenda Berita* (Sundanese News) see *Pemberita Betawi*, no. 185 (14 August 1903), and Pramoedya Ananta Toer 1988a:48-51. For the Sarekat Prijaji, its founding committee and its 700-strong priyayi membership see *Medan Prijaji* 3(1909):7-14 and Pramoedya Ananta Toer 1988a: 112-4.

Prijaji (Priyayi's Forum). This paper's circulation, with its political column (Bagian Politiek), soared to the unprecedented number of two thousand subscriptions. In April of the same year Tirto established the *Soeloeh Keadilan* (Torch of Justice), a monthly, like *Medan Prijaji*, that attracted monetary and moral support from well-placed *priyayi* civil servants, prosperous *haji* and wealthy Chinese alike. Equally well supported, with a financial contribution coming from the Dutch Queen Mother Emma von Waldeck-Pyrmont, was Tirto's women's periodical *Poetri Hindia* (Daughters of the Indies), appearing in June 1908.[10] All these pioneering developments caused Indonesia's foremost prose writer, Pramoedya Ananta Toer, to devote a political biography to Tirto in 1985 entitled *Sang Pemula*, The Initiator.

Tirto's endeavours focusing on the *priyayi* and their role as precursors of progress were not the only ones in the Dutch colony at that time. Wahidin Soediro Hoesoedo, a *priyayi desa* (village priyayi) by origin and a *dokter jawa* (Java-trained physician) by profession, was a spare-time journalist (in Djokja, he edited the Javanese journal *Retnodhoemilah*) who became a social activist. He functioned, in 1908, as the *pater intellectualis* behind the founding of Boedi Oetomo, a Javanist cultural association and very much *priyayi*-oriented (Shiraishi 1990:35, 38). R.M.T. Koesoemo Oetojo, Ngawi's *regent*, in the *Pewarta Prijaji* (Priyayi's Bulletin) he edited during 1901-1903, called for *priyayi* solidarity, for more Javanese schools, for scholarships 'for all *priyayi*', while devoting much of the journal's content to matters of interest to civil service *priyayi*.[11] He was also one of the influences in Boedi Oetomo's emergence and subsequent elitist conservatism, when younger, more progressive, founding members of the Soetomo and Tjipto Mangoenkoesoemo ilk lost ground to older, more entrenched *priyayi* interests. This trend demonstrated the generational and social gap between older, more traditional, high *ningrat priyayi* and young neo-*priyayi* or low *priyayi*. The former, at the apex of the Javanese social ladder, by virtue of closer contact with Dutch authorities and higher education, sensed the horizons of their class. But they remained more aware of the confining, even comforting, aspects of these boundaries than of their unifying potential. The neo-*priyayi*, however, taking advantage of the expansion of education, government, commerce and industry, became seri-

---

10   For the *Medan Prijaji* (Priyayi's Arena) founding see *Medan Prijaji* 3(1909):7-14, and Pramoedya Ananta Toer 1988a:55-8. For *Medan Prijaji*'s 2,000 subscriptions see Dr Rinkes' report to the Governor-General of 19 February 1912, in Pramoedya Ananta Toer 1988a:73. For *Soeloeh Keadilan* (Torch of Justice) see *Medan Prijaji* 4(5 March 1910):100, and Pramoedya Ananta Toer 1988a:56. For *Poetri Hindia* (Daughters of the Indies) see Pramoedya AnantaToer 1988a:88-93; for its catering to wives and relatives of highly placed *priyayi* see *Poetri Hindia* no. 1(15 January 1909), and *Medan Prijaji* 3(1909):744-5.
11   Nagazumi 1972:15. For Koesoemo Oetojo see bijlage of his son's (Moorianto) typescript autobiography, pp. 6-11.

ously involved in tapping the cohesive resources inherent in what was still a 'nation in embryo' – a 'nation', moreover, where both these elites accounted for but a minute section of the indigenous populace, while the masses of the people, the *wong cilik*, that is the illiterate peasants and labourers, were even more narrowly encapsulated in environments of near-feudal oppression and mounting economic confusion.[12]

The split within Boedi Oetomo

So, Boedi Oetomo, established in 1908 by young lower *priyayi*, intent on imparting more swiftly and widely the fruits of associationism that they themselves had enjoyed at the STOVIA, changed course. It was transformed into a mainly socio-cultural organization for mostly Javanese professional people and civil servants. It thereby repelled young and dissatisfied adherents, who soon began to involve themselves with other forms of political activity. The entrenchment of the old guard in Boedi Oetomo and the subsequent founding of the even more archaic Regentenbond (Regents' Union), later renamed Sedio Moelio (Sublime Aim), were developments much regretted by Mas Tirto, who, in protest, resigned from the Bandoeng Afdeeling Twee (second chapter) of Boedi Oetomo. He also wrote a 'Peringatan' (Reminder) in *Medan Prijaji*, warning his readers against Boedi Oetomo's appeal to upper-crust Javanese and lack of interest in the plight of the downtrodden.[13] His own Sarekat Prijaji, he stated, though resembling Boedi Oetomo in aim, was intended to appeal to a far broader audience than the upper-Javanese ethnic community alone. *Medan Prijaji*, in that effort, wrote in 'Maleisch' (the Indies *lingua franca*), instead of the Dutch or Javanese used initially in Boedi Oetomo's publications. He also attempted to dissuade *priyayi* youth from aspiring to become civil servants, and derided some civil servants for being *lintah darah* (bloodsuckers), and for prostituting their wives all too eagerly to the *galon-galon gondol* (the uniformed Dutch).[14]

Soon, Mas Tirto was to abandon all hopes of the *priyayi* heading a mass movement. The Sarekat Prijaji he had founded lapsed after a few years, so he searched for another cementing force to crystallize the aspirations of the *wong cilik*, the paupers of Java's crowded *kampung*, both urban and rural. He

[12]   This is the theme of Scherer 1975, particularly Chapter 1. For the 'nation in embryo' see Shiraishi 1990:32.
[13]   See Pramoedya Ananta Toer 1988a:119-21. Tirto's 'Peringatan' is in *Medan Prijaji* 3(1909): 151.
[14]   Tirto's advice to young *priyayi* is in *Medan Prijaji* 3(1909):613. For allegations against corrupt *priyayi* see *Pantjaran Warta* no. 192(28 August 1911), and *Medan Prijaji* 3(1909):759-60.

found it not in the civil service *priyayi* but in what he later termed the *kaum mardika* (free independent community): the middle class of traders, farmers, labourers and craftsmen, not in government service, adhering to Islam, the religion of the vast majority of the indigenous people of the Indies.[15] Here, he was predating Soekarno's *marhaen* concept of the late 1920s somewhat, though with Tirto placing more emphasis upon the crucial role the indigenous Muslim trading class was to play in the *pergerakan*. This was a class he was eager to link up with the more experienced, more professionally sophisticated Arab trading element of the colony to together stem the tide of growing Chinese commercial competition and to modernize the old mercantile standards still prevailing in the indigenous world of commerce.

The politicization of Islam

So, on Tirto's initiative, a meeting on 27 March 1909 at his house in Buitenzorg (or Bogor), attended by indigenous and Arab traders, saw the founding of the Sarikat Dagang Islamiah (Islamic Commercial Association, or SDI). The SDI aimed at 'serving Muslims of all races in the Indies' and at setting up branches 'anywhere in the Dutch East Indies'. In the SDI executive Arab traders were well represented. They were also the major financial donors, with four members of the well-established Badjenet family serving as president, treasurer and two of the commissioners. Tirto served in what Toer termed 'the comical twin position of secretary/adviser'.[16] On 5 April 1909, a building at Tandjakan Empang in Bogor was officially opened to serve as the SDI's head office. The ceremony was attended by all the important local authorities, led by Bogor's assistent-resident C.J. Feith. Feith was offered the position of patron of the SDI following the governor-general's recognition of the new association (Pramoedya Ananta Toer 1988a:123). Dr D.A. Rinkes of 'Inlandsche Zaken' (he was to succeed Hazeu as adviser of this bureau of 'native affairs' in 1913), never a supporter of Tirto, whom he considered a 'far too fraudulent troublemaker', claimed that the SDI, troubled by withdrawal of Arab donations, had stopped its activities within a few months of its inception (Van der Wal 1967:17). Rinkes, in the same missive to Governor-General Idenburg, asserted that the notion of mobilizing 'the nation in embryo' – a pergerakan concept Tirto had, editorially, done much to popularize – through the Islam trader element had come to nought. This

---

[15]   For Tirto's *kaum merdika* concept see Pramoedya Ananta Toer 1988a:121-2.
[16]   For the two quotes see *Medan Prijaji* 3(1909):190. For the Badjenet brothers see Pramoedya Ananta Toer 1988a:123-5, and D.A. Rinkes' 24 August 1912 letter to Idenburg, in Van der Wal 1967:91.

was denied by Tirto, in his periodical, claiming an overall Java membership of twenty thousand.[17] When Tirto became active in Solo during 1911, Rinkes was again swift to assert that, 'by using the more favourable situation in Solo to save his collapsed [Bogor] kongsie', and 'present it, there, as the mother organization of the Solo branch [...] Tirto managed to fool many people, the press, but above all, the Resident'.[18] It is no accident that Rinkes singled out Resident G.F. van Wijk, since it was Van Wijk who, instead of being fooled, asserted that it was Tirto and not Hadji Samanhoedi who stood at the cradle of what was to become Java's first mass party: the Sarekat Islam (SI, Islam Association). This was an opinion Soerakarta's resident shared with some prominent Javanese nationalists, familiar with the local socio-political scene.[19]

The Sarekat Islam: Java's first mass party

Originally stemming from needs among Arab, Sumatran and Javanese Islamic traders to protect their commercial interests against growing Chinese competition and hindrances, put in their way by the colonial administration, the association Jam Yat Khan was founded in Batavia around 1904-1905. This was followed by the Tirto-inspired groupings listed above. These latter initiatives, together with Tirto's continued dominance of opinion vented in the indigenous-language press, caused the colonial government to take steps to remove him from the political scene. Here the authorities pursued the same deradicalization measures that they had adopted earlier with Boedi Oetomo, with attempts to swerve the Sarekat Dagang Islamiah leadership toward more manageable and accommodating policies. Mainly through the machinations of the then acting adviser for 'native affairs', Rinkes, to whom Governor-General Idenburg lent an all too willing ear, Tirto was sent into exile to Ambon after being tried for libel: an action made considerably easier

[17]   See *Medan Prijaji* 4-9 (5 March 1910):105-6. The number of SDI members is exaggerated according to Adam 1984:224, note 44; for Rinkes's allegations see letter of 24 August 1912 in Van der Wal 1967:91.
[18]   Van der Wal 1967:87, 96. See also Verbaal 9 August 1913, B 13 letter Rinkes to Governor-General, 23 May 1913 and Verbaal 28 May 1913, no. 9, 'De Sarekat Dagang Islam in de Residentie Soerakarta', Mr. 2301/1912.
[19]   Solo's resident G.F. van Wijk contradicts Rinkes's opinion in two letters to the governor-general, dated 11 August and 11 November 1912 and states that Tirto founded the local SDI branch; see Van der Wal 1967:84, 96. Similar conclusions are held by Marco Kartodikromo in his 'R.M. Tirto Adhi Soerjo', *Sinar Hindia*, 12 December 1918 and by Tjipto Mangoenkoesoemo 1927: 10-1. For this source, though listed with its title incomplete, see Wertheim 1986 and Pramoedya Ananta Toer 1988a:139, 151.

by the draconian press laws of that time.[20] This, however, was not before he had formulated a new set of statutes for the association, to be named henceforth Sarekat Islam. He also authorized Hadji Samanhoedi to assume leadership of the association, a position Samanhoedi was to relinquish five years later in favour of the more charismatic Oemar Said Tjokroaminoto of Soerabaja. This shift, causing Soerabaja to become a Sarekat Islam stronghold, was keenly appreciated by the HBS student Soekarno, since he boarded during his entire HBS sojourn with the Tjokro family, first at Gang Peneleh VII, no. 29/31 just west of the European cemetery at Soerabaja's Kerkhoflaan and then at Plampitan, a stone's throw away from the former home, during the latter part of 1919 to mid-1921. Tjokroaminoto was a *priyayi/santri* inclined to politically exploit his double identity. It is to him that the young Soekarno owed his initial political grooming.[21]

Further growth and influence of Tjokroaminoto's Sarekat Islam

With the disappearance of Tirto from the socio-political arena, to which he had contributed through his writings and through the organizations he pioneered, a new era of Javanese awakening was truly ushered in. In his footsteps, mounting numbers of younger political activists and journalists – the young Soekarno among them – would come forward, more oriented to a Java-wide mass party, and excited by the emerging world of the *pergerakan*.[22]

By stressing Islam-inspired religious and socio-cultural traditions as opposed to Christian/Dutch authority, in league with the bureaucratized *priyayi/ningrat* upper layer of regents (*regenten*) and the economically stronger Chinese, Sarekat Islam managed rather swiftly to catalyse the many latent forces dormant among the urban and rural sectors of Java. This process was much aided by the *pergerakan* propaganda of SI party organs such as *Saroetomo* of Soerakarta, *Oetoesan Hindia* of Soerabaja, *Sinar Djawa* of Semarang, *Pantjaran Warta* of Batavia and *Kaoem Moeda* of Bandoeng. The Sarekat Islam leadership had indeed quickly grasped the potential of urban press outlets in Java's major cities. So *Oetoesan Hindia* appeared on 1 January 1913, as an official SI organ edited by Tjokro himself. In Batavia the SI-owned printing house Sedio Leksono purchased *Pantjaran Warta* from the Chinese Seng Hoat

---

[20]   For Rinkes's manipulations see in particular Pramoedya Ananta Toer 1988a:140-2, 153-65, 180. For the 'supervision' of the press see Verbaal 2 June 1913 no. 2 and Verbaal 9 July 1913 O 11, also Wertheim 1986:465.
[21]   Interviews with Anwar Tjokroaminoto and Roeslan Abdoelgani, Jakarta, 15 August 1971; also Amelz 1952, I:55, Soekarno's 12 May 1951 letter in Amelz 1952, I:11-2.
[22]   Tirto's crucial and trail-blazing role in the *pergerakan* has been acknowledged by Pramoedya Ananta Toer 1985b:Ch. 4. See also Wertheim 1986:459-61 and De Vries 1919:88.

publishing company on 21 June 1913 with Goenawan, a former employee of Tirto's *Medan Prijaji*, becoming its editor. A similar deal was struck in Semarang, where toward the end of 1913 the SI chapter bought the printing press and the newspaper *Sinar Djawa* from the Hoang Thaij concern. The Solo-based *Saroetomo*, edited from 1912 to 1915 by Marco Kartodikromo, developed into one of the most outspoken SI party organs. In Bandoeng *Kaoem Moeda* was founded on 2 April 1912 by the Sumatran Abdoel Moeis and the Bantenese A.H. Wignjadisastra, with financial backing from Arab businessman Mohammad Djoenas.[23] Another source of inspiration for grass-roots support came from the huge SI rallies, patterned after the Indische Partij (IP) rallies orchestrated by Douwes Dekker. Even the more culturally and modernist-oriented sister organization Moehammadijah, led by Hadji Achmad Dachlan in Djokjakarta, thought it wise to halt SI expansion in its own bailiwick by securing the SI chair (by Dachlan himself) in that city. By March 1913, at the first SI congress, held in Soerakarta, the number of SI branches had reached 48, of which 42, representing a total membership of 200,000, had sent delegates to the congress.[24]

However, all this did not mean that a cohesive organizational structure emerged at the same time. The regional distinctions, particularly in Java, were too great an obstacle to surmount. The initially strong *priyayi* element being whittled down by pressure exerted by the government, and the government's adoption of piecemeal legal recognition for local SI chapters, instead of granting immediate corporate status to a central SI executive body, naturally stood in the way of a strong organization developing. Organizational grip upon Java's rural sector after the first euphoric years also diminished rather rapidly. The social distance between Java's *desa* (villages) and the supra-village sphere remained too large a gap to bridge. Peasant resistance to private landed estates and the heavy burdens exerted by both European and Chinese landlords, and the general unrest in sugar-growing areas were issues the Sarekat Islam left largely unexploited.[25] To exert effective control over

---

[23]   *Bescheiden Sarekat Islam* 1913:9-11; *Pemberita Betawi*, no. 141(23 June 1913); *Sinar Djawa*, no. 19(24 January 1914); Letter of resident of Solo to Governor-General, dated 24 May 1913, no. 73/S, Verbaal 9 August 1913 B 13; Verbaal 8 May 1916, no. 55, Verbaal 8 December 1916, no. 58.

[24]   For Moehammadijah and the Djokja Sarekat Islam see letters resident of Djokjakarta to Governor-General, dated 20 April 1913 no. 4252/21a and 16 May 1913 no. 65, Verbaal 13 August 1913 B 13. For the first Sarekat Islam congress see Soerjosoeparta's 'Verslag van het Congres van de Sarekat Islam op Zondag 23 Maart 1913, gehouden in de Stadstuin Sriwedari te Soerakarta', dated 25 March 1913 in Verbaal 9 August 1913 B 13, and Sartono Kartodirdjo 1975:304-7.

[25]   For non-recognition of the Centrale Sarekat Islam see Verbaal 12 July 1913 no. 5 and *Javasche Courant* no. 56 (15 July 1913). For the private landed estates and the sugar-growing areas see, for instance, Verbaal 27 June 1917 no. 2 (about the Petodjo estate), and Besoeki's resident's report to director of Binnenlandsch Bestuur of 25 January 1917, Verbaal 5 September 1917 no. 20.

such a loose arrangement of urban and rural SI chapters remained an impossible task to perform, even for such a charismatic orator as Tjokroaminoto. Years later, on 17 March 1983 to be exact, Mohammad Roem confided to Bob Hering that prior to the political ascendancy of Tjokro, political speakers adapted their oratorical style to the *bangsawan* stage-plays, which in turn were largely derived from Western theatre, with gesture, facial expression and imagery being somewhat formal if not mechanical. The great innovation in verbal delivery made by Tjokro, and then adopted and further developed by Soekarno, was tuning their oratorical skills to the well-known fashion of recitation as performed by the *dalang* in the popular *wayang* theatre-plays. This novel approach ensured that both traditional imagery and traditional sonorities were utilized to the utmost, thus registering an unprecedented appeal to their audiences by these two masters of oratory.[26]

So, with this new technique and linked to the two important socio-cultural identities, *priyayi* and *santri*, Tjokro's prestige soared. No one ever dared openly confront him, nor did anyone question his rapport with the masses, causing Dutch opponents to label him 'the truly uncrowned king of Java'. Nonetheless, Tjokro was not able to achieve effective political control, even in his own bailiwick of Soerabaja (Tichelman 1985:39, 382). He chose, instead, to cultivate the image of the restrained, dignified and widely respected leader, responsible for party unanimity, often leaving thorny problems for others to solve. This was a pattern his first son-in-law Soekarno would adopt years later with some modification. Formlessness at the top adhered to by Tjokro, dependence on Arab and Chinese capital and the lack of a clearly defined social platform or of useful economic initiatives continued to plague the SI to the end (Mul 1988:32, note 1, 44; Tichelman 1985:37-8). KNIL captain W. Muurling, head of the colonial Politieke Inlichtingen Dienst (PID, Political Intelligence Branch), portrayed Tjokro as someone who

> cloaks his dignity in haziness [...] speculating simply upon his magnetic effect upon the masses [...] with an ill-defined attitude leaving anyone to guess what he really aims for, and yet with no one, except Semaoen, daring to resist him occasionally.[27]

For the abuse occurring on these estates see also Douwes Dekker 1908. See also for government reactions, Verbaal 12 October 1912 N 14.

[26]   17 March 1983 interview with Moh. Roem in Jakarta. See also Amelz 1952, I: 68, citing P.F. Dahler '[where Tjokro,] with his great and forceful baritone voice that carried easily over all those thousands, who, quite fascinated, hung literally on his lips, was able to get his message across convincingly and warmly', and claiming Tjokro as Soekarno's mentor in speech-making.

[27]   Politieke Inlichtingen Dienst (PID) report no. 154, 20 October 1917 in Verbaal 15 May 1918 no. 64.

Yet internal developments were to play a role in the growth of a complex of disparate urban SI sections, where some influential personalities such as Abdoel Moeis, Goenawan and Hasan Djajadiningrat carved out personal domains of their own. By the end of 1912, two important urban SI centres had emerged: one in Bandoeng, the other in Batavia, where Goenawan used Tirto's hotel Samirono as a base for his manifold political activities. An organizer of the Batavia SI chapter since late 1912, he also, in 1913, opted for membership of the Batavia branches of Boedi Oetomo and the Indische Partij. Through his initiatives in the area of cooperatives, and his popularity among white-collar civil servants, and backed up by his editorship of *Pantjaran Warta,* he gradually expanded his influence throughout West Java and South Sumatra, even to the extent of making that vast area an autonomous SI region under his personal sway. This attempt was finally frustrated by mid-1916 by combined forces marshalled by Tjokro, Abdoel Moeis and Hasan Djajadiningrat, with Hasan Djajadiningrat replacing Goenawan as the West Java regional head of the SI.[28]

In Bandoeng two SI chapters came into being, one founded by Samanhoedi's brother but soon overshadowed by the branch led by journalists, such as the radically inclined Pakoe Alam prince Soewardi Soerjaningrat. Soewardi Soerjaningrat, chairman of that chapter and also editor of Douwes Dekker's periodical *De Expres,* was soon to form with Douwes Dekker and Tjipto Mangoenkoesoemo the triumvirate leadership of the radical but short-lived Indische Partij.

In the SI chapter led by Soewardi, the more moderate Abdoel Moeis and A.H. Wignjadisastra, both co-founders of *Kaoem Moeda,* served respectively as vice-chairman and secretary. The branch, soon connected with the Indische Partij, developed a radicalism independent of Tjokro, with aims to transform the SI into a non-Muslim Sarekat Hindia. Such aims were also propagated by the branch's newly appearing journal *Hindia Sarekat.* However, these aims eventually drove Abdoel Moeis away and into the fold of the associationist centre. In 1916, after the fall of Goenawan, Moeis became vice-president of Centrale Sarekat Islam. In 1917 this was followed by membership of the Indië Weerbaar deputation to Holland and editorship of the Batavia-based *Neratja* (as of 8 September 1917), a journal inspired by Hazeu, founded by Hadji Agoes Salim and Soetan Toemenggoeng, an employee of Inlandsche Zaken, and subsidized by the colonial government. Moeis's Batavia moves were most likely inspired by the fact that the Volksraad was soon to open in that city.[29]

---

[28] *Sarekat Islam Congres* 1916:1, 62, 64, 89; Sartono Kartodirdjo 1975:7-15, 18-25; Mr. 615/1917; letters of resident Batavia to governor-general, 10 May 1913 and 27 May 1913, in Verbaal 9 August 1913 B 13.

[29] Soerjosoeparta's report in Verbaal 9 August 1913 B 13; Politieke Inlichtingen Dienst (PID)-reports: no. 127, 30 August 1917, no. 129, 5 September 1917, no. 130, 8 September 1917, no.

Yet, until 1917, and in spite of all its weak points, the SI, in its steady evolution toward a nationalist peoples' movement, so far had no serious competitor. However, it started to respond more and more to the criticism of the tiniest of all political groupings in the Indies: the small band of Dutch radical socialists organized in the Indische Sociaal-Democratische Vereeniging (ISDV, Indies Social Democratic Association).[30] With access to the Indonesian urban world of politics far out of proportion to its small membership, the ISDV, increasingly aware of the growing socialist-inclined core operating from within the SI itself, had hopes of gaining control of the still inert SI masses (Tichelman 1985:49; Mul 1988:45-6). For Sneevliet, the energetic leader of the IDSV, also quite active in the Semarang-based railway union, the Vereeniging van Spoor- en Tramweg-Personeel (VSTP, Association of Rail and Tramway Personnel), through his editorship of the VSTP organ *De Volharding* (Perseverance), one issue was primary. The fight against colonial/capitalist exploitation could be effectively waged only by class-conscious trade unions and political parties, representing the working masses of Java. The opinion that Sarekat Islam provided the key to such a development dawned slowly.

The pioneer here was Ir Asser Baars, a teacher at Soerabaja's Koningin Emma School, and Sneevliet's trusted lieutenant and theoretician at the ISDV. Adequately fluent in Malay, Baars was a frequent visitor at Tjokro's Gang Peneleh home, conversing often with the Indonesian inmates of Iboe Tjokro's boarding house, Soekarno among them.[31] To Baars, and somewhat later also to Sneevliet, it became clear that increasing Indonesian membership of such organizations as Semarang's VSTP[32] and propagating leftist ideals and principles among VSTP/SI members, facilitated infiltration into the SI. So, later in 1917, they erected in Soerabaja, and also in Batavia and Semarang, a sister organization of the ISDV, the Sarekat Rajat Sama Rata

---

137, 21 September 1917, no. 156, 25 October 1917 in Verbaal 15 May 1918 no. 64; *Oetoesan Hindia*, 14, 15, 17 September 1917, bijlage of Verbaal 20 April 1918, no. 28; *Sarekat Islam Congres* 1919: 109-13; Verbaal 20 June 1917, no. 5.

[30]   The 'people's movement' features of Sarekat Islam were recognized as early as 1913 by Snouck Hurgronje. See Gobée and Adriaanse 1962, III:2009. For the ISDV see Tichelman's superb documentary collection (1985).

[31]   Mul 1988:32, 44. Also A. Baars, 'Het S.I. congres te Bandoeng' in *Het Vrije Woord*, 25 June 1916:165-7. This was the first issue of *HVW* completely devoted to the SI and its congress, a congress attended by Baars and VSTP/ISDV/SI members Semaoen and Mohamad Joesoef. For Baars' visits to Tjokro's home and the influence exerted upon Soekarno, see Amelz 1952, I: 55; Legge 1984:54; McVey 1965:363, note 36 and Soekarno himself in his 1 June 1945 Pantja Sila address, included in Rachmawati Soekarno 1984:14.

[32]   For the VSTP see *De Volharding* 20 September 1917:1 and the issue of 20 April 1918:1, where numbers of Indonesian and European members are listed as follows: 4,075 and 834 in December 1916, and 4,521 and 609 in April 1918. For earlier VSTP developments and Semaoen's spectacular rise in it, see Peters-Hesselink 1971:3-9, 12-3, 24-5.

Hindia Bergerak (Peoples' League for the Common Struggle in the Indies). As its title suggests, it was a league of Indonesians to form a bridge to the ISDV; its clearly defined platform was something still lacking in the SI. Here, they were helped by the tendency among politically alert Indonesians to opt for dual or even multi-party membership.[33]

The challenge by the Indische Sociaal-Democratische Vereeniging

To challenge or inspire politically alert Indonesians to take the ISDV aims of struggle seriously, ISDV stalwart supporters stepped up opposition to the SI-supported indigenous militia (Indië Weerbaar, The Indies active and capable of self-defence) and Nationaal Comité plans. This latter short-lived platform had been initiated by Boedi Oetomo (BO) and aimed to coordinate the policies of BO, Centrale Sarekat Islam (CSI), Regentenbond (Union of Regents) and the four Prinsenbonden (Princes' Union of the Solo and Djokja courts) in view of the 1917 elections for the Volksraad (Larson 1987:79; Tichelman 1985:36, 559, note 56). However, the ISDV, prompted by news of the February revolution in Russia and Sneevliet's 'Zegepraal' article about it, started in earnest their struggle for control over the urban Sarekat Islam masses.[34] They achieved some measure of success.

The Semarang Sarekat Islam leadership changed hands from the more moderate VSTP/SI/ISDV member Mohamad Joesoef to the militant VSTP/SI/ISDV member Semaoen, Sneevliet's most adept pupil. The move was well prepared by the radical media of that city: *Sinar Djawa*, edited by Semaoen and Alimin, and also the region's Chinese-Malayan daily *Djawa Tengah*, sympathetic to the socialist cause. Semarang, with VSTP and ISDV party executive headquarters already located there, with Semaoen boosting the SI following from 1,700 (in 1916) to 20,000 in 1917, and with him leading a number of successful strikes, indeed looked like a 'red' bulwark. From here the SI elite was manoeuvred into accepting Semaoen on its Central Committee. The conflict between those who considered Islam the best basis for political action and the 'red Semarangers' who were against mixing politics with religion became serious.[35]

---

[33]   For the Soerabaja-based sister organization, see Mul 1988:51-3, and PID report no. 76, 21 May 1917, with bijlage, containing a police report of *assistent-wedana* Poedjo on that organization, dated 7 May 1917, in Verbaal 15 May 1918 no. 64.

[34]   Sneevliet's 'Zegepraal' article is reprinted in Tichelman 1985:464-7. For Indië Weerbaar see Teitler 1981:22-4; the PID reports no. 123, no. 127 in Mr. 177/1917, Verbaal 15 May 1918, no. 64.; issues of *Het Vrije Woord*, 10 October 1916:76, 10 February 1917:75, 10 March 1917:97, 10 May 1917:144, 10 July 1917:186-7; Mul 1988:46-9; Peters-Hesselink 1971:21-2.

[35]   See Peters-Hesselink 1971:25, 29; Mul 1988:62 and Semaoen 1966:61. For *Sinar Djawa*, later

At the same time some dents were made in Batavia and Soerabaja, Tjo-kro's Soerabajan Centraal SI bulwark. In the milieu of the Batavian SI, the ISDV initially gained influence through the regionally powerful SI vice-chairman Raden Goenawan, the 'Tjokroaminoto of West Java'. Goenawan, close to Semaoen and the SI's left wing, opposed the indigenous militia project and had joined the ISDV at the end of 1917. At that time, he had lost regional clout to Hasan Djajadiningrat, the brother of the *regent* of Serang (Banten). However, the Batavian SI/ISDV link remained intact, since Hasan Djajadiningrat joined the ISDV and was placed on that party's executive (at the fifth general ISDV meeting of 18-20 May 1918).[36]

Baars, the first of the ISDV to seriously tackle agrarian issues and eager to explore the SI's base of popular support, had meanwhile, together with J.H. Soeharijo, ex-chairman of the Soerabaja SI branch, stirred up action around the expulsion of peasants from private landed estates near Soerabaja. Soeharijo had left the SI in 1916 to become vice-chairman of the Soerabaja ISDV. Around the same time, the contacts with the Tjokro household, of which young Soekarno formed part, were laid. During his sessions with his two biographers Solichin Salam and Cindy Adams, Soekarno gives proof of the formative impact of these meetings with radical left foremen of the *pergerakan*, Dutch and Indonesian alike; he was particularly impressed by Baars and Alimin (Solichin Salam 1966:41-2; Adams 1965:40-1; Utrecht 1969:11).

At the time Soekarno also witnessed the founding of Soeharijo's association Porojitno (the forerunner of the Semarang-based Perhimpoenan Kaoem Boeroeh dan Tani, League of Workers and Peasants) which with its mouthpiece *Selompret Hindia* and ISDV organizations such as the Sarekat Rajat Sama Rata Hindia Bergerak and its newsletter *Soeara Merdika* began to rival the local SI organizations. In that city progress was also made toward organizing soldiers' and sailors' unions, a highly sensitive issue for the colonial authorities.[37] These developments boosted Sneevliet's popularity among Indonesian radicals, his esteem already heightened by his spirited defence of persecuted Indonesian journalists, notably Batavia's *Pantjaran Warta* editor Mas Marco Kartodikromo, formerly linked with Tirto's *Medan Prijaji* and SI's Soerakarta journal *Saroetomo*. Mas Marco had been a leading SI member during 1914-1915, but in 1918 had become an executive of both the Semarang ISDV branch and that city's daily *Sinar Djawa*. However, between June 1917 and February 1918 he had been persecuted and then incarcerated,

---

in 1918 renamed *Sinar Hindia*, and *Djawa Tengah* see 'Persoverzicht: Januari-medio Maart 1918' in Mr. 264/1918.

36   Document 101 and note 1 in Tichelman 1985:335-6, 57, note 71.

37   See PID reports no. 71 of 12 May 1917 and bijlage, and no. 76 and bijlage Mr. 99/1917 in Verbaal 15 May 1918 no. 64; Mul 1988:47-8, 51-3, 81-2; McVey 1965:42; *Het Vrije Woord* 25 July 1916:193, 25 October 1916:16 and 10 March 1918:136-7.

mainly due to his series of articles 'Sama rasa dan sama rata' appearing in the February 1917 issue of *Pantjaran Warta*, his brochure *Boekoe sebaran jang pertama* printed in The Hague in November 1915, and his article 'Boekan Persdelict tetapi Klachtdelict' where he defended Sneevliet's ISDV actions against the colonial government.[38]

As for Sneevliet, his prestige was further magnified by his 'Zegepraal' piece and the defiant defence of it during his trial, followed by his acquittal, which, however, solidified conservative opinion favouring his expulsion from the Indies. Years later, in 1929, Soekarno told Roeslan Abdoelgani in Bandoeng that to really understand him, 'you must first read *Het Proces* by Sneevliet' (Baars and Sneevliet 1991:xxxvi). Sneevliet's extradition finally took place by vice-regal fiat, on 20 December 1918,[39] in the wake of the establishment of the Soerabajan Soldiers' and Sailors' Council, labelled by PID chief Muurling as 'red guardist soldiers and sailors inspired by Soviet initiatives'.[40] Earlier, in September 1917, the Batavian right-wing faction, true to its so-called 'parliamentary' approach platform, had separated from the ISDV. It accused the ISDV of revolutionary anarchism and cavalier leadership, thus laying the blame on Baars and Sneevliet.[41]

The impact of the Volksraad upon local political organizations

Like the local and regional councils described earlier, the Volksraad was a product of both the decentralization furore and the ethically inspired associationism existing during the early years of the twentieth century. In 1916 the Dutch Minister for the Colonies introduced legislation for the creation of a Koloniale Raad (Colonial Council), a representative body to advise the governor-general of the Indies. It was to consist of representatives of the entire Netherlands East Indies community – Indigenous, Foreign Oriental and European – and would be freed as far as possible from constraints emanating from the immensely cumbersome overseas bureaucratic apparatus, seen by some as obstacles to the development of the Indies as a nation.[42]

---

[38]   Mr. 550/1917; Verbaal 8 May 1916 no. 55, Verbaal 8 November 1917 no. 36, Pramoedya Ananta Toer 1988b:200-9; *Indische Gids* 37(1917):1466-7, 1079-82.

[39]   Mr. 174/1918 in Verbaal 13 November 1918, Verbaal 14 February 1919 no. 20; Baars and Sneevliet 1991:xv-xxxvi.

[40]   Muurling's 'Geheim verslag' no. 41, 1918: 'Nota omtrent de revolutionnaire socialistische actie hier te lande', 29 May 1918, Mr. 258/1918, Verbaal 6 January 1919 no. 16; Mul 1988:83-5.

[41]   For the ISDV/ISDP split, see Tichelman 1985:108-10; *Het Indische Volk* 1-1(3 November 1917):1-2; PID reports no. 130, 8 September 1917 in Mr. 187/1917 and no. 134, 13 September 1917 in Mr. 190/1917, both in Verbaal 15 May 1918 no. 64.

[42]   Chailley-Bert 1900:311 termed Java as 'un paradis des fonctionnaires'; see also Fock in

The debate prior to ratification had mainly revolved around the extent of the power to be vested in the new council and the procedures of election and appointment to it. The Minister had envisaged the governor-general consulting the council as much as possible and being required to do so in matters of the budget and loans, but without any actual legislative powers residing in the new body. Some deputies were instrumental in obtaining a gradual extension of the body's jurisdiction, while others argued about the new council's electoral basis and about the educational requirements for electors. In the end consensus was reached on the new council, now renamed Volksraad (People's Council), following the example of South Africa's Volksraad, a body similarly racially and culturally diversified. It was to have 38 members, excluding the European chairman. Its members, half of whom were non-European, were to be partly elected by local electoral colleges and partly appointed by the governor-general. However, its electoral base, like the municipal and regional councils described earlier, was extremely narrow since only an infinitesimal number of electors were involved. For instance, in 1921, twelve Indigenous and twelve European and Foreign Oriental members of the Volksraad were elected by an electoral college of 594 Europeans, 451 Indigenous and 81 Foreign Orientals. It was therefore hardly representative, and with so little indigenous influence it deserved to be seen as no more than a council with some quasi representative features. It was at best an embryonic parliament where some independent opinions could be aired publicly. Moreover, the Volksraad, which was opened in May 1918 in Weltevreden, had little power: it was consulted on budgetary matters, it could give advice, but it had no decision-making powers at all.

Nonetheless, the Volksraad became the forum for the quite rapidly developing political associations of the Indies. Its establishment in 1916 had caused a relaxation of laws governing political activity similar to earlier developments with local councils. And so it encouraged the formation of new parties and the further politicization of existing parties. Prior to and during the elections for the first Volksraad, existing parties such as the SI, BO, ISDV and Insulinde intensified their activities. For instance, in 1916 the ISDV began to approach SI and Insulinde hoping to mobilize what Sneevliet termed 'indigenous revolutionary sentiments' (Cohen Stuart 1946:10). In response to that, prominent associationists like Hazeu and Van Hinloopen Labberton tried to tie the indigenous political leadership more firmly to the government by promoting schemes of an indigenous militia-based defence for the Indies – only to see their attempts countered by ISDV foremen claiming that such an indigenous mobilization could only be decided by a fully

---

Handelingen Staten Generaal Tweede Kamer 1916-17:62 and H.J. Benda's treatment of the *Beamtenstaat* in Benda 1972:236-52.

fledged representative parliamentary body (Tichelman 1985:23).

More mildly conservative elements formed the Nederlandsch-Indische Vrijzinnige Bond (NIVB, Netherlands Indies Liberal Union) in 1916, followed by two confessional parties: the Christelijk-Ethische Partij (CEP, Christian Ethical Party) in 1917, and the Indische Katholieke Partij (IKP, Indies Catholic Party) in 1918. Partly patterned after Dutch parties and ideologies, they were associationist in the sense of a gradual social development and of cooperation among all the ethnic groups of the colony. They also broadly supported a degree of autonomy for the colony – based, however, upon continuing solidarity between Holland and the Indies. They all allowed Indonesian membership. An indigenous Serikat Soematera (SS, Sumatra Association), supporting autonomy through a similar evolutionary process, was founded in 1918. In 1919 followed the founding of still more conservative parties, the Politiek-Economische Bond (PEB, Political Economic Association) and the Indo-Europeesch Verbond (IEV, Indo-European Union) (Van den Bijllaardt 1933:14-22). However, among the more radical European political sector a rift occurred in 1917. The Indische Sociaal-Democratische Partij (ISDP, Indies Social Democratic Labour Party), a right-wing rump of the ISDV, was established, thus demonstrating mounting concern about the radical direction adopted by the ISDV in the wake of the Russian revolution. Originally a section of the Dutch Sociaal-Democratische Arbeiders Partij (SDAP, Social Democratic Labour Party), it became an independent Indies party, but still based its programme on the 'colonial chapter' of the Dutch SDAP (Cohen Stuart 1946:8). Within a mere three years, this radical rump reorganized itself into Asia's first communist party, Perserikatan Komunis di Hindia (Communist League of the Indies, later renamed Partai Komunis Indonesia).

The parties NIVB, CEP, IKP and ISDP, all represented in the first Volksraad, in session during 1918-1921, though all multi-racial in composition, were in fact a reflection of the Dutch party system in the 'mother country'. The NIVB, with five European and five Indonesian members, formed the strongest bloc in the first Volksraad. Next came the other multi-racial parties: CEP with three members, IKP and ISDP with one member each, and the NIP with two (Tjipto and J.J.E. Teeuwen), and Insulinde with one (Abdoel Rivai). The wholly Indonesian parties Boedi Oetomo, Serikat Soematera and Sarekat Islam had four, one and two member-delegates, respectively. Not linked to any party were eight European, five Indonesian and three Foreign Oriental members.[43] According to the Volksraad secretary, that body 'left a progres-

---

[43]   *Tien jaar Volksraadarbeid 1918-1928*:53-65; *Indisch Verslag* 1924:23-7; 'De uitslag', *Indische Gids* 38(1918):715; 'Volkraads benoemingen', *Indische Gids* 38(1918):858; Visman 1941, I:82 reports that of the five NIVB indigenous members, two were also BO members and one an SI member.

sive impression, pressing for more reforms to be implemented, often quite vigorously' (Cohen Stuart 1946:9). Led by such speakers as Tjokro of the SI, Tjipto and Teeuwen of the NIP, Dr W.M.G. Schumann and Achmad Djajadiningrat (*regent* of Serang) of the liberal NIVB, and Ch.G. Cramer of the ISDP, the first Volksraad began to assert itself to such an extent that many within the European community, the government, and die-hard *sana* press circles feared to have drawn a Trojan Horse within the white-washed walls of the colonial edifice at Weltevreden's Pedjambon. Increasingly, there flowed within the Volksraad building a stream of criticism. This came from liberal and leftist deputies who made good use of the political immunity granted them and obviously were inspired by the dramatic revolutionary events occurring in Europe at that time. Teeuwen in particular linked the situation in Europe with the demand 'of guaranteeing for the Indies a politically independent peoples' existence'.[44]

Worried by a possible Troelstra-led socialist take-over in Holland, by demands for genuine reforms by the Cramer-initiated Radicale Concentratie and by the NIVB's 'urgency programme' demanding a directly elected Volksraad with extended powers, Governor-General Van Limburg Stirum issued the so-called 18 November declaration through his representative for general affairs in the Volksraad (Mr D. Talma). The declaration promised future modification of colonial administrative structures and foresaw – in vague wording – a shift in the centre of gravity in colonial matters passing from The Hague to Batavia.[45] Volksraad reaction was swift. It approved motions by Tjokroaminoto (and associates) and Achmad Djajadiningrat (and associates) seeking to establish full parliamentary powers for the Volksraad, with complete budgetary control and accountability of departmental heads to it rather than to the governor-general. The motions also insisted on guarantees for continuing decentralization and for a degradation of the Raad van Indië (Council of the Indies) to a mere advisery body serving the governor-general. A motion by Tjipto Mangoenkoesoemo (and associates) granting the right of inquiry was similarly referred to the Volksraad sections.[46] Despite the news of an improving situation in Holland, where the Troelstra-inspired agitation had quickly petered out, the Indies administration decided to placate aroused Volksraad tempers. So it first elaborated upon the very brief 18 November declaration as requested by the Volksraad and then appointed a Herzieningscommissie (Revision Commission of Inquiry) established by

---

[44] Visman 1941, I:79; *Handelingen Volksraad*, Tweede gewone zitting 1918-19:179, 206, 250.
[45] *Handelingen Volksraad*, Tweede gewone zitting 1918-19:209-10 for the NIVB's urgentieprogramma and Cramer's initiative. For Talma's statement: pp. 251-2 and Cohen Stuart 1938:295-8.
[46] For the Tjokro and Djajadiningrat motions: *Handelingen Volksraad*, Tweede gewone zitting 1918: Onderwerp 27, stuk 2 and stuk 4 respectively; for Tjipto's: Onderwerp 13, stuk 1.

Gouvernementsbesluit (Government Decree) of 17 December 1918, no. 1. This commission was to draft proposals for a further decentralization, a broader electoral base and the concentration of legislative powers in the Indies with a concise demarcation of the Volksraad's vested prerogatives and jurisdiction in these matters.[47] These concessions proved sufficient to cool down emotions in the Volksraad, particularly since the so-called democratic progressive bloc believed that victory had been achieved. Most of the Volksraad parties, with the NIVB in the forefront, welcomed the news of the Carpentier Alting commission. However, Abdoel Moeis (speaking for the Radicale Concentratie) was quick to point out that the promised reforms might well run the risk of being postponed indefinitely. This turned out to be a prophetic analysis, since Van Limburg Stirum found that his schemes – as well as most of the Herzienings Commission's recommendations – were ignored by the new conservative Minister of Colonies, the former BB director S. de Graaff.[48]

From Sarekat Islam to Partai Sarekat Islam

Meanwhile, within the Sarekat Islam camp, tension between the right wing led by Abdoel Moeis and Hadji Agoes Salim and radical left members under the sway of Semaoen, Darsono, Sosrokardono and Alimin increased. Also, Raden Pandji Sosrokardono, CSI secretary during 1916-1919 and founder in 1916 of the rather militant Perserikatan Pegawai Pegadian Boemipoetra (PPPB, Indigenous Pawnshop Workers), had in May 1919 at the PPPB congress, together with Alimin, proposed the establishment of a Vakcentrale (federation of trade unions). A federation of trade unions then called Persatoean Perserikatan Kaoem Boeroeh thereupon came into effect on 25 December 1919 in Djokjakarta (*Mededeelingen* 1920:4-5; Tichelman 1985:650).

All this faction-ridden potential was partly placated by the appeasing ploys of the centre, dominated by the chairman at that time, Tjokroaminoto. But the process eventually forced the SI chairman to depart somewhat from the road of accommodation and associationism in lieu of anti-colonial mass-party policies. During the third national SI congress held in Soerabaja, Tjokro announced plans to organize peasants and workers into trade unions, a move seen by most as a victory for ISDV members such as Semaoen,

---

[47]   *Verslag Commissie Herziening Staatsinrichting* 1920:xiii. Its preamble reflected the commission members' opinion: 'the course of political development lies in the direction of autonomy for the entire Indies' (p. 1); see also cable Van Limburg Stirum to Idenburg, 28 November 1918 about the commission's establishment chaired by mr J.H. Carpentier Alting, Verbaal 30 December 1919 T 11.
[48]   For Moeis: *Handelingen Volksraad*, Tweede gewone zitting 1918:520.

Darsono and Alimin. However, Tjokro in this matter was rather inspired by Agoes Salim. A trade union specialist, Agoes Salim had close ISDP contacts, particularly with Sam Koperberg, also referred to as Setan Merah, the Red Devil, in spite of his rather milder brand of socialism. Salim, probably urged by Koperberg, became an ISDP member in mid-1918.[49] The third SI congress, held in Soerabaja from 29 September to 6 October 1918, thus marked a significant shift to the left, with issues like independence, revolution and socialism being so widely stressed that it caused one conservative Dutch observer to remark that this congress marked the old SI as dead and buried (Petrus Blumberger 1920:25). The pendulum was to swing back, however, in the wake of the Toli-Toli (Central Celebes) and Garoet (West Java) disturbances, bringing disrepute to the CSI leadership and diminution of SI membership.

In Toli-Toli in the wake of a May 1919 SI propaganda tour by Moeis, some local people had refused to perform corvee duties, leading to the murder of a Dutch BB controller (*controleur*) when he attempted to enforce corvee obligations. Legal proceedings were commenced against Moeis for having instigated the assassination, while his credentials as a moderate CSI member were by now seriously questioned by many Dutch *ethici*, Hazeu and Rinkes among them. Far more serious were the disturbances in Garoet in July 1919, where a local *haji* named Hasan and his family resisted forced rice deliveries and were then shot and killed by police forces led by the *assistent-resident* of the Preanger. Further investigations in the area revealed the existence of a rather wide and secret SI network referred to as SI Bagian Kedoea or Afdeeling B (Section B), with clearly subversive aims. This discovery led to a massive police and judicial investigation now probing the existence of a possible Afdeeling B all over Java. This scenario did not materialize, but it did result in massive arrests and the closure of many local SI branches in West Java, as well as an exodus of many loyalist SI leaders and pious SI Arab and indigenous Muslim traders. All this truly shattered the lofty 'ethical' ideal of Indonesians being coached by the Dutch on the path of progress and assisted in that process by such enlightened and Western-oriented leaders as Tjokro and Moeis. In the wake of the Toli-Toli and Garoet upheavals, however, many Dutch *ethici* sincerely started to discredit Tjokro and Moeis, with the former being labelled as a 'dishonest, insincere, untrustworthy, weak and indecisive personality'. It is here that the knell was tolled of the 'ethical period' in the Indies.[50]

As to the faction-ridden climate within the SI, for a year or two some

[49]   *Sarekat Islam Congres* 1919; Petrus Blumberger, 'Hadji August Salim', Kabinet Nota, pp. 1-3, Verbaal 28 June 1930 D 15; Kwantes 1975:229.
[50]   For Toli-Toli and for the Garoet Afdeeling B and also for the resignation (in 1920) of Dr Hazeu, see *Mededeelingen* 1920:27-33; Hazeu Archief no. 72. For Tjokro and the disdain of the ethici for him, see Kwantes 1975:220-2.

sort of an uneasy truce existed between the two factions. Their differences of opinion, which Tjokro was unable to resolve, finally led to rupture brought about by the conservatives Salim and Moeis, both at that time linked with the government-sponsored periodical *Neratja*. With further radicalization and even militancy emerging under the banner of Indonesian communism and the young Indonesian trade union movement, a formal break with communist elements of the party became inevitable. In 1926, Soekarno, determined to bring Marxists and Muslims together again, recalled the split as follows:

> My heart is sad when I remember the dark and gloomy atmosphere in Indonesia some years ago, when I was witness to the outbreak of bitter hostilities between Marxists and Muslims, when I was witness to the division of our movement's forces into two warring factions. It is this struggle which fills the darkest pages of our history. It was this fratricidal struggle that dissipated all the force of our movement, which should otherwise have grown stronger and stronger. It was this struggle which set back our movement [by] several decades. (Soekarno 1969:50.)

In 1923 that process reached resolution when the Sarekat Islam changed itself from an open nationalist mass movement into a Pan-Islamic party with closed membership along religious lines, renamed Partai Sarekat Islam (PSI). With this move it restored cohesion among the remaining followers, but at the price of losing mass-party status and abandoning, forever, its position in the vanguard of Indonesia's political awakening. Their Marxist opponents, ideologically averse to communal politics, but ironically forcing upon Tjokroaminoto's Sarekat Islam that tighter girdle, were to fare no better. Pluralist-oriented calls for strikes and armed rebellion, where they struck root, were not able to stop the colonial repression unleashed by Governor-General Dirk Fock.[51] That these *pergerakan* activities ended in failure should not, however, be allowed to obscure the truly dynamic indigenous forces released by them. Nor should we ignore the achievements of the small band of men, both indigenous and expatriate, who were responsible for introducing and then spreading the message of revolutionary radicalism in the Indies. This message was not lost on the young Soekarno either, who would soon part ways in an ideological sense from his erstwhile political mentor, believing he was seeking refuge in a useless belief in cooperation – Tjokroaminoto's being willing to accept a Volksraad seat again if it was offered to him, for instance, while also turning the SI in a Pan-Islamic direction.[52] So, it was in Bandoeng, aptly termed by Soekarno 'the gateway to the West', that he, fur-

---

[51]   See, for instance, Koch 1950:88-92.
[52]   Dahm 1969:51 with Tjokro stating in his *Islam dan Socialisme*, Jakarta 1950, p. 111, that 'for achieving true socialism efforts must be primarily directed toward realizing the ideals of Pan-Islam'.

ther influenced by yet another brand of urban radical nationalists, conceived a non-cooperative political programme truly of his own making. Before we trace these developments in the next chapter devoted to Soekarno's Bandoeng years, we must first discuss the political role played in the Indies urban melting-pot environment by Indo and Chinese minority groups, small though they were, yet capable of rendering an impact.

The political emancipation of Indos and Chinese in the Indies

Smaller-scale mobilization, like Boedi Oetomo and Sarekat Islam, appealing to the interests of specific communities or socio-cultural groups, had occurred earlier. Again, the common generational factor, bringing increased numbers of school-age youth to the capital city and the major provincial cities, played a significant role. In these urban melting-pot environments the uniqueness of one's region or ethnic/cultural background combined with rising social expectations. Such feelings emerged, first of all, among mainly urbanized Indos[53] and Indonesian Chinese, both *singkeh* (newcomers) and *peranakan*. These two broad categories of Indonesian Chinese – 'pure' China-born *singkeh* and mixed-Indies born *peranakan* – were split not only by language but also by many other socio-cultural distinctions. Their elites had in the past carved out more or less secure niches, though at the lower rungs, in the colonial hierarchy, but felt aggrieved by developments in the wake of the 'liberal' policies after 1870, more particularly during the upward economic cycle of the 1890s. According to Veth, in 1900 there were 277,265 ethnic Chinese as against 28,746,638 indigenous people living in Java and Madoera. The 'more or less prosperous' layer of Chinese consisted of 66 owners of private landed estates, 320 sugar plantation entrepreneurs, and some 2,000 pawnshop and opium-distribution lessees, as well as 27,000 traders, the majority of whom were engaged in petty trade and peddling. During the 1890s, resentment against long-standing and new forms of racial discrimination accumulated, only this time it fuelled the emerging tide of ethnic consciousness.[54]

---

[53] For the Indo-European elite, a 'razor-thin part piercing the upper strata of the European group', see Van der Veur 1968.

[54] Veth 1899-1907, IV:105. For *singkeh* (pure) and *peranakan* (Indies-born, mixed) Chinese resentments see Go Gien Tjwan, 'Inleiding tot de memoires van Siauw Giok Tjhan', ms. Amsterdam 1981, pp. 39-41, and his 'Introduction' in Siauw Giok Tjhan 1982:v-vii.

Indo political consciousness grows

Among the Indos the 'May movement' of 1848 in Betawi had been a useful precedent. The years since that manifestation of Indo discontent had seen some positive signs of upward mobility along the colonial bureaucratic ladder (after 1864 *klein-* and *groot-ambtenaar* (junior and senior civil servants) exams were available in the colony through the Gymnasium Koning Willem III, and there was greater access to Dutch citizenship after 1892). However, these changes had not improved the lot of the majority of the Indo community, the little *bung*. In the second half of the nineteenth century, and beyond, they hovered around or even below the poverty line, forming seedbeds of discontent and leading to the formation of a 'pauperism commission' to probe their plight. Besides, these paupers and a far too tiny middle class above them with little access to civil service jobs began to feel economic competition from Chinese and indigenous Indonesians. Moreover, Indos were not allowed to own land.[55] Therefore, at the turn of the century feelings of resentment, embitterment and disquiet among Indos reached peak proportions. At that juncture the pauperism problem seemed further than ever from solution, while life in the Indies in all its aspects had been caught up in the 'maelstrom of modern times' (Vos van Zalingen 1973:3).

Some self-consciousness among Indos led – after the few moderately successful self-help organizations such as Soeria Soemirat and *kleine landbouw* (small farming) forerunners of the Giesting agricultural enterprise – to the founding by A. Bijvoet of the Indische Bond (Indies League) in Batavia on 4 October 1898. However, it scored but limited success in its efforts to 'promote the interests of the members and lend material and moral support to those needy among the European citizens of the Indies'. Instead, it 'chose to cultivate self-pity and malice' (against the Dutch) to 'vegetate into a small sleepy Indo club until it was absorbed in the early twenties by the ultra-conservative Indo-Europeesch Verbond' (Indo-European League).[56] The second Indo organization was the Bandoeng-based association Insulinde, founded in 1907 with the aim 'to better conditions, particularly among the Indies-born Europeans, but also among the so-called *blijvers* [permanently settled] of the [*totok*] Europeans' (Petrus Blumberger 1933:33). It was narrower in its appeal

---

[55]   For the 1848 May movement see Van Hoëvell 1849, I:84-93, 159-62, 220-4, 290-5, 440-1; II:79-80, 297-8, 335-6; also Petrus Blumberger 1918:752-61, 897-913. For Indo pauperism see *Pauperisme* 1901-02; Hoogendoorn 1900.

[56]   For the founding of the Indische Bond see Van der Veur 1955:138. For *kleine landbouw* (small farming) efforts, see Van Hinloopen Labberton and Van Brink 1904 and *Pauperisme* 1901-02, III: 9-51. For Soeria Soemirat led by the energetic preacher Dr Van Lingen: *Pauperisme* 1901-02, III:50, and Werkman 1976:17. The first quote is from Nomes 1978:8, the second from Vos van Zalingen 1973:35-6.

than the Indische Bond, where both *trekker* (wanderer) and *blijver* (*totok*) were welcome as members. Both organizations had an outspoken social character, although still able to influence political developments, as demonstrated by the Eurasian-led radical political interlude during 1912-1913 and 1919-1923.

The significance of Douwes Dekker's Indische Partij

The party that inaugurated the radical period of 1919-1923, the Indische Partij (IP, Indies Party), formed in many ways a reaction to the conservative and accommodating course set out earlier by both Insulinde and the Indische Bond. Faced by the quandary of a position between *inlander* (indigenous Indonesian) and European, between East and West, the Indos formed an intermediate group with all the problems attached to such a status. Normally, they chose, as demonstrated by Insulinde and the Indische Bond, the 'better party' or the white European group, although they were seldom accepted by the Europeans.[57] Rinkes of Inlandsche Zaken wrote a bulky report on the Indische Partij in January 1913, where he analysed the idea of striving for independence as an amalgam of Javanese Mataram and Modjopait traditions, the Praboe Djajabaja prophecies and European 'revolutionary' ideas. Douwes Dekker was portrayed as the best figure to propagate these ideas, having a degree of influence Rinkes compared to that of the Dutch socialist pioneer Domela Nieuwenhuis in the Netherlands.[58]

Indos on the whole felt superior to *inlanders*; toward the pure Dutch, however, attitudes of inferiority generally prevailed, causing Indos to feel ambivalent about Holland, feelings of bondage mingling with those of aversion to the 'mother country'. Nonetheless, they had difficulty opting for a distinct nationalism. Only with the Indische Partij (IP) would the political barometer register a clear rejection of Holland's role as the ruling colonial authority setting the pace of emancipation. The IP also made Indo-Europeans the true pioneers of Indonesian nationalism against the background of the 'rising expectations' prevailing in the colony. With the ideal of genuine independence as the principal aim, E.F.E. Douwes Dekker[59] tried to create a perspective of an *Indië voor de Indiërs* by which all those whose allegiance was to the Indies should be considered citizens of the Indies and be equal, irrespective of race

---

[57]   On the dearth of a sense of equality between Belanda and Indos, turn to Van der Veur 1969.
[58]   For Rinkes's report see Van der Wal 1967:101-29. Pramoedya Ananta Toer 1988b:156-65 suggests that the IP resembled a 'party of shadows', its strength only due to the novel concepts and ideas it spread. The title of Pramoedya Ananta Toer's novel may well have been inspired by Douwes Dekker's own 'Het glazen huis' in *De Expres* of 1 November 1912.
[59]   Biographical details about Ernest François Eugène Douwes Dekker are provided by Glissenaar 1999; Van der Veur 1958; Snoek 1995.

or ethnic origin.[60] E.F.E. Douwes Dekker, a grand-nephew of Eduard Douwes Dekker (as 'Multatuli' of anti-colonial publicist fame), thus introduced two new concepts to the political life of the Indies. Eurasians were to form the elite leadership together with other elites born in the colony.

All this impressed Western-trained Indonesians. In spite of the great mistrust vis-à-vis Eurasians and their leadership aspirations, hundreds of Indonesians, among whom were a number of future nationalist leaders, joined the IP or remained in contact with it. These Indonesians were, relatively speaking, of a higher intellectual level, such as Tjipto Mangoenkoesoemo and the Pakoe Alam prince Soewardi Soerjaningrat. They were capable of opting for the more sophisticated politically mature ideology of the IP, while many of the less well placed turned en masse to the Sarekat Islam. Indeed, the IP, and above all its party organ _De Expres_, appealed to the _bumiputera_ semi-intelligentsia. For that group it formed a major source of radical ideas about rallies, strikes, boycotts and organizational workings. The Indos of the IP belonged largely to the discontented group of lower-ranking officials working for the Indies railways, customs, and postal or other services. Augmented by the pauperized lumpenproletariat, they saw in Douwes Dekker's programme the articulation of their own, so often frustrated, aspirations. In Semarang, with 18% of total IP membership, about 90% were Indos, many of them already associated with the VSTP. Douwes Dekker, and later Sneevliet as well, were keen to exploit that Semarang 'revolutionary potential'.

The Chinese in the colony also showed interest, with Chinese seated in the party executives of Serang, Soerakarta and Ngawi. The initial enthusiasm, with Indonesians, Indos and Chinese fraternizing, was captured by one highly placed _priyayi_, Pangeran Achmad Djajadiningrat, brother of Hasan, and at that time the 35-year-old _regent_ of Serang. Douwes Dekker also cultivated contacts with both Boedi Oetomo and Sarekat Islam.[61] This broad, multi-racially inspired appeal – he was later to include Japanese as well – adopted by E.F.E. Douwes Dekker and later echoed by his young Javanese _priyayi_ comrades-in-arms in a broader Asian context, went much further than the inert social developments of that time.[62]

Douwes Dekker had planned the official founding of the IP to take place in 1913. However, the closure of the Koning Willem III gymnasium's section

[60] Early _Indië voor de Indiërs_ perspectives are aired in Douwes Dekker 1912a en 1912b, the latter address is also in _Het Bondsblad_ 15(10 February 1912):47-8.

[61] For Chinese IP membership see Van Ham 1913:118-9. For Douwes Dekker's contacts with BO and SI see Van der Veur 1955:164-5 and Vos van Zalingen 1973:39. For Djajadiningrat's euphoria at that time, see Djajadiningrat 1936:283.

[62] For these Pan-Asian notions see the Clignett nota (memorandum) in Verbaal 8 December 1916 no. 58.

'B', responsible for preparing predominantly Indo candidates for the Indies civil service, and the protest of the league of medical physicians against the admission of Indo candidates to the second medical college[63] forced him to move the founding ceremony forward to 25 December 1912.[64]

The wane of Indiërs-inspired radicalism and the brief regeneration of Insulinde

However, the vision of an independent Indië led by Indos and members of the Indonesian elite, inspired by Philippine and Latin American developments, had little chance of succeeding (Vos van Zalingen 1973:43). It overlooked the fact that among Filipinos, unlike the Indos, there was a significant class of landlords, and that both in the Philippines and Latin America mestizos and indigenous inhabitants generally shared the same homogeneous Iberian Catholic culture. Moreover, all the internal conditions needed to bring about the realization of that prospect, so dear to Douwes Dekker and his principal Javanese lieutenants, were lacking. Since the IP so clearly placed itself outside the programmes envisaged by the *ethici* of that time, Governor-General Idenburg denied it legal status. He moreover deemed it necessary to exile (in 1913, to Holland) its triumvirate leadership, ostensibly for publishing articles endangering public peace and order but also because of his fear of its moving into the top ranks of Sarekat Islam.[65] From this blow, Indo-inspired nationalism would never truly recover.

Insulinde, now harbouring some of the Indische Partij rump, was a mere shadow of the IP of the 1912-1913 period. Still, during 1914-1917 Insulinde was the only political group to struggle for nationalism and make political demands for it. The moderately liberal colonial administration viewed this group, therefore, as the most radical wing among the ethically inspired reformers. Insulinde was also willing to cooperate with the small band of Dutch socialists then politically active in both the Indische Sociaal-Demo-

---

[63]   For the discriminatory nature of the medical journal see *Bulletin van de Bond van Geneesheren in Nederlandsch-Indië* no. 52/3(1912):27-8.

[64]   Van der Veur 1958:554; Glissenaar 1999:82-3, 89; Nomes 1978:17-25. Van Niel and Muskens incorrectly list 12 December 1911 – the date of Douwes Dekker's 'Aansluiting tusschen Blank en Bruin' (Alliance between White and Brown) address to the Indische Bond – as the date of IP's founding (Van Niel 1984:63; Muskens 1969:105, 115).

[65]   For the denial of legal status see Verbaal 7 April 1913, no. 35 and Verbaal 18 April 1913, no. 67. For the internment and subsequent exile of the IP's triumvirate see Verbalen, 12 August 1913 H 13, 19 August 1913, no. 56; 25 September 1913, no. 56; 3 October 1913, no. 52; 20 November 1913, no. 38; 5 March 1914 P4/23; Glissenaar 1999:99-100. Also the exiles' own account in *Onze verbanning* 1913. For Governor-General Idenburg's fears of penetration in the SI and of IP taking over the SI leadership see 'Autobiografie', pp. 48d-49b, Idenburg Archief, Vrije Universiteit Amsterdam.

cratische Vereeniging and Insulinde. Not that the radical-socialist core was in favour of the ideals of independence. As Marxists they mistrusted petit bourgeois nationalist sentiments, but like Insulinde they sought freedom of opinion and representation on the municipal council.

So, Insulinde took part with the ISDV in municipal council elections. Here, Insulinde's platform, with voting rights for non-Europeans and demands for direct elections of all (not only the European) councillors, matched those of the ISDV. Moreover, Insulinde provided the socialists with a wider political range than the ISDV was capable of attracting by itself.[66] After the outcome of the municipal elections, however, they parted ways in 1917, partly because Insulinde opted for participation with the forthcoming Volksraad and a more moderate programme of reform. It was stung, as well, by the growing ISDV domination of the Semarang-based railway union, the Vereeniging van Spoor- en Tramweg-Personeel (VSTP), an association Insulinde considered its own bailiwick.[67] The ISDV, on the other hand, had difficulty with Insulinde's mounting Pan-Asian and pro-Japanese orientation.[68] It is no accident that Insulinde remained so sensitive to Pan-Asian notions. Here Douwes Dekker was an important source of inspiration. He had been the first nationalist to seriously study Asian nationalism, and he remained impressed until the early 1940s by Japanese developments.

However, on the eve of the Volksraad elections, with Sarekat Islam still loyal to colonial authority and direction, *ethici*, and particularly Dirk van Hinloopen Labberton, had made efforts, with the prospect of the new Volksraad in mind, to tie Indonesian and Eurasian nationalists more firmly to the colonial government through such schemes as Indië Weerbaar (The Indies active and capable of self-defence) and the so-called Inheemsche Militie (indigenous militia).[69] It seems to have worked, since the SI supported the associationist Volksraad and the Indië Weerbaar plans, although it had as yet fallen short of defining a sharp political platform of its own.

However, of all political groups, the SI remained the most omnipresent.

---

[66]   For the common municipal platform, see PID reports: 108-111 in Mr. 156/1917, Verbaal 15 May 1918, no. 64.

[67]   On the VSTP being a *twistappel* (bone of contention) between Insulinde and the ISDV, see PID report no. 130, 8 September 1917 in Mr. 187/1917, Verbaal 15 May 1918, no. 64.

[68]   For Insulinde's Pan-Asian notions see Japanese journalist Y. Minami's 'Kaloe orang Japan ditrima sebagi lid Insulinde', *Pertimbangan*, 24 June 1916 and the comments about it in 'Licht en donker', *De Locomotief*, 25 November 1916. For the editors of *Pertimbangan* the 'revolutionary nationalists' J.R. Razoux Kuhr (an ex-colonial administration [BB] controleur), the Javanese Darna Koesoema and the Chinese Nio Tian Pang, turn to Archief Sneevliet 1686/1 and the Clignett nota, pp. 3-10.

[69]   Van Hinloopen Labberton 1916-17; Mul 1988:46-7; Verbaal 15 November 1916 Q 14 listing correspondence of the Indië Weerbaar executives H. s' Jacob and H.G. Bandon with the governor-general and the minister of colonies.

Moreover, it had been instrumental in transforming Indonesia's socio-political features. Therefore, Insulinde, upon the initiative of ex-ISDV member Tjipto Mangoenkoesoemo, sought, with the same Volksraad elections in mind, closer cooperation with both the SI and Boedi Oetomo. This reflected the attitude of many politically alert Indonesians of that period, to whom dual or even greater combinations of party membership (BO, SI, Insulinde and ISDV) formed no obstacle at all. A nationalist consciousness, be it socio-cultural or economic and political, even when buttressed by Javanist or Muslim slants, was still some distance from maturing, causing Muurling of the PID to state that the *pergerakan* absorbed all kinds of streams (*aliran*). To him it looked like

> a bubbling witches' cauldron, with Tjokro being hazy and providing no arguments, but always relying upon his magnetic influence, with no one like Moeis and the *Neratja* group daring to challenge him, and with only Semaoen and Sneevliet really striving for purity of political purpose.[70]

So, the time for defining clear and sharp political distinctions, let alone for stating basic political ideologies, was still to come. ISDV chairman Henk Sneevliet, then a recent arrival in the colony, was deeply impressed by the 'nationalist explosion' of 1913. He often argued for a revival of that 'spirit of resistance' so keenly demonstrated by the little *bung* of 1913 and their Indonesian IP comrades.[71] The ensuing cooperation between ISDV and Insulinde, however, did not recapture the euphoria created earlier by Douwes Dekker's IP. Only during the radical period of 1919-1923 did the old IP spirit return somewhat among the Insulinde rank and file. But not before Insulinde, with a returned Douwes Dekker among its ranks, had set out on the path of moderation and associationism.

These policies resulted in Volksraad participation, with Tjipto Mangoenkoesomo and J.J.E. Teeuwen being appointed (by Gouvernementsbesluit – Government Decree – 23 February 1918, no. 2), and Abdoel Rivai being elected to represent Insulinde. In spite of its extremely limited representational character, the newly installed Volksraad seemed to most of the European *ethici* and to a majority of the Indies' indigenous elite to be a refreshing start of a new era. In reformist circles, therefore, a climate of associationist euphoria existed for some time. Within Insulinde this atmosphere reinforced the push for parliamentary reforms and caused Insulinde to join the Radicale Concentratie in the Volksraad. There, in a joint effort with the ISDP, Boedi Oetomo and Sarekat Islam, it endeavoured to stimulate further democratic

---

[70]   W. Muurling in PID report no. 154 of 20 October 1917, Mr. 240/1917.
[71]   H. Sneevliet letter, 17 February 1914, to F.M. Wibaut, reprinted as document no. 37 in Tichelman 1985:171-9 and Sneevliet's 'Herleving der I. P. ?' in *Het Vrije Woord* 4(1918):19.

and constitutional reforms and urged for rapid transformation of the Volks-raad into a genuinely representative body of the people.[72]

The brief 1919-1923 impact of the Sarekat Hindia/Nationaal-Indische Partij

However, during 1919-1923, under pressure to seek support among radic-ally oriented Indonesian activists and to disengage itself from the growing conservatism within the Indo community, Insulinde adopted a more radi-cal course. At its eighth party congress, held in Semarang, 7-8 June 1919, it renamed itself Sarekat Hindia/Nationaal-Indische Partij (SH/NIP, Indies Association/National-Indies Party). This congress reported a membership of 23,000; more than three times that of the Indische Partij of 1913.[73] Almost immediately SH/NIP waged a fierce campaign against the ISDV for influence in Sarekat Islam. Its radical activism was manifested in agitation around Solo (or Soerakarta, capital of the largest self-governing principality in Central Java). In this principality Tjipto Mangoenkoesoemo and Hadji Misbach, a *pesantren* (Islamic village school)-educated Islamic *muballigh* (propagandist), both fitting C. Wright Mills's label of 'managers of discontent', stirred up resistance of peasants and farm labourers against the land-lease regulations and corvees. Tjipto seen by many Dutch *ethici* as far too charmed by Douwes Dekker's 'wicked spirit', also organized strikes among his own professional colleagues, the *dokter jawa* (indigenous Java-trained physicians).

He also campaigned against the Soesoehoenan, Soerakarta's traditional ruler.[74] For Tjipto the causes of Solo's unrest and the ruler's abuses had to do with the outdated social structure of Java and the Soesoehoenan's old-fash-ioned administration. He felt that the institution of the Soesoehoenan needed to be overhauled and allowed sufficient latitude for arranging its own expen-ditures. Contradicting Soewardi and Soetomo, whom he felt overly idealized Javanese traditional institutions, Tjipto censured these structures emphati-cally, before the Volksraad for instance, in an effort to have them defeudal-ized.[75] The views he held at that time about his own society, quite unique for

[72]   See Tjipto Mangoenkoesoemo 1917. Insulinde's weekly *De Beweging* 1-21(24 May 1919) cites the party's annual (1918) report, claiming a climb in membership from 6,875 in January 1918 to just over 17,000 in April 1919.
[73]   For the statutes of the re-named party, still with Soewardi at the helm and Douwes Dekker serving as adviser, see Mr. 996x/1921. For the eighth party congress with the party now number-ing 23,000 members see 'Het achtste Indiërs Congres', *Indische Gids* 39(1919):1160-3.
[74]   For the unrest stirred up in and around Solo see Mr. 661/1920; Mr. 725/1920; Mr. 844/1920; Mr. 1090/1920; Mr. 1194/1920; Mr. 1235/1920; Mr. 20/1921; Mr. 62/1921.
[75]   See, for instance, Tjipto's 26 June 1919, comments before the Volksraad, in *Handelingen Volksraad* 1919:72-81.

a Javanese *priyayi*, were considered by the authorities as threatening to the established order. Misbach, on 29 February 1920 in Delanggoe, addressing a joint gathering of the SH/NIP, the Sarekat Islam and the Personeel Fabriek Bond (PFB, Field and Factory Workers' Union), went even further. He urged his audience to rid Java of the domination of both the Soesoehoenan and the colonial government, a speech which would land him in jail some months later.[76] Soerjopranoto, an older brother of the Pakoe Alam-related Soewardi, chairman of the Djokja SI branch and commissioner of the Centrale SI and since 19 February a member of Insulinde, had also clamoured for the native rulers to be pensioned off.[77] At the same time he transformed the PFB, which he had started in Jogja under the name of Adhi Dharmo (Exalted Duty), into a Western-style labour organization of field and factory workers associated with agricultural estates.[78]

With the radical *pergerakan* thus reaching critical *mogok* (strike) proportions due to support of the PFB by *raja mogok* (strike king) Soerjopranoto, now truly seen as Java's leading labour organizer outside the revolutionary socialist fold, Tjipto was finally banned from the Central Javanese principalities.[79] He settled in Bandoeng, a city that, like Soerabaja, Batavia and 'red' Semarang, had become a supra-ethnic educational and political melting pot. It was in Bandoeng where the young civil engineering student Soekarno was to undergo the influence of Tjipto, Douwes Dekker and Soewardi Soerjaningrat, causing him to steer away from and then break with Tjokro's political ideology altogether.

About this time, Douwes Dekker remarked in *De Beweging* (The Movement) that

> this [colonial] government needs to disappear to make room for a government of our own, using all moral means [in our possession]. If need be, even using illegal methods when morality – as is now the case in the Indies – has been placed outside legality.

These remarks would eventually lead to his incarceration during much of the year 1920. Miss Marie Vogel, a Eurasian *batik* entrepreneur and theosophist and soon to become Tjipto's wife (they married on 2 February 1920), made similar remarks, calling for a joint SI and SH/NIP effort to gain real freedom

---

[76] Letter resident A.J.W. Harloff to governor-general, 8 June 1920, Mr. 661/1920.

[77] McVey 1965:42-3; *Sarekat Islam Congres* 1919; *De Beweging* 1 February 1919:77.

[78] McVey 1965:42-3, but calling it Adidarmo 'the Army of Labour '; Shiraishi 1990:111 states that the army of labour (Arbeidsleger, also called Prawira Pandojo ing Joeda) was a branch of Adhi Dharma; Letter of R.A. Kern of Inlandsche Zaken to the governor-general on Adhi Dharma, 29 September 1920, Mr. 1248/1920; Tichelman 1985:666, note 9.

[79] For Tjipto's banishment from the Vorstenlanden see Mr. 20/1921, Mr. 62/1921.

for all the people; as did Soewardi Soerjaningrat, calling for 'taking the country back from a group of Dutch capitalists, who de facto owned Indonesia'.[80] Soewardi Soerjaningrat also called for an independent Indonesian system of education, and SH/NIP numbers, with an Indonesian-member majority, soared to 70,000, ten times that of the Indische Partij of 1913.[81] These huge numbers, led by charismatic men like Douwes Dekker, Tjipto and Soewardi, with a colonial resistance programme matching that of the militant Partai Komunis Indonesia and the equally restive trade union movement, may have caused the Indies government's frequent postponement of legal recognition of the SH/NIP statutes.[82] The postponement was also prompted by Muurling, now elevated from head of the PID to the position of government representative for general affairs in the Volksraad. In a missive to Governor-General Fock, where he drew a rather candid profile of the SH/NIP, Muurling also counselled patience in the hope that the SH/NIP, led by Volksraad members like J.J.E. Teeuwen and P.F. Dahler, would shift their party back to the associationist and non-revolutionary path of Insulinde again.[83]

In any case the measures against Douwes Dekker, Tjipto, Misbach and Soewardi Soerjaningrat – Soewardi Soerjaningrat was arrested for protesting in the *Persatoean Hindia* against Douwes Dekker's incarceration – led to a closed SH/NIP ninth party congress, in August 1920. With J.J.E. Teeuwen elected to the chair to succeed Soewardi, only two Indonesians, Tjipto and Aloewi Tjitroatmodjo, were elected to the party's main executive. The public tenth congress of 14-16 May 1921 in Semarang, with Douwes Dekker, Soewardi and Tjipto being absent, saw a further shift to the right. By mid-1921 the SH/NIP executive was dominated by still more moderate Indos, thus marking the decline of revolutionary fervour only recently so fiercely propagated by the SH/NIP 'managers of discontent'. So in the wake of the drastic, paternalistic changes wrought by Minister of Colonies De Graaff reducing the Carpentier Alting reform proposals to almost nil, the activist/nationalist fibre to counter this development did not truly display itself. Even the response conceived by Douwes Dekker, Van Hinloopen Labberton and Ir Fournier in the form of an Indisch Nationaal Eenheids programme – from which moderate autonomy platforms such as the Al-Indië congress and a revived Radicale Concentratie (of 12 November 1922) also sprang – did not stem the clearly reactionary measures assumed increasingly by the new

---

[80]   For Douwes Dekker's remarks see *De Beweging* 1-48(29 November 1919). For Miss Vogel's remarks see *De Beweging*, 25 October 1919 and for Soewardi's *De Beweging* 25 October 1919:1007-9.

[81]   A membership of 72,000 by May 1920 is listed by Van der Veur 1955:187 and *De Beweging*, 5 June 1920.

[82]   Van der Veur 1955:187; *De Beweging*, 5 June 1920.

[83]   Missive of Muurling to Fock, 13 February 1922, Mr. 343/1922.

Governor-General Fock.[84]

Finally, on 18 May 1923, just after recognition of its revised statutes was declined by Gouvernementsbesluit of 10 April 1923, the SH/NIP decided to dissolve itself. Its chairman in this final phase, P.F. Dahler, withdrew from the Volksraad. From then on, Indonesian activists left the SH/NIP, most likely in the direction of the PKI and the activist trade union movement. The PKI, with men like Semaoen, the soul behind the April 1923 VSTP railway strike, and with Darsono, who had brought the 'red sections' of the SI under the PKI banner, along with militant leaders like Sosrokardono, of pawnbrokers' strike fame, and *raja mogok* (strike king) Soerjopranoto, appealed to Indonesian activists far more than frustrated attempts for autonomy in a vaguely perceived commonwealth framework.[85]

By now it had become quite evident that Indos and indigenous Indonesians were not destined to work together to achieve the independence of their country. Also, since the militant years 1919-1922, the majority of the more literate Indos had decided to return to the policies of moderation and accommodation once advocated by the Indische Bond. And so in 1919 they established the Indo-Europeesch Verbond (IEV, Indo-European Union). This organization, together with the *totok-belanda* association founded much later (in 1929), De Vaderlandsche Club (VC, The Fatherland Club), was to exert heavy conservative, if not reactionary, pressure upon colonial policies. In years to come, its often paralysing influence thus seriously limited room for more flexible and imaginative colonial policies to emerge. This caused Mohammad Hoesni Thamrin to state in the Volksraad:

> [The IEV] seems to keep all the privileges of their father's side, that is to say the rights granted him by the constitution, his economic standing, and other racial prerogatives [...] along with the entitlements of their mother's side, such as the right to own land, but none of her obligations [...] [thus rendering Indo-Europeans in the archipelago] the most privileged of all races.[86]

What precisely the Indo contribution amounted to in that paralytic development remains difficult to fathom, although some observers considered a return to the Indonesian nationalists by the Indo group (now politically led by highly placed Eurasian colonial administration officials together with some intellectuals oriented strongly to the Dutch element) as psychologic ally no longer feasible (Kuiper and Surie 1967:99-101; Van der Veur 1955: 105-6).

---

[84]   See Koch 1950:80-4; and, also *Ontwerp Eenheidsprogram* 1921; *Eerste Al-Indië-Congres* 1922: 1-35; Van Hinloopen Labberton 1922:1-8.

[85]   See adviser R.A. Kern's Verslag to Governor-General D. Fock, 31 May 1921 in Mr. 641/1921. For Indonesian members joining the PKI see Tichelman 1985:19; Nomes 1978:108-9.

[86]   *Handelingen Volksraad* 1931-1932:808-9.

In any case, Douwes Dekker's daring appeal had fallen twice upon deaf ears among literate members of his own kin group. However, his initiatives, particularly of the 'revolutionary year', were to influence thousands of Indonesians and hundreds of *peranakan* Chinese for years to come. In the late 1930s, Mohammad Hoesni Thamrin, then Java's most influential indigenous Indonesian nationalist, described Douwes Dekker 'as capable of an old-fashioned chivalry, not fully understood by his time and of having such inner honesty and strength of character that it would earn him a solid historical reputation' (Douwes Dekker and Harumi Wanasita 1949:89). On 11 March 1956 at Bogor Palace, another prominent Indonesian influenced by Douwes Dekker, the then President Soekarno, would refer to him as his *sahabat karib* (great friend), his teacher, who did much to stir up nationalist feelings in his own heart. In front of the Gabungan Indo Untuk Kesatuan Indonesia (GIKI, Eurasian Grouping Promoting Indonesian Unity) executive and other key Indo figures assembled at the Bogor presidential palace, Soekarno saw fit to bestow upon Douwes Dekker the title of 'father of Indonesian political nationalism'. Thus, Soekarno paid tribute to the fact that Douwes Dekker not only stood for the nation in embryo, but that he was also a symbol for a history which was inevitably a nationalist history. In that context he was the first genuine 'Indonesian' nationalist to become part of the political and cultural credo of what eventually evolved into the independent Republic of Indonesia.[87]

Political emancipation of the Indies singkeh and peranakan Chinese

Another group equally responsible, but less flamboyantly so, for the socio-political awakening of their own kin were the Indonesian Chinese, both *peranakan* and *totok* (or *singkeh*, Hokkien for 'newcomer'). So far, attempts to assess their place in Indonesian socio-political emancipation have moved along isolated non-integrative lines. Only by dealing with the Chinese element as an integral part of Java's modern history will the more positive impact of the Chinese upon the early stages of the Indonesian emancipation movement in Java be recognized. It is our contention that their impact is still underestimated, and not even properly chronicled (Tichelman 1990:2). In the late 1850s, when dismantling of the Cultivation System made way for more liberal policies, some significant restrictions on laissez-faire market economics were retained. One of these was the specific curtailment of Chinese eco-

[87]   *Onze Stem* 33-2/3(15 March 1956):1, 7, and conversations with GIKI participants, at that time, of the Bogor conference, Ernst Utrecht (interview 5 July 1986), and U.C. Koot (interview 9 August 1990).

nomic activities. Measures were taken to keep the Chinese out of Java's interior as much as possible and concentrate them in the earlier established urban ghettos: the *pecinan* (Chinese quarters).[88] As we will demonstrate in the next chapter, the Soerabaja *pecinan* and the Indonesian quarter, where Soekarno dwelt with the Tjokro family, formed separate racially segregated segments, the 'other face' of that harbour city, so to speak. However, the economic policies referred to above could not always be strictly executed, and elements of the old administration were also kept in force. Taxes were still farmed out to a number of Chinese, while opium farmers were granted permission to travel in Java's interior. Chinese contributed substantially to the monetization of Java's hinterland. In retail and wholesale trade their contribution was also significant (Skinner 1963:98-101). However, the restrictive government policies did affect Chinese communities. The margin for assimilation was reduced. In fact, the Javanization process of Java's Chinese was consolidated, and instead a separate *peranakan* Chinese society and culture was increasingly cultivated. This development formed part of a larger process of pluralization, the outcome of both specific Southeast Asian conditions and peculiar Dutch colonial policies aimed to keep everybody in their own place.[89]

At the end of the nineteenth century new changes in colonial administration were extended and intensified. A new colonial ideology was adopted: the 'Ethical Policy', proclaiming more effective measures to improve the welfare of the indigenous population. In colonial Dutch parlance, this often meant greater hostility toward the Chinese, since they were seen as the prime cause of indigenous poverty and distress in rural Java. In the words of one *peranakan* the Chinese 'carried the sins for the miseries of an indigenous population exposed since 1870 to new forms of exploitation by modern capitalism'.[90] So, modern 'ethical' government gradually dismantled the Chinese-run revenue farms and replaced them with state institutions. These opium farms and pawnshops had formed the financial mainstay of the colonial state but had also provided the institutional support of *peranakan* Chinese economic activity. The loss of them deprived the Chinese of their access to Java's rural markets. Freedom of economic enterprise was further curtailed by more rigid enforcement of the pass (1897) and zoning (1900) regulations, the so-called Passen and Wijken-Stelsels (pass and ward systems, systems

---

[88]   See Go Gien Tjwan, 'Inleiding tot de memoires van Siauw Giok Tjhan', ms. Amsterdam, 1981, p. 33.

[89]   Tichelman 1990:4, but see also Veth's sociological analysis in Veth 1899-1907, IV:108, where he concludes that 'the regulations, hindering the Chinese from competing with the European [in the post Cultivation System period] on an equal footing, were acquiring repressive even hostile features'.

[90]   Go Gien Tjwan, 'Inleiding tot de memoires van Siauw Giok Tjhan', ms. Amsterdam, 1981, p. 40.

which had been in force since 1740 (for the *pecinan* ward system) and since 1816 (for the special passes) (Rush 1977:261-6; Abeyasekere 1987:109-10). Although this led to liquidation of many Chinese economic enterprises, the upward economic trend starting around the mid-1890s witnessed Chinese investment and entrepreneurship adapting to new opportunities, as they were no longer tied to revenue farming and were now joined by new waves of *singkeh*. The new policies did not, however, lessen Chinese resentment of long-standing and more recent forms of discrimination. Aware that they, vis-à-vis the indigenous population, were often in a better economic position, in spite of governmental discrimination, Java's Chinese felt the need to reconsider their social status. Moreover, in that quest, internal and external impulses were to fuel Chinese ethnic consciousness, both among *peranakan* and among *totok* (or *singkeh*).

The first wave of such Chinese socio-political awakening long predated external impulses emanating from mainland China around the turn of the century. As early as the 1860s, Chinese took part as typesetters in the then emerging Malay-language publications owned by Dutch and Indo-Europeans. In the same period, new Chinese socio-religious associations and cultural/cooperative organizations were set up. From the mid-1870s onward, wealthy men's clubs, temple associations, new private schools and also secret societies were founded. 1886 saw the start of a Chinese-owned Malay-language press, a medium that proliferated in the next two decades and was to play an important role in the rise of both Chinese and Indonesian nationalist awakening.[91]

Influence from abroad and the Tiong Hoa Hwee Koan

The rise of Japan as a strong modern state, and the subsequent 1899 decision by the Indies government to bestow 'European status' upon Japanese citizens of the Indies, also served as strong stimulants for Chinese emancipation. Some of the Indonesian Chinese also were affected by the rise of Dr Sun Yat-sen's revolutionary nationalist party T'ong-meng Hui in 1905. *Peranakan* and *singkeh* began to feel a common bond, a 'Chineseness', still tangible in spite of a generations-long separation, cemented further by the shared experience of humiliating socio-economic standards imposed by colonial authority. The same ingredients which had spawned indigenous Indonesian socio-political awakening among their *kaum muda* (young generation) were to enhance

---

[91] For Chinese ill-feeling see Fromberg 1926:405-55 and Adam 1984:120-3. For the importance of the Chinese to the vernacular press turn to Suryadinata 1971 and Adam 1984:118, 124, 127-38. Adam also discusses mid- and late nineteenth-century Chinese societies (Adam 1984:124-6).

Indonesian Chinese aspirations to modernity and their own ethnic identity. In the case of the Indonesian Chinese, Confucianism, formulated by Kang You Wei as the modernizing tenet of Chinese polity, would serve not merely for religious purposes but as a signifier of 'Chineseness', just as Christianity had served for the colonial Dutch, and Islam for the majority of indigenous Indonesians.[92] So, in 1900, the first modern association of the Chinese ethnic community in Indonesia, the Tiong Hoa Hwee Koan (THHK, Chinese Association), was formed in Batavia by *peranakan* and a few *singkeh*.[93]

The need of *peranakan* for an organization that would satisfy their quest for a Confucianist-based identity was mainly a response to late-nineteenth-century colonial structures, which had developed strictly along race and caste lines. However, the THHK was not as yet a manifestation of overseas Chinese nationalism. It had more of the hallmarks of a proto-nationalist endeavour, where a purified religious variant of Confucianism formed the ideological vehicle for a common struggle to reach 'respected' socio-economic status, equal to that enjoyed by the Dutch colonial establishment.[94] Hence the emphasis upon Chinese-language schools, the THHK Sekolah Tjina (Chinese schools), or Tiong Hoa Hak Tong, styled after modern Japanese standards, throughout Java. These schools climbed rapidly in number: from one in 1901 to fifty-four in 1908, prompting the colonial government to set up parallel Hollandsch-Chineesche Schoolen (HCS, Dutch Chinese Schools).[95] Chinese newspaper and publishing ventures proliferated too, as did Chinese commercial activity, now relaxed by valid one-year pass regulations (by 1904) in new ventures such as sugar plantations and cottage industries like *kretek* cigarettes and *batik* textiles. Here, the first clashes between Islamic entrepreneurs and Chinese traders occurred, with the former often receiving the support of the authorities.[96]

[92]   For Kang You Wei, see Go Gien Tjhan, 'Inleiding tot de memoires van Siauw Giok Tjhan', ms. Amsterdam, 1981, pp. 41-7. The comparison between *kaum muda* modernist strivings and those of the ethnic Chinese is made by Shiraishi 1990:32.
[93]   For the establishment of the THHK, for Pramoedya Ananta Toer, 'the first modern organization of the Indies' (Pramoedya Ananta Toer 1988a:110), see Nio Joe Lan 1940:Ch. I; Go Gien Tjhan, 'Inleiding tot de memoires van Siauw Giok Tjhan', ms. Amsterdam, 1981, pp. 50-6
[94]   Go Gien Tjhan, 'Inleiding tot de memoires van Siauw Giok Tjhan', ms. Amsterdam, 1981, p. 54.
[95]   For these schools see *Soerat kiriman* 1900, where the THHK executive sets out the founding of Chinese boys and girls schools as patterned after modern Chinese and Japanese standards with aims to teach the boys also Dutch and English. See also Nio Joe Lan 1940:202. Go sees their founding as a tactical manoeuvre to force the colonial government to open Dutch-language schools to the Chinese, see Go Gien Tjhan, 'Inleiding tot de memoires van Siauw Giok Tjhan', ms. Amsterdam, 1981, pp. 59-60. For the HCS, a reaction to the THHK schools, Van der Wal 1967: 44-8, 97-104.
[96]   For the relaxation of the pass system, see Shiraishi 1990:36; he also reports on the first economic clashes (pp. 46-8), as does Pramoedya Ananta Toer 1988a:160-4, who, however, blames Dutch official machinations for being behind these racial conflicts.

Another Pan-Chinese development was the formation, during 1907 and 1908, of Chinese chambers of commerce (Siang Hwee) in Batavia and other towns, with the *singkeh* members outnumbering *peranakan* (Suryadinata 1981:6). Strong sympathy among both *peranakan* and *singkeh* for the nationalist movement in China – in 1907 a branch of Sun Yat-sen's nationalist party was established in the Batavia *totok* quarter of Pintoe Ketjil, leading to revolutionary reading clubs (Soe Poe Sia) spreading all over the Indies (Suryadinata 1981:6, note 17) – and feelings of self-respect were stimulated by the Chinese revolution of 1911-1912, and the subsequent fall of the Ch'ing dynasty.

The split between Ko and Non-Ko Chinese associations

These developments not only sharpened differences between Pan-Chinese and Indies-oriented Chinese, culminating in the 4 November 1917 Semarang Conference, but also caused more egalitarian elements among all Indonesian Chinese to denounce the entrenched *peranakan* cooperation with the colonial government (Suryadinata 1981:21-5). To boost the *peranakan's* prestige, and their own as well, the colonial government further accelerated administrative reforms beneficial to the Chinese, though still denying them full 'European status'.[97] Chinese were also granted rather generous representation in the Batavia, Semarang and Soerabaja municipal councils, and later in 1918 in the first Volksraad. In these bodies they often voted with their Dutch counterparts against Indonesian interests (Abeyasekere 1987:112, 119). In that way Dutch-oriented *peranakan* became largely reconciled to the colonial regime. Remaining true to the tenets of ethically inspired associationism, that group – represented by politicians like Kan Hok Hoei, Dr Ir Han Tiauw Tjong[98] and Yo Heng Kam, and by the Chung Hwa Hui in Nederlandsch-Indië (CHH, Chinese Association in the Netherlands Indies) which they formed – continued to be wary of Indonesian nationalist aspirations. Following the example of the equally conservative Indo-Europeesch Verbond (IEV), the CHH, dominated by wealthy *peranakan*, obviously felt more secure under

[97]   Instead, the Indonesian Chinese were offered Dutch 'subject' (*onderdaan*) status. For the controversy around this and its repercussions, see Suryadinata 1981:26-38.

[98]   Han Tiauw Tjong, member of the Volksraad May 1924 to June 1929 and July 1938 to June 1939 and curator at the THS in Bandoeng from 1924 until his untimely death on 29 June 1940, was keenly remembered by Soekarno years later when his son Han Bing Siong, then a lecturer during Soekarno's first 1958 visit to the Fakultas Hukum dan Pengetahuan Masjarakat Universitas Indonesia at Salemba 4, was introduced to the president: 29 July 2000 letter by Han Bing Siong to Bob Hering; *Jaarverslag Technische Hoogeschool* 1940:55; *Handelingen Volksraad*, 6e vergadering of 2 July 1940.

continuing Dutch tutelage.[99] Yet the 1917 Semarang Conference, as did the Chung Hwa Hui congresses of April 1927 and April 1928, revealed some strong undercurrents still advocating basically Pan-Chinese, even Pan-Asian, orientations. That current of opinion, supported by influential dailies, such as the leftist *Sin Po, Sin Jit Po, Keng Po* and *Pewarta Soerabaia*, denounced colonialism, and with it the 'loyalist' stance adopted by the CHH, as harmful to 'genuine' Chinese interests. Kwee Kek Beng, editor-in-chief of *Sin Po* during 1925-1947 and a contributing editor to Soekarno's and Soetomo's *Soeloeh Indonesia Moeda* during the late twenties and early thirties, together with Dr Kwa Tjoan Sioe, an Amsterdam-trained physician, were the foremost supporters of Soekarno's PNI during that time, with Kwee often printing the PNI periodicals free of charge and distributing them as well.[100] This attitude, also supported by some Western-educated intellectuals, would bring its adherents somewhat closer to the 'Non-Ko' (non-cooperative) stances adopted by Indonesian nationalists in a phase of Indonesian socio-political radical behaviour still to come (Suryadinata 1981:21-4, 51-4).

---

[99] For the CHH congresses and the subsequent founding of the CHH, see Suryadinata 1981: 41, 49-63.

[100] Interview with Ir (Harry) Kwee Hin Goan, 15 February 1996. During that time the composer of 'Indonesia Raja', Wage Rudolf Supratman, was *Sin Po*'s city reporter. At the 28 October 1928 youth congress in Batavia, *Sin Po* printed 5,000 copies of 'Indonesia Raja' free of charge and distributed it among the congress audience, see Kwee Kek Beng 1948:35-6. As to Dr Kwa Tjoan Sioe see Kwee Kek Beng 1948:35; McVey 1965:335, 485 and Visbeen's police report listing Kwa as a PKI delegate at a closed 12 November 1922 Radicale Concentratie gathering, Mr. 1187/1922, Verbaal 3 November 1923 B 16.

CHAPTER III

Soekarno's Soerabaja and Bandoeng years of education and political apprenticeship

The Soerabaja scene after Soekarno returned

The harbour city of Soerabaja that Soekarno returned to after his rather secluded and sheltered experiences in East Java had taken on ever swifter socio-cultural and commercial dimensions during Soekarno's *windu*-long absence from it, the city of his birth. It had emerged not only as the Netherlands Indies' greatest harbour and naval base, but had since taken on the appearance of a truly bustling metropolis. And, like Betawi, Bogor, Semarang and Bandoeng, while incorporating essential elements of the traditional structure of the Indonesian *kota*, it exhibited a European countenance: train and tramway stations, hotels, banks and post offices, schools, theatres and cinemas, shopping areas, a network of main and side streets, and lively traffic (usually trams, horse carts, Europeans using their motorcars, and well-to-do Indonesians, with the young Soekarno among them, riding bikes).[1] However, in spite of this Western façade, Soerabaja, like these other colonial cities, remained 'a city of two faces'.[2] One historian characterizes Soerabaja as having 'a harsh colonial entrepreneurial atmosphere' with an expatriate upper class that is outspokenly

> unethical and hard [...] but still confronted with a new, rather turbulent and burst-open Indonesian world, where an indigenous local leader like Tjokroaminoto, through his Sarekat Islam leadership, the associated printing house Setija Oesaha and the daily *Oetoesan Hindia*, enjoyed great prestige among his stalwart followers.[3]

---

[1]   For the great proportions of its harbour and its engineering potential outstripping Batavia, see Abeyasekere 1987:82; *ENI* IV:31-3; *ENI* VI:153-4. For Soerabaya's European countenance, Jedamski 1998:168; Hermen Kartowisastra 1978:66; Labrousse 1986.

[2]   For Betawi's 'two-faced' countenance with crowded indigenous *kampung* clusters within or near the city limits, largely catering to a wide variety of demands made by the Dutch colonial establishment, but culturally still remaining a world apart, turn to Hering 1996:Chapter 1; and for Soerabaja with an equally 'split personality' to Marco Kartodikromo 1924; Romein-Verschoor 1978, I:48; Frederick 1989:3-5, 7-28.

[3]   Tichelman 1985:26 and Baars en Sneevliet 1991:xii. For this 'living and growing Indonesian

Our source further asserts that most *totok* Dutch businessmen and a score of sugar plantation managers, belonging to the Dutch upper-class Soerabajan Simpang Club, not only had but little affinity with current ethical policies, they often were to play first fiddle in the city expressing their rather conservative, even racist credo. They expected the indigenous people, especially the toiling masses in the sugar-growing industry, to remain forever submerged in a culture of silent obedience. This not only made the sugar industry far easier to handle, it also expressed the feelings of most of the Soerabajan sugar barons of fierce cultural arrogance and racial superiority. And then there was the sexual aspect. Historians and sociologists concerned with Indonesia seem to overlook how sexist an enterprise Dutch plantation colonialism in fact was. We refer here not just to the metaphor of a virile West penetrating the passive feminine East, as portrayed for instance in Edward Said's *Orientalism,* but to the lust blond-haired[4] planters exhibited toward brown-skinned women in their employ.

In this respect, white sugar-cane planters behaved like the medieval seigneurs of Europe's feudal past, enjoying, like them, a droit de seigneur and thus entering at will the *kampung* under their economic jurisdiction in order to seek their pleasure with young native maidens.[5] Even Baars, Soekarno's political sponsor in 1917-1919, sought pleasures with a fifteen-year-old indigenous servant maid in his employ, named Onok Sawinah; he did, however, marry her on 17 May 1921, after his marriage with To Cheriex had been dissolved on 9 July 1920 (Mul 1988:87, 98, 110). This blatantly expressed sexism did not easily find its way to the columns of the *Soerabaiasch Handelsblad,* since such behaviour was taken for granted and condoned as well. Instead, the editorials of the daily paper amply recorded the sugar barons' economic and business-like exploits and concomitant arrogance, faithfully penned by editor-in-chief M. van Geuns.

Van Geuns, a former schoolteacher, had made the Soerabajan daily into

---

society' existing in Semarang, Soerabaja and even Bandoeng, in contrast to Batavia without 'a true native world with some estranged Indonesian intellectuals', see PID head Muurling's rapport no. 127 of 30 August 1917 in Mr. 177/17, Verbaal 15 May 1918, no. 64. However, in report no. 41 of April 1918, Verbaal 6 January 1919, no. 16 Muurling contrasts the concentration of strikes in Semarang to the few occurring in Soerabaja and argues that the latter city had a more prosperous indigenous population with a more diverse industrial base, making it less affected by adverse economic conditions than Semarang.

4   Termed by Soekarno in his defence speech before the Bandoeng Landraad as *tuan-tuan rambut djagung:* see Soekarno 1961:131.

5   For this sexism demonstrated in Deli, another area ruthlessly exploited by plantation owners, turn to Hering 1988:201-2. For the Soerabajan case see Marco 1924. Long before Edward Said, the Dutch journalist Charles Boissevain coined the phrase 'imperial machismo', with the West being 'strong, energetic and logical while the Orient was weak, emotional and languorous', cited by Gouda 1995:175.

truly a 'mouthpiece of the sugar industry' (McVey 1965:13; Perthus 1976:91). The industry remained hypocritical and racist, despite its proud pretensions to epitomizing a dynamic world of Indies modernity. It was therefore no wonder that European panic reactions to the rather swift expansion of the Sarekat Islam were felt most strongly among the East Javanese planters, with their Sugar Syndicate headquarters in Soerabaja.[6] One such panic reaction resulted in the mid-1913 rumours spread by the Sugar Syndicate spy network about imminent riots and murder to take place in the sugar plantations surrounding Soerabaja, prompting the Syndicate to appeal to Governor-General Idenburg for a distribution of armaments. Idenburg and his advisors dismissed the appeal as a hysterical reaction by the Syndicate. Somewhat later, the Syndicate continued to agitate by issuing quite biased weekly reports on the 'native movement in the sugar-producing areas'.[7]

The impact of the European Great War

These sentiments may have been strengthened by the outbreak of World War I, a war which was to affect Soerabaja and its environs in a number of ways. For instance, with sugar prices booming as the war progressed, domestic rice harvests were poor and cheap rice imports badly impaired by shipping shortages, causing the price of rice to rise far too steeply. This caused further inflation and hence growing unrest among many indigenous urban and rural Soerabajans, with the intelligentsia among them starting to doubt the blessings of a foreign-controlled capitalist economy. The peasants in the sugar areas around Soerabaja also began to grumble about the low rents the sugar industry paid for irrigated land, causing Governor-General Van Limburg Stirum to morally support SI and ISDV demands (by Soekarno's HBS teacher of German, Coos Hartogh, for instance) for at least part of such land under contract to sugar plantations to be transferred to the peasantry for growing rice. The sugar lobby – recently reinforced by the Bond van Eigenaren van Nederlandsch-Indische Suikerondernemingen (BENISO, Union of Sugar Plantation Owners) and politically aligned with the equally conservative Politiek-Economische Bond (Political Economic Union) in the Volksraad – was loath to follow this proposal in anticipation of even higher sugar booms that might occur after the war.[8]

---

[6]	Tichelman ms 'Socialisme in Indonesië', third part. For the Algemeen Syndicaat van Suikerfabrikanten in Nederlandsch-Indië of Soerabaja founded on 1 January 1895 see *ENI* IV: 229 and Taselaar 1998:99, stating that it was 'for a long time the largest and most powerful employers' organization of the Indies'.
[7]	Tichelman ms, 'Socialisme in Indonesië', third part; Shiraishi 1990:68.
[8]	Taselaar 1998:102-3,108,306;McVey 1965:20,38;G.F.E.Gonggrijp 1991:1338,1949:154-8;*ENI*IV:

Just after the war, with Sneevliet being banned forever from the Indies, one S. Partoatmodjo saw fit to write that Sneevliet, whom he had admired for promoting the sugar-cane workers' interests, had merely been exiled for the benefit of sugar-cane capital (*diboewang lantaran pengaroe kapitaal riet*).[9] Another consequence of the war directly involving Soekarno was that the HBS he attended experienced an explosion of students, since many Dutch and Indo families preferred to stay in the colony instead of going on overseas leave. In 1915, the first grade had no less than seven parallel classes, and a total of 400 students, making the Regentstraat HBS one of the largest in the Indies (Vervoort 1975:27).

In Soekarno's own words, Soerabaja, the

> bustling, noisy port town, much like New York. [...] A key industrial area with fast turnover in sugar, tea, tobacco, and coffee, it had keen competition in commerce from the sharp Chinese plus a large influx of mariners and merchantmen who brought news from all parts of the world. It had a swollen population of young and outspoken dockhands and repair workers. [...] The town was seething with discontent and revolutionaries.

And he added: 'Into this atmosphere stepped a little mama's boy of 15 clutching a small suitcase',[10] thus demonstrating some keenly felt uneasiness about the startlingly new and rather bewildering world he was about to enter. As John Legge has it, 'he [Soekarno] was plunged into it [...] with acute homesickness' assailing him when he entered the Tjokroaminoto household at Gang Peneleh VII, no. 29/31. Soekarno as well attests to this: 'When I arrived I cried every day. Oh, I missed my mother so much. [...] Now, I had no mother, no adoring grandmother to spoil me, no devoted Sarinah to fuss over me. I was all alone.'[11]

184; Deliar Noer 1973:199. For Coos Hartogh's objections (introduced by him in response to the land rent problems at the ISDV 5th congress of 18-20 May 1918) see Tichelman's letter of 12 December 1998.

[9]   *Sinar Hindia*, 6-1-1919. Marco's contribution to *Sinar Djawa* no. 26 entitled 'Apakah pabrik goela itoe ratjoen boeat bangsa kita' (Are the sugar factories not poisoning our people?), cited in Soe Hok Gie 1990:7, 13 speaks for itself. Tjokro at the same time said in the Volksraad that 'hunger and illnesses in the sugar-growing areas drove some parents to sell their children for one and half to two florins per child', cited by Van Miert 1995:150.

[10]   Adams 1965:34. For Soerabaja's 'revolutionary potential and prominent labour agitation' during 1910 to 1920: Abeyasekere 1987:101, 107; Ingleson 1986:108-9, 133-46.

[11]   Legge 1984:51. For Soekarno's initial feelings of despair and loneliness, Adams 1965:37.

Early boarding-house years in the Internaat Soeharsikin

When our 'mama's boy' at the end of June 1916 crossed the threshold of the Internaat Soeharsikin, he found it located directly behind the front living quarters and the *pendopo* (veranda) of the Tjokro family at no. 29. Across a tiny courtyard was the *markas* (headquarters) of the Soerabaja Sarekat Islam at no. 31. The latter dwelling also served as a counselling office for the many indigenous folk who were simply looking for advice and guidance, oppressed as many felt they were by the all too stringent measures of the local and provincial colonial administrations.[12] Entering the Tjokro family, Soekarno learned that it consisted of Tjokro, his wife Soeharsikin, daughter of Raden Mangoensoemo, the *patih* of Ponorogo, married to Tjokro since 1905, and four children: two boys and two girls. The oldest was a rather pretty and slender girl named Siti Oetari, just about to turn eleven on 18 August 1916, four years younger than the handsome new boarder now facing her. She used the nickname Netty, given to her by one of her female Dutch teachers at the Instituut Buys she attended in Soerabaja. One of her sons reveals another nickname: Lok, derived from the Dutch word *verlokkend* (enticing), since 'she had naughty eyes'.[13] These nicknames continued to be used by the family; even Soekarno during his late teens often called her Lok. The oldest of the two boys was named Oetarjo Anwar and the youngest Harsono, also called Moestafa Kamil, aged five and three respectively. The youngest child in the family was a baby girl called Siti Islamijah. Oetarjo Anwar and Siti Islamijah were born in Soerabaja, while Siti Oetari was born in Ponorogo, at Iboe Soeharsikin's parental home, where she awaited the arrival of her first-born. Harsono was born in Glodog, near Madioen, where Iboe Soeharsikin's parents were then stationed. A third boy, the *anak bungsu* (youngest child), named Soejoed Ahmad, was born in Soerabaja in the third year of Soekarno's boarding at Gang Peneleh.[14]

Soekarno's own quarters, at the back attic of no. 29, where about twenty or so Internaat Soeharsikin boarders were accommodated, were quite tiny and dark. In the words of his former Modjokerto playmate Hermen Kartowi-sastra, a boarder of two years' standing:

[12] McVey 1965:363 note 36; Amelz 1952, I:55; Shiraishi 1990:54.

[13] For the Instituut Buys, an expensive private school for Dutch and non-Dutch children, see Siauw Giok Tjhan 1982:4; Von Faber 1931:253. According to Oetari's son Ir Harjono Sigit Bachrunsalam, she was born 18 August 1905 and died in Surabaya in 1994: see his 'Riwayat singkat Ibu Utari', ms of 3 October 1999, which on page 1 reveals the nature of the nickname Lok. Also mentioned in Erka 1978b:137, 140 with Soekarno naming her so.

[14] Interview Oetarjo Anwar Tjokroaminoto and Harsono Tjokroaminoto, 15 August 1971. See also Harsono Tjokroaminoto 1983:i; Amelz 1952, I:54; Gunseikanbu 1944a:292, 445; Soebagijo 1985:2-3; Proces-verbaal Tjokroaminoto in Mr. 184/1921.

I felt sorry for Soekarno not getting a good room, since most of the better rooms were by now occupied by students before he came to board with us. So his was quite dark since it had no windows, not even a door, forcing him to keep the light bulb alight during the entire day. But he took it all without any grumbling. (Hermen Kartowisastro 1978:66.)

But grumble he did, some fifty years later, to Cindy Adams, complaining he had no money to buy a light bulb, using a candle instead so he could study until deep in the night in his mosquito-ridden *kadang ayam* (chicken coop) (Adams 1965:34-5). And so Soekarno continued to sell to Cindy Adams the David Copperfield-like existence of his teens, an image he may have cherished since Dickens' classic was required literature during his years at the Regentstraat HBS, but which was also prompted by his own awareness of the rags-to-riches stories so appealing to large segments of the American public and to Hollywood.

Harsono Tjokroaminotopoetero, in his recollections, also describes Soekarno's poor quarters. He claims that Soekarno's small sleeping quarters had earlier been used as a *gudang*, a store-room for rice and other goods, and then cleared for Soekarno's occupancy in mid-1916. After a while, however, Iboe Soeharsikin felt sorry for Soekarno, being the youngest and skinniest of all her boarders, and had him moved to a bigger room at the front, close to the Tjokro family's own private quarters. It is in this room that Harsono recalls watching Soekarno in the late hours of the evening standing on a table and facing a huge mirror, speaking loudly to an imaginary mob while wildly gesticulating arms, hands and head at the same time. Some of the other boarders watched such theatricals at first, but soon got bored with them and preferred to stay in their rooms, often locking out Soekarno in the process. Hermen Kartowisastro relates that Soekarno was really a bright student, even close to being a genius in all kinds of fields of learning, and a fine artist as well. As to the artwork, Hermen recalls that J.W. Broekhuysen, the HBS art teacher, was so impressed by Soekarno's watercolour drawing of a dog-house that it was praised to the whole class and then put on permanent display (Hadi 1978:71). But here again, Soekarno's memory fails him; he describes to Cindy Adams an unnamed female art teacher who was pleased with the drawing, showing it to the class but refusing to give it back to him (Adams 1965:44).

In the boarding house, Soekarno was usually way ahead of the other boarders in finishing his HBS homework. Soekarno was then often eager to discuss all kinds of matters with his fellows, even if they were still busily engaged with their own homework. Some of these fellow boarders began to avoid him or even shut him out altogether.[15] As to his private theatrical

---

[15]   Hermen Kartowisastra 1978:70-1 and Hermen's contribution 'Pemuda Soekarno kawan sekolah dan kawan mainku selama 1909-1919' in *Simponi* 25 June 1978:8.

performances in his room, Soekarno himself describes them as being inspired by a HBS lecture about a people's tribune in ancient Greece – given by Soekarno's first-grade history teacher L.D.J. Reeser, ISDV's first chairman during 1914-1917 and a member of Soerabaja's municipal council during 1915-1918.[16] Reeser was known for standing on a table in his classroom to show historical figures theatrically, with the director of the HBS relishing these performances so much that he was often found eavesdropping at Reeser's classroom door (Vervoort 1975:26).

Soekarno, an avid reader of books in the Theosophical Library and the Freemason's Lodge (his sister called him a *kutu buku*, or bookworm),[17] was keenly impressed by some of Reeser's vivid performances, which brought to life some of the historical figures he had met in the library. However, Soekarno's own antics as well as his behaviour toward some of his fellow boarders, described by his Modjokerto pal Hermen, may have been ways to ward off strong feelings of despair and loneliness. As Tjokro was often on the move attending SI affairs, Soekarno may have felt robbed of having a father figure to lean on. He singles out one event when he was only fifteen, being taken by the Tjokro family to a Moehammadijah meeting-hall just across from their Peneleh dwelling, where 'because Father was not deeply involved in it, I discovered Islam myself'.[18] He may also be implying here that his foster father, Tjokro, more at home with Islamic matters than Soekemi ever was, had been preparing him for this unique new discovery. Harsono, however, remembers his father often taking the family and all their boarders, including Soekarno, to the indigenous clubhouse Panti Harsojo, located just around the corner from their home, to watch hours-long wayang performances. Their favourite was the Ramayana epic with Hanoman and his army of monkeys fighting off the brutal overseas king Dasamoeka, the abductor of Sita, Rama's young and beautiful bride. Tjokro compared it with the current struggle being waged by Indonesia's nationalists against their colonial overlords (Soebagijo 1985:11).

As for Soekarno, his situation at Peneleh improved in another sense as well. Having moved him to better quarters, Iboe Soeharsikin and Mbok Tambeng, a servant woman, were now often found preparing for the fifteen-year-

[16]   Harsono Tjokroaminoto 1983:35, also Hermen Kartowisastra 1978:71. For Soekarno's recollections of it see Adams 1965:39-40. For biographical data on Reeser: Tichelman 1985:124-5, Tichelman's 2 November 1993 letter, giving details about his 19 October 1970 interview with Reeser.
[17]   Saiful Rahim 1989:46, with his sister stressing the works of Gandhi, Krishnamurti and Annie Besant.
[18]   Adams 1965:113. Most likely the Moehammadijah meeting was held at the indigenous clubhouse Panti Harsojo at the corner of Gang Peneleh and the Kerkhoflaan. On a visit to Soerabaja on 14 August 1972 we discovered that the clubhouse had been converted to a hotel.

old Soekarno some of his favourite dishes, such as *gado-gado*, a vegetable dish with peanut sauce and *tempe* (soybean cakes) added to it, and *sayur asem*, a vegetable soup flavoured with tamarind. All this made Soekarno feel quite close to Mbok Tambeng, soon considering her as a substitute mother since Iboe Soeharsikin had little time for him, occupied as she often was in running her boarding house (Harsono Tjokroaminoto 1983:35; Adams 1965:37). However, on 2 May 1951, Soekarno did not dwell on this neglect at all but paid tribute to Iboe Soeharsikin, describing her as follows: 'I will never forget Ibu Tjokro, the wife of Pak Tjokro, a woman with a truly noble heart and with such deep insight and fine feeling. She indeed left a great and deep impression on me.' (Amelz 1952, I:13.)

As for Mbok Tambeng, she was to have a meeting years later with President Soekarno in Jakarta's Istana (Palace). Harsono, a second deputy prime minister in the Burhanuddin Harahap cabinet at that time, had taken her to the Istana since she had complained to him about suffering from quite bad eyesight and Harsono was sure that Soekarno would find a remedy. Learning of Mbok Tambeng's misfortune, Soekarno was instrumental in getting her a set of proper glasses, and sending her to a physician for a general check-up (Harsono Tjokroaminoto 1983:10-1; Soebagijo 1985:10).

Soekarno's early HBS years

After Hermen Kartowisastro's testimony of Soekarno being such a bright and well-read HBS pupil, comes another one by Joop Soetjahjo, like Hermen an alumnus of the Regentstraat HBS. Soetjahjo considered Soekarno a *blokbeest* (a cramming animal, or someone who studies a lot), with history being his favourite subject. Perhaps Reeser's vivid history lessons as described above did leave an indelible mark on the young pupil Soekarno. The same source, however, describes Soekarno as being quite discreet, even withdrawn, not at all interested in sports or in the dances at the occasional school parties in Soerabaja's Schouwburg (theatre for stage plays) or the HBS assembly hall, while another pupil has it that Soekarno was shy around girls, yet still adoring them from afar. Annie Verschoor comments that the classes were segregated by sex, with the girls occupying the front desks in the classrooms and the boys the desks at the back, with little contact between them even during free time. During the three daily breaks, the girls usually withdrew to their own space, the so-called *meisjestuin* (girls' garden), separated from the boys.[19]

---

[19]   Vervoort 1975:61; of Soekarno being shy but still admiring the cute *totok* and Indo girl students from afar but never getting seriously involved with them, let alone proposing marriage

Still another contemporary of Soekarno's records a different image altogether of the secondary school life as described by Soekarno in his sessions
with Cindy Adams (1965:43-4). This indigenous alumnus, named Max Soe-
marjo, recalls his experiences as follows:

> I have the most beautiful and pleasant memories of my time at the [Regentstraat]
> HBS in Surabaya. The most important reason for this was that I never experienced
> any discrimination during my entire time of study at the HBS, neither from my
> teachers nor from my fellow students. So I owe quite a lot, if not everything, to
> my study at the HBS in Surabaya. However, I was made cruelly aware of the fact
> that I still lived in a colonial country when after my final examinations I tried to
> get a job in the business world. It remained nearly impossible to get a proper job
> – mainly due to discrimination. (Vervoort 1975:59.)

Mas Soetjahjo confirms the above, stating that 'The HBS-Surabaya was for all
of us an oasis of *fraternité et égalité*'.[20]

Another student, a Dutch girl named Annie Verschoor, some years ahead
of Soekarno – she attended the HBS during 1907-1911 – vividly remembers
the huge *waringin* (*Ficus indica*) trees in the HBS front yard, with groups of
indigenous *kettingberen* (chained prisoners) employed daily to sweep the
shrivelled *waringin* leaves while rattling their neck and ankle irons in the
process. She also recounts that 'some of the teachers were anti-colonial or at
least inspired by the ethical ethos', the latter being a creed current in colonial
reformist circles at that time. One such teacher, responsible for Dutch literature, geography and bookkeeping, was Van Mook (father of H.J. van Mook),
also an alumnus, having attended the Regentstraat HBS during 1906-1911,
who demanded that his students memorize the following ballad of a colonial
army officer:

> In Atjeh [where a long brutal colonial war had been waged] we were, it was
> a wretched time, we burned down everything, the kampungs wide and far
> destroyed by our mighty cannons. Putting everyone to the sword (Romein-Ver-
> schoor 1978, I:55).

---

to one of them, we owe to an interview with Pauline Gobée, a HBS alumna, close to the Hessels
family and a niece of the former head of the Netherlands Indies Bureau van Inlandsche Zaken
during 1929-1937 Emile Gobée, Amsterdam, 6 June 1972. See also her contribution, where Soekarno paid tribute to her uncle, stating that 'he had a warm heart for Indonesia' in Vervoort
1975:47. For the separation between the sexes see Romein-Verschoor 1978, I:58. For Soekarno
recollections of Mien Hessels see Adams 1965:45-6.

[20]   Vervoort 1975:59. For Soetjahjo, three years junior to Soekarno, graduating from the
Ketabang HBS in 1925 (the Regentstraat HBS facing the Stadstuin (City Garden) had in 1923
become the new post office), attending the NIAS during 1926-32 and serving at Soerabaja's CBZ
(Central Civil Hospital) 1932-39 and finally becoming a pulmonary specialist, see Gunseikanbu
1944a:370.

And then there was T. Young, responsible for economics and history, a devout Christian but also a firm believer in 'a remarkable social Christian creed and, connected with it, an ethically inspired colonialism' (Romein-Verschoor 1978:55-6). Another HBS alumnus, named J. Turpijn (at the HBS from 1912 to 1917), opined that '[H.J.] van Mook and Soekarno were both taught the basic principles of constitutional history and national economy' by T. Young.[21] But the one teacher who really excelled, in Annie Verschoor's observations, at least, was Reeser. 'Red to the core [politically,] not at all tall, a bit obese, with a head resembling that of Jaurès, [...] always energetically challenging his classes to draw proper conclusions from his own vivid interpretations of colonialism, the abuse of power and the discrimination of women'. When Verschoor met him again after forty years, in 1952, she remembered Reeser as being 'the first one to awaken in me my own interest in history and colonial relations' (Romein-Verschoor 1978:56-7).

Soekarno's first quasi-political perceptions and club membership

As for Soekarno, his image underwent change as well. Whether influenced by his teachers – Soekarno himself gives but little detail about them to Cindy Adams, though paying tribute to his German language tutor Coos Hartogh[22] – or at home by Tjokro and Iboe Soeharsikin and the many politically aware supporters visiting Peneleh, he seems to have gradually stood out as someone keen to debate matters close to his own heart. It has been said that outside the HBS classes, at the usual Sunday meetings at Panti Harsojo, he was keen to test his own, still only quasi-political, perceptions, in debate or in speeches, 'with his listeners hanging spellbound on his every word as he spoke in fluent Dutch in a quite engaging fashion' (Vervoort 1975:61). There was also the HBS branch of Jong Java (Young Java), the student youth group that was the successor to Tri Koro Dharmo (Three Noble Aims, founded 17 March 1915 in Batavia; a Tri Koro Dharmo Soerabaja branch was founded soon after; the change in name to Jong Java was adopted during the first Tri Koro Dharmo congress in Solo on 12 June 1918 in order to attract non-Javanese as well), which met once a week. But that was considered insufficient by the young Soekarno.[23]

---

[21]   J. Turpijn's contribution in Vervoort 1975:23. For Young, see also Vervoort 1975:37.
[22]   Adams 1965:44, where Soekarno claims that he was Hartogh's pet and that this teacher also used to chair the (Thursday) meetings of Soekarno's HBS debating club. And that Hartogh was so impressed by Soekarno's debating skills that he 'told the 20 pupils collectively and me individually that I would be a great leader some day'.
[23]   Vervoort 1975:60. For Tri Koro Dharmo and Jong Java: *Gedenkboek Jong-Java* 1930; *Jong-Java's jaarboekje* 1923:115-7, 120-2; Rapport Hazeu and Rapport Nieuwenhuis about the Jong Java

So it was Soekarno again, most likely urged on by Dr Hartogh, who set up a debating club with some twenty-five Indonesian HBS students. He also moved it away from Panti Harsojo, since the clubhouse was suspected of being prone to unwelcome infiltration by Indonesian members of the Politieke Inlichtingen Dienst (PID, Political Intelligence Service), to a spare HBS room kindly provided by the Belgian teaching assistant of the HBS named Uijterelst, who could also be trusted to keep nosy strangers away (Vervoort 1975:61-2). Dr Ch.J.R. Both, the HBS director, was also impressed by Soekarno's debating club. During the only visit the '*dirk*' (Dutch nickname for *directeur*) ever made to the club, he was exposed to Soekarno debating 'The influence of Western civilization upon Native youth'. After it and during the usual question period, the students were amazed to see their *dirk* raise his hand. Addressing the chair in the Dutch polite form and Soekarno with '*mijnheer*' (Dutch for sir), Dr Both impressed upon his audience, while referring to his own experience, the importance of always making a clear distinction between genuine civilized forms and mere sham ones. And not to think of everything that was Dutch as being automatically proper or correct. To the students attending that evening's debate it was a revelation to see their *dirk* not automatically approving of all *belanda* (purely Dutch) ways.[24]

Some detail about Soekarno's fellow boarders

The boarders, coming from diverse parts of Java, and encouraged by Soeharsikin to mingle frequently with the many politically aware visitors at her boarding house, seemed, along with the visitors, to resemble 'a who's who of early Indonesian nationalism'. In this 'cradle of all the ideologies'[25] were boarders such as Mas Alimin Prawirodirdjo, two years older than Soekarno and hailing from Solo, and Moeso or Moesodo, a Pegoe-born Javanese from Kediri, four years older than Soekarno. Both were to become prominent members of Sneevliet's ISDV in 1917, while still retaining Sarekat Islam

---

congress of 8 July 1919 in Verbaal 7 October 1919 no 37. For Soekarno's early membership of Tri Koro Dharmo see Hermen Kartowisastra 1978:75. In an article 'Badan Persiapan Organisasi Ra'jat' in the 12 December 2602 (1942) issue of *Asia Raya*, p. 2, Soekarno is said 'to be known as Bhima by the association Jong Java during his student years', while in *Oetoesan Hindia* issues of 5 October 1920, of 14 December 1920, of 7 February 1921, of 21 March 1921 and of 7 April 1921 Soekarno and the Soerabaja branch were labelled as belonging to the radical wing of Jong Java.
[24]   Vervoort 1975:62. Soekarno, however, does not give details about it at all, dismissing Both as merely someone who considered him a source of mischief, see Adams 1965:43.
[25]   Legge 1984:54-5. For the pivotal role of Soeharsikin see Amelz 1952, I:54-5; Harsono Tjokroaminoto in our 15 August 1971 interview with him also referred to it, calling his mother's boarding house a 'Kawah Candradimuka', a true training school; see also Harsono Tjokroaminoto 1983: 4, where he adds that from that school a 'Gatotkaca Indonesia would rise named Soekarno!'

and Insulinde membership. Alimin, named by Soekarno as the one 'who introduced him to Marxism', was also instrumental in founding – at the end of 1917, together with Baars and Soeharijo – the Perhimpoenan Kaoem Boeroeh dan Tani (PKBT, an association promoting the interests of farmers and labourers in the sugar-producing areas, particularly since the sugar factories were paying far too small amounts to farmers for renting their land). Still later, in 1919, both he and Moeso were involved with the Preanger-based Sarekat Islam Section B, leading to brief terms in prison for both of them. These experiences made them swerve, after their release, in an even more radical direction and they became prominent members of the 1920 Perserikatan Kommunist di India (PKI), the successor to the ISDV and Asia's first communist party to boot. Alimin and Moeso were also among those who backed that party's fateful decision in 1926 to instigate armed rebellion.[26]

Other boarders in 1916 included less radical figures such as Raden Abikoesno Tjokrosoejoso, Tjokroaminoto's younger brother, four years senior to Soekarno, and at that time a pupil of Soerabaja's Koningin Emma School. Later, in 1923, he, like Soekarno in 1926, would become an architect, after graduating from the Polytechnisch Instituut in Arnhem. Always active politically in the Soerabaja branch of the Sarekat Islam, in 1932 he became the chairman of the Partai Sarekat Islam Indonesia (PSII), the successor to Tjokro's Sarekat Islam (Gunseikanbu 1944a:470). Other boarders were Mas Pangestoe, born 6 March 1897 in Oeteran near Madioen, and Mas Sigit Bachroensalam, born 31 December 1901 in the *desa* Gorang-gareng near Magetan. Pangestoe, after graduating from the Regentstraat HBS in 1918, served as an official at the Rechtsschool in Batavia, while Sigit Bachroensalam graduated from Soerabaja's Technische School in 1919. According to his son, he was never active in politics or in the *pergerakan*, the nationalist movement. During his final boarding years Mas Sigit had spent time coaching Oetari, then attending a Dutch ELS, in arithmetic. This was much to Soekarno's chagrin, since he was keen to appreciate female beauty and 'at that time had eyes only for her'. Mas Sigit won in the end, marrying Oetari Tjokroaminotopoeteri in mid-1923 after Soekarno had divorced her in 1922. This union lasted a lifetime and produced eight children.[27]

[26]   McVey 1965:168-9; Tichelman 1985:668; Harsono Tjokroaminoto 1983:4, 42-3, claims that Moeso did not board until the Internaat had moved to *kampung* Plampitan in late 1919; this was also confirmed by his father (see Verhoor Tjokro, 17 January 1921 at noon, p. 4, Mr. 184/1921), but Soekarno recalls debating with both Alimin and Moeso when still at Peneleh, though without making clear whether at that time they were boarders at the Internaat or just visiting it, Adams 1965:40-1. As to the backing of the 1926-27 revolt see Tan Malaka's criticism of Alimin's position in Tan Malaka 1991, I:136-7.
[27]   Gunseikanbu 1944a:13; Harsono Tjokroaminoto 1983:3-4, 37; Ir H. Harjono Sigit Bachroensalam's (Sigit and Oetari's sixth child) ms 'Riwayat singkat Ibu Utari', given to Bob Hering 3 October 1999 and his letter of 7 October 1999 to Hering in Stein. See further

Other boarders quite close to Soekarno were Raden Sampoerno, born in Salatiga on 21 July 1903, Raden Hernowo, born in Blitar on 2 April 1900, and the already mentioned Hermen Kartowisastro, born on 13 June 1900 in Modjokerto. Sampoerno, then attending a Hollandsch-Chineesche School in Soerabaja, left the boarding house in 1918, coming back to attend the Neder-landsch Indische Artsen School (NIAS, Netherlands Indies Medical School) in Soerabaja in 1924. Starting in 1934 he served as an Indisch Arts (Indies' Doctor), first privately and then in the service of the colonial government. The latter two attended the same Regentstraat HBS where Soekarno was also a pupil, though Hernowo was one grade ahead of him and Hermen two grades. After graduating from the HBS, Hernowo left Soerabaja to become a civil servant with the postal service in Batavia. Hermen Kartowisatro, after graduating from the HBS in 1919, left for Leiden University and graduated there as an *Indoloog* (Indologist) in 1923. He was also the first Indonesian (elected in 1921) to become a board member of the Indologen Vereeniging (Indologists Association), while in 1922-1923 he chaired the Indonesische Vereeniging (Indonesian Association), a student group and forerunner of the more radically inclined Perhimpoenan Indonesia (PI, Indonesian Associ-ation). After returning to Indonesia in late 1923 he served as a civil servant in a number of postings, ending up in 1939 as a *wedana* attached to the *resi-dent* of Pekalongan. During 1935-1939 he was a member of the Volksraad as well.[28] Harsono also mentions two other residents of the boarding house, boarding first at Peneleh and then by mid-1919 at Plampitan: one named Soepardan, a younger brother of Iboe Soeharsikin, and the other named Kardjono. Both were pupils of the Soerabaja Middelbare Technische School. After finishing the MTS, Soepardan became an engineering supervisor and Kardjono a chief train driver with the SS (State Railways) (Harsono Tjokro-aminoto 1983:41-2).

Soekarno's further political grooming and firmer participation in some associations

Among the Indonesian visitors to the boarding house and the Markas Sarekat Islam at Peneleh during Soekarno's first years of boarding were, first of all, the most stalwart of the SI supporters. These were figures such as Semaoen and Darsono, both representing the SI's radical left wing and from 1917 also members of the ISDV, and Soerjopranoto, a vice-chairman of the SI, and also chair of the Perserikatan Pegawai Pegadaian Boemipoetra (PPPB, Association

---

Oetari's recollections in Erka 1978b:142-5 and Soekarno's recollections rendering Sigit's name incomplete, Adams 1965:59.

[28]   Gunseikanbu 1944a:48, 212, 348. For Hermen's Indologen period see Poeze 1986:161-3.

of Native Pawnshop Workers, seen as a true SI bulwark), founded in 1916 by
Sosrokardono.[29] Sosrokardono, also a frequent visitor to Peneleh, was a radi-
cally inclined SI secretary during 1916-1919, and instrumental in laying the
foundations in Bandoeng in May 1919 – together with Alimin, Semaoen and
ISDV stalwart Pieter Bergsma – of a *vakcentrale*, a labour union federation, the
Persatoean Perhimpoenan Kaoem Boeroeh, afterwards located in Jogjakarta.
He was also deeply involved with the Preanger Section B of the SI during
that time.

Another person seen at Soeharsikin's boarding house or the Markas SI was
Soeharijo, president of the Soerabaja SI branch during 1915-1916, who in 1916,
together with Asser Baars, founded Porojitno, a Soerabaja-based organization
actively promoting the interests of the indigenous population living on the
private landed estates in the Soerabaja area. At the end of 1917, upon the initiative of Soeharijo – who by then had left the Soerabaja SI, taking the SI daily
Selompret Hindia (Trumpet of the Indies) with him, and by now an ISDV stalwart – transformed Porojitno together with Baars and Alimin into the Perhimpoenan Kaoem Boeroeh dan Tani (PKBT, already mentioned above). Soeharijo
would also, in May 1917, become treasurer of the Soerabaja-based Sarekat
Ra'jat Sama Rata Hindia Bergerak (People's League for the Common Struggle
in the Indies), the Indonesian sister organization of the ISDV, founded and led
by Baars since its inception in 1917; it had some 120 members, but petered out
after Baars quite suddenly left the colony in February 1919.[30]

As for Darsono, he moved to Soerabaja in March 1918 to become second
editor-in-chief of the weekly *Soeara Rajat,* a periodical founded by Baars on 1
March 1918, and for a while stayed in Baars' home as well, where Baars made
the talented young Javanese nobleman even more aware of the intricacies
of economics and politics. The two of them, members, together with Coos
Hartogh, of the ISDV Soerabaja branch daily executive, often visited Iboe Soeharsikin's boarding house. Baars at that time had closer contact with Tjokro,
then a member of the Volksraad, who used some radical language in the
Volksraad, putting the ISDV in a more favourable light (Mul 1988:68-9, 94).

Other boarding house visitors were Abdoel Moeis, representing the SI's
right wing, active in the Indië Weerbaar movement, and a 'fierce anti-social-
ist'[31] serving on the SI's main executive, and Tjokrosoedarmo and Tirtoda-

[29] Amelz 1952, I:55, 107, 112-3, 116; Tichelman 1985:384-5, 650, note 1, 651, note 7; Mul 1988:
84.
[30] Tichelman 1985:228, 269-71; McVey 1965:17-8. For Sosrokardono's involvement with Section B, see his Verhoor of 17 December 1920, in Verbaal 14 February 1923 no. 48, Mr. 93/1922. For
Baars' sudden decision to leave the Indies, leaving his wife and son behind, see Mul 1988:90-1.
[31] Tichelman 1985:26. Sneevliet's *Het Vrije Woord* 10 October 1917 contribution entitled 'De
heer Abdoel Moe s Volksleider' on p. 7 accused Moeis of having urged his removal from the
Indies during the 1917 Indië Weerbaar propaganda sojourn in Holland.

noedjo, like Moeis conservatives, both serving on the SI executive of the Soerabaja branch, Tjokrosoedarmo also being the editor of *Oetoesan Hindia*. Tjokrosoedarmo and Tirtodanoedjo, on 11 March 1917, had taken the initiative in forming the Djowo Dipo (Noble Java) movement, which had the aim of abolishing High Javanese (*kromo*, a register of speech dictating forms of studied politeness whenever an inferior addressed a superior) and instead promoting Low Javanese (*ngoko*, a register devoid of submissiveness used by superiors addressing an inferior) as the standard language. Using *ngoko* throughout, the founders hoped to promote a new sense of self-confidence among the Javanese masses. Tjokro and his younger brother Abikoesno served as honorary president and propagandist of the movement, respectively. Both were perhaps aware that this movement was a peculiar expression of Javanese democracy and would bring further benefit to the SI, being seen as evidence of a new spirit of socialism and democratic values while mobilizing dormant social forces (Tichelman 1985:651; Shiraishi 1990:105-7).

Also aware of this was Soekarno. A member since 1916 of Tri Koro Dharmo and its successor Jong Java, Soekarno now clashed repeatedly with the conservative *kaum ningrat* (aristocratic) leadership of these student organizations, particularly about the use of *ngoko*. It earned him the name of a relentless Bima, partly because the legendary figure Bima dared to address the gods in *ngoko* as well.[32] At a later stage, when he was in his late teens, he was marked as the 'red leader' of Jong Java's Soerabaja branch.[33] He remarked to Cindy Adams that eventually he became the secretary and then the chairman of the branch (Adams 1965:49).

Soekarno under the sway of Asser Baars' concept of cosmopolitan socialism

Naturally most of the figures described above were often in the habit of bringing along their expatriate colleagues-in-arms to the boarding house or to the Markas SI at Peneleh, and sometimes to the indigenous clubhouse Panti Harsojo at the corner of Gang Peneleh and Kerkhoflaan, since it had more space to offer. The clubhouse was used by Baars, among others, not only for frequent meetings with his Indonesian political comrades but also occasionally for staging demonstrations against colonial policies or against some of the right-wing stances of the SI.[34] This caused PID chief Muurling to comment:

[32] Onghokham, 'Bung Karno, Bima, Jawa', *Tempo* 3 May 1980:57 and Suprijatna 1981:105-6.
[33] *Oetoesan Hindia*, 5 October 1920.
[34] This Panti Harsojo meeting of 12 September 1917, attended by SI and ISDV stalwarts and some 1,000 people from the general public, was in response to the 31 August 1917 meeting in Soerabaja's movie theatre, the Oost Java Bioscoop, called by Baars' ISDV Soerabaja branch and the aligned Sama Rata Hindia Bergerak association to attack Moeis and the SI right wing for their

Sneevliet is in fact far less dangerous than Baars, who knows the native and his language [Malay] quite well. He is someone who does not tire the native with slogans which for the native have but little meaning, but instead makes connection through matters like cooperation, the problems around the privatized lands [Baars's concern about small farmers and low rentals paid for land used by white sugar planters] etc. and thus truly gaining the native's trust.[35]

It was under these circumstances that Soekarno, already influenced moderately by Hartogh and Reeser, fell under the spell of Asser Baars and Baars' indigenous companions, such as Semaoen and Darsono, and thus came to embrace a still more radical brand of socialism. Baars, of all the expatriate ISDV stalwarts the most fluent in Malay and a consistent and outspoken anti-nationalist, convinced Soekarno and perhaps even Tjokro, always trying to placate both rightist and leftist elements of his SI, in a way as well, to adhere to a more cosmopolitan socialism based upon humanism and solidarity with the outcasts of society. 'Do not believe in nationalism', argued Baars. 'Struggle instead for humanity and do not show any trace of chauvinism.' Years later, on 1 June 1945 exactly, Soekarno recalled this stage in his early political awakening as follows:

> I confess that when I was sixteen and at a [Dutch] secondary school in Surabaja, I was quite influenced by a socialist by the name of A. Baars, who taught me not to believe in nationalism but in the humanity of the entire world. 'Do not have even the least sense of nationalism' he told me! That was in 1917. However, in 1918, thanks be to God, there was yet another man who impressed me deeply, and that was Dr Sun Yat Sen. In his work *San Min Chu I*, or The Three People's Principles, I found a lesson which discredited the cosmopolitanism taught by A. Baars.[36]

This infatuation with cosmopolitan socialism first fading and then being rejected altogether was undoubtedly due to a set of new circumstances facing Soekarno in his now burgeoning politically aware life. First of all, his foster father was often away, attending sessions at Betawi's Volksraad. Tjokro had been appointed to that quasi-parliamentary body on 23 February 1918, and accepted in a letter to Governor-General Van Limburg Stirum dated 30

---

positive stance vis-à-vis the Indië Weerbaar movement, attracting some 800 people. For both these meetings see *Oetoesan Hindia*, 14, 15 and 17 September 1917 and Verbaal 4 April 1918. Baars' remarks there about the Indies government being *busuk* (rotten) and therefore not to be trusted to make Indië Weerbaar something worthwhile for Indonesians led to his dismissal from the Koningin Emma school on 24 October 1917, see Mul 1988:59 and Perthus 1976:158.

[35]   PID report of 12 May 1917 no. 71, Mr. 99/17, Verbaal 15 May 1918 no. 64.

[36]   Soekarno 1986b:147. Soekarno cites here, as he did in his defence plea before the Landraad in 1930, Sun Yat-sen's *San Min Chu I* of Shanghai 1928. Which edition he used in 1918 we have not been able to trace. Both Mul 1988:49 and Perthus 1976:154 maintain that Hartogh and Baars were instrumental in Soekarno's one-year-long infatuation with cosmopolitan socialism.

March 1918, after a narrow SI locals' referendum in which 27 voted for acceptance and 26 against. Another vote was held by the central body (CSI), with
six voting for it and five against,[37] thus favouring Moeis's view over that of
Semaoen, who had termed the Volksraad 'merely a nonsensical show and a
trick of the capitalists to deceive the Indonesian people in order to gain more
economic profit' (Pringgodigdo 1950:17). These narrow voting margins show
how strong the position of the young Semaoen had indeed become.

Soekarno once more changes course ideologically

As for Tjokro, during his occasional visits to his Soerabajan bailiwick, he
gradually entrusted Soekarno with some minor political duties and responsibilities. These the young pupil was only too glad to perform. He had watched Tjokro's charismatic handling of crowds before, had even emulated
Tjokro's oratorical performances in the privacy of his boarding room,[38] and
was now quite eager and ready to engage himself similarly – not just during
the weekly sessions at the school's debating society where he had tested his
oratorical skills, but also outside it in the wider world of indigenous politics.
He had been keen to embrace the philosophy of the Djowo Dipo movement,
a group for which Tjokro served as honorary president. And although this
was primarily a linguistic issue, Soekarno felt prepared to make use of the
political consequences of Djowo Dipo as well. This was demonstrated by the
clashes he would soon have with the conservative leadership of Jong Java.
where he was twice forbidden to reveal his criticism in *ngoko*, which led to
his storming out of the meeting hall. His performance, though aborted, still
added to his fame of being a relentless Bima and fearless to boot.

Bernhard Dahm alleges that it was Abdoel Moeis who was mainly responsible for Soekarno abandoning Baars' anti-nationalist brand of cosmopolitan
socialism. To strengthen this claim, Dahm cites the following remarks made
by Moeis at the SI's second national congress held in Betawi, 20-27 October
1917:

> Because our own conditions are now so miserable, they demand all our strength.
> They demand the effort of nationalists, whose force must not be dissipated. For
> the betterment of the whole world we need not begin by turning into internation-
> alists. [...] One who calls himself a leader of the people must [therefore] revive
> national feeling in the hearts of his countrymen. Only if we have that national
> feeling can we expect that our wish for independence [...] may soon be fulfilled.
> (*Sarekat-Islam Congres* 1919a:4-5.)

---

[37]　*Neratja*, 21 and 25 March 1918.
[38]　Oetari in *Sarinah*, 22 June 1987; Saiful Rahim 1978:48.

It was at this same national congress that the Semaoen-Darsono left wing was somehow brought into line by Tjokro's cementing clarion call of condemning 'sinful [meaning foreign or Western] capitalism' (*Sarekat-Islam Congres* 1919a: 83). As for Soekarno, it seems unlikely that, at the end of October 1917, he would have heeded Moeis' advice to abandon Baars's cosmopolitanism altogether. As Soekarno attested on several later occasions, his departure from Baars' ideas took place at the end of 1918 and not in the autumn of 1917. So the true source for Soekarno's changing ideological course lies elsewhere. It has in fact to do with a set of developments propelling the young Soekarno in the direction of political engagement, without any longer relying on Baars' ideology. First of all was the stance adopted by the SI during its third national congress, attended by Soekarno and held in Soerabaja from 29 September to 6 October 1918, an event that marked a significant shift to the left. Not entirely satisfied with the mere struggle against sinful capitalism and the idea of equality preached by Djowo Dipo – the use of *ngoko* was adopted by the congres (*Sarekat-Islam Congres* 1919b:40-3) – the SI left wing, spurred by recent European revolutionary upheavals, wanted still more emphasis on the concept of class struggle. This call was heeded by the SI executive, causing Petrus Blumberger (1920:25) to comment that 'the old SI was dead and buried' since the pendulum had now swung to 'issues of independence, revolution and socialism'. That the SI immediately joined the Volksraad's Radical Concentration of 16 November 1918, did not surprise Petrus Blumberger either. To his way of thinking, 'the end of the World War and the major political upheavals that preceded it did not fail to influence the spiritual currents in Java' (Petrus Blumberger 1931:68). Well aware of a certain drop in SI membership rurally, Baars, often carried away by events and not always having a proper sense of realism, immediately expressed his delight about the changes taking place within the SI's top ranks. With ISDV stalwart supporters such as Semaoen and Prawoto Soedibijo, now members of the SI executive, and Darsono, a paid propagandist, surely growth in urban membership of both the SI and the ISDV would soon commence, Baars thought. On 5 October 1918, in a letter to Sneevliet, he said: 'This morning's SI congress clearly shows that we do not need to busy ourselves needlessly since we already seem to posses the spiritual leadership. This congress was indeed not an SI but an ISDV congress!'[39]

However, faced with mounting marital troubles in his own household and with Henk Sneevliet's expulsion soon to occur, Baars was not to see any

---

[39]   IISG-Sneevliet archives, no. 48. Hazeu, the government's commissioner for Native and Arab affairs, was disturbed to see 'Baars so freely moving around the SI following at the congress, using his command of Malay to inspire some aura of confidence but [fortunately] not being seen by the entire assembly as the mediator', see Kwantes 1975:108.

solid results coming in the wake of the SI congress. An attempt by Baars to sway Tjokro in the direction of supporting a bolder course of action, such as promoting strikes in the sugar-growing areas, was neatly avoided by the SI leader (Mul 1988:90). Furthermore, when the revolutionary councils of the Soerabaja soldiers and sailors were smashed by the government in late November 1918[40] (though these had not been publicly supported by him), Baars was dismayed, being well aware that Sneevliet's earlier meddling with the restive soldiers and sailors had led to his expulsion. And so, with Sneevliet finally gone from the scene, Baars was left in charge of the ISDV. Firmly supported in that endeavour by Coos Hartogh and Barend Coster in particular, Baars seemed nevertheless to have lost control of his own situation, politically as well personally. Finding a passage on the steamer *Kawi* bound for Holland open, Baars suddenly left Soerabaja at the end of February 1919 on the *Kawi*. In a farewell note to *Het Vrije Woord* he alleged that 'ISDV power had been illusory all along, but that in Europe revolutionary upheaval was now near, and he clearly longed soon to be part of those events over there' (Mul 1988:90).

At this juncture Soekarno must have felt that Baars' role in the Indies had come to a definite end, and he may have turned once again to his HBS German language tutor, who was now in sole charge of the ISDV. While Soekarno maintained in June 1945 that by the end of 1918 he had abandoned socialist cosmopolitanism, it may well not have been until February 1919 that he made that fateful decision, after Baars had left the Soerabajan political scene. It is at that time that Soekarno was given a serialized account of Karl Kautsky's *Sozialismus und Kolonialpolitik; Eine Auseinandersetzung* – it appeared, considerably shortened, in the February-May 1919 issues of *Het Vrije Woord* – by his German language tutor.[41] Kautsky, described by Günther Roth as one who thought 'of no better form for the dictatorship of the proletariat than a powerful parliament, after the English pattern, with a social-democratic majority and a strong proletariat backing it',[42] would later exert a rather strong influence upon a more mature Soekarno. As for the more moderate Hartogh, Dahm asserts that he was from now on to influence Soekarno, though Dahm simply got some of the facts wrong. First of all,

---

[40]   For this unrest among the Surabaya soldiers and sailors, with the former attempting to occupy strategic locations in the city, a ploy aborted at once by the government and thus ending 'this revolutionary attempt in the Indies', see Verbaal 7 August 1919 no. 49, Mr. 461/18, 478/18.
[41]   Koch 1956:14; 15 August 1971 interview with Harsono Tjokroaminoto and 5 January 1952 interview with Marcel Koch. Kautsky's treatise, though considerably shortened, appeared in *Het Vrije Woord* of 22 February 1919:184-6, 15 March 1919:214, 29 March 1919:229-30, 5 April 1919: 241-2, 12 April 1919:254, 19 April 1919:262, 3 May 1919:276-8.
[42]   See Roth 1963:189, citing Kautsky's 8 July 1893 letter to Franz Mehring; also in Goldenberg 1933:15.

Hartogh did not leave the ISDV in 1917 in order to found the ISDP, as Dahm alleges (Dahm 1969:30, 42). Also, in choosing between nationalism and socialist class struggle, Hartogh, like Sneevliet, Baars, Coster, Stam and Bergsma ideologically, would always opt for the latter approach.

So Tjokro's approving the 25 December 1919 founding of the Persatoean Pergerakan Kaoem Boeroeh (PPKB, Association of Labour Unions) and the Persatoean Pergerakan Kemerdekaan Rakjat (PPKR, Association of People's Liberation Movements) and stating that 'socialism, though admirable, had to wait until after Java's liberation' were condemned by the ISDV top, since they were seen as merely nationalist rather than true socialist attitudes.[43] More *ethisch* (ethically) inclined socialists – such as Marcel Koch, the brothers Zadok Stokvis and Jozef Emanuel Stokvis, Daan van der Zee and Sam Koperberg – all of them rather sympathetic to Indonesian nationalist notions, clearly rejected the revolutionary class sentiments advocated by the ISDV. Instead, they would stress gradual indigenous development made possible through Western capitalism, in order to form a bridge to effective social legislation, and then (so they hoped) to more rapid development of indigenous capitalism (Perthus 1976:144-5; Koch 1919:48, 1956:5-8). As for Coos Hartogh, he remained in charge of the ISDV until the seventh annual congress of his party, where the name Perserikatan Komunis Indonesia was adopted, against his advice. He remained a member, however, until his sick leave in Holland commencing in 1921. Returning to the colony in 1923, he joined the ISDP, but was never in charge of it.[44] Some years before that time, and in the wake of some dramatic personal events at Peneleh, Soekarno changed tack, taking nationalist politics more seriously. In his own private life, quite a dramatic change was to take place as well.

Iboe Soeharsikin's death and the move to Plampitan

While Tjokro was away in the Preanger in order to smooth matters concerned with Section B of the SI, he received urgent calls to return home, since his wife and his *anak bungsu* Soejoed Ahmad had fallen seriously ill. Tjokro was back home at Peneleh on 6 March 1919. Diagnosed as having typhoid fever, Iboe Soeharsikin succumbed on 27 April 1919, while Soejoed Ahmad, one month after his mother's death, miraculously recovered.[45] Iboe Soeharsikin

---

[43]   McVey 1965:45, 62; Shiraishi 1990:114; Ingleson 1986:126-7.
[44]   McVey 1965:46-7. For Hartogh's wariness of Leninist Bolshevism see *Het Vrije Woord* 10 January 1920:113. For Hartogh's sick leave and 1923 ISDP membership: Tichelman's letter of 12 December 1998.
[45]   Verhoor (interrogation) Tjokroaminoto, 16 January 1921, p. 9, Mr. 184/1921, Verbaal 2 May 1923 D6; also Soebagio 1985:6-7 and Amelz 1952, I: 56, but citing 1921 instead of 1919.

was buried, with many SI followers attending her funeral at the indigenous cemetery at Botopoetih on the east bank of the Pegirian river, some three km to the northeast of Peneleh. One chronicler stated that 'Soerabaja was overcome by sadness, with tears flowing abundantly (*hudjan air mata*)', and that Iboe Soeharsikin 'had closed her eyes forever in order to save her son (*menutup mata setelah berpesan kepada anaknja jang laki laki*)' (Amelz 1952, I:57). Overcome by grief, Tjokro decided to leave his Peneleh dwelling soon afterwards. He settled with his family and his boarders, with Soekarno among them, in *kampung* Plampitan, just a stone's throw south of Peneleh, near a *warung besar* (a big provisions store) owned by the rather wealthy Pak Hadji Abdoel Gani, a faithful SI member (Harsono Tjokroaminoto 1983:36; Frederick 1989:26), whose son, then five years old, would years later become one of President Soekarno's closest political associates.

At his new boarding house, Soekarno was given a large room next to Tjokro. One of the new boarders at Plampitan was Soemini, a fifteen-year-old niece of Soekarno, then attending the Soerabaja MULO (Meer Uitgebreid Lager Onderwijs school, comparable to a US junior college) and later to enter the NIAS (Nederlandsch-Indische Artsen School, Netherlands Indies Medical School) in 1924. After her 1931 graduation from NIAS, she and her physician husband, Mas Moerdjani, after practising two years in Soerabaja, moved to Magelang and in 1939 to Bandoeng, where they joined M.H. Thamrin's drive for a genuine Indonesian parliament.[46] In that latter city Soekarno would use the *nom de plume* Soemini for his drawings, appearing on some of his 1932 *Fikiran Ra'jat* covers,[47] in order to honour his niece, who that year had been promoted to physician at the Soerabaja CBZ (Centraal Burgerlijk Ziekenhuis, Central Civil Hospital).[48]

Soekarno's marital engagement with Siti Oetari Tjokroaminotopoeteri

In order to bring some order into the new Plampitan household, Tjokro remarried a woman named Roestinah, a rather notorious *tandak* (professional dancer), in March 1920. The marriage remained without issue, and experienced some strain caused by the extravagant tastes and habits of the new wife.[49] It was around this time that Soekarno, most likely pressed by Tjokro's younger

[46]   For Soemini's boarding, see Harsono Tjokroaminoto 1983:37. For her and her husband's careers, see Gunseikanbu 1944a:334.
[47]   See for these *Fikiran Ra'jat* covers Soekarno 1965:180, 186, facing 214, 218, facing 226, 244.
[48]   Interview with Ibu Inggit Garnasih, 30 March 1971.
[49]   See Hadji Misbach's 'Semprong wasiat: Partij discipline S.I. Tjokroaminoto mendjadi ratjoen pergerakan ra'jat Hindia' (The magic lamp: Tjokroaminoto's party discipline has poisoned the Indies people's movement), *Medan Moeslimin* 1923-9:175-6.

brother Abikoesno, informed Tjokro that he would be pleased to become his
son-in-law by marrying Siti Oetari. Tjokro enthusiastically approved of the
proposal.[50] The exact date of the 'marriage' cannot be established since there
was no certificate ever issued of this *kawinan gantung* (literally, a hanging
marriage, but more like an engagement), which according to the two people
involved was never consummated, due to Oetari's young age. Since both
Oetari and Soekarno claim that the engagement took place when they were
fourteen and eighteen respectively, April 1920 seems to be the most likely
month, just before Soekarno's nineteenth birthday (Erka 1978b:140-1). The
Dutch journalists Otto Kuijk and Bart van Veen claim that the photograph
on page 76 of their book *Soekarno tabeh* shows Oetari and Soekarno in the
front row of a group of Indonesian HBS students in front of the entrance hall
of the Soerabaja Regentstraat HBS, while Giebels (1999:63) refers to it as the
photograph of their bridal engagement. Neither description is true. The girl
sitting next to Soekarno is not Oetari but a Miss Soekartini, a younger sister
of the later *Resident* of Soerabaja Raden Soedirman. The latter, during 1921 to
1924, was a revered member of Soerabaja's municipal council. After graduation, Soekartini became a school teacher and was posted to Makassar. In the
early fifties she held a senior post at the Department of Education (Vervoort
1975:61; Gunseikanbu 1944a:465). Fortunately, Oetari's son Ir Harjono Sigit
Bachrunsalam mailed an early 1920 photograph to me, showing a somewhat
older looking Soekarno standing behind his new young bride, who looks
slimmer, younger and more beautiful than Miss Soekartini of the HBS photograph. Ir Harjono dated the photograph at the beginning of the 1918-1919
Regentstraat HBS term.[51]

Soekarno's somewhat more positive involvement with nationalist politics

Soekarno, in his final year of HBS and a married man to boot, now divided
his time between preparations for the final and rather tough HBS examinations soon to come and getting politically involved more seriously than
before. Brief references were made above to the political clashes he had
with the *kaum ningrat* leadership of Jong Java, a leadership which he felt
was out of touch with the true spirit of the Indonesian *pergerakan*.[52] During
the annual plenary meeting of the Jong Java Soerabaja branch on 6 February
1921, Soekarno, in anticipation of Coos Hartogh's attendance as well as that

---

[50]   For Tjokro marrying Roestinah: Harsono Tjokroaminoto 1983:3. For Soekarno's and
Oetari's *kawinan gantung*, see Ir H. Harjono Sigit Bachrunsalam, 'Riwayat singkat Ibu Utari', ms,
p. 1; Legge 1984:61; Adams 1965:47; Solichin Salam 1966:43.
[51]   Letter of Ir H. Harjono Sigit Bachrunsalam to Bob Hering, 3 February 2000.
[52]   So described by him in *Das Parlement* 1958-18:209.

of a guest speaker, commenced his address on the educational system, using *ngoko*, the Javanese language form utilized by the Djowo Dipo movement he had supported since its inception. Soegito, who was chairing the meeting, promptly stopped Soekarno from speaking and ordered him to continue in Dutch, since Soekarno would not address the meeting in *kromo*. This Soekarno refused to do, and since his tutor Hartogh did not show up either, the meeting somewhat uproariously broke up.[53] Equally turbulent was the meeting of 20 March 1921, where once more it was Soekarno who caused tempers to flare. At this meeting, Soekarno proposed admitting to the membership not only secondary and intermediate school pupils but also pupils attending elementary schools, as long as they were competent to debate political issues. And he proposed that Jong Java's periodical should be published in Malay rather than in Dutch alone. The Djowo Dipo language issue also cropped up, with Soekarno now proposing the admittance of Malay during meetings. And again Soegito abruptly disbanded the meeting.[54]

At the fourth Jong Java congress held in Bandoeng from 12 to 15 June 1921 – labelled by some as the congress of the 'reds', since they were by far the most militant – Soekarno not only condemned *kapitalisme terkoetoet* (cursed capitalism) but passionately urged the audience to use *ngoko*, citing hereby the slogan of the French Revolution: *kemerdekaan, persamaan dan persoedaraan* (liberty, equality and fraternity). Also, the proposal for Jong Java to join with the Jong Sumatranen Bond (League of Young Sumatra) was strongly criticized by Soekarno and Soekartono (the latter also a member of the Jong Java Soerabaja branch), with Soekarno inveighing against it as follows: 'in order to improve the plight of the common people we ought to tackle economic problems first and not get involved with federative union'. Nonetheless, the *kaum ningrat* conservatives prevailed, and the plans for federation were approved.[55]

Soekarno's first newspaper articles and his search for a nationalist political concept

Some of Soekarno's views expressed during these Jong Java meetings and congresses were aired as well in *Oetoesan Hindia*. Soekarno was now a contributor to that daily and he was also no longer an unknown. At a huge May Day manifestation on 1 May 1921, it was reported in *Oetoesan Hindia* that 'walking through the masses with Tjokro toward the podium was the young and popular leader Soekarno'.[56] His first *Oetoesan Hindia* article about

---

53   *Oetoesan Hindia*, 7 February 1921.
54   *Oetoesan Hindia*, 21 March 1921.
55   *Sinar Hindia*, 22 June 1921; *Boedi Oetomo*, 20-27 June 1921; *Jong Java*, July 1921.
56   *Oetoesan Hindia*, 2 May 1921.

'Nasibnja S.I. Soerabaja' (S.I. Soerabaja's fate) he wrote together with SI member S.P. Soerdarjo in response to an SI meeting they had on 17 January 1921 with only a hundred showing up. Chairman Soekiran viewed the low attendance as a sign of little public interest in the SI. Soekarno and Soerdarjo then raised three questions about the poor attendance: 'Was it caused by Darsono's criticism of Tjokro; by the lack of zest demonstrated by the people at large or by the fact that the people were fed up with the current leadership and declined to be led by it any longer?'

As to the first, they held that Darsono's criticism had been ironed out by a subsequent well-attended meeting in Soerabaja. As to the other two issues, they did not feel that the public's gusto had been quenched, since a number of meetings had been attended by a thousand or more people. One such gathering, led by Soekarno's tutor Coos Hartogh, they held up as an example to follow. Hartogh had taken a public stand against the city government's plans to erect a *schouwburg* (theatre) at a cost of 400,000 florins, arguing that the plans would not benefit the welfare of the people at large at all. With all this in mind, Soekarno and Soerdarjo maintained that the next SI meeting would surely attract thousands as long as meaningful issues were seriously addressed.[57]

That the planned Jong Java-Jong Sumatranen Bond fusion stuck in Soekarno's throat was demonstrated by his contribution 'Intellectueelen?' (Intellectuals? – with the question mark speaking for itself). This, his second contribution to *Oetoesan Hindia*, immediately tackled the problem of what benefit such a federation would bring to the common people of these two islands. Soekarno noted that 'the Sarekat Islam planned to promote the welfare of the people of Hindia Belanda [Netherlands Indies], while the Perserikatan Kommunist India (PKI)[58] had those same aims in their banner'.

But having the same overall goal, Soekarno argued, did not mean that their methods were the same as well. As to the two student associations, with one striving for a Greater Java and the other for a Greater Sumatra, what did they hope to gain from such a fusion? Soekarno asked: 'Were these federation plans, soon to be decided on at Jong Java's fourth national congress, really worthy of pursuing? Did they not invite foggy and vague notions of sham greatness to emerge as a result of it?'

So, at the end of his article, Soekarno summoned 'the young intellectuals to aim for the only proper solution: instead of a useless federation they should devote themselves solely to the plight of the people and assist them out of their current miseries'.[59] Here, he seems to sympathize with the ideals

---

[57] *Oetoesan Hindia*, 21 January 1921.
[58] Not the ISDV, as Giebels 1999:64 states.
[59] *Oetoesan Hindia*, 7 April 1921.

of the young Marxists of the ISDV/SI, as expressed so far primarily by Sema-oen, Darsono and Marco.

Two weeks after his summons to the young intellectuals, Soekarno tackled quite a different problem: that of prostitution. The policy of Bandoeng's *Regent* Wiranatakoesoema to remove prostitutes from the city and relocate them elsewhere was, to Soekarno's mind, not the answer to the problem. As Mas Marco argued in 1924 with respect to Soerabaja's rather dismal city life, Soekarno dwelt upon the evils of Western capitalism and its dramatic impoverishing impact upon the indigenous labouring classes employed by that system. He described the condition 'as an urban master and slave rela-tionship, and in the rural sector as a landowner and serf one, bringing slave and serf to such poverty that their wives and daughters were often driven into prostitution'.

To end the poverty he called upon 'the SI and its womenfolk to continue the struggle of eradicating colonial capitalism, since that system was at the core of evils such as prostitution'.[60]

Soekarno's article also appeared on the front page of the Bandoeng peri-odical *Sama Tengah* of 9 March 1922, a rather neutral paper politically, edited by A.H. Wignjadisastra. Soekarno's piece being reprinted there serves as yet another indication of Soekarno's growing popularity, even in West Java.[61]

In two *Oetoesan Hindia* articles dated 22 April 1921 and 6 May 1921, deal-ing respectively with 'Zelfbestuur' (Self-government) and 'Hak memilih; Samboengan rentjana zelfbestuur' (Electoral suffrage; An appendage to the self-government scheme), Soekarno first dealt with the SI's aim to work toward self-government. In his view, the struggle of the SI in that sense was a *noodzakelijk verschijnsel* (essential phenomenon), but with the SI still some considerable distance away from realizing real self-government for the people of the Indies. Also, it required some time for the common people to realize that a government of their own needed to be based upon shared interests between them and such a government. For that to happen would require a learning process among the people of the Indies. Soekarno then dwelt with some detail on the democratically based electoral institutions in the Netherlands, contrasting these with the embryonic phase and far too narrow base of the electoral institutions in the Indies. And while he praised the current decentralization of these latter organs, he lamented the fact that they failed to sufficiently educate the common people in self-government. These councils at the municipal, regional, regency and Volksraad level did not truly represent the common people, neither were they quite in touch with them. So all these councils needed to be changed gradually to become true

---

[60]   *Oetoesan Hindia*, 21 April 1921. For Mas Marco see his *Roesaknja kehidoepan di kota besar*, 1924.
[61]   *Sama Tengah* no. 31 (9 March 1922).

representatives of the *kaum proletariaat* (proletariat), Soekarno concluded, asserting that it would take some time for the *pohon* (tree) of self-govern-ment to firmly take root. Such a government of the people would then bring about economic and political justice under the auspices of the Sarekat Islam. The people would be wise therefore to opt for Sarekat Islam membership, Soekarno concluded.[62]

In his next contribution, 'Hak memilih; Samboengan rentjana zelfbestuur', Soekarno elaborated somewhat on the nature of future elections to be held in the Indies. But first he briefly explained the nature of Dutch electoral insti-tutions and the way their membership was elected by direct and indirect elections, leading to a satisfactory system of proportional representation. He considered these developments quite useful in a homogeneous society such as the Netherlands, but not as yet suitable for Java, since the common folk in that diverse society needed to become more sophisticated (*kaoem kromo masih bodoh*). And here was another educational challenge for the Sarekat Islam in its efforts to make self-government feasible in the not-too-distant future. Also, Soekarno tended to distance himself from the SI radical wing in his support of the SI Agoes Salim-Moeis drive for party discipline, which was opposed by the communists since it would abolish their ISDV bridgehead within the SI. This issue was resolved in favour of the conservatives dur-ing the Soerabaja CSI congress of 6 to 10 October 1921.[63] Soekarno censured 'those SI leaders who were still far too eagerly following principles of other associations which were often in dire contradiction to the SI's own political and basic concepts'.[64]

As to future elections, Soekarno strongly opted for 'direct elections, since they were ideal for our folks living in the Indies, who by that time would surely be more sophisticated'.[65] In closing, Soekarno urged the SI,

> once the right conditions had been created and a proper parliament with true representatives of the people had been installed, to continue to work and agitate in order to reinforce democracy and Islam in the Indies so as to abolish capitalism, since what use is a government of our own if it is still controlled by supporters of capitalism and imperialism?[66]

---

[62]   *Oetoesan Hindia*, 22 April 1921.
[63]   McVey 1965:102-3 and *Overzicht CSI* 1922:44-57. With Tjokro in prison on charges of per-jury, Salim dominated the proceedings (*Overzicht CSI* 1922:48).
[64]   Beberapa pemimpin pergerakan Sarekat Islam menoeroet pendapatan atau azasjna lain-lain perhimpoenan jang atiap kali bertentangan dengan azasnja Sarekat Islam.
[65]   Rechtstreeksche verkiezing itoe jang baik sendiri bagi Ra'jat kita di Hindia [...] tentoelah Ra'jatnja soedah tiada bodoh lagi sebagai sekarang.
[66]   Djika wakil-wakil jang doedoek di madjelis itoe wakil Ra'jat jang sedjati, jang dengan sebe-toel-betoelnja bekerdja boeat Ra'jat kita... djanganlah Sarekat Islam berhenti ichtiar, Sarekat Islam akan teroes bekerdja dengan sekoeat-koeatnja akan menegoehkan democratie dan Islamisme di

From these statements several deductions can be made. First, Soekarno did concede that the Dutch still had a role to play politically and constitutionally in the colony, since the Indonesian people at that time still lacked sufficient sophistication for them to take sole charge of their own destiny. Here, the moderating influence of his German tutor Coos Hartogh and also of his father-in-law Tjokroaminoto come into play, since in both cases their criticism of the colonial system was often kept within certain limits. Also evident was Soekarno's perception of the role the Sarekat Islam ought to adopt in its drive toward genuine self-government. Becoming slowly more aware of the currents that formed the SI's mental make-up – nationalism, socialism and Pan-Islamism – he went somewhat further than the Sarekat Islam *azas-azas* (basic principles) did, by demanding the abolition of capitalism and imperialism the moment his country achieved self-government, thus following a purely Marxist maxim. Here we may well have arrived at the key to understanding the young Soekarno's political thinking at that time. The blending of nationalism, Islam and Marxism would only later – in Bandoeng, in October-December 1926, to be exact – be perfected, with him following more clearly the old Javanese dictum that, synthetically speaking, all matters were basically one.[67]

Soekarno's HBS graduation and the move to Bandoeng

It is no wonder that Soekarno's last contribution to *Oetoesan Hindia* occurred on 6 May 1921, since from that date onward he needed all his spare time for preparing himself for the tough final oral examinations of the Regentstraat HBS, still to come at the end of May. His final written examinations he had already passed in April 1921, during a lull between his 21 January and 7 April *Oetoesan Hindia* contributions and his stormy attendance at Jong Java congresses. On 10 June 1921 Soekarno received his final HBS diploma; all in all he had been examined in fifteen subjects. That he finished his HBS education in a mere five years – in spite of his being married during the final HBS years and in spite of the time-consuming political issues he was involved in – do mark him as a remarkably intelligent student. Of the 67 candidates, 52 received the diploma, with Soekarno being one of only three indigenous (and two *peranakan* Chinese) receiving it.[68]

Hindia ini, akan menolong Ra'jat jang menderita dan menghantjoerkan kapitalisme jang menindas, sebab apakah perloenja zelfbestuur djika tiada dengan haloean jang democratisch? Apakah ertinja zelfbestuur, djika jang mendjalankan zelfbestuur ini semoea dari pehak kapitalisme dan imperialisme? *Oetoesan Hindia*, 6 May 1921.

[67] See his articles appearing in *Indonesia Moeda*, nos 1-3, October-December 1926.

[68] Interview with Anwar and Harsono Tjokroaminoto, 15 August 1971.

That his parents as well as his in-laws did finally opt for his entry to the Bandoeng Technische Hoogeschool (TH, Technical Faculty) is not so strange a choice at all. In Soerabaja, still not too far from Soekarno's paternal home in Blitar, no *hogeschool* existed; there was only the one in Bandoeng. A university sojourn for Soekarno in the Netherlands, which had been the custom since the turn of the century for a small but growing number of high *priyayi* or *pangreh praja* offspring, seems to have remained beyond the financial resources then available to Soekarno's family circle. In 1964 Soekarno himself perhaps still felt inferior intellectually to indigenous graduates of Dutch universities, some of whom had become his political adversaries, and he implied to Cindy Adams that it was his mother – his theosophical father is not mentioned at all – who was dead set against her son going to Holland. Iboe Soekemi, hearing on 11 June 1921 that her son intended to go to a university in Holland, as quite a few of his indigenous classmates planned to do, told him that they financially lacked the resources for sending him abroad. Besides, he was better off attending the only university then existing in the Indies, 'among your own. Never forget, my son, that your place, your destiny, your heritage, is in these islands.' (Adams 1965:50.)

So, by the end of June 1921 Soekarno was enrolled, using the title of *raden*, at the Bandoeng TH for the academic year 1921-1922. He was one among six Indonesian students – with two Chinese and 29 Europeans making up the rest of that academic year's enrolment – in a city he described as being 'the Gate to the White World' (*Gerbang ke Dunia Putih*), perhaps a rather appropriate description at that time, since he had still to commit himself seriously to a career, let alone a political one. After he breezed into Bandoeng, he intimated to Cindy Adams, 'I was fairly pleased with myself. I even went so far as to affect a cigarette holder.' All this was 'due to my success establishing the *pitji*, that black velveteen cap which is my own trademark, as our symbol of nationalism'. He had unveiled it at

> a Young Java [Jong Java] meeting just before I left Soerabaja. Previously there had been much heated discussion on the part of the so-called intelligentsia, who resented the kerchief Javanese men wore with their sarongs, and the *pitji* that *betjak* drivers [*betjak*: a tricycle pedalled by its driver, carrying one to two passengers] and other humble people wore. In fact, they scorned all true Indonesian headgear, and went uncovered; it was their way of sneering subtly at the lower classes. They needed to learn that you can't lead the masses unless you're one of them. [...] I deliberately decided to link myself with the common man. At the next meeting I arranged to wear a *pitji*.[...]
>
> The name even devolved from our conquerors. The Dutch word '*pet*' means cap. '*Je*' being the diminutive implying 'little', the word is actually '*petje*'. [...] By the time I strutted off the train at the Bandung Railway Station with my *pitji* at a rakish angle, it was already the nationwide badge of the freedom fighter. (Adams 1965:51-2.)

This Bandoeng *pici* incident is also mentioned by Inggit in her recollections titled *Kuantar ke gerbang* (To the gate I escort you) (Ramadhan 1981: 5). But here, she and her biographer Ramadhan were obviously inspired by Soekarno's own 1966 reading of his breezing into Bandoeng in June 1921. Also, the title of Inggit's biography clearly reveals Soekarno's influence, since he was to refer to Bandoeng as a 'gate' as well, this time as a gate to the White World, while adding that it was 'with Inggit at my side, I stepped forward to keep my date with destiny' (Adams 1965:60).

However, the reality was far more prosaic. Naturally, at the time he imparted these rather sentimental outpourings to Cindy Adams, it was pardonable for him – being a president of twenty years' standing – to project onto his first entry on the Bandoeng scene such a daring and resolute political pioneering role as he was in fact to assume quite a few years later. As to the *pici*, moreover, such a head covering had been used by both Tjipto and Soewardi Soerjaningrat as early as 1913.[69] As to the *blangkok*, the Deppen photograph shows Soekarno among his HBS graduating class wearing one, as he still did at the 1926 family gathering on the occasion of his becoming an *Ingenieur* (Ir, engineer).[70] Also, J.E. Stokvis relates that, upon meeting him for the first time on 8 March 1923, after Stokvis had just given a lecture to the Bandoeng student members of the Tot Algemeene Ontwikkeling association (TAO, For Wholesale Maturity), Soekarno was still sporting a *blangkok*, while wearing a sarong as well. Only three years later, Stokvis, now speaking at the Bandoeng Study Club, recalls Soekarno wearing a *pici* and being dressed in a Western tailored white sharkskin suit.[71] Besides, Soekarno himself had enrolled at the TH as a *raden*, albeit with some compassion for the humble folk, while in 1926, when he graduated from the TH, he was proud to call himself Ir Raden Soekarno (Adams 1965:68). As late as 1944 Soekarno was still referred to as a *raden* in the Gunseikanbu data bank of prominent Indonesians living in Java at that time (Gunseikanbu 1944a:465).

Rather strange, moreover, is the story about the *pici*-wearing *becak* drivers. *Becak* drivers only appeared on the Indonesian city scene just prior to the outbreak of the Second World War, and were thus not at all a part of city life in the early twenties. Soekarno obviously mixed them up with the *sado* (from *dos-à-dos*, horse-drawn two-wheeled carriage) drivers seen everywhere in the city streets during his Soerabaja and Bandoeng student years, while Cindy Adams lacked sufficient expertise for checking the accuracy of

---

[69]   See *Bescheiden Indische Partij* 1913 executive photograph with Tjipto and Soewardi flanking Douwes Dekker, KITLV photograph, also shown by Glissenaar 1999:93.
[70]   See the third and fourth photographs in Adams 1965, placed between p. 156 and p. 157.
[71]   Stokvis 1931a:7-9 and Stokvis 'Indische brief' in *Het Volk*, 30 December 1926. For Stokvis' speech of 8 March 1923, see also *De Locomotief*, 12 March 1923 and 'Bandoengsche brieven' (by a special correspondent), *De Locomotief*, 13 March 1923. See also Glissenaar 1999:144.

Soekarno's story of the *becak* drivers. In his literary description of Mas Tirto
Adhi Soerjo's life, Toer describes city traffic at that time: 'Carriages [named
after their inventor Mr Deeleman], loading carriages [*grobak* after the Dutch
word *grootbak*], dos-à-dos, jalopies, landaus, victorias and dogcarts – all gifts
of immigrants – were busily riding in the streets'.[72]

Inggit Garnasih comes into Soekarno's life

Pak Tjokro, who, according to Van der Plas, together with Pak Soekemi and
Mas Poegoeh, had been responsible for covering Soekarno's TH fees,[73] had
further been instrumental in getting a dwelling for his son-in-law in Bandoeng. He had written to a friend in Bandoeng, Hadji Sanoesi, an SI prominent and rather well-to-do businessman dealing in building materials and in
rice storage on Bandoeng's wide Kebon Djati thoroughfare (Ramadhan 1981:
6), about Soekarno's pending arrival in the city. In the letter he had requested
Sanoesi to help Soekarno find some private rooms, since the latter was
soon to be joined by his bride. Soekarno, who had left Siti Oetari behind in
Soerabaja, had been eager, just as Tirto some ten years earlier, to come face
to face with the Preanger girls so famous for their beauty and their soft and
alluring *kulit langsep* skin, exposed as they were to the highland climate of
their area.[74] Little did he expect that immediately upon his arrival he would
meet such a beautiful Bandoeng woman, who not only would make him
forget the Sundanese girls altogether but would soon dramatically change
his private life as well.

Picked up from Bandoeng's railway station by Hadji Sanoesi, 'an elderly
man' (Adams 1965:52), Soekarno was escorted to Sanoesi's home just a stone's
throw south of the railway station. Soekarno learned there about Tjokro's letter of introduction and the request to help him look for appropriate rooms for
himself and his bride. To Soekarno's surprise, Sanoesi spontaneously offered
him and Oetari lodgings in one of the front rooms of his own house. But the
real breath-taking surprise was Soekarno coming eye to eye with Sanoesi's
wife Inggit Garnasih. Forty-five years later, his recollections of this meeting
are still quite vivid:

> standing in the doorway in the semi-darkness framed in a halo of light, a petite
> figure, a luscious red flower in her hair and a dazzling smile. [...] All the sparks

---

[72]   Delman, grobak, sado, bendi, landau, victoria, dokar – semua persembahan peradaban
pendatang beriringan di setiap jalan (Pramoedya Ananta Toer 1985a:5).
[73]   Interview Van der Plas, 14 April 1974; Ramadhan 1981:46
[74]   Pramoedya Ananta Toer 1985a:5; see also Soekarno about them in Adams 1965:52.

that can shoot out from a callow inexperienced boy of 20 to a matured, experienced woman in her 30s did. (Adams 1965:52.)

That Soekarno was so readily stirred up by his new landlady's stunning good looks at their initial meeting was most likely due to his own budding frustrations of being tied to a 'hung marriage'. In the months to come, Inggit's presence was to upset him continually, with only one new development bringing some relief to Soekarno's uneasiness about the feelings he harboured toward his alluring landlady.

Some detail on the Bandoeng Technische Hoogeschool

As to the TH, seldom in the Indies had such an academic project been tackled with such speed and success. The real initiative for it – the earlier ones mounted in 1912 and 1914 had all been abortive – occurred in 1917 when the Indies was facing dire shortages of highly skilled technical experts, and after the war the added nuisance of recruiting such experts in Europe for the Indies (*Mededeelingen* 1920:53). From the side of industry, trade, shipping and the plantation sector, a considerable amount of money had been collected for the project, amounting to three and a half million guilders by mid-1919. In the meantime, an association named the Koninklijk Instituut voor Hooger Technisch Onderwijs in Nederlandsch-Indië (Royal Institute for Higher Technical Education in the Netherlands Indies) had been formed in The Hague, and a Raad van Beheer (Board of Management) in the Indies to locally oversee the plans for building the TH. In September 1918 the 34-year-old Indo-European architect Henry Maclaine Pont, son-in-law of Raad van Beheer member Ir J.Th. Gerlings, had been contracted to commence with the architectural planning and building of the Bandoeng TH. The buildings and the parks around and in between them were to be located on a site of 30 hectares, donated by Bandoeng's municipality to the TH, in the northern part of the city, flanked by the Dagoweg (now Jalan Juanda) and the Tjikapoendoeng River (Van Leerdam 1995:116-7, 121, 128).

On 4 July 1919, four *waringin* trees were planted at the site, instead of the usual Western-inspired stone slab, on a piece of cleared ground which later would serve as a big central square flanked by the TH's library and main building.[75] Some years later, a still bigger park, named the IJzerman park (now Taman Ganeca) after Raad van Beheer chairman Dr J.W. IJzerman (not designed by Maclaine Pont but pushed by IJzerman himself), was cleared

---

[75]   Van Leerdam 1995:illustration no. 27; see also *Preangerbode*, 3 July 1920 and *De Ingenieur*, 28 August 1920.

south of the main entrance to the TH.[76] According to traditional Javanese ritual, the *waringin* trees symbolize hope, profound wishing and longing. The planting of these four *waringin* preceded the erection of the first two big TH buildings flanking the main entrance. Designed by Maclaine Pont, they were, specifically in the roof constructions, clearly inspired by the old Javanese *kraton* of Djokja and Solo.[77] Years later Soekarno, then exiled in Benkoelen and a Moehammadijah supporter, would renovate a local mosque incorporating Maclaine Pont's *kraton* roof design.[78]

On 3 July 1920, Governor-General Van Limburg Stirum opened the TH during a ceremony held in the most eastern of the two still unfinished buildings mentioned above. Anticipating that the first 1920-1921 academic year the school could not yet be housed in these two buildings, construction was started some months before the official opening on two far less grandiose complexes, with the one to the south to house the administration and the other to the north to serve as a provisional lecture hall.[79] That the TH in its early stages was quite small is demonstrated not only by the number of lecturing staff – 15 – but also by the student enrolment during the time Soekarno was at the TH (1921-1922: 29 Europeans, 6 Indonesians and 2 Chinese; 1922-1923: 30 Europeans, 8 Indonesians and 4 Chinese; 1923-1924: 10 Europeans, 5 Indonesians and 3 Chinese; 1924-1925: 20 Europeans, 8 Indonesians and 2 Chinese; 1925-1926: 10 Europeans, 3 Indonesians and 1 Chinese) (*Lustrumuitgave jaarboek* 1935:138). The drop in numbers after 1924, especially among the Europeans and the Chinese, was caused by the opening that year of the Rechts Hoogeschool (RH, Law Faculty) in Weltevreden. The TH's curriculum, dismissed by Dahm (1969:45) as one of 'purely a trade school', was rather tough. For the so-called *propjes* or *propaedeuse* I and II (first-year foundation course), thirteen preliminary examinations (*tentamen*) were required, and for the *candidaats* (college) degree, nine. The final examinations for the engineering degree consisted of six tough subject courses and a final written paper. In Soekarno's case his final paper concerned a harbour design. Throughout the entire four years, excursions were made to building projects of the Public Works Department (BOW) or the Billiton Tin Works, with students during their third-year break doing an internship with the BOW as extraordinary supervisors.[80] According to our source Nico Palar, himself a TH dropout, no discrimination existed at the Technical Faculty. Still, there was a TAO association, formed by indigenous-born and other Asian students, and a TH

---

[76] Van Leerdam 1995:133, see also illustration no. 47.
[77] Van Leerdam 1995:139, 173, 175; see also illustrations nos 37 and 50.
[78] See photograph in Fatmawati Soekarno 1978:105.
[79] Van Leerdam 1995:113-4, also illustration no. 27; *Preangerbode,* 2 June 1920; *De Ingenieur,* 18 September 1920.
[80] Interview with Nico Palar, Menteng, 7 August 1971.

Bandoengsche Studentencorps (Bandoeng Student Association), which was exclusively for European students (*Lustrumuitgave jaarboek* 1935:95). The latter club was seen by the Indonesians, including Soekarno, as an outlet for 'playing bridge and billiards, occasional dance festivities as well as drunken brawls' (Ramadhan 1981:52-3). Palar (a TH student during 1922-1923) also recalls Soekarno chairing the Jong Java branch at the TH, and notes that at the time Dutch was used far more often than *ngoko* at Jong Java meetings.[81]

Tjokro in jail and Soekarno's return to Plampitan to manage the household

After only a couple of months in Bandoeng, Soekarno, having been joined by Siti Oetari, was startled to hear the news of his father-in-law's sudden preventive arrest by the colonial authorities on 30 August 1921. Tjokro was held in a Weltevreden prison, while his incarceration would be prolonged monthly until matters had been cleared judicially. The charge was perjury committed during Tjokro's earlier interrogation sessions about the so-called Preanger SI Section B affair, and specifically about Sosrokardono's role in it.[82] In a way, Tjokro's arrest gave renewed lustre to his waning stature, caused mainly by the verbal attacks on his personality and financial management made by Semaoen, but specifically by Darsono. The latter had coined a new word, *mengtjokro* (literally, 'to act like Tjokro', soon, however, being bandied about in *pergerakan* discourses as meaning 'to embezzle like Tjokro') in view of Tjokro's purchase of a brand new car costing *f* 3,000, in addition to buying expensive jewellery for his new ex-*tandak* wife Roestinah with CSI funding.[83] Darsono demanded 'honest, selfless leaders [...] showing blameless conduct [...] being quite able to rectify errors by applying genuine self-purification'.[84] Imprisonment, however, turned Tjokro into an instant martyr of Dutch colonial oppression and offered him an excellent chance of ascetically purifying himself of whatever mistakes he had made in the immediate past.

In Sanoesi's home Tjokro's arrest and its impact on his family was debated at once by Inggit and Soekarno, with the former, obviously already quite enamoured of her young handsome boarder, counselling against his decision to leave Bandoeng immediately for Soerabaja in order to support the Plampitan household. Inggit warned of the danger of such an indefinite leave of absence impacting unfavourably on his TH studies, while she also stressed

[81]   Interview 7 August 1971.
[82]   See Verbaal 2 May 1923 D 6; Verbaal 14 February 1923 no. 48, and 'Het Regeeringsbeleid tegenover de inlandsche beweging', *NRC Avondblad*, 16 December 1922.
[83]   *Sinar Hindia*, 6-9 October 1920; Verbaal 4 January 1922 H.
[84]   *Sinar Hindia*, 9 October 1920.

that Roestinah, Tjokro's wife, had not even asked for Soekarno's return to Plampitan in order to support the family (Adams 1965:54; Ramadhan 1981: 14). Professor Ir J. Klopper, the TH *rector magnificus* (chairman of the first TH academic board), also seems to have warned Soekarno that a return to Soerabaja would possibly impair his academic studies, perhaps even permanently, while he wondered whether such a promising and gifted student should instead not be supported by the entire family in a *gotong royong* fashion. Soekarno ruled out this possibility at once, since he himself had from the start been aided by members of his own family, and now it was his turn to help his in-laws, who were presently in urgent and dire need of his support (Adams 1965:55; Ramadhan 1981:15). So, placing his loyalty to Tjokro and the Soerabajan household above his own academic ambitions, Soekarno, accompanied by Siti Oetari, hurried back to Soerabaja, arriving there 2 September 1921 (Harsono Tjokroaminoto 1983:37).

In Soerabaja, Soekarno was fortunate to readily find employment as an editing clerk by the State Railway and Tramway Services (SS, Staats Spoor en Tramwegen), receiving a monthly salary of *f* 165. For an HBS alumnus this was a rather good salary, since the standard starting SS salary for male HBS graduates at that time amounted to only *f* 110 (Giebels 1999:69). Most likely, Soekarno's status as a TH student and the promise of editorial skills put him in a higher wage scale. According to Harsono, the entire wage was handed over to Roestinah, a gesture Harsono characterized in his recollections 'as quite a marvellous act by Soekarno' (Harsono Tjokroaminoto 1983:37). In his own recollections Soekarno maintains that he kept *f* 40 for himself. He still took the entire family to cinema outings, coached the boys in their studies, clothed them, but also sternly disciplined them, using his own leather slippers to beat them when their behaviour threatened to get out of hand, and finally arranged for Anwar's circumcision ceremony to take place during a proper *selamatan* (religious meal).[85]

Fortunately for Soekarno, Tjokro was released from his Weltevreden prison on 5 April 1922, while on 16 August 1922 the Indies highest court (Hoog Gerechtshof) dismissed all the lower courts' allegations of perjury still pending against him.[86] By that latter date Soekarno and Siti Oetari had already settled back in the Sanoesi household in Bandoeng, and Soekarno was again enrolled at the TH (Ramadhan 1981:17). For Soekarno, however, the time had come to make some crucial personal decisions. Coming face to face with Inggit again after an absence of seven months, Soekarno realized that his feelings for his landlady were as strong as ever. Soon he would learn that Inggit's own romantic attachment to him had been growing as well.

---

[85]　Adams 1965:56. Confirmed by Anwar and Harsono, 15 August 1971 interviews.
[86]　See Mr. 991/1922, Verbaal 14 February 1923 no. 48.

Also, Soekarno's ties with Tjokro, his revered mentor, came under strain and must have weakened to some extent during Tjokro's long absence.

The private break with Tjokro and Soekarno's subsequent marriage to Inggit

In order to get his studies in good order again, since he had lost an entire year, Soekarno realized he needed to come to terms first of all with the personal dilemma facing him. The 'hung marriage' with Siti Oetari had shown him time and time again that his young bride was still some distance away from a physical consummation of their relationship. In his recollections of her while they lived with the Sanoesis, he consistently pictures Siti Oetari as a mere child eager to play with one of Inggit's nieces, living in a world of her own, not sharing his interests[87] or even the bedroom with him. Soekarno was not really bothered about it since he was no longer physically attracted to Siti Oetari but drawn rather strongly to someone else, not only in a physical but increasingly even in a spiritual sense. Siti Oetari and he were truly part of an 'older brother-younger sister relationship and no more than that', he told Inggit (Ramadhan 1981:10).

With Sanoesi often away on business deals or partaking in nightly gambling or billiard sessions, and with Siti Oetari not in the least suspicious of what was going on between her landlady and her handsome husband, the romantic attachment between the two reached boiling point. And so, after informing Inggit that he was going to return Siti Oetari to her father and that Siti Oetari knew and had agreed (Ramadhan 1981:20), Soekarno took Siti Oetari to her father in Soerabaja during the Christmas break of 1922. There he begged Tjokro to allow him to separate from Siti Oetari through the usual *talak tiga* (irrevocable repudiation) ceremony, a separation sequel common to both *kejawen* and *santri* Javanese when marriage ties prove not to be enduring. The Koranic *surah Al-Talāq* describes the procedure for *santri* Javanese. Tjokro naturally was pained by it, but in view of Soekarno's seven-month-long generous management of the Plampitan household while he himself was incarcerated, he agreed to it. Upon his return to Inggit, Soekarno told her that 'Tjokro still saw him as a son and someone whom he had emancipated politically, while he himself remained quite close to Tjokro and his family' (Ramadhan 1981:22; Adams 1965:58-9).

Soekarno soon after moved to consolidate his position toward his landlady by openly declaring his intense love for her and his determination to marry her as soon as Sanoesi agreed to let her go. Both decided to confront

---

[87]   Inggit related that Soekarno had frequent talks with both Douwes Dekker and Tjipto and was unable to impart their meaning to Oetari (Ramadhan 1981:19).

Sanoesi, first Soekarno all by himself and then Inggit to do the same. Sanoesi was not at all perturbed by the news and even imparted to Inggit that a match with Soekarno was the right one, since the latter would go far in life, urging her to make him into an important person.[88] Soon after this discussion, Inggit was repudiated by Sanoesi in a *talak* ceremony, thus freeing her to join with Soekarno matrimonially after the usual *idah* (a waiting period of 100 days for widows or divorcees before remarrying) (Ramadhan 1981: 42). She and Koesno, as she fondly used to call him throughout her recollections, moved to a simple Gang Djaksa dwelling just north of Bandoeng's race tracks, and on Saturday, 24 March 1923 they were married before an Islamic magistrate in Inggit's paternal home on Javaveem street. Inggit also relates that Pak Soemosoewo, a close family member of Soekarno's father, witnessed the wedding. Soekarno's parents were absent, though they had earlier approved of the union. On Inggit's side only her mother Iboe Asmi was present, since Inggit's father Bapak Jipan had passed away some twenty years earlier (Ramadhan 1981:42). In their Soerat Katerangan Kawin no. 1138,[89] Soekarno and his bride are listed as domiciled as *oerang desa* (Sundanese for district folks) of Kadjaksan. Soekarno's *pagawean* (Sundanese for occupation) was given as *moerid* (student) while his *oemoer* (age) was listed as 24 and that of Inggit as 23. Also, Inggit was listed as having been a *randa 4 boelan* (a divorcee of four months' standing) and had thus fulfilled the *idah*. Another Sundanese-language document, Kaoela Neda Panaksen no. 493, described Soekarno's obligations to his new wife.

Inggit and Soekarno's perceptions of their new marriage tie

Of interest are Inggit's and Soekarno's own outpourings about their new tie and the new responsibilities it would entail. She was quite aware of the big intellectual gap between them: a gap she feared was capable of separating them in the end. She regretted that the only education she really had was during her years of *madrasah ibtidaiyah* (basic religious school) as a youngster living in Desa Kamasan in the district of Bandjaran just south of Bandoeng. Another matter that worried her was the difference in age, she being eleven years older than her husband. As to the first, she would do the utmost to help him complete his engineering degree in the shortest time possible, even if it meant her working her fingers to the bone with her *jamu* and *batik* enterprises

---

[88]   Pasti bisa mendorongnya sampai ia menjadi orang penting (Ramadhan 1981:40).
[89]   A copy of the Sundanese-language Soerat Kawin was given to us by Tito Zaini Armen, a son of Ratna Djuami, in Bandung on 7 January 1988, four years after Inggit's death. See also Gatot Triyanto and Agung Firmansyah, 'Jimat itu mulai kecokelatan', *Tempo*, 6 February 1988:26 and H. Mahbub Djunaidi, 'Surat nikah Bung Karno', *Tempo*, 13 February 1988:112.

or keeping boarders to meet the daily household expenses. As for the age difference, she consoled herself that even Prophet Mohammad had married Siti Khadijah, a woman who was also much older than her husband.[90] Soekarno's recollections stressed the love, warmth and unselfishness Inggit gave him – something he needed badly and hadn't had since he left his mother's home[91] – as well as the camaraderie which from the beginning had existed between Inggit and him. However, he did make room for a psychological note about his marriage to a much older woman being possibly part of a lingering mother-complex. But he brushed that aside by saying that if he had married her for that reason, it was subconsciously so. Consciously, however, the sentiments she aroused in him were anything but filial (Adams 1965:60).

The adoption of Arawati and the encounter with Marhaen

Another factor heightening their bliss was the adoption early in 1924 of a baby named Arawati, a child of Inggit's older sister Moertasi. Such *anak angkat* (foster child) adoptions often took place in Javanese and Sundanese families, and sometimes in Eurasian families as well. Moertasi was quite willing to leave Ratna Djoeami, or Omi – so named by Koesno – with her younger sister and her new brother-in-law. Koesno, who quickly nicknamed the child Kroto (little ant), was particularly fond of her, playing with her whenever he could, even taking her to discussion meetings or on visits to friends. Inggit commented that their Omi was not only 'the pearl of the family but a source of energizing their own spirit as well'.[92] It was at that time that Soekarno, near the *desa* Tjibintinoe south of Bandoeng, met a farmer named Marhaen, a *tani sieur* (Sundanese for a chicken flea farmer) owning all the tools for working on his tiny plot of land with the crop being for his own use. Yet he was poor and destitute like the poor worker, the poor fisherman, the poor clerk, the poor stall vendor, the poor cart driver, the poor cab driver. They were all marhaen, Soekarno told Inggit, and marhaenism was truly Indonesian socialism, since it was practically everywhere (*marhaenisme adalah sosialisme Indonesia dalem praktek*) (Ramadhan 1981:62-3). To these paupers he would, years later, dedicate his 1933 treatise *Mentjapai Indonesia Merdeka*. At that time he considered the concept of marhaenism more fitting for a national ideology than proletarian class notions.

---

[90] Ramadhan 1981:43-4, 48-51. In the Koranic *surah Al-Duhā* verse 8, an allegoric reference is made to the rich widow Mohammad married around the year 595.
[91] This may indicate that Inggit was the first woman whom he had sex with.
[92] Ramadhan 1981:63-4; interview with Omi and her son Tito Zaini Armen, 7 January 1988.

The ksatrian spirit of Bandoeng and its growing influence upon Soekarno

Inggit relates that even before her marriage to Koesno, frequent contacts occurred between Koesno and Douwes Dekker (like Soekarno, a Soerabaja HBS alumnus) and Tjipto, then the Bandoeng-based leaders of the Sarekat Hindia/Nationaal Indische Partij (SH/NIP, Indies Association/National Indies Party) (Ramadhan 1981:19). This party, represented by Douwes Dekker and Dahler at a closed meeting held on 12 November 1922 in the Masonic Lodge at Weltevreden's Vrijmetselaarsweg (now Jalan Budi Utomo), chaired by Ir Ch.G. Cramer, was working with the SI (represented by Agoes Salim and Kadar), ISDP (with among others Cramer and Stokvis), PKI (represented by Semaoen, Dr Kwa Tjoan Sioe and Najoan), VSTP (with Dahlan and Marti-widjata), BO (represented by Dwidjosoewojo) and Sarekat Ambon (Dr J. Kayadoe and A. Patty) to revive a new Radicale Concentratie.[93] This caused Soewardi Soerjaningrat in Djokja to summon the *ksatria* (warrior nobles) to adopt non-cooperation and challenge the Indies government in a *sini* versus *sana* struggle (*sini*, literally, 'those standing here', and *sana*, 'those standing there', meaning the friends versus the foes of indigenous autonomy).[94] Earlier, on 3 July 1922, Soewardi had challenged the Indies government's educational policies as well, launching the Taman Siswa (students' garden) national school system, where truly indigenous values and the revival of a *roch kebangsaan merdeka* (free national spirit) were taught by Indonesian students as teachers of their own countrymen. Soekarno, in the wake of Taman Siswa's first congress, held in Djokja from 20 to 23 October 1923, was appointed as the Taman Siswa regional representative for Bandoeng (Tsuchiya 1987:55, 59-60).

As to the renewed Radicale Concentratie, now also joined by the Perserikatan Minahassa and Pasoendan, more closed meetings – soon to be labelled councils of war – were to follow: on 3 December 1922, at Weltevreden's Dordrechtlaan no. 4, and on 7 January 1923, at Kebon Klappa no. 17 (ISDP member H.R. Meyer's home) in Bandoeng. At the latter meeting, chaired by Alexander Patty of Sarekat Ambon, Tjipto (Douwes Dekker was absent due to a severe bout of malaria), Dr Ratulangi, Semaoen, Soetopo (BO) and Meyer were charged with preparing a manifesto to be discussed in a number of open *rapat* (rallies) in the big cities. Also, the Menadonese Najoan (PKI) was to foment actions in Soerabaja and Patty to do the same in Ambon, while Bandoeng was earmarked as a *brandpunt* (focus) of intense association activities still to come. However, the police reports of the time show awareness of growing disputes going on among the various party representatives.

---

[93]   Mr. 1187/1922, Verbaal 3 November 1923 B 16. For Patty and Kayadoe: Chauvel 1990:77.
[94]   For Soewardi's appeal for struggle see *Panggoegah*, 21 February 1923, a periodical edited by him.

They report that SI leaders such as Agoes Salim and ISDP prominents such as Cramer often absented themselves, wary as they were of Semaoen dominating the debates while seeking a key role for the PKI.[95]

Early public ksatrian activities of Soekarno

Still captivated by the new spirit, however, were Inggit and her Koesno, with Inggit recalling a dramatic key role played by Koesno during a Saturday, 20 January 1923 open-air rally of the Radicale Concentratie on Bandoeng's *alun-alun*. Koesno, not able to contain himself, climbed on the platform and started to loudly censure the colonial system in no uncertain terms. All this resulted in him being forcibly removed from the rostrum and the rally being disbanded on the orders of Bandoeng's police commissioner Heyne. Inggit also relates that Soekarno, because of the incident, was warned the following Monday by Professor Klopper not to engage himself in nationalist politics any longer and instead to devote himself to his studies.[96]

It seems Soekarno did not heed Klopper's advice, since during a PKI and SI Merah meeting in Bandoeng on 4 March 1923, held in the SI Merah School at Gang Sekolah, and attended by some two thousand people, Soekarno again took the floor, this time to defend Tjokro against the verbal attacks against his former father-in-law made by Hadji Misbach. Misbach had severely censured Tjokro's defence of the party-discipline issue and also reiterated the earlier criticism aired by Darsono about Tjokro's embezzling practices. The speech was repeatedly interrupted by shouts from the public like '*partij discipline maoenja Salim, complotnja Tjokro*' (party discipline was Salim's wish but engineered by Tjokro), and '*Tjokro maoe djadi radja*' (Tjokro wants to be king) and '*Oewang Tjokro kemana piginja?*' (Where did all Tjokro's money go?) and '*Tjokro main kedok-kedokan*' (Tjokro playing hide and seek). In reply, Soekarno referred to the *ksatria* spirit, censuring Misbach for not heeding that spirit, accusing a man (Tjokro) who was absent and therefore not capable of defending himself. Soekarno's defence of Tjokro drew warm applause as well, and caused Misbach to personally apologize to Soekarno,[97] which did not deter Misbach from renewing his attacks even more violently in an article titled 'Semprong wasiat: Partij discipline SI Tjokroaminoto mendjadi ratjoen pergerakan Ra'jat Hindia'. There, for instance, he accused Tjokro of using

95   Mr. 49/1923 and Mr. 59/1923, Verbaal 3 November 1923 B 16.
96   Ramadhan 1981:24-8. For the *alun-alun rapat* see *Pahlawan* of 21 January 1923, though it does not report that Soekarno was removed from the podium by commissioner of police Heyne, an incident reported by Soekarno in Adams 1965:63-5 and by M.Y. Nasution 1951:24.
97   See *wedana* Landjoemin gelar Datoe' Toemenggoeng of Inlandsche Zaken in a 23-page report, pp. 7-8, 10-1, Verbaal 1 October 1923 E 14.

party discipline as merely a ploy to deter other associations from entering the SI – since if they did, they would be only too glad to challenge Tjokro's own money-making ventures. And that was something Tjokro wanted to prevent at all costs, faced as he was with the desires and ambitions of his ex-*tandak* wife. Misbach concluded that the greed for money had truly corrupted Tjokro and in so doing had indeed poisoned the *pergerakan*.[98]

Soekarno moving closer to Tjipto and Douwes Dekker

Another event may have drawn Soekarno still closer to Douwes Dekker and Tjipto, labelled by Dahm as the two true *ksatria* responsible for a new Bandoeng spirit (Dahm 1969:46-7). Four days after his own Gang Sekolah performance, Soekarno witnessed a verbal clash between Jozef Stokvis and Ernest Douwes Dekker before an audience of Indonesian Technische Hoogeschool student members of the Tot Algemeene Ontwikkeling (TAO, For Wholesale Maturity) association. While Stokvis in his lecture had been critical of the colonial rela-tionship, he still admonished the students to work even harder and so prepare themselves to become the equals of the Dutch, who far too often had been placed in superior positions on the basis of race. Such a studious approach would lead to better interracial understanding and prevent feelings of hatred. All in all, it was a theme Soekarno had been exposed to before, through his mentors Hartogh and Tjokro, both of whom had not excluded some degree of European guidance. This theme was blasted that evening, however, by Douwes Dekker, who rejected any semblance of European guidance, since Europe was far too enthralled by capitalism, and capitalism was far too ster-ile to provide any culture at all. Douwes Dekker encouraged the students to devote more time to working for the political independence of their country and less time on their current academic studies.[99]

While all the events that evening may have impressed Soekarno, there is no mention of it at all in his own recollections. He does refer to Douwes Dekker in another context, however, with Douwes Dekker earmarking him 'already active in the SH/NIP [and] as a future successor leading the SH/NIP when he [Douwes Dekker] was gone' (Glissenaar 1999:144; Adams 1965: 50). As for Tjipto and Soewardi Soerjaningrat, no mention at all is made in the Soekarno autobiography. Also, Inggit, while relating the many contacts between Koesno and both Tjipto and Douwes Dekker, on the whole does not provide us with sufficient detail about the matters under discussion here, apart from the fact that their home and that of Tjipto gradually became a

---

[98]   That article appeared in *Medan Moeslimin* 1923-9:175-6.
[99]   *De Locomotief*, 12 March 1923:1-2, 13 March 1923:1; Dahm 1969:47-8.

focus for discussion and argument among Bandoeng's leading nationalists. However, during an interview with George McT. Kahin on 19 March 1959, Soekarno admitted that the trio who had been leading first the Indische Partij (IP, Indies Party) and then the SH/NIP had politically influenced him most.[100] In December 1927, moreover, Soekarno mentioned Tjipto as his 'Saudara Dr Tjipto – my chief, sebagai Gandhi diseboetkan oleh pengikoet-pengikoetnja' (Brother Dr Tjipto – my chief, just as Gandhi was called by his followers).[101] That this trio, two of whom lived near him (Tjipto in Tegallega at Pangeran Soemedangweg 89 and Douwes Dekker at Tjiateul 33)[102], were thus instrumental in maturing his radically inspired political credo remains therefore beyond dispute, with Tjipto, his 'chief' and, like him, a middle-class *priyayi*, being the most influential.

Even the dissolution of the SH/NIP on 18 May 1923[103] and the subsequent folding of the Radicale Concentratie, probably caused by too much bickering among the various prominent party leaders, could not deter the young Soekarno any longer from developing a political programme all his own. As Douwes Dekker and Tjipto took part in the final closed meetings of the Radicale Concentratie, Soekarno must have been informed by them of the growing polarization between the SI and the PKI. The first association was drifting from socialism to Pan-Islamism and the second to yet another Pan movement directed by Moscow, a body called the Communist International (Comintern).[104] In the Comintern, famous PKI exiles such as Semaoen and Darsono, then residing in Holland, would soon sit as delegates. As to the SI, however, it showed its truly vacillating character once again. First it had sacrificed its lofty independence aims on the altar of socialism, only to sidestep that once more by dedicating itself to yet another ideal – that of Pan-Islamism. It was at this latter juncture that Soekarno must have decided to break politically with Tjokro altogether. That he turned to the spirit of the IP and the SH/NIP, with two of their erstwhile leaders now being in close contact with him, is not surprising at all. He had been aware for some time that their slogans of strict non-cooperation, equality of the races, the struggle

---

[100] Stencilled note given to Bob Hering by George McT. Kahin.
[101] *Soeloeh Indonesia Moeda* no. 1(December 1927):30. Inggit relates that Tjipto was called by Soekarno 'my chief atau sepku' (*sep* being derived from the Dutch word *chef*): Ramadhan 1981:54.
[102] For these addresses, see Westenenk's 30 June 1927 'Bijlage' of *Indonesia Merdeka* contributors in Verbaal 4 July 1927 W 10.
[103] 'Nationaal Indische Partij dioerai' (The NIP dissolved) and 'Manifest N.I.P. (Sarekat Hindia) hal Non-Coöperatie' (Non-Cooperationist Manifesto NIP/Sarekat Hindia), Bandoeng 18 May 1923:1-7.
[104] Inggit relates a discussion on the League against Imperialism and Colonial Oppression, seen by many as a branch of the Comintern, in their home: Ramadhan 1981:76. The frequent talks Soekarno had with Tjipto and Douwes Dekker may have escaped Inggit, since most of these were held at the homes of Tjipto and Douwes Dekker.

against capitalism, had been steadfast while focusing on the one goal: that of national independence. And as Dahm has it, Soekarno 'found this goal more and more worth working for', while in Bandoeng it was Tjipto 'who made him into a convinced nationalist'.[105]

So it was particularly the highly principled and clear-thinking Tjipto who was to win his new and eager pupil Soekarno for the idea of unbridled non-cooperation. They both felt that politically active Indonesians should shun all forms of participation in the representative councils of the day and should lend no other service to the alien colonial authorities. Thus, when Soekarno in July 1926 received his degree as a civil engineer, he refused to enter governmental service and chose instead to join Douwes Dekker's *ksatria* school as a mathematics and history teacher, earning additional money in a private architect's practice. Douwes Dekker, robbed of a political platform, had decided to follow Soewardi's idea of a special educational system, but shunning the latter's blending of Tagore, Steiner and Montessori in order to identify himself afresh with his own culture and then attempt to rebuild that culture. Soekarno's stint as a teacher was cut short at the end of 1927 after a Dutch school inspector deemed him 'a well-meaning but quite inexperienced educator who needed a lot to make him fit for his task'. The inspector was not impressed by the other teachers either, including Douwes Dekker, and advised closing the institute.[106] This advice was not heeded by the colonial authorities, aware as they undoubtedly were that the demand for Western-style education continued unabated among the indigenous population. Douwes Dekker's Ksatrian Institute might not offer a superior, or in some respects even an adequate education, but it was cheaper and more easily accessible than Dutch-style public education.

So Douwes Dekker continued to inspire his students to adopt Western methods and techniques principally so that they could arm themselves better against Western domination. In that context Douwes Dekker is said to have imparted to Soewardi: 'Dressed with a *kain* [also indicating a sarong] and walking on bare feet, you will not be able to kick the Dutch properly, since for that you need trousers and leather boots' (Glissenaar 1999:144). As to the private architect's practice, Soekarno and his fellow TH graduate Ir Anwari established it right after their graduation on 26 July 1926. However, not much work was generated by the new practice, since both Soekarno and Anwari became politically involved in an endeavour which would consume most of their energies.

---

[105]   Dahm 1969:52. C.O. van der Plas was a major civil servant attached to Inlandsche Zaken in 1927, reporting that 'the influence of Tjipto westernized Soekarno and made him separate from the Muslims': Hering 1982:54, note 20a. Ruth McVey also refers to Tjipto as 'Sukarno's chief political mentor during the latter's student days in Bandung' in Soekarno 1970:62, note 47.
[106]   Inspectie-Mulo no. 2669 of 3 December 1927, pp. 2-3, Mr. 224/1928.

Founding the Algemeene Studie Club and the input of the Perhimpoenan Indonesia

Prior to his TH graduation, together with Leiden-trained lawyer Iskaq Tjo-krohadisoerjo (who became its first chairman), the veteran nationalists Tjipto and Abdoel Moeis, and the TH student Anwari, Soekarno founded the Alge-meene Studie Club (General Study Club) of Bandoeng, on 29 November 1925.[107] Tjipto remarked on 16 September 1931 that the Bandoeng General Study Club worked in a similar fashion as the Indische Partij, an association he once led in 1913, together with Soewardi and Douwes Dekker.[108] Inggit, too, in her recollections, describes the crucial role played by Tjipto during the deliberations that led to the founding of the General Study Club, causing her husband to state 'that the club they intended to erect in Bandoeng should be at once more challenging, more progressive and more far-reaching'[109]

As to the general idea of such study clubs, they had been primarily set up by returning Indonesian graduates who had studied in the Netherlands and settled in cities like Soerabaja, Bandoeng and Batavia, cities they had selected because there they were able to find jobs commensurate with their Western-oriented skills. That most of these returnees were quite politically motivated was due to some novel ideas they had picked up during their university studies in the Netherlands. There, a solid core of some thirty to forty politically conscious students, most of them engaged in preparing themselves for law, engineering and economics degrees, had been instrumental in turning their student association into a genuine reflection of the *pergerakan* being waged in their homeland. In late 1922, their student association was quick to support the views generated by the renewed Radicale Concentratie, while early in 1924 the name of the Indische Vereeniging (Indies Association, established in 1908) was changed to Indonesische Vereeniging (Indonesian Association) and then again to Perhimpoenan Indonesia, replacing the Dutch word *vereeniging* with the Indonesian term *perhimpoenan* on 3 February 1925.[110] Also, the name of its journal *Hindia Poetra* (Son of the Indies), established by Soewardi Soerjaningrat as early as 1916, was changed to *Indonesia Merdeka* (Free Indonesia), a title that indeed expressed Perhimpoenan Indonesia's goal of striving for a new independent Indonesia. *Indonesia Merdeka* soon found its way to Indonesia through seamen couriers or by being wrapped innocuously inside editions of the Dutch journal *Haagsche Post*, and so reached a growing

107   Most accounts list Sunday, 17 January 1926, the date of its first public meeting, as the founding date; however, its new newsletter *Indonesia Moeda* no. 1 of October 1926 lists 29 November 1925 as the founding date of the Algemeene Studie Club.

108   *Soeloeh Ra'jat Indonesia*, 16 September 1931.

109   Bahwa organisasi jang akan mereka dirikan di Bandung harus lebih meluas, lebih progresif dan lebih luas jangkauannja (Ramadhan 1981:53-4).

110   *Indonesia Merdeka*, February 1925:1.

number of Indonesian intellectuals and politicians, Soekarno among them.[111] Its clarion call, 'Strijd aan twee fronten' (Struggle on two fronts), demonstrates that the battle lines were now drawn and that no quarter would be given to those who still sided with the colonial power.[112]

These activities owed much to a Rotterdam University business student (since 1922, changing in September 1925 to the economics faculty of that university, to finally graduate there on 5 July 1932) named Mohammad Hatta. He was a native of the Sumatran Minangkabau area, and a Perhimpoenan Indonesia chairman from January 1926 to March 1929, contributing many articles to *Indonesia Merdeka*. In his own words he perceived Perhimpoenan Indonesia to be 'an advance post of the Indonesian national movement', and its members who had returned to their homeland as a vanguard to 'go to the masses and struggle with the masses'.[113] This perception often led him to actively meddle in the internal political affairs of his homeland, which as we will see below, did not always endear him to some leaders, Soekarno and Soenarjo among them.

As for the Indonesian graduates already back in Indonesia, it was Soetomo who on 11 July 1924 established the Indonesische Studie Club (Indonesian Study Club) in Soerabaja, a club which, similar to Perhimpoenan Indonesia, aimed to develop a new Indonesian nationalist ideology. Soetomo planned to use his new club to bring together educated Javanese and so make them conscious of Indonesia as a nation, while preparing them for leadership in a yet to be formed new national movement. As to his attitude toward the colonial authorities, perhaps aware of the need of Western-trained Indonesians still seeking jobs in the colonial establishment, Soetomo preferred to use non-cooperation merely as a tactic, a tactic occasionally useful for forcing the Dutch to see Indonesians more like their equals and to finally abolish the custom of obeisance expected of 'natives' by their Dutch superiors in the administrative apparatus. As to Boedi Oetomo, Soetomo, once a founding member of that Javanese association, now considered it as far too Java-oriented rather than Indonesia-oriented. At the time, the association had been labelled by one of Hatta's close contacts, the Betawi-based Department of Finance clerk Soedjadi,

---

[111]   Communication by John Ingleson, 8 May 1974. Inggit recalls her husband getting it as well: Ramadhan 1981:98.

[112]   *Indonesia Merdeka*, February 1925:3-5.

[113]   Hatta 1972:216. Also in a Hatta to Soedjadi letter of 18 May 1926, Verbaal 28 June 1927 M 10 Hatta mentioned the PI being an advance post idea while also stressing full PI-PKI cooperation, since the latter 'was truly a nationalist movement'. Hatta's revelations may well have been inspired by the Comintern's (using the code name Kijai) fifteen hundred dollar donations to the PI, and the fact of Semaoen and Koesoema Soemantri being the PI representatives in Moscow; see letter 30 June 1927 of the Ministry of Colonies Adviser for Students (L.C. Westenenk) no. 89, p. 1, Verbaal 4 July 1927 W 10; see also 8 November 1927 Hatta interrogation in Verbaal 16 February 1928 A 3, pp. 9, 11-2.

as being too much influenced by a Jan Compagnie (bourgeois) spirit.[114]

Soetomo's example was soon followed by a number of similarly inspired study clubs, the most important one being the Algemeene Studie Club (General Study Club) formed in Bandoeng. As in the case of Soetomo's organization, a phalanx of former Perhimpoenan Indonesia members were to join it. Another member was a Dutch national, the socialist Marcel Koch, a fierce critic of the policies of the colonial administration, who had befriended Soekarno in August 1925, a friendship that would span a lifetime.[115] Later, Soekarno would reveal that Dutch theosophists like Ir P. Fournier, Ir A. van Leeuwen and a Mrs Van Harteveld joined the General Study Club as well.[116] However, in the case of Bandoeng, radical nationalists of the ilk of Tjipto were involved, and that may be the reason that, of all the study clubs – including Soerabaja, Solo, Djokja, Bogor, Semarang and Batavia – Bandoeng was the most militant, imbued as it was with a strict non-cooperative stance.[117] The Bandoeng Study Club, with some seventy members, was earmarked by Soekarno 'as a springboard for a new party capable of filling the vacuum with young intellectuals not drawn to Marxist or Islamic inspired ideologies'.[118]

Comité Persatoean Indonesia and plans for a new nationalist party

Here again, it was Tjipto's home in Tegallega, along with Soekarno and Inggit's own house, where these new ideas were generated, and which also gradually became a beacon for new leaders wanting to guide future masses of Pendawa to become an army openly challenging the Rahwanan colonial establishment. Inggit recalls that the contents of Tan Malaka's new brochure *Massa Actie*, then passing from mouth to mouth, often formed the main topic of discussion at their homes (Ramadhan 1981:54-5). Mass action also became part of Soekarno's

---

[114]   31 May 1926 letter Soedjadi to Hatta, Verbaal 9 August 1927 G 13, with Soedjadi also reporting 'that Mr Soejoedi's efforts to get Boedi Oetomo's Djokja branch to adopt non-cooperation had been fruitless'.

[115]   Penbrook 1992:69-70. Koch, in his own recollections (1956:191-2), attests to Soekarno's preoccupation with Marxist literature during his Algemeene Studie Club years, often borrowing Koch's books about it and always returning these promptly; they also shared a love for negro spirituals. According to his friends, Koch's 'Marxist socialism was thoroughly an element of belief and of the eschatological expectations' he had harboured since his childhood: Mrázek 1994:51. There were also lectures by Koch's circle held in the Ons Genoegen clubhouse and sponsored by Soekarno; see *Kaoem Moeda* of 4 November 1926.

[116]   Soekarno's testimony before the Bandoeng Landraad as reported by the *Algemeen Indisch Dagblad* of 2 September 1930 and by *Pemeriksaan Soekarno* n.d:109.

[117]   For Tjipto's crucial role, Ramadhan 1981:53-4. See also note 105.

[118]   Organisasi itu menuju kepada pembentukan suatu partai yang akan mengisi kekosongan yang dirasa oleh pemuda-pemuda intelek yang tidak berpaham Marxisme dan juga tidak berideologi Islam (Ramadhan 1981:54).

programme – mobilization of the Indonesian people against colonialism. It was at this juncture that Soetomo, in order to regain the initiative, sent his club's secretary – a Leiden-trained lawyer named R.P. Singgih – on a mission urging closer Indonesian unity through the formation of more study clubs. Arriving in Bandoeng, Singgih found that the General Study Club, together with Pasoendan and Boedi Oetomo, were already engaged in discussing the creation of a more closely unified *pergerakan*.[119] During a closed meeting on 21 August 1926, it was resolved to set up in Bandoeng a Comité Persatoean Indonesia (Indonesian Unity Committee), with an executive to be composed of Sartono (chairman), Soeprodjo (vice-chairman), Soekarno (first secretary), Sjahboedin Latief (second secretary) and Raden Oesman Sastroamidjojo (treasurer), all of them members of the Bandoeng General Study Club. It was also resolved to encourage the setting up of such committees in Batavia, Djokja and Soerabaja.[120] Meanwhile, Iskaq had passed on the chair of the General Study Club to Ir Darmawan Mangoenkoesoemo, a younger brother of Tjipto and a recent graduate of Delft University. One of Darmawan's first decisions as chairman was to deny Bandoeng General Study Club membership to anyone belonging to the PKI, for fear that the Indies government would then extend its tough anti-PKI policies to Study Club members as well. This decision caused the ire of Mohammad Hatta, who at that time was still actively seeking to form a national bloc in Indonesia with the PKI fully participating.[121] Hatta, having now lived for some time in a democratically open society – he himself was soon to experience being acquitted of inciting an overthrow of Dutch authority in the Indies – was probably not sufficiently aware of the quite repressive anti-terrorist measures unleashed by Governor-General Dirk Fock. Hatta also urged Soedjadi, the official Perhimpoenan Indonesia representative in the Indies, to convert the Bandoeng General Study Club into the equivalent of the Perhimpoenan Indonesia, as a step toward yet another national party to be called the Nationaal Indonesische Volkspartij (Indonesian National People's Party).[122] Whether Soekarno was fully aware of all these plans cannot be determined, although in Hatta's mind it must have dawned that the Bandoeng Study Club, with a phalanx of Leiden- and Delft-trained Perhimpoenan Indonesia members at its core, could form the nucleus of a truly nationalist party in the Indies. Whether Hatta at this stage saw Soekarno as the obvious person to lead such a new party seems rather unlikely.

---

[119] *Bandera Islam*, 23 and 26 August 1926.
[120] *Bandera Islam*, 23 and 26 August 1926. See also 23 February 1926 letter of Sartono to Raden Ali Sastroamidjojo in Leiden, Verbaal 28 June 1927 M 10.
[121] See 2 June 1926 letter of Hatta to Soedjadi, Verbaal 28 June 1927 M 10, where Hatta condemns the Bandoeng Study Club for allowing membership to a *Belanda* (Koch).
[122] 2 June 1926 letter of Hatta to Soedjadi, Verbaal 28 June 1927 M 10.

Soekarno's Indonesia Moeda clarion call

With the founding of the Bandoeng-based Comité Persatoean Indonesia still fresh in his mind, Soekarno decided to strengthen the General Study Club's propaganda by issuing a new monthly in October 1926. Edited by Soekarno himself, and named by him *Indonesia Moeda* so as to stress the dawn of a new Young Indonesia, he submitted an essay titled 'Nasionalisme, Islamisme dan Marxisme', which duly appeared in the first three issues of *Indonesia Moeda*. This clarion call was to elevate Soekarno even closer to the centre of activities seeking to give renewed meaning to the course of Indonesian nationalism. Here, the ideas he had formulated in his *Oetoesan Hindia* contributions were refined to become, as he thought, a solid basis for the *sini-sana*[123] struggle yet to come. Already in its opening phrase, Soekarno hailed his new periodical as a genuine child of Bima:

> Like the son of Bima [Gatoetkatja, a famous hero of the wayang], who was born in an age of struggle, *Indonesia Moeda* now sees the light of day, at a time when the peoples of Asia are deeply dissatisfied with their fate, dissatisfied with their economic fate, dissatisfied with their political fate and dissatisfied with their fate in every other respect! The age of being satisfied with conditions as they are has definitely passed. A new age, a youthful age has arrived, like the dawn of a bright morning. The conservative philosophy which held that whoever is at the bottom must acquiesce, satisfied to sit in the background of historical events and therefore giving himself and the small goods he treasures to those who reside at the top, is no longer finding acceptance by the people of Asia.[124]

Here, Soekarno established right away that he was not at all addressing the older and more cautious members of the Indonesian political elite, for whom issues of regionalism and cooperation with the colonial authorities had often been so paramount in their programmes. His appeal was instead directed solely to the politically conscious of his own generation – youthful and modern – to those thinking in terms of a purely national rather than a regional identity and therefore far better equipped for the struggle for independence. For Soekarno this generation, though still small, was the sole source of his homeland's future leadership. However, he remained quite aware of its weaknesses, with energies being wasted through continual strife, and far too often fed by silly private or ideological differences. He made a dramatic

[123]   As to *sana* and *sini* (literally, 'those standing there' and 'those standing here'), in *wayang* terms the Kaurawa (99 male members and one female) feuding with the five all-male Pendawa over the kingdom Ngastina; for a short description of this epic struggle see Anderson 1965: especially appendix ii. Dahm 1969 uses this Pendawa-Kaurawa concept throughout, and perhaps with some justification, since Soekarno, as no one before him, employed *wayang* stories to cultivate unity and foster popular nationalism.
[124]   *Indonesia Moeda* no. 1 of October 1926, also reprinted in Soekarno 1959.

appeal to the three dominant political organizations to forget their differences and instead forge a still tighter unified front. Thus united, they would not only become a nearly unconquerable force struggling against the alien colonizers, but would one day be able to wrest control from the latter and thus fulfil the dream of an Indonesia Merdeka. Brushing aside all narrow-minded exclusionist ideas, whether of a purely nationalist, internationalist-Marxist or Pan-Islamic nature, he now pressed these divergent groups of the Indonesian *pergerakan* to adopt his own far more radical solution: that of unity at all costs in order to form a common resistance to a common oppressor. It remains striking that Soekarno addressed himself not so much to the West or to the oppressions of that world's colonial regime, but to what he saw as a basic deficiency among his own people. As we will see in the next chapter, he became increasingly convinced that without a firm base in popular support, the prospects of a vibrant nationalist and populist movement would be slim. However, let us return to his first political clarion call.

In our country, Soekarno argued, where Christianity had been the faith of the oppressor and Islam the faith of the underdog, Marxism and Islam ought to be natural allies. Islam was in fact nationalist since its religion was the religion of the underdog, while Indonesian Marxists were in fact nationalists since Marxism condemned the capitalist system of the alien oppressor and thus also sided with the underdog. As for the nationalists, they ought to recognize these nationalist tendencies in both Marxism and Islam, and thus unite with them in order to finally overcome the common enemy. Convinced that the pure nationalists of his generation would have no objection to following the precepts he was unfolding, his main thrust was to bring Indonesian Muslims and Marxists together. In this, he must have weighed the consequences following the recent organizational political split between them, but also the bare fact that in numerical strength they still topped all other political organizations in the country.

So he lectured indigenous Marxists and Muslims alike on the basic economic and sociological tenets they had in common but so far had been unaware of. He cited the Koran's *surah Âl'Imran* verse 129, and argued that surplus value seen by Marxists as rooted in capitalism was the equivalent of usury for pious Muslims[125] Citing yet another *surah, Al-Tawba* verse 34, Soekarno argued that both Muslims and Marxists were against capitalist hoarding of money. And he reminded his audience that the Islamic obligation to pay tithes, an obligation for the rich to share their wealth with the poor, essentially corresponded to the sharing of wealth required by Marxists in order to combat pauperization. Even when it came to the principle of liberty, equality and

[125]   Ia (the true Muslim) mengerti bahwa riba ini pada hakekatnja tiada lain daripada meerwaardenja faham marxisme itu!

fraternity (and here he referred to the Koranic *surah Al-Hudjarat* verse 13), Muslims and Marxists had the concept of fraternity in common. As to equality, that was taught in the Koranic *surah Al-Kahf* verse 10. Soekarno further distinguished between historical materialism and philosophical materialism, the basic maxims of Marxist theory, and held that they were not interdependent at all, since the former remained subject to change due to constant new historical factors emerging.[126] Therefore, Soekarno argued, the Marxist maxim that religion is the opiate of the masses had been superseded. Marx and Engels, if they were alive today, would surely have recognized that Islam was a victim of imperialist capitalism, just like the Western working classes. He stressed that today, Marxists no longer demanded that religion be abandoned, as the 1847 Communist Manifesto had prescribed.[127] He concluded that if Indonesian Marxists remained true to the new tactics and new theories of Marxism, they could surely be considered as true and valid defenders of the common people and truly be seen as the salt of the earth. However, if conservative Marxists stuck to outdated theories and tactics and therefore opposed unity or genuine cooperation with Muslims and nationalists, they should not be surprised to be called the opiate of the people.[128] It is here that the influence of fellow General Study Club member Marcel Koch comes into focus, someone who since mid-1923 had exposed Soekarno to a welter of Marxist thought and opinion, adding hereby to the earlier teachings of Coos Hartogh.

Yet the main thought emerging in Soekarno's *Indonesia Moeda* clarion call was that nationalism pure and simple – he cited the SH/NIP so recently disbanded but with its credo still so present in the minds of true nationalists – is what made the unity he craved a distinct possibility. Uppermost in his mind at that time was that the nationalist ingredients of both Marxism and Islam should be more than sufficient for channelling the diverse currents into one powerful stream. At the same time, some of his Javanese/Balinese temperament shone through his *Indonesia Moeda* essay. While the heroic struggle soon to come between *sini* and *sana* was portrayed only briefly by

---

[126] Kita haroes membedakan historis-materialisme itoe dari pada wijsgerig-materialisme; kita haroes memperingatkan bahwa maksoednja historis-materialisme itoe berlainan dari pada maksoednja wijsgerig-materialisme tahadi.

[127] Taktik marxisme-baroe terhadap agama adalah berlainan dengan taktik marxisme-doeloe. Marxisme-baroe adalah berlainan dengan marxisme dari tahoen 1847 jang dalam Manifes Komunis mengatakan bahwa agama itoe haroes di'abschaffen' atau dilapaskan adanja.

[128] Dan dengan memenoehi segala kewadjiban marxis-moeda tahadi itoe, dengan memperhatikan segala perobahan teori azasnja, dengan mendjalankan segala perobahan taktik pergerakannja itu. Mereka boleh menjeboetkan diri pembela rakjat jang toeloes-hati, mereka boleh menjeboetkan diri garamnja rakjat. Tetapi marxis jang ingkar akan persatoean, marxis yang kolot-teori dan koeno-taktiknja, marxis jang memoesoehi pergerakan kita nasionalis dan islamis jang soenggoeh-soenggoeh, – marxis jang demikian itoe djanganlah merasa terlanggar kehormatannja djikalau dinamakan ratjoen rakjat adanja!

naming Bima and his son, the stress on harmony and unity was paramount throughout Soekarno's appeal. And here we arrive at the heart of Soekarno's Javanist-inspired appeal. In the final passages he calls for an organizer who could make himself the Mahatma of Unity, while also pondering the question whether Mother Indonesia, with such sons as Oemar Said Tjokroaminoto, Tjipto Mangoenkoesoemo and Semaoen, did not also deserve a son who could become the champion of this unity.[129] Was Soekarno here not thinking of himself as someone who not only had restored the ancient Javanese dictum that, synthetically speaking, all matters were basically one, but also as someone deserving to become the future leader of a united *pergerakan*?

Developments leading to the founding of Soekarno's Perserikatan Nasional Indonesia

One of the first steps in promoting unity between Muslims and nationalists was Soekarno's moves toward his former father-in-law Tjokroaminoto. Together with Mr Sartono, a fellow member of the Bandoeng General Study Club who had become more and more a confidant, Soekarno made arrangements in December 1926 to edit a 'nationalist' section for Tjokro's new journal *Bandera Islam*. This new periodical displayed on its front page, along with the usual Muslim symbol of the crescent moon and star, the *kepala banteng* (wild buffalo head) of the nationalists.[130] Also, from now on, Soekarno and Tjokroaminoto were often seen appearing together at public platforms. Aware that nationalists of the older generation were still prone to succumbing to ideas of a greater Sumatra or a greater Java, and that even Jong Java was diametrically opposed to a 'revolutionary approach',[131] Soekarno's next influential move was the founding, on 20 February 1927, of a Bandoeng association called Jong Indonesia (Young Indonesia) for indigenous youngsters fifteen years of age and older.[132] Later, during its first congress on 28 December 1927, it was renamed Pemoeda Indonesia (Youth of Indonesia), and on this occasion Soekarno was the main speaker. This youth movement, followed by a brace of *kepala banteng* girls, and with nationalist boy scout associations being set up in the Preanger, caused some serious concern among a number of colonial civil servants.

However, the greatest stroke of luck for Soekarno's unifying campaign

---

[129] Persatoean itoe bisa berdiri; tinggal mentjari organisatornja sahadja jang mendjadi Mahatma Persatoean itoe. Apakah Iboe Indonesia jang mempoenjai poetera-poetera sebagai Oemar Said Tjokroaminoto, Tjipto Mangoenkoesoemo dan Semaoen, – apakah Iboe Indonesia itoe tak mempoenjai poela poetera jang bisa mendjadi kampioen persatoean itoe?

[130] *Bandera Islam*, 7 February 1927.

[131] 4 February 1926 letter of Oesman to his brother Ali Sastroamidjojo, Verbaal 16 February 1928 A 3.

[132] 23 February 1926 letter of Sartono to Ali Sastroamidjojo, Verbaal 16 February 1928 A 3; *45*

was the unexpected and yet rather swift disappearance of the Marxists from Indonesia's political scene. This may at first glance seem odd, since in his *Indonesia Moeda* contributions Soekarno had directed much of his efforts to bringing the Marxists under the unified roof he envisaged. Yet, aware of the bitter clashes between particularly the Marxists and the Muslims during the debates on party discipline, and then later during the closed sessions of the second but short-lived Radicale Concentratie, he must have doubted at times whether in a practical sense Muslim-Marxist unity could ever be achieved at all. But then, with the PKI deprived of its more experienced leadership and, contrary to Moscow's own directives, deciding on armed rebellion to be waged in Banten (November 1926) and West Sumatra (January 1927) – only to be swiftly overwhelmed by the far more powerful Indies army and police forces – Soekarno was left with a much less daunting unification problem. In the wake of the so-called 'communist' uprisings – in fact more an orthodox Muslim than a proletarian upheaval, having little local support – some 13,000 people were arrested on charges of being responsible or connected to it. Of these, some 4,500 were incarcerated, while some 800 so-called communist diehards were exiled to an internment site named Tanah Merah on New Guinea's Boven Digoel river, causing Hatta to remark 'that the ethical hand of [the new governor-general] De Graeff could strike a heavier blow than the fist of a born tyrant such as Fock'.[133] So the results were disastrous for the PKI, with the party being banned and remaining banned for the rest of the colonial period. The sole bright spot remaining for it was that key prominents who had fled the country such as Alimin, Moeso and Soebakat were now able to join leaders such as Tan Malaka, Semaoen and Darsono, already abroad, to continue some semblance of underground activity mixed with some propaganda efforts through the Indonesian Section of the Third International. These prospects, however, soon petered out altogether.[134]

Hatta's schemes thwarted and the founding of the Panitia Persiapan

Meanwhile, in the Netherlands, two plans were made to fill the vacuum: one submitted by Hatta to the PI executive on 23 November 1926 calling

---

Tahun Sumpah Pemuda 1974:43-4; Ramadhan 1981:75, with Inggit listing Soetan Sjahrir as one of its members.
[133]   Hering 1997:19. See also the Indonesian Information and Press Agency release 'After the insurrection in Indonesia', The Hague, April 1927 and Tjipto Mangoenkoesoemo (with a foreword by Ir Soekarno) 1927, where Tjipto echoes Soekarno's *Indonesia Moeda* essays calling 'all revolutionaries to form a united front against the Dutch' (p. 18). For Hatta's comment see Hatta 1972:387.
[134]   'Geheim overzicht van de Inlandsche politieke beweging in Nederlandsch Indië', up to 1 February 1928, Chapter III, pp. 3-4, Mr. 176/1928.

for the creation of an Indonesische Nationalistische Volkspartij (Indonesian Nationalist People's Party), and one by Semaoen submitted at the same time entitled 'Organisatie-plan voor onze nationale beweging' (Organizational plan for our national movement). Of the first, no copy of its detailed programme has been unearthed, though Hatta did give a summary of it during his 2 November 1927 interrogation by Dutch authorities. The party platform contained moderate political, social and economic points, with no explicit statement about Indonesian independence nor any mention of non-cooperation. It called for a national congress to be held in mid-1927 at which the party would be officially launched by PI members living in Indonesia.[135] Hatta even considered resigning in January 1927 from the chairmanship of the PI in order to return to Indonesia. However, his resignation was not accepted by the PI general meeting, partly in view of the 10-15 February 1927 International Liga congress to be held in Brussels, where Hatta was to lead the PI delegation (Hatta 1981:112). As to Semaoen's organizational plan, it was condemned by Hatta and not even submitted to the PI committee, mainly because it advocated violent underground activities with the aim of creating a state within a state.[136] During his interrogation sessions, Hatta indeed fervently distanced himself from Semaoen's plan – to no avail, however, since soon thereafter, authorities in both the Netherlands and the Indies were quick to link it with the alleged revolutionary intentions of certain old and new Indonesian nationalist associations. This official distrust may well have been fed by the rather odd convention signed on 5 December 1926 by both Semaoen and Hatta. This agreement was obviously designed to boost nationalist-communist cooperation in the wake of the suppression of the PKI in Banten. PI leadership was accepted by Semaoen, but he soon terminated the agreement (on 19 December 1926) after the Comintern had repudiated the convention.[137] As for Hatta, it showed his unfamiliarity with events in Indonesia, as did his next move: urging Soedjadi to found the Indonesian Nationalist People's Party in the homeland.

In Indonesia, where Soedjadi, together with Iskaq and Boediarto, in response to Hatta's prodding, tried to found this Sarekat Rakjat Nasional Indonesia, their efforts soon came to naught. Most of the leaders of the General Study Club believed at that time that they had a far better understanding of the Indonesian political scene than the PI executive in Leiden. Soedjadi reported to Hatta on 7 February 1927 that Hatta's concept of a new people's party had been rejected out of hand as being contrary to the spirit of

---

[135]   See 2 November 1927 interrogation Hatta, pp. 3-5 and 8 November 1927 interrogation Hatta, pp. 4-5, 32-3, 43, Verbaal 16 February 1928 A 3.
[136]   Interrogation Hatta 2 November 1927, p. 4, Verbaal 16 February 1928 A 3.
[137]   Bijlage A, Verbaal 16 February 1928 A 3. See also Westenenk report no. 88, 23 June 1927, Verbaal 28 June 1927 M 10.

non-cooperation and to the ideas expounded in *Indonesia Merdeka*.[138] Hatta was thus discouraged from directing political matters from his foreign location. This may well have dawned upon him as well. So, plans of a speedy return to his homeland were no longer envisaged: instead, he changed his course of study. Yet he still defended his aims in a letter dated 9 March 1927 to the Leiden-based law student Gatot Taroenamihardjo, whom he considered to be a staunch Marxist. In the letter, he even cited Semaoen's 'state within a state' concept, this time considering it to be quite appropriate for the situation developing in his home country. He also cited Semaoen's opinion that it was 'the only possible way to get the people on our side'. He ended his letter by expressing his surprise about the Batavia leaders 'judging it otherwise', while his and Semaoen's concept was so moderate, concluding that it was 'indeed quite difficult to understand each other when geographically we are so far apart'.[139] It is odd that Hatta here writes about Batavia and does not mention Bandoeng at all. Was he so far out of touch with Bandoeng? It seems unlikely, since he knew about the Comité Persatoean Indonesia being based there. And had he not earlier suggested making the Bandoeng Study Club a strong PI bulwark, eventually leading to the People's Party he envisaged, perhaps with himself as the future leader? Or did he pick on Betawi since Soedjadi, Boediarto and Sartono (all based there) had not fulfilled his dreams, and besides, had been wanting to get Bandoeng on their side for founding the People's Party he so cherished? We will never know, since the correspondence between his Indonesian following and Leiden soon petered out, and was further hampered by his own incarceration, on the charge that he and some of his closest colleagues were inciting an overthrow of Dutch authority in the Indies.

What we do know is that Bandoeng, even prior to Hatta's 27 September 1927 arrest, saw not only the birth of a vigorous new nationalist party but also the rise of an inspiring new leader, a twenty-six-year-old academic who had never been abroad. On 9 April 1927 a Panitia Persiapan (Preparatory Committee) consisting of Tjipto, Soekarno, Iskaq, Soenarjo and Boediarto met at Regentsweg 22 in Bandoeng to consider launching a new nationalist party. No chairman was appointed, but the senior member Tjipto remained dubious about the entire enterprise, since he feared it would be suppressed by the colonial government. He was overruled by the other four, however, who decided to go ahead with it.[140] The spirit of this preparatory committee

---

[138]   Verbaal 11 April 1928 G 6. In a subsequent 7 March 1927 letter to Hatta, Soedjadi reported having inserted statutes on non-cooperation and *kemerdekaan*, also labelling Soetomo and Agoes Salim (whom he called an agent-provocateur) as not suited to lead the *pergerakan*: Bijlage B i, Verbaal 9 August 1927 G 13.

[139]   Bijlage C u, Verbaal 9 August 1927 G 13.

[140]   Ramadhan 1981:88; interview with Mr Mas Soenarjo, 7 June 1971.

also found its way to the so-called 'question and reply evening' suggested by Soekarno and scheduled by the General Study Club to take place on 30 June 1927. On this occasion, Pan-Asianism was considered a greater drawing card for the common people than communism or Pan-Islamism. Tjipto and Tan Tek Ho, editor of the Betawi *Sin Po*, successfully defended the thesis of Asia against the Whites.[141]

From Pan-Islamism to the Partai Sarekat Islam's 'revolutionary nationalism'

The attempts of Tjokroaminoto and Agoes Salim to seek tighter cohesion through Pan-Islamism after the expulsion of the communists from their ranks showed but little sense of vision.

Even the disaster which ended in the near total destruction of the PKI did not seem to offer the SI – now renamed the Partai Sarekat Islam (PSI) – hope for a brighter future. As one observer had it, 'the CSI and Tjokroaminoto were caught in a political impasse, since their propaganda activities being solely for Islamism and against Communism had nearly exhausted them. And so the people's movement from now on circumvented the CSI.' (Petrus Blumberger 1931:83.) Some years later, the author of the September 1927 report on the 'Revolutionary direction of the PSI' described the party's decline at that time as follows:

> With the departure of Semoean and his following, the SI lost its best and most active members, a sheer bloodletting causing loss of vitality and leaving the SI to become a lifeless body not able to reorganize itself for at least another two years. Another factor in its rapid decline was that Moehammadijah, the modernist and fast-growing Islamic association, from a religious perspective but even more from a social one, took the wind out of the SI's sails.[142]

Due to the energies of Agoes Salim, however, the eleventh CSI congress on 8-10 August 1924 in Soerabaja was able to present a new political programme conceived by Salim himself. Here, all PSI activities were still considered as being solely backed by the singular and true tenets of Islam. Non-cooperation with the Volksraad was maintained, and more active propaganda against the communists was proposed. As to strictly religious issues, these were to

---

[141]   Poeze 1982:65, and 'Bestuursconferentie 1928; Overzicht van den inwendigen politieken toestand (Maart 1927-Maart 1928)', p. 25, Mr. 263/1928.
[142]   'Nota Revolutionnaire richting van de partij Sarekat Islam', parts one and two, sent by the General Secretariat to the 12 November 1927 extraordinary meeting of the Council of the Netherlands Indies, part one, p. 4, Mr. 1325/1927.

be reserved for the sister organization of the PSI, namely the Al-Islam congress.[143]

In spite of the efforts made by Agoes Salim, by far the brightest of all PSI leaders on the Pan-Islamic side, and by Mas Soerjopranoto in the field of national education and labour union activity inspired by Islamic tenets, the road to Pan-Islamic unity still seemed beset with thorny problems. Initially, Tjokroaminoto and Agoes Salim did gain some semblance of international and local stature through their sponsoring at home of so-called Al-Islam congresses; the first, with orthodox and modernist factions attending, was held in Cheribon from 31 October to 2 November 1922, and it became a permanent institution after the exclusively modernist second Al-Islam congress, held in Garoet from 19 to 21 May 1924, where Moehammadijah seemed to move closer to the PSI's social platform.[144] This institution, now named Al-Islam Hindia, with a chief executive consisting of the same members who sat in the Centrale Sarekat Islam (CSI) but also with some input from Moehammadijah prominents as well, promoted Pan-Islamic religious policies more rigorously, along with organizing a so-called Tanzim movement, where socio-economic and cultural perspectives were based exclusively upon strict Muslim tenets.[145] As to notions of 'liberating Islam from a position of submission to the West, these had found earlier inspiration by the Turkish victories of Mustapha Kemal Ghazy against the Greeks and Armenians', but had then been overshadowed by the fact that Turkey had abolished the caliphate in 1924 (Tjokroaminoto and Salim 1927:1-2).

And so, urged by the Soerabaja-based Arabic association Attadibiah, the PSI decided to press for a delegation to be sent to the Caliphate Congress to be held in Cairo in March 1925 in order to decide on the appointment of a new caliph, or at least a directorate to deal with all-Islam issues, particularly in the holy cities of Mecca and Medina. A Caliphate Committee was duly founded and then followed by an extraordinary Al-Islam congress held in Soerabaja from 24 to 26 December 1924, and attended by close to one thousand delegates representing the PSI, Moehammadijah and some smaller Java-based religious associations. According to the acting adviser of Inlandsche Zaken R.A. Kern, this congress was 'marked by a modernist spirit, with Salim being the soul of it' and with him 'idolizing Pan-Islamism in such a way that, aside from the caliphate issue, it was truly a question of Islam flexing its political power muscles'.[146] During the congress, the news

---

[143] See Inlandsche Zaken adviser R.A. Kern's report to Governor-General Fock, Mr. 793/1924.

[144] See Congress reports by Hoesein Djajadiningrat, 3 December 1922 no. 1128, Mr. 85/1923 and by Gobée, 11 June 1924 no. F 160, Mr. 460/1924.

[145] 'Geheim overzicht van de Inlandsche politieke beweging in Nederlandsch-Indië', Chapter II, pp. 5-6, Mr. 176/1928.

[146] Kern to Fock, 29 January 1925 no. G 55, Verbaal 15 December 1925 A 18.

broke that in the Hejaz, fighting between Sjarif Hoesein and Abdoel Azis bin Saoed had flared up, which then resulted in a unanimous Al-Islam congress resolution to dispatch Hadji Fachroedin, vice-chairman of Moehammadijah, Soerjopranoto of the CSI and Kijahi Hadji Abdoel Wahab Hasboellah of the traditionalists to the forthcoming Cairo congress.[147] However, this congress was postponed and replaced by the 1 June 1926 World Islam Congress (Moetamar Al 'Alam Al Islami 1344H) in Mecca, a change of venue to mark the inauguration of the new Wahabist leader Abd al-Azis bin Saoed as monarch of Arabia. After his victory, this man had made a start at purifying religious practices in line with his Wahabist teachings, measures which were partly welcomed in the East Indies but also partly rejected. In the East Indies, it was resolved, mainly by PSI and Moehammadijah consent, to charge Tjokroaminoto of the CSI and Mas Mansoer of Moehammadijah as delegates to the World Islam Congress in Mecca. The two delegates, during their sojourn in the Holy Land, would also investigate the possibility of a *hadj* organization, an institution to help Indonesian pilgrims overcome the usurious practices they were chronically exposed to both in the Indies and in Arabia. However, prior to their departure, a split occurred in the East Indies Muslim community. The traditionalists, led by Abdoel Wahab Hasboellah, during the fifth Al-Islam Hindia congress in Bandoeng on 6 February 1926, had submitted proposals to the effect that traditional religious practices, such as the erection of tombs on graves, the reading of certain prayers and the teaching of *madzahib* (orthodox schools), should be respected by King Abd al-Azis bin Saoed. These proposals were not adopted by the Bandoeng congress, which caused the traditionalists to angrily withdraw from the Caliphate Committee and instead form a Comité Meremboek Hidjaz (Committee for Discussing Hejaz Issues). This latter committee, during a meeting in Soerabaja on 31 January 1926, was transformed into the Nahdatoel Oelama (NO, Revival of Religious Scholars), an organization to resist the rise of modernism in Indonesian Islam and emphasizing direct recourse to the Koran and the Hadiths (sources of law), which largely dispensed with the learning of orthodox religious scholars. It quickly developed a strong following in East Java and southern Borneo.[148]

As to the Mecca world congress, it did not amount to much: the caliphate issue was barely touched upon and referred to a future Cairo congress. However, the fact that Tjokroaminoto and Mansoer had been sent to Mecca as 'representatives of the Muslims of the East Indies' caused the Al-Islam

---

[147]   *Bandera Islam* and *Hindia Baroe*, 9 January 1925.
[148]   *ENI* VI:272; 'Geheim overzicht van de Inlandsche politieke beweging in Nederlandsch-Indië', p. 8, Mr. 176/1928.

Hindia congress to become a section of the Mecca World Congress and to change its name to Moetamar al-Alam al-Islami far'al Hind asj-Sjarqyah (MAIHS, Islamic World Congress, East Indies Section).[149] After the return of the delegation, the PSI, in an obvious attempt to further monopolize the caliphate question, assumed sole representation of East Indies Muslims by transforming the MAIHS into a section of the PSI. This decision was immediately disapproved by the Moehammadijah and derided by the traditionalists.[150] The result was that Agoes Salim's visit to Mecca in 1927 for a second World Islam Congress was solely as a representative of the PSI. This second congress was a complete failure. Not only had Salim arrived late – after the pilgrimage – thus missing the delegates from other countries who had already gone home; these delegates had been undecided whether or not the congress should be continued in years to come (Tjokroaminoto and Salim 1927:5-6). Harry Poeze (1982:lxxviii) has commented on this that the PSI had indeed become 'increasingly isolated and not at all fit to be the leading and overall representative of the Islam pillar any longer'. The united Al-Islam Hindia front, with the traditionalists just having formed a new association hostile to the PSI-MAIHS, indeed crumbled even further, with the PSI taking disciplinary measures against its Moehammadijah members. This purge was similar to that carried out in the recent past against the then communist wing of the SI. Moehammadijah members were purged from the PSI or could still stay with it after having discarded Moehammadijah membership altogether. As for Moehammadijah, these measures did not really affect its growth. During 1927-1928 its membership almost doubled, to 17,000 members, while it directed 205 schools with 600 teachers supervising 16,000 pupils.[151]

Meanwhile, the PSI, during the 1-5 December 1926 MAIHS meetings in Bogor and a subsequent 13-16 January 1927 PSI-MAIHS congress in Pekalongan, approved a motion called 'Islam and Government involvement', signed by Tjokroaminoto but most likely drafted by Agoes Salim. Its main argument was that the colonial government's regulations concerning purely Islamic matters, such as Muslim marriages, the supervision of mosques and their councils, and Islamic religious teaching as a whole, were not in harmony with the guarantees for freedom of religious worship as laid down in both the Dutch and the Indies constitutions. Tranquillity and order (*rust en orde*),

---

[149] Tjokroaminoto and Salim 1927:3-4; 'Geheim overzicht van de Inlandsche politieke beweging in Nederlandsch-Indië', pp. 7-8, Mr. 176/1928.

[150] *Bandera Islam*, 13 June 1927; Tjokroaminoto and Salim 1927:5. For the Nahdatoel Oelama considering the Tjokro-Mansoer mission to Mecca a failure, see *Oetoesan Nahdatoel Oelama* no. 1 of 14 December 1928:10.

[151] Poeze 1982:lxxix. See also 'Bestuursconferentie 1929; Overzicht van den inwendigen politieken toestand van Maart 1928 tot December 1928', p. 20, Mr. 260/1929, for Moehammadijah causing the PSI to severely diminish its strength and appeal.

according to the motion, were sufficiently guaranteed without meddling and obstructing the exercise of religious rights of Muslims in the Indies. So all regulations violating these rights should be withdrawn without delay.[152] A first reaction to this was delivered on 2 July 1927 by Emile Gobée, acting adviser of Inlandsche Zaken, who held that:

> The disintegration of the communists and the internment of their leaders freed the PSI of its most dangerous enemy. So from there onwards, the PSI strove to occupy the place now vacated by the communists. [T]he motion approved at the MAIHS congress of 1-5 December 1926 in Bogor was indeed the first step to see how far it could go, as well as to show the extremists and other anti-government elements that they would find the PSI on the way to cooperating with them in a mutual sense. So, again, the PSI is trying to mobilize not only the economic and religious opponents of the government, but also the nationalists, under the PSI banner. [The motion was written] with great talent but exceedingly incorrectly, since the writers must have been aware that the objections they raised were not at all based upon the true facts.[153]

However, Gobée was quick to admit that the government, while deeming the motion improper and therefore not worthy of a reply, would nonetheless be willing to consider some of the objections raised and then take necessary corrective measures.[154] Perhaps alarmed by growing concern within the colonial administration about mounting PSI revolutionary postures, mainly reported by J.E. Jasper, *Resident* of Djokja, and by W.P. Hillen, governor of West Java,[155] Gobée undertook two lengthy official trips into Java's interior. Afterwards, both Gobée and attorney-general Duyfjes saw no imminent danger looming in the PSI actions and counselled that, for the time being, close supervision would suffice.[156] This opinion, however, was not shared by most of the colonial administration officials. Gobée still saw fit to caution the PSI leaders, 'since considerable distrust existed about the PSI's way of handling its propaganda and agitation' and that therefore 'not much was needed to cause severe measures to be taken against the association and its leaders'. In the same missive, Gobée warned the PSI 'not to get involved with the Liga, since it was quite clear that the latter was organized and financed by Moscow'.[157] Agoes Salim, and also Soekarno, an invited guest speaker at the PSI's 14th

[152] See Mr. 1022/1927 for the 18-page motion written in Malay.
[153] Letter of 2 July 1927 no. I/193, Mr. 830/1927.
[154] Letter of 13 September 1927 no. I/347a, Mr. 1147/1927.
[155] For Jasper see his letter of 10 May 1927 no. 39 G.E. to Attorney-General H.G.P. Duyfjes, Verbaal 15 November 1927 L 18. For Hillen's letter of 15 August 1927 no. G 5/60/21 to Governor-General De Graeff, Mr. 1249/1927, Verbaal 15 November 1927 L 18.
[156] 'Nota revolutionnaire richting van de Partij Sarekat Islam', part two, pp. 19-20, 24-5, Mr. 1325/1927.
[157] See Gobée's letter of 3 September 1927 no. I/329, Mr. 1074/1927.

congress, counselled not getting involved with the Liga for the time being, with the latter stressing that Indonesians in their quest for freedom needed to rely primarily upon their own strength. This, however, did not deter the Liga from wiring its congratulations to the PSI congress.[158]

Even before that 14th congress, with Pan-Islamism now being nearly dead and buried, PSI leaders had started to heed the advice of the Djokja-based Soekiman Wirjosandjojo, an erstwhile chairman of the Perhimpoenan Indonesia, to seek closer cooperation with the emancipatory nationalists. This, as we have seen above, had led to some semblance of cooperation, allowing a nationalist section edited by Soekarno and Sartono to appear in Tjokro's new periodical *Bandera Islam*. However, Soekiman Wirjosandjojo wanted to intensify such cooperation even further, as he testified first at the Djokja PSI leaders conference of 11 April 1927 and then at a 27 April 1927 meeting at his home attended by Tjokro and Mr Soejoedi. Here Soekiman was able to obtain firm authorization for seriously discussing the issue of unity with the Bandoeng-based emancipatory nationalists.[159] Soekiman had thus allayed the concerns put forward earlier by Agoes Salim, who in January of that year had fulminated against the westernized intellectuals and their study clubs. Agoes Salim noted that these associations had come to fruition outside Indonesia and failed to understand the true inner drives and desires of the Indonesian masses they intended to lead. These Netherlands-educated intellectuals often stressed anti-Dutch sentiments rather than love and self-sacrifice for their own people, and non-cooperation rather than *swadeshi* (self-help).[160] In the next chapter we will see that Soekiman's efforts eventually bore fruit. In the words of the author of the 'Bestuursconferentie 1929' internal political survey, it was clear

> That the slogan at the moment is *kemerdekaan* and not Islam, and that the nationalist leaders who aim at creating Indonesian unity prefer to see Christians, atheists, Hindu Balinese and Muslims all assembled in such a united front. [A]ll this is partly due to the leadership of Western-oriented intellectuals who are mostly hostile to Islamic decrees on marriage and interest levies since they impede real progress.'[161]

[158]   For its contents see Poeze 1982:129.

[159]   Algemeene Secretarie, 'Geheim overzicht van de Inlandsche politieke beweging in Nederlandsch-Indië', Chapter II, pp. 11, 13-4, Chapter IV, p. 9, Mr. 176/1928; 'Bestuursconferentie 1928; Overzicht van den inwendigen politieken toestand (Maart 1927-Maart 1928)', p. 18. With the die-hard governor of Djokjakarta J.E. Jasper soon labelling Soekiman Wirjosandjojo as 'the communist cell within the PSI': see Bijlage VII, p. 24 of 'Bestuursconferentie 1929; Overzicht van den inwendigen politieken toestand van Maart 1928 tot December 1928', Mr. 260/1929.

[160]   See Salim's 'Onze intellectueelen en de volksbeweging' (Our intellectuals and the people's movement), *Indonesia Moeda* no. 4/5 (January-February 1927).

[161]   'Bestuursconferentie 1929; Overzicht van den inwendigen politieken toestand van Maart 1928 tot December 1928', p. 21, Mr. 206/1929.

We will also learn in the next chapter that Agoes Salim continued to perceive Islamic tenets as quite interlaced with the nationalism he approved of. And this duly caused him to clash regularly with the *kebangsaan* notions of Soekarno and his followers.

CHAPTER IV

Soekarno's PNI and his brown front
Sini versus sana personified

Soekarno's Perserikatan Nasional Indonesia (PNI) and its objectives

On Monday, 4 July 1927, back at Regentsweg 22, Soekarno and Inggit met with Tjipto, Anwari, Iskaq Tjokrohadisoerjo, Sartono, Soendoro Boediarto, Soenarjo, Samsi Sastrowidagdo, Soedjadi (alias Soegito) and the Menadonese J.W. Tilaar, who were already assembled there. Soekarno immediately proposed that the time was ripe for establishing a new nationalist party. As Inggit has it: 'my husband could no longer contain himself and so he proposed that now was the time to found a party'.[1] And again it was Tjipto who cautioned that such a new party would be seen by colonial authorities as a mere substitute for the PKI and this would only court danger. Although some said that the new party now envisaged was not at all like the PKI,[2] both Anwari and Soekarno felt the risk should be taken for mounting it. Inggit quotes her husband as saying: 'Yes, so be it, the risks we must bear. We better be bold.'[3] All but Tjipto agreed, with Tjipto then stating he would not join it. Next, it was resolved to name the party Perserikatan Nasional Indonesia (PNI, National Indonesian Association). A board was chosen, with Soekarno as chairman, Iskaq as secretary/treasurer, and Anwari, Samsi, Sartono and Soenarjo as members.[4] Together with the latter, Soekarno would also, in May 1928, edit a new PNI periodical called *Persatoean Indonesia* (Poeze 1982:332).

---

[1]   'Suamiku sudah tidak tahan, ia menganggap sekarang waktunya untuk membentuk suatu partai' (Ramadhan 1981:90).
[2]   'Kita sama sekali berlainan dengan PKI' (Ramadhan 1981:90).
[3]   'Ya sudahlah, risiko apa pun kita tanggung, Kita harus berani' (Ramadhan 1981:90). Inggit expressed her admiration for Soedjadi, a colonial finance department official now joining a party which aimed to challenge the Indies government (Ramadhan 1981:89).
[4]   Ramadhan 1981:91. It is interesting to see that Iskaq's biographer does not mention the preparations made by both Hatta and Soedjadi. Iskaq, who graduated in law in 1925 and then returned to Indonesia knowing Hatta only by name, gives full credit to the lawyers residing at Regentsweg 22, to the *ingenieurs* Soekarno and Anwari, and to Dr Samsi, for having arrived independently at the idea of creating a nationalist party: Nalenan 1982:19-23. Also, Mr Soenarjo claimed that the actual formation of the PNI stemmed from the Bandoeng Study Club rather

That Soekarno, an *arek Soeraboyo*, was chosen to lead the new nationalist party in a region where the main language was not Javanese but Sundanese may seem strange to outsiders, but as Charles van der Plas, an Arabist then attached to Inlandsche Zaken,[5] was to put it:

> Bandoeng's population consists of a mixture of Sundanese people and itinerant Javanese and Minangkabau. The latter groups are as yet not firmly anchored in the society, while the Sundanese themselves are moving away from their traditional moorings. Therefore, all of these groups are liable to be influenced by unbalanced propaganda. Because the city of Bandoeng is the location of the State Railways [Staats Spoorwegen], and the Departments of War and of Government Enterprises, the number of Indonesian semi-intellectuals is quite high.[6] Difficulties arising between European and indigenous members of the colonial administration [BB, Binnenlandsch Bestuur], and the many dismissals among village [*desa*] heads have further decreased resistance to the mounting influence of fierce nationalist-inspired propaganda.[7]

The Preanger (now Parahyangan), belonging to what Professor Van Vollenhoven[8] had called the *adatrechtskring* (traditional/territorial jurisdiction) of West Java, was further noted for its individual and hereditary rights of disposal over land and the tendency – particularly around Bandoeng – to the formation of a wealthy class of landlords, which in turn caused proletarization and pauperization among the Sundanese *wong cilik* (the tiny landlords, the tenants and the sharecroppers already labelled by Soekarno as Marhaen[9]). During the late 1910s and early 1920s this situation was exploited by the PKI and its Sarekat Rakjat affiliates to their own benefit (Svensson 1983:98-112). After the suppression of these communist organizations, a

---

than from the Perhimpoenan Indonesia, see Legge 1984:90 and our own interview with Mas Soenarjo, 7 June 1971.

[5]　　The Kantoor voor Inlandsche Zaken (Office of Indigenous Affairs), next to the *adviseur*, was usually supported by a small, racially-mixed staff who acted somewhat as a socio-political barometer for the government, registering shifts in indigenous moods and matters of opinion: Hering 1985:2; Suminto 1985:99-198.

[6]　　On the development of Bandoeng as a growing government centre, see Oostingh 1970: Chapter 2.

[7]　　Mr. 547/1930, Verbaal 9 May 1931 C 9.

[8]　　Van Vollenhoven's teacher was Jacques Oppenheim, author of *The theory of the organic state and its value for our times*, Groningen 1893, who, as chairman of the so-called *Proeve Oppenheim*, a supplement to the *Herzienings Commissie*, held that the Volksraad should be based on corporations and communities (*lichamen en gemeenschappen*). Oppenheim's archaic tract on organic statism was frequently cited by Soeharto New Order ideologists such as Abdulkadir Besar and Hamid Attamimi and earlier in Professor Soepomo's explicit totalitarian prescription for an 'integralist state' before the Investigating Committee for the Preparation of Independence (Panitia Persiapan Kemerdekaan Indonesia, PPKI) on 31 May 1945.

[9]　　Soekarno's meeting with Marhaen has often been questioned, but for our purposes it remains a powerful symbol which he utilized to great effect in speeches throughout his career.

vacuum was created that was rapidly filled up again by Soekarno's own nationalist organizations. Soekarno quite often visited this area for propaganda and membership purposes, while his wife translated some of his speeches into Sundanese.[10]

Soekarno further perfected the Sundanese language through the friendship he and Inggit had struck up somewhat later with Soegondo and Soewarsih Djojopoespito, the latter being a Sundanese just like Inggit. The Djojopoespitos, both quite emancipated and operating outside the common norm (*buiten het gareel*) as teachers in the indigenous 'wild school' system of Ki Hadjar Dewantoro, often met at Karno and Inggit's *panggoenghuis* (house on stilts) at Astanaanjarweg 174. Soewarsih described Inggit as a charming, svelte and elegant woman well versed in and positively engaged in the Indonesian feminist movement as well as the nationalist party activities of her husband. Soewarsih herself admired him, not only for his fascinating personality but also for his smashing good looks, while her husband, a member of the PNI and the Perhimpoenan Peladjar-Peladjar Indonesia (PPPI, Union of Indonesian Students), admired Soekarno for the dazzling way he handled the audiences who came in droves to hear him speak.[11] E. du Perron, who wrote a foreword to Soewarsih's recollections, describes Soekarno's entry on the Preanger scene even more poetically:

> It is the dawn of primary education experienced by the Indonesian population, of whom the greater part are still quite illiterate: a romantic atmosphere [...] which by an Indonesian 'demagogue' such as Soekarno, who to some appeared as the Lassalle of Indonesia, was thus so nationally directed that it became ever more romantic, since it grew gradually into a truly politically coloured phenomenon. It was the time of strict non-cooperation, a time when Dutch aid and guidance were rejected out of hand so as to utilize one's own means spiritually, and all that despite one's own poverty, [...] a fashion further encouraged by Indonesian nationalists and always linked by them with the new norms of a bright political awakening. [...] The figure of Soekarno may have been sketched a bit pale [in Soewarsih's tale]; however, the influence he was to exert upon their world [of the Djojopoespitos] made quite a deep impact, [...] while the memory of the perspective opened by him would from now on always profoundly linger in their minds. (Soewarsih Djojopoespito 1947:7-8.)

Van der Plas in mid-1927 drew a profile of Soekarno which, though longer than the brief one rendered here by Du Perron, shows some interesting similarities:

> In the PNI two factions can be discerned: the group of engineers – Tjipto Mangoenkoesoemo is the spiritual father of this faction – and that of the jurists. In

---

[10]   Ramadhan 1981:73-4. See also Mrázek 1994:53.
[11]   On the contacts with the Djojopoespitos: Ramadhan 1981:58-60 and Soewarsih's own recollections (Djojopoespito 1947:48-58).

the former, the most important and interesting figure is Ir Soekarno, an extremely gifted orator, and an honest and courageous man who wears his heart upon his sleeve, though often somewhat careless and taking quite some risks giving his confidence to those he trusts. When he was a student he wavered between Islam-inspired political tendencies and the modern-nationalistic one. However, the influence of Dr Tjipto Mangoenkoesoemo westernized Soekarno and led him to separate from the Muslims. In my opinion Soekarno is a completely sound and pure figure, undoubtedly revolutionary – he acknowledges that himself – and since recently he is of the firm conviction that the liberation of Asia is near at hand. However, his fair-mindedness, coupled with his sensitivity and sunny candour, make him a person of whom, when older and more experienced with working toward a more meaningful future, it can be expected that he will be prepared to cooperate in a fruitful way.[12]

In a sequel to his report, Van der Plas expressed his fear that the PNI would grow in influence and that it had clearly taken over the political leadership of the Indonesian *pergerakan,* and should therefore be considered the colonial government's 'most dangerous opponent'. In contrast to the now banned PKI, the PNI expressly rejected the use of violence to achieve its aims. The PNI also stressed that no support from abroad was to be expected: no air-ships from Moscow or warships from Turkey nor an intervention by a *ratu adil* or a *mahdi.* The PNI also remained silent about the Liga (Van der Plas was obviously reminded of the PI-Liga ties existing in the Netherlands[13]). Van der Plas concluded this sequel with the observation that 'many of the well-educated academics among the PNI leadership had a completely different spiritual background when compared to the earlier PKI leaders. Therefore, feelings of responsibility differed and there was among the first a greater sense of reality and of the possibilities of the moment.' Van der Plas warned, though, that 'extreme nationalist preaching as done by Soekarno would ultimately strike deeper roots than had been the case with the communist cause'.[14] In yet another report, Van der Plas stated the PNI's views as outlined by Soekarno as follows: 1. no social or economic advancement is possible without achieving national independence first; 2. the Netherlands will never grant (Indonesian) independence voluntarily; 3. an entire nation, conscious of its right to freedom and proclaiming that right with a thunderous voice, will indeed become free; 4. every Indonesian at heart sympathizes with the PNI (here Van der Plas inserted that this was probably correct; it would include members of the indigenous administration and the police as well, but with them remaining silent about it since they earned a living from the Indies government). Van der Plas culled Soekarno's aims from the latter's

[12]   Mr. 457/1928, and Meyer Ranneft Collection no. 527, ARA.
[13]   For PI-Liga contacts: Hatta's interrogation, pp. 23, 26-8, 32-3, Verbaal 16 February 1928 A3.
[14]   'Rapport over de politieke toestand', pp. 1-8, Mr. 1083/1928.

address to the Jakarta PNI branch of 4 December 1927, as recorded in a report by Inlandsche Zaken's language specialist Dr L. de Vries. Soekarno's address on that occasion was considered by Petrus Blumberger, then one of the main *pergerakan* advisers to the Ministry of Colonies in The Hague, as 'the best ever manifestation of Indonesian nationalism pursued by the PNI'.[15] *Perniagaan* of 10 December 1927, drawing a comparison between the PNI and the NIP, expressed the view that the PNI leadership's sober and calm approach was quite different from the violent and bitter ways adopted by Douwes Dekker and its other leaders, whose writings were passionate but often marred with hatred toward the Dutch and their colonial policies. The writer in the end, however, feared that the PNI would depart from its present calm and patient ways and become as fierce as the NIP, since most of the *sana* press had termed the PNI a dangerous phenomenon.

Indian nationalist ideas influencing Soekarno's political programme

That Van der Plas in all of his reports so far did not dwell at all on the non-cooperationist aspects of Soekarno's programme, while Du Perron did, may well have been due to perceptions still cherished at the time by both Inlandsche Zaken and the new Governor-General De Graeff about guiding the nationalist *pergerakan* toward evolutionary rather than revolutionary courses of action (Hering 1996:81, note 96). That Soekarno himself was much taken with the idea of a rather strict non-cooperation we have already noted, citing Tjipto, Douwes Dekker and Soewardi Soerjaningrat as major mentors in that endeavour. Yet Soekarno was also much influenced by the tactics Mohandas Karamchand Gandhi employed against the British in India, a situation he followed closely by reading widely about it and often discussing it with his close friend Marcel Koch, the author of a pioneering study on Indian nationalism.[16] So, inspired by the political activities demonstrated by men such as Gandhi, Jawaharlal Nehru, Gopal Krishna Gokhale and Chitta Ranjan Das, Soekarno too stressed the need of wresting himself and his people from the beguiling enchantment with which colonial authority for far too long had entrapped its indigenous subjects. He had already referred briefly to the spirited activities of all these Indian nationalist leaders in his first *Indonesia Moeda* contributions late in 1926. Even the Indian poet Mrs Sarojini Naidu, infatuated with Mohammad Ali Jinnah, whom she saw as a future ambassador of Hindu-Muslim unity, Soekarno hailed elsewhere 'as a shining example for our own Indonesian women to emulate'.[17] In Soekarno's article

15   Mr. 1447/1927; Petrus Blumberger 1931:212.
16   Interview Marcel Koch, 5 January 1952.

'Lihat kemoeka' (Looking ahead) he again cited Sarojini Naidu: 'not a single people will fail to become free if its soul wills to be free. No tyranny can chain a spirit, if the spirit refuses to be chained [...]. [E]ven the gods cannot set free a slave if his heart is not aflame with the fiery desire to be free.' (Soekarno 1959:80.) So these words by her, and non-cooperation such as Gandhi's bold *satyagraha sabha* campaign against the Rowlatt Act (Nehru 1941:41) and the concomitant self-respect it had aroused among Indian masses, profoundly affected Soekarno. Moreover, he perceived these Indian demonstrations and sentiments as having something in common with his own ideas about Javano-Balinese spiritual power.[18] Perhaps this is not such a strange perception, since both Indian and Javano-Balinese traditions stem from a common cultural background, a tradition Soekarno had been exposed to by grandparents and parents alike during his own youth and beyond. So, strict non-cooperation and profound feelings of self-respect, even if they did not reap any immediate benefit in the realm of concessions and advancement – and here he truly had given the prime example – would ultimately, Soekarno felt, bring the much desired nationalist consciousness and self-esteem to all of his Marhaen.

However, he did not altogether approve of Gandhi's passive civil-disobedience campaign. Instead, he was in favour of Jawaharlal Nehru's demand for Gandhi to change the passive stance for a militant one.[19] Also, in terms of the potential impact of the Gandhi-inspired *swadeshi* (autarky, self-sufficiency of a nation's economy, from Sanskrit *svadeśi*[n], '[one's] own country') in order to hasten *swaraj* (self-rule), Soekarno sensed it would not as a whole apply to the Indonesian situation. Aware of the vast difference in imperialist methods utilized in India and Indonesia, Soekarno believed *swadeshi* could work with some measure of success in India since it would certainly cause rather serious damage to British imperialist economic interests. He thought, however, that it would not work at all in Indonesia, where what the Dutch ultimately profited from was the exploitation of resources upon which their colonial economy was mainly based – labelled by Soekarno

---

[17]	From Soekarno's address to Pemoeda Indonesia's second congress on 24 December 1928, Mr. 408/1929. For Naidu and a sample of the purple prose she addressed to Jinnah, see Bolitho 1954:21-2.

[18]	See V. Suryanarayan's presidential address, 'India and the Indonesian Revolution', *Indian History Congress Proceedings 42nd Session*, 1981, pp. 555-6; Bharadwaj 1997:102-4.

[19]	'Gandhi sendiri disebutkan "passive-civil-disobedience", jakni "tidak menurut, setjara passif". Jawaharlal Nehru sendiri [...] pernah minta kepada Gandhi supaja passive-civil-disobedience ini diganti dengan militant-civil-disobedience. (Soekarno 1959:194.) Some of Soekarno's criticism can be found in his foreword to Tjipto Mangoenkoesoemo 1927, where he states that 'The spiritually inclined Indian pays scant attention to the materialist side of the struggle [...]. [T]o have results, politics should be based on the real, concrete situation and never lose itself in vague clouds of philosophisms and abstractions. [...]. [E]ven Gandhi, brilliant though he is, sinned greatly against this, and so society turned cruelly against him.'

'a resources and capital investment imperialism' (Soekarno 1959:154) – rather than the colony providing markets for the mother country's manufacturing enterprises. Soekarno argued further that a considerable percentage of the Indies' resources and investment economy remained in the hands of foreign enterprises who did not give a hoot about indigenous people's interests.[20]

Somewhat later, Soekarno would stress the need for activities such as *massa-actie* and *machtsvorming* (mass protest and power formation) in the wake of efforts to make the populace more aware – concepts which we will meet below and where Gandhian influence exerted upon Soekarno as a young leader can be discerned. Gandhi's famous anti-salt-tax march in India and the Mahatma's advice of boycotting all government officials were militant activities Soekarno certainly did approve of (Soekarno 1959:163-6). At that time Soekarno was fond of decorating his *Fikiran Ra'jat* covers with Gandhian phrases such as 'Our people only know one kind of public safety and that is the public jail', with Soekarno adding 'that such a state of things was also common here in my own homeland'.[21]

Developments causing the PNI to grow and the PPPKI to be established

A windfall for the new PNI came in the form of the arrest and subsequent trial of some key members of the Perhimpoenan Indonesia (PI) executive committee in the Netherlands. The PI – perceived as an affiliate of the Liga and the Comintern (in PI correspondence referred to as Kiaji) – caused Dutch authorities first to search PI executive homes and then to arrest Hatta, Ali Sastroamidjojo, Mohammad Nazir Pamoentjak and Abdoel Madjid Djojoadiningrat on charges of scheming to overthrow Dutch rule in the Indies. Achmad Soebardjo, Gatot Taroenamihardjo and Arnold Mononoetoe escaped arrest since they were abroad, the first being in Moscow and the latter two en route to their home country (Hatta 1972:117, 119). In Soekarno's house this situation was debated right after the news reached Indonesia, and duly assessed as useful propaganda to exploit. So, a protest meeting scheduled by the PNI on 14 August 1927, where Soekarno condemned the house searches, was followed by another one on 25 September 1927 protesting the arrests and collecting money for the imprisoned students in Holland. So the arrests came indeed at an opportune moment for the newly established PNI, with its leaders using the issue to good advantage, holding protest meetings and

---

[20]   See Soekarno 1959:136-57, with Soekarno rendering ample evidence of Koch's influence by profusely citing the latter's treatise *Herleving*, 1922.

[21]   'Satoe-satoenja keamanan oemoem jang dikenal oleh bangsa kita hanjalah keamanan oemoemnja openbare gevangenis belaka!' and 'Soeatoe oetjapan jang djitoe. Jang tjotjok djoega dengan keadaan disini!' (Soekarno 1959:facing p. 226).

discussing the matter in their newspapers.[22] Soekarno, in an article titled 'Pemandangan dan pengadjaran' (A review and a lesson), after learning of their acquittal, was quick to point out that all the allegations made by Westenenk of so-called PI and Moscow links, and of plotting an uprising in Indonesia, had turned out to be unfounded. Soekarno also conjectured that if their case had been tried in Indonesia they would not have been so fortunate as to be acquitted. Nonetheless, he was quick to salute the two SDAP lawyers, Mr J.E.W. Duys and Mr T. Mobach, for having successfully defended the students for no fee at all (Soekarno 1959:68-70).

A blow, however, was Tjipto's sudden arrest by the colonial authorities. His medical practice at Pangeran Soemedangweg 89, where he had been searching for a new anti-tuberculosis remedy, was only a stone's throw from Soekarno and Inggit's home. The practice had for some time been closely watched by indigenous detectives of the Politieke Inlichtingen Dienst (PID, Political Intelligence Branch).[23] Soon after, he was accused of having a part in the so-called Soediro affair, for he had had some contact with Menadonese warrant officers of the Koninklijk Nederlandsch-Indisch Leger (KNIL, Royal Netherlands Indies Army). These warrant officers, following the intentions of the now incarcerated Soediro,[24] were believed to be planning an uprising among indigenous, mainly Menadonese, members of the KNIL 15th battalion located in Bandoeng and other units located in Meester Cornelis (now Djatinegara). Two of these Menadonese had contacted Tjipto at his Bandoeng home and may well have disclosed their insurgency plans. Whether Tjipto approved of these plans was never properly established; what he did was to give them ten guilders – one source reported twenty-five guilders[25] – to cover their transportation costs to Batavia. Official suspicion also arose about a Betawi municipal official with alleged communist sympathies named J. de Jeer, who stayed at Tjipto's house twice during May 1927. Tjipto replied that he sensed De Jeer was an undercover agent and that he therefore remained quite watchful in the conversations he had with his guest.[26] Nonetheless, in the wake of the swift suppression of military-inspired disturbances in Meester Cornelis and an aborted raid on the Bandoeng military pyrotechnical plant, Tjipto was summoned to appear before the Preanger *resident* to

[22]   Ramadhan 1981:98, 102-3; Hering 1985:35; Poeze 1982:97, 122.
[23]   On this omnipresent branch see Hering 1982:51 note 1 and Poeze 1994a.
[24]   On Soediro, a Semarang-based former PKI member who in 1924 founded a Muslim-oriented communist party and organized, before he landed in prison in January 1927, a revolutionary wing in some indigenous military units, Petrus Blumberger 1931:356-7; Poeze 1982:76-7; 'De samenzwering van de Soediro-Partij', part one and two in *Soerabajaasch Handelsblad*, 27 and 29 August 1927.
[25]   *De Courant*, 22 August 1927.
[26]   *De Locomotief*, 15 August 1927; *Algemeen Indisch Dagblad*, 13 August 1927; *De Courant*, 21 August 1927.

answer the usual list of questions the common ritual which always preceded banishment. To his close friend Marcel Koch, Tjipto intimated that he had nothing to do with the November PKI uprisings nor with the recent military riots. He added to his friend that 'if twenty years later an uprising would occur with some measure of success I would join it for sure'.[27] Prophetic words indeed. Koch tried to prove Tjipto's innocence by writing in the *Indische Courant* and by cabling the governor-general (Koch 1956:193). All to no avail. By government decree Tjipto and his family were banished to Banda on 16 December 1927.[28] At his departure by train from Bandoeng's railway station with the destination Soerabaja, he and his wife were bid farewell by Soekarno, Iskaq, Soenarjo and Samsi. In Soerabaja, Tjipto and his family had a farewell dinner with Soetomo and other prominent local nationalists at Hotel Victoria, where he and his family stayed overnight as well. The next day they boarded the steamer *Van den Bosch* at Tandjong Perak harbour, again escorted by some friends to the harbour, for the voyage to take him and his family to Bandaneira.[29] Before leaving Bandoeng, Tjipto had also written a brief farewell note to Soekarno, which the latter handed over for propaganda purposes to the *Algemeen Indisch Dagblad* to print.[30] In a *Soeloeh Indonesia Moeda* (Torch of Young Indonesia) article of December 1927, Soekarno further described his sorrow upon his mentor's departure:

> Our friend Tjipto Mangoenkoesoemo departed with his family and his brave undaunted wife, leaving us behind – we who had stood behind him with similar principles, with common objectives and common action for so many years. For the third time Tjipto is entering the life of an exile imposed upon him by the exorbitant rights of the rulers; for the third time, with head held high and a brave heart, he is offering his sacrifice for the country and for the people he serves. And we, the friends left behind, we, the Indonesian nationalists, the Sumatran nationalists, the Soendanese nationalists, the Javanese nationalists and all other nationalists – we wish him farewell also with heads held high. For the dawn has began to break; the cock, therefore, has begun to crow. Tjipto in exile or Tjipto not in exile [...] the movement will make progress toward its goal: without fail the sun will rise [...]. What lesson should we draw from comrade Tjipto's exile? What does it reflect? First of all: the manner in which comrade Tjipto underwent exile is a lesson that an endeavour to make the future bright is not at all easy, not a light task, but an endeavour difficult and heavy; an endeavour that does not accept half-hearted devotion; an endeavour that demands one's entire self, one's whole being. 'One must give oneself entirely, since heaven rejects half-hearted measures.' Tjipto has indeed shown us the way: the way to serve the people and the nation. (Soekarno 1959:41.)

---

[27]   Koch 1956:193. Tjipto also revealed his non-involvement to Stokvis, in a letter written in Bandaneira of 26 September 1930, Collection Stokvis, IISG.
[28]   Verbaal 25 January 1928 Q 1.
[29]   *De Indische Courant*, 2 January 1928; *Bataviaasch Nieuwsblad*, 3 January 1928.
[30]   *Algemeen Indisch Dagblad*, 23 December 1927.

Somewhat later, on 1 October 1928, to be exact, Tjipto issued a 'Ma'loemat' from Neira in response to the moves then afoot in the Volksraad to re-elect him to that body. In his 'Ma'loemat' Tjipto specifically stated his wish to become a member of the PNI the moment he arrived back in Java. Tjipto's decision to join Soekarno's PNI may well have been prompted by the notion that as a Volksraad member he would normally enjoy parliamentary immunity. He also referred to a set of cables he had received from Soekarno, Tjokro, Kaoem Betawi (led by Thamrin), Boedi Oetomo, Pasoendan and the Sumatranenbond welcoming him to the Volksraad. All this was of no avail, however, since the Volksraad, in spite of a spirited defence by Volksraad delegates such as Thamrin, Stokvis and Jonkman, decided against Tjipto having a seat.[31]

Long before these developments, Soekarno had been instrumental in further cementing nationalist unity. Invited to the PSI's 14th congress held in Pekalongan from 28 September to 2 October 1927, Soekarno urged the PSI to join the PNI and other *pergerakan* parties to form a united front. He referred in that context to H.C. Zentgraaff's call in the *Soerabajasch Handelsblad* to form a solid *blank front* (white front), a front that Soekarno said had initially not been supported by the *sana* press due to the fear that such a white front would certainly be opposed by a far stronger brown front. However, dailies such as the *Java Bode*, *Nieuws van den Dag*, *Algemeen Indisch Dagblad* and *De Locomotief*, which in the past had been sympathetic toward the *pergerakan*, were now often engaged in sowing disunity among the indigenous parties, Soekarno claimed. And with some justification. *De Locomotief*, for instance, worried about Gobée cabling De Graeff, who was touring on the government steamer *Wega*, that 'the congress had been satisfactory and not at all revolutionary in nature', and with Gobée also complaining about 'the rather false impressions made by most *sana* press editorials including those of *De Locomotief*'. In response, the daily cited the following statements. One by Agoes Salim stated: 'Soon, comrades, the time will arrive that we will have to take the reins into our own hands'; and by Tjokroaminoto: 'All slogans are false but one: chasing the alien oppressor away'. And another by Soekarno: 'Cooperation with the colonial oppressor? Never and unconditionally so!'[32]

As for Soekarno, he referred to the statutes he had designed and then circulated among the PSI congressional audience. In these statutes Soekarno called for a brown front to be formed, based upon a rather loosely formed

---

[31]   Tjipto's 'Ma'loemat' and supporting letters were given to me by Nico Palar during an interview with the latter on 7 August 1971. See also 'Tjipto en de Volksraad; Manifest aan zijn kiezers', *Java Bode*, 26 October 1928. For the Volksraad deliberations: *Handelingen Volksraad* 1928-1929: 2020-1, 2042, 2044, and the scathing comments of 'Bantengkop' about Tjipto being barred from a Volksraad seat in *Bintang Timoer*, 2 and 6 April 1929.

[32]   *De Locomotief Overzee-editie*, 18 October 1927:17-8. Also *De Locomotief*, 17, 18 and 19 August

federation of parties. This federation so formed, leaving each of its components to follow their own ideology, would be its strength, Soekarno stressed. Too tight a band among the parties involved would only harm the unity he had envisaged in his proposal. Paying homage to the Javano-Balinese dictum that synthetically all matters were one, he urged his audience to support the federation without abandoning each one's own individuality. In practical terms that would mean that all federated components had to demonstrate consensus (*moefakat*) only in matters concerning them all, such as the incarceration of the students in Holland, the struggle against the penal sanctions, and against the governor-general's exorbitant right to – without a court decision – exile people from the Indies if they were regarded as dangerous to public peace and security. Soekarno said these issues could only be resolved by a common vote of all delegates so federated, following the traditional *permusyawaratan* (general discussions for resolving opposing views through compromise) principle until *moefakat* (consensus) had been reached.[33]

The brown front taking shape with Non-Ko and Ko parties participating

It was this call by Soekarno which on 17 December 1927, six months after the PNI's inception and prompted by Soekarno's own initiatives,[34] led to the founding convention of the Permoefakatan Perhimpoenan-Perhimpoenan Politik Kebangsaan Indonesia (PPPKI, Consensus of Political Associations of Indonesia), with seven of Indonesia's most prominent political organizations – both of a Ko or Non-Ko inclination – joining it: Perserikatan Nasional Indonesia, Partai Sarekat Islam, Boedi Oetomo, Pasoendan, Sarikat Soematra, Kaoem Betawi and Indonesische Studieclub. Persatoean Minahassa and Sarekat Ambon, Ko parties to the core, led respectively by Dr Ratulangie and Dr Apituley, chose not to join the PPPKI. Somewhat later Sarekat Madoera, Perserikatan Celebes and the Bantenese association Tirtajasa joined the PPPKI as well.[35] In the permanent advisory council (Madjelis Pertimbangan), located in Bandoeng with Mr Iskaq serving as chairman and Dr Samsi as secretary, each of these seven member organizations was represented. A first initia-

---

1927, in a three-article series titled 'Hoog spel' (A bold game), proposed having the leaders put away rapidly since their resistance and their call for action was far too pregnant with danger.

[33]   Gobée, 'Verslag congresvergaderingen PSI te Pekalongan 28 September-2 October 1927', pp. 19-21, Mr. 1252/1927, and 'Bijlage 4', draft of statutes for the Sarikat Partij-Partij Politiek Indonesia (SPPI, Association of Indonesian Political Parties), pp. 1-2.

[34]   Gobée, 'Verslag congresvergaderingen PSI te Pekalongan 28 September-2 October 1927', also Soekarno's speeches reported by Gobée in Mr. 1252/1927 and Mr. 1447/1927.

[35]   Pringgodigdo 1978:74. See also *Fadjar Asia*, 21 December 1927.

tive of the Madjelis Pertimbangan was to issue a manifesto saluting Tjipto with a farewell but also wishing him a speedy reunion within the fold of the PPPKI.[36] So Soekarno had accomplished the unique feat of theoretically overcoming all contradictions earlier seen as insurmountable, but also of combining in one political organization Javanese, Sumatrans, Madurese, Bantenese as well as Celebes (now Sulawesi) people. And along with all this, also achieving Semaoen's 'state within a state' notion, an ideal also cherished by Mohammad Hatta. At this juncture Soekarno's thoughts must have dwelt on the earlier unification attempts by his former father-in-law, which ended in failure due to Tjokro's radical allies, who had followed Marxist proletarian tenets far too rigidly instead of making use of practical and traditional Indonesian approaches. With some relief Soekarno must also have pondered the fact of the outlawing of the PKI giving him the unique chance of uniting the *pergerakan* so smoothly within a year after the PKI's forced removal from the Indies political platform. Be that as it may, in his keynote address Soekarno stressed yet another Indonesian approach, overlooked in the recent past:

> Let us refrain from matters that could stand in the way of consensus. Let us, therefore, not discuss cooperation and non-cooperation – the question whether we are to work with the government or not. But let us above all seek that which brings us together. Let us put into the foreground all that unites us.[37]

It was this optimism and the clarion call for consensus that brought Mohammad Hoesni Thamrin closer to Soekarno, so much so that in the months to come, a kind of symbiotic political relationship would evolve between these two exponents of Indonesian emancipatory nationalism. The former, by far one of the most consistent left-of-centre adherents of a cooperationist-inspired nationalism, and the other, representing a more radical non-cooperationist wing of the *pergerakan*, would during 1928-1933 each leave their stamp upon Indonesian politics.[38] Thamrin, a Batavia-born Indo-European, who in the twenties and thirties often visited my parents' and grandparents' homes in Betawi, enthralling our family with his sensible political credo, had earlier entered the wider field of Indonesian politics. He had used that arena to refine his arguments on behalf of his regional bailiwick both in the Batavian Gemeenteraad and the Volksraad with increasing effect, with him being by far one of the most eloquent speakers the Volksraad had harboured

---

[36]   See 'Bestuursconferentie 1929', pp. 11-2, Mr. 260/1929, and 'Overzicht van de inwendigen politieken toestand van Maart 1927-Maart 1928', pp. 29-36; *Fadjar Asia*, 21 December 1927; *Soeloeh Ra'jat Indonesia*, 28 December 1927; *Darmokondo*, 26 December 1927; *Bintang Timoer*, 30 December 1927 and 19 January 1928 considered the PPPKI 'being the proper answer to Treub's *Het gist in Indië* proposals' and ridiculed *sana* press suspicions about the PPPKI.

[37]   *Soeloeh Indonesia Moeda* no. 2(January 1928):51.

[38]   On that relationship Hering 1996:Chapter Five.

so far. However, with his own municipal council Kaoem Betawi delegation reduced a number of years before from three to one (Hering 1996:81, note 100), he may have realized that local patriotic interests were far better served within the context of a consensual bloc. With the local inter-party bloc, the so-called Inheemsche Fractie (Native Faction), which he had led during 1927-1928 in Batavia's Gemeenteraad, the daring step to join a nation-wide federation seemed only too logical. In order to deepen his own nationalist perceptions, Thamrin had also frequented meetings and rallies where the young PNI chairman figured as the keynote speaker, sometimes taking my grandfather and father along.[39] At these meetings, like many of his countrymen, Thamrin had become increasingly impressed by Soekarno's vision, with its main thrust toward solid syncretist bloc-formation. From now on, Thamrin would speak in the Volksraad of the Ko and Non-Ko ingredients of Indonesian nationalism in anticipation of governmental and his own understanding that both steadily represented evolutionary nationalism as conceived by Governor-General De Graeff and Inlandsche Zaken. The new governor-general, in his inaugural oration during a special Volksraad session on 7 September 1926, stated that he would distinguish between anarchic anti-government revolutionary nationalism, which he would fight 'with all legal means' open to him, and evolutionary nationalism, which he 'as a right-minded Dutchman could only have respect for' – a ploy Hatta dismissed as ethical clap-trap and a return to the old divide-and-rule policy.[40] De Graeff's early 1927 clamouring for a Volksraad 'indigenous member majority' (*Inlandsche meerderheid*), reversing the earlier adopted Feber amendments ensuring a European member majority, was also a step toward meeting cooperationist nationalism at least half-way. After the proposal carried by thirty-four to eighteen votes, De Graeff listed the no voters in a 30 December 1927 letter to his predecessor Van Limburg Stirum as follows: 'the Kali Besar group [the big business district in Betawi's *benedenstad* (downtown)], the fascist Meijer Ranneft, PEB, excluding s'Jacob, the Indos of the IEV and in the Catholic Party, all voted against it since they all feel so threatened by it [the indigenous majority]'.[41] In yet another letter to Van Limburg Stirum, De Graeff stated that he was 'practically all alone with my few supporters, not being able to withstand any longer the rowdy yells coming from

[39] At these meetings Thamrin was often accompanied by his ISDP friends and the acting adviser of Inlandsche Zaken (Native Affairs) Emile Gobée, a *neo-ethicus* and a staunch proponent of De Graeff's evolutionary nationalism concept, a man hailed by Du Perron (1946:178) as 'one of the noblest figures ever known in our colonial history of recent years'.
[40] *Handelingen Volksraad* 1926:6. For Hatta's remarks: Hatta 1972:393.
[41] *Handelingen Volksraad* 1927-1928:2483-90; De Graeff's comments are in Van der Wal 1965:46. De Graeff's labelling of Dr J.W. Meijer Ranneft, chairman of the Volksraad during 1929-1933, as a fascist was not a slip of the pen. As late as 1938 the latter sat in the honoured guests section of the Nazi Parteitag in Nuremberg: see Hering 1996:186, 259.

the entire European public and from most of the European press [...]. [T]he European [community of the Indies] has now clearly taken sides and feels that thoughtful natives do not exist, since they merely are all inferior beings who cannot be trusted and need thus to be kept in check at all costs.'[42] It remained to be seen whether the Volksraad or the European community at large would follow De Graeff's reformism or would instead heed the mainly negativist opinions so whipped up by *sana* circles ever since the start of De Graeff's tenure. And as Volksraad ISDP member Stokvis was to put it so succinctly after the battle over the indigenous majority had been won:

> The once tranquil meadow of ethical colonialism has become a battlefield, with the contrast of race and interests raised implacably in a very short time. The European community, never in love with ethical colonialism, as well as the Indonesian world, will from now on rely solely on their own strength, no matter how uneven the chances or the possibilities still are.[43]

Nonetheless, De Graeff kept his nerve. As late as 20 August 1928, in a letter to hard-liner P.J. van Gulik, Governor of Central Java, he maintained that there were grounds for believing that Soekarno's PNI would eventually swerve in an evolutionary direction, since the PNI would come to realize that no colonial government would allow revolutionary strivings to develop in the Indies.[44] De Graeff admitted that it remained a speculation, but went on to state that:

> Given the widespread nationalist sentiments, given also the fact that there are many natives who on the one hand think that Soekarno and his associates have gone too far and are striving after ideals as yet unattainable, but on the other hand do tacitly sympathize with the ideals which Soekarno brings out into the open (no matter whether they see it as something wrong) – given all that, we remain convinced that an internment of Soekarno *cum suis* at this time will only result in all nationalist elements, including the more sober and loyal segments, coming together in one front.[45]

As to the brown front, Thamrin, who had consistently championed the

---

[42]   Letter of 26 October 1927, in Van der Wal 1965:29-30. As his supporters, De Graeff mentioned K.F. Creutzberg, E. Gobée, H.G.P. Duyfjes (Attorney-General), Dr H. Kraemer and BB officials J. Tideman, A.J.L. Couvreur and W.Ch. Hardeman. *Bintang Timoer* of 12 June 1928 saw De Graeff as 'not influenced by the interests of capital but more attentive to common interests and the maintenance of peace' and referred to the appointments of Kiewiet de Jonge as government spokesman in the Volksraad, Resident Hardeman as Governor of East Java, Resident Tideman as Governor of Palembang, as 'civil servants not at all liked by European papers such as the *Nieuws van den Dag* and the *Java Bode* since they were too ethical'.
[43]   Stokvis 1931b:825 and calling it 'De Graeff's difficult but still beautiful first year' (p. 830).
[44]   Mr. 823/1928 and Hering 1985:118.
[45]   Hering 1985:118-9. De Graeff, too, must have welcomed the opinions of his new Attorney-

Volksraad indigenous member majority issue, began increasingly to see himself in symbiosis with Soekarno, by far the most radical of the Non-Ko group,
as an indispensable *trait d'union* not only between Non-Ko and Ko factions of
the nationalist *pergerakan* but also between the federated Indonesian movement and the government spokesmen in the Volksraad. That lofty endeavour of generating mutual respect and understanding between all these elements, as we will learn later, failed to be realized due to circumstances much
beyond Thamrin's and Soekarno's control. As for now, with both the PNI
and the PPPKI forming the backbone of the brown front, and with Thamrin
increasingly becoming a spokesman of that front in the Volksraad chambers
at Betawi's Pedjambon (also named Hertogspark, after a former KNIL army
commander, the Duke of Saxony Weimar-Eisenach), the *pergerakan* seemed to
enter a more solid future. In the first issue of Soekarno's and Soetomo's new
journal *Soeloeh Indonesia Moeda* in December 1927, Soekarno's speech held at
the PSI 14th Congress was printed in Dutch and especially directed toward
sana hard-liner H.C. Zentgraaff, who had called earlier for a 'white front' to
be established. Although this appeal had not been heeded, it had still led to
a growing *sana* versus *sini* controversy in the Indies press on both sides of
the divide.

*Concern about the brown front and the steady growth of the Partai Nasional
Indonesia*

As to the *sana* press and their racist stirrings (*gestook*) that Soekarno had referred
to at the PSI Pekalongan congress, these became even more sensational in the
wake of Soekarno's formation of a solid brown front, which he outlined in
the first issue of his and Soetoemo's new periodical *Soeloeh Indonesia Moeda* in
December 1927. The outline was entitled 'Naar het Bruine Front!' (Toward the
brown front!), and Soekarno deliberately published it entirely in Dutch (also
in Soekarno 1959:37-40). After its appearance a large segment of the *sini* press
became increasingly aware of the *sana* press stirrings and provocations being
aired. Editor Karel Wijbrands, nicknamed KaWe, the '*kijaji* of Kali Besar', was
reported as being a staunch '*inlanderhater*' (hater of the natives). He and his
successor Van Dijk (of *Het Nieuws van den Dag*), J.H. Ritman (of the *Bataviaasch
Nieuwsblad*) and H.C. Zentgraaff (of the *Soerabajaasch Handelsblad* and soon
co-founder of the ultra-conservative and reactionary Vaderlandsche Club, or

General Mr J.K. Onnen, who in a letter of 18 June 1928 expressed his conviction that the PNI
aimed at 'a liberation by means of a revolution' but that the 'PNI action was no danger to the
state as yet', also stating 'not to declare that being a civil servant is inconsistent with the membership of that party', see Mr. 649/1928.

Fatherland Party) were seen by many of the *sini* press editors as the main agitators in the *sana* camp. *Fadjar Asia* of 30 March 1929 referred to the *pena lancang* of KaWe, the 'wild sensationalism' of Karel Wijbrands; and *Sedijo Tomo* on 20 April 1929 asserted that 'the mounting anti-Dutch feelings were in fact due to the provocative actions of Wijbrands, Zimmerman and Zentgraaff and associates'. *Bintang Timoer* of 27 May 1929 spoke of 'the kings of the agitators, Ritman and Zentgraaff', labelling the actions as 'Moscow's newest offensive' (in *Soerabajaasch Handelsblad* of 22 June 1929), and 'Z' linking 'the PNI and the PPPKI with the communist Liga' as yet another crude and poorly informed example of *sana* stirrings. *Keng Po*'s S. (Saeroen) in its 1 July 1929 issue accused *Het Nieuws van den Dag* of uttering dangerous lies by stating that the founding of the PNI was 'merely a camouflage for the erstwhile so notorious PKI'. *Keng Po* also ridiculed that paper's 'reliable sources' for stating that 'the PNI was plotting a revolution'. *Darmokondo* of 22 February 1929 compared the untruthful reporting and slanted reports of the *sana* press to poison, and in its 21 February 1929 issue carried a long article about the *modus operandi* of the *Java Bode*, where dubious reporting was common in order to provoke the PID and other colonial authorities to take sterner measures against the PNI. *Perniagaan* of 22 February 1929 declared that the *kijaji* of Kali Besar would never miss an opportunity of stating that 'natives formed a notoriously dangerous element in our society of the Indies'. *Bintang Timoer* of 27 December 1928 lamented the fact that 'there is no truly neutral European daily any longer, as a paper such as *De Locomotief* [then edited by the ethically inspired Stokvis] used to be'.[46] The latter daily's main editor, a strong supporter of the associationist principle, had been sacked by the financial backers of *De Locomotief* the year before (Van der Wal 1965:29).

These *sana* stirrings were no doubt inspired by the views of such authorities as Professor Melchior Treub, chairman of the Dutch business association, and Hendrikus Colijn, an oil magnate and the club's spokesman, who from the start of its existence had fulminated against the workings of the Volksraad. Almost at the same time, Treub's treatise, carrying the loaded title *Het gist in Indië* (The Indies in ferment), appeared along with Colijn's book, *Koloniale vraagstukken van heden en morgen* (Colonial problems of today and tomorrow). Treub argued that every activity advocating Indonesian independence needed to be crushed forcibly and immediately, while Colijn charged that the Volksraad was rotten to the core, a hotbed of unbridled critics and misled agitators in urgent need of being replaced as soon as possible by 'island councils' representing the several main islands of the archipelago (Colijn 1928:49, 59, 71). These regions would then gradually be steered toward positions of responsibility with the final aim of creating

46   For these press releases see my clippings archive.

locally restricted autonomies. This was clearly a divide-and-rule proposition to keep the Indies forever and firmly under Dutch control. Soekarno seemed to be well aware of this as well, and he dismissed these reactionary proposals as rubbish in a *Soeloeh Indonesia Moeda* article entitled 'Djerit-kegemparan' (A cry of consternation). Soekarno greeted with 'a smile the threat uttered by Treub that all activities intended to bring about Indonesia's independence must be suppressed if necessary by brute force'.[47] And Soekarno continued: 'We, the Indonesian nationalists, regard this cry of consternation by Professor Treub as a sign, as a symptom, since it indicates that our opponents truly do feel the ground shaking beneath their feet'.[48] Earlier in his article Soekarno had asserted that 'the colonial problem is essentially not an issue of rights but rather an issue of power',[49] an issue he linked at the end of his paper with the key for nationalist victory:

> Viewed from the angle of self-defence and self-preservation, the rulers' side has the right to obstruct, oppose and pursue our movement, but, seen from the angle of self-preservation, we equally have the right to take action, the right to seek power to release ourselves from present conditions, the right to seek liberty. Their right in this matter is opposed to ours; their right of reaction is diametrically opposed to our right of action [...] and this matter of right confronting right at once becomes an issue of one power confronting another power, of *macht* opposing *macht* [...]. However, it is indeed difficult for the colonizing people to take the correct attitude with regard to our movement. Our movement advances when it is not suppressed; but our movement also advances when it is suppressed. And that indeed remains the colonizers' dilemma.[50]

Earlier, in his Brown Front article aimed at *sana*, Soekarno had stated 'the sooner and the more sharply the antithesis is posed, the more clear-cut the struggle will be'[51] As Dahm correctly viewed it: 'Treub and Colijn, to the extent that they helped to strengthen the antithesis, were, for him [Soekarno], more partners than opponents' (Dahm 1969:94). As for the *sana* press editors, the majority of them would persist in assessing the Colijn and Treub treatises as quite proper and wise and as a model for the Indies colony to be emulated as soon as possible.

Van der Plas and Gobée were concerned about these frequent *sana* press

---

[47]   'Semua aksi, jang bermaksud mendatangkan kemerdekaan Indonesia harus ditindas, kalau perlu dengan kekerasan. Kita bersenjum.'
[48]   'Kita, kaum nasionalis Indonesia memandang djerit-kegemparannja Professor Treub itu sebagai suatu tanda, sebagai suatu gedjala. Ia menandakan, bahwa memang benar-benar lawan kita ini merasa tanah bergojang dibawah kakinja.'
[49]   'Soal djadjahan itu pada hakekatnja bukanlah soal hak; ia soal kekuasaan; ia soal macht'.
[50]   *Soeloeh Indonesia Moeda* no. 3/4, 1928, also reprinted in Soekarno 1959:51-5.
[51]   'Hoe zuiverder en eerder de antithese is gesteld hoe karaktervoller de strijd wezen zal' (Soekarno 1959:38).

provocations and reported their findings to De Graeff.[52] De Graeff himself and his new representative in the Volksraad Mr Ir H.J. Kiewiet de Jonge, a *neo-ethicus* of the Van Limburg Stirum variety, were wary of it as well, something which was widely reported in several *sini* press releases. Commenting on De Graeff's mid-year opening address to the Volksraad, *Keng Po* of 17 June 1929 noted that De Graeff had 'not yielded an inch to the ravings of the *sana* press' and was quite in tune with 'the spirit of the times'; *Sin Po* of 15 June 1929 expressed similar sentiments. *Warna Warta* of 16 June 1929 recognized that De Graeff's administration had been accused of widening the rift between *sini* and *sana*, but approved of De Graeff's 'not yielding a millimetre in spite of the blatant criticism still emanating from the *sana* press'. *Bintang Timoer* of 15 June 1929 was also impressed by De Graeff's address, stating that it was 'a courageous exposé [...] a real piece of statesmanship' and above all proving that the governor-general had 'remained a radical to the core'. *Pertja Selatan* of 27 June 1929 asked what the critics of the *sana* press really wanted to achieve: 'Go back to Fock? To the iron fist? We have all seen the results of that repressive regime.'[53] De Graeff, right up to the end of his term in office, was stung seeing so much of that *sana* die-hard counsel being elevated to rare samples of wise and responsible governance by a number of *sana* press editorials, editorials that were sensation-seeking if not blatantly racist. He was irritated by the fact that most of his own efforts of moderation were often dismissed in the editorials as being too weak, and lacking in moral strength and patriotic fibre. To his predecessor, Van Limburg Stirum, like him ethically inspired to the bone, he described the *sana* community of the Indies as follows:

> It is a terrible shame that just at this moment, with the indigenous nationalists calming down, the Dutch of this country have seen fit to form the Vaderlandsche Club, a Dutch nationalist movement to confront the indigenous nationalists. Essentially, the VC is as extreme as the PNI. However, I do consider the VC, with its exclusively negative programme, a stillborn child, only able to spread some influence during the forthcoming [Volksraad] elections; but for now the harm has been done and relations have been damaged. It seems that a curse rests on the European community in this country, which has always been characterized by such short-sightedness and sheer stupidity. It is far too often led by silly sentiments which manifest themselves in a very unfortunate way at the most inopportune moments. I have long since given up fighting this force so clearly marked by stupidity.[54]

On the other hand, De Graeff was quite warmed by Thamrin's and Stokvis'

---

[52]   Mr. 561/1929.
[53]   My clippings archive.
[54]   20 August 1930 letter to Van Limburg Stirum, Archief De Graeff, ARA.

frequent support of his moderating addresses to the Volksraad and the general drift of most of his domestic policies, as well as by the positive *sini* press editorials we sampled above.

The PNI and PPPKI first national congresses

As for the PNI and the PPPKI, they steadily established a more urban-centred cohesive organization to appeal to the urban masses they hoped to win for their cause. The PNI, now renamed Partai Nasional Indonesia, declared at its first congress held in Soerabaja from 27 to 30 May 1928, in its new programme, its intention to further promote economic and social progress of the indigenous people. It was also resolved to more strongly support monogamous practices and to abolish the practice of child marriage.[55] During the 1 July 1928 PNI meeting in Pekalongan, Soekarno would refer to the issue of monogamy versus polygamy, stating that 'the PNI does not regard polygamy as illegal but it is eager to promote monogamy. Just ask our sisters whether they would like to be a *getjandoengd'* (cut off by a *candung*, a sword, in this case cut off from a marriage). Soekarno then pictured how it felt for 'these sisters to be divorced by a man who would then marry again until he divorced the new wife, repeating this pattern time and time again'. So Soekarno asked himself whether 'it was not better to keep several lawful wives at the same time instead of disposing of them one after the other'.[56]

However, at the PNI congress the more serious social problem of loosely maintained marriages was not touched on at all, perhaps an attempt to placate the Muslim PSI, one of the new pillars of the PPPKI united by Soekarno. The PNI's statement of principles (Keterangan Azas PNI) and its working programme had been adopted during three closed PNI leaders' meetings held in Bandoeng from 24 to 26 March 1928 for consideration at the first congress.[57] In an ensuing PNI Soerabaja branch meeting held at Ketabang Kemoeningweg 9 on 22 April 1928, the chairman, Mr Gatot Taroenamihardjo, reported on the proceedings of the Bandoeng leadership conference, discussing as well his difference of opinion with both the PNI's main executive in Bandoeng and the Djokja branch (Mr Soejoedi) regarding the path to be pursued by the PNI to

---

[55]   See *Fadjar Asia*, 1 June 1928 with 'Penonton' (Spectator) accusing Soetomo of assessing the PNI's raising of that issue of child marriages as merely a propaganda stunt.

[56]   See Mr. 772/1928, where a translation of Soekarno's address is printed.

[57]   See *Soeloeh Ra'jat Indonesia*, 4 and 11 April 1928 and *Persatoean Indonesia*, no. 1, 1928. The PNI's working programme is also listed in 'Bijlage' of the March 1928 'Politiek-Politioneel Overzicht', dated 22 April 1928, Mr. 442/1928.

realize revolution.[58] Gatot Taroenamihardjo, though seen by his former fellow-students and close friends Iwa Koesoema Soemantri and Achmad Soebardjo, as well as by some members of his own family, as a genuine radical, nonetheless held that the PNI at this stage should adhere to a peaceful and mainly educational approach and thus spurn the more aggressive methods advocated by Bandoeng and Djokja.[59] In Soerabaja that day, Gatot Taroenamihardjo's views were endorsed; he was also confirmed as branch chairman and may well have been the real architect of the more moderate direction henceforth associated with Soerabaja. Resident Hardeman welcomed this, stating that Gatot Taroenamihardjo 'did not support a revolution at any price since a revolution primarily needed to be born out of the proper circumstances'.[60] As we will see below, Gatot Taroenamihardjo's vice-chairman Ir Anwari, too, would adopt a less defiant and less noisy approach.

At the congress the PNI's working programme and statement of principles were adopted. It was also resolved to issue a new PNI periodical titled *Persatoean Indonesia*, to be edited by Soekarno and Soenarjo and to be printed by the Keng Po printing house. Soekarno himself, during that first congress, stressed that 'any colonization was an injustice to the autochthonous population – even immoral – though the colonizers interpret it in a different way. They deny the profit-seeking economic objectives they are solely after, while colonization is explained as a mission to raise the country's level of civilization by means of developing popular education and prosperity.' Soekarno then went on to say: 'the Dutch shifted from their original economic objectives to a strategy of gradually gaining full political power in Indonesia. So the country's products were bought up by the Dutch government at low prices and then transported to Holland only to be brought back here and sold at a high profit.' All this Soekarno called 'modern imperialism, which squeezes (*mengisap*) the country, strangles its industries and ruins its economy' and 'since Great Britain, the United States and others are investing capital here,

<hr />

[58]   *Pewarta Soerabaja*, 23 April 1928 lists Gatot as chairman, Anwari as vice-chairman, Mohammad Joesoef as adviser and Santoso as secretary of the Soerabaja PNI branch, and reports that the first PNI congress will be held in Soerabaja by next May.
[59]   Letter of Gatot Taroenamihardjo's sister Titi, of 18 April 1926, Bijlage B, Verbaal 9 August 1927 G 13. The Soerabaja branch meeting was infiltrated by two police spies, S 2 and S 5, both also members of the branch. See their report no. 61/S, Mr. 558/1928. Gatot Taroenamihardjo is sometimes confused with Gatot Mangkoepradja (see Hering 1991d). The former faded out of the PNI at the end of 1929, to appear again briefly as a witness in the PNI trial. He was the first *jaksa agung* (attorney-general) in Indonesia's first cabinet (1945) and served in that capacity again in the first *kabinet kerja* (working cabinet) of 1959, only to be pushed out by General A.H. Nasution because Gatot Taroenamihardjo had commenced investigations of army staff officers involved in the so-called Tanjung Priok barter. As to the PNI's working programme, see *Sin Jit Po*, 27 April 1928, and on the *Keterangan Azas* PNI, *Persatoean Indonesia* no. 1(15 July 1928):2.
[60]   Hardeman to De Graeff, 22 May 1928, pp. 2-3, in Mr. 558/1928.

the PNI feels that international imperialism needs to be opposed firmly as well. The Asian people therefore need to collectively combat these imperialists who are constantly expanding their influence in Asia.'[61] The reporter of the Soerabajan weekly *Pemberita Kemadjoean* was so enthralled by Soekarno's speech that he felt 'already freed, not sensing his poverty, in spite of having not one cent in his pocket'.[62] *Pewarta Soerabaja* was enthused about the fact that 'PNI leaders devoted fifty percent of their time to party matters, some like Soekarno even one hundred percent'.[63]

In spite of all the rather strong talk used by Soekarno during the congress, Gobée in his report to De Graeff reported that 'the theme that formed the warp and weft of Soekarno's speeches was above all the development of a genuine national consciousness, a national sentiment he feels is very much alive among the entire population', a sentiment, Gobée argued, 'that needed only to be converted into what Soekarno termed the national will'. Soekarno 'had been so sure about the people being serious about their aspirations to be free that no power on earth would be able to prevent the national will leading to national deeds'. And this, through 'a process of sacrifice, of subordinating self-interest to the common interest, of preferring a life of deprivation to the convenience of a comfortable life in government service, will ultimately lead to victory over all the obstacles on the road to freedom'. Gobée closed his arguments by saying, 'even if one assumes that the idealism of people like Soekarno is so strong that they consider it feasible to achieve independence through a peaceful process, which they see at the same time cannot be realized through phases of gradual economic construction and political emancipation, there still remains a wide difference between ideals and reality, especially in this country'. Gobée was quite aware of the fact that the PNI at this stage was still rather urban-centred, and he feared that the plan announced by the PNI leadership of campaigning in the countryside would certainly pose problems in the near future. Less-educated rural leaders would then come to the fore, propagating the call for freedom and influencing their audiences in their own manner, thus making it far more problematic for the government to handle, as had been the case so far with the present Western-trained PNI leadership. As to the present size of the PNI organizationally: nine urban PNI branches were established in Batavia (Jacatra) with 643 members, Bandoeng with 400, Djokja (Mataram) with 110, and Soerabaja

---

[61] Gobée to De Graeff, 19 July 1928 and minutes of the first PNI congress, Mr. 749/1928; see also Hering 1979:7-16 and Poeze 1982:329-33. In *Soeara Publiek,* 2 June 1928 the Pan-Asiatic ideals of Soekarno were discussed.

[62] *Pemberita Kemadjoean*, no. 22 of 2 June 1928. This Soerabajan weekly was renamed *Indonesia Bersatoe* on 16 June 1928 with Mr Gatot Taroenamihardjo urging in that latter issue the formation of a PNI labourers union as soon as possible.

[63] *Pewarta Soerabaja*, 29 May 1928.

with 482 members, plus Pekalongan and Cheribon each with 30 members, all located on Java.[64] Further, there were three branches in Makassar, Palembang and Padang (in Celebes and Sumatra) with no member totals being given. In spite of these gains, the PNI leadership was well aware of the serious short-age of capable second-echelon leaders. To relieve the shortage, PNI branches were urged to develop politically conscious leaders through special courses or debating club meetings.[65] All in all, the first PNI congress had been a suc-cess, with close to two thousand people attending it each day. In his closing words, Soekarno cited Gandhi: 'People who dare to live also dare to die', and said that 'sacrifices need to be made, but let us not be afraid, for we all know that we possess *aji-aji tondo biworo* (Javanese for the charm of one dead three born, three dead five born).[66] Soekarno was implying by this that the Brown Front of his making would always far outrun the numbers *sana* was capable of assembling.

As to the PPPKI, its Madjelis Pertimbangan was now located in Soera-baja, with Soetomo as chairman and Ir Anwari (vice-chairman of the PNI Soerabaja branch) serving as secretary. The PPPKI also held its first congress in Soerabaja from 30 August to 2 September 1928. The congress was well organized and led by Western-trained leaders who kept a rather strict sched-ule, with the public meetings starting and finishing right on time. These meetings, like the PNI congress, were attended by close to fifteen hundred people. Expectations were high about the 'more opportunistic and subtle Dr Soetomo being the one leader capable of uniting more firmly the hetero-geneous parts of the federation' founded by Soekarno.[67] As to its proceed-ings, the congress devoted an entire day to national education, with Ki Adjar Dewantoro as main adviser, while another day was devoted to discussion of economic problems, with Dr Samsi Sastrowidagdo as the moderator. During the closed meetings, the founding of a national bank was proposed and a committee appointed to look into it. Also, a committee to study the national education plans of Ki Adjar Dewantoro was set up, with Mr Singgih, Soeki-man Wirjosandjojo and Mr Soejoedi as members, and another committee to coordinate and plan future PPPKI activities. Appointed to the latter com-

---

[64]   'Bestuursconferentie 1929; Overzicht van den inwendigen politieken toestand Maart 1928-December 1928', p. 8, Mr. 260/1929.
[65]   See note 102.
[66]   'Bestuursconferentie 1929; Overzicht van den inwendigen politieken toestand Maart 1928-December 1928', pp. 7-8, 16, Mr. 260/1929.
[67]   'Bestuursconferentie 1929; Overzicht van den inwendigen politieken toestand Maart 1928-December 1928', p. 12, Mr. 260/1929. In that context *Pemberita Boedi Oetomo Tjabang Betawi*, no. 6, 1928 stated that the PNI was strictly NonKo while Soetomo's Soerabaja Studieclub adopted a give-and-take attitude, working in councils solely to promote indigenous interests. For wel-coming this first PPPKI congress see Soekarno's 'Menjamboet Congres PPPKI', *Soeloeh Indonesia Moeda* September 1928:207-10.

mittee were Soekarno, his former father-in-law Tjokroaminoto, Oto Soebrata (of Pasoendan) and Mohammad Thamrin (of Kaoem Betawi), the latter two being firm Ko adherents.[68]

On the final day, a cultural (*pertunjukan seni*) evening show was held in the Stadstuin theatre, opposite Soekarno's former alma mater, the Regent-straat HBS (which at that time served as Soerabaja's post office), organized by Abdoel Gani (of Pemoeda Indonesia), Tjindarboemi (of *De Indische Courant*), Koentjoro Poerbopranoto (of Jong Java), Setyono (of Jong Islamieten Bond) and Askaboel (of the Indonesische Studieclub) (*PPPKI Congres* 1928:1). A variety of Sundanese, Javanese, Minahasan, Timorese, and Ambonese *menari* (dance), *cakakele* (war dance), *wayang* (puppet show), *joged* (dance) and *pencak* (martial art) performances were held. It all ended with a farewell song:

> Unity starts as of now; at sea and at land in this overseas country; to reach what is still rare; so that freedom will not fail; Indonesia will be free.
>
> In closing we'd like to say; a united Indonesia to be realized; with matters still not right to be solved; in order that our ideals will be reached and Indonesia will be free.[69]

As to the reactions of the *sini* press to the PPPKI's first congress, *Darmokondo* of 6 September 1928 hailed it as a vivid expression of the Groot-Indonesië (Great Indonesia) concept, while *Bintang Timoer*'s editor-in-chief Parada Harahap, in an article entitled 'De kloof tussen sana en sini' (The rift between *sana* and *sini*), recalling the stirring words of Soekarno's main address, wrote that it was

> with joy that the PNI views the existence of the PPPKI, since a line, a clear distinction, is drawn by it, to separate *sana* from *sini*, to divide friend from foe. The notion of cooperationist association is indeed a thing of the past. The division having now been drawn, the PNI accepts it wholeheartedly, because from it power and self-confidence will truly take root.[70]

---

[68]   'Bestuursconferentie 1929; Overzicht van den inwendigen politieken toestand Maart 1928-December 1928', p. 12, Mr. 260/1929; Poeze 1982:384-5 and *Soeloeh Rajat Indonesia*, 22 August 1928.

[69]   Bersatoe moelai dari sekarang; Dilaoet didarat ditanah seberang; Boeat rapat barang jang djarang; Soepaja kemerdikaan djangan terkarang; Indonesia merdika.
Boeat penoetoep kami oetjoepkan; Indonesia sepakat diharapkan; Barang bernoda segera hapoeskan; Soepaja kesempoernaan kita didapatkan; Indonesia merdika. (*PPPKI Congres* 1928: 10.)

[70]   *Bintang Timoer*, 6 and 7 September 1928.

Soekarno's growing radicalism leads to a variety of responses

As to the PNI, during a Grissee propaganda meeting on 30 August 1928, Soekarno was reported by Inlandsche Zaken to have spoken in a much sharper tone than had been the case before. This may have been caused by several incidents occurring before the meeting in Grissee, such as the brief detention of Mr Ali Sastroamidjojo by police, as well as the confiscation of issues of *Persatoean Indonesia* and the harassment of PNI members in Grissee itself just prior to the meeting. Van der Plas, urged earlier by Soetomo to investigate these matters, did censure the police tactics as quite silly in his report to De Graeff. The change of location to Grissee, once the cradle of Soenan Giri and other *wali songo* (Muslim saints), Van der Plas considered a smart move, but the actions by the local police he regarded as rather unwise. He argued that 'tolerating the *patih*, chief of the local police, clapping his hands in approbation during Ir Soekarno's fierce and hostile speech and then detaining some of the local organizers on grounds of not having announced that the meeting was an open one showed an amazing lack of consistency'.[71]

Soekarno himself, facing a crowd of a thousand people, was quick to point out that only an independent Indonesia would guarantee an economic and educational system suited to the real needs of the Indonesian people. Then, he continued,

> we will not be bothered any longer by such regulations as no. 161 bis or 152 bis and ter. Present conditions do not permit us to speak our minds a bit loudly, for if we do, immediately Digoel is our lot![72] (thunderous applause.) It does not matter whether you are a member of the PKI, a nationalist or a Muslim, as soon as you display some deep commitment to your country, you will be Digoel-ed. We have seen that with Dr Tjipto, with Patty [with Soekarno ignoring the fact that at the time the former was exiled to Banda and the latter to Benkoelen and then to Palembang]. We must all think about this over and over again. Not until Dutch rule has disappeared can we improve our economic situation. Do I have to give you evidence of the truth of this statement? Take for instance rubber cultivation. As soon as indigenous people set up a rubber plantation, the government imposes

---

[71]   Van der Plas to De Graeff, 31 August 1928, Mr. 868/1928; Hering 1991b:17-23.

[72]   Boven Digoel was a hastily prepared internment camp in the malaria-infested southeast corner of western New Guinea in the wake of the PKI disturbances. Article 153 bis and ter and 161 bis were conceived in the wake of early 1920s labour unrest. The first reads as follows: 'whoever by word or picture wilfully states an opinion whether directly or indirectly which advocates anything disruptive of the public order or which impedes or violates Netherlands or Netherlands Indies authority or which incites thereto shall be sentenced to an imprisonment term not to exceed six years', and the second reads as follows: 'whoever causes or aids work stoppages or in defiance of the public order obstructs work with the intention of causing public disturbance or economic disruption shall be sentenced to an imprisonment term not to exceed five years'. Bis is a Dutch term for first supplement and ter for second edition; see Hering 1991a:37.

export duties exclusively on rubber produced on indigenous land allotments [Dutch: *bevolkingsrubber*]. Another example: the cases of long-lease contracts on land [*erfpachtsuitgiften*] in Ranau and Tasikmalaja, by which our land is cut up and divided as if it were a loaf of cake (loud applause). Therefore, we have to be free first of all. Only when the Dutch government and Dutch rule have vanished from this country will we be able to make progress. Holland will never voluntarily grant national independence to Indonesia. Think of Professor Melchior Treub: *Indonesia merdika, negri Blanda bankroet!* [Indonesia free, Holland bankrupt]. [...] The PNI does not care to be called a non-cooperator. The real non-cooperator is the [Dutch] government. Did the government ever consult us when it was drawing up articles 161 bis and 153 bis and ter? [...] [W]e do not mind being dubbed by whatever name. If people want to indicate our action by some outlandish name, then they better use the word self-essentials, while we have plenty to do in our propaganda work in the villages and the mountain areas. We will go to the kampungs and to the hilly areas to clearly disseminate our ideas and then to try and amalgamate the thoughts of all our brothers and sisters. You, too, go to the countryside and into the mountains and bring the people the message that we, Javanese, Madurese, Sundanese, and all of us are one people – Indonesians. Unless we tie together our *lidi* [palm leaf ribs] into one *sapoe* [broom], we shall always be the losers. [...] Everybody is welcome with us, in particular women, for they are the nurturers of future generations. [...] [Y]ou must keep in mind that your obligation is to work for your progeny. What would you answer if your children and grandchildren, in distress because of your lack of forethought, were to ask you, 'Father why are we living in such dismal conditions?' (Thunderous applause, in which the *patih* joins.)

Soekarno was also pleased to see quite a few Chinese brothers among the audience. Addressing them, he stated that in Indonesia 'imperialism is international in character, with England, the United States of America and even Japan investing capital. Therefore, China has the same enemies as we have, and so has Egypt, so has India. Pan-Asianism is therefore what we see as an ideal.'[73] In an article appearing in July 1928 in *Soeloeh Indonesia Moeda* and titled 'Indonesianisme dan Pan-Asiatisme', Soekarno had argued that:

> In opposing British imperialism and others of the kind, the Egyptian people, the Indian people, the Chinese people, the Indonesian people face a single enemy. [...] therefore we should all forge one Asian community and oppose the foreign strongholds of imperialism. [...] [T]hat is the reason why we must adhere to the principle of Pan-Asianism. [...] [T]he times demand that we reach out our hands to the banks of the Nile, or to the plains of the land of the Dragon or to the country of Mahatma Gandhi. Soon the times will call upon us to bear witness to a fierce struggle to be waged in the Pacific Ocean between the imperialist giants America, Japan and Britain. [...] Will our country, situated right on the outer fringes of the

---

[73]   Hering 1991b:20. In his 1 July 1928 address in Pekalongan, Soekarno invited Mr Tan Ban Tiam to come to Bandoeng to see the portrait of Dr Sun Yat-sen hanging there on one of the walls of his house, see Mr. 772/1928 and Hering 1985:94.

Pacific, not be dragged into the clash of these giants? Let us be prepared if our enemies soon fight each other in a life-and-death struggle close to our homeland, perhaps even within the borders of our own country [...] so by closing ranks with other Asian nations we may prepare ourselves and determine our attitude to this coming commotion. (Soekarno 1959:69-71.)

Prophetic passages indeed, and a message Soekarno would often repeat.

While the PNI meetings in Grissee and the meeting on 15 July 1928 in Batavia had not generated any serious governmental repercussions – the meeting in Batavia was described by Gobée as being quite wary of the use of violent means[74] – the PNI propaganda meeting in Semarang on 14 October 1928 was abruptly aborted by police authorities. This move demonstrated that regional officials still commanded considerable liberty of action. While such officials could not instigate actions against parties like the PNI without De Graeff's approval, nor start criminal proceedings against individuals without the Indies attorney-general's consent, they were still able to endorse lesser measures such as harassment, refusal to allow public meetings, early closure of such meetings or exerting pressure on PNI members who happened to be civil servants. As to the PNI branch meeting in Jacatra on 15 July 1928, celebrating the PNI's first anniversary and attended by some fifteen hundred people, *Fadjar Asia* reported, through Hadji Agoes Salim, a man by no means favourably inclined toward Soekarno, that Soekarno's speech was often interrupted by applause and signs of approval. Agoes Salim also recorded that vivid interest of the public was clearly demonstrated by an incident when Soekarno lost his voice due to a recent bout of influenza. When Soekarno asked for a quarter-hour break before continuing his address, *Fadjar Asia* (16 July 1928) reported 'the audience during that interval did not stir from their seats at all, in spite of the fact that it was stiflingly hot in the meeting hall on account of the low zinc roof'.

As to Semarang, the police stopped Soekarno from completing his speech, since he had referred to *kemerdekaan* (independence) and *pemerasaan* (exploitation). The chairman of the PNI's Mataram (Djokja) branch, Mr Soejoedi, who chaired the Semarang proceedings with some two thousand attending, after stating that Soekarno had used these phrases over and over again at some fifty similar gatherings, then disbanded the meeting.[75] The *Fadjar Asia* reporter argued that the police had in fact 'committed a serious political mistake', while Soekarno had gained a 'moral victory by wiring the adviser of Inlandsche Zaken about the incident'.[76] The next day Soekarno

---

[74]   Gobée to De Graeff, 19 July 1928, p. 1, Mr. 749/1928; *Persatoean Indonesia*, no. 1, p. 1, article '4 July'.

[75]   Hering 1985:145-50; Mr. 1181/1928; *Algemeen Indisch Dagblad*, 17 October 1928.

[76]   *Fadjar Asia*, 17 October 1928, see further *Bintang Timoer*, 20 October 1928 calling upon the Hoofdparket (prosecutor's department of the Indies attorney-general) to censure the Semarang

attended a so-called branch-installation meeting in Solo, with a thousand people present. Twice during these proceedings Soekarno was warned by police authorities to moderate his words.[77] In the wake of these incidents the Regeerings Gemachtigde voor Algemeene Zaken (RGAZ, Government Representative for General Affairs) Ir Mr H.J. Kiewiet de Jonge said in the Volksraad that, while recognizing 'the PNI's independence aims', he felt obliged to advise PNI leaders 'to use more moderation, since if they did not they would be held responsible if matters got out of hand' (*Handelingen Volksraad* 1928-1929:1647-8). This was obviously a veiled threat aimed at Soekarno's recent behaviour in Central Java. However, De Graeff took some of the venom out of Kiewiet de Jonge's warning, not only by condemning the Semarang incident but by thus questioning the Central Java governor's die-hard police measures as well. And by December 1928 De Graeff drafted a letter to the *Residenten* ordering them to refrain from taking ill-considered measures against Soekarno's PNI.[78] This was most likely prompted by the incident in Solo, where Soekarno was forbidden from using such words as *merdeka* (free), *kemerdekaan* (independence) and *pemerasaan* (exploitation), terms the authorities on the spot considered not permissible.[79] De Graeff, in another missive to Van Gulik, also maintained that he still saw Soekarno's PNI as a fact which the Indies government needed to heed since it was essentially

> a movement which in itself was a natural phenomenon but also made possible and allowed to progress by our own colonial policies of the last ten years. [...] [T]herefore it should at the moment not be driven by governmental measures in a revolutionary direction, while there remained still a fair chance for the greater majority [of PNI nationalists] to finally opt for the evolutionary option.[80]

Soekarno's rebuke of Agoes Salim's 'Kebangsaan' and the notions behind it

Kiewiet de Jonge's warning, however, may well have been inspired by a close friend's assessment of Soekarno's recent behaviour. Hadji Agoes Salim,

---

police authorities for the actions it took, recommended also by *Bendee*, a Solonese Japanese/Malay weekly no. 40, of 3 October 1928, which asserts that Indonesian officials were made increasingly aware of the fact that higher authorities did not want them to join the PNI. *Pewarta Soerabaja*, 29 September 1928 reports the sacking of Raden Pandji Djatmiko as editor of the Semarang daily *Medan Doenia* as a sign thwarting the founding of a PNI branch in Semarang.

[77] *Fadjar Asia*, 17 October 1928 states: 'the words *kemerdikaan, merdika, pemerasaan* were not tolerated by the police'.

[78] Missive of De Graeff, 28 December 1928, Gobée Collection, KITLV.

[79] *Soeloeh Ra'jat Indonesia*, 24 October and 7 November 1928.

[80] First Government Secretary to Central Java Governor (P.J. van Gulik), 5 January 1929, Mr. 21/1929 in reply to Van Gulik's 4 December 1928 letter to Governor-General, Mr. 21/1929.

who like Mohammad Hoesni Thamrin and Soekarno often paid nocturnal
visits to the RGAZ's home at the Kramatlaan,[81] saw Soekarno 'turning the
Indonesian fatherland into an idol [*afgod*], with a nationalism not in the least
tempered by Muslim precepts and thus leading to an imperialistic nationalism quite similar to that propagated in the distant and recent past by such
figures as Louis XIV, Napoleon, Bismarck and Mussolini'.[82] These allegations
by Salim were immediately refuted by Soekarno in an article titled 'Kearah
Persatoean! Menjambut tulisan H.A. Salim' (Toward unity! A response to
an article written by H.A. Salim). Soekarno's rebuttal appeared in *Soeloeh
Indonesia Moeda* in September 1928:

> Hadji Agoes Salim forgot to state that the nationalism adhered to by Soekarno is
> a nationalism which is not aggressive, not on the offensive and not at all driven
> by the desire to hold an arbitrary sway over the world. Our nationalism remains
> inwardly directed and not outwardly. Hadji Agoes Salim also forgot to state
> that Asian nationalism, which inspired Mahatma Gandhi, C.R. Das, Aurobindo
> Ghose, Mustafa Kamil and Dr Sun Yat-sen and also inspires our own Indonesian
> nationalists, is part of a nationalism which differs totally from the Western brand
> of nationalism which, as Bipin Chandra Pal alleged, is truly a worldly national-
> ism. It is, moreover, an imperialistic nationalism which fights to the death among
> itself. [...] So we must refer to the nationalism of the Asian champions we cited
> before, since they view their nationalism as we do, like a religion, and by turning
> – as we do – our followers into worshippers of the country they love and there-
> fore truly idolize. Must we then term this latter nationalism that dwells happily
> in the souls of those heroes and leaders of mankind an enslavement to matter?
> Must we then term this Asian nationalism of these champions – a nationalism
> far more sublime than the imperialistic nationalism of the Western nations that
> still keep fighting among themselves – must we view that nationalism as based
> upon mere worldliness? However, if we must truly call it so, if this is so-called
> idol worship, if this is making oneself into a slave to matter, if this is called basing
> oneself on notions of worldliness – then we, Indonesian nationalists, are indeed
> only too proud to call ourselves idol worshippers or to call ourselves slaves of
> matter basing ourselves on issues of worldliness! We remain convinced that the
> nationalism of our Asian champions, in origin and nature, in no way differs from
> our own nationalism. Moreover, both remain a noble nationalism to the core. [...]
> This, then, is what we would like to add to Hadji Agoes Salim's article.[83]

Censuring Salim in this manner may also have to do with the fact that
Soekarno's erstwhile political mentor Tjipto, Soekarno himself, Anwari and
Soetomo were all more or less tainted by the theosophical brush. These prom-

[81]   Hering 1992:ix, xvii, note 14. See also *Bataviaasch Nieuwsblad*, 19 August 1930.
[82]   An article entitled 'Tanah Bangsa dan Tanah Air' (Nation and Fatherland*)*, *Fadjar Asia*, 26
July 1928.
[83]   *Fadjar Asia*, 18 August 1928 and *Soeloeh Indonesia Moeda* September 1928:223-8; also in
Soekarno 1959:104-6.

inent politicians took the view that all religions are inherently good and that everyone therefore should be left free to choose the religion most fitting to him or her. This notion, however, was totally unacceptable to revelation religions like Islam. And, as Van der Plas had it, 'these theosophically inclined leaders are, though admitting that circumstances for the moment favour cooperation with Islamic leaders, not kindly disposed toward Islam. They therefore were averse to a man like Agoes Salim.'[84] In his report on the Second Indonesian Youth Congress, Van der Plas also stressed the animosity between theosophist and Muslim delegates.[85] Around that time Raden Soeratmoko, a PNI treasurer and chairman of the Soerabajan theosophical association Mardi Kasoenjatan, and like Anwari employed by the Job and Spree architectural bureau, started a new PNI monthly called *Rasa*. In a preface Soeratmoko explained that *Rasa* 'would maintain a neutral stance and remain open to views of all religions and philosophical convictions', while also cherishing the belief that 'adherents of several religious and philosophical beliefs can be brought together in an atmosphere of mutual appreciation and respect'.[86] However, Van der Plas alleged that *Rasa*'s editorial staff remained 'dead set against Agoes Salim and other Muslim modernists, since they were in the habit of maintaining that cultivation of mystical practices and the lingering influence of Hinduist and Buddhist ideas caused the slackening of Islam on the whole, but in particular on the island of Java'.[87] Gobée, after having analysed the contents of the first issue of *Persatoean Indonesia*, informed De Graeff about Soekarno 'turning away from Islam' since the PNI chairman believed strongly in the power of the indigenous culture to absorb it.[88] A young woman teacher named Seti Rahajoe, in an article dealing with the feminist movement, accentuated a growing aversion in her circles to Islamic tenets as propagated by Hadji Agoes Salim.[89] Salim, while agreeing with Soekarno that PSI and PNI agreement on aims and tactics of the presently united *pergerakan* made it quite explicit, noted that there were some basic differences in principles between

---

[84]   See Van der Plas' 173-page analysis, p. 31, Mr. 457/1928. In the ten letters Tjipto wrote, nine to Soekarno and one to Iskaq, up to Soekarno's Landraad trial, Tjipto was often quite adamant about Salim's and Tjokro's deceptive behaviour toward the nationalists. See for a summary of these letters, *Algemeen Indisch Dagblad*, 4 and 7 September 1930 and one quoted in full, addressed to Soekarno, dated 5 March 1928: *Algemeen Indisch Dagblad*, 20 September 1930.

[85]   See Van der Plas 3 November 1928 report to De Graeff, p. 5, Mr. 1066/1928.

[86]   *Rasa* no. 1(June 1928):1. See also 'Bestuursconferentie 1929; Overzicht van den inwendigen politieken toestand Maart 1928-December 1928', p. 21, Mr. 260/1929.

[87]   Van der Plas report, p. 31, Mr. 457/1928.

[88]   Gobée to De Graeff, 19 July 1928, Mr. 751/1928. As early as late 1926, Soekarno had argued that 'true nationalists perceive their nationalist feeling as a divine inspiration [*wahyu*] and express it through acts of devotion [*bakti*]'; powerful ingredients of the Javano-Balinese culture, see Soekarno 1959:5.

[89]   *Persatoean Indonesia*, 15 July 1928.

the Muslim and the secular nationalists. PSI ideology was based on Islamic tenets, with the aim of bringing about the Society of God in the Indies: 'we indeed value unity since it is a command of God, but we are not merely a slave to unity but rather a slave to God'. Gobée had earlier reported to De Graeff that Salim, with his 'critical and analytical mind saw the purification of the indigenous movement as his main task, and because of that was dead set against the unity aims of the nationalists, even when he was still trying to cooperate with them'.[90] Salim, nonetheless, became increasingly critical of the PPPKI, deeming it far too susceptible to PNI ideology and direction. Therefore, he pointedly refrained from attending PPPKI meetings any longer. As we will discuss later, Tjokro was to join Salim's criticism during the year to come. All tentative signs now indicated that the nationalist/modernist Muslim rapprochement achieved by Soekarno a year ago had acquired several cracks, despite declarations denying it.

The path-breaking Second Indonesian Youth Congress in Weltevreden

Two months after Soekarno's response to Hadji Agoes Salim, the PNI chairman cabled a congratulatory message to the PPPI's Second Indonesian Youth Congress held in Weltevreden. This Congress met first at the Katholieke Jongelingen Bond (Catholic Youngsters Union) clubhouse at Waterlooplein and the Oost Java movie theatre at Koningsplein Noord on 27 October 1928, and then at the Indonesian Club building at Kramatweg 106 on the evening of 28 October 1928. The PNI was represented during the Youth Congress by Mr Soenarjo and Mr Sartono, while Soekarno's close Bandoeng friend Soegondo Djojopoespito, a PNI/PPPI prominent, chaired the congress proceedings (Ramadhan 1981:108-9; *45 Tahun Sumpah Pemuda* 1974:61-3).

Van der Plas reported that 'the political character of the second youth congress was apparent and quite in tune with the influence exerted by the PNI [...] through Mr Sartono and Mr Soenarjo'. Van der Plas noted 'the clashes between the theosophists and the Muslims', referring to the 'recently fierce opposition waged by the Perhimpoenan Indonesia against the theosophists

---

[90]   For Salim's paper see *Fadjar Asia*, 20 August 1928. For Gobée's remarks to De Graeff, 20 March 1928, p 2, for his letter about the 26-29 January 1928 PSI congress in Djokja celebrating its fifteenth anniversary, Mr. 332/1928. The congress was poorly attended (by some one hundred people) and with only eighteen delegates out of the total of forty being present; see attached report, p. 1, Mr. 332/1928. Agoes Salim stressed that 'Islam was the law for the entire society including politics' and Soerjopranoto stated that 'Islam still needed to resist Christianity and Theosophy since they were out to destroy Islam, the most precious fundament of the indigenous community [...] while Buddhism was like a poison eroding the spirit of the Javanese to be strong'; p. 6, Mr. 332/1928.

and the so-called Orde der Dienaren van Indië [Theosophical Order of Servants of the Indies] with Soedjadi and Hatta taking the initiative to destroy 'these enemies of Indonesia', causing the latter to be expelled from the Orde der Dienaren and thus widening the chasm even further.

The Inlandsche Zaken official also ridiculed Soegondo's efforts, using the Bahasa Indonesia term meaning 'as far below par', while 'Soegondo further lacked any authority for chairing the congress properly'.[91]

Nonetheless, two dramatic events of symbolic significance for Indonesian unity were to mark this Second Youth Congress. First was the so-called Soempah Pemoeda (Oath of Indonesia's Youth), with the delegates rather jubilantly pledging 'to unify under one country, one people and one language' (Bahasa Indonesia). The second was that *Sin Po* reporter Wage Rudolf Soepratman's tune 'Indonesia Raja', so very much the poetic version of the newly emerging Indonesian consciousness, was proclaimed by the youth congress to be Indonesia's nationalist anthem.[92] That Soepratman's tune was described as a nationalist and not a national anthem was perhaps an effort not to unduly provoke the *sana* press. *Sana* did react, however, in the wake of De Graeff's 18 October 1929 circular stating that the tune was a club song and not a national anthem and could be sung at gatherings even with audiences standing at attention. If the latter was the case, the circular urged civil authorities who were present to politely stand up as well.[93]

Urged by Soekarno, 'Indonesia Raja' would from that time onwards also be sung at PNI gatherings and other nationalist occasions. Another song soon to be sung together with the PNI's party tune was 'Partai kita' (Our party), composed by PNI member Inoe Perbatasari, one of the *jempolan* (champions) of the Bandoeng branch and a close friend of Soetan Sjahrir since their AMS (Algemeene Middelbare School, general intermediate school) years in Bandoeng.[94] In the wake of that decision came a spate of negative *sana* comments, both in press circles and in the Volksraad. The *Algemeen Indisch Dagblad* of 26 October 1929, for instance, stated that 'no Indonesian people existed and therefore the tune ['Indonesia Raja'], just like the lullaby 'Nina bobo', did not need to be revered at all'. In the Volksraad Thamrin was quick

---

[91]   Van der Plas, 3 November 1928 report no. J/302 to the Governor-General, pp. 2, 4-5, Mr. 1066/1928.

[92]   Ramadhan 1981:110-2, *45 Tahun Sumpah Pemuda* 1974:69-73; Van der Plas, 3 November 1928 report, p. 3, Mr. 1066/1928. For Hatta being an Orde member and then being expelled, see De Tollenaere 1996:348-9.

[93]   See, for instance, letter of the government's secretary to the heads of the regional administration no. 314, Verbaal 9 May 1931 C 9. For the outcry about 'yet another cave-in by De Graeff' see *Bataviaasch Nieuwsblad*, 20 October 1929; *Algemeen Indisch Dagblad,* 26 October 1929; *De Locomotief,* 27 and 31 October 1929.

[94]   *Algemeen Indisch Dagblad.* 6 November and 6 December 1929. For the connection with Sjahrir, see Mrázek 1994:77.

to ridicule these *sana* arguments that 'singing or even the humming of this popular tune formed a threat to peace and good order'. He himself had in the past seen no signs of order being disrupted by the use of Soepratman's 'Indonesia Raja'.[95] What seems to be at the core of *sana*'s concern was not so much the song but the radicalization of urbanized nationalist youth being stirred up under the auspices of Soekarno's PNI, causing the Second Youth Congress – even though Soekarno was absent – to adopt the unitary prin-ciples he had promoted so vigorously in the past few years.

Nationalist concern about Soekarno's radical approaches

Earlier concern expressed by the Soerabaja branch about Soekarno's approach was noted above. In the wake of Mr Gatot Taroenamihardjo's objections, notions ignored by Soekarno at the time, others followed, with some counsel-ling restraint and two even suggesting that Soekarno step aside for a while and go abroad for study. These suggestions Soekarno could not leave unan-swered; his leadership seemed to be at stake, particularly since several rather strong objections had been raised by his former political mentor Dr Tjipto, the lonely exile of Bandaneira. Besides, even some of the *sini* press started to circulate rumours of the imminent internment of Soekarno, with *Matahari Indonesia* suggesting that Soekarno appeared on a list of persons to be interned or exiled. 'Semprot', in the same issue, aired dismay about this since 'if the government carries through with it, the reins of the PNI will then surely fall into the wrong hands'. Some three weeks later *Bintang Timoer* echoed these concerns as well, as did *Medan Doenia*, with the latter counselling and perhaps also lecturing the *sana* outlets at the same time 'that it is no use at all pestering the current leader of the nationalists with the intention of thereby crushing the populist movement to death [...]. [T]he nationalist movement is not just a demand made by a Soekarno but it is truly a sign of the times.'[96]

As to Tjipto's suggestions to temper the situation, Soekarno was quick to respond, urging his former mentor to be more supportive of the so-called Bandoeng approach. He was aware of some objections to his approach by Anwari, who in 'a poisonous letter' to Soekarno said he was speaking on behalf of Soetomo, Thamrin and Soebrata as well.[97] So on 5 October 1928 Soekarno wrote to his exiled mentor:

[95]   *Algemeen Indisch Dagblad*, 26 October 1929. For Thamrin, see *Handelingen Volksraad* 1929-1930:139-40.
[96]   *Matahari Indonesia*, 24 November 1928; *Bintang Timoer*, 14 December 1928; *Medan Doenia*, 8 and 10 January 1929.
[97]   Van der Plas,'Gegevens ten behoeve van een Regeeringsbeslissing inzake de PNI leiders', p. 9, note x, Mr. 547/1930, Verbaal 9 May 1931 C 9.

Well, you may by now understand what Bandoeng wants. Prepare and prepare once again, together with constant agitation, so that on the day of great unity we truly are able to mount one great manifestation. I am thinking of organizing a huge open-air meeting on that great day, followed by a large demonstrative march (unless of course the *kaoem kekoeasaan* [the ones holding power] prohibits it). We can only count upon success if we carefully prepare the ground beforehand. The large turmoil of open-air meetings and the noise of marches is like the rice needed for the political education of the common folk. The common folk do not have a thinking mind but they have a temperamental heart. By bringing them to move, Gandhi, Lenin, Garibaldi, Young Egypt, Young China etc. were able to ignite the common folk with a huge spirit.[98]

Still, in a 6 November 1928 letter, Tjipto reiterated his concern, advising Soekarno as follows: 'I am very concerned about you. Half a year ago I already made known to you my objections about your actions in the PNI.' (It is this letter of half a year earlier which may have prompted Soekarno's remarks of 5 October 1928 printed above.) 'You have not trained a deputy or a successor as yet, and if you fall, the PNI will be without a leader. Should you not moderate yourself? I think there are sufficient grounds for taking such a course.'[99]

From the Netherlands as well, some objections were raised to Soekarno's approach. Mohammad Tabrani, a Madurese activist and theosophist who had chaired the First Youth Congress, held from 30 April to 2 May 1926, and had known Soekarno since 1920, when they were both members of the Soerabaja branch of Jong Java, wrote in December 1928 from The Hague 'that one [the Indies government] is out to catch you', and counselled Soekarno 'to stay behind the scenes' or even better 'to leave the country for a while'.[100] This appeal was echoed by Mohammad Hatta, in a letter addressed to Soekarno (dated The Hague, 4 February 1929, and sent by way of Sartono's mailing address in Batavia):

The danger of a government decision to exile you is now quite imminent. As you know yourself, Zentgraaff has mentioned several measures which the government is likely to take against you. And you are, just as I am, aware of the fact

[98]   Van der Plas, 'Gegevens ten behoeve van een Regeeringsbeslissing inzake de PNI leiders', p. 10, Mr. 547/1930, Verbaal 9 May 1931 C 9, where Van der Plas comments that these remarks by Soekarno did not show violence as being an aim of the PNI at all.
[99]   Van der Plas, 'Gegevens ten behoeve van een Regeeringsbeslissing inzake de PNI leiders', p. 6, Mr. 547/1930, Verbaal 9 May 1931 C 9. Van der Plas also refers to a 2 July 1928 or 1929 communication of Tjipto to Soekarno stating that 'When I urge you to moderate, I am led by opportunism'.
[100]   Van der Plas, 'Gegevens ten behoeve van een Regeeringsbeslissing inzake de PNI leiders', p. 6-7, Mr. 547/1930, Verbaal 9 May 1931 C 9. For Tabrani being a member of the Orde der Dienaren van Indië see *45 Tahun Sumpah Pemuda* 1974:316.

that Zentgraaff represents the semi-official voice of the government [...]. I have received confirmation of the above from a reliable source in this country. Darsono, the exiled PKI leader, has heard similar things and so came to me straight away. We have discussed the matter with several other people and have formed the opinion that your safety is at stake and that therefore it is necessary to seek cover. We are also of the opinion that – since we are now at the stage of organizational build-up of the PNI – your exile would become too much of a sacrifice. Not that we are so opposed to our leaders being exiled, but for now that must be prevented, since we do not want any stagnation to occur to our organization. Darsono, who has had practical experience in the Indonesian revolutionary movement, is therefore of the opinion that you should, for the time being, not appear in public, and should withdraw for the moment from the front line of leadership, leaving this to some other person or persons. In times that danger threatens, such a manoeuvre is necessary. We fully agree with Darsono. Therefore, brother, please restrict yourself during the next few months to the training of propagandists. Also, in connection with the threatening danger, it would be desirable if you were to leave Indonesia for a little while, for instance using the pretext of a study tour about trade-union movements and cooperative systems in Europe. All this would connect rather well with my previously made suggestion that the PNI send a special delegate to the forthcoming world congress of the Liga [...]. Independent of the PNI's decision whether or not to send representatives to Brussels, it is in my opinion very desirable that you disappear from Indonesia for some time. It is in the interests of the sound development of our national freedom movement, a movement which is now being threatened by danger, that I give you the above to seriously consider. Expecting a speedy reply, I sign with brotherly greetings.[101]

In a postscript to the letter, Hatta said that he was quite prepared to cover Soekarno's travel and living expenses while in Holland.

Hatta's motives for expressing his concern about Soekarno's PNI

It seems quite clear that Hatta was not so much concerned about Soekarno's well-being as that he wanted Soekarno out of Indonesia as soon as possible in order to forestall colonial government repression of the PNI or of the entire Indonesian *pergerakan*. With the PNI then left alone by the colonial government, Hatta may have considered the possibility not only of having a substantial future directing role in the party himself – his letter is replete with matters he sees as essential for the PNI, while he was not even a member of that organization – but also of there finally being a chance of the PNI leader-

[101]   Hatta's letter was attached to advocate-general Mr G. Vonk's 4 June 1930 missive to De Graeff about Vonk being criticized by some other members of the government, no. 1127/AP, p. 13, also in Mr. 559/1930. An English-language translation of Hatta's letter is in Hering 1985:25-6, while a Dutch-language copy of it was printed in the *Algemeen Indisch Dagblad*, 4 September 1930 during Soekarno's trial before the Bandoeng Landraad.

ship falling into less flamboyant and more cautious hands, which would be more amenable to his own directives and ideas. Sending the letter to Sartono's mailing address instead of Soekarno's own Bandoeng address was obviously a step in that direction. Also, the offer to pay Soekarno's expenses while abroad, coming from a man whose family in Minangkabau was quite wealthy, must have been an affront to Soekarno, dependent as he was on the irregular seventy-five-guilder monthly stipends he received from his PNI lawyer colleagues and the steadier but modest income from his wife's *batik* and *jamu* enterprises. It is therefore no wonder that Soekarno did not honour Hatta's letter with a reply. Soekarno may have been stung further by the fact that Hatta, as recently as 29 October 1928 in a letter addressed to him, had praised him to the hilt 'for his fine efforts in training future leading cadres through courses', and now, barely three months later, was counselling a swift departure from that scene.[102] On the other hand, Hatta could not entirely be blamed for composing the 4 February 1929 letter the way he did. As a somewhat staid and rather reserved man himself – characterized by one person as being far better as a writer than as a speaker[103] – Hatta failed to truly come to terms with Soekarno's vibrant and dominating personality, which was accompanied by such charm and humour that it drew the masses to him like flying ants to a flaming torch. So, by suggesting Soekarno leave the scene, Hatta was simply unaware of one crucial fact: that Soekarno derived immense personal satisfaction from thundering out his protests and claims before huge indigenous mass audiences. As D.A. Low has attested:

> Sukarno's principal gift – in which he had no equal either in Indonesia or in India – was his oratory. He could capture and stir huge audiences in a way no other leader – certainly not Hatta – ever did, and he combined this not merely with a considerable personal nationalist fervour but with acute political sensitivity as well. (Low 1986:126.)

Naturally, Hatta had as yet to witness these grand crowd-pleasing performances of Soekarno in action: only a glimpse filtered through the correspondence Hatta had with his small following in the homeland. So Hatta had little inkling that this theatrical side of Soekarno's personality did indeed demand

[102]   Soekarno's testimony before the Landraad, reported by the *Algemeen Indisch Dagblad,* 4 September 1930. As to Hatta's 29 October 1928 letter, he may have been inspired by Soekarno's efforts training second-echelon leaders during the Bandoeng closed course meetings of 19 October and 26 October 1928, each attended by two hundred course students; see Poeze 1982: 440. During the latter meeting it was further resolved to start a debating club as well, with three of them meeting in Bandoeng 26 October, 9 November and 7 December 1928, Poeze 1982:464-5 and Gobée Collection KITLV no. H 795/11.
[103]   De Jong 1969-91, XIa:326. Also Saeroen, one of the *sini* press's top reporters, felt that 'Hatta, unlike Soekarno, had never been able to employ an effervescent, stirring style of oratory'; Hering 1996:182.

the spotlight, and not the empty wings that Hatta had so amply suggested in his recent letter. As for Soekarno, it graced him to still allow Hatta space in the PNI's periodical *Persatoean Indonesia* for writing a four-part essay titled 'Boeah pikiran politik' (On the subject of political thought). Beforehand, the two had discussed the possibility of Hatta becoming more actively involved in contributing articles to *Persatoean Indonesia,* but Hatta claimed he was far too busy with Liga executive affairs to submit a contribution as yet.[104] Yet Hatta did ask Sartono afterwards to supply him with more details about the PNI and the PPPKI, their numbers and their appeal.[105] As a result, Hatta submitted the above-mentioned essay on political thought, which appeared in subsequent issues of *Persatoean Indonesia:* 1 January, 1 February, 15 February and 1 April 1929.

Hatta's blueprint for the future

In his essay, Hatta first discussed the PPPKI, making it clear to his readers that his was essentially a voice from overseas but that he meant well, since he had been closely observing the *pergerakan* with immense sympathy, particularly the attempts to achieve unity. Yet he found the PPPKI still wanting in the realm of political clout and organization, and therefore admonished it to become instead a Dewan Rakjat, a people's council representing all shades of socio-political opinion current in the Indonesian nationalist *pergerakan*. Hatta cherished this concept since it fitted in with his own frequently expressed views of establishing 'a state within a state' where one would strive to uplift indigenous socio-political and economic structures so as to parallel the ruling colonial administrative edifice. That would offer the only true foundation for a brighter future, blessed this time with genuine independence. He then turned to the Indian National Congress and reviewed its habit of mounting grand annual congresses. He held it up as an example to be emulated quickly by the Indonesian PPPKI. In closing, however, Hatta cautioned that the PPPKI would only achieve real momentum if its constituent nationalist parties were willing to gain strength and organizational cohesion all by themselves. Hatta then turned his attention to Soekarno's PNI, naturally his main concern.[106] Again, as in the opening stages of his arguments, Hatta held that despite his criticism of the PNI, he was not assailing its existence as such, reminding his readers that the PNI's principles were quite close to those of

---

[104]   Letter from Hatta to Soekarno, The Hague 29 October 1928 printed by *Algemeen Indisch Dagblad,* 4 September 1930.
[105]   Letter from Hatta to Soekarno, The Hague 27 November 1928 addressed to Sartono.
[106]   *Persatoean Indonesia,* 1 January 1929.

the Perhimpoenan Indonesia. He also stressed the fact that he had always urged members of the Perhimpoenan Indonesia to join the PNI as soon as they returned to the homeland.[107] Yet he was disappointed to see that the PNI was still in its demonstration stage, a preliminary phase where it had also failed to sufficiently emphasize the role of education. Therefore, the PNI should leave behind that phase swiftly in order to move on to a more genuine stage of still tighter and more solid organization. Aware that at such a stage, mere mass membership would clash with a tightly and centrally controlled politically-aware membership, Hatta was undecided about which approach should be adopted in the advanced stage he was fond of envisioning. So he tried another tack in his arguments about the PNI's chances to grow in strength. He urged the PNI to become a large people's party with millions of members, thus challenging the colonial government and showing *sana* its true purpose and determination. In other words, to truly become a powerful 'state within a state'. Tempering this view, he cited his own observations that so far, while thousands of people indeed attended the many PNI meetings, they did not bother to become members. This he deemed a clear sign of weakness or even failure of the organization, but above all of a lack of genuine leadership. As well as being organizationally weak, Hatta considered the PNI to be far too short of capable second-echelon leaders able to create and than sustain an active politically conscious mass membership. Hatta also urged the PNI not to draw such leaders from the westernized educated sphere alone, but to recruit them from every sector of society. These leaders would then be charged to maintain close contact with the masses and at the same time imbue them with the PNI's political doctrines.[108] And here Hatta took Soekarno to task, adopting some of Soekarno's verbose style in the process:

> When Soekarno speaks, it is not enough for the audience to noisily applaud him. It is not enough that people merely become Soekarnoists. What is needed above all is that every PNI member becomes a Soekarno in his heart. In short, it is not enough if there is only one Soekarno, rather there must be thousands and later millions of Soekarnos. Soekarno's spirit must permeate the whole of the PNI. If all PNI people work in this fashion, there will be a new power and a new large party emerging and we will be able to force the [colonial] government to heed our demands.[109]

[107] As late as 22 July 1931, Hatta maintained: '*Dan djoega maksoed saja akan masoek dalam PNI kalau saja kembali di Indonesia*' (It is also my intention to join the PNI the moment I am back in Indonesia); see his open letter (*surat terbuka*), Rotterdam 22 July 1931 printed in *Bintang Timoer*, 3 August 1931.

[108] Hatta seems to ignore here the useful start Soekarno had made by enlisting such leaders through Bandoeng bi-weekly debating club meetings attracting some 87 candidates during sessions on 26 October, 9 and 23 November, and 7 December 1928; see also note 102 and Poeze 1982: 440, 464-5.

[109] *Persatoean Indonesia*, 1 February 1929, also Ingleson 1979:83.

To some extent Hatta's criticism is unjustified and insufficiently backed up by facts. Also, a few of his arguments are open to contradiction. In terms of organizational matters, Hatta overlooked some crucial factors facing the PNI's central executive at that time. Aware of the dangers it was running in building up the PNI as quickly as possible, and of the pitfalls the PSI and PKI had encountered before when lower-level activities occurred outside central executive control, the PNI central executive had indeed taken steps since November 1928 to tighten control over its own rank and file (Poeze 1982:464). Also, the fact that the PNI had been trying, through so-called candidate memberships, to achieve a more politically conscious following seems to have escaped Hatta altogether, as well as the efforts demonstrated in that field by the PNI's Tjahja Volksuniversiteit (Radiant People's University), Douwes Dekker's Ksatrian Institute and Mr Soejoedi's Comité Penjedar Perasaän Boemipoetera Djocjakarta (Committee to Raise the Consciousness of Yogya's Native Sons).[110] Finally, Hatta's call for some million members to come forward – while having first backed the politically-conscious and educational approach – demonstrates how far out of touch he indeed was with some of the immense difficulties faced by the PNI and by every other indigenous nationalist association at that time. Fortunately for him, he was brought rather quickly to his senses in 1932, when ideas of his joining the PNI, let alone the prospect of tighter unity, were rapidly abandoned. Coming face to face for the first time with the harsh reality of a nationalist leader operating in a 'near police state'[111] colony, Hatta opted for a mere thousand politically advanced followers, only to see them crushed at the start of 1934 by a relentless colonial authority led by a new governor-general.

Soekarno and PNI and PPPKI developments during the first half of 1929

The year 1928 ended with the PPPKI Bandoeng branch meeting in that city on 16 December 1928, with Soekarno 'speaking with great caution and not in a seditious sense', declaring that 'if the spirit remains alive, we of the PNI, the PSI and Pasoendan trust that one day our wishes will come true. Even if it takes ten, twenty or a hundred years, Indonesia Merdeka will come.'[112] That same month, the second Pemoeda Indonesia congress was held in Weltevreden from 24 to 28 December 1928, with the aim of fusing together

---

[110]   Poeze 1982:388. For the Tjahja University of Bandoeng being established with branches in Batavia and Djokja, see Poeze 1982:466-7; Mrázek 1994:42.
[111]   For the 'police-state' label see Onghokham 1987:52-4; Hering 1996:186, 201, 213 who cites Cees Fasseur and Henk Maier, and Wiranata Koesoemo's *Polizei-staat* (police state) label, *Handelingen Volksraad* 1929-1930:82.
[112]   Letter Van der Plas to De Graeff, no. J/322, 18 December 1928, p. 1, Mr. 1199/1928.

all Indonesian youth associations. As was the case with Pemoeda Indonesia's first Bandoeng congress, Soekarno delivered the key address, this time on the topic of emancipating Indonesian womanhood.[113] Soekarno said, 'feminist activities in Eastern countries had for some time lagged behind that of women in the Western world, though recently considerable progress had been made in the East'. Here Soekarno was referring to the emancipatory activities of Sun Yat-sen's widow Soon Chin-ling of China, Sarojini Naidu of India, and Halide Edib Hanum and Nakie Hanum of Turkey; he encouraged Indonesian women 'to emulate the shining example set by these Eastern feminists'. Referring then to the *wayang* repertoire, he urged 'Indonesian women to become like the courageous Srikandi, the second wife of the noble Ardjoeno, who both had closely cooperated in reaching victory over alien intruders'.[114] The issue of Indonesian feminism was again dealt with, this time by Gatot Mangkoepradja, secretary of the PNI's main executive, during the 24 March 1929 PNI meeting held in Bandoeng's Empress movie theatre and attended by some fifteen hundred persons. Gatot stated that 'the women's movement was indeed a vital part of the national *pergerakan*'.[115]

In the letter written to De Graeff about this meeting, Van der Plas indicated that 'the PNI has taken sides with the PPPKI executive against the PSII [since January, 'Indonesia' had been added to the name of Tjokro's association], while also repudiating Salim, without however naming him specifically'. As for Soekarno, he was reported as citing Sun Yat-sen in encouraging his compatriots to, 'like the Chinese leader, erect propaganda outlets abroad in order to promote the nationalist cause'. Soekarno added that such activities would also 'enable us to lift the lid of all the vile garbage accumulated here in this colony, such as the penal sanctions, the forced labour services, the Digoel concentration camp and the penal code articles 161 bis and 153 bis ter'.[116] Soekarno also felt that all that would strongly promote the cause of pan-Asianism, but here he warned that such 'must be done exclusively on our own, with no support or payment by others or by sending a delegate abroad on behalf of an association which is in fact against our Indonesia Merdeka ideals'.[117] By acting on our own, '*rukun agawé santosa* [Javanese for

---

[113] See Inlandsche Zaken A. Cense's report, Mr. 408/1929 and *45 Tahun Sumpah Pemuda* 1974: 74-5.

[114] See Inlandsche Zaken A. Cense's report, pp. 2-3, Mr. 408/1929.

[115] Van der Plas to De Graeff, no. 441, 26 March 1929, p. 2, with 'Bijlage' about the PNI meeting's deliberations also written by Van der Plas, Mr. 314/1929.

[116] This prompted the journalist Parada Harahap to write articles on 'The land of the penal sanctions' in *Bintang Timoer*, 13 and 14 May 1929.

[117] Van der Plas, 'Bijlage', p. 3, Mr. 314/1929, in which Van der Plas boldfaced the latter part of Soekarno's appeal and added in the margin that this was done to penalize and ridicule Agoes Salim.

'unity brings peaceful security'] will be our lot'. Soekarno also regretted the
circulation of 'rumours stating that the PPPKI was about to fall apart and
that even the PNI would soon leave the federation'. Van der Plas, in yet
another margin of his report, stated that the rumours had been circulated
by the PSII periodical *Fadjar Asia* and the PSII executive. Soekarno, on behalf
of the PPPKI federation, rather vehemently denied the rumours. At the end
of the PNI meeting, two motions were adopted: one that 'Perhimpoenan
Indonesia needed to continue doing its nationalist propaganda, or at least
that propaganda outlets be erected elsewhere in Europe', and the second,
that 'the PPPKI was vital in the struggle for Indonesian freedom'.[118] As to the
first motion, the PPPKI conference held in Djokja on 29 and 30 March 1929
resolved that Perhimpoenan Indonesia was its representative in Europe, and
thus charged with waging nationalist propaganda activities overseas.[119]

These issues and the latent hostility expressed toward the PSII may well
have been prompted by an PSII congress held earlier, from 16 to 23 January
1929 in Batavia, attended by some 350 persons. In his report to De Graeff, Van
der Plas, now in charge of Inlandsche Zaken due to Gobée's well-earned leave
of absence, stated that 'the congress was a flop, showing that the political significance of the PSII has indeed dwindled considerably', with 'the truly faithful getting increasingly fed up with the notions expressed by the adventurers
of the PSII', and where 'motivations of pan-Islamic action clearly clash with
the notions of pan-Asianism as adhered to by the PNI'.[120] As to the latter, Van
der Plas noted that 'Dr Soekiman Wirjosandjojo, on the one day he visited the
congress, demonstrably joined PNI guests Mr Sartono and Mr Soenarjo and
sat with them throughout the session'.[121] Also, the poorly attended provincial
East Java PSII congress held in Soerabaja from 25 to 27 April 1929 (where
Soetomo, chairman of the PPPKI, in a guest address, ridiculed 'the PSII pan-
Islamic action as being outdated and useless since in all Muslim countries
nationalism dominated all other issues') was, according to Van der Plas, 'a
bitter pill for PSII leaders to swallow'.[122] The pill may have been made even
more difficult to digest since the Soerabaja PNI meeting held 14 April 1929 in
the Stadstuin theatre, chaired by Mas Roeslan Wongsokoesoemo, drew some

---

[118]   Van der Plas, 'Bijlage', pp. 4-5, Mr. 314/1929. The propaganda plans were welcomed by
Bintang Timoer, 27 March 1929 and by *Fadjar Asia*, 28 March 1929 with Salim agreeing with
Soekarno on this issue.
[119]   Letter from Attorney-General Verheyen to De Graeff, nr. 606/A.P., 12 April 1929, Mr. 352/
1929. *Djanget* (Djokja-based PNI periodical edited by Mr Soejoedi) of 18 April 1929 lauded the
PPPKI resolutions, as did *Bintang Timoer*, 10 April 1929 and *Soeloeh Ra'jat Indonesia*, 10 April
1929.
[120]   Van der Plas to De Graeff, no. 449, 27 March 1929, p. 1, Mr. 334/1929.
[121]   Van der Plas to De Graeff, no. 449, 27 March 1929, p. 2, Mr. 334/1929.
[122]   Van der Plas to De Graeff, no. 722, 24 May 1929, p. 1, Mr. 492/1929.

three thousand *arek Soeroboyo*. Soekarno clearly set out once again the aims of his party, calling members 'to concentrate all forces under the red and white banner and the Banteng head of the PNI'.[123] Even Pekalongan's 5 May 1929 PNI branch meeting, chaired by Lawi and attended by two thousand people including Soekarno, Gatot Mangkoepradja, Mr Soejoedi and Maskoen, was seen by some of the *sini* press as a sign of a 'remarkable revival of the PNI in that semi-rural area of Central Java'. *Sedijo Tomo* stressed 'that Pekalongan had long been considered by the authorities as being *angker'* (Javanese for dangerous) and rightly so, 'since repression and improper intervention had been conducted all along by police and civil authorities as had been the case earlier in Semarang, once the red capital of Java'.[124]

So, in contrast to the PSII, the PNI meetings earlier in the year, and particularly the well-attended second PNI congress held in Batavia from 18 to 20 May 1929, showed a vibrancy characterized by Van der Plas as being 'optimistic and cheerful but also close to exuberance [...]. The great public interest in the congress was due to the fact that the PNI singularly stood at the core of all nationalist action, causing hundreds to join it even after the congress had ended, thereby throwing all caution to the wind.'[125] This analysis was shared by most of the major *sini* press editorials. *Bintang Timoer,* in response to *Java Bode*'s main article accusing 'the PNI congress of mere rabble rousing', held that the congress 'commanded great general respect and that when Soekarno was barked at [by the *Java Bode*] it was a clear sign that the *pergerakan* was well on its way to ultimate independence'. *Darmokondo, Sedijo Tomo, Swara Publiek, Djanget* and even *Zaman Baroe*, a conservative Christian weekly, though not agreeing with 'Soekarno's revolutionary goals', felt that the congress was a sign that the PNI had 'progressed from being a movement of intellectuals to truly becoming a populist party'.[126] Attorney-General R.J.M. Verheijen, in his congress report to De Graeff, also mentioned the upsurge in numbers flocking to the PNI, estimated by him to 'be close to six thousand, with many silent sympathizers to boot, due to the diligent *kampung* propaganda exercised by active PNI leaders [with the] Bandoeng course meetings alone attracting close to eight hundred members'. Another concern listed by Verheijen was 'the current interest showed by the PNI in engaging in labour union activ-

---

[123]   *Bintang Timoer,* 18 April 1929; *Pewarta Soerabaja,* 15 April 1929.
[124]   *Bahagia,* 7 and 8 May 1929; *Bintang Timoer,* 7 May 1929; *Sedijo Tomo,* 3 and 10 May and *Sipatahoenan,* 18 May 1929.
[125]   Van der Plas to De Graeff, no. K 59, 5 June 1929, pp. 1-2, Mr. 561/1929, and his attached survey about the congress proceedings, pp. 3-4.
[126]   See *Bintang Timoer,* 22 and 27 May; *Darmokondo,* 24 May; *Swara Publiek,* 27 May; *Sedijo Tomo,* 28 May 28, 1 June: with a 'Mr S' (Soejoedi?) stating that 'the congress was *summa summarum* a great succes in spite of the reproaches made by the *pers putih pembohong* [lying white press]'; *Djanget,* 6 June and *Zaman Baroe,* 31 May 1929.

ities and so-called *tani* [peasant] unions'. He suggested the likelihood of the PNI engaging in possible union and even strike activities in tandem with the recently (8 July 1928) established Liga-connected Sarekat Kaoem Boeroeh Indonesia (SKBI, Labourers Union of Indonesia) of Soerabaja.[127]

Meanwhile, at the congress, Soekarno needed to change venues in order to absorb the huge audiences flocking to hear him speak. After delivering his major address at the Thamrin-owned Gedong Permoefakatan Indonesia (House of Indonesian Consensus) at Gang Kenari 15, Soekarno was rushed to the Rialto movie theatre in the suburb of Senen to repeat his address. On the closing day he stated that 'eventually a Pacific War will occur, with America, Japan and Britain fighting each other, which will mark our own historic moment. We will then be *ramai* [cheerful] and finally take our own destiny in our own hands (thunderous applause).'[128] And while this may well demonstrate Soekarno's growing popularity, it also revealed some inherent weaknesses of his party's programme as well of his own individual approach. In the stirring speeches he gave throughout the congress proceedings – a performance he was to repeat at various PNI assemblies during the remainder of 1929 – it became quite apparent that his own provocative style was the PNI's sole means of ensuring some kind of momentum. The momentum, however, was curtailed rather severely by colonial regulations disallowing genuine indigenous political emancipation while restricting outpourings of such emancipatory sentiments in crowded public meeting halls with rather vague references to an indeterminate future when the country would finally attain *merdeka*. Here, we touch upon the Achilles' heel of the PNI programme, namely the sheer lack of attainable targets short of Indonesia Merdeka itself. This course was promoted by some of the moderate PNI leaders situated in Soerabaja and Betawi, but not seriously considered by Soekarno. Moreover, while we noted above how Soekarno was duly impressed by the nature of Gandhi's *swaraj* (self-rule) campaign against the British in India, he and his party remained rather incapable so far of organizing massive civil disobedience campaigns, salt marches and the like in order to keep up momentum and solidify member enthusiasm. Instead, in the wake of the second congress, Soekarno and his PNI hoped to gain a credible mass membership in order to make increasing use of the provocation tactics and actions verbally outlined by Soekarno to pressure the colonial government into making some valid concessions (Ingleson 1979:90-1). In a 7 June 1929 letter to Tjipto Mangoenkoesoemo,

[127] See Verheijen to De Graeff, no. 1160/A.P., 6 July 1929, pp. 2-3, 9, Mr. 650/1929. As to a possible PNI-SKBI union and strike activities, see Verheijen to De Graeff, no. 1160/A.P., 6 July 1929, pp. 3-4, Mr. 650/1929, his letter to De Graeff about the significance of the SKBI, no. 803/A.P., 15 May 1929, Mr. 627/1929. As to PNI trade and peasant unions, see his letter nr. 1448/A.P., 12 August 1929 to De Graeff, pp. 1-3, Mr. 766/1929.
[128] Van der Plas to De Graeff, no. K 59, 5 June 1929, pp. 3-4, 16, Mr. 561/1929.

Soekarno said: 'In 1927 the PNI brought the idea of self-strength and ability; and at present that idea is almost like a religion, and such a faith will lead to power; if that happens, our movement will be truly irresistible.'[129]

Soekarno's activities during the remainder of 1929

Exactly a month later, on 7 July 1929, with the PNI now commemorating its second anniversary, the party held crowded meetings in Weltevreden chaired by Mr Sartono and in Bandoeng with Maskoen, one of Inggit's boarders, in charge.[130] In Weltevreden Sartono stressed that the PNI had now entered a new phase, in which it was 'achieving socio-economic activities like erecting a library, a medical clinic, a consultation bureau to help the fight against usury, a reading club [...] and a transitional school [Pergoeroean Rajat] where no politics were taught but purely educational matters with a fund established to support needy students'. He lamented the fact that there were still people who 'assailed the PNI for doing so little', obviously a dig at Hatta's recent PNI analysis, while others held that the PNI's 'constructive efforts were all financed by Moscow'. He vehemently denied that 'the party received one penny of support from outside sources' and said that 'party funds had been built up from the small two-and-a-half cent and five-cent contributions coming from the membership'. He also called Perhimpoenan Indonesia the European-based propaganda outlet of the PPPKI and the PNI, a fact endorsed by the PNI but still giving cause for *sana* to comment that it was all part of a sinister communist plot due to the close links the Leiden-based student association had with the Liga.[131] Yet Sartono's conduct of the meeting was hailed by Van der Plas as 'rather business-like and conciliatory, which could not be said of the speeches made by Soekarno and Iskaq at the Bandoeng meeting, being mainly repetitive and reminiscent of old lectures'.[132]

However, Soekarno, perhaps thinking of his recent 7 June message to Tjipto, reminded his audience that two years ago the PNI was born and 'that our destiny does not depend on the *sana* party but that it lies in our own hands'. In answer to a speaker hoping that the PNI would last two hundred years, Soekarno noted 'that such was not necessary since twenty years would be sufficient to free Indonesia of the foreign imperialists'.[133] Also, 'the PNI

---

[129] 'Nota' Van der Plas on the PNI arrests, Weltevreden, 31 May 1930, p. 11, Mr. 547/1930.
[130] For Maskoen boarding at Soekarno's and Ingitt's home, see Ramadhan 1981:93.
[131] Van der Plas survey about the Weltevreden meeting, pp. 1-7, Mr. 709/1929, also in Hering 1985:193.
[132] Letter Van der Plas to De Graeff no. K 81, Weltevreden, 10 July 1929, p. 1.
[133] This caused *Bintang Timoer*, 9 July 1929 to print a heading 'In 20 years Indonesia will be independent'.

did not believe the promises of *sana* nor the stories spread by *sana* about our immaturity [...] [W]e instead continued our work, and with the *kaum buruh* [workers] in Europe we will try to make contact through [the Leiden-based] Perhimpoenan Indonesia. In the case of no such contacts occurring, we shall all the same achieve Indonesia's freedom through self-activity.'[134] A fortnight later, at a 21 July 1929 PNI meeting in Pekalongan's Royal Cinema theatre, while addressing close to two thousand people, Soekarno spoke in the same stirring vein, stating that 'we have some contact with the Liga exclusively to expand our working sphere in order to achieve our aims and strivings'.[135] That he did so may well have to do with the warnings issued by Peka-longan's *Resident* and by Inlandsche Zaken prior to his address, in which he and his executive were told 'to remain responsible for the behaviour of the [PNI] branches, and if such behaviour prompted intervention by the authori-ties, the [PNI] executive committee need not flatter itself with the hope that it would be spared'. The warnings were issued because local PNI branch lead-ers had allegedly used far too provocative language during a recent course meeting. Gobée, now back at Inlandsche Zaken, also added that:

> The PNI's aversion to violence will only be given credit if every direct or indirect preaching of violence is forcefully objected to in public, as well as within its own inner circles [...]. If that is not the case, the disastrous consequences attendant to such courses of violence need to be clearly understood [...]. Taking into account the seriousness of these warnings, I must view as very unsatisfactory what has been said in Pekalongan [...]. Ir Soekarno's speech did not differ in the least from his previous addresses; the bare statement that the PNI does not want violence, therefore, does not mean anything.[136]

Drawing Soekarno so negatively may well have to do with a degree of irrita-tion that had crept in about the PNI chairman's posture ever since the PNI's second congress. Van der Plas reported that 'Soekarno began to lose his nerve due to the pressure of continuous espionage, the fear of internment and the sense of standing rather powerless against a huge organization [the colonial government]'.[137] Yet the *patih* at the disposal of Inlandsche Zaken,

---

[134]   See Inlandsche Zaken survey written by Landjoemin gelar Datoe' Toemanggoeng, p. 1-11, Mr. 709/1929.

[135]   'Kita berhoeboengan dengan Liga tegen koloniale onderdrukking itoe, tida lain hanja boewat meloeaskan djadjahan kita agar dapat mentjapai tjita tjita kita', Verheijen to De Graeff, no. 1448/A.P., 12 August 1929, pp. 6-7, Mr. 766/1929, in which Verheijen states that Soekarno referred here to the PPPKI propaganda mandate given to the Liga-connected Perhimpoenan Indonesia and not to any direct contact existing between the PNI and the Berlin-based Liga. Verheijen also felt that Soekarno, in Pekalongan in the wake of the SKBI house searchings, needed to demonstrate 'his courage in public and, indeed, also to the authorities'.

[136]   Gobée to De Graeff, no. 1124, Weltevreden, 25 July 1929, pp. 1-2, Mr. 739/1929.

[137]   Van der Plas to De Graeff, no. K 59, p. 2, Mr. 561/1929.

the Minangkabau nobleman Landjoemin gelar Datoe' Toemenggoeng, in his report on the Pekalongan meeting, paints Soekarno as follows:

> The soul of the meeting was Ir Soekarno, as indeed at all PNI assemblies I have attended in the recent past, and this was again clearly demonstrated in Peka-longan. There, many country folk assured me that the large attendance was owing exclusively to rumours spread beforehand that Soekarno was to speak among other matters about the warnings issued by the *Resident* and by Mr Van der Plas. However, not a word of protest about these threats materialized, since according to the branch leaders I spoke with, both Ir Soekarno and Mr Iskaq firmly ruled it out in order to maintain calm. Both gentlemen, and also some of the branch leaders concerned, positively claimed to me that the much denounced and incen-diary words had not at all been spoken by them at the relevant course meeting. Strong proof in their possession about it seems to suggest that they were falsely accused by members of the local police. I was further assured by several members of the Native Administration that the accusations launched by the police against the Pekalongan PNI leaders were indeed quite exaggerated [...]. The interest in the PNI in Pekalongan therefore has been growing. The number of members amounted to eight hundred by the end of May, and more than a hundred persons have since enrolled. I expect that still more new members will come forward in the wake of this meeting.[138]

Naturally, these candid revelations, while relished by the *sini* press, were going to add still more fuel to the ire already expressed by most of the *sana* press editorials and to the objections about Soekarno and his PNI raised by die-hard segments of the colonial administration and the Indies War Department. West Java's governor J.B. Hartelust, in a letter to De Graeff, had counselled 'making PNI membership incompatible with a paid civil-service vocation', because 'PNI propaganda had become fiercer and PNI member-ship in Bandoeng and Batavia had risen considerably'.[139] Such a ban, how-ever, was seen by Gobée, Verheijen and Mühlenfeld (the new BB director and a social-democrat to boot) as a curtailment of civil rights, causing De Graeff to reject Hartelust's proposal.[140] Also, the fact that the Leiden-based Perhimpoenan Indonesia functioned as the advanced 'European front' unit of the PPPKI, and was therefore charged with raising wider concern about the Digoel internment camp, the Coolie Ordinance and the Penal Code articles, caused some official and press *sana* circles in the colony to suggest that it was merely a plot instigated by the Dutch Communist Party, the SKBI led by Marsoedi, an ex-PKI man, and the Berlin-based Liga. Furthermore, the Dutch

---

[138] See survey of Pekalongan PNI meeting of 21 July 1929, drafted by Landjoemin gelar Datoe' Toemenggoeng, pp. 11-3, Mr. 739/1929. *Bintang Timoer*, 30 July 1929 reported growing PNI mem-bership 'in the town and the kampongs nearby'.
[139] Letter Hartelust to De Graeff, no. G5P/41/24, 16 August 1929, Verbaal 13 March 1930 N 5.
[140] Verheijen to De Graeff, 16 September, Gobée to De Graeff, 23 September, Mühlenfeld to De Graeff, 19 November 1929, Verbaal 13 March 1930 N 5.

communists, the Perhimpoenan Indonesia, the Liga crowd, the PPPKI and the PNI's periodical *Persatoean Indonesia* had recently been supporting the 'Los van Holland Nu' (Free of Holland Now) slogan. This slogan, according to Professor J. van Gelderen, one of the few leftist-oriented members of the colonial administration and a faithful visitor of recent PNI assemblies, had been made 'into an up to the minute, more or less revolutionary demand by anti-imperialistic forces'.[141] Somewhat later, Agoes Salim, then on a European trade-union fact-finding tour, claimed that the desire to be freed from Holland was 'certainly alive in all ranks of the Indonesian political community' and that 'if freedom were to arrive today, all parties federated in the PPPKI would be among the first to welcome such an event'. In conclusion he added: 'Immediate freedom was the wish of all; it is only concerning the possible approaches that Indonesian political opinion remains as yet divided'.[142] Around the same time, the ties between the Leiden-based Perhimpoenan Indonesia and the Liga were somewhat jolted by what Hatta termed the 'Frankfurt betrayal'. After attending the second Liga Congress, held in Frankfurt from 20 to 31 July 1929, where Russian communist delegates successfully got the upper hand, pushing the Liga toward a Bolshevik construction rife with communist/anarchist tendencies, Hatta reported that in his view 'The Liga was facing a great crisis'. He believed there were 'only two possible consequences to be faced; either the Liga goes back to its original premises where it championed all races and all nationalities, in which case this kind of Liga will always find our warm support. Or the Liga becomes merely a tool of Moscow and the Comintern. In that kind of Liga there is really no room for us at all.'[143] However, Hatta did not leave the Liga nor did he withdraw the Perhimpoenan Indonesia from the Dutch branch of the Liga, as a recent biographer suggests (Rose 1987:50). As a matter of fact, Hatta remained a Liga member until March 1931, when he was expelled by the Liga for being 'a bourgeois reformist' (Mrázek 1994:76; Van Vugt 1987:82). Long before that expulsion, Hatta did join a 26 August 1929 meeting in The Hague called by the Liga affiliate of that city to lodge a firm protest against the measures taken by the Indies government to curb the Liga-connected SKBI. After that meeting, he seems to have been instrumental in sending a Perhimpoenan Indonesia manifesto to his followers in his homeland stating that 'a new offensive by Dutch Colonial Imperialism has been issued against the most active part [the SKBI] of the Indonesian revolutionary movement!' Attorney-General Verheijen condemned this action, since Hatta and his Perhimpoenan Indonesia followers should have known better, and were

---

[141]   See Van Gelderen letter to J. Oudegeest, 16 December 1929, p. 2, IISG archives.
[142]   Salim's 19 October 1929 article in *De Socialist*, pp. 3-4.
[143]   *Persatoean Indonesia*, 15 October 1929, also reprinted in 'Bijlage' 8, Mr. 1016/1929.

'contradicting the PNI's attitude, since that party, after all, did not make any attempt to protect the SKBI'.[144] In the Volksraad, Kiewiet de Jonge claimed that the PNI had instructed its members in East Java not to have relations with the SKBI and that the latter, while seeking relations with the PNI, had not had any success establishing such contacts.[145] Let us therefore briefly sketch SKBI developments and the government's response to these.

As to the SKBI organization, it managed to set up small branches in Soerabaja (two hundred members), Banjoewangi (150), and in Bangil, Tjepoe, Pekalongan, Meester Cornelis (now Djatinegara) and Medan, each having some forty to fifty members. These developments gave the PNI some pause for thought, since Mr Iwa Koesoema Soemantri had founded the SKBI Medan branch.[146] The SKBI, however, overplayed its hand, contacting both the Liga and the Shanghai-based Pan Pacific Trade Union Secretariat, and then joining the Liga on 1 April 1929. Yet Van der Plas, the first official to hint at possible SKBI-Liga connections, cautioned against government intervention, arguing that of the main radicals, Iwa Koesoema Soemantri, who moreover had been loath to set up a PNI branch in Medan due to his rather busy trade union activities, seemed to be the only nationalist intellectual involved. Also, Van der Plas held that the SKBI leadership was of such low calibre that it was better to leave it unmolested for fear that better equipped cadres would move in.[147] Van der Plas' call for caution was initially respected by Attorney-General Verheijen, but not for long. Warned off by Soerabaja's *Resident* A.H. Moreu about Liga-SKBI connections, Verheijen decided in favour of massive SKBI house searches and subsequent arrests in Soerabaja, Solo and Medan. In Medan, Koesoema Soemantri was detained on evidence of contacts by letter with Moscow, which eventually led to his being exiled to Bandaneira. In fact, Hatta himself may well have aroused the colonial administration's suspicions of Koesoema Soemantri as early as December 1927 by branding the latter together with Semaoen as Moscow-based communists during the Hatta interrogation sessions of 8 November 1927.[148] As to Verheijen's measures, Volksraad members W. Middendorp of the ISDP and Thamrin of the Kaoem Betawi seriously began to question the government's motives for

---

[144] See 'Bijlage', pp. 1-2 attached to letter Verheijen to De Graeff, no. 1836/A.P, 26 September 1929, Mr. 905/1929, Verbaal 8 April 1930 S 7, with the manifesto also appearing in the August number of the Dutch leftist periodial *De Nieuwe Weg*. For Verheijen's reproach, see p. 2.

[145] See *Handelingen Volksraad* 1929-1930:607, 743. *Sedijo Tomo,* 3 August 1929 reported that the PNI had no connections with the SKBI, and *Bintang Timoer,* 5 August 1929 quoted Mr Soejoedi as saying that 'PNI members with SKBI connections would be expelled'.

[146] See Van der Plas' SKBI Nota of 25 April 1929 to De Graeff, p. 1, Verbaal 30 September 1929 O 10.

[147] Van der Plas to De Graeff, 22 June 1929,Verbaal 30 September 1929 O 10.

[148] Interrogation Hatta, p. 33, Verbaal 16 February 1928 A 3.

intervention, since the SKBI arrests were followed almost immediately by the freeing of 23 out of 26 detainees in Soerabaja and all 20 in Solo. Moreover, contacts with Soetomo in Soerabaja revealed that SKBI leader Marsoedi, who apart from being called an undercover agent if not a police spy, was the only one who had requested Liga affiliation in writing.[149]

As for Soekarno, although in Pekalongan and again in Soerabaja during the 28 July 1929 open-air meeting of the Indonesische Studieclub he had hinted at making some contacts with the Liga through the Leiden-based Perhimpoenan Indonesia, he appears to have abandoned these plans if he ever had them. Thamrin and Middendorp, always in close contact with the PNI leader, believed that the sudden spate of raids and arrests of SKBI members, alleged to be in close and secretive collusion with Moscow and the Berlin Liga, were merely attempts by the government to placate some of the 'hard-liners' at the top levels of its own administration, in addition to serving as a strong warning to nationalists of Soekarno's ilk to heed the government's line (Hering 1996:93-4). In the Volksraad, on 9 August 1929, Kiewiet de Jonge saw fit to distinguish between communism and extremism in the following fashion:

> [B]y communism is commonly meant that trend which directly or indirectly is inspired by Moscow, while extremism is seen as the extreme outgrowths of the nationalist movement [...] and against that extremism the government wishes to explicitly warn the PNI for the final time [...]. If, however, the government's expectations are not met or if the government feels that the [nationalist] leaders – either deliberately or by their own weakness – fail to prevent their actions from acquiring a provocative tone, or if they refuse to openly and explicitly distance themselves from any thought of violence, then intervention must occur and strong measures will have to be taken against these leaders and perhaps also against the movement itself.[150]

These admonitions directed at Soekarno's PNI must still have placated the *neo-ethici* such as Mühlenfeld, Van Gelderen and Gobée in De Graeff's bureaucratic establishment as well as Volksraad members such as Thamrin and Middendorp, since the warnings did not entirely close the door on the PNI's executive exercising self-correction and overall restraint.

Kiewiet de Jonge and Gobée in particular were to flavour their views about Soekarno and his PNI in a somewhat more positive sense. Both seem to have been influenced by developments in which Thamrin, Hatta and Soekarno

---

[149]   See Middendorp's 29 October 1929 SKBI report and the Mollen report attached to it. ISDP archive, IISG; Thamrin's written request 31 July 1929 to the Volksraad and the reports in *Fadjar Asia*, 30 July and *Oetoesan Sumatra*, 8 August 1929.

[150]   See *Handelingen Volksraad* 1929-1930:734-5. *Bintang Timoer*, 7 August 1929 suggested that 'it was time for the nationalist intellectuals to support the work of the cooperationists in the Volksraad, such as Thamrin and Middendorp', while the issue of 10 August 1929 assessed 'the RGAZ's statement [as] strong and not weak, as so many in the *sana* editorials suggested'.

played rather crucial roles. Thamrin, with the fracas about the SKBI now behind him, had been instrumental in assuring the RGAZ in the Volksraad that the PPPKI and the Perhimpoenan Indonesia were not at all tinged by communist influence. As for Hatta, he wrote to Soekarno, perhaps to counter the effect caused by the PI's pro-SKBI manifesto in late August, that he planned to 'form an international counter group of Indonesian, Chinese and Indian members outside the Liga'. Soekarno declared himself quite willing 'to meet Bandoeng *Resident* Kuneman to agree on proper conduct to be adopted at PNI meetings'. Kiewiet de Jonge commented 'that all this certainly did not indicate that the nationalists were striving to aggravate the [political] situation'.[151] As to the Inlandsche Zaken reports on the PNI meeting on 25 August 1929 in the Tanah Abang suburb of Weltevreden and the subsequent PNI meetings on 27 October 1929 held in Batavia and Bandoeng, they all evince a rather positive attitude toward Soekarno's party. The first *patih* attached to Inlandsche Zaken stated that 'the meeting was not meant as a protest against the detention of Mr Iwa Koesoema Soemantri, although the case caused surprise, but that instead the PNI took that matter with the necessary patience, since the party did not stand for violence'. The *patih* also stressed that 'the PNI would always attain its ideals without the force of arms'.[152] As to the Batavia and Bandoeng meetings, Gobée stressed 'the extraordinary large measure of sympathy these meetings were able to command', and noted that in the latter city 'the meeting hall after a well-attended meeting with close to two thousand spectators, was again filled to capacity immediately afterwards in the ensuing second meeting of that day'. He also reported Soekarno's protest 'against the opinion held by *Fadjar Asia* that the PNI was hostile to the tenets of Islam'. Soekarno is reported to have stressed once again 'that it was far from his intention to contest the teachings of Islam; he merely questioned some of the applications of those teachings'. Gobée added that 'all that was in accordance with Soekarno's remarks made earlier in Bandoeng – namely that the PNI did not aim to eradicate polygamous practices but that it rather wished to promote the cause of monogamy and make this latter practice more popular'. Gobée also stated that 'Tjokroaminoto considered the PNI stance as hostile to his own association', but 'that Soekarno in this matter, in accordance with the PPPKI's principles, would strive to avoid disunity at all costs'.[153] Gobée and Van der Plas somewhat later even attested to feelings

---

[151]   Letter Kiewiet de Jonge to De Graeff, Weltevreden, 19 October 1929, p. 2, Mr. 1016/1929.
[152]   Letter Gobée to De Graeff no. K 101, Weltevreden, 4 September 1929 and 'Bijlage', pp. 1-2 in Mr. 854/1929. In his defence plea before the Bandoeng Landraad, Soekarno (1931:104) would cite the *patih* as well.
[153]   Letter Gobée to De Graeff no. K 115, Weltevreden, 5 November 1929, pp. 1-2, Mr. 1080/1929.

within the PNI swerving toward *kooperasi*.[154] So with these progressive key members of the Indies signalling the PNI's moderating trends, room for some compromise seemed clearly to be in the offing.

The demise of Soekarno's PNI and its aftermath

However, by the end of 1929 those hopes were dashed and doomed to failure – and not because perceptions of Indonesian reactions had been ill-founded or because efforts for compromise displayed at the eleventh hour by a number of well-meaning individuals had been lacking in drive or intensity. On the contrary, the nationalist side, notably Soekarno and Thamrin, and the opposite side, with Kiewiet de Jonge, Gobée, Kuneman and Van der Plas figuring in it, actually made serious attempts at compromise as late as mid-December 1929. These were mainly attempts to clear the air in the Preanger area, since lately these districts had been riven by rumours of upheavals to take place in the year to come. Even a government-sponsored periodical *Poestaka Soenda* of December 1929 stated that: 'During this year the entire population of Pasoendan was stirred up by the news that in 1930 something important was to happen'.[155] Urged by Thamrin, Soekarno and Kiewiet de Jonge met five times, with the latter arranging for Soekarno and *Resident* Kuneman to meet and arrive at a modus vivendi the moment Soekarno returned from Solo and Djokja on New Year's Eve. During the fifth meeting with the RGAZ, Soekarno asked to be given 'a chance to organize the masses, but if something still goes awry I will still take full responsibility for it', and the RGAZ replied: 'Ir Soekarno, this is indeed a royal gesture I will be glad to relay to the government'.[156] Later, on 2 December 1930, in his defence plea before the Bandoeng Landraad, Soekarno would cite Datoek Toemenggoeng, Gobée and Van der Plas, all attached to Inlandsche Zaken, as well as the RGAZ, as being quite convinced of the PNI's aversion to violence at that time. That same day in court, Soekarno referred to a story appearing in *De Locomotief* of 28 December 1929 in which it was reported that the PNI condemned violent revolution (Soekarno 1931:104-5, 1978:144-5).

---

[154]   Hering 1985:14, note 33; Gobée's letter to De Graeff no. 93 K 2 on the 25 December 1929 PPPKI congress in Solo, p. 2, Mr. 72/1930, also in Hering 1985:248. Soekarno's defence plea (1931:104) also refers in that context to Gobée and Van der Plas.

[155]   Cited by Soekarno 1931:90, 1978:125-6.

[156]   Soekarno's testimony before the Landraad on 18 December 1930 see *Pemeriksaan* n.d.:10; *Bataviaasch Nieuwsblad*, 19 December 1930 with the headline 'Mr. Kiewiet De Jonge en PNI'; *Algemeen Indisch Dagblad* of the same date with the headline 'De Regeering en de PNI'. Marcel Koch, in a letter of 20 August 1930 to the latter accused it of departing 'from the good journalistic adat' and stated that the RGAZ's 'efforts were highly commendable and a worthy example for others to follow' (see my clipping archive).

Therefore, the sources exerting pressure on the colonial government to nonetheless act firmly and unilaterally against Soekarno's PNI at the end of 1929 must be sought elsewhere. We have already dwelt on Governor Hartelust's 16 August 1929 proposal to bar all civil servants from joining the PNI being dismissed by De Graeff. In spite of this decision, Hartelust still pressured De Graeff on 2 October 1929 for his consent to issue a circular banning all West Java police from joining the PNI. This was soon followed by army commander H.A. Cramer's circular prohibiting not only the military from joining the PNI but their families, housekeepers and servants as well. Since both these bans involved so-called *gezagsapparaten* (apparatuses of authoritative power), Verheijen departed from his earlier civil rights stance and was moreover able to persuade De Graeff to support his view and that of the army commander. Gobée and Mühlenfeld were not consulted on either of these proposals, although the latter wrote to De Graeff as late as 9 November 1929 that 'while army, navy and police personnel naturally ought to be devoted and obedient to the government, it remained questionable whether the PNI was indeed guilty of being so subversive'. Mühlenfeld argued that 'not the PNI leaders alone, but also some other parties recruiting their members exclusively from the European population are guilty of repeatedly criticizing the government', and 'authority-undermining elements are to be found among all sectors of the population', while 'it is open to question who during the last ten years has done more harm, the extremists of the right or those of the left'. In conclusion he proposed not to single out the PNI or to name it, and to only issue the bans in a general sense if urgency demanded it, a situation which he felt had not as yet developed.[157] As to these so-called PNI circulars, Middendorp was foremost in condemning them, along with many of the *sini* press outlets. *Sipatahoenan* of 15 October 1929 called it 'a matter of racist discrimination with an army colonel De Winter remaining a member of the Vaderlandsche Club'. *Timboel* of 20 October 1929 registered 'surprise at the sudden reversal of a governor-general so well disposed toward the nationalist movement', a surprise shared by *Soeloeh Ra'jat Indonesia* of 23 October 1929, but rejected by *Darmokondo* of 15 October 1929, which concluded that 'Hartelust and De Graeff after all represented one and the same repressive system' and that both would have been 'far more honest by openly declaring the PNI as dangerous'. *Banteng Priangan* of 15 November 1929 printed a PNI circular of its own, namely a PNI executive memo for 'police and army PNI members not to leave their jobs for the sake of the party, but to simply await the authorities' explanation about dismissal'.[158]

---

[157] Mühlenfeld to De Graeff, Weltevreden, 9 November 1929, no. G x 1/3/20, Verbaal 31 March 1930 N 5.
[158] See Middendorp's 19 November 1929 letter to the SDAP, IISG archive, and his article in *Het Indische Volk*, 19 November 1929. The *sini* press reactions are also in Hering 1996:98.

However, with De Graeff and Verheijen now obviously bent on calling a halt to further compromise and obviously not quite aware of last-minute attempts by their own officials to moderate the situation, the next steps taken against the PNI were all but predictable. In the face of persistent rumours of upheavals to occur in 1930,[159] and with the *gezagsapparaten* about to be cleansed of PNI-contaminated elements, massive house searches and arrests of PNI foremen were undertaken during the night of Sunday, 29 December 1929. In Soekarno's case he was arrested at Mr Soejoedi's home at Toegoe Kidoel Djokjakarta and, as the 'Ma'loemat kepada Ra'jat Indonesia dari Pengoeroes Besar Partai Nasional Indonesia' (Declaration to the Indonesian people from the main PNI executive) issued by Mr Sartono and Ir Anwari of 9 January 1939 had it, 'the entire branch executive of the Pekalongan PNI and nearly all of our executive Bandoeng branch were detained'.[160] All this, it seems, was intended to ward off the expected 1930 insurrection. The Leiden-based Hatta suggested close to a fortnight later 'that the [colonial] administration indeed made clever use of the rumours of insurrection in 1930, probably spreading them through its own undercover agents, to beat down the PNI once and for all'.[161] However, this time the police break-ins and searches – one of them so vividly described by Soekarno's wife at the time[162] – together with Mr Roskott's substantive summary of the investigation, after sifting through some 68 interrogation reports, failed dismally to yield convincing evidence of planned or underground PNI activity. Hatta again hinted 'that the car-loads of confiscated papers may well prove a blunder and a fiasco for the [colonial] government'.[163] Even so, the suspected subversive PNI activities were dismissed as early as 30 December 1929 by a *Timboel* manifesto which also declared 'to no longer regard the Indies government as a pillar of credibility'. PNI subversion was further denied on 2 January 1930 by *Sin Po*, and by S(aeroen) in a *Keng Po* editorial the next day 'as mere gossip induced by *sana* and government circles to harm the PNI'. The January 1930 issue of *Soeloeh Ra'jat Indonesia* posited that 'if the PNI leaders were really out to plan rebellion, they would not have been in Solo at the PPPKI congress'.[164] With all this coming to the surface, the question arose what to do with Soekarno and his principal lieutenants (Gatot Mangkoepradja, Maskoen and

---

[159]   For these rumours turn to Poeze 1983:xix. A more plausible source for those not involving the PNI is Van der Plas' 'Nota': 'De huidige politiek van de Agama Djawa Soenda Pasoendan', alleging *ratu adil* revivalist-inspired disturbances to start by 1930, Mr. 115/1930.

[160]   Stokvis collection IISG, for an English-language rendering of it: Hering1991b:58-9.

[161]   *De Socialist*, 10 January 1930.

[162]   Ramadhan 1981:133-4, and Gatot's contribution 'Sepatah kata sambutan' in Dachlan 1954: 12-6.

[163]   *De Socialist*, 10 January 1930.

[164]   Hering clippings archive.

Soepriadinata), who, after being detained by the police in Djokja, were now languishing in custody within the walls of Bandoeng's Bantjeuj prison. They initially shared their fate with Iskaq, Inoe Perbatasari, Moerwoto, Soeka, Soekemi and Soebagio, who however were released from Bantjeuj after one month of interrogation by *jaksa* (public prosecutor) Hendarin.[165] As for the Hoofdparket, it seemed set on having the PNI share the fate meted out to the PKI just two years earlier, while acting Attorney-General G. Vonk, not in the least embarrassed by the paucity of solid incriminating evidence, clamoured for a 'noiseless' punishment of exile for Soekarno and his followers by De Graeff's fiat.[166] This stance, however, met with resistance from some members of Batavia's official establishment, who upon De Graeff's request counselled an open and fair trial, or even acquittal, to be considered as useful options for the Indies government to pursue.[167] Eventually, De Graeff, ignoring Vonk's advice and the majority opinion of the Raad van Nederlandsch-Indië (Council of the Indies), decided in favour of a judicial trial rather than internment and exile (Hering 1982:iv, viii, notes 69, 70). For most *sana* press circles and other conservative opinion, by now well embedded organizationally in fascist or semi-fascist groupings such as the Nederlandsch-Indische Fascistische Organisatie (NIFO, Netherlands Indies Fascist Organization) and the Vaderlandsche Club, De Graeff's decision was quite unacceptable. They preferred to view the events merely as displays of PNI duplicity encouraged as usual by the government's lack of firm resolve (Hering 1991c:ix-x).

Meanwhile, in the Volksraad, during the first session of the new year, RGAZ Kiewiet de Jonge stoutly defended the preventive actions taken by the colonial administration against the PNI (*Handelingen Volksraad* 1929-1930: 1597-601), without, however, revealing his own surprise at the suddenness of the measures taken that eventful night.[168] Nor did he elaborate on the Thamrin-arranged meetings he had had at Soekarno's private Bandoeng residence just prior to the PNI leader's detainment.[169] The RGAZ issued his statement right after chairman Meijer Ranneft's word of welcome, because the administration was considering a 3 January 1930 College of Delegates' motion requesting immediate disclosure of the government's motives for its actions against the PNI (*Handelingen Gedelegeerden* 1929-1930:184-6). After

---

[165]   Gatot Mangkoepradja's 'Sepatah kata sambutan', in Dachlan 1954:22-4.

[166]   For the Hoofdparket's and Vonk's scenario see Hering 1982:i and Vonk's letter of 13 May 1930, Mr. 491/1930.

[167]   For that counsel rendered by Gobée, Schrieke and Kiewiet de Jonge, see letters of 21 and 27 May and 1 June 1930, Mr. 547/1930.

[168]   His 14 January 1930 letter to his parents, p. 1, IISG archive.

[169]   However, these meetings were revealed by 28 November 1930 in *Het Volk* of that date, causing Stokvis, then back in the Volksraad, to comment that 'with [these] talks still afoot with Soekarno as late as 9 December 1929, the alleged plausibility of PNI's disquieting stirrings look thin indeed': *Handelingen Volksraad* 1930-1931:1875.

stating that only the PNI had been targeted and no other nationalist association, the RGAZ declared that persistent rumours of disturbances planned for
early 1930, followed by well-documented reports indicating evidence of PNI
involvement, had been the prime reason for the government to act as it had.
By doing so the government 'had been faithful to the separation it had consistently drawn between socially productive and socially destructive forces
and to its promise to ward off revolutionary tendencies harmful to healthful
political growth of the indigenous community' (*Handelingen Volksraad* 1929-
1930:1600). During the ensuing debate, opinions of right-wing members and
the ten indigenous members now united in a brown-front-like Nationale
Fractie (nationalist faction) chaired by Thamrin predictably clashed about the
preventive actions taken by the government.[170] While announcing the formation of the faction, Thamrin elaborated that this nationalist grouping would
henceforth aim 'to attain Indonesian independence as quickly as possible'.
It would therefore 'devote all its activities toward constitutional reforms
and strive to abolish all political, economic, and intellectual discrimination
caused by the colonial antithesis'. It would do so 'by applying all legal means
open to it'.[171] So, faithful to the tenets of his friend Soekarno, now in jail,
Thamrin cast the die, with the dividing line separating *sana* and *sini* factional
aspirations for Indonesia's socio-political future thus distinctly drawn. That
he chose to establish the brown-front faction in the Volksraad precisely at a
time when the nationalist *pergerakan* was so severely rocked by amputation,
disarray and indecision demonstrates not only his pluck, but above all his
determination to steadfastly continue the nationalist movement's struggle in
spite of Soekarno's absence from the political scene.

That Thamrin, of all the *pergerakan* leaders, continued to keep faith with
Soekarno was demonstrated by his organizing a PPPKI protest meeting in
the Gedong Permoefakatan Indonesia as early as 12 January 1930, by his
frequent visits to Soekarno in jail whenever he had the time to do so, and
by his eliciting of outside and foreign concern for Soekarno's plight. On 24
March 1930, for instance, he submitted a written question to the government
complaining about the small (1.5 by 2.5 metre) dimensions of Soekarno's
prison cell (number five, block F). In the text, he argued that political prisoners such as Soekarno ought not to be treated as common criminals.[172] Copies

---

[170]   *Handelingen Volksraad* 1929-1930:1637-738, where Middendorp supports the PNI (pp. 1710-
4), and Ratulangi of Persatoean Minahassa, not belonging to Thamrin's Nationale Fractie, considered the government's actions as 'a blow to all nationalists' (pp. 1716-7).
[171]   *Handelingen Volksraad* 1929-1930:1646. Its members were Koesoemo Oetoyo, Mochtar
Praboe Mangkoenegara, Dwidjosewojo, Datoek Kajo, Nja Arif, Soangkoepon, Pangeran Ali,
Soetadi, Soeroso and Thamrin.
[172]   *Aanhangsel Handelingen Volksraad* 1929-1930:37. Soekarno's letter about his life in jail in *Het
Indische Volk* June 1931:105 and Inggit's description in Ramadhan 1981:243.

of this he mailed to both Stokvis in Holland, who passed it on to Dutch daily papers, and the Indonesian-language press at home. As to the PPPKI protest meeting, 'an air of renewed unity seemed to prevail', with Soetomo concluding that 'the well-attended meeting signified that feelings of anxiety (*angstneurose*) have now evaporated'. Others during the meeting viewed the RGAZ's 10 January 1930 statement of PNI culpability as extremely doubtful, and the government's measures as lacking in sufficient legal credibility.[173] In closed sessions, decisions and motions were adopted about a Fonds Nasional (national fund) to aid members and their families recently victimized by the police measures and about the PPPKI's firm will to wage actions in the ongoing fight for national freedom. Another motion labelled the government's measures as patently wrong.[174]

However, soon after this manifestation of renewed unity, PPPKI resolve seems to have evaporated rather swiftly. Thamrin, for instance, must have sensed that with the PNI's imaginative and cohesive leadership gone and its propaganda machine gagged, divergent forces within the PPPKI were bound to emerge, along with efforts to exploit the present vacuum in Indonesia's body politic.[175] The PSII, with the word 'Indonesia' now proudly added to its name, had been quite aware that for some time the PNI had been making inroads into the overall urban sector. PSII's rural position, especially in the Preanger, so close to Soekarno's political nerve centre located in Bandoeng, had always been shaky. Moreover, the PSII had been plagued by intellectual nationalist allegations that its social record was not up to par as compared to that of the PNI, Soetomo's Studieclub or even the progressive, Islamic-oriented Moehammadijah. So, as one keen conservative observer predicted: 'the federationist roof constructed in the past by both the PSII and the PNI is about to collapse, because the pillars of Indonesianism and Islamism diverge rather sharply' (Petrus Blumberger 1931:274). No wonder the PSII, with the PNI's future prospects now hanging much in the balance, considered the time ripe to recoup its losses and to restore some of its injured prestige. On 28 December 1930 it withdrew from the PPPKI, giving the reason that PPPKI

---

[173]   See Mr. 79/1930, for an Inlandsche Zaken report on it.
[174]   See Mr. 79/1930, for an Inlandsche Zaken report on it. *Bintang Timoer,* 13 January 1930 prints these motions and decisions, while in its 17 January issue it cites Salim about the government relying only upon *kabar angin* (rumours) and *surat kaleng* (anonymous letters). In its 27 January 1930 issue it hailed Iskaq's release and hoped 'that the *kepala banteng* [Soekarno] will be freed soon as well'; *Timboel,* January 1930 issue felt that 'confidence in the government has melted as snow in the sun'.
[175]   19 January 1930 letter to Stokvis, file 115, IISG archives.

unity was more of a sham than a fact.[176] Soetomo, faced with similar waxing PNI prospects in his own urban stronghold and with plans afoot to turn his socially and economically constructive Indonesische Studieclub into a full-fledged political party, saw chances looming his way as well.[177] That party, named the Persatoean Bangsa Indonesia (PBI, Indonesian People's Union) and seeing itself as an alternative to the PNI, came into being on 11 November 1930.[178] Even Hatta in far-away Holland, after initially making some positive comments about Soekarno and his PNI, soon embarked upon a strongly critical campaign meant to ridicule Soekarno's erstwhile federationist and party constructs. Here Hatta can be seen as rekindling earlier efforts for a party of his own making, and his broadsides can thus be interpreted as preparing the ground for such a Hatta-led grouping to emerge the moment he returned to his native soil (Hering 1991b:ii, vi, notes 11, 12). These developments, as well as those concerned more directly with Soekarno's experiences during 1930-1934, are dealt with in the next chapter.

---

[176] 'Makloemat L.T. PSII tentang fasal jang djadi pembitjaraan dalam actie oemoem pada 28 Desember 1930', *Lasjkar*, no. 4-5, 1930.
[177] Letter to Stokvis, 2 February 1930, p. 2, file 115, IISG archives.
[178] *Soeloeh Ra'jat Indonesia*, 12 November 1930.

CHAPTER V

Soekarno's trial, Soekamiskin and the Partindo years
A tryst with destiny?

The road to Soekarno's trial

In the wake of Soekarno's arrest, the soul of the emancipatory nationalist movement seemed to evaporate, and as Jan Pluvier stated a generation later, 'a pensive stillness' set in after years of fiery, Soekarno-inspired anti-colonial agitation (Pluvier 1953:4). However, some of the spirit rekindled at the time of the Bandoeng Landraad (district court) trial of Soekarno and associates. In the 1930-1931 Volksraad, Governor-General De Graeff, on 16 June 1930, stated that Soekarno, Gatot Mangkoepradja, Maskoen and Soepriadinata were thought to have been in violation of articles 153 bis and 169, and that hence their case would be tried before the Landraad court.[1] In the Volksraad, the nationalist faction members Thamrin and Dwidjosewojo responded to these decisions. Dwidjosewojo, reiterating Thamrin's complaints about the small dimensions of Soekarno's Bantjeuj cell, held that Soekarno, 'like a true ksatria, would undergo this shabby treatment'. He further endorsed the views of a *De Stuw* article that the '29 December 1929 activities of the government were in no proportion to what the PNI was now charged for'.[2]

As for Thamrin, he argued that the duumvirate De Graaff-Fock and De Graaf-De Graeff had merely taken an increasingly stiffer approach toward

---

[1]   *Handelingen Volksraad* 1930-1931:9-10. Article 153 bis made it a crime to contribute by speaking or writing, directly or by implication, to the disturbance of public order or to impede or to violate Netherlands Indies authority. Article 169 prohibited organizations which encouraged their members to commit felonies or misdemeanors.

[2]   *Handelingen Volksraad* 1930-1931:122. The *De Stuw* article appeared in the 20 June 1930 issue. *De Stuw* was a moderately progressive association formed – the day after Soekarno's arrest – by European ethically minded civil servants and college professors from the Leiden School of Snouck Hurgronje and Van Vollenhoven and strove to promote a policy of emancipation in order to ultimately establish an 'independent Indies commonwealth'. Due to its sympathy for Indonesian nationalism it was labeled from the start by most of the *sana* press as 'extreme leftist': Locher-Scholten 1981:118-9.

the *pergerakan*. He also felt that by abandoning the initial charges upon which the 29 December actions were founded and then pulling out of the hat new penal articles such as 153 bis and 169, the government showed how ill-timed and wrong it had been. Moreover, by using article 169 the government showed its intent to label the PNI a criminal association, thus paving the way for the party to be banned. He therefore asked what steps would be taken against the persons in the government who were responsible for this blunder. He further stressed that the *pergerakan*, though quiet at the moment, was tired of undergoing all these futile experiments cooked up by legal experts. In this connection, he argued it would be far better to have the PNI culprits heard by a more neutral and higher court such as the Supreme Court (Hooggerechtshof), since 'there the right of a defence and a justification of motives would be far better guaranteed than in the case of the simpler procedures followed by a Landraad'. In the latter case, '[the government] probably wishes the Landraad to establish whether a party striving for national independence is often also a party deemed to commit crimes', and here Thamrin asked 'whether such a delicate political issue needed to be determined by the lower court at all', since 'a lower court judge in any case ought not to function as an inquisitor, neither is it the task of the government to do so; on the contrary, they should both honour the liberty of conscience of all individuals under their jurisdiction'.[3]

These fears, as we shall see below, were confirmed all too clearly by the authoritative and inquisitorial behaviour displayed by Landraad president Mr R. Siegenbeek van Heukelom and his star witness, Bandoeng's police commissioner H.H. Albreghs. On 26 July 1930, the PNI leaders in Bantjeuj prison were served with an indictment charging them – in addition to the charges announced earlier in the Volksraad (articles 169 and 153 bis) – under article 171 (an article which deals with false reports deliberately aimed at disturbing public peace and order), article 110 *oud* (which deals with collusion in revolution and of illegally overthrowing the Netherlands Indies form of government), articles 108 and 109 *oud* (dealing with revolution and criminal activity) and article 163 bis (dealing with inciting other persons to carry out deeds with implements sufficient to accomplish such tasks).[4] On 4 August 1930, PNI defence attorneys Mr Soejoedi, Mr Sartono, Mr Sastromoeljono and Raden Idih Prawiradipoetra were finally allowed to enter Bantjeuj

---

[3]   *Handelingen Volksraad* 1930-1931:123-6, 131. On 31 July 1931 Thamrin moved to state 'the raids to be ill founded': *Handelingen Volksraad* 1931-1932:602-3, his motion did not carry (p. 640). Thamrin's objections concerning the lower court were later vindicated by RHS law professor Julius Schepper; see note 24.

[4]   Dachlan 1954:34, 36; *Bataviaasch Nieuwsblad*, 26 July 1930 with the heading 'De acte van verwijzing; De PNI gekwalificeerd als opvolgster der PKI' (The act of committal; The PNI qualified as the successor of the PKI).

prison in order to discuss the case with the four PNI leaders.[5]

Meanwhile, Soekarno's wife Inggit was having a difficult time. At first she was not allowed to make any visits to her husband in Bantjeuj at all. Later, often accompanied by Omi and Gatot's wife, she was allowed to take some food to the prison, but still not to meet her husband face to face, under the pretext that interrogations of Soekarno and his co-defendants were still going on. Finally, after more than a month, she and Omi were able to meet him face to face in the visitors' room and to take him some of the delicious food he was so fond of. Another visit was marred by the news of Omi having typhoid fever and thus not able to see her adopted father for a while. After Omi recovered and was again visiting him together with Inggit, he almost broke down upon seeing her so thin and so weak in outlook. Also, Soekarno showed increasing anxiety about Inggit managing matters adequately at home. Inggit told him not to worry, since she was coping as well as she could, now being an agent selling soap, cigarettes and even chopping-knives (*parang*), in addition to a small income from mending clothes. Moreover, she pressed him 'to stay firm and not to give up the struggle even if matters look a bit grim at the moment'.[6] In talking to him that way, Inggit must have sensed how deeply her erstwhile *singa* (lion) on the podium was wrestling with the misery of isolation. Years later, Soekarno said: 'it was a shattering experience. [...] I could not take the isolation, rigidity, filth, the rigidity, the million little humiliations of the lowest form of prison life' (Adams 1965:97). However, Inggit mentioned a Dutch warder named Bos, who was married to a Sundanese and had a child attending a Taman Siswa school. This official often had friendly talks with her husband and provided the latter with several *sini* papers, such as the Sundanese periodical *Sipatahoenan* and the Chinese daily *Sin Po*.[7] When the Landraad trial finally started on 18 August 1930, Inggit again displayed her undaunted spirit by being there throughout the entire trial proceedings near the front row. There, she and Omi were often accompanied by Thamrin, Tjokroaminoto, A. Hassan, Soewarsih and Soegondo Djojopoespito, as well as by members of the families of Gatot Mangkoepradja, Maskoen and Soepriadinata. During breaks, Soekarno and the co-defendants, in a separate room of the Landraad, were allowed to mingle more intimately with their families and with some good friends such as Thamrin and Stokvis (Ramadhan 1981:177-8; Stokvis 1931a:11).

[5]   Gatot Mangkoepradja in Dachlan 1954:24; Paget 1975:lxxiii.
[6]   'Tegakkan dirimu Kus tegakkan! Teruskan perjuanganmu! Jangan luntur karena cobaan semacam ini!', Ramadhan 1981:145-7, 157-8, 160-2, 168-9.
[7]   Ramadhan 1981:170-1; Gatot Mangkoepradja in Dachlan 1954:25. In a 28 October 1931 letter to Stokvis, Soekarno stated in Bantjeuj 'socio-political works, daily papers and periodicals were to reach me': Hering 1991b:28.

Some observations about Soekarno's trial

From the start of Soekarno's trial, it was clear to him, his co-defendants and their defence attorneys that the prosecution would cling to legal etiquette and procedure. The fact that Soekarno and his associates had been hauled before the Landraad on an even greater number of charges of subversion than earlier was the case made them perfectly aware that the whole legal process was a pre-arranged ploy by the colonial authorities and that they were in court merely to receive a heavy sentence. Accordingly, it must have dawned on Soekarno that, rather than wasting his time on defending himself against the charges, it was better to go onto the offensive by laying bare all aspects of the racist colonial system. And as we will see below, this tactic reached its climax in his ably prepared marathon defence oration, a plea which was to become known later by its title 'Indonesia Accuses!' and has since become a key historical document for the future of the Indonesian people.[8] But long before the two-day delivery of his defence plea, Soekarno was able to touch on the real political issues, and so he often outsmarted the prosecution, whose main initial intent was merely to taint the PNI as the banned PKI's successor as well as having intimate contacts with communist-contaminated associations such as the Leiden-based Perhimpoenan Indonesia and the Berlin-based Liga. The president of the Landraad and then its star witness, police commissioner Henri Hubert Albrechs, tried for days on end to establish these links – obviously with article 153 bis in mind, since it was that article of the Penal Code that had originally caused the PKI to be banned.

Even Kiewiet de Jonge confided to De Graeff, then on a three-week state visit to Siam, his concern about the approach taken by the Landraad president, who acted as both judge and accuser.[9] Mainly, since the latter, during a dinner in Bandoeng's Preanger hotel with the RGAZ and Mrs Titia Kiewiet de Jonge-née Jelgersma,

> tended strongly to the views held by Mr Vonk (who moreover ignored my advice) of consulting an expert sociologist to assess why former PKI members joined the PNI and why there was a relation between the Leiden-based PI and the PNI. If he had looked into them, these relations would have proved to be quite normal and not necessarily criminal.

Also, Kiewiet de Jonge found it 'indeed remarkable that the notorious Organization plan [drafted by Semaoen and found during the police search of Perhimpoenan Indonesia's office in The Hague on 10 June 1927] and some

---

[8]   For this shining example of a nationalist rebuttal of the racist colonial regime see the excellent translation of it in Paget 1975:1-142.
[9]   For this label see also Jonkers 1940:53.

other documents which have been available for some time were only on 15 October brought into a case that started on 18 August'. So he wondered whether

> such withholding of important documents by the prosecution, which were already known to it at the start of proceedings, was indeed justified, given what is stated in article 277 of the Inlandsch Reglement [Native Regulations]? Even more questionable, I think, about such withholding is that now, by the suggestion of a climax, many will a priori tend to see this late-produced material as most import-ant documents for proving the defendants guilty. And that is indeed the highest trump card played in this game by the prosecution.[10]

These objections by the RGAZ do seem to help explain the court's accept-ance from one expert witness, Albreghs, of fourteen days of largely unreli-able hearsay testimony that had been extracted from a succession of rather humble PNI members. These members were paraded before the Landraad terrified and often utterly confused, and forced again to make vague state-ments about their understanding – or indeed lack of it – of the PNI's capacity for fomenting unrest in unison with persons already tainted by communist beliefs. As one expert had it in 1975, it all amounted to:

> Sweeping vague charges mostly based upon hearsay evidence, imputations of guilt by association, blatant reliance upon agents provocateurs, and expert testi-mony admitted to record though riddled with conjectural opinion – such were the techniques of the prosecution and the disposition of the court. The defence was as easy as it was irrelevant to the outcome, and, knowing the verdict beforehand, the four lawyers played a different game. Unctiously deferential to the judges, they proceeded meticulously, point by point, to demolish the prosecution's case. At every opportunity, however, they would appear to step back from their material and, still in deferential posture, tutor the judges in elementary judicial procedure. Sastromoeljono, for example, would cite Mr I.A. Nederburgh, professor of law at the University of Utrecht, in one instance, on the most basic principle of what kind of evidence and opinion from an expert witness constitutes admissible testi-mony. In this light, the court's acceptance, from one expert witness, Henri Hubert Albreghs [...] was made to appear patently ridiculous. [...] One can only imagine the extreme irritation of the judges and the glee of the nationalists as the trial turned into a spectacle. (Paget 1975:lxxii.)

Along with that of their lawyers, the PNI leaders' own defence, particularly that of Soekarno, proved to be quite spirited and more than a match for the prosecution. During hours of extensive cross-examination, they ably frus-trated all the efforts of the court to label their party as being linked with

---

[10]   Private survey sent to De Graeff, at the Paruskawan Palace, Bangkok, by RGAZ Kiewiet de Jonge, 15 November 1930, Collection Kiewiet de Jonge, IISG archives. For article 277 see Poser 1927:84-5.

the banned PKI, the Liga or the Comintern, or as being merely a source of fomenting strife and unrest. Instead, they demonstrated that the PNI had remained within the bounds of Netherlands Indies law, and had never planned or advocated armed uprisings against the colonial government. This point was further substantiated by the testimony of a highly placed representative of the government, the RGAZ Mr Ir Kiewiet de Jonge, who stated from the witness stand on the fortieth day of the trial on 21 October 1930, that 'Soekarno had asked permission to denounce the rumours of an uprising and was further willing to have discussions with Bandoeng's *resident* about quelling it' since the PNI 'did not want these incidents'. A discussion was arranged but, according to the RGAZ, did not eventuate, due to Soekarno's being detained.[11] Even a last-minute trump card produced by the court to establish definitively that Soekarno had advocated a resort to force in writing, when investigated by a handwriting expert (the military apothecary H.E. de Zoete) proved not to be written by Soekarno at all.[12] As to the many rebuttals made by the defendants and their lawyers during most of the 84 days in court, they lacked the substance and grandiose delivery of the masterly performance of Soekarno's own 170-page defence plea, delivered in Indonesian (labelled Malay by the *sana* press)[13] on 1 and 2 December 1930.

Soekarno's preface to his defence plea

Well aware of the fact that he was awarded centre-stage during these two days, Soekarno, with all the dexterity of his oratory, delivered a marathon and rather clever defence plea studded with official and other irrefutable data in order to render its message in still more potent terms. It had been prepared during the seven and a half months of detention between Soekarno's first day in Bantjeuj prison and the start of his trial the following August. It was in many ways an impressive soliloquy, with Soekarno clearly presenting a cogent set of Indonesian arguments, though always closely wedded to the vernacular of European and other Western sources of political thought. It communed more with the spirit of the West than with echoes of Indonesian intellectualism, replete as it was with reference to European social-democratic and trade-union tenets being the PNI's intellectual guide and not at

---

[11]   *De Locomotief*, 22 October and *Java Bode*, 23 October 1930, with the latter reporting that the RGAZ saw 'Soekarno as prone to some Marxist ideas but also thinking as a liberal democrat', an observation which caused the Landraad president to retort that the RGAZ 'was now moving into the field of the defence'. In reply the RGAZ was 'still convinced that Soekarno's mass organizations followed the pattern adopted by the social-democrats'.

[12]   *De Locomotief*, 7 November 1930; also cited by Dahm 1969:125, note 226.

[13]   See for instance *Algemeen Indisch Dagblad* and *De Locomotief*, 1 December 1930.

all the views of the banished PKI. It was an effort to further undermine the thrust and parry of the prosecution, taking the wind out of its sails. From the outset of his delivery, Soekarno maintained in his preface that this 'was indeed a political trial and therefore one needed to understand that political issues could not be separated from the fact that these formed the foundation of the PNI's character as well as being the source of its basic aims'. Also, these issues were the basis not only of the thought but also of the soul of the four defendants. And so he trusted that the judges, with

> we, the defendants, arriving later to explain these issues more fully, not only would maintain strict neutrality but also be cognizant of the fact that we are not making propaganda just for the sake of our political beliefs. On the contrary, we would like you to learn about the aims, the nature and the actions of the PNI so that you can judge and understand our own political views as well as the signific-ance and intention of our statements and actions. This and this alone is the aim of my plea.

Soekarno then tackled the elasticity of the articles of law he and his co-defend-ants had been charged with, reminding the judges that 'from the onset of their publication, articles like 161 bis and 153 bis had been criticized by him and other Indonesian politicians since we consider them a real impediment to the freedom of assembly'. The so-called hate-sowing articles prohibiting the spreading of hostile opinions also fell into that category, and here he asked if 'the hate-sowing articles gained fame as the worst of all elastic regu-lations, what label should then be given to an article such as 153 bis, which as early as 1926 had been labelled by Mendels in the Second Chamber of the Dutch parliament as a horrible criminal law the likes of which he had not seen in recent years?' Soekarno continued, citing Mendels as stating: 'this is not only illegality pure and simple, but terror with the law on its side'. Then, referring to law professor David Simons, Soekarno noted that, 'aside from the elastic articles there is another problem: to what extent and in what fashion does criminal law have to take into account the beliefs or convictions of the accused?' Soekarno concluded his preface by stating:

> It therefore remains imperative for us, the defendants, to elaborate on all of the most essential features of our political convictions, in addition to the relevant aspects of our nationalist movement, in order that you, honourable judges, will clearly understand that the PNI and we as individuals are not guilty at all of the charges now brought against us. We beg your honours' pardon if for our defence we are obliged to require many hours of your time. We further beg your honours' pardon if now and then we draw upon passages from learned books and sources. We offer these to assist us in demonstrating that what we are stating is outside the realm of fabrication – particularly when it touches upon matters which may be bit-ter and painful – and represents our own honest views based upon the perception of wise and upright men. To but one of the President's questions of interrogation,

we answer that no matter how objective we are, as standard bearers of the left we indeed observe much more evil than good in the present state of our nation and our people. So we are known as being severe critics of the miserable condition this country and its people has been put in. And indeed we think we had cause to be critical. Yet by doing so we have never uttered falsehoods nor did we stray from justice.[14]

The main thrust of Soekarno's defence plea

In the next five parts of his plea, Soekarno dealt with Imperialism Old and New and its Outgrowth Capitalism; Imperialism in Indonesia; The Indonesian Movement; The Partai Nasional Indonesia; The Violations of Articles 169 and 153 bis.[15] In the first two parts he noted that imperialism, which he saw as 'an economically determined requirement', had been practised throughout the centuries 'by white-skinned, yellow-skinned, black-skinned and even by brown-skinned people like ourselves, as was demonstrated by the lust for gain and empire by such Indonesian states as Modjopahit and Sriwidjaja' (Soekarno 1931:9, 1978:10). As to modern imperialism, and here Soekarno cited J.S. Bartstra, 'it was truly a drive toward unlimited colonial expansion from 1880 to the present that was adopted by most great civilized nations in order to secure their own industrial gains and banking capital'. While it 'brought some knowledge, progress and civilization, its primary motives remained in the realm of making profit'. Then, referring to Abraham Kuyper's book *Antirevolutionaire staatkunde*, Soekarno argued that in such a process 'the relationship is and will remain a purely mercantile one, enriching the colonizer but more often than not impoverishing the colonized indigenes'. Soekarno concluded that 'for his PNI, the roots of colonialism pure and simple were vested in materialism and the insatiable lust for profit' (Soekarno 1931:13-4, 1978:16-8).

In the next part Soekarno dwelt on the evils of that drive, as recently experienced in his homeland. He argued that 'open-door' imperialism had formed a constant drain by alien capitalist forces sapping the far weaker indigenous resources. This process started in the seventeenth and eighteenth centuries, when monopolistic enterprises such as the East Indies Company successfully enslaved indigenous kingdoms one after the other outside and inside Java, enabling them to extract – by means of levies and quotas – agri-

---

[14]   Soekarno 1931:5-7, 1978:5-7; *Pemeriksaan* n.d.:242-3; *Algemeen Indisch Dagblad*, 1 December 1930.
[15]   Soekarno 1978:123 adds to the chapter heading of this part of Soekarno's plea the words *Adalah mokhal* (They [the articles] are absurd) while Soekarno 1931, translated from Indonesian into Dutch by Soetan Sjahrir, does not.

cultural produce from the indigenous population through the medium of indigenous chiefs. This population's own economy was stifled by the East Indies Company's monopolistic methods, and the levies soon came close to being economically exhausted. After the demise of the East Indies Company at the end of the eighteenth century, the system found a worthy successor in the nineteenth century with the introduction of the so-called Cultivation System. This system, Soekarno noted, was 'one of massive forced labour far more cruel, far more oppressive and truly slashing like a whip on the backs and shoulders of our people' (Soekarno 1931:18, 20, 1978:23, 26). Drawing on a host of authorities, he then elaborated upon the dire consequences for his people during the entire period of the Cultivation System.

Referring to Karl Kautsky's *Sozialismus und Kolonialpolitik* (Socialism and colonial policies), H.E.B. Schmalhausen's *Over Java en de Javanen* (About Java and the Javanese) and G.F.E. Gonggrijp's *Schets eener economische geschiedenis van Nederlandsch-Indië* (Survey of the economic history of the Netherlands Indies), Soekarno held that the increase in production facilitated by modern transport facilities did indeed benefit public progress, though nonetheless causing movement of private capital to that rapidly expanded and branched out. And in the process, this caused quite severe disruptions of the common people's means of livelihood. As Kautsky noted, 'under these circumstances technological progress became indeed a means of agricultural plunder and impoverishment'. Schmalhausen wrote that: 'Java possesses railways and streetcars, but an extensive part of its tenured land has been both exploited and reclaimed. Also, many sugar-cane and indigo plantations have been started', and then asking: 'Has all this really been able to keep the well-being of these areas from deteriorating instead of advancing?' Gonggrijp concluded that 'world market mass production together with all the modern means of communication as yet have not succeeded in making a clearly visible impact on the welfare of the indigenous masses'. Soekarno made a dig at article 161 bis in stating that 'this article forbids the right to strike and so, with no protective labour legislation existing in our country, our labourers are exploited at will, making the capitalists feel they are living in a heavenly paradise'.[16] At the end of this part of his plea, Soekarno, after citing Boeke's and Huender's description of the increasing poverty among the indigenous masses,[17] made the following observations:

---

[16] Soekarno 1931:25-6, 1978:33-5. As to Karl Kautsky, he was the theorist Soekarno valued the most, since through him Soekarno came in touch with Western explanations of Indonesia's plight and of the political ends of by Indonesian nationalism, see Paget 1975:xxxxvii.

[17] Soekarno 1931:32, 1978:42. Boeke stated that 'the impoverished Javanese farmers could not exert any influence on improving their miserable existence ever', while Huender established 'the income of an average indigenous family of five as being eight cents a day'.

Modern imperialism has made our indigenous people into a nation of paupers, and our nation into a pauper among nations! And about our paupers, respected judges, their wages indeed amount to subsistence wages. The economy in which they live is indeed a mere subsistence economy! No wonder our national spirit rebels against the evils of such a modern imperialism! Moreover, who will ever restore the wealth removed from Indonesia by private coal- and oil-mining prospectors! Who is able to return this mineral wealth? This source of wealth will never again be ours, since it has disappeared into the pockets of the shareholders of these imperialist enterprises! And, as Professor Van Gelderen puts it, 'mining operations will sooner or later exhaust their sources of wealth [...] and the object of all these coal and oil activities will then be irretrievably lost!' Lost forever – indeed not such a happy prospect to ponder [...] still, there may be something else to offset these harsh economic realities. What about the rights enjoyed by our people? Could granting such rights be a means of hopefully lifting their grieved national spirits somewhat? Let us see, by tackling education first. Alas, what do we see here in this civilized century of ours: only seven per cent of our males are literate, while of our females only a half per cent are so endowed. [A]s to the right to strike, a given in all civilized countries, that right in our country, because of article 161 bis, has gone up in smoke. As to freedom of the press, of association and of assembly – can we really maintain that our people enjoy these rights? Of course not; these rights do not exist under a Penal Code allowing unlimited interpretations of the elastic hate- and discord-sowing articles, and the even more elastic 153 bis/ter article, which is a menace to our journalists and political leaders who can be gagged at will [...]. Are our rights not violated when a mere critical observation in public is liable to severe reprimand or even arrest, where police spies attend our public meetings, where our leaders are being tailed and our meetings disbanded out of hand or even prohibited altogether, and where even our confidential letters are opened at will? What remains of our rights when police spies' reports and anonymous letters are considered sufficient justification for house searches to be carried out, for detaining dozens of our leaders or for sending some of them into exile? At times, the iron fist of the law has been felt by our journalists; almost every one of our Indonesian leaders has once or twice been incarcerated, while nearly all of the Indonesians starting a radical struggle have been labelled as dangerous to the public order! Truly no rights have been granted to the Indonesian people, rights badly needed to counteract the catastrophic havoc wrought upon our society and upon our livelihood. (Soekarno 1931:34-6, 1978:45-8.)

In the next part, dealing with the Indonesian *pergerakan*, Soekarno dwelt on how and why this movement had come about. After briefly sketching how through the centuries freedom movements, including the Dutch struggle to liberate themselves from Spanish oppression, had arisen in Europe, and more recently in Africa and Asia, Soekarno maintained that his own country since 1908 had responded in that way as well. Quoting the Dutch Second Chamber member J.W. Albarda as saying that the Indonesian *pergerakan* 'will go forward and will no doubt reach its ultimate goal: liberty of the Indonesian people from foreign colonial rule', Soekarno, sensing that his judges would dismiss this observation coming from a socialist, then quoted Dr H. Kraemer, 'by no means an adherent of socialism'. Kraemer denied 'the widespread conception of the Eastern awakening being limited since it involved only a thin layer of indigenous intellectuals whose numbers were moreover quite negligible. The "silent masses", willing or not, find themselves therefore in a melting pot.' Professor Snouck Hurgronje, also mentioned as a source who did not belong in the camp of the dogmatists, was quoted:

the seedbed, then as now, was never the overbreeding of some thousands of Western-schooled indigenous intellectuals not absorbed by their own indigenous society, but rather the wish, deeply cherished everywhere, and sometimes openly expressed but more often hidden, the wish to oppose being ruled by people of another 'bangsa' [race]. (Soekarno 1931:36-8, 1978:49-52.)

Then Soekarno, repeating one of the opening phrases of his own 1926 landmark address, told the judges: 'the sun rises not because the cock crows; the cock crows because the sun rises!' And he continued,

As for those who still doubt the authenticity of the freedom movements, we quote Jean Jaurès, the great leader of the French labour movement, who spoke to the National Assembly as follows: 'How blinded are you as to suggest that only a few sparked the present universal evolution? Are you then not touched by the world-wide evolution of the nationalist movements which at the moment are blossoming everywhere in all those countries which are still not free? In the last ten years it is no longer possible to sketch the history of Egypt, India, China, the Philippines and Indonesia without recording the story of their nationalist movements! [...] In the presence of these developments, is it still proper to suggest that these movements are caused only by a few troublemakers? These provocateurs, as you call them, are given far too much credit by you, since it is not through their efforts alone that this powerful movement was unleashed, but by the roots of it. And these roots of the movement are to be found in the depths of events themselves; they stem from the infinite sufferings of those who had not joined forces until they found some relief in the promise of a call which promised to set them free. The truth is that, in Indonesia, the nationalist movement arose from the imperialist system so adored by you, and from the concomitant system of economic drainage operating in this country for centuries. Imperialism is thus the great troublemaker and the great provocateur – so much so that it should be hauled before the gendarmes! [...] Indeed, haul it before the police and before the judges! And yet [...] not imperialism, not the imperialists, not the friends of imperialism, not Treub, not Trip, not Colijn, not Bruineman, not Fruin, not Alimoesa, not Wormser are hauled before the court, but rather the four of us who stand here before you: Gatot Mangkoepradja, Maskoen, Soepriadinata, and Soekarno! Alas, we accept our fate, since that is the consequence of our being leaders! Moreover, we do not feel guilty of having committed the crimes we are here accused of. So we therefore expect a verdict of not guilty![18]

---

[18]   Soekarno 1931:38-9, 1978:52-3. As to Colijn and Treub, we have met them before; Bruine-

In the next part, also the most lengthy of the six sections of his plea, Soekarno devoted himself largely to the Partai Nasional Indonesia. This is no doubt the heart of his entire plea and was aimed to convince the judges about that party's lofty aims to guide and prepare its followers for a cause which, though it was revolutionary in concept, did not engage in criminally subversive activities. From the outset, Soekarno stressed that the principles of his party were basically not different from those held by the labour movements of Europe and the United States, in the sense that labour had to gain power politically before socialism could be realized. Here he cited section eleven of the information manual of the Dutch SDAP: 'by gaining political power the proletariat will break capitalist resistance to the transfer of the means of production from private to public control'. In other words, 'only by gaining power politically will a colonially dominated people ever manage to break imperialist resistance to indigenous reconstruction' (Soekarno 1931:41-2, 1978:57-8).

Therefore, Soekarno's PNI, for the purpose of securing that lofty aim, would function as the primary agent of change. Although envisaging a large-scale revolution and systematic evolution, the PNI would remain wary of turning it into a bloody transition. This absence of violence he stressed, since 'our struggle will not be fought with swords or rifles or with bombs or through the violations mentioned in articles 153 and 169'. And although the 'PNI, from the start, was indeed a revolutionary party, it did not wish to wage a rebellion nor did it wish to break the law. [It] was radical and not moderate, since it wanted to accelerate reform.' Citing Kautsky's *Der Weg zur Macht*, (The road to power) Soekarno pointed out that

> the social-democratic party was indeed revolutionary, but not a party waging a revolutionary rebellion. [It] is not because the PNI is a revolution-making party, it is because the PNI is out to abolish anything that may hamper the evolution of our people. [...] To say it once again, the PNI is revolutionary and we are revolutionaries with the sole purpose of creating a rapid *Umgestaltung von Grund aus* [complete transformation]. [...] So, what is the use of bombs and dynamite if we of the PNI are already convinced of reaching our aims through our spiritual organization of power?

Here he referred to the 'Srikandi of India', the poetess Sarojoni Naidu, who maintained: 'Who can ever chain a people when their spirit refuses to be chained? Who can ever destroy a people when their spirit refuses to be destroyed?' (Soekarno 1931:53-4, 60-2, 1978:75-6, 84-7). In the final section of this part devoted to the PNI, Soekarno dealt first with the so-called 'spiritual

---

man, Fruin, Alimoesa were right-wing Volksraad members, Trip a bank president and Wormser a *sana* press magnate.

organization' and then expounded on the actual moves in realizing the 'outward manifestation of the PNI's organization of power'.

In order to build up that spiritual awakening, 'the PNI would devote all its efforts to promoting the fervour for freedom among our people. Moreover, our tormented people share that fervour for freedom with the proletariat of the industrialized states.' However, perhaps mindful of Cramer's advice he had cited earlier, Soekarno was quite aware that class conflict due to the exploitation of the labouring classes in Europe and America was gradually being reduced due to the growth of trade unions and by emerging political parties of a liberal or social-democratic ilk. Therefore, 'in his country the PNI ought to awaken the nationalist spirit mainly because here no such evolution has as yet taken place, due to the fact that the white colonial upper class, faced by a brown mass of toilers, deemed the latter to be distinctly inferior'. Another point Soekarno made was that in the industrialized nations such racist elements did not occur, since on both sides people belonged to a single race, while in his country it was a conflict between white and brown, between East and West, between colonized and colonizer. So in order to lift up his people spiritually, 'a three-pronged approach was needed for the PNI: first, to make the brown Indonesian masses quite aware of their glorious past which, though feudal in nature, was still capable of inner growth; secondly, to remind them that their present plight is empty and sick and not generating any growth; and lastly, to confront them with the promise of a bright future soon to dawn'. Here, Soekarno told his judges 'that the PNI's entire effort had been to create a tight organization of men working steadfastly to realize tomorrow's promises'. 'As to the outcome of these, that was no longer a riddle, since our people, who flourished so well in the past, though they are now nearly lifeless, will still be capable of reviving the grandeur of their past and indeed will surpass it!'[19]

Coming back to the present, Soekarno held that 'the imperialist system in our country not only initiated a policy of divide and rule, a policy of sowing discord, but also deliberately kept our people in a state of backwardness, in addition to creating the myth of white superiority, with a belief that a policy of association would bring unity between the white and brown races'. All this was anathema to him, and he said that his PNI was dead set against these policies and would instead lift up his people:

> So far we have created a spiritual organization of power with the aim of recreating some unity among our people, of warding off intellectual decay and feelings of inferiority, but now we must achieve a more concrete physical organization to reach out to the masses [...]. The PNI's conception of such is a movement capable of arousing thousands, ten thousands, even hundreds of thousands of our people.

---

[19]   Soekarno 1931:63-7, 1978:88-93. As to Cramer see Soekarno 1931:55, 1978:77.

(Soekarno 1931:67-8, 71-4, 1978:94-5, 101-5.) […]

So what about this PNI's physical organization of power: it is like a national freedom movement and a reform movement all in one [...] as Albarda suggested in his address [of 19 December 1919] to the Second Chamber of the Dutch parliament: 'the indigenous movement, like social democracy, has a twofold target: it strives to realize its aims for the future while at present it attempts to achieve improvements for the masses whose ideals it serves. As with social democracy, it hopes by struggle to achieve improvements of conditions rapidly, as well as raising intellectual standards and training of the masses whose goals it serves'. [S]o our movement, while striving toward freedom, is also active in getting reforms for our people realized in the present. […] However, mass protest, with a view to the immediate future, lacking theories, courses, brochures, news outlets and other organs, is indeed a mass protest bereft of a soul or a will. And yet it is the will that is the genuine driving force for mass protest to succeed! (Soekarno 1931: 79-80, 1978:111-3.)

As Karl Kautsky, the famous theoretician of proletarian mass protest in Europe, writes in his *Der Weg zur Macht*:

The will to fight is determined firstly by the price of it being worthy to struggle for, secondly by the combatants' own sense of power, and lastly by the real strength of their power. The higher the price the stronger the will, the more daring the combatants the more energetically they will bundle their strength to secure the price. [Also] theory remains essential for raising the strength of the people's power [...] since theory not only enlarges the active potential of the people but also expands their perception of being powerful.

Turning to his judges, Soekarno stated that his own PNI

teaches theory through its courses, brochures and news outlets, dealing with the impact of imperialism, the problems faced by our own movement and by those of similar organizations abroad. […] However, these theoretical topics, though useful for expanding our people's mental potential, need to be augmented to inspire our people toward genuine mass protest. Such protest, put into action, will stimulate our people to become energetic, determined and strong. (Soekarno 1931:81-2, 1978:113-5.)

Referring again to Karl Kautsky's *Weg zur Macht*, Soekarno told his judges:

What the common people still lack is awareness of their power. So what social democracy has done so far is to raise this consciousness of power among the common people – here again, mainly through theoretical counsel, but also by something else! Far more useful than all kind of theories for lifting mass consciousness were continuously led actions speaking louder than words. By waging such energetic actions, social democracy would reveal to the common people what their real source of power was, while also enhancing the people's own individual sense of power. Naturally these actions were guided by a theory making it possible for involved and organized parts of the proletariat to exert at all times the maximum of its newly won power. [...] Thus, trade union activities were initiated and inspired by social democracy, together with other gains realized in and out-side parliaments, causing the proletariat to sense its power, not only in the form of material rewards secured by a few, but mainly by the fact that the impoverished masses, once feeling so fearful and hopeless, were now part of a force which cou-rageously fought against the ruling powers, gaining victory after victory, while being nothing more than an organization made out of mere have-nots [...]. Not always did these struggles bring important material gains to the proletariat, and not seldom were the gains out of proportion to the sacrifices made. Yet when a struggle did end in victory, it immediately showed a powerful upsurge in the proletariat's dynamic strength. And nothing is more feared by our enemies than the growth of this sense of power! They are aware that this giant presents no dan-ger to them as long as it remains unaware of its inherent power. So their greatest concern is to limit that power; material concessions made by them they dislike less than being faced by the prospect of the proletariat's moral victories, heightening the latter's sense of power. (Soekarno 1931:82-3, 1978:115-6.)

Turning to his judges, Soekarno maintained that in

Indonesia such a giant as yet unaware of its power posed no threat so far to the imperialists, but not for long, since my PNI would make this giant aware of its enormous power by theorizing about it and by waging actions to further clarify it. [...] Are you surprised that the Indies newspapers, being cohorts of imperial-ism, so loudly urge you 'to condemn Soekarno and his ilk, to exile Soekarno and his followers, and to ban the PNI at once'? Are you surprised, your honours, that they even went so far as to attempt to prejudice this court? [...] However, we will not be provoked; we will stay within the bounds of the law. (Soekarno 1931:83-4, 1978:116-7.) [...]

   We wish to experience rapid change, since the PNI is a revolutionary party in the sense that it wants reforms to be established sooner rather than later, with the hope of seeing these reforms realized without any bloodshed. [B]ut what about the imperialists? To the latter we say: it is you who planted the seeds of untold misery, it is you who stifle our community, and it is you who keep planting the seeds of revolution. So, before it is too late, cease your odious work that is driv-ing our people to misery, and instead pay serious attention to the wishes of our people. For if because of your blind craving for profits and due to your own hell-ish behaviour the spectre of revolution comes to reign in our country, a thousand PNIs will then be unable to prevent it from happening. And as Karl Kautsky had it, 'We do know [...] that we are unable to create this revolution, just as our oppon-ents are unable to prevent it', and as Professor Bluntschli warns us, 'he only means to prevent a revolution is timely and fundamental reforms, since as soon as hope for reforms begins to wane among the people, the spectre of revolution will wax. So the main culprits are found among the power brokers and not among the badly governed people who demand a natural and improved legal system. It is therefore a rather silly perception which assumes that revolutions of our century are merely caused by a group of conspirators.

Concluding this part of his plea, Soekarno said:

> Indonesia will be free! That we know for sure! It poses no problem: not for us,
> nor for the Dutchman who cares to be honest about it. The entire history of the
> world and that of mankind cannot present one single case of a people being ruled
> forever. On the contrary, it shows that such people have always managed to free
> themselves from being chained. If therefore the Indonesian people aim at seeing
> the end of foreign rule, and if the PNI and all of us crave for that freedom to occur,
> then what we do is nothing more than fulfilling our historic task, a mission which
> always will be just. But, as to the fashion in which Indonesia will be freed, the
> way the chain of foreign domination will be broken, this lies entirely in the hands
> of the imperialists. So the final word rests not with us, nor with the Indonesian
> people, but with imperialism and the imperialists alone! (Soekarno 1931:86-7,
> 1978:119-22.)

The final part of Soekarno's plea dealt with articles 169 and 153 bis and
included much repetition from earlier parts. Crucial matters, such as Kiewiet
de Jonge's testimony, the positive comments about the PNI by key officials
of Inlandsche Zaken reporting on the meetings in Pekalongan and Solo, and
the spreading of rumours about a 1930 upheaval by government-sponsored
periodicals, were all dealt with again by Soekarno. This final part of his plea,
however, did contain some novel aspects. He first repeated that 'the unrest
of the people and the rumours concerning 1930 were not caused by us at
all. [A]s a matter of fact our movement dismissed the rumours as lies, and
we warned and taught our people that these 1930 predictions were utterly
groundless! So the suspicion that we instigated these we must reject absolutely and positively!' Then Soekarno turned to a discussion of the spectre of
a future war in the Pacific.

   Though not entirely a novel topic, his reference to a host of foreign experts
and to recent developments in the Pacific are worthy of notice. First he asked
'whether the problem of a coming Pacific war would not offer evidence that
we are spreading lies to create unrest among the people and so affirm that we
indeed did violate article 171 of the Penal Code'. But this cannot be true, since
'the predictions of a future Pacific war were first aired by a host of European
scientists', while 'we discussed it not to create unrest but to steel our people,
soon to become a nation, to be strong and prepared!' (Soekarno 1931:91, 1978:
127). Citing foreign forecasters of that future war such as Ernst Reinhard,
Karl Haushofer and Hector C. Bywater, Soekarno marshalled a host of unde-
niable facts about the strong naval and military build-up in the Pacific, noting that 'anyone who has read these predictions must conclude that a Pacific
war will some day erupt!' He referred to the Washington Conference, which
limited the tonnage of battleships and cruisers, and how each participant
dodged the regulations by building smaller but more efficient cruisers and
submarines. He pointed out that new naval bases had been erected stretch-

ing from Panama to Pearl Harbor, from Malta to Singapore, stating that 'like three lions ready to pounce upon each other [...] like three octopuses stretching their tentacles in order to destroy the enemy, in that way the English prepare themselves in Singapore, Japan prepares at home and in the Marianas, Marshall and Bonin island groups, and America prepares in Dutch Harbor, Hawaii, Tutuila, Guam and Manila' (Soekarno 1931:92-3, 1978:128-31).

Turning to his judges again, Soekarno maintained: 'we are not the ones stating that the Pacific conflict will erupt this year or that it will occur soon, we only sense that with the rivalry existing between America, Japan and England, war will be inevitable! Here in Indonesia we are not the only ones who feel that! Dr Ratulangi in the Volksraad session of 14 June 1928 spoke of a future Pacific conflict long before we did; somewhat later the *Algemeen Indisch Dagblad*, the *Preangerbode* and the *Javabode* wrote about this coming conflict! Were they spreading false information? Was their purpose to disturb the public order? [...] Why is such information, the moment we report it, automatically perceived as false information or as an attempt to disturb the public order? Just because we lend force to it, does such information become liable for prosecution under article 171 of the Penal Code?' (Soekarno 1931: 95-7, 1978:133-5.)

In Soekarno's *penutup* (closing argument), after once more stressing Kiewiet de Jonge's testimony and the PNI's honest attempts (together with the RGAZ and other sincere officials) to temper the emotions concerning the 1930 rumours, he turned to his judges:

> Your honours, the Indonesian people await with a pounding heart the moment the sun will rise. Together with the Indonesian people we wish to suffer, and together with them we wish to share their joy. With the Indonesian people we await your honours' verdict. Indeed, we stand here before your court not as Soekarno, not as Gatot Mangkoepradja, not as Maskoen or Soepriadinata, we stand here as members of the suffering and miserable people of Indonesia, and also as devoted sons of Iboe Indonesia. Therefore, our voice in this court room will not simply roam within these four walls here. Our voice will be heard by the people, a people we are devoted to. This voice will penetrate everywhere across the plains, the mountains, the seas, from Kota Radja to Fak-Fak, from Oeloe-Siaoe near Menado all the way to Timor. The Indonesian people, hearing that voice, will then tremble as if hearing their own voice. Your honours' verdict on our efforts will thus be a verdict on the efforts of the Indonesian people themselves. A verdict of not guilty will delight the Indonesian people; a verdict of guilty will truly sadden them. We urge you to take all these matters into consideration. And so, with our hearts as one, united with the hearts of the Indonesian people, and humbly swearing to be faithful to our beloved Iboe Indonesia, we truly hope that both the Indonesian people and Iboe Indonesia will proceed on the way to greatness. As to whatever fate will befall us, your honours, you will find us prepared to hear your verdict. (Soekarno 1931:111, 1978:154.)

The verdict and reactions to it

It took Soekarno's judges only twenty days to deliver a 66-page verdict of guilty, announced on 22 December 1930. On 17 April 1931, in spite of Soekarno and associates' appeal, the verdict was upheld by the Raad van Justitie (Court of Justice) in Batavia. Soekarno and associates were charged with having violated articles 153 bis, 169, first clause, 108 *oud*-110 *oud*, 161 bis and 171 (Schepper 1931:7), and were sentenced to a four-year gaol term for Soekarno, two years for Gatot, twenty months for Maskoen and fifteen for Soepriadinata, to be served (except for Soepriadinata) in the modern Soekamiskin Prison located near Bandoeng's southeast city limits. Since the time served in preventive detention was counted as well, Soepriadinata was released after the Court of Justice's confirmation of the verdict.

This latter verdict caused Sartono to abolish the PNI and to instead found a new party named Partai Indonesia (PI, Partindo) on 1 May 1931 in order to once more solidify the leaderless brown front.[20] The solidity of that front was soon tested by the Hatta group in the Netherlands, which for some time had been critical of the feeble posturing of the PPPKI and Sartono's 'undemocratic decision to dissolve the PNI'. Hatta's group not only disputed Sartono's Partindo's claim to the mantle of Soekarno's PNI, but formed several Golongan Merdeka (Free Groupings) in the main cities of Java and Sumatra. These steps led steadily toward the establishment of a new cadre-party founded by Hatta and Sjahrir after their return to their homeland.[21]

Meanwhile, in the Volksraad, Thamrin, shocked by the severity of the sentences, announced that protest meetings all over Java would be organized by him and the PPPKI. A committee for that purpose was set up, with Mr Hadi of Kaoem Betawi, Mr Soepomo of Boedi Oetomo, Oto Iskandardinata of Pasoendan and Hadji Dahlan Abdoellah of Sarekat Soematra and chaired by Thamrin. As a matter of fact, nineteen such meetings were held in West Java and nine in East Java.[22] As for the *sini* press, *Sin Po* of 23 December 1930 felt that 'the heavy penalties would increase the masses' love and respect for Soekarno and see him and the other leaders as martyrs'. *Keng Po* of the same date compared it 'with the Hatta case' but still anticipated 'a different verdict from the Council of Justice'. *Swara Publiek* of 22 December found 'the sentence far too heavy for someone who spoke so frankly', and considered

---

[20]   Gobée to De Graeff, letter 4 May 1931 and bijlage to De Graeff, Mr. 491/1931.
[21]   *Indonesia Raja*, August 1931:399-400, 421-5. For the Partindo and Golongan Merdeka groups see Mr. 794/1931 and Mr. 1148/1931, with the latter first public meeting on 1 November 1931 at Betawi's Gedong Permoefakatan being reported on by Gobée and Datoek Toemenggoeng in Mr. 1148/1931 as well. *Daulat Ra'jat* started on 20 September 1931 as the Golongan Merdeka's Batavia-situated newspaper at Gang Lontar, where Soedjadi alias Soegito also lived.
[22]   Gobée to De Graeff no. K 15/3, 16 May 1931, p. 1, Mr. 491/1931.

that 'Soekarno could not be sentenced according to article 161 bis since he did not lead a trade union'. *Sinar Deli* of 23 December cited Soekarno's conclusion: 'if I am to be judged guilty, the people will pray to God, in the case of my acquittal they will thank God'. *Darmo Kondo* of the same date maintained that 'Soekarno, in spite of the sentence, is still a great man, and though his PNI will be disbanded, it will not stop the people's push toward progress'. *Pewarta Deli* of 24 December considered 'the grounds for the verdict as quite inadequate, especially in view of the material indirectly gained by Albreghs'. In its 25 December issue, the paper cited Soekarno, who is compared to Gandhi and Sun Yat-sen, as follows: 'we are part of the people, and our voice is truly the people's voice'. *Pewarta Deli* advised that 'the people ought to think about these words'. *Kristen Djawi* of 27 December, after briefly summarizing Soekarno's defence plea, concluded that 'he indeed is a great leader deserving praise, and so every one should bare his head and consider above all that he demonstrated his love for his country and people; in our esteem he is far above the other leaders'. *Sipatahoenan* of 29 December reported the reactions in the Landraad building, 'with the PNI leaders and Mrs Soekarno not looking sad but rather defiant, though several in the room, mainly women, were upset, with some of them weeping quietly'. *Sedio Tomo* of the same date questioned whether 'violation of articles 169 and 153 bis has been proven and if so, why only now, instead of at the founding of the PNI? Why is it that only now the PNI is deemed to be so bad?' *Bintang Timoer* of 5 January 1931 stated that 'the verdict will not silence or force back the *pergerakan*. Even the PSII seems to have risen from the grave. Action shall continue in both the Ko and Non-Ko camps, and will prove wrong the predictions of the *sana* press outlets that the *pergerakan* will become less active.'[23]

However, the most stringent criticism of the verdict came from members of *De Stuw* group. In its periodical of 1 January 1931, an article titled 'De veroordeling te Bandoeng' (The Bandung verdict), most likely written by Mr J.M.J. Schepper, then a law professor at Batavia's Law Faculty, expressed the hope that 'the government would never again feel the need to shift its own responsibility for having acted against such associations [the PNI] following art. 169 onto the shoulders of a judge'.[24] As for Mr Julius Schepper, he commenced his working life as a civil servant in the Finance Ministry in The Hague, to leave it for the vocation of *zendingsconsul* (official representative of the Protestant Church Mission serving on the governor-general's staff)

---

23   Hering clippings archive.
24   *De Stuw*, 1 January 1931:4. In his brochure Schepper (1931:20) argued: 'When the government left the judgement of the PNI's political policies to a common judge and declared it would respect the latter's verdict, the government expected and demanded something such a judge could not accomplish at all'.

starting in Batavia in 1918. Having left this job in 1922, he went on to teach penal law, criminology and philosophy at the newly opened Rechtshooge-school (RHS, Faculty of Law) from February 1925 onwards (Leclerc 1986: 91).

It is from his pen that the most critical review of the verdict flowed. Inggit commented: a legal expert [...] Mr Scheffer (sic) heavily criticized the verdict since it did not deal with justice at all.[25] In a privately issued booklet titled *Het vonnis in de P.N.I.-zaak* (The verdict in the PNI case), Schepper argued that 'the first clause of article 169 (being part of an association which aims to commit felonies) formed the basic construction of the verdict'. The verdict, he said, 'looked at some points more like the closing speech of a public pros-ecutor than like a proper judicial decision' (Schepper 1931:8). More directly, he accused the Landraad president of 'ignoring the fourteen witnesses à décharge since they were unreliable due to the position they held in the PNI organization'. Like Soekarno's defence attorneys, Schepper deemed the Landraad president 'to base his judgement upon suggestions instead of the bare facts ensured by established legal practice'. Further he held that 'it indeed requires some extraordinary courage to critically review or even weigh the Landraad's considerations, since if one does, one gets choked in a mish-mash of mere assumptions, syllogisms and suggestions, causing the real facts to remain hidden [...]. So the proven facts upon which the verdict rests are over-run by the lush flora of the argumentation.' (Schepper 1931:10.)

As to the PNI, Schepper argued that the Landraad had failed 'to arrive at something concrete from all the material made available by defendant and witness testimony and by a score of documents presented as evi-dence. Instead, 'it used hints and parallels based upon such documents as Hatta's brochure *Indonesië vrij*, Semaoen's organization plan, Tan Malaka's *Massa-actie in Indonesië* and the articles appearing in *Indonesia Merdeka*, the Perhimpoenan Indonesia's periodical'. The Landraad decided that

> the ideas, the suggestions, the methods and plans explored in these publications ran parallel to the organization, the working methods, the activities and practices of the PNI. Not as the PNI officially and publicly pretends it to be but as it really is in spirit, in nature and in intention. The Landraad saw all of that confirmed by the score of documents confiscated during the house searches, as well as by the PNI's lectures, courses and candidate-member examinations. From all these so constructed 'hints', the Landraad 'deduces' its 'concrete facts' in any way it sees fit. In that fashion, spiritual and essential PI–PNI solidarity is seen as reflected in the intentions of these organizations. Likewise, the very close ties between the PNI

---

[25]   Ahli hukum. [...] Mr. Scheffer menyatakan kritik keras karena keputusan dirasakan sangat tidak adil (Ramadhan 1981:241).

and the disbanded PKI proves, on the whole, the connection with communism and communist elements. Finally, by the already mentioned brochures, the PNI is clearly identified as the 'nationalist association' to reach Indonesia's freedom by means of an armed rebellion and an overthrow of the Netherlands Indies government. With all these 'hinted' and 'deduced' facts, the Landraad believes it has solid evidence for its case against the PNI. (Schepper 1931:11-2.)

And while Schepper understood that the Landraad needed to 'gather political data from a wide spectrum of governmental information services, among which the Hoofd Parket [Prosecutor's Department of the Indies Attorney-General] by far formed the pivot', he doubted 'whether the judge was truly equipped for critically assessing such data'. Also, 'nowhere in the entire verdict was any trace of such an objective assessment found'. Therefore, 'the Landraad simply relied upon the Hoofd Parket's instructions and acted accordingly'. Schepper concluded the main thrust of his objections to the verdict with a plea to have some of the Indies penal legislation changed. 'Political delinquents ought not necessarily to be treated as ordinary criminals', and yet, 'the former are punished the same way as the latter and put in a common gaol. Such a situation certainly does not satisfy our sense of justice [...]. Is it therefore not more to be recommended to isolate political delinquents in separate institutions and not just in common gaols housing criminals?' (Schepper 1931:21-2.)

Schepper's message also reached the Volksraad, where conservative members clashed with Thamrin's faction, ISDP member De Dreu, and *Stuw* member H.J. van Mook. De Dreu started the debate stating 'that the change in attitude toward the people's movement at the end of 1929 heralded the destruction [of the PNI], a scheme that had been in the wings for some time, supported as it always had been by right-wing elements and by most of the [*sana*] press'. As for Schepper, he praised 'the brilliant and courageous brochure which had clearly proven without any doubt that the sentence was not based upon any legal foundation', concluding that 'in this country we are dealing not with a classic kind of justice but with a racist kind of justice' (*Handelingen Volksraad* 1931-1932:69, 79). Van Mook supported De Dreu's view, adding that 'Soekarno deserved a more chivalrous treatment, since a criminal mentality was quite foreign to him'. He also ridiculed Kiewiet de Jonge's allegation that 'the Landraad president combined three functions: that of public prosecutor before the start and during the public court session, that of judge during the entire session, and lastly, when weighing the sentence, as some kind of defence counsel'. Van Mook quipped that 'all that was quite beautiful but that no one would assume that a Landraad president would, like *maitre* Jacques in Molière's *l'Avare* [The miser], simply change jackets from cook to coachman and back again. [T]he more so, since we all know by now that the Landraad president and the Hoofd Parket cooperated so closely that the latter can truly be viewed as being the real prosecutor.'[26]

Soangkoepon, Iskandardinata, Soekardjo Wirjopranoto, Mochtar Praboe Mangkoenegara and Thamrin of the Fraksi Nasional were all deeply impressed by the contents of Schepper's brochure, with the first three also condemning Mr A. Mieremet, one of the editors of the *Indisch Tijdschrift van het Recht* (Indies Law Periodical) for refusing to place Schepper's piece in that periodical purely on political grounds. On the whole, Thamrin's faction hailed Schepper's contribution as being to the point, and considered it a courageous and unbiased piece of scholarly expertise (*Handelingen Volksraad* 1931-1932:92, 106, 159, 164, 179).

The heart of Schepper's observations found its way as well into a much smaller and less technically legal brochure written by J.E. Stokvis, Due to the long and often close relationship he had with Soekarno and his kin, Stokvis' contribution provides us with warmer, though sometimes biased detail. Some of it we related above, in quoting Stokvis' description of the cordial meetings he had with Soekarno from 1923 onwards, as well as the talks he had with both Soekarno and Inggit during the short breaks in the long Landraad session. Subtitling his brochure *De rechters veroordeeld* (The judges condemned), Stokvis, a long-time critic of colonial government policies, clearly showed where his sympathies lay. De Graeff and the entire colonial system he belonged to were condemned in no uncertain terms. De Graeff had been 'outwitted by the attorney-general', whom Stokvis saw as 'the true ruler of the police and therefore the actual ruler of this land'. The latter had 'for some time prepared the house searches without informing the government or its political advisors about it', then 'catching De Graeff completely by surprise, giving him only one day to decide on these measures. So on that fatal 29 December a heavy blow, if not a mortal one, was dealt by the Prosecutor's Department and the Police to an administration already under fire for quite some time.' (Stokvis 1931a:5.)

As for the police, Stokvis posited that 'anyone knowing something about the Indies reign of terror must be aware of the role the colonial police play in it, with the most extreme examples of it coming to light all the time. In a country saturated with an army of spies manned by unsavoury and not too bright characters – with even Soekarno having warned the government about them – these elements [used by the police to spy on Soekarno's PNI] were thus all too keen on proving their point! One can conclude therefore that the raids and detentions were nothing more than a reckless police manoeuvre.' (Stokvis 1931a:2.) Stokvis also ridiculed the erratic course adopted by government officials before the Volksraad, where the government first stated

---

[26]   *Handelingen Volksraad* 1931-1932:111, 519; for the RGAZ's comments on the three functions of the Landraad president *Handelingen Volksraad* 1931-1932:461.

that 'the raids were needed even in the case of insufficient material being produced, since no risks could be taken', only to moderate 'this view again the next day with the government then confirming that if these interventions were shown to be wholly or partially unfounded, the Volksraad would be notified at once and measures taken accordingly, obliged as the government was by a higher morality common to all governments. [...] During the next Volksraad budgetary deliberations, the government was forced to admit that materials produced during the raids did not yield anything of importance. [...] Nonetheless, Soekarno and his associates were not released but vanished behind bars.' (Stokvis 1931a:4.)

Turning to the Landraad, Stokvis argued that such 'a body with a European always presiding over it, though assisted by indigenous judges who, however, all had served or still served in the administration, would practically yield a one-person verdict: that of the president! The latter had a decisive preponderance due to his race and his legal expertise, making the indigenous judges meekly follow him, accustomed as they were to being obedient and subservient to their white-skinned masters.' (Stokvis 1931a: 9.) Moreover, 'the Landraad's administration of justice – in criminal cases already marked as a murky source – in a politically laden lawsuit would, as it were, readily invite injustices to be committed. In such a case inevitable political passions would come into play, whereas this is precisely where a strong guarantee of impartiality was called for in order to protect a judge from yielding to his own personal frailties. Moreover, such impartiality was needed for a case dealing with one race confronting another race.' (Stokvis 1931a:9-10.) Stokvis then took the president of the Landraad to task following Schepper's arguments. Since these were elaborated above, we will not deal with them again, closing this part now with Stokvis' main conclusion:

> This PNI verdict is implausible judges' work. It is contrary to the writings of the law and contrary to the intentions of the law. It goes against a clear sense of justice, since it was directed solely at the matters incriminating the defendants, while totally ignoring all evidence in their favour. Everything was aimed at charging them without having any grounds or events to support such charges. So the law has spoken, but justice has not prevailed. [...] Soekarno and his friends are now behind bars [...] but no one assessing and understanding their ideals will view them as criminals. Even the governor-general saw that at last. So while on the verge of returning to the Netherlands, he used his right to pardon them [...]. Soekarno's term being halved, he will be freed at the end of this year [1931]. [A]ll this is of great significance since the judges who punished Soekarno and his friends are by now themselves morally condemned [...] while the governor-general now understands that the law spoke in the past but that no justice was ever served. However, the political consequences of the raids and their aftermath will not cease. The rift between strong genuine segments within the nationalist movement on the one hand and Dutch authority in this country on the other hand is by

now quite complete. That latter authority has thus committed a grave assault on itself. (Stokvis 1931a:15.)

Prophetic words indeed, as we will see later in this. But before we become involved with these events, we need to devote some time to Soekarno's experiences in prison.

Soekarno's Soekamiskin experiences and emotions about it outside his jail

Just before Soekarno was moved from Bantjeuj to Soekamiskin, he received the following message from Alexander Patty, then exiled in Roeteng on the island of Flores:

> Dear brother, although in a material sense we are separated far apart, in a spiritual way we are close together, are we not? Roeteng is quite a distance from the move-ment, and communications are not as they should be, since the boat only comes twice a month. The most recent daily from Soerabaja was dated 3 December 1930. Fortunately, it contains some news about your defence plea and those of the other brothers appearing before the court. It is for that reason that I send you this letter, declaring that Mother Indonesia should be justly proud to have you brothers as her sons. No matter how our cause may end, we are convinced that our pure and exalted strivings will be a remedy for our sufferings. With national greetings to you, brave brothers, I sign, Patty.[27]

Soekarno himself was writing to his kindred outside as well. He wrote to Stokvis on 8 January 1931 expressing his views about the sentence and regretting that the judge did not heed some of his good intentions. He maintained this correspondence throughout his detention.[28] Just after his move from Bantjeuj to Soekamiskin, he wrote to an unnamed friend on 17 May 1931 about the horrifying experiences he had had in the new penal institution. There he was 'clothed in the blue denim prison attire', his 'head shaven and then put to work in the prison bindery, where he had to prepare reams and reams of paper day after day, working himself to the bone'. In the evening, 'his harsh daily tasks behind him, he was given six minutes to bathe and clean himself of all the persistent oil spots on hands, feet and cheeks'. Then, after finishing 'his plateful of unhusked rice and some other sober fare, he was glad to be back in his tiny one-and-a-half by two-and-a-half-metre cell to rest his body from the fatigue experienced during the day.

[27]   *Sin Tit Po*, 3 January 1931 printed Patty's letter dated 23 December 1930.
[28]   The Stokvis-Soekarno correspondence is lodged in the IISG archives. English-language translations of it are in Hering 1991b:21-2, 23, 27-8.

Psychologically, he was then so spent that his brain seemed to be in a dulled state of lethargy.'[29]

Yet there were some bright spots as well. He loved the sporadic visits of Inggit and Omi, with the former taking him a copy of the Koran, some hard-boiled eggs and baked cakes with some money hidden in them. The money he needed to bribe some of his warders for getting news from the outside world, since, unlike his Bantjeuj experience, here he was prohibited from reading any newspapers or books of a political nature. However, he seems not to have been successful in getting any news, and he remained quite unaware of political developments beyond Soekamiskin. So he started to deepen his knowledge of Islam and the Muhammadiyah, telling Inggit on one of her visits: 'Inggit, it is so true that big ideals come to me during the quiet moments of my life here. [...] As of now I am deeply engaged in reading and analysing the Koran from the moment I wake up, and then sensing the greatness of God.'[30] Another lift to his spirits during his gaoled existence was the fortnightly letters from his kindred in both Holland and Indonesia and visits of the delegation of the Nederlandsch Verbond van Vakvereenigingen (Netherlands League of Trade Unions), first to Inggit's home and then twice visiting him in Soekamiskin. The three delegates, P. Moltmaker, E. Kupers and P. Danz, were in Indonesia from 22 May to 18 September 1931 in order to give impetus to the Indonesian trade union movement and to strengthen possible ties with Dutch trade unions. Of the three, Moltmaker was the most outspoken about Soekarno's plight in prison. In an interview with an *Algemeen Indisch Dagblad* journalist, and after having seen Soekarno twice on 19 and 29 June 1931, he stated that 'the SDAP planned to have the latter [Soekarno] freed as soon as possible'. As for himself, he felt that 'Soekarno had been convicted for the wrong reasons and should have been granted a reprieve right away even if he did not request it'. As to Soekarno's reputation, Moltmaker saw it 'as not tarnished, because his imprisonment had made him into a freedom fighter'. During his trip to Bandoeng and his visit to 174 Astanaanjarweg, he was quite impressed by the size of Soekarno's library, which he assessed as 'one truly worthy of an intellectual'. He was also 'amazed seeing so many photographs of Soekarno on display in the tiny dwellings of *kampung* folk in and around Bandoeng!'[31]

---

[29] *Nieuwe Rotterdamsche Courant*, 8 August 1931 with English-language renderings of it in Hering 1991b:20 and in Sukarno 1966:107-9.

[30] Enggit, benar, cita-cita yang besar datangnya pada saat-saat yang sepi. [...] Sekarang aku benar-benar mulai membaca al-Quran, menelan al-Quran... Kalau aku terbangun, maka aku membacanya. Lalu aku memahami Tuhan itu. Ramadhan 1981:247-9; our interview with Inggit, 15 December 1971.

[31] *Nieuwe Rotterdamsche Courant,* 8 August 1931; *De Telegraaf,* 3 September 1931; *Het Volk,* 8 and 10 July 1931; *Het Indische Volk,* 12 and 13 June 1931; *De Strijd,* 4 December 1931, and *Timboel,*

That both the SDAP and the ISDP wanted to do something positive for Soekarno was demonstrated by correspondence of Stokvis, who after May 1931 was back again in his home country. Before Stokvis left Indonesia, Soekarno had written to him on 10 April, stating that his

> repatriation meant a great loss to our people, and to myself the loss of a friend. [F]or the remainder of my life I will cherish the fact of you being present during several sessions of my trial and how your attendance there was felt by me as the presence of an old friend. As for my wife, I must convey similar feelings of grati-tude. She too is profoundly thankful, and as grateful as a sorely tried wife can be. She is a courageous woman; I do not hesitate to call her heroic.

Back in The Hague and unknown to Soekarno, Stokvis had been instrumen-tal in getting Soekarno a reprieve by arranging for him a Labour seat in the Second Chamber of the Dutch Parliament. This scheme was supported by both Alberda, a member of the parliamentary SDAP faction, and Ankersmit, editor of *Het Volk*. In Indonesia the ISDP was involved as well, and Bob van Gelderen was instructed by Stokvis to commence priming Soekarno for the scheme through letters and visits to him in Soekamiskin.[32] However, all these SDAP/ISDP initiatives to involve Soekarno did not materialize, since he was suddenly granted a reprieve by De Graeff. It seems that De Graeff was induced to make this move in view of Schepper's and the NVV's argu-ments about the Soekarno case. So a draft of De Graeff's government decision was duly sent to the Raad van Nederlandsch-Indië, which approved it, since 'political upheavals had by now considerably quieted down in the colony'. De Graeff did not bother to inform colonial minister De Graaff beforehand, nor his own successor De Jonge. On 3 September 1931 De Graeff signed the decision freeing Soekarno on 31 December 1931, making it public the next day and then wiring De Graaff about it. The contents of the wire implicitly criticize the Soekarno case verdicts of both the Landraad and the Raad van Justitie since 'they had not sufficiently taken into account, no matter how reprehensible and unlawful his [Soekarno's] behaviour, and how rash and impetuous his methods had been, that this condemned man had been led purely by idealistic motives'.[33]

As to Soekarno's own reactions to this, among the first to hear was his old flu-ridden comrade-in-arms in a 28 October letter to The Hague. A highly

---

no. 14(29 August 1931):218-20 in an article titled 'Hoe vrije mannen spreken over de zaak Soekarno' (How free men speak of the Soekarno case).

[32]   See Stokvis collection IISG archives, 16 July 1931 letter to Bob van Gelderen; an English-language translation of it is in Hering 1991b:24-6.

[33]   Leclerc 1986:91; 'Boeng Karno dapat gratie', *Persatoean Indonesia* no. 102 (16 September 1931):253-4; De Jong 1969-71, XIa:354-5; De Graeff to De Graaff, Wire no. 219, 4 September 1931, Verbaal 8 September 1931 X 15.

spirited Soekarno thanked Stokvis, also on behalf of Inggit, for his congratulations on the reprieve. As for Inggit, Soekarno cited Mazzini, who had personal experience of being supported by an inwardly strong spouse. She had given him spirited support while charting her own way in such a courageous manner. However, with his freedom soon to be restored, Soekarno turned to politics. Soedjadi had sent him a post card congratulating him, but concluding his scribble with the words 'salam nasional dari saudaramoe di-loear golongan Sartono' (national greetings from your brother who is outside the group of Sartono). Soekarno was puzzled by it and wondered whether there had been a rift in the movement; Sartono, too, had been silent about it in his last communication to Soekarno. Not anticipating any clarification, Soekarno turned to the translation of his defence plea, soon to go to the presses in Holland in a Dutch-language version. He was aware of the troubles Stokvis had had with the translator of it, and hoped that matters would turn out right in the end, though so far he had not received any request for approving the translation. However, what mattered most was that his ideas were represented accurately. As to Stokvis praising it as a choice piece, Soekarno felt it to be a flattering compliment, since to him it was somewhat mediocre, partly because, while preparing it in Bantjeuj, he was unable to check it, since the literature he needed for it was denied to him.[34]

As to the Dutch-language translation of Soekarno's defence plea, Thamrin had been instrumental in sending the Indonesian version of it (printed by the PPPKI Fonds Nasional) to Stokvis. Stokvis found the Arbeiderspers (Labourers Press) willing to print it, and Sjahrir prepared to translate it into Dutch. Somewhat later, around the end of July 1931, with Sjahrir having finished the draft and titling it *Indonesië klaagt aan*, Stokvis became annoyed about Sjahrir's laxity in mailing the proofs to Soekarno first for corrections. Letters to Sjahrir to meet him at the office of the Arbeiderspers to resolve that issue remained unanswered, and so *Indonesië klaagt aan* got printed without Soekarno having seen the proofs at all and with Stokvis writing to Thamrin that he had withdrawn his involvement.[35] Sjahrir stated in his introduction that he had had

> to delete some of its digressions and repetitions to make it more accessible to Dutch readers. [Yet] it did not diminish the impact of Soekarno's original plea, since the greatness of Soekarno as a speaker and a leader was the close comradeship and the oneness he had with the millions of Indonesian paupers [and because] he uses their language and their images, sweeping the young and the old, the intellectual

---

[34]   Soekarno to Stokvis, Soekamiskin, 28 October 1931, IISG Stokvis collection. An English-language version is in Hering 1991b:27-8.

[35]   Stokvis to Thamrin, The Hague, 18 August 1931, p. 1 with the former writing that the title *Indonesië klaagt aan* was not his doing at all but Sjahrir's: IISG archives. Sjahrir's involvement is also in Bondan 1992:78-9.

and *kromo,* all to the highest of peaks. [A]ll that cannot be rendered into Dutch at all [...] so the translator is quite aware of the fact that the beauty of the language has been lost, yet even through our translation, Soekarno radiates [...] so much so that even in the many citations making the book in Western eyes so useful and worthy, his voice prevails! Through him therefore the voice of the Indonesian people also reverberates in defiant defence and accusation! (Soekarno 1931:3-4.)

The awe for Soekarno expressed here was reflected in some of Sjahrir's letters, even if he did not adopt Soekarno's political credo, as we will see below. As to the appearance of the Dutch-language version of Soekarno's *Indonesië klaagt aan,* a big chest containing a huge number of copies arrived in Batavia by early February 1932 addressed to Bintang Merah, the ISDP bookshop run by the wife of Professor Bob van Gelderen. These were confiscated at first, since the front cover, showing former Governor-General Van Heutsz looking down at a number of coffins, was considered to be in violation of article 157 of the Indies Penal Code. After consultation with the Arbeiderspers, the offending front covers were removed, after which the distribution of the brochure proceeded smoothly.[36] It seems strange, however, that the back cover, showing a number of pre-teenage Indonesian children busily preparing straw hats, was not considered to be offensive at all at that time.

Outside Soekamiskin, the news of the reprieve was predictably hailed by *sini* and condemned by most of the reactionary *sana* elements and the *sana* press outlets. The news was greeted by loudly applauding indigenous workers at Batavia's Gambir main post office, as well as at Gambir's Koninklijke Paketvaart Maatschappij (KPM, Royal Packet Lines) headquarters, while most of the *sini* press outlets printed special issues with the heading 'Boeng Karno dapat gratie' (Soekarno received a reprieve).[37] Thamrin, in a 29 December 1931 letter to Stokvis, remained somewhat hopeful that the *pergerakan* with Soekarno back would soon become united again. Yet he had misgivings. He intimated to his former Volksraad comrade and sponsor:

Tomorrow I leave for Soerabaja for the Indonesia Raja Congress. I will be the proposer for several motions concerning the reorganization of the PPPKI. [...] All hopes are set on Soekarno. The meeting has been postponed in order for Bapak Soekarno to be able to attend, and all the proposed regulations will be subject to his judgement. I myself find that a great honour for Karno, but I feel sorry for him as well. I am afraid that too great expectations are being nourished and when later these hopes vanish into thin air, Soekarno will be ruined. If I had my way I would like to make him temporarily the secretary of the reorganized PPPKI, then he would have an opportunity to reorient himself and, for the time being, be out of

---

[36]   See the question of VC member Hamer about the issue and Kiewiet de Jonge's reply to it during the 29 February 1932 Volksraad session: *Handelingen Volksraad* 1931-1932:2483-4; *Het Volk* 1 March 1932 with an article titled 'Soekarno's brochure: Vragendag in den Volksraad'.
[37]   *Sin Po,* 5 September 1931; *Persatoean Indonesia* no. 102 (16 September 1931).

harm's way. I visited Karno in Soekamiskin a week ago and conveyed to him your regards. He returns these greetings gladly. Will you also greet Kupers, Moltmaker and Danz on behalf of him and myself?'[38]

Even Sjahrir, now in Indonesia and having just established the Pendidikan Nasional Indonesia (Indonesian National Education, soon to be called the PNI Baroe) party, confessed in a letter on 4 January 1932, to his Amsterdam-based lover and former hostess Maria Tas-Duchâteau, after first complaining about possible closer Soekarno/Thamrin/PPPKI links, that 'we cannot drop him [Soekarno]. For a few years now he has fascinated the people and will continue to do so; for the time being he will remain dominant. To oppose him would endanger the situation and could well lead to an isolation of our own ideas or even the political death of Hatta.'[39]

Soekarno's return to a divided pergerakan and his failure to unify it

And fascinate the people he indeed did! Picked up by Inggit and Thamrin from the gates of Soekamiskin on New Year's Eve, Soekarno, heading a motor-car procession into Bandoeng to Gatot's home, was greeted everywhere by enthusiastic crowds of people welcoming him back. Even Pendidikan Nasional Indonesia members like Soeka, Maskoen, Inoe Perbatasari, Moerwoto and Hamdani were among the crowd at Soekamiskin's gate to meet him. At two well-attended Balai Pertemoean (public meeting) receptions arranged by Thamrin at Gatot's and Inggit's home until the early hours of the next day, Soekarno vowed that he 'again stood before his people as a leader who, like a recently purified *keris*, had been drawn from its sheath far sharper than ever before'. The next day he, Inggit, Omi, Soekarmini and some of his followers travelled by train to Soerabaja, meeting cheering crowds wherever they made a stop. In Djokja he was honoured to be greeted by one of his early political mentors, Ki Hadjar Dewantoro, while at the final stop at Goebeng's railway station he was met by a huge crowd of *arek Soeraboyo*, who accompanied him, the guest of honour and his entourage to the first Indonesia Raja congress, then in session at the Gedong Nasional Indonesia (Home of Nationalist Indonesia) on Soerabaja's Boeboetan thoroughfare.[40] Inside the congress hall, after he was carried on the shoulders of some attendants to the dais, Dr Soetomo introduced him 'as someone who had been the

---

[38] Stokvis collection IISG archives, an English-language translation is in Hering 1991b:56.
[39] Verheijen to De Jonge, letter 19 August 1933, no. 4131/A.P, Verbaal 19 October 1933 O 24.
[40] Ramadhan 1981:258-9, 263-7. For Soekarno and associates being at the prison gate to welcome him see Mrázek 1994:88. For Soekarno's reference to the *keris*: *Soeara Oemoem*, 5 January 1932.

victim of unjust punishment, but who had sacrificed himself as a true *ksatria*. [In] the hearts of the people you will always remain the *banteng*, a faithful comrade and a beloved hero.' Soetomo then turned to Inggit and asked her to rise from her seat. He introduced her to the audience as being 'a true Srikandi, who had been patient and given her husband strong moral support while he was in prison'. Mr Ali Sastroamidjojo was able to talk to Inggit as well, confessing that 'Actually the PPPKI is as good as dead. This effort is thus to bring it to life again. So that it gets new blood and is able to breathe again'.[41] She was worried about this description and felt sorry for her Koesno, but this mood vanished after she heard him speak to the congress the next morning. That next day, 2 January 1932, it was Soekarno's turn to electrify his audience as of old with a *wejangan* (a message). Comparing himself to *wayang* hero Kokrosono (also named Wesi Drolodoro), who had returned from his Argo Songo exile with his magic powerful weapon Aloegoro only to find his relatives Banowati and Irowati divided, an obvious reference to the current Partindo/PNI Baroe schism, he vowed to unite them in a reinvigorated and powerful radical brown front.[42]

True to his promise, Soekarno approached Sjahrir the moment he returned from Soerabaja on 4 January 1932. With tactful understanding, he urged Sjahrir to join a joint Partindo/PNI Baroe radical front against *sana*. That he made these moves was truly a token of his consensual style; that Sjahrir and his friends did not reciprocate was a token of their style. As for Hatta, he had earlier, immediately in the wake of Sartono's founding of Partindo, declared his unwillingness to join that party. In a letter to the *sini* press, Hatta declared that he planned to formulate a socio-pedagogic programme the moment he returned to Indonesia.[43] Hatta was also stung by recent allegations made by fellow Sumatran Dr Abdoel Rivai, a well-known Minangkabau journalist and editor of *Bintang Timoer*, who considered Hatta unfit to dabble in Javanese nationalist politics, since as a Sumatran he was culturally and ethnically at a disadvantage and should therefore stick to being a *saudagar* (trader) instead. Rivai also felt that Hatta was unable to get along with his people due to his long absence abroad. Yet he advised him that if he still wanted to dabble in politics and come closer to his people, to

---

[41]   Sebenarnya PPPKI ini sudah hampir mati. Ini usaha untuk menghidupkannya kembali. Supaya berdarah lagi, supaya bernafas lagi.

[42]   *Soeara Oemoem*, 5 January 1932; this *wejangan* (message) of Soekarno was also reported in full by Gobée to De Jonge in a letter 16 January 1932, no. KI/III to 'counter the unreliable reports which appeared in the European press about it'. For Ali Sastroamidjojo's reference to a dying PPPKI, see Ramadhan 1981:267-8.

[43]   Hatta's letter in *Sin Po*, 10 June 1931 and in *Siang Po*, 4 August 1932, with comments about it in *Bintang Timoer*, 11 and 12 June 1931, *Sipatahoenan*, 15 June, *Boedi Oetomo*, 10 August and *Oetoesan Sumatra*, 17 August 1931, with some stating he had lost his touch due to his long absence.

then live in Sumatra and seek election to a Volksraad seat to represent them.[44] Also, Sjahrir, perhaps being a bit ill at ease about their future prospects due to their long absence, labelled Hatta as 'our most Europeanized intellectual [...] with more respect for the Dutch than Thamrin ever had', while saying about himself: 'I feel so at ease in Holland that it seems like a homecoming'.[45] So, Hatta and Sjahrir were in a sense tortured persons, victims of a Mannoni-like acculturation syndrome caused by their long study sojourn abroad in a cultural environment they both intensely admired but never could become wholly part of. No doubt all that frustrated them. It also made it difficult for them to reconcile themselves with their own people, as Rivai remarked. Of the two, Sjahrir was the more cynically articulate about the degree of aliena-tion both he and Hatta suffered. Their recent expulsion from the ranks of the Leiden-based Perhimpoenan Indonesia, a move most likely instigated by fel-low Minangkabau Roestam Effendi and approved by Sartono and associates, may also have been instrumental in their not cooperating with Partindo after their return to Indonesia.[46]

So, bent on impressing their peers in Holland and Indonesia, and aware that they possessed an intellect at par with the best in the West, they were quick to formulate a socio-pedagogic political agenda for the achievement of Indonesian nationhood. Their platform was naturally laced with more than ample reference to Western European writings. However, here they basically failed to comprehend that their Western-oriented blueprint would remain largely irrelevant in the minds of the one ethnic group capable of making ultimate *merdeka* a reality: the Javanese. As the Australian Brian May put it so succinctly some six *windu* later:

> Neither [Hatta nor Sjahrir] had the capacity to make contact with the masses, nor, being Sumatrans, could they understand that Javanese mysticism made their pol-icies impracticable. [...] It would have been astonishing if Sjahrir, a Minangkabau looking at Java through European spectacles, had been able to see the road to independence with Sukarno's clarity. Ridiculing Sukarno's widely loved evoca-tion of the image of Ibu (Mother) Indonesia, with its beautiful landscape and fer-tile soil, he said: 'Mother Indonesia as a mystical experience is outside the realm of practical politics'. This gibe might have won an approving smile among dons; but it disqualified him as a leader of the Javanese, who, in addition to being mystical, were well described by Sukarno as an *artiestenvolk* [a people of artists]. Sukarno did not appeal to the people's emotions simply because he was himself emotional,

[44] *Het Vaderland*, 21 August 1931, Aneta's cable of 26 August 1931; Parada Harahap 1939:146; Rose 1987:55, with her commenting 'there was a ring of truth in Rivai's words, as Hatta was to discover over the years'.
[45] Sjahrazad (Sjahrir's pseudonym) 1945:9, 172, 161.
[46] Rose 1987:55-6; Poeze 1986:246-7; Tas 1969; for Hatta's dejection and Sjahrir's nonchalant defiance at the Perhimpoenan Indonesia expulsion.

but above all for practical reasons. [He] knew what had to be done and that his
talents suited him for the task. (May 1978:52-3.)

And yet, in an article for *Daulat Ra'jat* titled 'Faham persatoean... sepandjang strategie, Faham persatoean... sepandjang taktiek' (The unity notion
seen strategically and tactically), Sjahrir, while maintaining that the differences between the Pendidikan Nasional Indonesia and Soekarno were of a
fundamental character, still did 'not rule out a fusion with the latter – but
then only as a tactical and temporary measure'.[47] He even invited Soekarno
to be a guest speaker at the Pendidikan Nasional Indonesia's first congress,
held in Bandoeng 23-26 June 1932, where Sjahrir was elected chairman. On
that occasion Soekarno stated that 'so long as his blood flowed in his veins
he would back the *kaum marhaen* and he hoped that all marhaenist parties
would eventually fuse with a nationalism based on Marxism, with the distinct aim of becoming one with the people and for the people'. In spite of
these lofty aims, which Soekarno hoped would ease unification in the near
future, he was not allowed to join the closed sessions.[48] Still, immediately
after Hatta's return to his homeland on 24 August 1932, Soekarno visited him
at the Boenga Hotel on Bandoeng's Grote Postweg thoroughfare. Apparently
Hatta had gone to Inggit's and Soekarno's home, and, not finding them there,
had left a note about his whereabouts in Bandoeng. According to both Hatta
and Soekarno, that first meeting did not deal at all with important matters,
due perhaps to the fact that they were joined there by a *haji* named Oesman,
owner of a Padang shop in Betawi's suburb of Kramat, who had driven
Hatta in his motor car from Betawi to Bandoeng. As Soekarno later related
to Inggit: 'There was someone else there I did not know very well, so we did
not talk about serious matters at all.'[49] Yet Soekarno, true to his promises of
pergerakan reunion, tried again to meet Sjahrir, Hatta and some of their followers in order to discuss a possible Partindo/PNI Baroe fusion; he had also
joined Sartono's Partindo on 1 August 1932. However, Sjahrir and Maskoen
declined to meet Soekarno and Sartono, so Hatta went alone to see them in
Bandoeng on 25 September 1932.[50] This meeting failed to bear any fruit, possibly because of the animosity the Hatta forces had held now for some time
against Sartono. So, at last, Soekarno learned that the proud promise of uniting the two parties made after his release was a task beyond even his char-

[47]　*Daulat Ra'jat*, 10 February 1932.
[48]　See Van der Most report about that first congress attached to Verheijen to De Jonge, 29 July
1932, no. 3521/A.P., pp. 13-4, Mr. 830/1932.
[49]　Ada orang lain Kus tidak mengenalnya benar. Jadi kami tidak bicarakan hal-hal yang penting (Ramadhan 1981:276-7).
[50]　Interview with Hatta, 25 June 1976; Hatta 1981:139. Neither Rose nor Mrázek mention this
second meeting.

ismatic powers. He thus decided to devote his energies solely to Partindo, while Thamrin, a close associate of his over the past years, would endeavour to bring Partindo into a reorganized PPPKI as soon as possible.

The ultimate clash between Soekarno and the PNI Baroe

While the reasons for the clash were many and various, not least including some bitter personal antagonisms, the main issue between them, ideologically and politically, was how best to face the current task of reinvigorating the *pergerakan*. Even before Soekarno joined Partindo in his *Makloemat dari Boeng Karno kepada Kaoem Marhaen* (Brother Karno's announcement to the Marhaen), he insisted that both Partindo and PNI Baroe were in fact the only parties representing marhaen (Soekarno 1959:167-70). Even this last attempt to leave the door open to future compromise was hotly rejected by the small Hatta faction. They instead insisted that both Soekarno's political credo and the attendant propaganda methods were far too harmful an opiate for *marhaen* to absorb at this time. While both factions claimed to represent the interests of these Indonesian paupers, Hatta expected them 'to merely fall thoughtlessly in line behind Soekarno like ducks quacking in unison' (*membebek*) (Hatta 1976:105). Only through select PNI Baroe leadership cadres would these paupers, ill-prepared as they were intellectually and organizationally, slowly but surely be guided toward organizations where democratic freedom of expression and critical political thought would prevail. By contrast, Soekarno, while acknowledging that cadre formation remained essential, argued that the PNI Baroe cadre schemes would lead to elitism and ultimately to the loss of intimate contact with the Indonesian masses, which he considered to be the most important link to any meaningful confrontation with the Dutch. The PNI Baroe leaders in return rejected Soekarno's charisma, which they considered to be too exclusively linked with Javanese mystical notions and the delusions of the *wayang* to get the masses to back him.[51] Moreover, they viewed Soekarno's continual attempts to unite the secular and religiously oriented segments of the *pergerakan* behind him as shallow, superficial and a waste of time. Termed by Hatta a sociological monstrosity, these schemes of Soekarno's and his efforts at unification merely resembled a *per-sate-an* (hodge-podge) and should instead be aimed at a rationally and politically well-educated, stable, small cadre-like *persatuan* (unity) front.[52]

[51]   'Hatta, 'Sekali lagi Noncooperasi dan Tweede Kamer', *Daulat Ra'jat*, 30 January 1933.
[52]   Hatta on the PPPKI's loose unity: 'Persatoean ditjari, Per-sate-an jang dapat' *Daulat Ra'jat*, 20 April 1932. *Per-sate-an* refers to the separate pieces of broiled meat skewered together in that well-known Indonesian dish *sate*.

Their own PNI Baroe hoped to achieve just that through strict training and education, even to the extent of entering, if the need arose, Dutch parliamentary institutions.[53] They further discounted Soekarno's and Partindo's desired association with the union forged by the PPPKI. In fact, they viewed it as a transgression of marhaenist principles and a true sample of a Soekarno-woven *per-sate-an*, bringing the masses together in unholy alliance with the bourgeoisie and the *ningrat*.[54] Such a state would only result in the interests of *marhaen* being trampled upon and jeopardized. Moreover, it would reinforce the cooperationists and Thamrin's position in the PPPKI, and thus drive that Soekarno-inspired constellation even further from the *marhaen*.[55]

For Soekarno these PNI Baroe considerations were indeed in dire contrast to his own views. Moulded as he was by the syncretism and principles of *rukun* (harmony) inherent in the Javano-Balinese worldview, Soekarno regarded his efforts to unite all factions in the PPPKI as echoing his first political clarion call. In that 1926 address, he had proclaimed himself to be at once a Nationalist, a Muslim and a Marxist, quite capable, so he thought, of forging within himself all the *aliran* that struggled for political expression. It appears that here we have arrived at the crux of the matter underpinning the ideological and structural distinctions between the two factions. On the one hand was a tiny but highly organized cadre party, perhaps wary of irritating colonial authorities unduly, hence the mention of education (*pendidikan*) in its name instead of party (*partai*). This also explains that not once was the *sana* versus *sini* conflict, the confrontation so dear to Soekarno's rhetoric, mentioned by the PNI Baroe. This was dismissed by Sjahrir as a dangerous effort

---

[53]   It refers to Hatta's November 1932 initial decision (he later withdrew it) to accept candidacy for an OSP Dutch Second Chamber seat. Hatta saw it as an 'honour' (Dahm 1969:161) and in accordance with a 1929 tactic adopted by the PI, see *Daulat Ra'jat*, 30 January 1933. It caused a bitter Soekarno-Hatta debate, see the former's 'Sekali lagi tentang sosio-nationalisme dan sociodemokrasi' in Soekarno 1959:187-91, and Hatta's 'Sekali lagi Noncooperasi dan Tweede Kamer' in *Daulat Ra'jat*, 30 January 1933 and Soekarno's 'Djawab saja pada Saudara Mohammad Hatta' in Soekarno 1959:207-9. Hatta's about-face is described by L.N. Palar in *Kentering* 11-6:90 as 'Soekarno defended non-cooperation with great passion against Hatta, who wanted to use it as a tactic'.

[54]   *Ningrat* is a term to describe members of the higher Central and West Javanese aristocracy. Some of these highly placed persons (mainly serving in the *pangreh praja*) stemmed from families like Djajadiningrat, Widjojodiningrat and Djojoadiningrat.

[55]   It seems odd that the PNI Baroe leaders singled out Thamrin as Soekarno's wicked and contaminated associate; see Sjahrir's article 'De Indonesische beweging op een dood punt; De uitweg', *De Nieuwe Weg* August 1931:4. Thamrin's trade links were well known but so were Hatta's and Sjahrir's, and like the former, Thamrin had cordial relations with Dutch socialists and was viewed as a possible candidate for an SDAP Tweede Kamer seat at one time; Letter Stokvis to Van Gelderen, 16 July 1931, pp. 1-2, IISG archives. As to the Thamrin/*ningrat* link (Djajadiningrat, Wiranatakoesomo, Koesoemo Oetoyo) that was one with the most liberal of regents; Sutherland 1979:79.

One of the few photographs showing Soekarno as a Modjokerto primary-school pupil seated at right in the back seat of the carriage. This picture somewhat belies the poverty-stricken David Copperfield image he created years later for Cindy Adams during the preparations for his biography. (Collection Mas Guntur Sukarnoputra.)

Tjokroaminoto's house at Gang Peneleh VII, where Soekarno by mid-1916 boarded together with some twenty-five Indonesian pupils. The house was only a stone's throw from Gang Lawang Sekereng, where Soekarno was born 6 June 1901. At Pak Tjokro's house (Tjokro was then in charge of Sarekat Islam, Indonesia's first mass party) the young Soekarno met the founders of the first truly nationalist Indische Partij: Ernest Douwes Dekker, Tjipto Mangoenkoesoemo, Taman Siswa chairman Soewardi Soerjaningrat alias Ki Hadjar Dewantoro, and the Dutch Marxists Henk Sneevliet and Asser Baars. So it may be assumed that in Soerabaja the foundations were laid for Soekarno's political and revolutionary moulding. (Collection Rob van Diessen.)

Soekarno sitting at left during his third year of HBS (Hogere Burger School, Dutch-language secondary school) in Soerabaja with a gathering of Indonesian HBS pupils in front of the Indonesian club building Panti Harsojo, a small Indonesian enclave just around the corner from Soekarno's boarding house. Next to him, also in Javanese traditional clothes, is his former Modjokerto pal Hermen Kartowisastro. (Collection Hering.)

Another photograph of the Indonesian pupils, this time in front of the HBS, taken during Soekarno's fourth year, with him sitting second from left. The girl sitting next to him is Soekartini, a sister of Mas Soedirman, a member of Soerabaja's municipality at that time and later the first resident of that city during the famous October-November 1945 battle against British forces. (Collection Ir. H. Sigit Baruchsalam.)

Engagement photograph of Pak Tjokro's daughter Oetari and Soekarno, then in his final year at the HBS (Collection Ir. H. Sigit Baruchsalam)

Photograph of Soekarno during his first year at Bandoeng's Technical Faculty (THS, Technische Hoge School) (Collection Mas Guntur Sukarnoputra)

Ibu Inggit Garnasih coming into Soekarno's life (Collection Ibu Inggit)

Ir. Soekarno after graduating from the THS as an engineer (Collection Idayu)

Ir. Soekarno sitting second from right with a member of Dewantoro's Taman Siswa
school in Bandoeng at a Taman Siswa meeting, early 1926 (Collection Oedaya)

The leaders of the Partai Nasional Indonesia (Collection Hering)

Second PPPKI congress, held in Solo, 25-27 December 1929 (Collection Hering)

Soekarno in front of the Bandoeng Landraad during the 1930 PNI trial. From left to right: Maskoen, Gatot Mangkoepradja, Soekarno, their three lawyers, and Soepriadinata. (Collection Hering.)

Soekarno just released from Soekamiskin jail delivering his welcoming speech to the delegates of the first Indonesia Raja Congress, 2 January 1932, in the Gedong Nasional on Soerabaja's Boeboetan thoroughfare. (Collection Ibu Inggit.)

Soekarno, now vice-chairman of Bandoeng's Partai Indonesia (Partindo) branch,
flanked by Inggit during an 15 August 1932 gathering of the party
(Collection Ibu Inggit)

Soekarno, now chairman of Partindo, at that party's congress, mid-April 1933
(Collection Ibu Inggit)

Soekarno at Soerabaja's harbour on the way to the steamer Jan van Riebeeck, 17 February 1932, where he together with Inggit, his mother-in-law Iboe Asmi, and their adopted daughter Omi would be transported to Ende on the island of Flores (Collection Ibu Inggit)

Soekarno flanked by Inggit and Omi, with another adopted daughter Kartika sitting
in front of Soekarno at their second place of exile, Bencoolen, in 1939
(Collection Ibu Inggit)

Fatmawati with her parents in Bencoolen. She would become Soekarno's third wife in Jakarta during the Japanese occupation and bear him five children.
(Collection Ibu Fatmawati.)

'We Indonesians will continue to collaborate with Japan...'

The first picture shows Soekarno and Fatmawati entertaining some Japanese officers in the back yard of the Pegangsaan Timoer 56 home in Djakarta.
The bottom one shows Hatta, Soekarno, and Mas Mansoer with two Japanese Diet members during their visit to Japan. (Collection Idayu.)

Soekarno at left, flanking Tojo, with Hatta partly seen behind Soekarno, during the visit to Japan (Collection Idayu)

Members of the Choo Sangiin photographed after a meeting in front of the Pantjasila Building (Collection Hering)

Soekarno with his newly gained Japanese decoration, flanking his father Soekemi a few months before the latter's death on 8 May 1945 (Collection Idayu)

Soekarno and Hatta having proclaimed Indonesia's independence in the early hours of 17 August 1945 at Pegangsaan Timoer 56, watching the red-and-white banner being hoisted, with Fatmawati and Trimoerti watching it at right (Collection Kempen)

Street scene in Jakarta, August 1945 (Collection Hering)

Soekarno and Soebardjo with Soedarsono behind them at Pegangsaan Timoer 56 just before assembling Indonesia's first presidential cabinet (Collection Kempen)

Soekarno on his way to Ikada square on 19 September to address a huge crowd there. In a brief speech Soekarno called for calm, in a performance to show both the Allied powers and the Japanese that his Republic meant to stay alive even if it had to fight for it. (Collection Kempen.)

Yet another photograph of the Ikada square mass meeting on 19 September 1945, with Soekarno here addressing the huge crowd (Collection Hering)

Iboe Fatmawati, at Pegangsaan Timoer just before Soekarno and Hatta left for Djokjakarta (they arrived there by train on 18 December 1945). Only the seat of the Republican cabinet now led by Soetan Sjahrir would stay in Djakarta in order to negotiate matters with both the Dutch and the British. As some historians allege, the move was to avoid possible indictment of both Hatta and Soekarno for their collaboration with the Japanese during the occupation years. (Collection Ibu Fatmawati.)

Soetan Sjahrir, now premier of the first parliamentary cabinet, meeting Lt. Gen. Christison and H.J. van Mook, representing NICA (Collection Hering)

Soekarno and Fatmawati (pregnant again), with their son Goentoer in the Djokjakarta residence (Collection Hering)

to blow the dissimilarities between East and West out of proportion, a *'wasiat* [mythical exhortation] [...] and magically established as *hoekoem hikmat* [a law of fate], something beyond the capacity of mankind to change' (Sjahrir 1933: 18-9). So the PNI Baroe association continued to be inspired and driven by socialist concerns of a rationalist progressive and utilitarian humanist nature then current in Western left-wing circles.[56] The PNI Baroe thus welcomed hearing that their Dutch friends – such as Piet Schmidt, Sal Tas and his wife Maria Duchâteau, Jacques de Kadt, Edo Fimmen and Henriette Roland Holst – had split from the SDAP to form their own Onafhankelijke Socialistische Partij (OSP, Independent Socialist Party). This party considered the PNI Baroe to be the 'Indonesian revolutionary avant-garde' and thus a far cry from the indolent SDAP which, with its own colonial twin the ISDP, had ideologically harboured many who were close to the Soekarno camp.[57] So the PNI Baroe was reinforced by all that remained to hope for its concepts to be embodied in the foundations of a future Indonesian democratic society, no matter how long or slowly that lofty event would be in coming about. Also, since it seemed to believe that the Dutch would remain in control for some time, the PNI Baroe felt it had ample time for propagating its credo to Indonesian society as a whole.[58]

On the other side was a man just as intrigued by visions of 'a golden bridge' of self-determination for Indonesia, but far more centralist and Javanist to the core in his approach for turning that venture into a reality for his people. At once more Javanese, if not yet Indonesian, and surely more nationalist than universal, Soekarno saw himself as playing a pivotal role. He alone employed that emotion-laden Javanese word *manunggal* (to become fused as one), wished to become one with the people and in that stance achieve unity among his countrymen. Moreover, he alone was *sembada* (whole), and, so he thought, poised to unleash the very forces for making Indonesian independence feasible, while also restoring a primordial oneness long since lost among his people as a result of the far too disintegrative power of Dutch colonial overlords. To Soekarno, bred in relative provincial isolation and steeped in Javanese syncretist modes, the notions of Western-style gradualism therefore remained anathema. The class struggle notions of the Hatta/Sjahrir faction were thus rejected by Soekarno in favour of the wider though surely less cohesive brown front concept of pitting *sini* against *sana*. To Soekarno, that contradiction, far from being a *wasiat* or a *hukum hikmat,* was solely based upon racially inspired struggle; that struggle remained far more appealing to him and, so he thought, to the Indonesian masses, than questions about what

---

[56]   Hatta, 'Kearah Indonesia Merdeka' in Hatta 1953:61-2.
[57]   *Daulat Ra'jat,* 10 May 1932 and the OSP periodical *Fakkel,* 17 January 1933.
[58]   Benedict Anderson's introduction to Sjahrir 1968:1-2.

shape a future Indonesian state would finally assume. So, versed in Javanese magico-mystical perspectives that call for a cyclic recurrent development, with the *cakra manggilingan* (wheel of history) appearing to oscillate between periods of disorder and order, with power ebbing and flowing and reflecting the leader's own lack or abundance of *wahyu*, and being keenly aware of the presence of such a rhythm emerging in the *windu* of his own life, Soekarno in 1932, nearing the fourth *windu* after his birth, felt the time was ripe to reach out for his 'golden bridge': the *zaman mas* (golden era) to end years and years of *zaman edan* (era of insane instability). That this goal had little chance of achieving even partial success at that time did not much matter. If it failed, it would merely show the immense strength still wielded by Dutch *rahwanan* power; more importantly, though, it would demonstrate the *ksatrian* pluck of a Soekarno who dared again to challenge that power. Details of all this we will see later in the chapter.

Soekarno's efforts to reorganize the PPPKI and the tumult about the Wild Schools Ordinance

Bound as Soekarno was to the PPPKI, which, inspired by Thamrin, had been instrumental in giving him strong support from the moment he stepped outside Soekamiskin jail, Soekarno found Thamrin prepared to help reconstruct the brown front along these lines. For Thamrin, used to the frustrations of tiny cadre parties like his own Kaoem Betawi, PNI Baroe's narrow Marxist orientation had but little allure. Open as Thamrin had always been to the reformist appeal of his more moderate Dutch socialist acquaintances, he stuck to multi-party consensus politics in order to extract for his side and that of Soekarno concessions he considered feasible. More attuned to Indonesian domestic political realities than most of his peers, particularly those still abroad or having recently arrived home, he continued to opt for the political style based on the cordially constructed brown-front factions of his own making at municipal and quasi-parliamentary levels. At these councils he took full advantage of the liberty of speech extended to him, and of those crucial rights to challenge and question the government whenever its policies were deemed by him as harmfully exploitative to his people. Whatever brown-front support would be mobilized outside these narrowly enfranchised colleges he sat in, Thamrin not only welcomed but keenly stimulated Soekarno, who was often at his side in that challenging endeavour.

Soekarno, as well, perhaps prompted by the Hatta-Sjahrir cabal's ongoing criticism of Thamrin and the PPPKI, became aware of the fact that the PPPKI was in need of reorganization. With Thamrin as *praeadviseur* (main proposer) for such a renewal, moves were made in that direction with Soekarno as an invited guest, charged during the 30 April-1 May 1932 rally in Solo's Habi-projo clubhouse to draft such a PPPKI reorganization scheme. The rally was chaired by Dr Soetomo, however, who was 'not showing any signs of internal solidarity', as Soekarno put it. Soekarno also blamed the PPPKI for not bring-ing the PSII back, while other parties such as Partindo and PNI Baroe also stood aloof. These remarks made by an invited visitor caused Soetomo to offer his immediate resignation, causing even more turmoil among the deleg-ates, divided as they were into two camps, for and against Soetomo. After a break, Soetomo's resignation was honourably accepted and Thamrin elected as chairman, with Oto Iskanderdinata as secretary, and the PPPKI executive office (Madjelis Pertimbangan) moving from Soerabaja to Betawi also being approved. As for Soekarno, he was given four months to hand in his reorgan-ization proposal, which would then be discussed during a PPPKI assembly.[59] This occurred during the PPPKI conference at the Taman Siswa School in Djokja on 12 November 1932, where his draft was adopted to serve as a basis for new statutes and by-laws by a committee made up of Mr Wongsonegoro, Mr Soemardi and Mr Singgih. At that meeting Dr Soetomo was not present, a fact deplored by Soekarno and Thamrin. In all probability, the leader of the PBI had not managed to banish from his mind the disagreeable memories of the emotional Solo conference of the past April. Also at the Djokja meeting and the subsequent Solo PPPKI conference of 30 April-1 May 1933, where Partindo membership of the PPPKI was finally adopted, a meeting also shunned by Soetomo, the PBI delegation took recourse to belittling Soekarno and Sartono.[60] So Hatta's prediction of PPPKI unity being a sham was not far off the mark and, as *Soemanget* of 7 May had it, the PPPKI still looked 'like an empty barrel'. However, *Bintang Timoer*, *Sinar Deli* and *Sediotomo* of 4 May, and *Sipatahoenan* of 7 May 1932 all praised Thamrin's leadership, while seeing Soekarno as a possible bridge between Ko and Non-Ko elements of the *pergerakan*.

These *sini* views of Soekarno and Thamrin were confirmed somewhat by the tumult which occurred around the so-called Wilde Scholen (wild schools) ordinance of 15 September 1932, an issue which Dewantoro himself had raised at the recent Djokja PPPKI meeting, while also referring to the passive resist-ance campaign he had started by cabling to Governor-General De Jonge on 1 October stating his firm opposition to the ordinance. This ordinance, in the face of depressed economic conditions, was an attempt to curtail the spread of education by privately sponsored schools such as Taman Siswa, using the

---

[59]   See for that rally Mr. 545/1932.
[60]   Verheijen to De Jonge no. 123/A.P., 7 January 1933, Mr. 52/1933; A.W. Soentoro's report, no. 244/S, Mr. 52/1933; Verheijen to De Jonge no. 2681/A.P., 8 June 1933 and enclosed report by A.W. Soesilo, Mr. 775/1933.

pretext that these schools on the whole provided substandard education. The ordinance further required teachers of these private schools to obtain written permission to teach from local district government officials. Such permission would be granted to holders of a certificate from government or government-subsidized institutions, provided they could also convince local officials that they not would pose a threat to *rust en orde* (peace and tranquillity) through their teaching.[61] This led to retorts by Dewantoro and others that substandard education was better than none, while they also worried about the basis upon which Dutch standards were to be determined. They viewed the ordinance as a basic threat to their own educational aspirations, with Dewantoro viewing it as 'a comprehensive, if not draconian, measure to oppress indigenous-led education'.[62] Yet, in order not to provoke matters unduly, Dewantoro issued a 4 October 1932 manifesto to all *pergerakan* leaders asking them to avoid agitation or active resistance, in addition to requesting financial support for any victims of passive protests. These passive resistance measures brought Soekarno, Soetomo and Thamrin together, declaring their support for launching protest rallies about the issue, partly in order to bring Ko and Non-Ko together again. As the IPO survey of 17 December 1932 had it: 'in contrast to a few months ago when every one was against every one, all matters of disunity disappeared, and this strengthened the Indonesian movement in its opposition to the ordinance'.[63] Since at no time in the *pergerakan*'s history had one single issue galvanized such overall vehement opposition coming from all sides of the Indonesian community, all parties involved decided on a compromise. So, Dewantoro and Kiewiet de Jonge engaged in some private talks in Djokja on 19-20 October 1932, and then, after having exchanged letters about the issue on 21 and 27 October 1932, a Volksraad compromise was finally reached, requesting the government to suspend the ordinance for the time being.[64] To Soekarno and Thamrin, aware that passive resistance had led to success and, moreover, had been capable of restoring *pergerakan* solidarity, the final months of 1932 indeed held some promise of better things to come. Soekarno transformed Partindo into a still more powerful instrument than the expired PNI had ever been, and Thamrin was at the helm of a reorganized PPPKI; they both nourished hopes of *pergerakan* unity and steadfastness becoming a more permanent reality in the coming year. So soon after the solid successes they had achieved toward the end of 1932, they could hardly have foreseen that many of their own and other *pergerakan* achievements would be so seriously undermined by the harsh political realities of mid- and late 1933.

[61]   Soentoro's report, pp. 17-9, Mr. 52/1933.
[62]   *Poesara; Madjalah persatuan Taman-Siswa,* September 1932.
[63]   *Overzicht Inlandsche pers* 1932-50:385-6.
[64]   For these talks and letters see Kiewiet de Jonge collection, IISG archives and Hering 1991c: xiv, 83-5.

Partindo growth stimulated by Soekarno's inspiring leadership

Partindo, led by Sartono and Ali Sastroamidjojo and with young leaders such as Amir Sjarifoedin and Mohamad Yamin in influential positions, up to the time Soekarno joined it, had held some well-attended meetings. First, during the Betawi meeting on 24 April 1932, the party discussed the decision of the US Congress to grant the Philippines self-determination in 1940, thereby stressing the democratic and non-racist content of American educational and governmental policies and contrasting them with the situation in Indonesia.[65] Next came the First Partindo Congress, also held in Betawi, from Saturday to Tuesday, 14-17 May 1932, attended by some 2,500 people. Gobée commented

> that it was primarily to show the outside world the extreme radical character of the party so as to undermine the PNI Baroe's allegations that Partindo was merely a half-baked association, politically speaking. Fervour and an irreconcilable attitude permeated the association's conduct during its sessions, fed by the principal ideas of aloofness and self-help cherished by Sartono and associates for some time now. [Yet there is] no reason to take special measures against Partindo, even in spite of the negative views printed by some of the European dailies about the congress. [The] special branch reports of closed Partindo meetings have not revealed any indication that Partindo was moving along illegal ways at all or making any attempt to disturb public peace and order.

On the final day of the congress, after Soekarno in a short speech had hailed party chairman Sartono for his efforts, Soekarno again stressed the extreme left nationalist character of his party, which therefore formed no obstacle at all for other radical nationalists to join it, an obvious dig at the small PNI Baroe clique. With the PNI Baroe not exceeding a mere thousand, and Partindo with twenty branches in most of the important cities and towns of Java, Sumatra (Medan and Palembang), Celebes (Makassar and Menado) and Roeteng on Flores, all representing close to five thousand people, Sartono commented that 'our people still possess the strength to mount great activities for achieving our ultimate freedom'.[66] As to Bandoeng, its membership soared, surpassing Batavia's Partindo branch numbers. Soekarno, a Partindo

---

[65] Gobée to De Jonge, no. K 18/III, 3 May 1932 and report Datoek Toemenggoeng, Mr. 475/1932.
[66] Gobée to De Jonge no. K 20/III, 31 May 1932 and report of G.F. Pijper and Datoek Toemenggoeng, Mr. 607/1932; Verheijen to De Jonge, 21 May 1932 no. 2347/A.P. and a police intelligence report made up by Visbeen, Mr. 536/1932; Verheijen to De Jonge, 4 June 1932 no. 2549/A.P and Verheijen to Van der Hoek, *Resident* of Batavia, 4 June 1932 no. 2541/A.P.; Van der Hoek to Verheijen, 25 May 1932, no. 1271/F., all in Mr. 616/1932; Verheijen to De Jonge, 8 July 1932 no. 3197/A.P. with a Hoofdparket intelligence branch report made up by B.R. van der Most about Partindo, Mr. 721/1932.

member since 1 August 1932, was made vice-chairman of the Bandoeng branch and put in charge of propaganda on Partindo's Central Executive as well. From that day onwards, Soekarno devoted himself to promoting Partindo in Bandoeng and the rest of the Priangan in much the same fashion as he had done for the PNI in 1928 and 1929. As propagandist, he made promotional trips to Central and East Java during August and September 1932, claiming to have talked to some thirty thousand people at public meetings and member rallies.[67]

Partindo's Djakarta branch meeting of 16 October 1932, attended by three thousand people, was completely devoted to the Wild Schools Ordinance. Gobée commented that 'Sartono's mild objections about that issue were well founded'. The meeting also held a one-minute silence to honour Patty, who had been moved from Roeteng to the Boven Digoel concentration camp. The Djakarta branch counted three thousand members, owned thirty primary schools and some nine buildings divided over as many districts, and held weekly study course meetings attended by some six hundred people. Mochtar Loetfi, member of the Persatoean Moeslim Indonesia (PMI, Union of Indonesian Muslims), executive at Sumatra's West coast residency, expressed the hope that Partindo/PMI endeavours would result in Indonesia Merdeka. Citing some Koran verses and written traditions, Loetfi held 'that Islam, far from censuring nationalism, in fact welcomes and supports it'. During the closing session, Soekarno reported that a new Partindo daily called *Indonesia Berdjoeang* (Indonesia Fights) would be started soon.[68]

The Second Partindo Congress, with Soekarno now chairman, affirmed Sartono's prediction made on the final day of the First Congress. The Second Congress, held in Soerabaja 14-19 April 1933, elicited the following comments from Gobée:

> Partindo has proved to be quite a lively and well-organized association, having in Java and Madoera alone 43 branches catering to some 20,000 members. [...] Looking at its programme of action, one sees how well organized it is and how well prepared it is in working toward making the masses politically conscious of the aims which well up in the minds and the hearts of its leaders. The speech made by Ir Soekarno shows how passionately he pursues his mission.[69]

---

[67] *Inlandsche Pers Overzichten* October 1932:14, Mr. 1231/1932. As to the Bandoeng numbers, they soared from 226 in August 1932 to 3,762 in July 1933, with the Priangan area also showing numbers equal to those of Bandoeng; Albreghs' survey about Soekarno's political conduct during 31 December 1931 to 31 July 1933 notably in the Priangan, p. 80, Mr. 1276/1933.

[68] Gobée to De Jonge, no. 1666/K-III, 24 October 1932, pp. 1-2 with bijlage, pp. 1-3, 8, Mr. 1078/1932.

[69] Gobée to De Jonge, no. K 21/III, 2 May 1933, p. 1; attached to it is a report written by the language specialist of Inlandsche Zaken, Dr L. de Vries, Mr. 554/1933.

Soekarno, in an address titled 'The great contours of Indonesian society as pursued by Partindo', first explained the notions of socio-nationalism and of socio-democracy adopted as basic principles by the congress. These notions were

> part of and identified by marhaenism and partindoism, and as such these notions confront capitalism and imperialism. Since the founding of Partindo, all who are prepared to open their eyes and ears know that the democracy and nationalism of that party are part of the real marhaenism. And yet, two years after its founding, there are still people (because they are stone deaf) who feel that Partindo is a bourgeois party paying homage to capitalism (loud applause).

In contrast to these allegations, and with the *sana* press outlets also labelling 'our nationalist activity as inspired by communism', Soekarno cited Jawaharlal Nehru and Dr Sun Yat-sen in arguing that

> one did not need to be a communist to assail the present system. A democratic system such as the European and American ones was not Partindo's ideal, therefore, but one based economically and politically upon our socio-democracy with our people getting human rights in the widest sense. [...] At the moment Partindo is striving for a free Indonesia and accentuating the national element in that struggle for freedom. All capitalists, even the ones who belong to our own people, we need to fight against. Partindoism educates *marhaen* not to tolerate the present system and prepares *marhaen* to replace it by *sama rasa – sama rata*, a *rasa keoemoeman* (equal rights – equal burdens, a feeling common to us all). So Partindo's nationalism is an intrinsic kind of nationalism, a nationalism inspired by humane feelings, a *marhaen* nationalism of the hungry, of the ones feeling they live in squalor. Not a nationalism of the leaders alone but also of the people. Thus not a reformist kind, not a mealy-mouthed kind of a movement (*pergerakan apem-apeman*, literally a movement made of rice-flour cakes), not a weepy kind of movement, therefore, but a movement truly inspired by a courageous and radical kind of nationalism. [...] Let us therefore rid ourselves of the weakening impact of the *adat* [traditional system of law] and leave all the crying behind us. *Marhaen* live in poverty, but will not cry or complain about it any longer. Those times are behind us. We have cried enough. Partindo shall lead us all to a free Indonesia. So unite and make the Partindo banner known to all our people, whether they are working on the land or in the factories.[70]

Developments leading to Soekarno's second incarceration

Darkening clouds were gathering slowly but surely to curtail Soekarno's political impact, perhaps for good. During the tumult caused by the mutiny

---

[70]   De Vries report, pp. 14-6, Mr. 554/1933.

of the iron-clad vessel *De Zeven Provinciën* from 4 till 10 February 1933,[71] initial moves were prepared by the colonial government in that direction. It was alleged that Hatta's PNI Baroe was involved in the mutiny, and a decree was issued on 27 June 1933 forbidding all government crew officials, not only those in the military branches, being members of the PNI Baroe (Mrázek 1994:115). Gobée, however, on 17 March 1933, counselled moderation in view of intolerable breaches of the right of assembly committed by police and interior administration officials during Partindo and PNI Baroe meetings. Thamrin questioned the government on these breaches, on 24 March in the Volksraad. *De Stuw*, in its 16 April 1933 issue, discussed the matter, urging the government to look beyond its reactions to Partindo and PNI Baroe and devote some genuine concern to the entire Indonesian community. Mr G. Vonk, the government's police affairs representative in the Volksraad, argued that, on the whole, these police activities had produced calm instead of spreading tension, an argument met by loud approval from most of the *sana* in the Volksraad and outside the Pedjambon building. In reply, Thamrin vowed to calm down his own side and, though still blaming the police and *sana* for having created undue unrest in indigenous quarters, he decided not to submit a motion about it.[72]

In some circles of the colonial government, concern about Soekarno's Partindo activities had mounted. Officials were alarmed first by an article that had appeared in Partindo's periodical *Soeloeh Indonesia Moeda*, entitled 'De koelies' (The coolies; in this case, the contract labourers working in the tobacco-growing area of Deli in the Sumatran East Coast residency). This article was not even written by Soekarno, but he allowed it to be published in Partindo's periodical. It was held to be inflammatory in character, ignoring the fact that it had been written some thirty years ago by the jurist/journalist Mr J. van den Brand. Only this time, the allegations of Van den Brand of scandalous and often criminal behaviour committed by Dutch planters and their subordinates against the male and female coolies they supervised did not evoke an official condemnation (as it had in 1903 by the investigator J.T.L.

---

[71]   The mutiny was sparked by 7% wage cuts in the navy, with some 180 Indonesian and 50 European naval ratings involved. Mutineers sailed the vessel toward the Soenda Straits, leaving behind the ship's captain and nearly half of its officers in Koetaradja, with the captain later following the ship in a government steamer. The mutineers' plan to sail the vessel to Soerabaja to peacefully join their naval trade unionists there came to an abrupt and violent end on 10 February 1933, when in the Soenda Straits a Dornier Wall sea-plane bomber dropped a bomb on the vessel, killing sixteen Indonesian and three European crew members. Blom 1983:40-53, 74-6, 163, 289; De Jonge 1968:160-3; Mrázek 1994:112-3.

[72]   Gobée to De Jonge, 17 March 1933, Mr. 363/1933. For Thamrin's interpellation, see Volksraad Zittingsjaar 1932-1933, Onderwerp 147, Stuk 1, pp. 1-7 and for Thamrin and Vonk clashing about the issue, *Handelingen Gedelegeerden* 1932-1933:327-34, 343-51; for Thamrin not tabling the motion, *Handelingen Gedelegeerden* 1932-1933:350-1.

Rhemrev), but served now, in 1933, as a reason to accuse Soekarno and his followers of sowing feelings of hate and discord among the diverse ethnic communities of the Indies archipelago (Hering 1988:200). The wheels of justice not only grind slowly, but behave in strange ways indeed.

However, even greater governmental concern appeared in the wake of a ringing Soekarno brochure called *Mentjapai Indonesia Merdeka* (To achieve Indonesian freedom). He had composed the brochure while resting a few days in the Priangan town of Pengalengan just after finishing a hectic Central Java tour, which according to his foreword attracted 89,000 people. The booklet, appearing at the beginning of April 1933, was by far Soekarno's most important contribution to the corpus of indigenous nationalist polemical writing since his release from Soekamiskin prison. As such, it bore a strong resemblance to his 1930 defence plea. Like that 60,000-word plea, Soekarno's *Mentjapai Indonesia Merdeka* marshalled a vast array of official data to lend his arguments substance. In it, Soekarno exposed the evils he felt surrounded open-door imperialism, while condemning the entire colonial system. This system, with the economic recession now deepening, continued to allow foreign surplus capital to ceaselessly multiply by systematically draining far weaker indigenous potential and resources. And so, in the 1933 brochure, as in 1930, Soekarno argued with still greater intensity that the nationalist struggle, supported strongly by concerted indigenous mass protest, remained the appropriate method to counter capitalist power. The more so, since it was now facing a governor-general who made it his task to advocate undiluted Dutch domination and capitalist exploitation. So, replete with modern images of a reunited brown front locked in struggle with a white one, of *sini* in diametrical opposition to *sana*, Soekarno, enriched as he was since his youth by the vast imagery of the Javano-Balinese *wayang*, took recourse to stirring up more ancient and therefore more meaningful images from a glorious past similarly rife with violent and relentless strife. Hence, by evoking Ramawidjeje slaying a usurping and overseas alien Dasamoeka, and by recalling the magical powers of *aji-pancanesa*, of *aji-candrabirawa* and of *jemparing*,[73] Soekarno, as he had on so many occasions before, tried to revitalize modes of nationalist political expression, far too long rendered sterile and ineffective by alien intrusion. That Soekarno's message was not lost on some of the colonial authorities was demonstrated by the swift official reactions which greeted its appearance in the Indonesian-speaking world. Not only was it suppressed and barred from a third printing, but zealous civil

---

[73]   Based on the Ramayana epic with indigenous prince Ramawidjeje using his magic bow *jemparing* to slay the ten-faced Dasamoeka, who had violated Sita (Iboe Indonesia, Rama's bride) – all obvious references to the two-faced alien Dutch intruders; see Hering 1991a:35, note 12. As for the two *aji*, they are *mantra* (magic formulas) assuring immortality and reincarnation respectively; see Hering 1991a:37, note 38.

servants were quick to make a Dutch-language copy available to their overseas superiors in The Hague. The Hoofd Parket also commenced to prepare
an indictment of Soekarno, basing it in legal terms on the grounds of sedi-
tion allegedly contained in his brochure (Hering 1991a:i). Some of the Dutch
colonial officials at that time translated *mencapai* as a '*grijpen naar*' (a grab
for) Indonesia *merdeka,* obviously trying to create the impression of Soekarno
and associates working toward a revolutionary '*greep naar de macht*' a grab for
power.[74] Most Indonesian-language dictionaries, however, translate *mencapai*
as 'to achieve, to attain'.

In any case, administrative measures aimed at curbing the radical Non-Ko
pergerakan, or even squelching it, now continued in rather rapid succession.
Not only Partindo, but also Hatta's tiny PNI Baroe and the West Sumatra
and Tapanoeli branches of Persatoean Moeslimin Indonesia (Permi) and
the Partai Sarekat Islam Indonesia (PSII) received special attention by the
authorities. The activities of the non-cooperationist Permi and PSII were
watched closely, because these Sumatran areas were known to have been
prone to violent rebellion in the recent past. So, internment of Permi leader
Moechtar Loetfi was decided upon, and civil servants were prohibited from
joining Permi, the PSII, Partindo or the PNI Baroe.[75] The PNI Baroe, with its
Marxist-tinged message, had remained highly suspect in the eyes of the colonial administration ever since the party's inception. Also, Hatta's recent business trip to Japan upset the colonial government. In Japan, Hatta was hailed
by the local press as the Gandhi of Java, while the *Osaka Jiji* of 9 May 1933 and
the *Osaka Mainichi* of 15 April 1933 linked him with an upsurge of Indonesian
national chauvinism in the wake of the miscarried *Zeven Provinciën* mutiny.[76]
References to Japan by Thamrin and other members of his party as a sample
of Asian self-reliant industriousness to be copied, had earlier caused irrita-
tion among colonial authorities, and would henceforth colour official attitudes toward Indonesian sympathizing with that powerful Asian country.[77]
Even Boedi Oetomo and Dr Soetomo's PBI were to become suspect in the
eyes of officials dealing with their activities. In Soetomo's case, the Roekoen
Tani (farmers' union) activities of the PBI in the sugar-growing areas around
Soerabaja were reported upon with growing alarm by Soerabaja's *resident*

---

[74]   See Mr. 970/1933 and Mr. 990/1933, and the Dutch cabinet 'Nota' 'Oriënteerende aanteeke-
ningen betreffende de interpellatie Cramer', p. 7.
[75]   See 'Nota' of August 1933 in Verbaal 19 October 1933 O 24; Verheijen to De Jonge, 13 and
23 July 1933, respectively in Mr. 849/1933 and Mr. 920/1933.
[76]   See article 'Gandhi of Java entertained' in *The Japan Times,* 19 May 1933; for the *Osaka Jiji*
and *Osaka Mainichi* reports see J.C. Pabst to Minister of Foreign Affairs, 5 May 1933 report, p. 5
in Verbaal 27 July 1933 Q 18, Verbaal 7 June 1933 Q 13 and Mouw's 2 June 1933 survey 'Bezoek
Moh. Hatta aan Japan' to De Jonge, a survey also citing the 5 May 1933 *Japan Advertiser* report of
Hatta visiting Ras Bahari Bose, the Indian radical activist living in exile in Japan.
[77]   For these Thamrin references, see *Handelingen Volksraad* 1931-1932:1843; 1933-1934:154-5.

A.H. Moreu.[78] Moreu's concern reflected widespread administrative fears of the radical nationalist parties Partindo and PNI Baroe, like the PBI being in fact urban-based organizations, becoming involved in mobilizing rural masses, while specifically exploiting anxieties in Javanese sugar-growing and other rural areas. The more so, since it was in these areas that the economic recession had led to sharp reductions of labour and land rental income.[79] A subsequent police report discussing the PBI's 8-9 July 1933 Roekoen Tani Congress in Soerabaja held that most of the farmers' union leaders were not even *tani* (farmers), but members of the unemployed Soerabajan middle class. Subsequently, Soetomo's Gedong (national clubhouse) was closed by local administration officials, causing *De Stuw* to comment that this was yet another example of *politieke plagerij* (political harassment).[80]

Meanwhile, in an effort to challenge the Indies government even further, Soekarno, on 9 July 1933, proposed scheduling two Partindo public propaganda meetings to be held simultaneously in Batavia and Bandoeng on 31 August 1933, the Dutch Queen's birthday. These proposals of intensified and simultaneously planned radical *pergerakan* meetings[81] caused Thamrin in the Volksraad to appeal for moderation. Thamrin stated that, although he and his party faction had recently labelled the government's police activities as unnecessarily rigorous and provocative, his side would try to heed objectivity and not seek fault exclusively with others. Thamrin further admitted that his view of the situation and his estimation of the mental subtlety of some of the popular leaders had perhaps been too optimistic. He urged, however, that the government's representative recognize that his personal view was that the government's measures were inexorably leading to inevitable disaster (*Handelingen Volksraad* 1933-1934:571-5). Thamrin quite deeply abhorred the impending violent confrontation, and called on both the government and the *sana* press to think of their political opponents as decent and well-meaning people, instead of labelling them as 'troublemakers, haters of Europeans, underminers of state authority, extremists' and the like (*Handelingen Volksraad* 1933-1934:574). Also, the leaders of the *pergerakan* were far too often portrayed as 'self-seeking, ambitious, politically exploitative' people, while a whole army of Indonesians chose to see them as 'selfless and imbued with

---

78 Moreu to Kuneman, 26 June 1933, Mr. 1847/1934.
79 Memorie van Overgave Soerabaja, pp. 46-9, Mr. 1004/1935; Memorie van Overgave Oost Java, pp. 80-7, Mr. 847/1933; Memorie van Overgave Solo, pp. 133-5, Mr. 415/1937; Memorie van Overgave Cheribon, Mr. 1124/1933; Van der Plas to Governor West Java, 5 November 1932, Mr. 71/1932 and Van der Plas to De Jonge, 7 December 1933 and attached report, pp. 2- 10, 12-4, Mr. 1226/1932.
80 Poeze 1988:295, for the congress Poeze 1988:295-6. 'Politieke plagerijen', *De Stuw* 16 July 1933:173. Soetomo's *Soeara Oemoem*, too, was bridled by Gouvernments Besluit, 23 June 1933, no. 6.
81 For these meetings planned by Soekarno, see Poeze 1988:297-8.

service to their people and ready to sacrifice financial and other benefits'
(*Handelingen Volksraad* 1933-1934:574). Thamrin was immensely hurt by all
the diatribe, and regretted that those fine indigenous leaders were not sitting
next to him, although he respected their wish not to partake in the Volksraad
or any other council. Thamrin closed his remarks as follows:

> Mr Chairman. Let us, the government's representative and I, no longer make
> promises. We are both people of our time and of our own milieu, and quite unable
> to truly control events. Allow me, therefore, to express only the hope, and I speak
> here from my heart and as man to man, that henceforth both my peers and I will
> be better understood. I will thus quietly await the future development of true
> mutual understanding. (*Handelingen Volksraad* 1933-1934:574.)

However, it was to no avail. The deeds ensued swiftly enough, but were
hardly taking the course Thamrin had anticipated in the wake of his 26 July
Volksraad appeal for seriously meant moderation on both fronts. On the
night of 31 July-1 August 1933, Soekarno was arrested on the front lawn of
Thamrin's private residence at the Sawah Besar thoroughfare in Batavia. The
colonial police had been waiting patiently for him outside Thamrin's house,
while a meeting of Partindo's main executive was under way inside. During
the evening meal, hosted by Thamrin, Soekarno's political actions and the
overall precariousness of the situation had been scrutinized. Soekarno
had been urged by Thamrin and others to take a more moderate political
stance.[82] The meeting held at Thamrin's home demonstrated once again
Thamrin's crucial go-between function between extreme and moderate elements of the *pergerakan*. Even Governor-General De Jonge, in justifying the
administration's measures against Soekarno, Partindo, Permi, PSII and PNI
Baroe, seemed aware of Thamrin's key position and of the fear of escala-
tion expressed by this important nationalist member of the Volksraad (De
Jonge 1968:191). In his memoirs, De Jonge cites Thamrin's 26 July Volksraad
address, where the Fraksi Nasional chairman had vented concern about the
imminence of violent clashes, together with his somewhat diminishing lack
of confidence in some of the *pergerakan* association leaders' mental stability.
De Jonge had decided, therefore, that the right time had indeed arrived for
action in order to avert violence and to curb further agitation (De Jonge 1968:
191). Obviously pleased by seeing Soekarno placed behind bars once again,
De Jonge, however, could not resist speculating about Thamrin as well. So,
in his memoirs, he muses:

[82]   Comments by editor G. Boon in *Soerabajaasch Handelsblad*, 1 August 1933. A copy of it was
shown to us during an interview with J.H. Ritman on 2 April 1979. Ritman himself in *Bataviaasch
Nieuwsblad*, 1 August 1933 praised 'the government's moves against Soekarno since it showed
confidence and dash'. See also De Jonge 1968:191.

Would we ever be able to catch Thamrin? He was the worst of the lot, competent and clever; I did like him in a way, but I would very much like to have seen him safely put away in Banda or somewhere else. It was not to be; he did not give me a chance. (De Jonge 1968:191.)

In a letter dated 23 August 1933, after he had expressed his joy to De Graeff's successor, De Jonge, for having placed Soekarno behind bars again, Simon de Graaff disclosed that he had discussed Soekarno with De Graeff; the latter had then mused that things could have turned out in a more positive way if only the PNI leader had been financially supported to leave the Indies for studies in Holland. The ex-minister of colonies considered this to be a 'naive' suggestion. Naive or not, in the hothouse and repressive atmosphere of what remained of the 1930s, moderating qualities as displayed formerly by De Graeff and then often afterwards echoed and further elaborated in the counsels of Gobée, Pijper, Kiewiet de Jonge, Mühlenfeld, Van der Plas and the two brothers Schrieke, were well-nigh rendered inaudible in a sea of counter-reformist and repressive legislation. Even the Bureau voor Inlandsche Zaken, considered by De Jonge a superfluous institution too expensive to be maintained any longer, would have been scrapped were it not for the younger Schrieke's spirited defence to keep it operating.[83]

Totalitarian methods and principles were to have great and continuous appeal for De Jonge, an ardent advocate of undiluted Dutch domination, and it is no wonder that he accorded such a warm welcome to the Dutch Nationaal-Socialistische Beweging (Dutch Nazi party) leader Anton Mussert on the occasion of the latter's quite successful fund-raising campaign in the Indies. Evolutionary nationalism, a term once coined by his predecessor, De Jonge relegated to mere *gebral* (rantings) about misconceived Western-imported slogans, uttered in his view by a group of agitators far out of touch with the masses they professed to lead. Of course, not all of the reactionary obscurantism of those days should be laid at the feet of De Jonge. As the guardian of Dutch colonial policy, he had to abide by the general rules of capitalist exploitation, a task not made easy by the constant bickering of Minister of Colonies Colijn and the decision of the Dutch home government to adhere to the gold standard. Furthermore, the previous liberal experimentation, under admittedly more intelligent and more attractive viceroys, became almost impossible in the face of growing economic depression and the concomitant hardening of attitudes within European (*totok belanda*) and Eurasian *colon* communities (Hering 1987:296). Considering these developments, one can perhaps muse that Soekarno, now barred from contact with the world

---

[83]   See Hering 1987:296. For the isolation of his position vis-à-vis De Jonge, see Gobée to De Kat Angelino, 25 March 1936, Collection Gobée, KITLV H 795/27.

outside his cell, was spared from a more sinister fate. Would he, had he still been free, have refrained from condemning the colonial establishment as he found it? Of course not; true to his spirit, he would have continued condemning the colonial system in every way possible. He would most likely have found himself, like Thamrin, operating under growing clouds of official suspicion and perhaps, like Thamrin, been driven to a premature death. All this remains mere speculation. We must therefore come back to earth and ponder Soekarno's true fate, facing his interrogators in Soekamiskin gaol and the about-face he sprung on them at the end of these sessions.

Soekarno behind bars and the emotions around his letters for mercy

Soekarno was charged with having violated article 153 bis of the Penal Code, for the writing and the distribution of his brochure *Mentjapai Indonesia Merdeka*, but was allowed to defend his recent political activities during several interrogation sessions. These were held under the supervision of deputy chief-*jaksa* Raden Hendarin, assisted by Mr P.H.C. Jongmans, at that time attached as deputy attorney-general to the attorney-general, while occasionally the *controleur* for police and legal matters of Bandoeng's local administration, R.W. Kofman, was involved as well. Thus, here again, as it was during the Landraad trial, an entwining of the colonial justice and administration departments occurred. Also, while Hendarin's signature appeared in most cases at the bottom of the interrogation sessions, it was Jongmans who led most of the interrogations. Starting on 17 August 1933, there were three more sessions during August (on 18, 28 and 29) and four sessions during September (on 8, 9, 13 and 14). After these eight sessions, it would not be until 23 November 1933, that Soekarno was brought to face M.F. Tydeman, the *resident* of the Priangan, for a so-called *verhoor op vraagpunten* (questioning). At this time, Tydeman put 34 questions to Soekarno, which he duly answered. The usual colonial procedure for political culprits on the eve of their extradition, the questionnaire is the only ARA document so far in the massive dossier on Soekarno's interrogation to show Soekarno's genuine signature.[84]

In the earlier series of sessions during August, Soekarno appeared quite confident, even being defiant at times in the matter of his brochure and other issues. However, during the latter two sessions of September, he suddenly changed tactics. He regretted 'using metaphors which were too steep, while admitting that hate against Europeans had never been part of his propaganda and that his struggle had been directed against the system, not against

[84] Mr. 1502/1933, with Hering 1991a:105-8 providing an English-language translation of it.

persons'. But he was aware now that 'his brand of politics contained much which was mistaken, and that in general all his actions and remarks had been rash'. Even 'in matters of non-cooperation and mass protest, while he still felt that they were legitimate, he had tended to the extreme'. He maintained that 'he had never had a good word for the government, and failed therefore to explain more fully our political principles'. Having admitted all that, he had resigned from the *Fikiran Ra'jat* and stated thrice in succession his intention to withdraw from politics altogether. Concluding the 14 September session, Soekarno promised that he, 'when freed, would live in seclusion away from the world, and would try earning a living practising as an engineer and architect, with his wife supporting his earnings if need be by trading in kains [batik cloth]' (Hering 1991a:104).

One may well wonder what drove Soekarno to make these rather startling confessions at the very end of his interrogation. Perhaps the key to it all can be found in the four letters, probably urged by Jongmans,[85] that Soekarno was compelled to write to the colonial attorney-general. In these letters, the first two of which, written 30 August and 7 September 1933, overlapped the interrogation sessions, he begged the latter, in quite a passionate manner, to set him free and to accept his well-meant proposals to mend his ways. Soekarno described his intentions as being in the realm of completely leaving politically inspired activities and devoting his life henceforth in a purely civilian capacity suited to his academic skills. If he was to breach these promises, Soekarno maintained that the government was free to 'publish these lines' and 'immediately intern' him. Also, publication of the letter would 'surely spell his social death' and cause 'Indonesian society to cover him with scorn and spit on him'. These proposals Soekarno further embellished by begging the attorney-general to pay heed to the plight of Inggit and his mother-in-law, who needed him home and were reasons for him not leaving the country or settling abroad. Also, his mother, to whom he now owed it 'to start a completely new life', had 'become ill' finding him in jail again. To both his parents, who had worked 'their fingers to the bone in order to allow him to become an engineer', he felt it now his duty 'to keep them free from sorrow in their old age'. So he beseeched the attorney-general and the government to be merciful to him, his family and his parents, while at the end of this 30 August letter he again implored the attorney-general 'to release him as soon as possible from the nerve-racking state of confinement in which he now dwelt'. He added a postscript to that first letter that he was 'willing to sign a declaration'.[86]

---

[85]   For Jongmans' involvement, see Ramadhan 1981:295-6. Inggit revealed that it was an 'Utusan Pemerintah' (governement's delegate), though later, in our 15 July 1976 interview with her she recalled that it was Jongmans (Hering 1991a:x).

[86]   Mr. 1276/1933. For English-language translations, see Hering 1991a:109-10.

Hardly a week had passed when Soekarno, perhaps worried about not having had a reply to his first, wrote his second letter. He reiterated all the promises made in his first letter, and the sorrows he had caused his family and his parents, but this time he beseeched the government, concerned as he was about not having rendered his intentions sufficiently clear in his first letter, to publish a statement as follows: 'The government has received a request from Ir Soekarno for him to be released, on the promise that he will refrain from all further political activity'. Soekarno concluded: 'Allow me to return to my wife and child, allow me to kiss my old mother's feet. I prostrate myself before you and the government seeking forgiveness.'[87] As to his third letter, Soekarno enclosed two letters, one addressed to his wife and one to the main executive of Partindo, explaining to the attorney-general that these two letters revealed his 'purpose of severing all political ties with the *pergerakan*'. The letter to his wife instructed her 'to close the doors of our house to politics', while the letter to Partindo's main executive announced 'my resignation as chairman of the main executive and my resignation as a party member'. He 'courteously requested the attorney-general to forward these letters' and stressed to him that 'from now on I am no longer a political person'. In closing, Soekarno wrote: 'I sob out my appeal before you and the government: allow me to return to my wife and child and mother.'[88] In the fourth letter, while admitting that it was perhaps 'improper to frequent the attorney-general and the government with letters', he deemed himself to be 'in a state of most grievous suffering' and wished to prostrate himself 'again and again before those he sought mercy from'. He further announced his resignation as editor-publisher of *Fikiran Ra'jat* and his willingness, if the government so wished it, of 'submitting articles in the Malay language, guiding today's people's movement toward more constructive ways'. He added that such articles, 'written in bondage, would perhaps wield little effect since they represented the ravings of a demoralized man, who is now trying to curry favour with the government. [...] Articles written by a free man have more effect.' Soekarno further understood that the government would refuse to 'strike a bargain' with him, though he added, 'there is no question of a deal with the government, only a case of a deeply unfortunate man who, in sorrow, begs for forgiveness and who is furthermore prepared to accept any demand'.[89]

That the Indies government, while not responding at all to these pleas, refrained from making them public is to its credit. All that may well have been motivated by overall governmental intention, though not legally con-

---

[87]   Mr. 1276/1933 and Hering 1991a:110-1.
[88]   Mr. 1276/1933 and Hering 1991a:111.
[89]   Mr. 1276/1933 and Hering 1991a:111-2.

firmed as yet, to keep Soekarno politically isolated by swiftly banishing him outside Java. Such a measure had in the recent past been successfully employed with troublemakers of Soekarno's ilk such as Tjipto, Patty and Iwa Koesoema Soemantri. Due, however, to the letters Soekarno himself had managed to get to the outside world about his Partindo and *Fikiran Ra'jat* resignations, and the visits he had with Thamrin and Inggit, his about-face reached the Indonesian world outside Soekamiskin like a blast. Foremost in the attacks made to discredit Soekarno was Hatta. The latter gave vent to his own pent-up frustrations in two articles, one titled 'Tragedie Soekarno' and the other 'Sikap Pemimpin' (Attitude of a leader), arguing that the former Partindo leader was as good as dead politically, and thus no longer of any use to the *pergerakan*. So, with reports of the dramatic moves made by Soekarno surfacing, two streams of opinion emerged in *sini* daily comment. One, clearly a minority view, doggedly defended Soekarno. The other, with Saeroen in *Pemandangan* and Hatta in *Daulat Ra'jat* taking the lead, condemned Soekarno in no uncertain terms. However, more open views about Soekarno's about-face came to the surface in the wake of Thamrin's 10 September 1933 visit to Soekarno and Sanoesi Pane's *Bintang Timoer* disclosures made in that paper on 24 November 1933. It seems that during Thamrin's visit, Soekarno had revealed his plans to change course politically and to walk the road of cooperation, and that he had informed both Verheijen and his interrogators about this. Even Ritman, who often met Thamrin in the Volksraad public gallery, knew about these new approaches being made. As for Sanoesi Pane, he revealed that as early as May 1933, Soekarno and Thamrin had visited him, with Soekarno declaring that he was quite prepared to muster sufficient moral courage to become a cooperationist, as he saw the need for such a tactic.

Tjipto, writing in Dutch in *Soeara Oemoem*, regretted that so many *sini* columns did not rise above the 'usual coffee house gossip' when commenting on Soekarno's 'perfidy that had culminated in the decision to leave the pergerakan at a decisive moment'. Tjipto argued that the indigenous press, in so quickly passing a verdict on Soekarno's conduct, had in fact judged and sentenced itself. Tjipto then subjected Soekarno's actions to a psychological analysis. Ever since he had been released from Soekamiskin due to De Graeff's reprieve, Soekarno (according to Tjipto) had been a 'psychiatric patient'. An overseas trip then suggested by Thamrin would, in Tjipto's opinion, have been quite justified for Soekarno's sake. But the party's inner circle did not like it: 'the *pergerakan* needed him day and night, a trip abroad was a sign of cowardice'. To Tjipto, all that was empty talk of some 'so-called chauvinists who, when matters really counted, preferred others to make the sacrifice for them on behalf of the fatherland'. Sanoesi Pane, in a Dutch-language letter to *Soeara Oemoem* (12 January 1934), and like Tjipto's a veiled attack on Hatta's comments about Soekarno, reiterated Tjipto's more direct verdict on the *sini* press. In Pane's opinion, the indigenous press had failed to devote even a word 'to the man Soekarno, to his brilliant soul, his courage, integrity, his deep inner life'. Further, no evidence of 'individual psychological insight into his character nor of his many-faceted spirit' had been given. Nor was 'a social-psychological consideration of Soekarno as a historical phenomenon' to be found in the majority of the *sini* newspapers. Moreover, and in Pane's view even worse, Indonesians themselves had failed to show any sense of moral fibre:

> As a mass we have not proven to possess at this moment in time great moral capacities [...] while in the attitude expressed by many of our press vis-à-vis Ir Soekarno, our spiritual poverty, our impotence for subtle dialectics, has been in evidence. This attitude is certainly a reflection of our disrupted national life.

The *Bataviaasch Nieuwsblad*, whose editor-in-chief J.H. Ritman had closely followed the Soekarno case, was also more open in his views about Soekarno. In a lengthy article he wrote that:

> Soekarno really intends to mend his past mistakes. [W]e have some recent and reliable information that lends more credibility to this than we had before. [Q]uite different circumstances clearly show that Soekarno, lonely in his cell and also due to his isolation, has come to see the error of his ways. [...] He fears the prospect of internment, and from the first moment of his arrest he dreaded the possibility of exile. In a most humble way, he then turned to the government to request to be shielded from such a fate. [...] His conversion is not merely a matter of just today or yesterday, in fact it started during the first hours of his detention. [...] On behalf of the public, we deem it important that the government not simply reject in advance Soekarno's overtures to the judicial authorities.[90]

Stokvis, then on a short fact-finding tour in Indonesia, wrote in a report to the SDAP on 22 January 1934 that:

> The reports concerning a strong change in his [Soekarno's] political ideas are for the greater part correct. [...] A most reliable source [Thamrin, most likely] assured me that some time before his second arrest Soekarno had begun to doubt the tenability of his strict non-cooperationist views. [...] I also learned that Soekarno has informed the attorney-general of his changed convictions. [...] The nationalist press reproached Soekarno bitterly; fortunately, there were also some milder opinions aired by the press. My own opinion is that this man has struggled for his cause in a pure, courageous and talented way. Gaining a different view regarding the rightness of one's method for carrying out the struggle – anything different is out of the question – is understandable and should be respected. But even if weakness has crept in, even then one should realize that no single individual can

---

[90] Ritman, during an interview in Voorburg, the Netherlands, 2 April 1979, showed us his copy of the *Bataviaasch Nieuwsblad*, 24 November 1933, and revealed that he had been in close contact with Thamrin before he wrote the article.

carry all the burdens all the time and also remember that Soekarno, in any case, did accept and perform a gigantic task indeed.[91]

However, all these views were to no avail. The government, departing from the course of events adopted by the previous administration, where De Graeff, only after a detailed exchange of letters with his closest advisors, decided to try Soekarno, did not worry about such niceties this time. In short order the Raad van Indië was consulted about the Soekarno letters and the letters sent to his wife and Partindo's main executive.[92] In its 13 October 1933 recommendation, the Raad van Indië counselled against freeing Soekarno because he would 'always remain to endanger public peace and order'. Also considered doubtful were the promises he had made to adhere to a new course, since, as the Raad had it, Soekarno 'possesses a weak and uncontrollable nature and will, in spite of his good intentions and promises to moderate himself, again fall victim to the cheers of the public and break these intentions of good will'.[93] On 23 November 1933, Soekarno was subjected to a final interrogation following a pre-set questionnaire (*verhoor op vraagpunten*). On 28 December 1933, by governmental decree no. 2z, the town of Endeh on the island of Flores was indicated as Soekarno's place of exile. So, finding colonial officials unplacated by his conversion, Soekarno, ever mindful of Kokrosono and the ancient familiar Javanese saying *waninglah dulur weksane* (one with courage to make concessions will turn the tables in the end), came to terms with the inevitable.[94]

Initially, most *sini* papers copied Aneta's report on Soekarno's exile without comment. Later, after the appearance of Tjipto's and Pane's letters, the *sini* press described Soekarno's conduct more positively.[95] *Soeara Oemoem* of 20 February 1934, noted that 'in the past he was the engine and the soul of the movement and responsible for tumbling the walls which separated the diverse ethnic groups. Many of the Javanese, Sumatrans, Amboinese and Menadonese, *marhaen* and *ningrat*, welcomed him, Boeng Karno, as the champion of freedom.' It hoped, therefore, for his early return, 'purified and stronger'. *Pewarta Deli* of 22 January 1934, opined that most intellectuals had shown 'a despairing lack of responsibility, since they, not the masses, had let Soekarno down'. *Bintang Timoer* of 30 and 31 January 1934, went so far as 'blaming Thamrin for deserting Soekarno by not adopting a principled stand

---

[91]   Report to SDAP, Batavia, 22 January 1934, pp. 4-5, Collection Stokvis IISG archives file 961.

[92]   Raad van Indië, Advice 13 October 1933, no. xi, pp. 1-5, Mr. 1276/1933. In the 'Kommissoriaal' (committee deliberations) of 29 September 1933, letter WW, to the Vice-President of the Raad van Indië, the letters to Inggit and to Partindo's executive are mentioned.

[93]   Raad van Indië, Advice 13 October 1933, no. xi, p. 3, Mr. 1276/1933.

[94]   For that Javanese saying and Soekarno's motives, see Hering 1991a:.iv, note 39, xii-xiii.

[95]   Pluvier 1953:63, maintains that Tjipto's 'passionate plea' may well have caused respect for Soekarno to endure.

and for not having resigned from the Volksraad in protest'. *Sikap* of 5 January 1934, expressed sorrow and respect, and hoped that Soekarno would 'still be of use to his people and his country'. *Oetoesan Indonesia* of 11 January 1934, wrote that he 'had fallen for Iboe Indonesia' and that his 'sacrifice was not made in vain, since the masses would learn from it and still go forward'. The nationalist Soerabaja paper *Berdjoeang* of 21 February 1934, shared that opinion, and hoped that 'his exile to Endeh will still inspire *marhaen* to strive for a more unified and a better organized *pergerakan'*. The same paper also had an interview with Inggit held in a Tasikmalaja hotel, and opined that reports of her influence upon her husband's political conversion were quite unfounded. *Pemandangan* of 8 January 1934, concluded that it was not Soekarno's acts which had caused the conversion, but 'the jubilation of the masses'. However, on 16 February 1934, it opined that he had made 'marhaen conscious and had closed the gap between marhaen and the intellectuals [...] a tour de force which would never reach the *Staatsbladen* [statutes] like the key role of Thamrin in the Volksraad or Dr Soetoemo's promotion of people's security schemes, but was important nonetheless'.[96] On 17 February 1934, Soekarno, with a small coterie of relatives – Inggit, his mother-in-law Iboe Asmi and his adopted daughter Omi – boarded the KPM steamer *Jan van Riebeeck* for the voyage to Endeh.[97] Did Soekarno, watching the city of his birth slowly disappearing from sight, look upon the entire Partindo period as having been a tryst with destiny?

[96]   Extracted from Hering clipping archive and *Overzicht Inlandsche pers* no. 9, 3 March 1934.
[97]   *Overzicht Inlandsche pers* no. 9, 3 March 1934:133; see also the photograph of that departure in *Spiegel Historiael* January 1993:39.

CHAPTER VI

Soekarno's Endeh and Bencoolen years
1934-1942
A windu of semadi and reflection

Some statistics about the island of Flores

The district of Flores, consisting of the island of that name and the nearby Solor and Alor islands, fell under the jurisdiction of an *assistent-resident* based at Endeh close to *kampung* Amboegaga, where Soekarno, his family and his servants were to settle during their stay on Flores. Flores, so named by the Portuguese explores after the flowers they admired along the beaches of the island, with an area of 17,150 kilometres, was mountainous, volcanic and densely forested. Its main crop was corn (*jagung*), while some sandalwood, copra and tamarind fruit were exported as well. The census held in 1930 lists a population of 716,165 souls, with 174,136 indigenous, 1,529 Chinese, 305 Europeans and 195 so-called Foreign Orientals. As to religion, the census listed 436,587 pagans, 210,604 Christians and 69,945 Muslims, with the Muslims mainly situated in Endeh and further along the coastline. As to the christianization of the island, it was boosted in the wake of the Roman Catholic mission operating on the island, first by Jesuits and then, after 1914, by the German/Dutch Congregation of the Fathers of the Divine Word of Steyl. On 1 July 1933 the number of Roman Catholics was estimated at 197,000, with 94 Catholic churches and 380 prayer houses catering to their religious needs. At that time the Congregation of the Fathers of the Divine Word consisted of 64 missionaries and 30 brothers, all serving under the jurisdiction of the Ndona-based (near Endeh) Apostolic Vicar, who also held the personal title of Bishop of Arcis. In its work the congregation was further assisted by 56 sisters of the order of Servants of the Holy Ghost of Steyl. In 1933 a great seminary was founded in Toda Bèloe (Ngada). Here, seven youngsters, after having finished their small seminary (also in Toda Bèloe since 1925), were trained for the priesthood (*Flores* 1935).

Soekarno's first impressions of Endeh

As Dahm had it, Soekarno was quite at a loss during his first weeks on Flores, where 'hardly a trace of the civilization he so valued was to be found'. Years later, Soekarno, in an article titled 'Kilatan djiwa' (A glance at my soul), recalled these first experiences as follows:

> During my early period in Flores, only one or two people dared to come near me. Most of the people, whether old, young, men or women, Muslim, Christian or pagan, were all too shy to come near me, perhaps being afraid of the local authorities. [...] Only toward the end was I able to have a circle of friends totalling some forty people.[1]

Inggit as well reports their initial sense of loneliness and their being bereft of any local friends, though it tightened their family bonds. So, she and Kusno, pleased by the roomy size of their Amboegaga dwelling and the rather generous monthly stipend of *f* 150 granted to her husband, turned to some intensive gardening. They managed to grow all kinds of vegetables, such as cabbages, radishes, endive, beans, peas and spinach, causing the *raja* of Endeh to admire their garden and sample some of its harvest. At that time the Soekarno family befriended a Javanese couple hailing from Banjoemas. Mas Atmosoedirdjo, employed as an Openbare Werken (Public Works) land surveyor, together with his wife Chotimah and six-year-old daughter Soekarti, visited the Soekarno household regularly. Their friendship was further strengthened when Iboe Chotimah revealed to Inggit that two of her children had died at quite a young age and that she was in constant fear that such a fate would befall Soekarti as well. The upshot of all this was to ask whether Soekarti could be loaned (*meminjamkan*) to the Soekarnos, also since Omi (Ratna Djoeami), though six years older than Soekarti, had become quite fond of her new playmate being around so often. All this was arranged, with Soekarti now renamed Kartika by Soekarno. Inggit further relates how happy Omi was at not being alone any longer, and that the household had indeed become lively (*ramai*), partly because two Sawunese had joined it, a woman named Bertha and a man named Riwoe, the latter becoming Soekarno's faithful servant and the former aiding Inggit in running the household. Somewhat later, a young Bandoeng teacher named Asmara Hadi moved in

---

[1]   For Dahm citing Soekarno see Dahm 1969:179. For Soekarno's early recollections: 'Pada waktoe saja beloem lama di poelau Flores maka hanja satoe doea orang sadjahlah jang berani menghampiri saja. Semoea orang, toea, moeda, laki, perempoean, Islam, Sarani, Kafir, sama-sama takoet mendekati saja, oleh karena ditakoet-takoeti oleh pemerintah disana. [...] Achirnja dapatlah saja membentoek satoe lingkoengan sahabat, jang djoemlahnja koerang-lebih empat poeloeh orang', *Asia Raya*, 10 October 2602(1942):1 left column.

as well, since he had been contracted to teach Omi and Kartika.[2] Inggit tells of family trips to nearby beaches and also to Kelimoetoe, the inland volcano, 60 kilometres north of Endeh, with its three mountain lakes, of red, green and blue-coloured waters [3] In spite of all the bliss and *ramai* now reigning in the Amboegaga household, Soekarno, still shunned by most of the Florenese, turned to seek intellectual stimulation elsewhere. And so he strolled, after his gardening and his reading of papers and books were done, to the Roman Catholic mission compound a bit to the east of *kampung* Amboegaga.

Soekarno and the Fathers of the Divine Word

Meeting these fathers at first periodically and later almost daily, Soekarno was struck by the fact that they were quite happy to have conversations with him on topics close to his own intellectual standards and interests. The father in charge of the Immaculata parish, the bearded and lanky G. Huytink, became one of his best friends, often leaving Soekarno the key to his own room when he was engaged elsewhere. As to the provincial prior and learned scholar Father J. Bouman, he soon became Soekarno's most intellectual sparring part-ner on a variety of topics of interest to both of them. Also, it was Bouman, rec-ognizing Soekarno's keen intellectual appetite, who was to provide Soekarno with almost daily access to the well-stocked mission library. Another mis-sionary who befriended Soekarno was the easy-going brother Lambertus, the parish carpenter, who somewhat later would construct some of the props for the stage performances Soekarno was to mount under the auspices of his *kelompok sandiwara* (drama club), named Kelimoetoe, in the Immaculata par-ish. Also, visitors to the parish such as Father M. van Stiphout, just back from a visit to Rome and now on the way to his new post at the Toda Bèloe semi-nary, were showered by Soekarno with questions about Mussolini, a man Soekarno considered to be the reincarnation of Garibaldi (Giebels 1999:208-9; Seda 1981:72-4). Outside the parish, Soekarno's contacts with all these fathers and brothers were noticed as well. A Father G. van Velsen, head of the Nado-based Schakelschool (a Dutch-language primary school), invited Soekarno to his school after having first informed his mainly indigenous pupils of the forthcoming visit of a 'political exile, a communist and an enemy of the Dutch government'. One of these pupils, the ten-year-old Christian Timorese Frans Seda, was to greet the mysterious visitor on behalf of the Nado Schakelschool with the popular Dutch jingle '*Een haantje en een hennetje, die lopen in de wei*'

---

2   Ramadhan 1981:313, 315-17, 323; Kartika Uteh's nine-page manuscript 'Kisah sejati', sent to me by way of Ramadhan, 1 August 1999, pp. 1-3.
3   Uteh, 'Kisah sejati', pp. 4-5; Ramadhan 1981:321.

(a young rooster and a young chicken, strolling in the meadow). Soekarno, according to the recollections of that youngster, praised him loudly in the Dutch language for that performance.[4] All these were signs that the mission priests did not ignore the famous exile as so many of the Florenese still did. So Soekarno, quite ignorant of Roman Catholicism, let alone its missionary workings, encountering almost daily the mission's dedication to lift up their flock spiritually and materially, began to wonder whether Islam was capable of matching this fine example. As he was allowed to correspond with some friends outside Flores, he embraced the idea of attempting to learn more deeply about Islam. He had before, during his Soekamiskin episode, managed to somewhat deepen his knowledge of the Koran in order, as he said then, to bring himself closer to Allah. But that effort had to do with his own feelings of despair at that time and not so much with an effort to understand the *fikh* or *fiqh* (Islamic jurisprudence) and the *ubudijah* (strict religious matters), or the *ijtihad* (right of individual interpretation), together with the socio-political ramifications derived from all these. So, he decided to begin what was to become a rather long chain of communications with the revered Persatoean Indonesia (Persis) leader and Islamic theologian Ahmad Hassan, a man he had met before in Bandoeng together with the much younger Persis member Mohammad Natsir. After writing his first brief note to Hassan, Soekarno had to write to his former wife Oetari first, since he had learned of the death of her father H.O.S. Tjokroaminoto on 17 December 1934, only 52 years old. According to Oetari's own recollections, she was quite moved by Soekarno's written expression of deeply felt grief, and his reminding her of one of her father's famous sayings: 'everyone who is a good Muslim is also a socialist at heart, and that is why Muslims are truly socialists'.[5]

Soekarno's motives for writing to Ahmad Hassan

Perhaps recalling his former father-in-law's saying about Muslims and socialists, Soekarno, in search of a deeper analysis of the socio-political tenets of Indonesian Islam, began his correspondence with Ahmad Hassan on 1 December 1934. Ahmad Hassan, considered by Dr Pijper to be 'the most recognized, astute and scholarly leader of the purely Indonesian brand of Muslim reformism embodied by the Bandoeng-based Persatoean Islam

---

[4]   Seda 1981:72-4. Frans Seda, later to become Minister of Plantations in Soekarno's Dwikora cabinet, also recalls Soekarno's 1951 visit to Endeh, where Soekarno met Huytink and bestowed Indonesian citizenship on Huytink (p. 74).
[5]   On Tjokro's death, see Amelz 1952, II:157-62. For Oetari on Soekarno's letter, see our interview with her on 15 December 1976, and her contribution to the periodical *Sarinah* of 22 June 1987.

(Persis)' (Pijper 1950:248), was born in Singapore in 1887 of mixed Indian and Indonesian parentage. Hassan's father Ahmad, also called Sina Vappu Maricar, was a renowned writer and scholar in Muslim and Tamil literature. Hassan's mother was from a Soerabajan family of very modest means. Hassan, who never finished elementary school, took on several jobs in Singapore, first as a teacher and a textile trader, and then as the editor of the *Oetoesan Melajoe* daily, where he was mainly concerned with ethical questions. He obtained his religious education from his father, 'who placed emphasis on language, and so Hassan learned Malay, English, Arabic and Tamil as well as the usual religious subjects' (Federspiel 1966:19). In 1921, he moved to Soerabaja and then to Bandoeng, where he stayed with Hadji Moehammad Joenoes, one of the founders (12 September 1923) of Persis. It was here that Hassan, having joined Persis in 1924, became convinced of the reformism then propagated by Persis through its periodical *Pembela Islam* (Defender of Islam, starting circulation in 1929), with Hassan the same year being put in charge of special classes for young Persis members who had studied at Dutch schools, one of these being the Jong Islamieten Bond (Union of Young Islamists) member Mohammad Natsir.[6] The reformist ideas of Hassan, stressing the importance of *ijtihad* (the right of individual interpretation) as distinct from such original sources as the faith, the Koran and the Hadiths (codified statements and actions of the Prophet), and his condemnation of the *taqlid* (the acceptance of established *fatwa* – authoritative religious interpretation by religious scholars – and other established practices as final and binding) appealed to Soekarno, as we will see below. However, recognizing that intellectually his standard in these matters was not on a par with that of the Bandoeng-based scholar, who was 14 years older than the writer, Soekarno's first letter was simply a request for a number of scholarly works to be mailed to Amboegaga. He added, perhaps as an opening gambit to the dialogue yet to come, that 'People who hold that Islam recognizes an "aristocracy of Islam" are in error, since there is no other religion seeking equality of standing more than Islam does'.[7]

The theological and socio-political drift of Soekarno's letters to Hassan

In his second letter, of 25 January 1935, Soekarno, having sampled the works Hassan had mailed to him, regretted not having Buchari's (sic) work at hand since the Hadiths collected there were considered to be authentic (al Bukari (AD 810-870) had collected more than 600,000 traditional records of the

---

[6]   It is about that time that Hassan and Natsir frequented Soekarno and Inggit's home; see Ramadhan 1981:119-22.

[7]   Tersesatlah orang jang mengira, bahwa Islam mengenal suatu 'aristokrasi islam'. Tiada satu agama jang menghendaki kesama-rataan lebih daripada Islam. (Soekarno 1959:325.)

words and deeds of the Prophet, a collection revered by orthodox Muslims as second in authority only to the Koran). However, another source, by an English Islamologist Soekarno did not name, stated that even in al Bukari's collection 'dubious Hadiths had slipped in' causing Soekarno to add that 'the decline of Islam, its conservatism, its pollution, and the superstition of its followers are mainly caused by those dubious Hadiths – which are often more "in demand" than the Koranic verses'.[8] So, here, Soekarno set the tone in condemning Islamic orthodoxy in all its facets, in the hope of, together with Hassan, arriving at some terms for an Indonesian Islam that were more in touch with the present times.

In the third letter, of 26 March 1935, Soekarno reiterated his conviction that while there was 'no religion more rational or simpler than Islam'[9], weak and false Hadiths had been responsible for the obsolescence and the conservatism now reigning within Islam, thereby closing the gates to the *Bab-el-idjtihad* (individual interpretation and investigation of the Koran and Hadiths by oneself). But Soekarno went further, stating that it was his deep conviction that the Hadiths should not be seen as having absolute authority, even though investigations had determined them to be authentic. According to Soekarno, 'human reports cannot be absolute; what is absolute is only the word of God'.[10] In the fourth letter, 17 July 1935, Soekarno allowed Hassan some glimpses of his own circumstances and feelings at that time. He continued to study, but regretted the lack of a collection of books since

> all the books I have, have all been 'consumed'. The fact is that after my daily chores, weeding our garden and chatting with wife and child to cheer them up, I turn to reading again. [...] In Endeh itself there is not a single person whom I can question, for all of them indeed lack knowledge (as is usual) and are die-hard conservatives to the bone, with only one or two having a little knowledge. [...] In Endeh there is only one *sayid* with some education, but even he is not able to satisfy me. [The Muslims here] live and die with the *kitab fiqh* and so they remain conservative, dependent, unfree, faithful but blind followers. [...] Similarly, the world of Islam is now half dead, it has no soul, no spirit, no fire, since its flock is totally devoted to that "book of fiqh", and refuses to fly like the garuda in the skies of Living Religion. Alas, that is my situation in Endeh; with me wanting to increase my knowledge [of Islam], but lacking guides to do so properly.[11]

---

[8]   Kemunduran Islam, kekunoan Islam, kemesuman Islam, ketachajulan orang Islam, banjaklah kerena hadits-hadits lemah itu – jang sering lebih laku dari ajat-ajat Qur'an (Soekarno 1959:326).
[9]   Tak ada agama jang lebih rasional dan simplistis daripada Islam.
[10]   Berita jang datang dari manusia tak bisa absolut; absolut hanjalah kalam Ilahi (Soekarno 1959:327).
[11]   Begitu pula, maka dunia Islam sekarang ini setengah mati, tiada roch, tiada njawa, tiada api, karena ummat Islam sama sekali tenggelam didalam 'kitab-fiqh' itu, tidak terbang seperti burung garuda diatas udara-udaranja Agama jang Hidup. Nah, begitulah keadaan saja di Endeh; mau menambah pengetahuan, tetapi kurang petundjuk. (Soekarno 1959:328.)

In his next letter, of 15 September 1935, having looked at some of the brochures Hassan had sent him, Soekarno turned again to the situation in Endeh. This time he reported rather extensively on the workings of the Fathers of the Divine Word, 'with whom I often exchanged ideas'.

> You know that the island of Flores is a 'mission island' of which the missions are very proud. Certainly it is quite fitting that they are so proud of their work in Flores. I myself have observed how they 'work to the bone' to develop their religion in Flores and I duly respect them for their love of work. We greatly disapprove of the missions – but what labour do we do to propagate the religion of Islam and to strengthen the religion of Islam? That the missions spread Roman Catholicism, that is their right, and we may not condemn or complain about it. But as to ourselves, why are we so lazy, why are we so negligent, why do we not wish to work, why do we not care to be active? Why, for example, is there not one single Islamic preacher in Flores from some known Islamic association (Moehammadijah, for instance) to make propaganda for Islam there among the pagans? In just a few years, the missions have been able to convert some 250,000 [sic] pagans in Flores – but how many pagans are there in Flores who have been drawn to Islam? All this being considered, certainly all of that is simply our own fault and not the fault of someone else. (Soekarno 1959:330-1.)

The next letter to Bandoeng did not deal with Islamic issues at all, but contained a brief acknowledgement of Iboe Asmi's death on 12 October 1935, following an illness of only four days. Soekarno, quite fond of his mother-in-law, was deeply moved by her passing away and stilled his grief by constructing a tombstone for her grave out of stones he had collected from a river near Pantai Kumba. He became rather angry about some so-called Hadramautists of Flores censuring him for not having had a *selamatan tahlil* for his deceased mother-in-law.[12] In a postscript to his next letter to Hassan of 14 December 1935, he lashed out at these ultra-conservatives sticking to such rituals and being ignorant of the fact that Inggit and he prayed to Allah at least five times a day for mercy upon Iboe Asmi, ending this short note with: 'May Allah pour His mercy and His blessing upon her who, old though she was, yet followed me into the loneliness of exile!'[13] The letter also confirmed receipt of Hassan's earlier communication, stating his view that both the Koran and the Hadiths were inviolable. This was obviously a cautious attempt by the Bandoeng scholar to soften Soekarno's opinion about Hassan's articles of faith, which his Endeh-based pupil had so quickly rejected even though some

---

[12]   Ramadhan 1981:327-9. Hadramautists were orthodox Muslims who believed that everything in the Hadramaut, the centre of Wahabist ritual, was perfect and should be copied. The *selamatan tahlil* is a religious meal where the Muslim confession of the faith *la ilaha illa'llah* is pronounced; this also happens at a ceremony forty days after a Muslim's death.
[13]   Moga-moga Allah melimpahkan rahmatNja dan berkatNja, jang ia, meski sudah begitoe tua, toch mengikut saja kedalam kesunnjiannja dunia interniran (Soekarno 1959:333).

of these had been considered authentic. Yet, while Soekarno admitted in his letter that Hassan's arguments were indeed convincing, he still felt there were grounds for assailing another traditionally revered institution, the *taqlid* – the unquestioning acceptance of religious interpretion by well-known and revered Muslim jurists such as al-Sjafi'i, Ahmad ibn-Hanbal, Malik-ibn-Anas and Abu-Hanifah, commonly referred to as the Four Imams, or four leaders, while their branch of *fikh* was called *madzhab* (school), thus for instance al-Sjafi'i was the imam of his *madzhab* and henceforth named *madzhab* Sjafi'i.[14] Al-Sjafi'i's influence persisted down to the time of Soekarno's exile in Flores and beyond it among members of Nahdatoel Oelama.

To return to Soekarno, he condemned the *taqlid* since it did not adhere to *tarich*, the grounds of *sejarah*, the grounds of history. And so he held that when 'looking at the course of Muslim history it was evident that *taqlid* references had caused a line of decline up to the present time'. Most

> religious leaders and scholars did not have any inkling at all of history, let alone understand the minor patterns of it. So the deeper parts of history, the so-called forces of history causing progress or decline to occur in nations, did not attract them at all. And yet it is here that we touch upon a field of investigation important to us all. What are the causes of decline and why do they happen in one nation at a particular time? [...] So we should constantly turn to these whenever we study the ups and downs of history.
>
> Still, Muslim scholars and leaders, while 'knowing the Koran by heart', are not at all familiar with history's earth-shaking events. 'At best they know the history of Islam, and then only derived from antiquated sources which are not able to stand the test of modern science. [A]ll that proves that the world of Islam has declined greatly since the appearance of the rule of *taqlid*.' While promising Hassan to write an article soon on *taqlid* rule, Soekarno concluded 'that the genius of the world of Islam has been dead ever since the opinion arose that no independent expert on Muslim law would ever match the Four Imams, therefore forcing all Muslims to blindly follow religious leaders and scholars belonging to one of the sects of those Four Imams!'[15]

In the 22 February 1936 letter, Soekarno regretted not yet having finished the promised article on the *taqlid*. He told Hassan of having met two *pesantren* teachers from Java, one belonging to the *kolot* (conservative) type of Djakarta training school, the other being more *maju* (progressive), hailing from Banjoewangi. While they were in Endeh for trade, they visited Soekarno

---

14   See Gibb and Kraemers 1953:106, 562-4 on the blind acceptance of the *taqlid* due to *madzhab* conservatism; Alfian 1969:116-7, 119; Shadily 1973:583.
15   Bahwa dunia Islam adalah mati geniusnja, semendjak ada anggapan, bahwa mustahil ada mudjtahid jang bisa melebihi imam jang empat, djadi harus mentaqlid sahadja kepada tiap-tiap kjai atau ulama dari sesuatu madzhab imam jang empat itu! (Soekarno 1959:332-3).

night after night, discussing Muslim issues and asking Soekarno for his judgement. His judgements frequently startled the older of the two, hailing from Djakarta. But it was the younger one who pressed Soekarno, faced as he was by political exile, 'what should be the strategy to bring back the past age of Islam's greatness?' Soekarno responded, 'Islam must dare to catch up with the times'. With this as an opening, Soekarno started to lecture Hassan that it was not a matter of returning to former glory, to the age of the caliphs,

> but simply of racing ahead, of catching up with the times – that is the one and only way to become glorious again. Why, then, are we always taught to copy the age of the caliphs? Presently it is the year 1936, and not the year 700, 800 or 900. Society is not just a vehicle we can turn back at will. Society demands progress, and an advance to a newer stage; society refuses to be pushed back, to retrace its steps and return to the past. [...] The struggle to thrust orthodoxy behind us in order to pursue the age of the future – that is the struggle Kemal Atatürk had in mind when he stated that 'Islam does not order people to sit meditating the entire day in the mosque counting their beads, on the contrary Islam means struggle'.

Soekarno added, 'Islam means progress!' He concluded his letter saying that 'the aim of struggling to catch up with the times, of making comparisons and innovations up to the very standards of modernity, the aim of struggling against everything that will humble Muslims into humiliation and contempt' needed to be adhered to from now on (Soekarno 1959:333-4).

In his ninth letter Soekarno acknowledged the news of Hassan's having opened a new *pesantren*, adding right away the suggestion that the new institution should incorporate more emphasis on 'Western knowledge'. This Soekarno deemed essential, since 'our scholars of Islam are still so very deficient in the field of modern science'. He admitted that Hassan's *pesantren* was not a university, but added how great it would be if nonetheless more Western science were taught there. Soekarno even speculated on what a great fortune it would be to have *muballigh* (propagandists) of high quality, like Mohammad Natsir, a graduate of Hassan's new *pesantren* in a not too distant future. He stressed once more his conviction that Islam in this country and even throughout the whole world would not shine again if 'we Muslims remain fixated on the *kolot* attitude to life, rejecting everything that smacks of being Western or modern'. Aware of Hassan's stand on the Koran and the Hadiths as being inviolable, Soekarno maintained that these could well become bearers of progress if 'we were to read the Koran and the Hadiths together with some general knowledge to back up its standards'. 'Islamic science is not merely the knowledge of the Koran and the Hadiths all by itself; Islamic science is knowledge of the Koran and the Hadiths plus general knowledge!' Soekarno closed his diatribe on taqlidism with a personal note:

as an educated man I only gained respect for Islam after having read books on Islam which were scientific and modern in outlook. I know now why so many educated Indonesians are not pleased with Islam. That is due to Islam not keeping up with the times, and the errors made by those who propagate it. The latter are far too conservative and orthodox, they are anti-knowledge and superstitious, instructing their flock to only follow the *taqlid* and the faith, thus piling corrupt teaching upon corrupt teaching!

Soekarno closed his letter as follows:

Both of us belong to the anti-*taqlid* group. As for me, anti-taqlidism stands not merely for getting back to the Koran and the Hadiths, but turning to the Koran and Hadiths through the medium of general knowledge. Mr Hassan, please forgive me for going on like this. It is really a chat, but a chat coming from the depths of my heart. I hope you may heed it also in connection with your new pesantren.[16]

Soekarno's next communication to Bandoeng was devoted solely to the translation of H.C. Armstrong's *Lord of Arabia: Ibn Saud*, which Soekarno had just undertaken to render into Indonesian. He was quite impressed with the Wahabite leader now reigning in Arabia, admiring his personality because he 'towers above all Muslims of his time; a tremendous man, vital and dominant [...] truly a giant thrown up out of the chaos and agony of the desert, to then rule it according the example set by his great teacher, the prophet Moham-mad'. And though Soekarno did not approve of the entire system of Saudism he stood for, which was indeed still largely feudal, he was still gripped by admiration. So much so that he prayed to Allah to help him finish the transla-tion, and asked Hassan to circulate it when it was done. Many Indonesians reading it might then be inspired by it as well (Soekarno 1959:337-8).

In the eleventh communication to Bandoeng, of 18 August 1936, Soekarno commenced by thanking Hassan for looking for a publisher for the 400-page manuscript now in Hassan's hands. This would mean that Soekarno had finished his translation in record time, though whether Hassan ever found someone to publish it has indeed never been established.[17] In his letter, Soekarno once again devoted much of it to Islam's need to modernize and to use wider scientific knowledge in order to reach a progressive level. And

---

[16]   Tuan Hassan, maafkanlah saja punja obrolan ini. Benar satu obrolan tapi satu obrolan jang keluar dari sedalam-dalamnja saja punja kalbu. Moga-moga tuan suka perhatikannja berhubung dengan tuan punja pesantren. (Soekarno 1959:335-7.)

[17]   In *Bung Karno* 1988 no mention is made of a published Indonesian translation of Arm-strong's Ibn Saud biography by Soekarno. However, in his Panca Sila speech of 1 July 1945, Soekarno urged his audience to read Armstrong's Ibn Saud, telling of a rather backward state managing to become free, see *Birth of Pantjasila* 1958:12. Soekarno's article on the *taqlid* did not appear in print either; there is no mention of it in *Bung Karno* 1988.

true to the tone he had set in most of his letters so far, Soekarno lashed out first at the outdated and backward state of affairs in his country, followed by suggestions for improving its mental attitude. In other words, Soekarno was not so much out to widen theological subtleties, as to find ways of preparing Islam in a socio-political sense to become a meaningful part of a future Indonesian nationalist revival. Here, he simply extended the conditions featured in 1926 in his clarion call. This time, however, being 35 years old and having sampled a wider range of knowledge about Islam, he did not, as in 1926, shackle it to a Javanese syncretic model, but urged that it be progressive and in tune with modern science.

Soekarno ridiculed Muslims as being

> far too lavish with the term *kafir* (infidel) and to stamp it on nearly everything not to their liking since it was merely *kafir*. Western science and technology was *kafir*; radio and medical science were *kafir*; trousers, necktie and headdress were *kafir*; spoons, forks and chairs were *kafir*; Latin script was *kafir*. In fact, everything connected with people who are not Muslim was *kafir*![18]
>
> 'Good God forgive me! Is this Islam? Is this the religion of Allah? Is it really so? Branding knowledge and education as non-Muslim, radio and electricity as non-Muslim, indeed everything modern and up-to-date as non-Muslim? [...] To stay conservative and backward in order to keep on going by camel and to keep eating without spoons, as during the days of the Prophet and his caliphs? And getting angry and furious upon hearing news about new regulations being instituted in Turkey, in Iran, in Egypt or in other Muslim countries in the West?

And so Soekarno turned to his earlier arguments of Islam standing for progress as well, and that as such it formed no opposition to the revered articles of the Faith. So 'progress due to religious obligations and due to the regulations of the *Sunnah* [practices of the Prophet], but progress being broadened and rendered as well by the free play of rules, such as *dja'iz* [matters allowed to be decided upon by oneself; Soekarno in this communication revealed to Hassan that he was about to write a brochure on *dja'iz*] and *mubah* [refers to neutral ethics neither being rewarded nor being punished], the breadth of which exceeded the bounds of time'. Soekarno ended this letter as follows:

> Truly, Mr Hassan, for some time we both felt the need to eradicate the notions of all progress and education being outside the pale [of Islam], stamping all desire for progress as 'forbidden' and 'inadvisable', while instead such should be determined by oneself or by matters we are allowed either to do or not to do – purely

---

[18]   Rojal sekali dengan perkataan 'kafir', gemar sekali mentjap segala barang jang baru dengan tjap 'kafir'. Pengetahuan Barat – kafir; radio dan kedokteran – kafir; pantalon dan dasi dan topi – kafir; sendok dan garpu dan kursi – kafir; tulisan Latin – kafir; ja bergaulan dengan bangsa jang bukan Islam-pun – kafir! (Soekarno 1959:340.)

dja'iz or *mubah* alone! God willing, my brochure [about *dja'iz*] will be ready in two to three months![19]

In his final letter, of 17 October 1936, Soekarno acknowledged the arrival of two letters from Hassan, and granted Hassan's request for permission to print the letters Soekarno had submitted thus far, at the Persis printer shop. It is a pity that Hassan in that planned brochure did not print his own communications as well, robbing us of the opportunity to become acquainted with his own ideas, which we may assume were far less didactic in tone than the ones penned to him by Soekarno. Perhaps Hassan did so in deference to his young pupil, whom he, like so many of his countrymen, considered to be a Kokrosono now in exile but bound to propagate his political message as soon as his exile was lifted, wishes that, as we will see below, were cherished by many. On the other hand Hassan, aware of the fact that his Preanger-based organization was a tiny one surrounded by far larger and more orthodox Muslim organizations, may have been hesitant to expose his private ideas. As to Soekarno, he said in his last communication to Hassan that he had dropped parts of his heart, his spirit as well as his soul into these letters, his soul being first:

> A soul [at first] only superficially Islam, had turned into a soul becoming more convinced of Islam, from a soul being aware of the existence of God but not as yet acquainted with God, to a soul coming face to face with Him every single day. From a soul philosophizing much about belief in God but not believing in Him, into a soul paying homage to Him daily. (Soekarno 1959:325-6.)

The circulation of this volume of letters, printed at the end of 1936 under the title *Soerat soerat Islam dari Endeh dari Ir. Soekarno kepada T.M. Hassan, goeroe 'Persatoean Islam'*, naturally caused a stir among many Indonesians far beyond the confines of Endeh. The popular *regent* of Bandoeng, Wiranata-koesoema, said that Soekarno had written 'a thorough study on Islam', while being 'a member of Persatoean Indonesia'.[20] That same year, during the mid-August departure proceedings of Governor-General De Jonge, the *regent* had mused about the fact that under De Jonge's tenure the 'dangerous extreme-leftist political activities had indeed been curbed but that nonethe-

---

[19]   Sesungguhnja, Tuan Hassan, sudah lama waktunja kita wadjib membrantas faham-faham jang mengafirkan segala kemadjuan dan ketjerdasan itu, membelenggu segala nafsu kemadjuan dengan belenggunja: 'ini haram, itu makruh' – padahal dja'iz atau mubah semata-mata! Insja Allah, dalam dua-tiga bulan brosjur itu selesai (Soekarno 1959:340-1). Just like the *taqlid* article, there is no reference to Soekarno's *dja'iz* brochure being printed in the bibliographies we consulted.
[20]   *Verslag conferentie van de gouverneur-generaal met gouverneurs, residenten en regenten op Java*, 18 August 1936, Mr. 954/1936; Kwantes 1982:352.

less the intellectuals among the population were consciously moving in the direction of the realization of their political ideals'. And against 'this natural way of things', Wiranatakoesoema said, 'no administrative tactic' would ever be effective (cited in Van den Doel 1996:247). No wonder some politically inspired and more neutral Muslim circles considered whether a future role for Soekarno in some Muslim organization would indeed be feasible. Some of these trends we will discuss later in this chapter.

For now, we need to examine yet another Soekarno-inspired preoccupation; this time not his socio-political interests but his activities in the realm of fine arts. In his artistic endeavours he owed much, morally as well spatially, to the kind and eager support of the Fathers of the Divine Word. But also to his near expatriate following of some fifty people and to members of his own household, who worked enthusiastically to make these artistic endeavours a success.

Soekarno's preoccupation with the drama club Kelimoetoe

Perhaps inspired by the multi-coloured lakes surrounded by Flores' most dominant mountain range, Kelimoetoe, Soekarno, in addition to the letters penned to Hassan, wrote a series of eight stage plays, varying in composition and nature. Honouring the name of his *kelompok sandiwara* (drama club), one stage play was duly named 'Hantoe Kelimoetoe' (The evil ghost of Kelimoetoe), dedicated to a haunting spirit. This was a performance – all were held in the Immaculata parish building – that kept the audience spellbound. Frans Seda remembered it well, along with another musical play called 'Rendo Endeh' being one of his favourites. This play was a love story about a Portuguese naval captain Don Louis Pereira, enamoured of a dazzling Florenese beauty named Rendo, trying to kidnap her. His ploy was aborted by the missionaries, causing the Portuguese Don to wreck the mission compound with the guns of his man-of-war (Seda 1981:73; Ramadhan 1981:343-4). However, the most compelling of the stage performances was the six-act play entitled 'Dokter Sétan' (The satanic doctor), an interpretation in which Soekarno had rather closely followed the Dr Frankenstein story, the Hollywood movie version with the movie star Boris Karloff as the notorious doctor being quite popular at the time, though not as yet seen in Endeh, which had no movie theatre. Indeed, the absence of such a theatre caused Soekarno's plays to become cultural highlights, with many prominents and also quite a few humble people flocking to the parish hall to view them (Ramadhan 1981: 345). Soekarno's play about the evil doctor, here named Dr Marzoeki, bringing a dead man to life again was the main attraction, causing some to suggest that it symbolized Indonesia that would one day wake up again out of its deathly slumber. Frans Seda recalled that each performance opened with singing to the tune of 'Indonesia Raja', but replacing the refrain 'Indonesia Raja Merdeka' (Indonesia great and free) by 'Indonesia Moelia Moelia' (Indonesia noble, always noble), since singing 'Indonesia Raja Merdeka' would be considered an affront to the local authorities.[21] Even J.J. Bosch, the Koepang-based *resident* of Timor, under whose jurisdiction Flores fell, reported that the 'politically inactive Ir Soekarno had organized stage performances with his drama club Geli Moetoe which were performed twice a month to packed audiences in the Immaculata parish'.[22] Another play staged by Soekarno with some politically tinged symbolism, which like that of his main play of six acts may well have escaped even his well-versed audience, was entitled 'Tahoen 1945'. Uncanny foresight was demonstrated here by the Kelimoetoe stage director, since in this play it was suggested that freedom would reign in that year. Written by Soekarno, he was clever enough to leave the direction of it to another expatriate, the Filipino Nathan, a member of a travelling theatre company.[23]

However, these plays, so enthusiastically hailed by Soekarno as 'Come, let us erect such a comedy! With us providing the world with our plays', were followed by Soekarno having some severe bouts with malaria and fits of depression.[24] Hurt by the news that De Jonge, during interviews on 4 April 1936 with the *Deli Courant* and *Sumatra Post* and with the British journalist Bruce Lockhart, had declared that 'We Dutch have been here for three hundred years; we shall remain here for another three hundred. After this we can talk [about independence]', Soekarno said to Inggit: 'Governor-General De Jonge [his remarks] really cause me to be quite upset'.[25] Inggit was quite concerned about Soekarno's sagging spirits, and was glad to hear the news of Thamrin's attempts to have Soekarno moved from Endeh (Ramadhan 1981: 348).

[21] See Seda 1981:73. Seda intimated to Giebels that the Endeh-based *assistent-resident* named O. Schumacher always absented himself when it was sung, and returned to his seat only after the singing was finished; Giebels 1999:214. On the neutral conduct of officials and on 'Indonesia Raja': H.C. Marcella to Tjarda van Starkenborgh Stachouwer, no. 4541/A.P., 5 December 1939, Mr. 125/1940.

[22] Politiek verslag van de Residentie Timor en Onderhorigheden over het eerste halfjaar 1937, 2 October 1937, p. 9.

[23] Uteh, 'Kisah sejati', p. 5; Giebels 1999:212.

[24] Ayo, kita dirikan perkumpulan itu. Sandiwara! Kita penuhi dunia ini dengan sandiwara; Ramadhan 1981:343, 346.

[25] Gubernur Jenderal de Jonge itu tambah mengganas saya (Ramadhan 1981:346). For De Jonge's remarks see De Jonge 1968:351, note 774.

Attempts to settle Soekarno and his family elsewhere

Thamrin, well aware that the new governor-general A.W.L. Tjarda van Starkenborgh Stachouwer intended to continue the rather repressive policies of his predecessor, nonetheless did his utmost to resettle exiles such as Soekarno, Hatta, Sjahrir and Tjipto to more congenial sites. In Soekarno's case, Thamrin approached RGAZ H.C. Hartevelt in October 1937 with a letter from Soekarno in which the exiled leader pleaded for an internment site closer to Java. According to Soekarno, Flores was bereft of any 'spiritual traffic', while a place nearer to Java would open possibilities for Inggit to 'occasionally visit her family without incurring too much cost'. Such family contacts Soekarno deemed 'of great benefit to his wife's psychological well-being'. Thamrin requested the Indies government to consider a study sojourn in Holland for Soekarno, a tour Thamrin himself was prepared to finance. Thamrin was also quite certain he could enlist some of 'his Dutch acquaintances to employ Soekarno part-time, which would enable him to continue his studies'.[26] On 7 January 1938 Thamrin met Hartevelt again, with the message that this time the main executive of the Muslim association Moehammadijah – chairman Kijahi Hadji Mas Mansoer and secretary Hadji Hasim – were going to approach the government with a request to have Soekarno employed as a technical subjects director at one of its schools in the Vorstenlanden (or Principalities, of Central Java).[27] In his advice to Tjarda, Hartevelt rejected both the Thamrin and the Moehammadijah overtures in favour of a more suitable residence for Soekarno outside Java. That Soekarno still favoured a study sojourn in Holland was demonstrated by his appeal to Thamrin to involve Stokvis to press for his '*externering* [banishment] to Holland for study'. The failure of the Indies government to consent to this was a chance missed forever for turning the tide of history in another direction altogether.[28]

Motives for the Indies government to keep Soekarno outside of Java

That the Indies government declined to have Soekarno settle in Java had much to do with nationalist political developments in Java at the time, particularly in the Vorstenlanden. With the radical Non-Ko associations

[26] Hartevelt to Tjarda van Starkenborgh Stachouwer, nr. 66/2-1, Weltevreden, 6 November 1937, pp. 2-3, Mr. 150/1938.
[27] See Mansoer and Hasim to Tjarda van Starkenborgh Stachouwer, Djokjakarta, 23 January 1938, pp. 1-2, Mr. 150/1938.
[28] Thamrin to Stokvis, Batavia Centrum, 17 September 1938, p. 2, IISG archives.

banned for good and their leadership languishing far beyond Java in Boven Digoel, Bandaneira and Flores, a new constellation of Ko associations named Partai Indonesia Raja (Parindra, Greater Indonesia Party) was established on 28 December 1935. An elitist bourgeois-inspired nationalist front consisting of Dr Soetomo's Persatoean Bangsa Indonesia (PBI), Boedi Oetomo (BO), Kaoem Betawi (Batavia Group, founded by Thamrin in 1923), Sarikat Soematra (Sumatra Union), Partij Sarikat Selebes (Union Party of Celebes), Partij Rakjat Indonesia (Indonesian People's Party) and the small Banten intellectuals' organization Tirtajasa, Parindra was led by Dr Soetomo, with the influential Solo-based *pangeran* (prince) Woerjaningrat as vice-chairman.[29] The core of Parindra in fact consisted of an alliance of Soetomo's following in Soerabaja and the *kraton* (palace) politicians led by Woerjaningrat in Solo. And although Parindra's central administration was located in Soerabaja, Solo (always perceived by the Javanese as the political centre of Java) was by now seen as Parindra's adjacent branch. After Soetomo's death on 10 May 1938, Woerjaningrat became chairman, and with six of the eleven central administration members hailing from Solo, Parindra was now formally situated in that *kraton* city. Thus, with a prominent ideological stamp of the Solo elite, Parindra attempted to unite all strata, from the common people to the nobility at the top. Japan served as the prime example, with the veneration of the emperor and the *samurai*, the traditional class of military/rulers who came to power in 1868, responsible not only for modernizing the country but also for starting it on the way to world-power status. Even before Parindra had been formed, two popular movements bringing the elite and the common people together were instituted in both the *kraton* cities of Soerakarta (Solo) and Djokjakarta. Mainly to overcome the enduring economic crisis, which had particularly hurt the countryside of the Vorstenlanden, the Pakempalan Kawoelo Ngajogjakarta (PKN, League of Subjects of Djokjakarta) was established upon the initiative of Prince Soerjodiningrat on 29 June 1930. In just four years, this association became Indonesia's biggest socio-economic mass party of the thirties and early forties, having a membership of 250,000 by 1934. As was the case with earlier mass parties – such as Sarekat Islam – messianic expectations were involved, with Soerjodiningrat being labelled as a future *ratu adil*. All this was much to the chagrin of the Indies local authorities.

In Solo itself, on the initiative of Mr Singgih, who had withdrawn from Boedi Oetomo because it was not militant enough, the Pakempalan Kawoelo Soerokarto (PKS, League of Subjects of Soerakarta) was established on 5 May 1932. This party never matched the numbers of the PKN; it had some 50,000 members in 1935, dwindling to 10,000 by September 1939. The PKN

---

[29]   *Soeara Oemoem Extra Blad*, 28 December 1935; *Soeara Parindra*, January 1936.

in July 1941 numbered 262,852, and was thus still the biggest mass party of Indonesia.[30] In Solo, where both Parindra and the PKS were prone to follow the Japanese model, this pronounced affection for Japan was seen by the colonial authorities with growing mistrust and alarm, especially since the enduring economic crisis had caused the Indies to be swamped by cheap Japanese-made goods. Not only did colonial officials fear economic penetration – a copper-mining licence was granted in April 1937 by the Mangkoenegaraan to the Ishihara company – their foremost concern was the growing political influence exerted by Japan in the Vorstenlanden, an area where colonial authority was relatively weak. In Solo, contacts were made by the business club De Japansche Vereeniging (The Japanese Association), through the owner of the Fujiyoko shop, a Japanese named Sawabe, with princes such as Parindra prominents *pangeran* Soerjohamidjojo, *pangeran* Koesoemojoedo, *pangeran* Hadiwidjojo, the prominent leader of the *kraton's* anti-Dutch clique, and *pangeran* Poerbanegoro, the commander of the *kraton* bodyguard. Solonese colonial officials, alarmed by all these moves, were further disturbed by a Japanese report confiscated by police authorities during a search of the Japanese journalist Kubo's home in Batavia in June 1939. The report referred to a 'secret leaders' conference' where Prince Soerjohamidjojo was featured as the future *ratu adil* of Java. So, next to the Djokja-based Prince Soerjodiningrat, in Solo *ratu adil* messianic expectations came to the fore as well.[31] Even more turmoil came with the formation of the Gaboengan Politik Indonesia (GAPI, Indonesian Political Federation) in May 1939 on the initiative of Thamrin; it called for an Indonesian parliament to be established now that Soetardjo's 15 July 1936 petition proposing that Indonesian autonomy be implemented by way of gradual reforms within ten years had been rejected by Royal Decree of 16 November 1938.[32] With all this going on, it is clear why the colonial authorities did not allow Soekarno to be resettled in the Vorstenlanden. Aware as they were of his own predictions of Japan's role in a future Pacific war, and Javanese ideas of him being the *ratu adil*, they were keen not to have yet another *ratu adil* settle in an area so prone to ancient forebodings.

[30]   Hering 1998:45-9; Larson 1987:155-63, 168-73, 182-3; Vonk to Governor-General no. 1736/ A.P. bijlage 'Overzicht politieke beweging in Soerakarta en Jogjakarta' by Van der Most of 10 May 1936, Mr. 602/1936; Governor H.H. de Cock to De Jonge no. 24/G.E., 15 October 1934 with De Cock's 58-page report on PKN and its chairman Pangeran Ario Soerjodiningrat, Mr. 1179/ 1934; Governor of Jogjakarta Bijleveld to Vonk no. 764, 5 July 1935 on PKN and its chairman Pangeran Ario Soerjodiningrat, pp. 1-8, Mr. 840/1935.
[31]   See the sources cited above in note 30. An English-language translation of the Kubo report is in Hering 1996:378-84.
[32]   See for these developments Hering 1996:242-4.

Soekarno's road to Bencoolen

After having first considered Makassar in southwest Celebes and Bandjer-masin in southeast Borneo as sites for Soekarno, the government in the end decided on the town of Bencoolen in southwest Sumatra to be the new internment site for Soekarno, his family and his servants. The news quickly reached the Soekarno household by way of his tailor Darham, who had picked it up listening to the radio of Lie Siang Tek, the owner of a shop called De Leeuw (The Lion) (Ramadhan 1981:349). The decision may well have been motivated by governmental intentions to somehow appease the non-political and largest Muslim association, Moehammadijah. The government had first thwarted a technical-directorship for Soekarno with the Djokjakarta-based Moehammadijah, but Bencoolen, a growing Moehammadijah bulwark with 41 branches in that residency, would, according to some in colonial govern-ment circles, give Soekarno opportunities to engage in non-political affairs within that association. Also, they thought the socio-economic climate in Bencoolen, being far more sophisticated and more open to all kinds of daily news reporting, would perhaps open avenues to the famous exile in an architectural or even a harmless journalistic direction. The Moehammadijah had only recently been instrumental in the non-political Nahdatoel Oelama and the politically inspired PSII establishing the Madjlisoel Islamil A'laa Indonesia (MIAI, Indonesian Muslim Supreme Council) during the 18-21 September 1937 deliberations of Mansoer of Moehammadijah, Wahab Hasboellah of Nahdatoel Oelama and Wondoamiseno of the PSII. This was seen by governmental sources as a good sign, bringing together feuding modernists and traditionalists to find common grounds for cooperation.[33]

As for Soekarno and Inggit, with their adopted daughters and Riwoe, they boarded the steamer *De Klerk* with Soerabaja as destination. There they were taken by train, in a separate compartment with a police escort, to Batavia. In Batavia Soekarno was allowed to talk with Thamrin, with Ahmad Hassan, who had travelled from Bandoeng to Batavia to see his former pupil, and with Sjafei, also of the Persis, a visit Dr Pijper of Inlandsche Zaken had arranged.[34] Inggit, Omi and Kartika stayed at Thamrin's Sawah Besar 32 residence, and would first go to Bandoeng to visit Inggit's relatives and join

[33]   Interviews with G.F. Pijper and Ch.O. van der Plas on 10 and 18 May 1978 respectively in Amsterdam, and on 14 and 17 April 1974 in The Hague; Alfian 1969:532; Pijper's 'Verslag van de reis van de Adjunct Adviseur voor Inlandsche Zaken naar Bengkoelen', with Pijper meeting Oei Tjeng Hen, chairman of the Bintoehan Moehammadijah branch, p. 22 a man who would later become a close friend and even a business associate of Soekarno, Mr. 1500/1933; 'Soekarno en Moehammadijah', Mr. 580/1938; Abdul Karim 1982:60.
[34]   Pijper to Tjarda van Starkenborgh Stachouwer, nr. K-29/K-II, 8 June 1938, Mr. 506/1938; an English-language translation of this report is in Hering 1991b:183-4.

Soekarno later in Bencoolen. After his Batavia talks, Soekarno and his faithful servant Riwoe, again under police escort, took the train to Merak to board the steamer *Sloet van de Beele* for the crossing to Teloek Betoeng on Lampong Bay. Here the two of them (under police escort) boarded the South Sumatran railway to the bus stop at Loeboek Linggau, to arrive on the Autodienst Staats Spoor (State Railways Bus Service) in Bencoolen on Monday evening, 28 March 1938. Soekarno stayed in the Centrum Hotel, since the home allocated to him at Anggoet Atas road needed to undergo some repairs first.[35] L.G.M. Jaquet, then a BB *aspirant-controleur* (trainee controller), reported in his recollections that during the entire South Sumatra train trip, Soekarno's 'charisma was such that the generally loyal population at all the railway stations went down on their knees, making the signs of *sembah*'.[36]

This BB official was also responsible for delivering Soekarno's monthly allowance of *f* 150, while the two of them also developed a somewhat cordial relationship socially. This was due to the fact that in Bencoolen, inhabitants of a certain academic standard crossed racial barriers to socialize with each other, as was often the case in provincial towns in the Indies at that time.[37] Jaquet recalls how Soekarno on his first evening, during his courtesy visit to the Jaquets' home, stayed for close to four hours, engaged as they were in discussing the BB official's dissertation about Japan's industrialization as well as the issue of the authority of the *adat*. Jaquet was quite impressed by Soekarno's arguments about Japan. Soekarno stated that 'Japan, being a poor country, would turn the clock back if it came to rule over the Indies, since it would exploit the labour force and the cheap raw materials instead of investing in policies to the benefit of Indonesia itself'. Several visits from house to house were to follow, with Jaquet calling Soekarno's 'library by far the most extensive in Bencoolen at that time'. Jaquet was also responsible for getting Soekarno advance credit for a piano he had bought for a Bencoolen drama club led by Manap Sofian (Jaquet 1978:19-21). Another rather cordial relationship Soekarno struck up was with a young Dutch plantation employee named Jaap Kruisweg, who took Javanese lessons from Soekarno in order to better communicate with the Javanese labourers under his supervision. This employee, on the occasion of his wedding to Resident Hooykaas's daughter, invited Soekarno to be a guest at the wedding reception. Kruisweg also gave Soekarno two dachshunds, since Soekarno refused to be paid for the Java-

---

[35]   'Bung Karno dalam pembuangan di Bengkulu', manuscript written by Salmiah and Muhammad Ali Chanafiah, Stockholm, 1995, p. 8. This wedded couple were Bencoolen-based Taman Siswa teachers during Soekarno's stay there. Salmiah was a younger sister of Sanoesi Pane, a close friend of Soekarno's and a Gerindo stalwart.

[36]   Jaquet 1978:23. The *sembah* is a token of deep respect, bringing the hands together in front of one's head just below the mouth, see Poerwadarminta 1982:904.

[37]   On this socializing, see Abu Hanifah 1972:93-6; Jaquet 1978:20.

nese language lessons. Always fond of dogs, Soekarno named these Ketoek
Satoe and Ketoek Doea (Knock One and Knock Two) and took them all the
way to Java with him when he was freed by the Japanese (Jaquet 1978:23;
Adams 1965:144; Ramadhan 1981:396, 415, 418).

Soekarno's early activities in Bencoolen

Immediately upon arrival, Soekarno was met by Muhammad Ali Chanafiah,
his wife Salmiah, and Kakoeng Goenadi – all Taman Siswa teachers and
members of the leftist Ko association Gerakan Rakjat Indonesia (Gerindo,
Indonesian People's Movement, founded 23 May 1937 by former Partindo
stalwart Amir Sjarifoeddin, and led by Sumatran intellectuals such as Amir
Sjarifoeddin, Adnan Kapau Gani, Sanoesi Pane, Mohamad Yamin and Ipih
Asmara Hadi). That Bencoolen Gerindo members were among the first to
meet Soekarno had much to do with Gerindo considering itself as the true
and sole heir to Soekarno's Partindo, while Parindra was not. Gerindo specifically stated that it was 'a leftist-oriented correction of Thamrin's *fraksi* and
the "bourgeois" Parindra'. Such views were ventilated by Gerindo's periodical, *Plopor Gerindo*, appearing for the first time in September 1937, with Ipih
Asmara Hadi serving as its editor.[38] In Bencoolen, the Gerindo threesome,
coming face to face with their idol, questioned him about what an internee
was allowed to do and what not, and to what extent he was able to move
around. Soekarno answered: 'Everything is allowed! As long as I do not
meddle with politics, leave the area by sea, or distance myself beyond 40
kilometres from the city of Bencoolen.' After this, aware of the fact that Soekarno, known to be a movie fan, had not been able to see a movie during his
Endeh years, they took him to Bencoolen's Royal Cinema.[39]

A few days later, Soekarno was reunited with Inggit and their adopted
daughters at the Centrum Hotel. The family moved shortly thereafter to their
newly restored and roomy home at Anggoet Atas, causing Soekarno to burst
out singing 'Io vivat, Io vivat, nostrorum sanitas', and then taking them for

---

[38]   Poeze 1994b:175-6. Pijper was not fooled by Gerindo's autonomy aim (instead of *merdeka*)
nor by its Ko stance. He stated to Tjarda that 'the tone not the spirit had changed': Pijper to
Tjarda van Starkenborgh Stachouwer, no. K-55/K-3, p. 3, 10 October 1938, Mr. 961/1938.
[39]   Boleh semua! Asal tidak berpolitik dan keluar dari daerah dengan batas lautan dan di darat
tidak melebihi jarak 40 km dari kota Bengkulu; the Chanafiahs' manuscript 'Bung Karno dalam
pembuangan di Bengkulu', pp. 9-10. As for Kakoeng Goenadi, during the Japanese occupation
he was a member of the Menteng 31 *asrama*, and during the Indonesian *revolusi* a prominent
leader of the Barisan Pelopor Istimewa and a member of the short-lived Serikat Rakjat Indonesia
(Serindo, Union of the Indonesian People) which was to fuse into the post-war PNI, founded 29
January 1946; see Sidik Kertapati 1964:48-9.

an evening stroll (Ramadhan 1981:356-7). Inggit, particularly, while finding Bencoolen not quite like Bandoeng, found the people in her new environment, especially the women, her kind of women. The women of the town took her into their circle, while she seems to have gained their confidence, skilful as she was with a needle and knowledgeable about a lot of matters the Bencoolen women had never heard of. Inggit soon formed a small club for women and girls. She became the talk of the town when, together with her husband, she walked out of a Moehammadijah meeting in January 1939 because a *tabir*, a veil-like curtain, separated the men from the women. Soekarno had protested against the *tabir* in a Moehammadijah meeting on a previous occasion, since he regarded it as a symbol of the enslavement of women (Ramadhan 1981:358; Bharadwaj 1997:129-30).

Here, Soekarno was adopting the same disdain he had demonstrated in Endeh toward orthodox behaviour, being, however, unaware that local Moehammadijah circles at that time were probing cautiously to win over orthodox circles to their reformist ideas. Yet the *tabir* incident hit the *sini* press, with a correspondent of Antara (the Indonesian news agency) interviewing Soekarno at the end of January 1939 in relation to Soekarno's article named 'The curtain is not ordained by Islam' in the 21 January 1939 issue of *Adil*. In that interview Soekarno praised Agoes Salim, his former opponent, who 'once tore the *tabir* apart in a public meeting, showing great moral courage', while he himself 'did not display that kind of courage but merely left the meeting as a token of protest – like a cowardly dog!' Soekarno also revealed to the Antara journalist that in Bencoolen during Idulfitri – also known as Lebaran, marking the end of the Muslim fasting month of Ramadhan – following his own suggestion no *tabir* was hung (Soekarno 1959:349-51). However, having thus made his point locally, Soekarno still decided to address an open letter to Moehammadijah chairman Mas Mansoer in order to once again clarify his motives for having acted against the use of *tabir*. In that letter, he, on behalf of the so-called *kaum intelektuil Indonesia* (Indonesian intellectual community), urged Mansoer to make his arguments on the *tabir* issue known to Moehammadijah members soon to convene at that association's congress in the city of Medan (Soekarno 1959:353-4).

There is no record of Mansoer himself responding to Soekarno's open letter, nor did the *tabir* issue find its way to the Bencoolen monthly political reports drafted by the Javanese police assistant *wedana*, Raden Soekarta Martaatmadja. The latter, finding it a purely Muslim theological issue, may well not have realized its potential political benefits to Soekarno. As for Soekarno, we have noted earlier that purely theological subtleties were merely one means he used to broaden nationalist political concerns. As for Soekarta Martaatmadja, it dawned on him as late as 28 January 1940, that Soekarno 'so far did not meddle openly with political activities but still exercises political clout quite indirectly'.[40] Soekarno, serving as Ketoea Dewan Pengadjaran (chairman of the education council) of the non-political Moehammadijah Bencoolen branch since September 1939, and active in a Comité Pembangoen Mesdjid Djamik (Committee for restoring the local Djamik mosque) as well as doing weekend teaching at home of the Taman Siswa girls guide group led by his daughter Ratna Djoeami, a pupil at that time at the local Katholieke Vakschool (Catholic Trade School), had thus far kept away from politics as much as possible. Soekarno was also instrumental in getting Oei Tjeng Hien (alias Abdoel Karim) to move from Bintoehan to Bencoolen on 6 October 1939 to become advisor for the Moehammadijah in Bencoolen. In Oei Tjeng Hien's recollection, he made this switch because Soekarno had offered to become a business partner in Oey's furniture shop, now relocated from Bintoehan to Bencoolen. Soekarno often produced all kinds of tables, chairs and cabinets in the new enterprise, now called Peroesahaan Meubel Soeka Merindoe dibawah Pimpinan Ir Soekarno (Furniture Shop 'In love with longing', led by Ir Soekarno). Another of Soekarno's occupations was membership on the editorial board of the local weekly *Penaboer*, as of October 1939. He wrote a biographical article appearing in the 26 October 1939 issue on Adolf Hitler, with the rather unflattering subtitle 'Koeasanja kerongkongan' (The power of the throat), suggesting that 'the activities of Germany's dictator stem purely from an inherent inferiority complex'.[41]

Soekarno gradually expands his socio-political role

Soekarno, who had dwelt on Hitler recently, may well have pondered whether his own country would get embroiled as well, with Germany now at war with France and the United Kingdom, and united since 1936 with Japan in the Anti-Comintern pact. Japan had also left the League of Nations in the wake of the so-called Mukden Incident of September 1931. Japan occasioned yet another incident six years later, the so-called China Incident. In the wake of the China Incident, Japan started her drive to the south toward the *omote Nanyo* (Japanese for the 'front South Seas': the region including the Dutch Indies, the Philippines, Thailand, Indo-China and Malaya) by occupying the island of Hainan in the Gulf of Tonkin on 10 February 1939. After France's surrender to Germany, Japan, after first fomenting Thai irredentist claims in

---

[40]   Politiek-Politioneel Overzicht van de Residentie Benkoelen over de maand December 1939, p. 1, Mr. 290/1940.
[41]   The Chanafiahs' manuscript 'Bung Karno dalam pembuangan di Bengkulu', pp. 15-6; Politiek- Politioneel Overzicht van de Residentie Benkoelen over de maand September 1939, pp. 1, 10, Mr. 1313/1939; Politiek-Politioneel Overzicht van de Residentie Benkoelen over de maand October 1939, pp. 1-2, 14-5, 17, Mr. 1416/1939; Abdul Karim 1982:57-60.

French Indo-China, then mediated in the ensuing Franco-Thai war, forcing the French to cede some border provinces of Indo-China to Thailand. Japan itself was allowed to station army units in the northern border provinces of Indo-China. As we will show below, Japan, by mid-1941, would also extract the right to station large units of its army, navy and air force in the rest of Indo-Chinese territory. All these incidents made a mockery of the name Showa (Shining Harmony) given to the period of rule of Tenno Heika Hirohito (1926-1989) (Sluimers 1996:21-2, 1998:344-6; Zwitzer 1995:23, 25).

Such concerns Soekarno would soon deal with in a number of articles devoted to the European war and to Japan. For now, he became increasingly preoccupied with Indonesian developments in the wake of the outbreak of the war. Soekarno was reported to have expressed his opinion about recent Gapi activities on 27 November 1939 to Mohamad Noen, treasurer of the local Parindra branch, and to the Ambonese G. de Queljoe, former editor of *Soeara Benkoelen*, as 'not having his approval since they were far too meek and therefore of little use'.[42] In a subsequent Gapi branch meeting held on 17 December 1939 in the Royal Cinema theatre and initiated by the local branches of Parindra, Gerindo and the Partai Islam Indonesia (PII, Indonesian Islam Party), Soekarno, his wife and his daughter Ratna Djoeami were also present among the 1,200 people attending. This time, Soekarno, while not participating at all in the debate about the 'Indonesia Berparlemen' issue, tapped the floor with his walking stick several times to show his approval. Also, during the singing of 'Indonesia Raja', Soekarno, together with all those present, stood at attention. In the wake of this meeting, Soekarno was visited on 28 December 1939 by Roeslan Wongsokoesoemo and Soedjono, both executive members of the Soerabaja Parindra branch, together with local Parindra members A. Khahar and Ibnoe Hadjar Rasjid. All these visitors expressed the hope that Soekarno would be freed from his internment soon, while also expecting him to render advice to Parindra in writing, or even correcting the local Parindra branch when the need arose. At the end of the visit, Soekarno stressed that he stood squarely behind the Gapi actions, though warning his visitors to be quite cautious during public-speaking sessions. That same evening Soekarno attended the public Parindra meeting, again standing at attention during the singing of 'Indonesia Raja'. This meeting was held in the Glorie movie theatre and was attended by some thousand local people. Since this meeting was disbanded by local police authorities, Soekarno was met the following day by Semaoen Bakry, the local PII chairman, Zoelkefli Darsjah, Parindra's local secretary and leader of the local Soerya Wirawan (the youth affiliate of Parindra), Oei Tjeng Hien and Jahja, both of the Bencoolen

---

[42]   Politiek-Politioneel Overzicht van de Residentie Benkoelen over de maand December 1939, p. 1, Mr. 290/1940.

Moehammadijah branch. Soekarno cautioned them once again not to provoke the local colonial authorities unduly.[43] As to Moehammadijah activities
involving Soekarno, he was speaking in his capacity of Ketoea Dewan Pengadjaran (chairman of the education council) at a so-called *tabligh akbar* (exalted
announcement ceremony) on 24 December 1939, held in the clubhouse of the
association in Kebon Roos (the local Rose Garden), attended by some thirty
members. Soekarno revealed new plans in the education sector. The former
standard school would be replaced by the Ibtidaiah, with history and geography being added as new subjects, and this school would be the forerunner
for the secondary Whoestho. The Whoestho final certificate would form the
useful gate to the so-called Moealimin college, catering to a future crop of
Moehammadijah teachers.[44]

Soekarno as a publicist and his clash with Mohammad Natsir

At several public occasions during early 1940, Soekarno urged audiences to
discuss the situation in Europe, while emphasizing the importance of linking
these overseas events with current political issues at home. Because the local
periodical *Penaboer* had stopped its circulation due to a lack of finances,[45]
Soekarno submitted a number of articles to Java-based *sini* periodicals about
the war and its political impact on the local Indonesian scene. Even during a visit to the local Roman Catholic parish on 23 January 1940, Soekarno
discussed the 'Indonesia Berparlemen' issue, while at the same time censuring the local police authorities for disbanding the Parindra meeting of 28
December.[46] In February 1940 Soekarno was instrumental in getting approval
for a public Moehammadijah *tabligh* where European developments and the
cooperation issue could be discussed. That *tabligh* took place in Kebon Roos
on 9 and 10 February 1940, with some 80 people present. It caused the *assistent
wedana* of police to state that 'the politicization of the local Moehammadijah
has become a fact' and that 'Soekarno is striving to use the Pan-Islamic revival as a useful backing for his own political ideas'. Soekarno's address during
the Kebon Roos meeting stressed 'the need for Indonesia's youth to become
fired up idealistically, since this would make it possible to shift mountains'.

[43]   Politiek-Politioneel Overzicht van de Residentie Benkoelen over de maand December 1939,
pp. 2-6, 12-3, 24, 26-7, 35, Mr. 290/1940.
[44]   Politiek-Politioneel Overzicht van de Residentie Benkoelen over de maand December 1939,
p. 35, Mr. 290/1940.
[45]   Politiek-Politioneel Overzicht van de Residentie Benkoelen over de maand Februari 1940,
p. 29, Mr. 570/1940.
[46]   Politiek-Politioneel Overzicht van de Residentie Benkoelen over de maand Januari 1940, p.
3, Mr. 410/1940.

Such pronouncements, together with the fact that he often sought the company of such youngsters as Ali Chanafiah and Kakoeng Goenadi, caused the police *wedana* to add that Soekarno was 'again publicly airing his ideas in a political sense'.[47] An Indonesian local source, however, praised Soekarno and his family as an example to follow:

> Simply through his fellowship he moved the society of the city of Bencoolen at that time. Yesterday evening he stirred the people then present at Kebon Roos, while today, together with his wife, he moved the people of Tengah Padang to support the restoration of the Djamik mosque.[48]

During the first half of 1940, confronted with the news of Germany controlling Denmark and Norway and by May and June the Low Countries and France, Soekarno expressed his views in several *sini* press outlets. Some of these were devoted to the war situation, though Soekarno found time to devote articles to Muslim issues as well (Ridwan Lubis 1987:114-5). In a number of issues of the Medan-based *Pandji Islam* (Banner of Islam), under headings such as 'Me'moeda'kan pengertian Islam' (Rejuvenating the concepts of Islam) in *Pandji Islam* of 25 March and of 1, 8 and 15 April 1940; 'Masjarakat onta dan masjarakat kapal oedara' (Camel society versus aeroplane society) in *Pandji Islam* of 22 April 1940; 'Apa sebab Turki memisahkan agama dari negara?' (Why has Turkey separated religion from the state?) in *Pandji Islam* of 20, 27 May, 10, 17, 24 June and 1 July 1940; and 'Sontoloyo Islam' (Worthless Islam),[49] Soekarno reiterated the state versus religion and modernity versus *kolot* issues he had written so passionately about while in Endeh. This time, however, with his status as a Moehammadijah educator well established, and seen by some as the future leader of a nationalist/Islamic revival, Soekarno's views appearing in *Pandji Islam* were challenged at once by one of his former Bandoeng acquaintances: Mohammad Natsir, seven years younger than Soekarno and by now in charge of Persis. Natsir claimed that Soekarno had derived his ideas exclusively from Muslim reformists, since like them he favoured abandoning several revered Muslim tenets. But instead of supporting himself on sound and proven theological grounds, Natsir argued, Soekarno made almost exclusive use of recent socio-historical developments in westernized Muslim nations to back up his arguments. On the question of religion and state, however, Natsir pointed out that Muslims did adhere to a philosophy of life or to a political ideology, just as a number of Western

---

[47] Politiek-Politioneel Overzicht van de Residentie Benkoelen over de maand Februari 1940, pp. 2-3, 17, Mr. 570/1940.
[48] Politiek-Politioneel Overzicht van de Residentie Benkoelen over de maand Februari 1940, p. 25, Mr. 570/1940.
[49] These are all listed as well in Soekarno 1959:369-445, 483-506.

states were in the habit of doing. Yet, in the case of Muslim nations, political ideology rightly remained embedded in the principles and laws of the Koran and the Sunnah (Natsir 1973:437-44, 447-50). He acknowledged that much of *kolot* or so-called *sontoloyo* superstition could still be eliminated by some disciplined intelligent study. But here restraint was needed, since freedom without discipline or authority would easily invite confusion or anarchy to surface.[50]

Natsir also ridiculed rather severely Soekarno's deeply felt admiration for the Turkish leader Kemal Pasha. Quoting Chalide Edib Hanoum's works, *The Turkish Republic* and *Turkey faces West*, Natsir held that 'Hanoum lodged a sharp protest against dictator Kemal's government, where so-called freedom of religion essentially amounted to the suppression of religion altogether' with 'Kemal Pasja thus fettering religious life in Turkey' (Natsir 1973:478-9). Natsir further noted that Soekarno's lack of understanding of a *sensus fidei* (feeling for religion) caused him to seek solutions merely in the socio-political sphere. As Soekarno stated in *Pandji Islam* of 22 July 1940: 'In a future state there are only two alternatives politically: unity of religion and state without democracy, or democracy with the state separated from religion! That is the reality!'[51] It was at this reality that Soekarno would arrive on 1 June 1945 with a concept of state of the latter category.

Concern about Japan and growing pro-Japanese sentiments in Indonesia

As to the European war, here as well, Soekarno revealed his rather deep concern about that conflict, demonstrating his disdain for the fascist systems in Germany and Italy. Some people found it strange that he did not embrace Dr Pijper's proposal to have him moved back to Java on the condition that he would write some pro-Dutch articles.[52] Yet, in the wake of the German occupation of the Netherlands, Jaquet, during a brief visit to Bencoolen, described the situation there as follows:

> I met there a European society which had completely gone bizarre, with the mood being fearfully emotional. [...] This affected Soekarno as well, since the Dutch community feared that Japan would exploit the bad situation in Europe and use that for some adventurous military probe toward Southeast Asia. In view of such an invasion, Soekarno was considered to be a potential danger. This analysis was

---

[50]   Natsir 'Sikap Islam terhadap kemerdekaan berfikir', *Pandji Islam*, April-June 1940.
[51]   Buat negeri jang demikian itu hanjalah dua alternatif, hanja dua hal jang boleh dipilih diantaranja: persatuan negara-agama, tetapi zonder demokrasi, atau demokrasi, tetapi negara dipisihkan dari agama! Inilah realiteit!; 'Saja kurang dinamis' (Soekarno 1959:452).
[52]   Jaquet 1978:20; interview with Pijper, 10 May 1978 in Amsterdam.

deemed right. So the way to cope with it was as follows: the moment some bad news came from the European front, a police car would drive to Soekarno's home – not because he had done something wrong but merely since he was deemed to be potentially dangerous. Then, he would be carted off to the police barracks and kept there until the air had cleared again. This procedure was adopted several times in the wake of some bad news reaching Bencoolen again. (Jaquet 1978:24.)

Some reasons for expecting a Japanese invasion had trickled through to Soekarno as well, due to the contacts he had with Thamrin. Thamrin, together with Ratulangi and Soetardjo, had seen Ototsugu Saito then accredited as Japanese consul-general to the Netherlands Indies, as early as 4 October 1939. Saito probed his visitors about the military and naval potential of the Indies. All three maintained that 'the indigenous element of about 75% serving in the Royal Netherlands Indies Army [KNIL] would hardly put up a fight'. Unaware of Saito's wire to Tokyo that 'a mere force of 20,000 troops would suffice to overwhelm the Dutch Indies' – a cable intercepted by the Indies army decoding sources – the threesome within a week after the Saito meeting requested of US consular staff that an American protectorate be established over the Indies.[53] In their eyes such a guarantee would thwart the plans of Saito and be in the best interests of their country. These overtures, however, remained unbeknown to Dutch Indies army intelligence. The US protectorate guarantee was not forthcoming. The threesome were disappointed that no concrete constitutional concessions to their side were considered by the Dutch, let alone ensuring Indonesian independence in an immediate future, and they pondered whether Japan would be able to transform matters in their country in a constitutional sense. Also, increasing indigenous Indonesian power commercially, educationally and politically had for some time been goals for both Thamrin and Soekarno, and for most of their following of Indonesian prominents. That this number turning to Japan had grown steadily was not so surprising in the light of the colonial government's own unprecedented and rather huge recent concessions made concerning crude oil deliveries to Japan. If colonial authorities saw fit to gain financially and diplomatically from such deals – a second round of Dutch East Indies trade negotiations with Japan was scheduled for early 1941 – why should Indonesians of Soekarno's and Thamrin's ilk not engage in relationships similarly beneficial to themselves?[54] Ever since the onset of global economic depression, thousands of their indigenous countrymen sought to cushion their economic well-being or even their chances of financial sur-

[53] For the decoding assessment see Haslach 1985:130-1. For the 4 October 1939 US consular staff contacts see Hering 1996:251-3.
[54] For Thamrin assessing oil deliveries benefiting *sana*, see his two articles in *Berita Oemoem* of 14 and 15 October 1940; summarized in *Overzicht Inlandsche pers* 42, 19 October 1940, pp. 978-80.

vival by catering to Japanese dealers and traders in their search for cheaper textile, utensil and other imports. On top of this, numerous other contacts deemed beneficial to Indonesians were made during the late 1930s and early 1940s. For instance, together with the bureaucratically highly placed Hoesein Djajadiningrat, Thamrin and Koesoemo Oetojo were involved in plans, using credit from Japanese bankers, to erect a Japan-based trading firm of Indonesian importers. The plan misfired due to supposed restrictions by the Dutch barring import licenses to Indonesians (Kanahele 1967:8, 246). In the same vein, the one-time political tutor of Soekarno, E.F.E. Douwes Dekker, a self-confessed japanophile of long standing, had been instrumental in placing Indonesian graduates of his Ksatrian Institute – where Japanese was taught along with other Asia-oriented subjects – in firms connected commercially with Japan (De Bruin 1967:2). That a growing number of Indonesian national-ists turned to Japan was attested by Sjahrir as early as 26 June 1936:

> That our nationalists sympathize with Japan is not surprising in view of their recent and growing grievances against white rule – while Japan continues to act in so charming and obliging a fashion toward them and even grants autonomy to Korea! That there is a definite line and intent behind all the efforts to win the sympathy of the oriental people remains all too obvious. Unless I am very much mistaken, these efforts during the last few years have succeeded in turning our middle-class and white-collar people more and more toward Japan for the sake of educating their sons and daughters there, apart from nourishing their own cultural interests in that country. It has even become fashionable to go to Japan for a holiday.[55]

After that entry in Sjahrir's pre-war reminiscences, not only students but scores of Indonesian politicians, businessmen, journalists, teachers and tour-ists visited Japan, a country which began to loom for them as the cultural and spiritual centre of Asia.[56] And as was demonstrated earlier in this chapter about the Vorstenlanden and the contacts there with the Japanese, outside that politically sensitive area similar groups trading or dealing with Japanese residents of the colony were equally drawn to the promise that such contacts were not only mutually beneficial commercially or otherwise but perhaps even capable of furthering Indonesian nationalist aspirations. Even Nico Palar, during an orientation tour of his country, considered pro-Japanese sentiments to be present in most of his country's nationalist political circles outside Gerindo, 'the party with strong socialist traits and in everything unfavourably disposed toward Japan'.[57]

---

[55]   Sjahrazad (Sjahrir's pseudonym) 1945:100-1. An English-language rendering of it titled *Out of exile* by Charles Wolf Jr (1949) cites the wrong date (28 June instead of 26 June 1936).
[56]   RGAZ H.J. Levelt reported to Tjarda van Starkenborgh Stachouwer on 15 October 1940 on 'a Tokyo-based extreme-leftist radical group of Indonesian students'; see Hering 1996:299, note 170.
[57]   Palar 1939:794. M.A. Chanafiah's manuscript cites a late 1939 visit by A.K. Gani to

Even in Bencoolen Soekarno was made aware of these pro-Japanese sentiments, reported to him by local and visiting members of Parindra and Gerindo members. Soekarno also sent one of his protégés, a 23-year-old Sumatran youngster named Anak Marhaen Hanafi, to Batavia to assess the situation politically. This protégé would soon become a Gerindoist, while during the Japanese occupation he, together with two other former Bencoolen Gerindoists, the already mentioned Kakoeng Goenadi and M.A. Chanafiah, would join the Menteng 31 Asrama Angkatan Baroe Indonesia (Boarding House of the New Indonesian Generation). Also, Asmara Hadi, betrothed to Soekarno's adopted daughter Ratna Djoeami and affiliated with Gerindo, kept his future father-in-law abreast of the Javanese political scene.[58]

Soekarno's final Bencoolen year and his anti-fascist diatribe in the press

With the European war still widening and with Soekarno most likely realizing that Japan was to play a role in the destiny of his own country as well, Soekarno wrote most of his 1941 *sini* press contributions in an anti-fascist vein. Already in the final months of 1940 he had censured 'the Führer principle as an ideology quite opposed to the Indonesian spirit'. Its 'spirit was one of people's rule, a spirit fond of *moeshawarah* [deliberations] and of *moefakat* [consensus]'. Taught by Islam, Indonesians were

> aware of *wa amruhum sjura baihanum! Wa sjawirhum fil amri!* (One ought to consult together! One must consult others about one's affairs!). [Fascism was] essentially a spirit leaving everything to the private notions of just one man demanding blind obedience (*Kadavergehorsam*). [...] enthroned on the peak of the *Kadavergehorsam* structure reigns the supreme leader Adolf Hitler. [He] did not allow democratic rights or free spirits to dwell in his own country, and he was 'always right' (*Hitler hat immer Recht!*). [...] And today that fascist sword unleashed by him flashes fire [...] having struck Poland, Denmark, Norway, Holland, Belgium and France. [...] So, Siegfried's sword has indeed run amuck, like Rahwana [the abductor of Rama's bride Sita] once ran amuck when possessed by greed. [...] Indeed, we and fascism are like water and fire. Our spirit is the spirit of democracy, the fascist spirit is the spirit of tyranny. For that reason, we cannot and must not regard the present conflict as a conflict that does not concern us, directly or indirectly. (Soekarno 1959:457-8, 460-1, 465, 472.)

Soekarno, at which Soekarno was informed of an anti-Japanese motion adopted during the Palembang Gerindo congress, 'Bung Karno dalam pembuangan di Bengkulu', p. 27.

[58]   Hanafi 1988:viii, 17; Ramadhan 1981:224, 392, 404; Lucas 1986:181, 252, note 20; Anderson 1972:421, though listing Hanafi's departure in 1938 and not in 1940; our interview with A.M. Hanafi, Paris, 3 March 1999. Hanafi was also Soekarno's representative during Thamrin's burial at Karet on 12 January 1941. For the events leading to Thamrin's death, see Hering 1996:313-5.

Were these outpourings by Soekarno a balm for his earlier refusal of Pijper's request to write pro-Dutch articles?

On 14 June 1941, Soekarno became a *pembantu tetap* (regular contributor) to the *sini* periodical *Pemandangan*, Indonesia's biggest daily at that time. In his first contribution, called 'Mendjadi pembantoe Pemandangan' (Becoming a Pemandangan contributor), he lashed out against fascism again.

> Everyone in Indonesia hates and loathes fascism. Anti-fascism, anti-nazism, anti-Hitlerism have now become indeed the ideological slogans of our people here. [...] Now that war has broken out, now that Hitler is overhauling Europe, the eyes of our people have been opened. God be praised, I say! Better late than blind forever!

Paying tribute to his erstwhile teacher Coos Hartogh, who acquainted him early on with the theory of Marxism, Soekarno revealed that

> long before the Nazis came to power, before Hitler's name was widely known, he, Soekarno, had already understood the evils of fascism'. [...] My hatred for fascism was thus not caused by the Tenth of May [the date of Germany invading Holland] alone, but grounded upon awareness and conviction. All this has indeed been one of the services rendered by Marxism to me.

Soekarno concluded his remarks by referring to his former father-in-law's book *Islam dan sosialisme*, which had persuaded him to remain a nationalist, a Muslim and a Marxist (Soekarno 1959:511-2). He had first revealed this in his 1926 Indonesia Moeda clarion call.

Another article, written two days after Hitler's armed forces using the code name Barbarossa invaded the Soviet Union, showed Soekarno to be truly alarmed. With uncanny foresight, stunned by Hitler's newest onslaught, Soekarno in this article, titled 'Djerman versus Russia, Russia versus Djerman', wondered whether some counterforces like the British, the Americans and even the Russians would finally stop German aims of world hegemony. Though unsure when such a combination would come about, Soekarno remained convinced that such a 'a counterforce will break Hitler inevitably, just as day follows night!'. He repeated this prediction in the next article, entitled 'Batoe oedjian Sedjarah; Hitler, engkau segera dapat engkau poenja bagian!' (The test of history. Hitler, you will soon get your due)[59] With the Soviet Union now locked in a life-to-death struggle with Nazi Germany, Soekarno may well have wondered whether the South and Southeast Asian states would escape being embroiled. So, while 'hailing the courage of the heroes of both the British and Russian air forces and naval forces' in an August

---

[59]   Kombinasi itu akan mematahkan Hitler, pasti, tidak boleh tidak, pasti, sebagai matahari mengikuti malam! (Soekarno 1959:520, 531).

1941 article titled 'Beratnja perdjoangan melawan fasisme' (The difficulty of the struggle against fascism), he showed his awareness of the long way ahead toward victory and toward the freeing of colonial peoples (Soekarno 1959: 547). He turned to his own Asian continent in two articles titled 'Inggeris akan memerdekakan India?' (Will Britian free India?) and 'India-Merdeka, dapatkah ia menangkis serangan?' (Could a free India ward off attacks?). His arguments in both contributions centred on the war, wondering whether colonial peoples with such a great past history behind them were to be blessed by freedom and independence in the immediate post-war era. This message was thus directed to his own homeland people, or even to the Dutch colonial authorities. Aware as he was of self-rule developments in the Philippines, India and even Korea, he may have cherished hopes of a modern Modjopahit to emerge in his own country as well.[60] For example, Soekarno states:

> The bullets, the bombs, the dynamite that exploded and lit up the earth and skies of Europe, exploded and lit up as well the hearts and minds of people. [...] Albion, which always said 'not yet' [to Indian freedom], was thus forced to adopt a different attitude due to pressures of deadly necessity, even though it was not admitted publicly. [...] But if it is so that India will be free at the end of the war, then this freedom is basically and in the first place due to the struggle of the Indian people themselves [...] due to their own struggle, their own efforts, their own perseverance![61]

In the second article devoted to India, where he for the first time made some mention of Japan, Soekarno posed the question whether India would be able to successfully ward off an enemy invasion of its territory. Here, he again introduced the issue of freedom. Though acknowledging that Japan possessed a navy second only to that of the British and the American fleets, he maintained that India, once freed, would be quite capable of organizing and building up a military and naval apparatus as formidable as that of Japan and perhaps even more so. But for now, Soekarno argued that India, though not independent, but with huge mountain barriers flanking it and the vast Indian Ocean at its southern frontier, would make any invasion nigh impossible. And whereas

---

[60] In the wake of the German occupation of Holland, most of the *sini* press censured the German attack, even calling for a modern Modjopahit to be revived by the Dutch government, and the queen to settle in Indonesia instead of London, see Hering 1996:269-70.
[61] Peluru dan bom serta dinamit jang meledak dan mengkilat didalam bumi dan angkasa Eropah itu, meledak dan mengkilat pula didalam dada-dada orang dan ingatan-ingatan orang. [...] Albion jang senantiasa berkata 'belum' [untuk memerdekan India] itu, terpaksalah bersikap lain karena desakannja doodelijke oorzaak itu, meskipun belum diakuinja dimuka umum. [...] Tetapi kalau benar India sehabis perang ini akan merdeka, maka pada hakekatnja kemerdekaan itu pula tempat jang pertama adalah hasil perdjoangan rakjat India sendiri [...] karena perdjoangan sendiri, tenaga sendiri, keuletan sendiri! (Soekarno 1959:568.)

both Germany and Japan were still quite strong, Soekarno felt sure that in the end, the combined strength of the Allies unified in an American-British-Chinese-Dutch front would sooner or later break both Germany and Japan (Soekarno 1959:370). That Soekarno referred to this latter front may well have to do with the menacing situation developing in Southeast Asia at the time.

The road to war in the Southeast Asian theatre

Quite soon after Germany's occupation of the Netherlands, the Japanese made the opening gambit in their drive to create a so-called Co-Prosperity Sphere in the *omote Nanyo*, by some more crudely seen as the *Nahsin-ron*, the expansionist drive to the south. With Holland now occupied, the Japanese government on 16 July 1940 presented the Dutch ambassador in Tokyo with a declaration, stating that it wanted to send a delegation to Batavia in order to open trade negotiations in that city about strategically important products such as oil, tin ore, nickel, rubber, scrap iron and bauxite. These negotiations, according to Japan, would lead to a new economic treaty and would also be part of a more general political deal supporting the Co-Prosperity Sphere so dear to Tokyo's heart. Between 16 September and 12 November 1940, the Japanese trade delegation led by Ichizo Kobayashi negotiated with a Dutch delegation led by Van Mook, head of the Indies Department of Economic Affairs. On the whole, the negotiations did not move smoothly, primarily because Van Mook was faced by a USA memorandum finding the Japanese demands excessive. Van Mook thus left the oil negotiations to be dealt with by the various US and British oil companies. who could be trusted to be pressed by their respective governments not to concede too much to Japanese demands. In spite of this, the Japanese delegation was able to receive delivery by contract of 700,000 tons of oil. Also, the promised deliveries of rubber, scrap iron, tin ore, bauxite and nickel were quite large. Since the political agenda incorporating the Netherlands Indies in the Co-Prosperity Sphere was firmly rejected by Van Mook, Kobayashi returned to Tokyo on 12 November 1940 (Van Mook 1945: 49-53; Hering 1996:281; Zwitzer 1995:26-8). Yet Japan was not to give up easily. Within a few weeks it announced the dispatching of a new leader of the delegation, former Japanese foreign minister Kenkichi Yoshizawa, to Batavia, mainly with the purpose of drawing the Indies into an Asian Co-Prosperity Sphere. As before, Van Mook, perhaps also pressed by the Americans – he repeatedly consulted the American consul in Batavia, Walter F. Foote – procrastinated in such a way that on 17 June 1941 the negotiations were broken off. Yoshizawa feared serious loss of face if his delegation were asked to leave the Indies (Zwitzer 1995:28).

    In the remaining months of 1941 tension mounted in the *omote Nanyo*, with

Japan again taking the initiative, pressuring the French Vichy government to allow Japanese army units to camp near Saigon and to open the naval base at Cam Ranh Bay to Japanese fleet units. Vichy complied with these requests to on 21 July 1941, signing a mutual security pact with Japan, while Japan gave a solemn pledge to respect French sovereignty. Great Britain and the USA responded immediately, by freezing all economic and monetary assets with Japan, while also ceasing all oil deliveries. The Netherlands Indies followed suit on 28 July 1941, issuing a memorandum announcing far-reaching measures to restrict exports to Japan. Japan's prime minister Prince Fumimaro Konoye and his government were quite surprised by these strong reactions of the Western powers. A subsequent high-level meeting in Tokyo came to the disquieting conclusion that Japan's oil resources would last for a mere two years. So the country was now faced with two alternatives: negotiations or war. Under pressure from the Naval Department, the first choice was taken, with Admiral Kichisaburo Nomura, Japan's ambassador in Washington, joined somewhat later by Saburo Kurusu, opening negotiations with the US government. These came to an end when the two Japanese ambassadors handed in the Japanese declaration of war to the US State Department on 7 December 1941 at 14.00 hours local time. A fuming Cordell Hull lambasted them for delivering it hours after the sneak attack on Pearl Harbor. Unknown to Hull, the decoding of the declaration at the Japanese embassy had taken such a long time that it had been impossible to present it prior to the Pearl Harbor attack according to Emperor Hirohito's explicit wishes.[62]

The Japanese thrust into Indonesia

Even during the Nomura and Kurusu negotiations with the US government, Japan had been busy making preparations for war. In the wake of locating army and naval units in French Indo-China, the Japanese mounted a number of operational plans and so-called sandbox exercises of attacks directed at Malaya, the Philippines and the Netherlands Indies. Also the navy's air arm, using a mock model of Hawaii's Pearl Harbor naval base in a southern bay off the island of Honshu, practised a number of torpedo and bombing drills, according to a plan which had been conceived as early as January 1941. By

---

[62]   Geoffrey Blainey, 'The origins of the Pacific War', *The National Times*, 26-31 July 1976, p. 26, where he quotes an English colonel saying that among 'the start of European wars between 1700 and 1870 only one war out of more than one hundred had begun with a formal declaration of war'. Blainey also states that even The Hague convention regulating the commencement of war does not insist that 'a nation should issue or declare fair warning before attacking an enemy. [...] Even if Roosevelt had received that warning hours before the Japanese aircraft reached Pearl Harbor, US naval losses would have been just as crippling.'

mid-October, Prince Konoye was replaced as prime minister by General Hideki Tojo, a former minister of war and a known hard-liner. On 2 November the Tojo government decided to approach the US with a final proposition allowing Japan to create a Southeast Asian Co-Prosperity Sphere. If that was not forthcoming, Japan would then decide on war. US demands were clear: cessation of the war in China and Japanese withdrawal from Indo-China, while maintaining the status quo in the entire Pacific. Thus, the die was cast. On 5 November 1941, during a Japanese imperial conference, it was decided to start hostilities after 25 November, while during a subsequent imperial conference on 1 December 1941 it was decided to declare war on the US, Great Britain and the Netherlands.[63]

In the wake of the Pearl Harbor disaster, the Dutch East Indies government, pressed by the London-based Dutch cabinet, was quick to take up the gauntlet and declare itself at war with Japan. Whether this was a wise decision has been questioned by some who would have preferred to take such a step only after Japanese forces had violated Indies territory. 'By siding at once with Great Britain and the USA, the Dutch government, not used to reasoning like Churchill in terms of "raison d'état", dealt an important trumpcard [...] thus dealing a card which appeared to be a black jack.' (Zwitzer 1995: 32-3). Be that as it may, the Japanese gave short shrift to the so-called ABDA forces they encountered in the Indies archipelago. This American-British-Dutch-Australian Command, conceived by Churchill and Roosevelt during their meeting at the end of December, came into being on 15 January 1942. The commanding officer was British field marshal Sir Archibald Wavell, with his headquarters located at Lembang in West Java. His task was to hold the so-called Malayan Barrier, a bastion stretching from Singapore, the Palembang oil fields, Java, and Timor to Darwin. This line was drawn in answer to the first successes of the Japanese forces, who had captured Tarakan on 12 January 1942 and had landed airborne troops in Minahassa on 11 January, causing KNIL forces to withdraw to central Celebes. Meanwhile, Balikpapan fell to the Japanese on 24 January, while on the same day the important air base Kendari in South Celebes was captured by the Japanese. On 7 February, Ambon fell into Japanese hands, while on the 18th of the same month Japanese forces landed in Bali, having it all under control by the next day. The eastern wing of the Malay Barrier had thus been punctured. The western wing crumpled as well, with Palembang being taken by the Japanese on the same day that Singapore surrendered, 15 February 1942. These defeats showed the fallacy of the ABDA strategy. Java was now surrounded by superior Japanese

---

[63]   For the minutes of the imperial conferences (called imperial because the emperor was in attendance) an English-language rendering is provided in Ike 1967. For the fateful decisions turn to Blainey's 'The origins of the Pacific War', *The National Times*, 26-31 July 1976, pp. 29-30.

forces, which also had command of the air space. Wavell himself, on 18 February, admitted that Java could not be adequately defended any longer, and so on 25 February 1942 the ABDA command was dissolved. Java, now also closed off from reinforcements – Australian and British units on the way to Java were diverted to Suez or to the Burmese theatre of war – had to face the enemy by itself, together with a small contingent of Australians, British and Americans commanded by the English major-general H.D.W. Sitwell and the Australian brigadier A.S. Blackburn. The latter would command the so-called Blackforce brigade, with a core of seasoned veterans of the Syrian campaign. Meanwhile, a small Dutch-British-American-Australian flotilla of cruisers and destroyers tried in vain to intercept the Japanese invasion transports guarded by heavy cruisers. In the so-called Battle of the Java Sea, most of the Allied units were sunk or heavily damaged. This enabled units of the Japanese invasion forces, from 28 February to 1 March, to land almost unhindered at four sites on Java's northern shore. Only at one landing site, the Bay of Bantam, a brief battle ensued between two Allied cruisers, a Dutch submarine and the invasion forces. The Japanese commander-in-chief General Hitoshi Imamura and his staff had to swim to shore, since their transport ship was sunk during the battle. The Allied cruisers did not survive the encounter, but the Dutch submarine escaped, to reach Colombo later on. One of the few units which had been able to inflict heavy casualties upon the Japanese regiment confronting it was Blackforce – for two days, in Leuwiliang in West Java. In spite of this success, the situation further to the northeast in West Java worsened considerably. Japanese units landing near Cheribon on 1 March 1942 had captured the air base Kalidjati, 40 kilometres north of Bandoeng, on the same day. Counterthrusts by KNIL units to dislodge them had all failed, causing Blackforce and several of the KNIL regiments to fall back on Bandoeng. From Kalidjati the Japanese had mounted attacks on the fortified positions just north of Bandoeng. These were broken through and Lembang was then occupied by units of the Japanese regiment led by Colonel Shoji on 7 March. At that time, overtures were made by the KNIL command for a ceasefire, which led to the overall capitulation ceremony on 9 March held in Kalidjati.[64]

Factors leading to Soekarno's return to Java

For Soekarno, one of the first signs of the Japanese coming closer was a request made to him and his close friend Oei Tjeng Hien by *Resident* Maier

---

[64]   Zwitzer 1995:33-4; L de Jong 1969-91, XIa:740-3. A more detailed report of these developments is in Nortier, Kuijt and Groen 1994:58-9, 61, 67, 83-5, 106-9, 114-54.

to organize a so-called Penolong Korban Perang (Pekope, or Aid to War Victims). They both agreed, and so the Pekope was set up, with Oei Tjeng Hien functioning as chairman and Soekarno as vice-chairman. Soekarno seems to have departed from his stand of not writing pro-Dutch articles at that time. After Pearl Harbor's Day of Infamy, he told Maier that his ideas about Japanese fascism had not altered. He even approached the Indies government with a proposal to support it in its struggle to ward off the Japanese, mostly in the form of newspaper articles, in exchange for a return to Java. Soekarno may have preferred a still safe and well-defended Java to a rather weakly defended Bencoolen. However, Tjarda did not accept Soekarno's offer, feeling it was better to leave Soekarno where he was (Abdul Karim 1982:72; De Jong 1969-91, XIa:983-4). On top of these concerns, Soekarno had been plagued by a growing problem in his own household for some time. In his capacity of Ketua Dewan Pengadjaran (Chairman of the Education Council) of the Bencoolen Moehammadijah branch, he had been contacted way back in 1939 by a Moehammadijah foreman named Hassan Din who was concerned about his daughter's educational prospects. So a meeting was arranged with Hassan Din, his wife Chadidjah, and his daughter Fatmah to discuss whether Fatmah could enrol in the Roman Catholic Vakschool (Trade School) together with Ratna Djoeami. Since Fatmah had only managed to reach the fifth grade of the Hollandsch-Inlandsche School, it was decided to leave her at Anggoet Atas with Soekarno to upgrade her learning so she could join Ratna at the Vakschool later on. Fatmah, renamed Fatmawati by Soekarno and sharing a bedroom with Ratna, settled in, to the joy of her parents, while both Soekarno and Inggit came to see her as a third adopted daughter (Ramadhan 1981:365-6; Fatmawati Soekarno 1978:26-7).

Somewhat later, Fatmawati left Anggoet Atas to stay with her grandmother, who lived close to Soekarno's home, after a falling out she had with Ratna; Inggit also seemed annoyed about Soekarno being far too kind to her. Fatmawati did well at school and so she was able to finish the Vakschool just after she turned seventeen. Soekarno then started to frequent her grandmother's home in order to upgrade Fatmawati's command of the English language. His continuing involvement with her caused some concern to Inggit, who felt that he often sided with her during discussions when Fatmawati was visiting them. Yet Inggit left Bencoolen to arrange Ratna's entering the Taman Siswa teachers college in Djokja and then stayed in Bandoeng with her relatives for close to a month. After her return to Anggoet Atas, she felt a distinct change of atmosphere; her Koesno looked withdrawn and was often quiet for long periods. She often wondered whether Soekarno had been seeing Fatmawati regularly while she was away. Still, the ties between Soekarno's family and the Hassan Din family were further strengthened when one of Soekarno's nephews married an aunt of Fatmawati's. Around that time Soekarno finally confided to Inggit that he wanted to have children. When she retorted that he already had two daughters, he responded that he wanted children of his own. He also admitted that he was attracted to Fatmawati, and even discussed the possibility of having her as a second wife. He even wrote to Ratna in Djokja stating that, at forty, he really cherished the idea of having children of his own. And when Ratna returned to Bencoolen for a brief visit, he revealed that desire again to her, only to have both his adopted daughters chastise him and side with Inggit (Fatmawati Soekarno 1978:26-7; Ramadhan 1981:368-71, 373-4, 380-2, 390). Soon, however, developments in Bencoolen forced them to set this problem aside for a while.

News had reached Soekarno's household that Palembang had been captured by Japanese forces and that the key town of Loeboek Lingga was also within their reach. Some observers have it that Soekarno wired Tjarda requesting that he and his family be evacuated to Australia on an Australian warship. This request was confirmed by BB official B. Oldenburger, who was informed by Soekarno about this request when they briefly met at Bencoolen's residency office. Soekarno told the BB official that he feared repercussions if the Japanese caught him, since he had written anti-Japanese articles. Also, World War II historian L. de Jong states that Soekarno, in the wake of Palembang's fall, had requested evacuation 'in an emotional wire' to Tjarda.[65] Other sources, like Dahm, Wehl and Alers, however, question the validity of Soekarno's request, seeing it as a product of a defamation campaign instituted after the war. Dahm states that there 'is not the slightest evidence for it either in contemporary sources or in Sukarno's basic attitude'. All this should be weighed carefully: even Van Mook, upon his return to Indonesia after the war, alleged that Soekarno's *minta ampun* letters 'included an offer of collaboration by Soekarno to pass on all the secrets of the national movement to colonial authorities'.[66] Most likely, in the sauve qui peut to Padang, Soekarno and his family were taken along as well, in the hope of getting transportation to some safe haven outside the Japanese orbit. That these hopes were dashed by the swift Japanese advance in the remainder of north and central Sumatra made the Soekarno family await the future with some resignation. In Padang they were housed in Dr Waworoentoe's home, where Kartika befriended their host's daughters. It is from this city that Soekarno, on 17 March 1942, was escorted by a French-speaking captain named Sakaguchi to meet the Japanese area commander Colonel Fujiyama in Boekittingi.

---

[65]   De Jong 1969-91, XIa:984, who also cites Oldenburger referring to Jaquet 1978:26. De Jong, however, also refers to Tjarda van Starkenborgh Stachouwer's unpublished interrogation before the Enquête Commission punt n, vraagno. 28933, where Tjarda states that he wants 'Soekarno to stay put in Bencoolen'.
[66]   Dahm 1969:217; Alers 1956:47; Wehl 1948:10, for Van Mook's allegation see Van der Wal 1971-73, I:85.

There, Fujiyama, who spoke in Japanese through an American interpreter captured in Singapore, told Soekarno that if he desired future independence for his fatherland, such could only be achieved through cooperation with Dai Nippon. Therefore, General Imamura, the Saiko Sikikan (Commander-in-Chief) of Java, wanted him and his family to come to Djakarta in order to achieve that cooperation. And so, escorted by the Japanese, Soekarno, Inggit, Kartika and Riwoe and the two dogs Ketoet Satoe and Ketoet Doea – going by way of Bencoolen (where they briefly visited Oey Tjeng Hien) and Palembang – boarded a ship for the crossing to Djakarta. They arrived there on 9 July 1942, where they were reunited with Ratna and her husband Asmara Hadi. Soekarno, soon after, had discussions with his former political foes Hatta and Sjahrir (Ramadhan 1981:405, 411-24; Adams 1965:156-66). With them, Soekarno would start the quest for Indonesian independence.

CHAPTER VII

Soekarno's quest for Indonesian independence during the Japanese occupation period 9 July 1942 - 1 June 1945

Initial relations between Java-based nationalists and the Japanese authorities

In the few months before Soekarno's return to Java, General Imamura, perhaps surprised by the joyous reception granted by the Indonesian populace to his invading forces, seems to have adopted a soft-line policy during the first weeks of his brief reign in Java as the Saiko Shikikan (Highest Commander). Ably assisted in this matter by his senior political adviser Count Hideo Kodama, an old-style foreign-office official, he adhered to two major policy aims set up earlier in Tokyo for the Southern Regions, namely to win the trust of the indigenous population and to involve existing indigenous administration structures as widely as possible.[1] In a 17 March 1942 address Imamura said that

> the people greeted us with warm admiration and acclamation. Therefore our prime objective must be to allow these obedient people to bathe in the genuine Imperial graces. [...] We must allow them to share happiness with the Japanese. It is wrong to see them as an object to be exploited by the entire Japanese population. It was the exploitative policy of the Dutch that caused the total disaffection of the native people.

---

[1]   Indische collectie NIOD 004861/5089; Benda, Irikura and Kishi 1965:1, document 1. For Imamura's 'soft line' induced by the support of the indigenous population, see Reid and Oki 1986:31, 54. On page 54 Imamura refers to Senjinkun, a code of conduct he drew up in 1940. In essence the soft line and his own code also meant keeping a considerable number of Dutch experts at jobs useful to the Japanese and overall Japanese paternalism toward the Javanese, with the latter being encouraged to address their Japanese superiors as *saudara tua* (older brother); see Mrázek 1994:220. As to Dutch experts, Imamura insisted that they should retain their positions for the time being and that prisoners of war were to be treated according to the Geneva convention; see Nakamura 1970:12. For Dutch experts being utilized in restoring railtracks and bridges until 1 October 1942 see Kurasawa 1996:637-8.

As to the warm and widespread reception by the Indonesian populace, described by a high-ranking Japanese naval officer as 'a frantic atmosphere of welcome',[2] it had been stimulated by the numerous pamphlets dropped by Japanese airplanes during the landings on Java showing both the Indonesian and Japanese flags with the message 'we are both of one colour and of one race'. Other Japanese pamphlets even invoked the Djajabaja prophecy, carrying the message: 'His Majesty Djojobojo said the yellow-skinned people will come from the north to liberate the Indonesian people from the slavery of the Dutch. So look for the yellow-skinned people.'[3] One Indonesian observer reported the entry of Japanese units in Batavia on 5 March 1942 with their trucks and armoured vehicles draped with the Japanese flag and the *merah-putih* (red and white) and with posters carrying the message 'Satoe warna satoe bangsa' (one colour, one race) and 'Hidoep Asia Raja' (Long live Greater Asia). He observed that many Indonesians offered the Japanese drink, food and fruit, since they felt that Nippon had freed them from the Dutch yoke. Such feelings were further reinforced when the Japanese on 9 March 1942 appointed Dachlan Abdullah as mayor of Batavia and Tan Eng Hok as vice-mayor, and on 17 March Atik Soeardi and Raden Pandoe Soerhadiningrat as governor and vice-governor of West Java. This caused Soetardjo Kartohadi-koesoemo to say to his fellow countrymen that 'we are on the threshold of Indonesia Merdeka since Nippon has freed us from the tutelage of the Dutch and is now exhorting us to rely on ourselves'.[4]

Other main cities welcomed the entry of elements of the Sixteenth Army with similar outbursts of enthusiasm. In Soerabaja, for instance, the Parindra executive reported the overall joy of the people now that Dutch authority had been destroyed: 'Soerabaja came to life again with all its main thoroughfares crowded with people awaiting the entry of the heroic Japanese Army, while the red and white and the Nippon flag are flying from the roof of our own Gedong Nasional Indonesia [Indonesian National Home]'. In Soerabaja, as in Batavia, discussions took place between enthusiastic local nationalists and Japanese officials as to how to support the Japanese in their efforts to normalize the situation. In Solo, Parindra chairman Woerjaningrat also urged

---

[2]   Imamura's 17 March address was printed in *Sekidoho* of 18 March 1942. The naval officer Rear Admiral Tadashi Maeda, a former naval attaché in The Hague, was one who during the Japanese occupation was to acquire great prestige among young Indonesian nationalists, also playing an important role in the Indonesians attaining independence. For his comments on the March 1942 frantic atmosphere of welcome, see Indische collectie NIOD 005302.

[3]   Abdulgani n.d.:5-6; Groen and Touwen-Bouwsma 1992:65-6; Brugmans et al. 1960:99.

[4]   Pakpahan 1948:4. For the entry in Batavia and the eager services offered to the new occupiers: De Bruin 1982:58-9. For the mayoral and gubernatorial appointments: *Berita Oemoem*, 9 and 17 March and Pakpahan 1948:15. For Soetardjo's clarion call see *Berita Oemoem* of 19 March 1942; he himself would be elevated to *shochokan* (*resident*) of Djakarta residency on 1 December 1943, see *Djawa Baroe* 1(December 1943):8.

the people to support the Japanese in the common task of building a new society. Here, with Mr Singgih, Ki Hadjar Dewantoro and Mr Soejoedi, it was decided to present the Japanese government with a list of Indonesian leaders such as Soekarno and Hatta, probably with the intention of involving all of them in a new Indonesian government under Japanese auspices (Hering 1992). Somewhat later, a Dutch observer, Mr Dr Leo F. Jansen, a former acting secretary of the Raad van Indië (Council of the Indies) and since 31 May 1942 employed by the Japanese Overseas Broadcasting Service, due to his fluency in the Japanese language, confided to his diary the initial widespread anti-Dutch sentiment among Indonesians. Dr Hoesein Djajadiningrat, once the prime example of an Indonesian who had done well in the colonial establishment, told him that 'the Dutch would never be able to return to Indonesia'. Former Rechts Hoogeschool (RHS, Faculty of Law) law professor Willem Wertheim, one of the most sensitive and attentive commentators on the Indonesian scene at the time, wrote about Hoesein and his ilk as follows: 'they bowed quite readily to their new masters, these old-fashioned aristocratic civil servants, these crown jewels of feudal society. They had been yes-men before – and they were yes-men now.'[5]

As to Imamura's initial soft line, one has to consider that he was now only in charge of Java and Madoera – Sumatra and Java/Madoera were under the jurisdiction of, respectively, the Twenty-Fifth Army with headquarters in Shonanto (the Japanese name for Singapore) and the Sixteenth Army with headquarters in Djakarta. Borneo, Celebes, the Moluccas, the Lesser Sunda islands, and New Guinea resorted under the Third Fleet with headquarters in Makassar. Imamura's Sixteenth Army, which had the code name of the Osamu group (the pacifying group), soon bereft of the veteran 2nd and 38th divisions, thus consisted of a military force equal in numbers to the defeated KNIL (Nugroho Notosusanto 1979:27-8; Reid and Oki 1986:55, 220). Also, the Japanese contingent of administrative personnel at Imamura's disposal was quite small. The transport carrying the bulk of these military administrators had been sunk just prior to the Japanese landings in Java, with only a few surviving. Also, Imamura was robbed of utilizing the 1,700 Japanese who had lived on Java for many years, since the Dutch had removed them to Australia at the end of January 1942, where they were interned at Loveday camp in southern Australia.[6] However, some notable experts did make it to Java during those early days in March 1942. One was Parindra member Mr

---

5   Jansen 1988:2, 16, 28, 36, 38. For Wertheim's comments: Wertheim 1946:17-8.
6   Poulgrain 1993:142-5. In August 1942, 834 Japanese were repatriated, of whom 115 (including the naval spies Shigetada Nishijima and Tomegoro Yoshizumi) in that repatriation exchange preferred to go from Australia by way of Lourenço Marques to Java, where they arrived according to *Pewarta Perniagaän* on 30 September 1942 in Batavia; see Zwaan 1981:82. The former naval spies fluent in Dutch and Indonesian started up a special school for Indonesian independence

Raden Soedjono, a Leiden-trained legal expert, who since 1938 had taught Indonesian in Tokyo. He arrived with the Japanese landing forces as an officer in their army and would act as an adviser to Imamura (Gunseikanbu 1944a:17). Another was the Japanese Hitoshi Shimizu of the Sendenbu (or Barisan Propaganda, propaganda department) who was later to turn Muslim. He was viewed by one historian as someone who 'went native, learning to speak fluent Indonesian, mixing in Islamic circles, sitting at the feet of Professor Purbotjaroko, and nurturing a young group of Indonesian protégés [...] the precise equivalent of a man like Charles van der Plas'. While another historian who interviewed him on 4 to 5 June 1968 relates that five days after landing on Java Shimizu exhorted Indonesians and Japanese to *sama-sama tidur, sama-sama makan* (sleep together and eat together) – translating literally a common Japanese expression that conveys the notion of intimate fraternal community. Indonesians replied laughingly: Eat together, yes; sleep together no. The idea struck Indonesians as ludicrous, yet Simizhu had won their goodwill for trying the language as well as wearing local clothing.[7] With such a reputation it is no wonder that Shimizu stood at the cradle of the Tiga A Movement, as we will see presently.

Another group akin to Indonesia's main religious culture was the small contingent of Japanese Muslims arriving with the invasion force. Indonesians in Batavia – the name Djakarta would be used after the first anniversary of the outbreak of the Pacific War on 8 December 1942 – were startled to see these Japanese Muslims in army uniform attending services at the Kwitang Mosque only a week after the fall of the capital city.[8] The Japanese, well aware of Islam's strength and its specific demands during the colonial period in the realm of socio-political and religious reform, may have been using the goodwill to achieve closer contact with the Islamic world. On 16 March a colonel named Choso Horie, not a Muslim himself, arrived at the same mosque with a group of seven Japanese Muslims, and he addressed the flock of Indonesian Muslim worshippers in Japanese.[9] On 28 March, all these activities culminated in the establishment of the Kantor Oeroesan Agama (Office of Religious Affairs, Shomubu in Japanese), with Colonel Horie heading it. Its first task

---

established under the authority of Rear Admiral Maeda, Poulgrain 1993:148. For short biographies of these spies, see Sluimers 1978:152-3.

[7]   Anderson 1966b:16. Dr Raden Mas Ngabi Poerbotjaroko, a Solonese aristocrat, born in Solo on 1 January 1884, who obtained a Leiden University PhD in 1926, served in the Indies' Oudheidkundige Dienst (Archaeological Service) and during the Japanese occupation was a member of the Indonesia go I'inkai (Indonesian Language Commission). He authored an impressive list of scientific works and academic papers; see Gunseikanbu 1944a:423-4. As to the other historian citing Shimizu, see Friend 1988:149.

[8]   *Berita Oemoem*, 12 March 1942; *Pemandangan*, 12 March 1942.

[9]   *Berita Oemoem*, 16 March 1942.

was to put all mosques and also the rural *ulama* (Muslim teachers) under the control of the Japanese army.[10] The Shomubu staff consisted of the following Indonesians: Dr R. Prijono, formerly a lecturer in Indonesian languages at the Batavia Law Faculty (RHS) under Dutch rule, Raden Hadji Hoesein Iskandar, Abdoellah Aidid and Mr Raden Soebagjo Djojowidagdo – all formerly associated with the Dutch Kantoor van Inlandsche Zaken – and Mas Soewirjo.[11] On 9 May 1942 Horie ordered the abolition of the Partai Sarekat Islam Indonesia (PSII); on 20 May the more moderate Partai Islam Indonesia (PII) was prohibited.[12] These moves, as we shall see presently, were part of a wider plan to curtail Indonesian political ambitions.

In its activities catering to Muslim concerns, Horie's Kantor somewhat resembled the colonial Kantoor van Inlandsche Zaken, led by such Islamists as Snouck Hurgronje, Gobée, Van der Plas and Pijper. Another Islamist, Dr Harry J. Benda, suggested that Horie's Kantor was intended to divorce Indonesian Islam from politics, just as Snouck Hurgronje had done in the past. Yet the Shomubu's policies to a large extent showed a direct reversal of that of Japan's colonial predecessors in Java. Instead of maintaining mere neutrality toward the Islamic religion as the Dutch had done, the Japanese from the very outset were quite determined to turn the Muslim leaders of Java into staunch allies of their military administration. And in Benda's view, such an abrupt reversal was due to the primary concern of the Dutch being the maintenance of law and order and the continuation of the status quo, whereas the Japanese were out to mobilize an entire population in the support of their war aims. For this, the new rulers of Java needed to accelerate production of food supplies and the recruitment of labourers. To elicit such support from the Javanese peasants it remained essential to involve rural Muslim leaders, who for centuries had been the major counsellors and spiritual guides of Javanese villagers. It was to these thousands of Muslim leaders of the Javanese countryside that Horie's Shomubu was to give its primary attention.[13]

Indonesian political ambitions dashed and a turn to the Gerakan Tiga A

As to the events curtailing Indonesian political ambitions, these were inaugurated by overtures made by a number of prominent Indonesian politicians

---

[10]   *Berita Oemoem*, 28 March 1942.
[11]   Gunseikanbu 1944a:425, 435, 430 and 8, respectively, for these appointments. For Mas Soewirjo's see Benda 1958:233, note 26.
[12]   *Asia Raya*, 12 May and 5 June 1942; Van Nieuwenhuijze 1958:134.
[13]   Benda 1958:109-10, 1955:352-4; Van Nieuwenhuijze 1958:116-8. For Snouck Hurgronje's views see Snouck Hurgronje 1926:225-306.

after their talks with the Japanese colonel Yasuto Nakayama as early as 9
March 1942. These discussions, in Nakayama's view, at least solved the problem of the current shortage of administrative personnel, hence his request for
a list of useful persons to invite. The Indonesian prominents involved were
Abikoesno Tjokrosoejoso of the PSII, the non-partisan Ir Soerachman and Dr
Ratulangie of the Persatoean Minahassa. These three men, like some others
of their ilk in Soerabaja and Solo described above, were obviously under
the impression that some kind of Indonesian self-government was about to
emerge. Apparently, the three Batavia-based Indonesian prominents were
quite keen to exploit the shortage of local Japanese administrators as well.
As the Japanologist Laszlo Sluimers has it, 'they wanted to strike the iron
while it was hot'.[14] In the wake of his talk with Colonel Nakayama, that same
day Abikoesno of the PSII was quick to present a list of ministerial candidates
for an Indonesian government and their assistants (during the transition
period). The list was drawn up in Djakarta at a meeting of delegates from
the central executives of the PSII, Gerindo, Parpindo, Pasoendan, Persatoean
Minahassa, Partai Arab Indonesia, Perhimpoenan Peladjar-Peladjar Indonesia and MIAI. While this seems to imply a modicum of unity, it remains
strange that the Parindra was not invited to the meeting of delegates, while
only one of its members, Mr Raden Soedjono, appeared on Abikoesno's list
of ministerial candidates. That this Parindra member was listed was likely
due to his being one of Imamura's top Javanese advisers. So, on Abikoesno's
list Mr Raden Soedjono, just returned from Japan, was given the portfolio
for foreign affairs; Mr Moh. Yamin for domestic affairs; Hatta for economic
affairs; Dr Aboetari for commercial and maritime affairs; KNIL major
Santoso for national defence; Ki Hadjar Dewantoro for training and education; Dr Ratulangie for finance; Mr Maramis for justice; Hadji Mas Mansoer
for Islamic affairs; Dr Soekiman for social affairs; Dr Boentaran for health;
Abikoesno himself for transportation; Ir Soekarno for press and propaganda
and Mr Djoko Soetomo for arts and science (Sluimers 1968:366-7).

Parindra, apparently stung by it all, presented in its periodical *Berita
Oemoem* of 12 March 1942 yet another cabinet, with Dr Ratulangie for foreign
affairs; Parinda-prominent Soekardjo Wirjopranoto or Soetardjo for domestic
affairs; Moh. Yamin or Professor Mr Raden Soepomo for justice; Ir Soerachman for economic affairs; Drs Hatta for finance; Ir Teko for agriculture; Ir
Notoningrat for transport and communications; Soewandi for education;
Pandji Soeroso or Hindromartono for labour; and Ir Soekarno, Mr Soemardi

---

[14]   Sluimers 1968:347. Kanahele 1967:260, note 82, following an interview he had with
Nakayama on 15 June 1964 in Tokyo, maintains that the colonel, who spoke neither Indonesian
nor Dutch, may have had a less than competent interpreter and thus did not grasp the real intentions of the three Indonesians confronting him.

and others as ministers without portfolio. Also, on that date Raden Mas Winarno wrote in *Berita Oemoem* that it was time for Soekarno and Hatta to form a ministerial cabinet, while commenting that Indonesians did not need the Japanese as substitutes for the Dutch, since 'we are able to govern ourselves and therefore there is no need at all for foreign rulers or even for brothers to fill that role'. *Berita Oemoem,* however, had completely miscalculated the situation, since the 'new masters used the same methods as the former masters'.[15] Still, all that seems not to have sunk in, since the next day Abikoesno in *Tjahaja Timoer* retorted with yet another cabinet listing, this time with him as premier and Soekarno as vice-premier. This was also the first mention of the posts of premier and vice-premier. The other posts were as follows: Dr Ratulangie for finance; Hadji Agoes Salim for social affairs; Mr Raden Soedjono for foreign affairs; Drs Hatta for economic affairs; Hadji Mas Mansoer for Islamic affairs; Goesti Mohammad Noer for transport and communications; Mr Moh. Yamin for justice; Professor Mr Raden Soepomo for arts and science; KNIL major Santoso for national defence and Parada Harahap for press and propaganda.[16] The startling thing in Abikoesno's second list was the elevation of Soekarno to vice-premier. However, even more startling was Abikoesno's 13 March revelation cited in *Tjahaja Timoer* that all this had come about at the urging of the Japanese authorities.

The appearance of these three lists coming out in such short order keenly demonstrated that unity between the two major Indonesian political constellations had evaporated, prompting an upsurge of the old rivalry between the cooperationist Parindra and the non-cooperationist PSII as it had existed in the final days of Dutch colonialism. As for the Japanese authorities, they were quick to set the record straight as to Abikoesno's claim of having acted with their blessing. They stated 'that following the reports in some dailies about a meeting between Japanese army authorities with some prominent members of the Indonesian people's movement to arrive at the appointment of these Indonesian prominents to act as advisers or intermediaries, [these reports] have no grounds at all'. Also, the head of the Sendenbu, Colonel Keiji Machida, was quick to announce in the daily *Berita Oemoem* of 14 March that the appointment of Indonesian advisers was not true.[17] And to bring an end to all Indonesian illusions, the Japanese authorities on 20 March 1942 issued Oendang-Oendang (Regulations) no. 3 stating: 'For the time being, all kinds of discussion, actions, and suggestions or propaganda pertaining to the state regulations or the form of government are prohibited'. The same day Oendang-Oendang no. 4 implicitly prohibited the showing of the Indonesian

---

[15]   *Berita Oemoem,* 12 March 1942; De Bruin 1967:14. For Winarno's views see Zwaan 1981:36.
[16]   *Tjahaja Timoer,* 13 March 1942; De Bruin 1967:17.
[17]   Sluimers 1978:158; Machida's announcement was reprinted in *Kan Po,* Nomor Istimewa, 9 March 1943:38.

red-and-white banner by declaring that 'In the case of hoisting the official flag at office buildings or at houses during festival days, only the flag of Nippon need be used' (Gunseikanbu 1944b:8). In the wake of these regulations, one after another Indonesian *pergerakan* office closed its doors, thereby signalling the sad termination of the pre-war constellation of Indonesian political parties. How nonplussed some Indonesian prominents still were was demonstrated by Soetardjo Kartohadikoesoemo, who in *Berita Oemoem* on 19 March still maintained that 'a new Indonesia would emerge and that all indigenous civil servants and other officials who were in function during the Dutch reign before 8 March 1942 had to resume their duties and strive therefore for only one national party'. *Berita Oemoem* on 23 March reported that Mohammad Hatta had arrived in Batavia, causing chief editor Winarno to suggest in the 25 March issue that 'it would not be a disappointment if Soekarno and Hatta were given the leadership of the new party suggested by Soetardjo'.[18] As for Hatta, he had arrived in Batavia from Soekaboemi on 25 March and had talks with Imamura's deputy chief of staff Major-General Harada and Colonel Nakayama the following few days. These talks resulted in Hatta becoming a general adviser of the Japanese military administration and heading a *kantor penasehat umum* (general advisory office), also referred to by the Japanese as the Hatta *kikan*. Hatta's contact person was Shunkichiro Miyoshi, a former vice-consul in Soerabaya who was fluent in both Dutch and Malay and was known to have had contact with Soekarno and Hatta during his vice-consular period in the 1920s.[19] In his *kikan*, soon to be divided into two divisions – an advisory and a complaints branch – Hatta was assisted by Mr Abdoel Karim Pringgodigdo, Professor Soepomo, Mr Soejitno Mangoenkoesoemo, Mr Soenarjo Kolopaking, Ir Soerachman, Margono Djojohadikoesoemo and Mr Soewirjo, all of whom were Western-trained, with the first six having occupied rather high offices during the Dutch colonial period (Hatta 1981: 203-9, 1979b:401-6, 413-4).

As to how the *pergerakan* would be utilized by the Japanese authorities from now on, there are opposing views by two scholars. The Islamist Benda sees it as having been used primarily in Japanese ventures attempting to play off Islam against the secular nationalists, under a policy of divide and rule. One of Soekarno's biographers, Bernhard Dahm, on the other hand, maintains that Japanese army headquarters wanted to bundle all nationalists, secular and Muslim, behind it in an effort closely supervised by the Japanese. It seems that Dahm's view is closer to the truth than Benda's (Friend 1988:

---

[18]   *Berita Oemoem*, 19, 23 and 25 March 1942, also cited by De Bruin 1967:14.
[19]   Masuda 1971:123, with our thanks to Fujimoto Fumio of Teikyo Junior College Holland in Maastricht for translating that part of Masuda's book for us. For Hatta's *kikan* see also Miyoshi's contribution in Reid and Oki 1986:114-5, and Pakpahan 1948:14.

91; Sluimers 1978:159). However, as Laszlo Sluimers points out, 'there was little indication at the start of the occupation that the Japanese military administration wanted to foment Indonesian independence movements'.[20] While the army authorities on 20 March 1942 had thus quelled the political aspirations of both secular and Muslim Indonesian nationalists, some in the Japanese establishment were still keen not to alienate them and to involve the nationalists in ways useful to the Japanese administration and the war effort. One man within the Japanese administration who saw this quite clearly was Sendenbu member Shimizu. Another was Colonel Horie, in charge of the Shomubu, who was quite content to leave the task of establishing a new Muslim organization for the time being to Shimizu's initiative.[21]

And so, in an atmosphere of incipient disillusionment still reigning in most nationalist circles both Muslim and secular, 'some Japanese and Indonesians around the end of March or at the beginning of April 1942 inaugurated the so-called Gerakan Tiga A [Triple A Movement; or, in Japanese, San A Undo]'.[22] However, there was no public opening ceremony and so the exact beginning date of the Triple A Movement remains obscure. The question who was the real initiator of the Gerakan Tiga A remains equally dim.[23]

The Gerakan Tiga A and the subsequent arrival of Soekarno on the Javanese scene

Berita Oemoem, Parindra's official daily edited at Batavia, had already announced on 1 April 1942 the coming of the Triple A Movement and stated the next day that the V (for Victory) symbol of the Allied powers was now to be replaced by the AAA emblem of the Japanese. AAA stands for 'Asahi Akari no Asai' (Japan, Light of Asia), 'Asahi Amijiban no Asai' (Japan, Protector of Asia), 'Asahi Aniki no Asai' (Japan, Elder Brother of Asia). However, the Gerakan Tiga A was certainly not a propaganda movement to counter the

[20]   Sluimers 1996:26-7, where he cites the Main Points for the Execution of the Administration of the Occupied Territories established by the Imperial Headquarters coordination conference of 20 November 1941; paragraph 8 clause 4 stipulates that: 'Natives and aborigines shall so be guided as to induce them with a sense of trust in the imperial forces while premature encouragement of their independence movements shall be avoided'.
[21]   Benda 1958:113. While Horie had established contacts in early May with the MIAI and had toured the main Muslim centres of Java together with a three-man MIAI delegation, he awaited Shimizu's efforts with the Tiga A affiliated Persiapan Persatoean Oemmat Islam, and so for several months the MIAI suffered an eclipse.
[22]   Mr Samsoedin (who was to lead the movement), 'Pertemoean antara Poetjoek Pimpinan Pergerakan "Tiga A" dan pemoeka-pemoeka rakjat jang ada di Betawi' (Meeting between the Main Leadership of the Triple A Movement and the people's leaders of Batavia), NIOD Indische Collectie 030724.
[23]   See note 26.

victory symbol of the Allied powers. Its main aim was to generate a series of social organizations modelled on the total-mobilization groupings in Japan, covering a wide range of activities, excluding politics, in both urban and rural areas (De Bruin 1967:7-8, 16, 1982a:62; Sato 1994:46). Shimizu formulated the aims of the Triple A Movement as 'The ideology of the movement is based upon the consideration that we want to implant an ideologically based Asian information service on Indonesian soil' (Sluimers 1978:161). He also asserted that 'As far as I was concerned, the aim of the Tiga A was to unite all Asians in a fraternity of friendship'.[24] The Shimizu-inspired slogan of Asian solidarity under the auspices of Nippon aimed to open Gerakan Tiga A membership not merely to Indonesians but also to members of minority groups such as Chinese, Arabs, Indians and Eurasians.

Actually, the Chinese, who in 19 May 1942 had formed a Tiga A-affiliated Hua Ch'iao Tsung Hui (Chinese General Association), and the Arab community, who in 26 May 1942 had formed the Perkoempoelan Dagang Bangsa Arab (Arabian Trading Association), were used mainly as expedient sources of money, while the few Eurasians and Indians joining the Tiga A were obviously driven by aims of security and protection. As for the Indonesian Muslims, since July 1942 they were affiliated with the Tiga A through the Persiapan Persatoean Oemmat Islam (Preparation for the Unity of the Islamic Community), which superseded the Madjlisoel Islamil A'laa Indonesia (MIAI, Indonesian Muslim Supreme Council) for a while. A Tiga A youth affiliate, the Barisan Pemoeda Asia Raja (BPAR, Greater Asia Youth Corps), was established on 11 June 1942 with the Parindrist Soerya Wirawan at its core. Also, Dewantoro's Taman Siswa schools reopened under the aegis of the Tiga A, with its pupils being members of the Barisan Pemoeda Asia Raja. On 25 June 1942 in Meester Cornelis (now Jatinegara), Colonel Machida, head of the Sendenbu, opened the San A Seinen Korensho (Japanese for Triple A Youth Leaders' Institute). A similar institute for youth leaders was opened on 11 July 1942 in Mataram, the new name for Djokjakarta. On 5 August 1942 the Menadonese youth association Maesa joined the BPAR. During the month of August most of the Indonesian secondary schools were reopened in Java and Madoera, and that was an opportunity to get more pupils to join the BPAR. The teachers of these secondary institutions were given a brief period of instruction at the San A Seinen Korensho in order to get their pupils to become BPAR members.[25]

---

[24]   Kanahele's 20 April 1964 interview in Tokyo with Shimizu, see Kanahele 1967:270, note 28.
[25]   Suryadinata 1979:70, 78; De Bruin 1982a:65-6. For large Chinese money donations made to the Tiga A Movement, see Hatta 1979b:416; Sato 1994:40. As to the plethora of Tiga A affiliates see Sato 1994:46. For the San A Seinen Korensho and the steady growth of the BPAR see De Bruin 1967:17, 19-20.

All these multi-racial and unity-promoting features linked to the Tiga A Movement were a further guarantee against too far-reaching demands even from the side of Parindra. That Shimizu used members of Parindra was another safety valve, since they formed the most conservative segment among the nationalists and were therefore less prone to engage in adventurist ploys. So, referring to the merits of outstanding Parindrists such as the late M.H. Thamrin and Mr Raden Soedjono, Shimizu, the real sponsor of the Gerakan Tiga A and the one pulling the strings behind the scenes, chose the 34-year-old Leiden-trained Parindrist and former Volksraad member Mr Raden Samsoedin as chairman of the movement.[26] On 14 April 1942, the headquarters of the Tiga A Movement was inaugurated at Koningsplein West 2 in Batavia. Serving under Samsoedin in the executive were other Parindra prominents such as Soetan Pamoentjak, Mohammed Saleh, Drs S.H. Soebroto and Dr Slamet Soedibjo.[27] In the regions outside Batavia, Parindra prominents Gatot Mangkoepraja, Dr Soewondo, and Oto Soebrata chaired the Tiga A branches in Tjiandjoer, Tasikmalaja and Tjiamis respectively. This preponderance of Parindra members may be explained by Samsoedin's preference for his own party friends and by their willingness to cooperate with the Sendenbu (Kanahele 1967:271, note 36). Absent from the central leadership of the Gerakan Tiga A were the names of the more prominent nationalist leaders. One reason for this was that at the time the Triple A Movement was launched, Soekarno was still in Sumatra. Hatta, already employed in Batavia, refused 'to participate in a crude and inept propaganda exhibition', according to one source,[28] but another has it that he was acting as 'an adviser of the Three-A-Movement for economic affairs' (De Bruin 1967:16). Soetan Sjahrir, Dr Tjipto Mangoenkoesoemo and Mr Amir Sjarifoeddin, all three in the capital city at that time, desired to remain in the background. The first two were prompted

[26] De Bruin 1967:15; Sluimers 1978:160; Pakpahan 1948:13. However, Shigeru Sato, citing Shimizu, claims that it was Samsoedin who initiated the Tiga A by approaching the Sendenbu with an offer 'to conduct a movement for Asia Makmoer (Prosperous Asia)', stressing that such a movement 'was not created by the Japanese for the Japanese, but that it was a movement for Indonesia by the Indonesian people'. In fact, membership of the movement 'excluded Japanese, although Shimizu's leadership, or co-leadership, was hardly ever disguised and the movement was partly funded by' the Sendenbu; see Sato 1994:39. Gunseikanbu 1944a:462 states that Samsoedin, during 2602 (1942), was 'beberapa boelan mendjadi Poetjoek Pimpinan Persiapan Pergerakan A.A.A.' (for a few months leader of the preparations for the AAA Movement), thus suggesting that the Japanese military considered the Tiga A Movement to be a trial balloon without any official status.

[27] Gunseikanbu 1944a:462, 283, 347, 199, 357 respectively. For Koningsplein West 2, see De Bruin 1967:16. Volksraad member Mr Samsoedin, together with members of the late Thamrin's Volksraad faction, had formed the so-called Fractie Nasional Indonesia on 15 July 1941, with the single aim of striving for Indonesia Merdeka, see Hering 1996:318.

[28] Kanahele 1967:47 and note 38 on p. 271 where he refers to a 12 May 1965 interview with Hatta.

by their rabid anti-fascist inclinations while the latter, an anti-fascist as well, was involved in an underground organization led by Dr Charles van der Plas just prior to this colonial official's departure for Australia (Kahin 1952:111-2).

Both De Bruin and Nugroho Notosusanto consider the Triple A Movement to have been disappointing to the Indonesian nationalists in the end. De Bruin remarks that along with the sense appearing in it, the 'non-sense' prevailed. The nationalists 'did not expect the formation of a Japanese military government that would rule the Indonesian population in the same manner as the Dutch did in pre-war times. [...] Indonesian nationalists were disturbed by the triangular AAA symbol with one A on the top supported by two A's forming the base, thus suggesting that the top A indicated Japanese superiority over the base representing the native Indonesians and the foreign orientals.' (Foreign Oriental was the Dutch colonial term for the Chinese and Arabs then living in Indonesia.) 'This Tiga A propaganda had stepped hard on the soul of the native and expatriate Asians living in Java.' (Kahin 1952: 7, 14; De Bruin 1982a:65.) Nugroho Notosusanto, citing some Japanese views as well, posits that 'even for the Japanese the Triple A Movement was not a success, while the Indonesian nationalists, given their state of mind of disenchantment and distrust vis-à-vis the new rulers, often could not swallow the bombastic propaganda generated by the Sendenbu'. The 'elder brothers' did not behave like elder brothers at all, but rather like successors of the Dutch, treating the Indonesians as people of a lower race. Meanwhile, according to Nugruho, the Tiga A Movement was obstructed by another branch of the Japanese occupation forces, the Gunseikanbu (Military Administration Headquarters), although the issues were not entirely clear. Nugruho sees it as a case of interdepartmental rivalry which he deems to be quite common in the Japanese hierarchy.[29] Sluimers refers to unnamed elements within the Japanese military administration being against Shimizu's creation, while he cites Miyoshi as saying that the movement had some significance when it began, but would finally be doomed to disintegrate. This disintegration had much to do with the Tiga A not being able to penetrate the countryside, where the Kenpeitai (military police corps), fearing that peasant radicals would get the upper hand, was not averse to ruthlessly eliminating a number of Tiga A rural branches. The Tiga A in the cities remained too much identified with Parindra to ever become a significant factor in the Javanese urban world as a whole (Sluimers 1978:161).

---

[29]   Nugroho Notosusanto 1979:41. Sato 1994:48-9 details the rivalry between the Sendenbu and the Gunseikanbu. Miyoshi labels 'the Tiga A as an infantile "ding-dong party" for publicity, with no objective, no principle, and no organization, only to some extent successful in relieving the boredom of the people at a time when there was no entertainment. [T]hough it was preparing itself to act as an intermediary between the people and the government, the occupation government eventually repudiated it.'

As Nugroho somewhat theatrically mused, the Japanese had to understand that Indonesia was 'no empty vessel, where the wine of propaganda only needed to be poured in to get everyone drunk with joy at the arrival of the new masters. These new overlords had to realize that there was an Indonesian nationalist movement nurtured mostly by Western-educated intellectuals which had put down roots particularly in Java.' (Nugroho Notosusanto 1979:41.) This may well have led to the Japanese overtures to get Soekarno back from Sumatra to Java. Laszlo Sluimers suggests that Miyoshi, already connected with Hatta's *kikan*, may well have been the source for persuading Saiko Shikikan Imamura to assent to it. Imamura, already criticized by the Shonanto-based Count Hisaichi Terauchi, commander of the Southern Army Group, as being too lax toward Indonesians in the Sixteenth Army area, was warned by the latter that if Soekarno, the 'secessionist', was allowed to return to Java, some trouble might well be in the offing. Terauchi further suggested to Imamura that it would be like having 'his hands bitten by his own pet'.[30] As to the Tiga A Movement, the Poetjoek Pimpinan Pergerakan (main leadership of the movement), represented by Madjid Oesman and Rachman Tamin, had left Java for Palembang, urging the Tiga A leaders there to facilitate Soekarno's speedy return to Java. This was obviously a ploy to win Soekarno for their movement as well.[31]

Soekarno arrives in Batavia and strikes a bargain with Saiko Shikikan Imamura

Despite Terauchi's warnings, Imamura persisted in getting Soekarno back in Java and so Soekarno, after some considerable delay in Palembang, arrived by motor barge in Pasar Ikan, the fishing village just north of Batavia, on 9 July 1942. There he was met by Hatta, Soekardjo Wirjopranoto, Anwar Tjokroaminoto, Soendoro, his adopted daughter Ratna Djoeami and her husband Asmara Hadi, with some Kenpeitai officers staying in the background. *Pandji Poestaka* of 11 July 1942 carries two pictures: one of Soekarno together with his family and friends, and another of Soekarno flanked by a Kenpeitai member who according to *Pandji Poestaka* had escorted him from Palembang to Pasar Ikan (Zwaan 1981:69). That same evening Soekarno, together with Asmara Hadi, met Hatta and Sjahrir at Hatta's home. After dinner the four of them discussed opportunities for cooperating with the Japanese in an effort

---

[30] Sluimers 1978:162. On Imamura being bitten, see Kanahele 1967:52 and Brugmans et al. 1960:480.
[31] 'Kembalinja Ir Soekarno; Dioesakan oleh Poetjoek Pimpinan Pergerakan Tiga A' (The Return of Ir Soekarno; Being undertaken by the Main Leadership of the Triple A Movement), *Asia Raya* (the new name for *Berita Oemoem*), 9 June 2602(1942):1.

to rebuild the people's movement. Hatta stressed the point that the Japanese military government would not allow the Indonesian movement to progress and that therefore he had accepted an appointment as adviser to the Japanese government in order to reduce the impact of its oppressive policies toward the Indonesian people. Sjahrir added that both Hatta and Soekarno should not avoid cooperating with the Japanese, while he himself would stand aside since he was not so well known anyway. He also felt that Soekarno 'regarded the Japanese as pure fascists and felt that we must use the most subtle counter-methods to get around them, such as giving the appearance of collaboration'. Sjahrir also realized 'that the Japanese would try to capitalize [on Soekarno's] popularity for their own propaganda purposes' and so they all 'agreed that political concessions from the Japanese for the nationalists [needed to be] pressed for in return'. Hatta did not want Soekarno to join the Tiga A Move-ment; Soekarno stated that he would do so in order to abolish it from within (Hatta 1979b:415-6; Sjahrir 1949:246). On 11 July 1942 a huge crowd assembled in front of Gambir Koelon 7 (formerly the Holland House at Koningsplein West 7) to welcome Soekarno. Both Samsoedin and Shimizu were foremost in welcoming Soekarno and his family being free again to mingle among their own people after an absence of nearly ten years. In a thank-you speech Soekarno, now flanked by Hatta, promised to work together with Hatta to improve the people's welfare. Soekarno also gave due credit to the Japanese authorities for enabling him and his family to return to Djakarta.[32]

Soekarno had some crucial meetings with Imamura. The first occurred (according to Imamura) on 3 July 1942, two days after Soekarno had been involved in a nightly encounter with a Japanese captain who had slapped Soekarno's face for not following the black-out regulations then in force. Soekarno accepted the apologies of the captain involved, and the next day, in his first encounter with Imamura, gracefully admitted that he himself had been wrong in not adhering to the black-out regulations.[33] However, the date is not right, since on 3 July Soekarno was still en route from Palembang to Java.[34] The real first encounter between Imamura and Soekarno took place on 10 July 1942 in Meester Cornelis (now Jatinegara) during a visit to the San A Seinen Korensho, a Tiga A youth training facility, at which time Imamura invited Soekarno for a talk at his headquarters.[35] During that first interview at headquarters in the presence of the Sixteenth Army Head of the General Affairs Department, Colonel Nakayama, Imamura was probed by Soekarno

---

[32]   'Perdjamoean dengan Boeng Karno' (A reception with Soekarno), *Asia Raya*, 13 July 2602 (1942):2.
[33]   For this incident see Reid and Oki 1986:61-2; Ramadhan 1981:436-7 and Adams 1965:180.
[34]   See 'Keberangkatan Ir Soekarno dari Palembang' (Ir Soekarno leaving Palembang), *Asia Raya*, 1 July 2602(1942):3.
[35]   De Bruin 1968:18-9; *Asia Raya*, 11 July 2602(1942):2.

about the future status of Java. According to Imamura's account, the general replied through an interpreter that he did not know precisely what Tokyo's plans were, but that his administration would grant wider political participation as well as greater welfare to the people of Java than had been the case during the Dutch period. Also, Imamura said it was up to Soekarno to either cooperate with the Japanese or to watch matters from the sidelines. If the latter avenue was chosen, Soekarno's honour and property would be fully protected. What Imamura would not allow, however, was Soekarno in any way obstructing the Japanese administration or Japanese objectives through his behaviour or through press releases. But even if Soekarno chose to do so, Imamura had no intention of putting Soekarno in prison as the Dutch had done. Soekarno was then granted ample time to think about the future position he would take toward the Japanese. Imamura, perhaps having Hatta's collaboration in mind, suggested that Soekarno should first consult his closest comrades thoroughly.

Four days after this first interview, Soekarno, through Colonel Nakayama, indicated that he was indeed willing to cooperate with the Japanese administration throughout the war, but that he reserved the right to choose another alternative if need be after the end of the war. To some European scholars Soekarno's and Hatta's willingness to cooperate with the Japanese occupation authorities could be equated to collaboration with the German occupation authorities in Western Europe. Only one scholar, Japanologist Laszlo Sluimers, firmly rejects that comparison, since it implies that the national interests of the former colonies in Southeast Asia ran parallel with those of the former colonial rulers, which he finds a silly conclusion in the light of developments in Indonesia during 1938-1940. Moreover, we would like to add here that in the case of German-occupied Holland, the Dutch actually had been independent since the sixteenth century, while in Indonesia independence was still a dream cherished by a handful of Indonesian intellectuals. So the latter had every right, in view of the tardy developments Sluimers referred to, of using the Japanese occupation authorities to make their dream a reality. Dr Leo Jansen (1988:85) of the Djakarta Overseas Broadcasting Service observes:

> We ought to start all over again being friendly and making concessions [toward the Indonesians and their leaders] in an effort to forget the Japanese. In the unity forged from Hoesein [Djajadiningrat] to Soekarno one thing has been clearly established, and that is that returning Westerners cannot accuse some leaders of being traitors since practically everyone here has backed Soekarno. [After the war we] therefore need to arrive at a completely different course and work closely with both Soekarno and Hatta, the leaders of the people's movement.

One result of Soekarno's agreement with Imamura was that he was given an office, automobiles, a staff and a new housing site away from the prestigious Oranje Boulevard.[36] As to the latter, Inggit and Soekarno preferred a dwelling at the more modest Pegangsaan Timoer 56, in Dutch colonial times the house of Mr P.R. Feith, partly since it had an attached dwelling where Asmara Hadi and his family could live. An immediate result of all these facilities was that Soekarno, together with Inggit, Mr Sartono (who acted as his secretary) and Mohammad Djoeli (as his interpreter for Japanese), went on a Java-wide tour. They visited Bandoeng, Soekaboemi, Solo, Djokjakarta, Soerabaja, Semarang, Kediri and Blitar from 16 July to 28 July 1942. In all these cities Soekarno and his entourage were met by large and enthusiastic crowds. In Soekaboemi, where he paid his respects to Mohammad Thamrin's widow and to Tjipto Mangoenkoesoemo who had recently moved there, Soekarno was saluted by one thousand people singing the officially banned 'Indonesia Raja'. In Djokjakarta he stayed with his old mentor Ki Hadjar Dewantoro from 20 to 22 July 1942, and it may have been here that the idea of an Empat Serangkai (four-leaf clover) was born. While in Blitar Soekarno and Inggit were to stay for a few days with Soekarno's parents and with Soekarmini Wardoyo's family before returning to Pegangsaan Timoer 56 in Djakarta.[37] Thanks to Imamura, for the first time in nearly nine years Soekarno toured Java free to mingle intimately with the common people from whom he always drew his inspirational strength. His eminence as a nationalist leader seemed to be re-established, a situation he was to exploit to the full in the years ahead. Also, after this Java-wide tour Soekarno was made an adviser to the prestigious Department of General Affairs and granted a monthly wage of 750 guilders.

Imamura, too, became aware of Soekarno's mass appeal and so they both continued seeking each other's company during the few months Imamura was Saiko Shikikan of Java and Madoera. Some of the meetings were instigated by Soekarno. For example, he approached Imamura to ask if he was willing to pose for a painting to be made by Basoeki Abdullah, who Soekarno said was a nephew of his and one of Indonesia's best Western-style painters. After

---

[36]   As to the Soekarno-Imamura agreement and the facilities accorded to Soekarno, see Imamura's account in Reid and Oki 1986:72-3; Brugmans et al. 1960:480; Kanahele 1967:54-5. As to Sluimers' argument, see Sluimers 1978:230. The European scholars are Lambert Giebels and L. de Jong, with the former citing Legge somewhat sloppily as follows, 'He [Soekarno] went further [much further] than the cooperators of the thirties, whom he once critisised [criticized] so vigorously' (Legge 1984:176-7). For De Jong, turn to De Jong 1969-91, XIb:273, where he states that 'Soekarno's far-reaching collaboration with the Japanese has always been a fact'; he also cites Legge describing Soekarno in early 1943 arguing with the students Soedjatmoko, Soedarpo and Soebadio, stating 'that the Japanese were likely to win the war', Legge 1984:167.
[37]   See 'Soekarno berangkat ke Bandoeng dan Mataram; Samboetan Ra'jat di Soekaboemi', *Asia Raya*, 18 July 2602(1942):3; 'Boeng Karno di Bandoeng', *Asia Raya*, 21 July 2602(1942):3; 'Ir Soekarno tiba di Djokja', *Asia Raya*, 24 July 2602(1942):3; 'Boeng Karno di Blitar; Bersoedjoed kepada ajah dan boendanja; Disamboet oleh riboean rakjat', *Asia Raya*, 27 July 2602(1942):3.

four sittings at intervals of two or three days, Imamura was presented with the portrait set in a fine hand-carved frame. At that last meeting, in the presence of Colonel Machida, Shimizu, Soekarno, Hatta and Basoeki Abdullah, the painting was handed to Imamura as a gift from Soekarno. Imamura's offer to buy the painting from Basoeki Abdullah was politely refused. And so Imamura accepted Soekarno's gift in order not to give the impression by refusing it of judging it inferior. Later, however, Imamura gave an adequate present to Basoeki Abdullah in return for the fine painting.[38]

MIAI is tolerated and the Empat Serangkai aims at a mass organization

During the large sports meeting organized by the Ikatan Sport Indonesia (Indonesian Sports Federation) held in Gambir from 5 to 9 September 1942 and attended by some 5,000 athletes from all over Java, Imamura asked Soekarno to read the translation of the Saiko Shikikan's speech at the opening ceremony. This is a clear indication of how both men had begun to respect each other. This mutual respect had grown into mutual affection and this was to influence Soekarno's positive relationship with the Japanese administration as well as Imamura's coming to terms with the nationalists of Soekarno's ilk. After having delivered Imamura's welcome address at Gambir, Soekarno spoke as well, ending his speech with cheers of *banzai*, with the huge crowd responding enthusiastically (Sato 1994:48). A week after his Gambir performance, Soekarno, always out to seek rapport with the youth movement, attended a BPAR rally on 11 September 1942, urging the youth association to support their leaders in their quest for the rebirth of Java. With these two performances Soekarno seemed to have temporarily assumed the leadership of the Gerakan Tiga A, though at that juncture it was already in decline. One of the last positive activities of the Gerakan Tiga A was a conference it held from 4 to 9 September 1942 bringing Japanese authorities of the administration and the Shomubu (the Japanese Office of Religious Affairs) together with various leading *ulama* (Muslim scholars) in order to recognize the existing federation of the Java-based Islamic organizations grouped in the Madjlisoel Islamil A'laa Indonesia (MIAI, Grand Islamic Assembly of Indonesia). The main speakers at that conference were Colonel Horie, Shimizu, Mr Samsoedin and Soekarno, with *Asia Raya* headlining its report of the first day as follows: 'Together with Japan toward glory. The

38   See Imamura's account in Reid and Oki 1986:74-5. Basoeki Abdullah was no relative of Soekarno's, however, but a favourite and protégé. Born in 1915, he studied at the Academy of Arts in The Hague and had become established as Indonesia's leading portrait painter before the outbreak of the Pacific War. The painting showing Imamura appeared on the front page of *Pandji Poestaka*, 12 September 2602(1942).

time of destruction is over, now is the time for organization.' Soekarno in his speech was quick to comment that 'in former times we had a campaign for non-cooperation, but now, with the Japanese cause being identical with ours, synthesis and close cooperation reign.'[39] After the conference was over, lavish Japanese hospitality was accorded to the Muslim leaders in Djakarta as well as elsewhere. So MIAI was propelled, or rather given a chance, to once again become the leading central organization of the Muslim community of Java and Madoera, with its seat now in Djakarta. Its first president was Warchadoen Wondoamiseno, with Harsono Tjokroaminoto serving as first secretary and a board of directors including both Indonesians and Japanese. However, MIAI remained completely controlled by the Japanese, with its finances drawn from the government's budget and MIAI placed as a simple government apparatus under the Shomubu. MIAI was not allowed to gather all the rural *ulama* and *kiyayi* under its roof, since the Shomubu was to establish direct control over these crucially important Muslim village teachers. However, a different treatment was reserved for the predominantly urban-based Moehammadijah. That organization had cautiously but stubbornly continued its work in schools and hospitals with no interference by the authorities. The Japanese Gunsei on 22 October 1942 even officially granted Moehammadijah a permit to continue its activities. In a similar fashion, the mainly rural-based Nahdatoel Oelama held its own. Official and general recognition of Moehammadijah and Nahdatoel Oelama, both of which had stayed outside MIAI, duly followed when MIAI was dissolved on 24 October 1943 by its chairman, stating that MIAI's 'objectives as formulated at its rebirth could not be attained'. Under Japanese auspices a new Muslim umbrella organization was formed on 22 November 1943, the so-called Madjelis Sjoero Moeslimin Indonesia (Masjoemi, Indonesian Muslim Consultative Council) with Moehammadijah, Nahdatoel Oelama and MIAI now being absorbed by Masjoemi.[40] As stated in Masjoemi's programme, it aimed to consolidate the ties among all the Islamic associations of Java and Madoera in order 'that the entire Muslim community may render aid and exert its energies toward realizing the Greater East Asia Co-Prosperity Sphere under the leadership of Dai Nippon, as truly accords with the wishes of Allah as well'.[41] Mas Mansoer, for years the Moehammadijah chairman and the Muslim delegate in the Empat Serangkai, in his initial statement about Masjoemi used more sober words: 'Without relinquishing Islamic teaching we ought to attempt to adjust our present way of life and views to the new

---

[39]   *Asia Raya*, 5-9 September 2602(1942):2.
[40]   Benda 1958:115-7, 148; Van Nieuwenhuijze 1958:141-2, 147, 154; Gunseikanbu 1944a:445-6; Pakpahan 1948:40.
[41]   *Asia Raya*, 21 December 2603(1943):1.

era we now face and bring all that into harmony with it'.[42] Mansoer's words reveal a deep concern for the religion he adhered to, since for him the Japanese were only out to manipulate his religion for their own purposes. Why the Japanese at that time decided for the merger to take place is best explained by Shimizu, who in a post-war statement declared: 'the kijais attempted to involve themselves in politics and we, the Japanese, did not like that at all'. As Bernhard Dahm neatly sums it up: 'By the erection of a centralized organization, the Japanese hoped to establish better control over the practices of religious teachers in the countryside, and to prevent them from stirring up internal resistance against the "infidels" who worshipped a man [Hirohito] as a god.'[43] How Masjoemi was to function further will be discussed below.

After the Gerakan Tiga A was finally repressed, the Japanese administration, backed by Imamura, started preparing a new mass movement under the auspices of more influential nationalists such as Soekarno, Hatta, Ki Hadjar Dewantoro and Mas Mansoer. The movement had already been known since 4 November 1942 as the Empat Serangkai (literally, four-leaf clover, but also meaning the quadrumvirate, the big four, in Japanese the *shi i-in*). Since no official decree about it appears in *Kan Po*, its origins, at least officially, are somewhat hazy. Yet in the Indonesian press it had been revealed that Ki Hadjar Dewantoro and Mas Mansoer had moved to Djakarta to work with Soekarno and Hatta in early October. *Asia Raya* of 5 November 1942 held that it was Soekarno's idea from the start and that he had set it up on 4 November 1942. In any case, the quartet to act as the collective leadership for the Indonesian community of Java and Madoera had been established, with Imamura and several other top Japanese authorities in Java soon readily acknowledging the pre-eminence of Soekarno in the Empat Serangkai. His primacy derived from the bare fact that Soekarno almost invariably acted as the chief spokesman when Gunsei (military administration) public announcements were made through the Empat Serangkai. Another set of new developments toward that end had been the Poesat Kesenian Indonesia (Centre for Indonesian Arts), set up on 7 October 1942 under the direction of Soekarno and the Komisi Bahasa Indonesia (Indonesian Language Commission), founded on 20 October 1942, with Soekarno again serving in a key role. Though the actual work of the first was done by a number of well-known Indonesian artists with the aim of achieving new art forms unique to Djawa Baroe (the New Java), the domination of nationalists serving in the general executive – including Soekarno, Soetardjo Kartohadikoesoemo, Maria Ulfah Santoso, Soerachman and Soebardjo – was quite apparent.[44] The second com-

---

42   *Asia Raya*, 24 November 2603(1943):2.
43   Dahm 1969:262; he also cites Shimizu and Mas Mansoer.

mission was primarily to boost Bahasa Indonesia, now the only official language in Java besides Japanese, through formal training and the distribution
of a modern normative grammar and other means of popularizing the new
language. Several well-known literary figures, including Takdir Alisjahbana,
Sanoesi Pane and Parada Harahap, worked on the commission, while Soekarno and Hatta also served as members to lend added prestige.[45] Through
both these cultural institutions, an immediate further boost was given to the
Java-based nationalist consciousness in a broader and more meaningful way
than the Gerakan Tiga A, now defunct, had ever accomplished.

In the more sensitive political arena, Imamura had been instrumental in
erecting the Java Gunsei's first advisory council, named the Komisi Menjelidiki Adat-istiadat dan Tatanegara (Committee for Studying Traditional
Customs and State Forms, or Kyukan Seido Chosa Iinkai in Japanese) just
before he was to be transferred to Rabaul on 11 November 1942 to take
charge of the Japanese Army Group facing Australian and American forces
in the Melanesian area of the southwest Pacific.[46] This committee consisted
of ten leading Indonesian figures; from politics it included Soekarno,
Mohammad Hatta and Soetardjo Kartohadikoesoemo; from religion, Mas
Mansoer, Hoesein Djajadiningrat and Warchadoen Wondoamiseno; from
education, Ki Hadjar Dewantoro, Todoeng Goenoeg Moelia and Koentjoro
Poerbatjaroko; and from law, Soepomo with fourteen Japanese representatives of the military administration, completing the Japanese delegation with
Kyojiro Hayashi, a former ambassador to Brazil, as chairman of the committee. Kanahele viewed it 'as an unobtrusive but fairly effective liaison between
the nationalist leadership and the Japanese'.[47] It thus provided a useful medium between representative Indonesian prominents and Japanese administrators, giving the former the opportunity to air some grievances and the
latter improving their understanding of Indonesian affairs. Meetings were
held thrice a month between 7 November 1942 and 4 October 1943, when
the committee was replaced by its expanded version, the Central Advisory
Council (Choo Sangiin).[48] At the very start of these meetings the Indonesian

---

[44]   *Asia Raya*, 7 October and 13 December 2602(1942).
[45]   *Kan Po*, no. 9, 25 December 2602(1942):7. For the Komisi Bahasa Indonesia members as
listed in the text see Gunseikanbu 1944a:280, 423, 284, 466, 451.
[46]   *Asia Raya*, 9 November 2602(1942); Reid and Oki 1986:73-4; Hatta 1979b:418-9; Kanahele
1967:66-7. Imamura's successor was Lieutenant General Kumakichi Harada serving as Saiko
Shikikan until April 1945; for Harada's tenure (11 November 1942-28 April 1945), see Zwaan
1981:89; Brugmans et al. 1960:639. Dahm, citing *Asia Raya* of 25 May 2603(1943), makes the rather
startling observation that Harada arrived in Java on 25 May 1943, see Dahm 1969:251, note 88.
[47]   *Kan Po*, no. 7, 25 November 2602(1942):3 and Gunseikanbu 1944a:465, 451, 48, 438, 434, 446,
387, 398, 423, 159 for the ten Indonesian members listed in the text. For Kanahele's observation
see Kanahele 1967:67.
[48]   *Jawa Nenkan*, p. 28; Sato 1994:50-1.

members introduced the notion of establishing and leading an exclusively Indonesian cooperative mass movement, and Pakpahan (1948:20) reported that 'on 20 November 2602 [1942] the Japanese authorities charged Soekarno, Hatta, K.H Dewantara and K.H.M. Mansoer [of the Empat Serangkai] to erect a people's united front in order to assist the war effort'.

The tortuous road of the Poesat Tenaga Rakjat

The first public announcement of such a movement was in *Asia Raya* of 21 November 1942, while *Sinar Matahari* of 27 November 1942 referred to a Gerakan Persatoean Tenaga Rakjat Didalam Masa Perang (Movement for Uniting the People's Power in Wartime), which led to Soekarno and Hatta meeting with Colonel Nakayama, Miyoshi and Saito at that time. Soekarno and Hatta, according to the historian Shigeru Sato, were seen as far 'more tenacious negotiators' than Samsoedin ever had been. Both nationalist leaders were quite adamant in desiring a nationalist movement centring around the idea of Indonesia with a national anthem (Indonesia Raja), a national flag (the red and white banner), and an exclusively autochthonous Indonesian membership. However, this four-point request was clearly rejected by the three Japanese negotiators. The term Indonesia the Japanese considered inappropriate, since the Sixteenth Army military administration was geographically limited to Java and Madoera and a reference to Indonesia would only create undue restlessness in the Outer Islands, which were under the jurisdiction of the Twenty-Fifth Army and the Third Fleet. As for the national anthem and the national flag, the Japanese rejected these two basic symbols of Indonesian nationalism as well, considering them too nationalistic and not at all appropriate for the cooperative movement they had in mind. Finally, the Japanese wanted a movement that included all the indigenous population groups, not merely the autochthonous ones.[49]

In order to put more pressure on the Japanese, Soekarno and Hatta utilized the Empat Serangkai to bring a future Persatoean Tenaga Rakjat into line with their own nationalist views and demands. So on 8 December 1942, commemorating the anniversary of the Greater East Asia War, Soekarno, on behalf of the Empat Serangkai, announced the birth of a new Organisasi Rakjat (People's Organization), an organization Soekarno said the Japanese military authorities would like to see placed entirely in the hands of the

---

[49] Sato 1994:51; Shunkichiro Miyoshi, 'Jawa Senryo Gunsei Kaikoroku', *Kokusai Mondai*, no. 70:69. With thanks to Mr Fujimoto Fumio of Teikyo Junior College Holland in Maastricht for translating Miyoshi's paper for us.

people and their leaders. However, Soekarno at that time failed to reveal the new organization's specific aims and programme, explaining that all such details would be clarified at a public rally scheduled for 1 January 1943. A few days later, on 12 December 1942, it was revealed that a Badan Persiapan Organisasi Ra'jat (Preparatory Board of a People's Organization, also referred to as the Panitia Sebelas, or Eleven Members Board) had been set up in Hatta's office, consisting of the Empat Serangkai together with the following members: Mr Samsoedin, Mr Sartono, Mr Soemanang Soerjowinoto, Mr Amir Sjarifoeddin, Soetardjo Kartohadikoesoemo, Oto Iskandardinata and Soekardjo Wirjopranoto.[50] With all this going on, the Empat Serangkai was then requested to meet with Gunseikan's Lieutenant General Okazaki and Colonel Nakayama at the Selabintana Hotel near the mountain resort Soekaboemi for a two-day conference on 28-29 December 1942 to finally come to agreement about the new people's organization. However, due to some profound clashes about the blueprint, the movement's official inauguration was postponed several times. At the Selabintana Hotel – once the meeting place between Van Mook and Kobayashi back on 14-16 October 1940 – the Japanese again rejected the Empat Serangkai's demands for a purely nationalist format, conceding only an all-Indonesian membership (thus barring 'foreign orientals' – Chinese, Arabs, and Indians – and Japanese).[51]

The furore about Tojo's declaration on Burmese and Philippines independence

A further blow to Indonesian radical nationalist aspirations was the 28 January 1943 radio announcement by the Japanese prime minister General Tojo about granting independence to Burma and the Philippines within the year without making any reference to Indonesia (Brugmans et al. 1960: 555). Soekarno and Hatta approached Miyoshi and Major General Okazaki immediately after Tojo's announcement was released. Both nationalist leaders bitterly complained about the injustice done to Indonesia, especially since Indonesians had so warmly welcomed the Japanese forces liberating their country and since they had so faithfully cooperated with the Japanese

---

[50]   *Asia Raya*, 9 and 12 December 2602(1942):2; the headline is: 'Badan Persiapan Organisasi Ra'jat, terdiri dari 11 pemoeka Indonesia' (A Body Preparing the People's Organization made of eleven Indonesian prominents); *Djawa Baroe* no. 1:4-5 carries the headline 'Menoedjoe ke pembangoenan Djawa Baroe dengan membantoe Dai Nippon' (Toward the awakening of a New Java with the support of Dai Nippon); Sato 1994:242, note 89; Pakpahan 1948:21; De Bruin 1982a:86, though the latter source forgets to mention Mr Amir Sjarifoeddin.
[51]   Brugmans et al. 1960:554; Benda, Irikura and Kishi 1965:350; Kanahele 1967:73-4. However, Nishijima's and Kanahele's description of the Japanese attending the Selabintana conference differs from that given by Brugmans and by Sato 1994:52.

military administration. All that was to no avail, and Gunseikan's Okazaki reminded the two leaders that he could be of no help, since major policy matters such as these belonged to the realm of the Tokyo government (Kanahele 1967:90). Not since the initial furore over the banning of the Java-based indigenous political parties had a Japanese decision so provoked the nationalists. For those who had opted to closely collaborate with the Japanese military administration in the firm belief that their nationalist cause would be best served, Tojo's decision was indeed a bitter pill to swallow. However, while Soekarno and Hatta did consider Indonesia pre-eminent in matters of national independence, they still had to learn that it came last for the Japanese. Neither Soekarno nor Hatta had figured out that the logic behind Japanese motives was that independence was not necessarily a reward for good behaviour but simply an expedient against imminent danger. In the case of Burma, deadly danger loomed, with Japanese forces engaged at close quarters with the Allied enemy. As to the Philippines, it remained riddled with anti-Japanese guerrillas. Compared to these two countries, Java posed as yet no threat, either internally or externally (Friend 1988:106). Only later, when Java seemed to become a danger zone, were both Soekarno and Hatta able to gradually extract concessions.

Returning to the furore in the wake of Tojo's declaration, it came at a moment when Indonesian nationalists were becoming irritated by the tortuous and heavy-handed way the Japanese were handling the formation of the new Java-based people's movement. Some Japanese officials in Djakarta were, in turn, becoming apprehensive about this growing Indonesian nationalist dissatisfaction, and signalled their concern to Tokyo. Therefore, in early May Kazuo Aoki, Minister for Greater East Asia Affairs, the Dai-toasho, was dispatched to Java – the first time ever that a Japanese minister was to visit Java. In discussions with Hatta – Soekarno could not be reached since he was on a tour of Java – Aoki and Hatta worked out an agenda whereby Aoki would convey Hatta's views to Tojo. As to Hatta's views, apart from demanding a future status equal to that of Burma and the Philippines, he reiterated the wishes expressed by the Empat Serangkai at the Selabintana Hotel in late December 1942. For Nishijima, the former naval spy, back in Djakarta since 30 September 1942, this 'direct petition to Prime Minister Tojo was one of the highlights in the wake of my return to Indonesia'. However, the Liaison Conference, which met shortly after Aoki's return to Tokyo to discuss Indonesia's status, immediately reached an impasse due to strong opposition mainly from army and navy representatives. The latter argued in unison against granting Indonesia any semblance of political control, since it would endanger Japanese efforts to exploit the region's rich natural resources. The army and navy delegates also maintained that by holding on to authority Japan would be in a better bargaining position if it came to peace talks. In the end a compromise was reached, whereby the present overseas military governments would function as usual, though allowing some increased Indonesian participation in the administration of Java and Madoera.[52]

As for the promise of increased Indonesian participation, Dr Hoesein Djajadiningrat was the first to be appointed to high office. On 1 October 1943 he replaced Colonel Horie as the first Indonesian head of the Shomubu, and Mas Mansoer was attached to it as *komon* (adviser), a function Dr Hoesein Djajadiningrat had held since 26 March 1943 to assist Colonel Horie. Around that time some Indonesians were appointed to head residencies – on 10 November 1943, Mas Soetardjo Kartohadikoesoemo became *shochokan* (*resident*) of Djakarta Residency and Raden Mas Toemenggoeng Ario Soerjo *kencho* (regent, or *bupati* in Indonesian) of Magetan – while just prior to that an advisory council with Indonesian participation was installed, with Soekarno as chairman.[53]

Returning to Hatta, the talks with Aoki had a nasty aftermath involving the Kenpeitai. Hatta had written a memorandum about the issues he had aired recently with Aoki, and then sent it to Aoki in Tokyo, obviously in an attempt to pin the minister down on the explicit wishes he had expressed during their talks. The fact that the letter had been carried to Tokyo by a returning naval officer without the approval of Gunsei authorities made Hatta suspect for the Kenpeitai. The Kenpeitai already considered Hatta somewhat of a communist, ever since 8 December 1942, when he told a wildly applauding crowd of a hundred thousand 'to rather view Indonesia at the bottom of the seas than under another colonial regime'. Now keeping Hatta under close surveillance, the Kenpeitai went so far as to design a plot to have Hatta killed by framing a car accident in the hilly area of the Poentjak range near Soekaboemi. However, due to the timely intervention of Colonel Moichiro Yamamoto, who instructed Miyoshi to have Hatta meet with the head of the Tokko (an acronym for Tokubetsu Koto Keisato, Thought Control Police) division of the Djakarta Kenpeitai headquarters, Captain Mitsuo Murase, the plot to kill Hatta was aborted. The meeting with the Tokko captain seems to have cleared the air somewhat, with Hatta admitting that he had criticized Japanese imperialism before the Pacific War occurred and with Murase arguing that Japan had started the Greater East Asia War to liberate

---

52   Kanahele 1967:91-3; Reid and Oki 1986:271. Friend 1988:106 concludes that 'with vague promises and exhortations, the Japanese temporized for another year and a half'.

53   For the Shomubu appointments see *Kan Po*, no. 28, 10 October 2603(1943); Benda 1958:126, 136. For the *shochokan* and *kencho* appointments see *Kan Po*, no. 31, 25 November 2603(1943); *Djawa Baroe* 1-23, 1 December 2603(1943):8-9; Gunseikanbu 1944a:48, 96. During the entire Japanese occupation only one other *shochokan* was appointed, Raden Pandji Soeroso in the Kedoe residency; see *Pandji Poestaka* 23-2, 15 January 2605(1945). For his qualifications see Gunseikanbu 1944a:468.

the Asian peoples from Western capitalism and imperialism. The Tokko captain advised Hatta to read and study the *nippon seishin* (the Japanese spirit) as well as the *koodo seishin* (spirit of the imperial way). Apparently the opportunity to study the *nippon seishin* and the *koodo seishin* was one of the reasons for inviting Hatta to visit Japan, as we shall see presently.[54] However, we must first discuss the establishment of the Poesat Tenaga Rakjat.

Poetera is established

The preparatory committee for the new movement led by the Panitia Sebelas set up on 12 December 1942 completed its preparations on 22 February 1943 (Pakpahan 1948:21, 26; Sato 1994:53). And so on 9 March 1943, one year after the Dutch surrender, the Poesat Tenaga Rakjat, or Poetera (Concentration of the People's Energy, with the acronym Poetera meaning native son), was inaugurated with some 200,000 people in attendance. Yet in spite of Soekarno's fiery exhortations that day about the new spirit now to grow in Djawa Baroe, there were serious doubts about the future. All the idealism featured in the many attempts before had waned, if not come to naught altogether. Not a word was said about an independent Indonesia being in the offing, though much was said about the necessity to impel the common people toward responsibility and dutiful behaviour in a new and reborn society under the inspiring leadership of the Empat Serangkai and the Japanese authorities. Even Soekarno's earlier statement of non-interference by the Japanese occupation authorities was not honoured, since several Japanese – Miyoshi, Saito and Shimizu – served as advisers to the Poetera Guidance Board (Minshu Shidobu) and Poetera's main council included some Japanese as well.[55]

Poetera's original aim of mobilizing the population of Java and Madoera in a number of ways was stated specifically in its statutes, proclaimed on 10 March 1943. Poetera was to carry out activities to ensure that the people were made ready to build a Djawa Baroe. American, British and Dutch influences were to be eliminated right away, while the defence of Greater East Asia was to be paramount. Further, it was stipulated that Poetera's activities would be harmonized with those of the military administration to improve and stimulate the common people spiritually. Poetera also had the task of

---

[54]   Kanahele 1967:91-2, 95; Hatta 1979b:425-7; Friend 1988:191-2. Friend calls Murase a lieutenant colonel; he was not; as a major Murase was executed by the Dutch in Jakarta's Glodok prison on 3 November 1949; see *Kenpeitai* 1986:34, note 35; for the Tokko division *Kenpeitai* 1986:32-3.

[55]   Sato 1994:243, note 98. Sato concludes that all that 'had resulted in a unilateral and total compromise on the Indonesian side [...] with no hint of Indonesian nationalism' appearing in Poetera's statutes or regulations, Sato 1994:53; Benda, Irikura and Kishi 1965:136-9; *Jawa Shinbun*, 10 March 2603(1943).

advancing mutual understanding between the Japanese and the Indonesian peoples, one way of doing this being to encourage the study of the Japanese language and of Indonesian. Also, matters such as promoting hygiene and health among the populace as well as increasing productivity and labour all needed to be tackled quickly (Benda, Irikura and Kishi 1965:136-7).

Shortly before Poetera's inauguration, in early March 1943, Colonel Yamamoto arrived in Djakarta to act as the new Somubucho (head of the general affairs department of the military administration), replacing Colonel Nakayama. The new man, a hardliner, stated his views on Poetera as follows:

> The nationalists had organized the movement expecting to make it the core of their independence campaign. [...] The Sixteenth Army, however, had no plans at all in that direction at the time. Therefore, after I arrived in Java, I urged the nationalists to lead their movement more spiritually in order to combine all powers of the [indigenous] inhabitants according to the directions of the Japanese administration. Naturally, the nationalists were quite disappointed. (Brugmans et al. 1960:561; Sato 1994:53-4.)

Yamamoto added that: 'Since Tokyo would not allow any nationalist movement to occur, the Poesat Tenaga Rakjat [Poetera] had to assume the form of a Total Spiritual Mobilization.'[56]

Yet after the war Yamamoto came to a different conclusion, with the stage set

> for a continuous round of friction between the [Indonesian] radical nationalists and the [Japanese] Sixteenth Army. The former demanded immediate independence throughout the entire war period, causing us to be greatly embarrassed. The war situation forced us to outwardly preserve some unity, but in reality it amounted to a fierce struggle, and if the word struggle cannot be used, then to endless negotiations between the two parties. This quite tense situation lasted until Japan's capitulation. (Brugmans et al. 1960:547.)

However, these conflicting views raise the question whether Yamamoto was indeed, as some observers have implied, so keen on 'aiming the administration's figurative guns on Poetera and its nationalist political elite, thus rendering Poetera and its members no fair chance of survival' or even behaving like lame ducks from the start. Bill Frederick goes so far as to posit that Yamamoto 'either was unable or did not care to hinder Poetera's development between its founding and the official opening of its headquarters on Friday, 16 April 1943', noting that Hatta, in his Poetera reports, 'would surely have mentioned such activity [by Yamamoto] had it occurred'.[57] Secondly,

---

[56]   Sato 1994:243, note 99. In Japanese, Poetera was known as Jawa minsho soryoku kessho undo (Movement for the Total Mobilization of the People of Java).
[57]   William H. Frederick's introduction to Hatta 1971:18.

despite the claims made by such scholars as Bernhard Dahm and Harry Benda, it remains quite doubtful whether the Japanese Djakarta government was indeed so readily prepared to fan opposition to Poetera among the *sho-chokan* (*residenten*) and *pangrèh praja*. Official Djakarta remained quite wary of meddling in *sho* (residency) affairs and even insisted upon autarchy of the residency. Java itself at that time was in many ways more decentralized under Japanese rule than had previously been the case.[58]

Be that as it may, on 9 March 1943 the Poesat Tenaga Rakjat, or Poetera, was officially inaugurated by the Gunseikan's Major General Okazaki during a public rally at Ikatan Atletik Djakarta square (Ikada is the Djakarta-based Athletic Union) with some 200,000 people attending. Soekarno, perhaps still smarting from the fact that Indonesia had not been granted any form of independence in the near future, addressed the huge crowd. In his speech he tendered his usual expressions of gratitude to the new masters, but he also interspersed these with a strong appeal to the crowd's nationalist spirit:

> Fifteen years ago we reiterated the fact that our Indonesian nationalism needed to be oriented broadly, like a nationalism that was part of an international Asianism. At that time we held that when the Chinese dragon works together with the white elephant of Siam, with the sacred cow of India, with the sphinx of Egypt, with the *banteng* [wild buffalo] of Indonesia, and when such orientation is further warmed by the sun of Japan, then imperialism will be destroyed in all of Asia. So through the will of Allah and the wisdom of Japan, the cooperation of all Asian forces has indeed become a fact. The Japanese defence chain stretching from Manchukuo in the north, to Indonesia in the south, to Burma in the west, to the Philippines in the east, has indeed become one great bulwark. So, my dear brothers, do not forget that we Indonesians form a link in that chain, but that such a chain is only as strong as it weakest link. [...] Brothers, we have deliberately called our movement Poesat Tenaga Rakjat and we have abbreviated it to Poetera, to 'native son', so we are all native sons, a poetera of the new times, a poetera of the new struggle, a poetera of the new society, a poetera of Indonesia. I am as well a poetera, since I was born here, I was raised here, I eat and drink here, and shall be buried in the womb of this land.[59]

[58]   Both Benda (1958:140) and Dahm (1969:246-7), stress that Poetera and its members were curtailed from the beginning and doomed to failure by Japanese authorities scheming to arrive at such a goal. This view is somewhat corrected by Frederick's introduction to Hatta 1971:18-9, where he doubts whether Yamamoto was out to curb Poetera at all.

[59]   *Asia Raya*, 9 March 2603(1943):1; Brugmans et al. 1960:557-8. Both L. de Jong and Giebels refer to Hatta having spoken on 9 March 1943 as follows: 'Indonesia has been freed from Dutch imperialist domination, and that is why Indonesia does not want to be colonized again. Everybody, young and old, has a strong feeling about this matter. The Indonesian youth prefer to see Indonesia sink to the bottom of the sea rather than be colonized again.' See De Jong 1969-91, XIb:285, note 1, and Giebels 1999:291. However, these words were spoken by Hatta on 8 December 1942, as attested by his Indonesian-language *Memoir* (Hatta 1979b:419), his English-language *Memoirs* (Hatta 1981:212-3) as well as by *Asia Raya*, 9 December 2602(1942):2.

This was a clear appeal by Soekarno for Indonesia to be treated like all the other Asian countries now under Japanese rule. To that theme Soekarno would return again and again. As to the Poetera General Secretariat, the main chairman was Soekarno, with Hatta, Dewantoro and Mansoer serving as vice-chairmen. The department for planning and development was led by Hatta, that of cultural affairs by Dewantoro, that of propaganda by Soekarno, while Mansoer was in charge of the public welfare department. (Hatta 1971:40-1.)

Poetera's first six months and Tojo's short visit to Java leading to the Choo Sangiin

Poetera did not actually begin to function until its headquarters opened on 16 April 1943 in a former Roman Catholic high school, the Strada Mulo at Djalan Soenda 18 in the Menteng suburb of Djakarta. After Soekarno's welcoming speech at the opening, the Gunseikan, in front of 300 invited guests, admonished Poetera leaders to assist the Sixteenth Army in erecting a Greater East Asia and in particular a New Java (Djawa Baroe). The Somu-bucho (head of the general affairs department of the military administration), Colonel Moichiro Yamamoto, urged the assembly to assist the Japanese army in the present war, with the ultimate goal of destroying British, American and Dutch power. As for Poetera and its leaders, the Sombucho implored it to be aware of its responsibilities toward that end, urging it to maintain the clos-est possible contact with the military government. Next came Naimubucho (head of the internal affairs section of the military administration) Colonel Masatomi Hatakeda, expressing hopes that the Poetera leadership would work fruitfully with all elements of the *pangrèh praja*, and that Poetera would fully cooperate to make final victory a distinct possibility.[60] That the Naimubucho referred to cooperation between *pangrèh praja* and Poetera may well have been inspired by Soekarno's promise made at the Ikada square gathering on 9 March 1943:

> The *pergerakan* people will sincerely extend their hand to the *pangrèh praja*, asking them to work harder with us to guarantee the well-being and greatness of our land. I, therefore, hope that the *pangrèh praja* will sincerely accept the people's hand as well.[61]

---

[60]   Hatta 1971:29-30, 63. As to Soekarno's and Hatta's speeches at that formal opening, both stressed their appreciation for 'their elder brothers'. Hatta stated that they were 'happy about realizing the ideal of an Asia for the Asians, for the sake of which one must also swallow bitter-ness'; see *Asia Raya,* 16 April 2603(1943):1 and *Djawa Ba*roe 1-9:5.
[61]   *Asia Raya,* 9 March 2603(1943):2.

That the Poetera nationalist leadership was admonished to work closely with the *pangrèh praja* may well be related to the fact that during the Dutch era, relations between the Non-Ko nationalists and the *pangrèh praja* were far from cordial, the nationalists often regarding the *pangrèh praja* as mere handmaidens of the Dutch colonial administration.[62] Under Japanese rule the relationship was to worsen when the Japanese attempted to involve both groups in their mass mobilization campaigns. The nationalist intellectuals tried, though with little success, to extend Poetera's influence in the countryside, while the *pangrèh praja* often considered such efforts to be undesirable meddling in their own traditional sphere (Sato 1996:604). An added factor to that clash was that the Japanese, through the rural-based *shochokan* (Japanese civilian heads of residencies) in Java and Madoera, relied rather heavily on the *pangrèh praja* to get some grip on the situation so foreign to them in their new areas of jurisdiction (Kanahele 1967:60-1). (Toward the end of 1942 several Japanese homeland administrators not at all familiar with Javanese administrative practices had arrived from Japan to expand Japanese administration facilities in the countryside.) The situation was further complicated by the Gunsei's demands for increased production and by the drive for *romusha* (indigenous labourers) and *heiho* (indigenous auxiliary soldiers) volunteers. All these factors led to the *pangrèh praja* and the *shochokan* often forming a common front against the policies urged by Poetera's urban-based leaders.

And so the most pressing dilemma facing Poetera from the start was that posed by the *pangrèh praja* not really coming to terms with the urban-based nationalists and activists of Poetera. In his Poetera reports, Hatta therefore aims his most virulent charges against the *pangrèh praja*, even blaming them of often collaborating with the Japanese *shochokan* to obstruct Poetera's aims. Hatta goes so far as to suggest that an entente between the Japanese and the *pangrèh praja* was 'formed against the political and social activists of Poetera, while not recognizing that the latter were seen by the common people as being their true leaders'. In other words, Hatta asserts that the feudal spirit stemming from Dutch colonial times still in fact reigned, and that the *pangrèh praja* therefore stood in the way of Poetera. And so, 'psychologically the former, sometimes hidden, sometimes openly, would continue to resist Poetera's search for a meeting ground between Poetera and the *pangrèh praja*'. As to Poetera, Hatta concludes, it would not cease trying to win the *pangrèh praja* over to its side, but without pressure being exerted by the Japanese, the

---

[62] Even after the demise of Poetera, Hatta maintained publicly in a radio speech of 5 March 1944 that 'the gulf between the *pangreh praja* and the people exists because the *pangreh praja* official was used as a mere tool by the Netherlands East Indies government. [...] Indeed his only interest was giving orders to the people, without taking their circumstances into consideration'; see Sato 1994:224, note 115 and Hatta 1971:64.

pangrèh praja 'will only have smiles on their faces and burning resentment in their hearts' (Hatta 1971:36-7). Hatta blamed the Japanese for not exerting some pressure on the *pangrèh praja*, but Japanese authorities, aware that a divide-and-rule tactic would serve their ends, considered that in the rural districts the administration was better left in the hands of the *pangrèh praja*. This conviction was held with some strength, and caution was exercised not to unduly demoralize or alienate the *pangrèh praja*, who were after all vital to the smooth functioning of rural Java. So, the Japanese deemed *pangrèh praja* rural administration incomparably more important than the small bunch of urban-based Poetera intellectuals who busied themselves maintaining the Indonesian identity through schemes of their own. Poetera, and particularly Soekarno as head of the propaganda department and by far the main crowd pleaser, were thus manipulated to promote Japanese/Indonesian mobilization efforts almost exclusively in urban centres. Such propaganda efforts were further facilitated by the Japanese erecting radio poles, often referred to as 'singing towers', on urban main streets, thus exposing the *wong cilik* (ordinary people) to the radio.[63]

So, geographically, Poetera's activities remained confined largely to urban areas. Also, since in its statutes it was stated that ten local leaders were to be appointed in each residency (*sho* in Japanese) and three in each regency (*ken* in Japanese), none would be appointed at lower levels such as the *wedana* (*guncho* in Japanese) or the *camat* (small village, or *ku* in Japanese) level. So the nationalist Poetera leaders were cut off from ever establishing administrative contact with the subdistrict populace. As Hatta, Sato and De Bruin note, Poetera's activities at the village level were limited to propaganda tours only, which in turn the *pangrèh praja* usually sabotaged by pressing their country folk to ignore them. As Hatta indicates, the Poetera nationalists viewed the conflicts between themselves and the *pangrèh praja* as the most damaging schism within Javanese society (Hatta 1971:36-8, 63; Sato 1994:55-6; De Bruin 1982a:90-1). As to the appointment of chairpersons of local branches – the Empat Serangkai planned to establish residency branches in the seven largest urban centres of Java, assured as they were of firm nationalist support in these districts – these proceeded quite sluggishly due to long appointment procedures involving the approval of the *shochokan*. Since the Japanese *shochokan* often did not know the nominees, they relied upon the advice of lower Javanese officials, who were often biased against the *pergerakan* people. In any case, during the period 4 June to 18 August 1943, Poetera residency

---

[63]   Both Sato and Kurasawa, however, question the impact of the singing towers due to the fact that ordinary people speaking regional languages such as Javanese, Sundanese and Madurese barely understood the formal Indonesian used by Poetera leaders. See Sato 1994:58 and Kurasawa 1988:545-6.

branches were established in Djakarta, Priangan, Djokjakarta, Semarang, Soerabaja, Solo and Malang. Three more were added later, on 8 December 1943 in Pekalongan, on 11 December 1943 in Kediri and on 28 December in Kedoe. Some ten more were being prepared but were never established. So, at its official dissolution on 29 February 1944, Poetera had only ten branches in urban centres. The tardy pace at which these branches were established caused Hatta to blame the *pangrèh praja* and the Japanese *shochokan*, since both were 'frequently prejudiced against nationalists' of Hatta's ilk (Hatta 1971:63, 72-3; Sato 1994:59).

According to several sources both indigenous and foreign, these were signs that in the long run Japanese-inspired determination was to render Poetera into a subservient puppet, partly since the Japanese authorities never really trusted it fully. The Japanese were well aware that Poetera, far more than the Gerakan Tiga A, was led by a group of more prominent nationalists, and the Gunsei put it under stricter control by holding the purse strings while exercising tight overall control over Poetera's varied activities. Yet paramount among Poetera's aims, as Soekarno had stressed in his 9 March 1943 address, was Poetera's willingness to assist and support Japan in achieving final victory and to participate in the defence of Greater East Asia. His address was followed by several Poetera rallies held in Djakarta to commemorate the Emperor's Birthday (Tencho Setsu), and then in Bandoeng, throughout the principality of Djokjakarta, and in Soerabaja, all with the main theme being to 'Destroy the Allied Powers' and to 'Live simply and increase agricultural production', on 29 April, 1 July, 28 July to 2 August and 18 August 1943. During the Tencho Setsu rally in Djakarta, Soekarno used the notorious jingle 'Amerika kita setrika, Inggeris kita linggis' (America we will pulverize and England we will break apart) for the first time. These well-attended Poetera rallies – in Bandoeng Soekarno's address was heard by 100,000 persons[64] – may well have led to some concessions being made by the Gunsei.

As for the Poetera nationalist leadership's thirst for more consequential participation in government, this was quenched somewhat by several events. Following the decisions of the Imperial Conference, Premier Tojo reconfirmed in the Diet on 16 June 1943 the granting of independence to Burma and the Philippines, while he also promised 'to allow some political participation by the people of Java'.[65] To welcome Tojo's statement, a Poetera rally was held

---

[64]   For these rallies see Hatta 1971:49, 92; *Asia Raya*, 30 April 2603(1943):1 and 5 July 2603 (1943):1.
[65]   *Asia Raya*, 17 June 2603(1943):1. For reactions to it, see Soekarno's pledge made at a special ceremony held at the Saiko Shikikan's residence: 'we will work together with the forces of Dai Nippon with all of our power, and march united to reach the day of final victory', *Asia Raya*, 18 June 2603(1943):1 and *Djawa Baroe* 1-13:3, listing Soekarno's short speech as a *sumpah bantuan* (oath to support). As to Tojo, in the Diet he promised 'political participation within this year

at Taman Raden Saleh on the evening of 24 June 1943, with Soekarno offering the following resolution:

> Prime Minister Tojo has explained in the Diet that the political principles being followed by the Japanese Empire remain firm and unchanged: They are to free all of East Asia from American and British oppression, and to give a suitable place and position to each country in the area. In addition, he made clear that the necessary steps will be taken to insure that this year we will have an opportunity to participate in determining internal policy.[66]

Soon afterward, on 7 July 1943, Tojo paid a visit to Java, and Soekarno as the representative of the people (*sebagai wakil penduduk*) thanked him for his statement before the Diet, as well as declaring that:

> Our loyalty to Dai Nippon grows by leaps and bounds since we are truly convinced that the present war waged by Dai Nippon for a Greater Asia is in fact a Holy War. A War that will give Asia back to the Asian communities, a War that will give Asian countries back to the individual communities. A War that surely will tie all our Asian countries firmly into one family with a strong common well-being under the leadership of Dai Nippon.[67]

However, during his brief visit Prime Minister Tojo made no new promises about Indonesia's future status at all, nor did he clarify the political participation issue, other than to state that the promise he had made in the Diet needed to be understood as a way to bring a Djawa Baroe into being. This did mean, however, that all efforts should be directed economically and culturally in support of the Japanese armed forces, since these forces would devote themselves to defending Asia Timoer Raja against the Americans, the British and the Dutch. So, no private interviews were granted and no firm assurances given. Instead, Tojo referred to the southern regions, and did not speak of the Indonesian people but of the people of Djawa Baroe.[68] Thus, both Hatta and Soekarno, obviously shorn of all illusion, waited to see what

---

to Malaya, Sumatra, Java, Borneo and Celebes', thus studiously avoiding the term Indonesia, Kanahele 1967:93. Kanahele also cites the *Asahi Shimbun*, 17 June 2603.

[66]   Hatta 1971:50; *Asia Raya*, 25 June 2603(1943):2.

[67]   *Asia Raya*, 8 July 2603(1943):2-3; *Djawa Baroe* 1-14:11-2 headlines Soekarno's welcoming speech as 'Oetjapan terima kasih oleh Ir. Soekarno sebagai wakil pendoedoek' (Statement of thanks by Soekarno being the representative of the people) and Tojo's speech as 'Oetjapan Perdana Menteri Todjo dalam rapat pernjataan terima kasih rajat' (Statement by Prime Minister Tojo about the meeting expressing the people's gratitude).

[68]   See for Tojo's views, headlined as 'Keterangan Perdana Menteri Todjo tentang perlawatannja (Views of Prime Minister Tojo during his visit), *Djawa Baroe* 1-15:3-4; Abdoel Rasjid, 'Perasaan pendoedoek aseli tentang koendjoengan P.M. Todjo di Djakarta' (Feelings of the autochthonous population about Prime Minister Tojo's visit to Djakarta), *Pandji Poestaka* 21-20/1, 1 August 2603(1943).

the Java-based Gunsei, after being informed of Tojo's drift, would now have in mind for the New Java. Colonel Yamamoto interpreted Tojo's intentions as follows:

> Since these first measures are not altogether in agreement with Prime Minister Tojo's declaration at the 82nd session of the Diet, they must be regarded none-theless as a first step by the government toward more generous prospects in the future. For this reason alone, this first step will be a test of the [Javanese] people. If they are prepared to work loyally and willingly at this first opportunity, more generous measures are bound to follow.[69]

Barely a month had passed since Tojo's visit when, on 1 August 1943, the Saiko Shikikan, Lieutenant General Harada, announced that a central advis-ory council would be established, thus allowing prominent Indonesians to participate in the policy-making process. He stressed that the new measures were to facilitate the people of Java becoming inwardly and outwardly one with Japan and the Japanese.[70] Soekarno, with the recent views expressed by Colonel Yamamoto still in mind, responded to the Saiko Shikikan's announcement somewhat guardedly. He noted that, in evaluating the pro-posed council, it was necessary to distinguish the realities of today from the possibilities of tomorrow.[71]

The Choo Sangiin at work with Soekarno as chairperson

On 4 October 1943 the Choo Sangiin (Central Advisory Council), together with residency advisory councils (*sho sangakai*) in the seventeen residencies and the special city advisory (*tokubetsushi sangikai*) in the Special City of Djakarta, were established, while seven Indonesian advisers (*sanyo*) were attached to the departments in the Gunseikanbu. Soekarno was attached to the Department of General Affairs, Professor Soepomo to Justice, Abdoel Rasjid to Health, Mohamad Yamin to Propaganda, Soewandi to Education,

---

[69]   *Asia Raya*, 3 August 2603(1943):1; *Djawa Baroe* 1-15:4 with the headline 'Balaslah kepert-jajaan Perdana Menteri Todjo; Pidato radio Jamamoto Somoeboetjo' (Reaction to the views of Prime Minister Tojo; A radio speech by SomubuchoYamamoto).
[70]   *Asia Raya*, 2 August 2603(1943):1.
[71]   See Soekarno's 'Oedjian pertama oentoek bertindak menanggoeng djawab!' (The first test of the promised measures), in which Soekarno reminds the readers of Yamamoto's recent analysis: 'Keterangan Somoeboetjo ini perloe kami peringatkan disini, soepaja orang djangan melebih-lebihi harapannja bagi waktoe sekarang. Kita haroes membedakan realiteit sekarang dan kemoengkinanan dimasa datang' (We must here remember the Somubucho's statement in order that the people will not raise their hopes too high at present. We must therefore distin-guish the realities of today from the possibilities of the future), *Djawa Baroe* 1-18(15 September 2603(1943)):4.

Prawoto Soemodilogo to Industry and Mochtar bin Praboe Mangkoe Negara
to Transport. They also met in the Council of Advisers (Sanyo Kaigi), where
they discussed the major occupation policies passed by the Choo Sangiin.[72]
As for the Choo Sangiin, which some compared to the Dutch colonial Volksraad, it comprised 43 members, of whom 23 were appointed by the Saiko
Shikikan, Lieutenant General Harada, 18 elected by members of the regional
advisory councils, and two chosen by the Solo and Djokjakarta principalities. Among those appointed and elected to the Choo Sangiin there were 13
and 8 nationalists, respectively. Thus the composition of the Choo Sangiin
represented some sort of a victory for the Poetera nationalists, especially
since Soekarno was made chairperson (*gicho*) of the Council.[73] At the first
meeting of the Choo Sangiin, Soekarno stressed that more extensive concessions with regard to Indonesian autonomy would surely depend on the success of the present experiment. Yet he ended his speech with his usual touch
of independence: 'This is not a test imposed merely by the Gunsei. It is a
test of History. Let us undertake to face this test of History with spirit.'[74] As
for the Muslim and *pangrèh praja* members, they numbered 6 and 8, respectively. Compared to the Volksraad, which since 1927 had a so-called 'native
majority' of 30 with a nationalist segment of 9 or 10 against 25 Dutch and 5
so-called Foreign Orientals, the Choo Sangiin, having no Japanese members,
was almost entirely Indonesian. The three non-Indonesians were Chinese
appointed by the Saiko Shikikan: Liem Thwan Tek, Oei Tiong Tjoei and Oei
Tjong Hauw – all top executives in the Japanese-sponsored Overseas Chinese
Association, Kakyo Sookai.[75]

Though there were no Japanese members, the general work of the
Choo Sangiin was methodically carried out by a Japanese-dominated general secretariat (*jimukyoku*), thus belying the claim that the Choo Sangiin
responded spontaneously to Indonesian wishes and proposals. The secretariat, chaired by a Japanese and functioning as a watchdog, always passed on
all the Saiko Shikikan's questions or proposals, usually prepared by Colonel
Yamamoto, that were put to the Choo Sangiin some ten days before every
session. These, in turn, were read during the session by chairman Soekarno.
After that procedure, the Gunseikan or the Somubucho would further elaborate as to how the Gunsei expected the Choo Sangiin to respond, especially
in view of defence and production efforts. So Japanese officialdom methodi-

[72]   For the seven Indonesian advisers (*sanyo*), Pakpahan 1948:35; *Djawa Baroe* 1-19:7.
[73]   *Asia Raya*, 16 October 2603(1943):1; Sato 1994:61-2, 245, note 3; Kanahele 1967:99-101;
Friend 1988:92-4; Dahm 1969:251-4. For the 23 members appointed to the Choo Sangiin see
Djawa Baroe 1-19:6-7.
[74]   *Asia Raya*, 17 October 2603(1943):2; also cited by Bharadwaj 1997:181 and Legge 1984:175.
[75]   For the Chinese, appointed by Lieutenant General Harada, turn to Suryadinata 1972:21,
26-7. De Jong 1969-91, XIb:930 oddly enough refers to five Chinese delegates.

cally sought ways to influence all the Choo Sangiin sessions to its own benefit, as well as allowing no criticism whatsoever of the Gunsei's own policy
measures. Bernhard Dahm (1969:254-5) concludes that even the rather impo-
tent Dutch colonial Volksraad seemed to have surpassed the Choo Sangiin in
importance. However, he recalls 'how painfully little the Indonesian nationalists were able to achieve in the Volksraad in the entire twenty-three years
of its existence, despite the privilege of criticism and (after 1927) the so-called
co-legislative function [and] the [Volksraad] nationalists never achieved a
majority in the VR' (Dahm 1969:254-5). As to the Choo Sangiin, with the
Japanese-dominated secretariat ignoring the many Indonesian-member
proposals and only passing on to chairman Soekarno a few deemed appropriate, one should take note of some distinctly positive factors as well. First,
as Miyoshi attests, the secretariat was regularly flooded with Indonesian-
member requests concerning the use of the red and white flag and the official
singing of the 'Indonesia Raja' anthem, as well as with demands for realizing
the territorial unification of Indonesia in order to ultimately achieve national
independence.[76] Even though these Indonesian demands were not passed
on by the secretariat, they did show spirit and testified to a firm belief that
ultimately these wishes would be realized in a not-too-distant future. That
the Choo Sangiin, with an overwhelmingly Indonesian membership led by
Soekarno, existed at all, always fuelled hopes that all its efforts, though as of
now still Gunsei-inspired, would eventually slide into the bright promise of
an independent Indonesia. As to the Choo Sangiin's obvious shortcomings,
historians have evaluated it rather positively, since in their estimation the
nationalist leadership involved in the Choo Sangiin was above all a way to
acquire some valuable political expertise (Kanahele 1967:98-9; Herkusumo
1984:108-9; Aziz 1955:215-6). This fact in itself outweighed the demands of
the Gunsei to focus primarily on finding practical means for enhancing the
Javanese populace's loyal support of the Japanese in the Greater East Asia
War. As Shigeru Sato attests, this Japanese-inspired demand was posed in the
1 October 1943 session of the Choo Sangiin, with the following seven – up to
the last one held 18 to 21 June 1945 – merely being slight variations of that
first request (Sato 1994:62). And yet, in the long run, the Choo Sangiin led
by Soekarno was to develop in directions not originally anticipated by the
Gunsei, since it deliberately moved toward gradually placing more emphasis
on the vital interests of the Indonesian inhabitants of Java and Madoera. As
Bernhard Dahm (1969:255) says: 'behind decisions by the Council [Choo
Sangiin] which appear on the surface to serve Japanese interests exclusively,

---

[76]   Shunkichiro Miyoshi, 'Jawa Senryo Gunsei Kaikoroku', *Kokusai Mondai* no. 75:81. Thanks
are due to Mr Fujimoto Fumio of Teikyo Junior College Holland for translating Miyoshi's contribution for us.

there was often an explanation having a distinct social character, and aimed at reducing, rather than adding to, the burdens placed on the population by the war'. Also, John Legge posits that Soekarno, after years of imprisonment and exile, suddenly had a position and responsibility, even though at the same time he was involved in performing unpopular tasks to suit the Gunsei. Yet, Soekarno justified himself while doing these things that he was still serving long-term Indonesian interests, appealing to his followers to be patient in order to obtain 'what we all desire so deeply in the end'. John Legge notes Soekarno's frequent use of the Javanese word *gembleng* (meaning 'to harden oneself', but also 'to come together in unison'), conjuring up images of steel and of welding and forging, so as to coax his people to prepare and harden themselves for a brighter future bound to come. And even if Japanese wishes or demands had to be followed, this was always done in the hope of receiving brighter future benefits in the long run. This view is in accordance with Soekarno's keeping his position at all costs, while preventing nationalist sentiment from expressing an anti-Japanese mood until the time was truly ripe for it.[77]

Efforts to prepare and strengthen the Javanese home front

Just now, however, there were other pressing objectives, such as furthering mutual understanding between Indonesians and Japanese, as well as increasing agricultural and textile production, promoting public health and physical training, and coming to terms with the *pangrèh praja* and with the inadequate rice distribution in the Javanese countryside. The Javanese rice harvest had miscarried in 1943, causing widespread rural unrest due to the lack of price controls and proper execution by the Beikoku Kai (Rice Corporation) and by the Beikoku Oroshisho Kumai (Central Association of Rice Traders), resulting in hoarding and price inflation, mainly on the part of Chinese traders, who controlled some 95% of the ice-husking plants. This all caused rampant black marketeering among people engaged in every stage of production and distribution. However, peasants as well engaged in smuggling rice in the richest rice-producing areas to destinations as far away as Merak and other harbours in Banten or even to Palembang in South Sumatra. However, the black marketeering by rice millers and retailers was on a larger scale, with smuggling sometimes done by Chinese in cooperation with Japanese army units. Faced with such autarchy, military units had to acquire goods from Chinese dealers at black-market prices. Also, rice illegally siphoned off was

---

[77]   Legge 1984:174-5. For *gembleng* see *Asia Raya*, 7 and 9 December 2602(1942) and 6 October 2603(1943).

sold at high black-market prices, or was held back to await even higher black-market prices to come. All that, together with the Gunsei demand that the residencies were to become self-supporting districts, clearly disturbed the traditional trade arrangements existing between rice-surplus and rice-short-age areas.[78]

Rice requisitioning differed little from indigenous male labour requisitioning. Corvée labourers were encouraged to see themselves as *sukarela* (volunteer) workers helping to construct a New Java, while the Gunsei termed them *romusha* (war effort labourers). These youths, mostly of peasant stock, were utilized in all kinds of construction projects, first in Java as early as August 1942, and then both in Java and overseas, where they were boxed 'like oxen and horses', similar to what Dutch and Allied prisoners of war were experiencing at the time. Both Japanese and Indonesian government officials undertook widespread compulsory recruitment of *romusha* in order to meet the demands made by their immediate superiors. *Romusha* were often carted away in military lorries without even being informed of their final destination. So from *sho* (residency) to *ken* (regency) to *gun* (district) and finally to *ku* (village), there existed a massive systematic official complicity which, through requisitioning of food (mainly rice) left many of the poor starving and, through the requisitioning of *romusha*, left many bereaved. As to the massive recruitment of *romusha*, in the opinion of the liberal-minded Shunkichiro Miyoshi, that was 'a great blot on the record of the military administration'. Another Japanese, the historian Shigeru Sato, reveals that approximately 2.6 million *romusha* were in the employ of the Japanese on the island of Java in November 1944. And he believes this number to be under-estimated, since there was 'much labour, including child labour, mobilized for civil projects not appearing in the statistics' (Friend 1988:162-4; Sato 2000: 6-7). So the Gunsei got Indonesian rural males involved in the Japanese war effort by drafting them into massive forced labour schemes as well as by gradually enlisting more educated Indonesian males into military establishments of their own. One source concludes that 'this heavy-handed attempt at manipulation was inspired as much by the necessity to accommodate the nationalists as by a desperate need to mobilize all-out Indonesian support for the [Japanese] war effort' (Kanahele 1967:78). Manipulation or not, nationalists of Soekarno's ilk still saw a distinct benefit accruing from the Gunsei

---

[78] Brugmans et al. 1960:489-99; Kurasawa 1996:112-4. Kurasawa (p. 114) concludes that 'rice was worth its weight in gold in those days and was a prime item for speculation. This exacerbated the shortage even more.' See also Kurasawa 1993:Chapter 2. She was right; it exacerbated the shortage in 1944 as well, with all the problems she listed coming to the fore again; see Anderson 1966a. Also, during the 1944 main harvesting season, the largest rebellion of the entire occupation period took place in one of the major rice-growing areas (Indramajoe regency), as has been analysed by Kurasawa 1983:52-72. This rebellion will also be touched upon below.

emphasis on mass forced labour and indigenous military preparation, since both helped instil in the Indonesian people a consciousness and mental readiness for an independence yet to come. Soekarno referred to these sentiments in a text serialized in *Asia Raya* as *jadilah banteng* (do become and act like wild buffaloes). Hatta, always prone to express matters less dramatically, considered that the 'people's consciousness was finally freed from a sense of inferiority. In contrast to the Dutch, the Imperial Japanese forces have taught us to be courageous and to see ourselves on our own merits.'[79]

Naturally, in the long run, the recruitment of *romusha* forced labour did provoke resentment, but here as well, Soekarno was able to confront the Gunsei with stronger pro-Indonesian demands. So, at the first session of the Choo Sangiin, the establishment of a Badan Pembantoe Pradjoerit (Body to Aid the Fighters) was proposed in order to aid *romusha*, war volunteers, and their families. Thus, both Soekarno and his fellow nationalists were initially prepared to support the Japanese both with *romusha* labourers and with a Java-based indigenous military back-up as long as aid was forthcoming to the families of these workers. Yet, because the Poetera leaders were incapable of exerting sufficient influence in the countryside, they were never sure whether this aid did indeed materialize. That Soekarno, Sartono and Oto Iskandardinata registered themselves as *romusha* while asserting that to be a *romusha* was indeed a heroic activity was not only an example of blatant propaganda or blarney, but was also a sign of their inability to assert themselves at all in rural areas. Soekarno, who had figured for some time on a well-distributed poster clad as a *romusha*, was therefore challenged by Tan Malaka when both he and Hatta met the challenger during a Gunsei-inspired propaganda trip to Bayah in southern Banten. Tan Malaka, who had returned to Indonesia in early 1942, worked as an incognito clerk at the rather immense Banten Bayah Mines and Bayah-Saketi rail project from late 1943. During Soekarno and Hatta's propaganda visit, Tan Malaka said to both nationalist leaders that the plight of the *romusha* at Bayah was far from rosy and that the treatment of them was downright criminal. For both Soekarno and Hatta,

---

[79]   For Hatta's remarks see Hatta 1981:40. For Soekarno's see *Asia Raya* with the headline 'Djadilah banteng!! Pidato Pemimpin Besar "Poetera" pada 3 November 2603' (Become a wild buffalo!! Speech of the Great Leader of Putera on 3 November 2603), serialized in the issues of 5 to 11 November 2603(1943), where he, like Hatta, touched upon becoming brave ('haroes menoedjoe keara kebranian') and upon training your consciousness and your thoughts ('melatih kita poenja djiwa dan fikiran'), but also reminding his people that the Greater East Asia War was not only Dai Nippon's war but also our own war ('boekan sadja peperangan Dai Nippon tetapi djoega peperangan kita'), *Asia Raya*, 9 November 2603(1943):2. In that context Soekarno referred to the PETA as follows: 'Tentara Pembela Tanah Air itoe adalah langkah pertama kepada latihan kemiliteran oemoem jang mendjadi idam-idaman kita!' (The army to defend our fatherland is the first step toward training a public military force which fulfils our own deepest ideals!), *Asia Raya*, 6 November 2603(1943):2.

Tan Malaka's criticism was hard to swallow. Hatta, moreover, was in charge, together with Wilopo, of *romusha* affairs in the Badan Pembantoe Pradjoerit Pekerdja (BP3, Aid Organ for Labour Combatants).[80] Having agreed to work with the Gunsei and having accepted positions of at least nominal authority, both Soekarno and Hatta had put themselves in a position of acquiescence in, and even enthusiasm for, the entire *romusha* system. Soekarno recalled a date never to be forgotten – Sunday, 3 September 1944 – when he and other nationalist leaders, together with some five hundred members of the *kaum terpelajar* (learned people), all marched together to the Tanah Abang railway station in Djakarta amid cheers of 'long live the *romusha* volunteer corps'. After this they went by train to some defence installations outside the capital city for a day of hard labour on these sites.[81]

However, when pressed by Cindy Adams, Soekarno years later yielded, and came out with the following somewhat dramatic outpouring:

Dai Nippon preferred to lure *romushas* with promises of enticing wages and the title 'Heroes of Labor'. In reality they were slaves and I was the one assigned the task of enlisting them. Thousands never came back. They died in foreign lands. Often they were treated as inhumanly as the prisoners of war with whom they were shackled [...]. Yes, I knew about them. Yes, yes, yes, I knew they'd travel in airless boxcars packed in thousands at a time. I knew they were down to skin and bone. And I couldn't help them. In fact it was I – Sukarno – who sent them to work. Yes, it was I. I shipped them to their deaths. Yes, yes, yes, yes, I am the one. [...] I had pictures taken near Bogor with a tropical helmet on my head and a shovel in my hand showing how easy and glorious it was to be a *romusha*. With reporters, photographers, the Gunseikan – Commander-in-Chief – and Civil Authorities I made trips to Banten, the western tip of Java, to inspect the pitiable skeletons slaving on the home front down deep in the coal and gold mines. It was

---

[80] For Soekarno, Sartono and Iskandardinata see *Djawa Baroe* no. 7:16-7. For Tan Malaka arriving in Indonesia and then becoming an incognito clerk at Bayah, see the introduction by Helen Jarvis to Tan Malaka 1991, I:lxx-lxxi; Oshikawa 1990:14 and Poeze 1999:274-5, 299, 301. For Tan Malaka challenging both Soekarno and Hatta at Bayah see Tan Malaka 1991, II:173-5, and Poeze 1999:312-3. Kurasawa 1988:213-4, 228-30 states that the majority of the Java-based *romusha* were put to work at the Saketi/Bayah project, since that part of South Banten was sparsely populated; 100,000 of these labourers were working there in November 1944, of whom only 10,000 survived the Japanese capitulation. As to Hatta's Badan Pembantoe Pradjoerit Pekerdja see his detailed account of it in *Indonesia Merdeka*, 10 May 2605(1945):5-6. As to the title of *prajurit pekerja* (hero of labour) that was officially bestowed on labourers of all kinds during the Choo Sangiin's fourth session of 11-14 August 1944, *Djawa Baroe* 2-17 (1 September 2604(1944).

[81] *Tjahaja*, 5 September 2604(1944):1; *Soeara Asia*, 6 September 2604(1944):1, with the headline 'Rombongan pertama barisan Romusha dibawah pimpinan Ir. Soekarno berangkat ke medan perdjoeangan' (The first group of romusha led by Ir Soekarno left for our front of struggle); Pakpahan 1948:74. It is on that occasion that Soekarno is viewed in the famous poster giving instructions to *romusha*; see *Djawa Baroe*, no. 19, 1 September 2604(1944); see also Zwaan 1981: 197. Giebels 1999:316-7 also refers to it, citing Brugmans et al. 1960:360, yet on that page there is no reference to Soekarno and the *romusha* trip at all.

horrible. Hopeless. And it was I who gave them to the Japanese. Sounds terrible, doesn't it? They tell me the people won't like to read this – is that right? Well, I do not blame them. Nobody likes the ugly truth.[82]

As to the military back-up, yet another burden placed upon the people by the Gunsei, it did not at first involve the *heiho* (indigenous auxiliary soldiers, also called *genjomin gunta* (indigenous troops) by the Japanese), since they served under the jurisdiction of the Seventh Area Army and the indigenous troops were always led by Japanese officers. In the instance of the Java-based and purely Indonesian-officered indigenous militia (*milisi*), later called the Tentara Pembela Tanah Air (PETA, Army for the Defence of the Fatherland), it was Soekarno's former PNI stalwart Gatot Mangkoepraja who stood at the cradle of the PETA. Once a visitor to the November 1933 Pan-Asiatic Congress in Tokyo, an experience that made him an enthusiast Japanophile, he seems, through contacts with Captain Motoshige Yanagawa and Major General Kotoku Sato, to have written a report about the planned *milisi* on 7 September 1943, signing it with his own blood. This was followed by dozens of similar letters all over Java, some of them also written in blood.[83] Also, early in September 1943, Mas Soetardjo Kartohadikoesoemo and Dr Boen-taran Martoatmodjo, both on a trip to Japan, had requested the Japanese government to introduce compulsory military service for a *milisi* in Indonesia in order to support Japan in the efforts to win the Greater East Asia War. As to Yanagawa, who later would become an Indonesian citizen, he served as a member of the Tokubetsu Han or Beppan (acronym for this Japanese counter-intelligence and special forces unit which also had some experience training Indonesians for intelligence work), in January 1943 he was charged with leading an Indonesian youth training centre named Seinen Dojo (drill hall for young men) at Tangerang, just west of Djakarta, with about 40 Javanese trainees. In June of that year a second group of some 60 trainees was trained until October, with the graduates being sent to Bogor to form the first 100 cadets for the PETA officer corps.[84] The Gunsei acceded to the formation of the PETA in order to maintain an indigenous military force to fight the Allied forces if and when the need arose. The Gunsei apparently thought it would be preferable to shed Indonesian blood rather than Japanese (Adams 1966:186). Nugroho Notosusanto states that Japanese strategic concepts prescribed Indonesians to be used as the first line of defence at Java's

---

[82]   Adams 1965:192. Tan Malaka would have agreed fully with all that, but in 1966 when these outpourings came into print he had been dead for close to 16 years.

[83]   Gatot Mangkupradja 1968:117, 121; Nugroho Notosusanto 1979:70-1; Soehoed Prawiroat-modjo 1953:30; Pakpahan 1948:35-6.

[84]   *Tjahaja*, 8 September 2603(1943):2; Nugroho Notosusanto 1979:61-2.

beaches, with the Japanese forming a second line for frontal encounters, to finally engage together with Indonesians in mountain guerrilla operations (Nugroho Notosusanto 1968:289).

According to one American historian (Kahin 1952:109) the Indonesian nationalists viewed the PETA differently, since 'the continuous objective of Soekarno, Hatta, and other Poetera leaders was to indoctrinate PETA members with a pro-Indonesian point of view and only outwardly a pro-Japanese and anti-Allied orientation'. Abu Hanifah in his recollections (1972: 128) maintains that: 'The Japanese needed a good defensive organisation to fight beside their troops in case of an Allied attack. But gradually it became clear that the PETA troops were more nationalistic and less pro-Japanese than expected. There was among them also a strong anti-Dutch feeling.' Soekarno himself seems to have convinced the Gunsei that the PETA would turn into a reliable defensive organization as long as its rank and file as well as its officers were inspired by an aroused national awareness. Thus he was allowed to speak to various PETA units, 'inflaming them not against the Allies alone, but against imperialism in general. Many PETA members had no difficulty in equating Japan's activities with imperialism by themselves. To most of the less astute, this connection was soon made clear by the veiled innuendoes dropped by Soekarno and Hatta in their speeches.' (Kahin 1952:109.) Soekarno, who hailed the PETA as 'a useful springboard for eliciting the support of the Indonesian people for the nationalist *pergerakan*', as well as a first step in 'the welding of the Indonesian nation based on our own people',[85] allowed the following lines to appear in his autobiography (Adams 1965:186):

> As for me, I recognized this as an opportunity for our ragged flock to become proficient in soldiering. For the first time Indonesians would learn to handle guns, to defend themselves. They were taught army discipline, guerrilla training, how to ambush, how to fire a rifle from a crawling position, how to fashion home-made grenades from a coconut shell filled with petrol. They learned how to fight the enemy – whoever the enemy might be.

Prophetic words indeed, in view of the rather gallant struggle which ensued from August 1945 to June 1949. But was Soekarno here not thinking as well about the PETA-inspired revolt in Blitar, with the Japanese then surely being the enemy? On the other hand, these outpourings may well have formed an *imbangan* (counter weight) to the blame he so clearly took upon himself in the case of the pitiful *romusha*. Alas, let us now return to the PETA and also briefly discuss the advent of some other youth organizations.

These developments, with the PETA's final 1945 enlistment rising to 38,000 – 'four times the actual combat strength' of the Java-based Sixteenth Army

[85]   *Asia Raya*, 6 October 2603(1943):2.

– were to imbue Javanese youth with a new self-confident spirit. This spirit was also found in such earlier conceived all-Indonesian Java-based paramilitary organizations as the Seinendan (youth corps) and the Keibodan (auxiliary police corps). The Seinendan and the Keibodan, with males ranging in age from 14 to 25 years, though never armed except for some bamboo sticks, received only some self-defence training (*taisho* in Japanese), since they were to mentally and technically prepare themselves as a home guard to aid the Japanese war effort by keeping law and order, particularly on the Javanese rural home front. They were both inaugurated on the occasion of Tencho Setsu, Emperor Hirohito's birthday on 29 April 1943, with the Seinendan assisting efforts to increase production by repairing roads or by preparing land for cultivation and the Keibodan being an auxiliary to local police forces at the city and village level to maintain law and order under the direction of the local police chief. Organizationally, members of both the Seinendan and the Keibodan were spread geographically all over the urban wards and rural villages of Java and Madoera. By the end of the Japanese occupation, Seinendan had approximately half a million members, while the Keibodan numbered more than a million.[86] So, with the PETA in the offing and the Seinendan and the Keibodan already functioning on the Javanese home front, these youth formations seemed prepared to assist the Japanese whenever needed. In order to understand this Japanese emphasis upon overall Indonesian mobilization for the Greater East Asia War, we need to briefly sketch the military developments facing Japan in the mid- and southwest Pacific.

Japan loses the military initiative in the mid- and southwest Pacific

As to military developments, Japanese forces in the southwest Pacific had occupied Tulagi on 3 May 1942 as part of a plan approved 28 April 1942 in the wake of lengthy general headquarters meetings in Tokyo. There, Admiral Isoroku Yamamoto, the pioneer of carrier warfare, had been given approval to attack Midway in order to exert still greater pressure on Pearl Harbor.

---

[86]   Nugroho Notosusanto 1979:44-5, 63; De Bruin 1968:25, 28, 34. De Bruin (1968:21-2), however, lists 17 November 1942 as the start of a Semarang-based forerunner of Seinendan; also confirmed by *Asia Raya*, 17 November 2602(1942):2. But this branch was incorporated on 29 April 1943 by the Djawa Rengo Seinendan (De Bruin 1968:26). In Djatinegara, at the former Tiga A youth training facility, leaders of the regional Seinendan were undergoing 3- to 4-month courses to prepare them for their tasks (De Bruin 1968:26). PETA finally numbered 38,000, Seinendan and Keibodan numbered close to one and half million, and Barisan Pelopor and Hizboellah numbered 60,000 and 50,000 respectively. These youths, together with some 25,000 Java-based *heiho*, formed the nucleus of the military resistance against Dutch post-war attempts to subdue the Indonesian Republic, Nugroho Notosusanto 1979:44, 46-7.

This man, the architect of the 7 December 1942 attack on Pearl Harbor, an operation which will always stand as his crowning achievement, was well aware that Japanese superiority over the Americans at sea was only transitory, unless the US Pacific fleet could be annihilated. But in the Pearl Harbor raid on 7 December 1942, the US carrier fleet of five carriers had escaped being demolished. Two had left for the Atlantic, one had still been on the west coast of the USA, while the two still stationed at Pearl Harbor had been engaged in naval exercises 200 miles west of Pearl Harbor (Willmott 1982: 131, 133). However, after the Pearl Harbor debacle, the Americans redeployed the two carriers from the Atlantic to join the three in the Pacific. So it remained paramount for Japanese planners to destroy the US carriers in the Pacific. Another reason for the Japanese Midway operation was inspired by the daring US attack launched by Lieutenant Colonel James Doolittle on the Japanese homeland, when sixteen twin-engined B-25 Mitchell bombers took off from the aircraft carrier *Hornet* on 18 April 1942 and bombed oil, military and factory installations in Tokyo, Kobe, Yokohama and Nagoya, with most of the Mitchell bomber crews and Doolittle himself able to find refuge on the part of the Chinese mainland not controlled by the Japanese. While the damage wrought by Doolittle had been quite minimal – Japanese propaganda dubbed the raid a 'do-nothing raid', a pun on the name of its leader – its impact in a psychological sense had been great. With Midway in Japanese hands, the Tokyo planners believed such surprise attacks on the Japanese homeland would be highly unlikely in the future (Willmott 1982:448-9).

In the southwest Pacific the occupation of Tulagi and of Port Moresby would be the opening gambit for further extending the Japanese sphere as far as New Caledonia, Fiji and Samoa, in order to cut off US-Australian lines of communication. If all these plans materialized, and with Midway firmly in Japanese hands, Admiral Yamamoto believed Japan would be in a strong enough position to open peace negotiations. However, the Japanese overseas thrust to Port Moresby did not materialize, due to the sea battle in the Coral Sea from 7 to 8 May 1942 between Japanese and American aircraft carrier forces. Already in April, the American navy had been aware (after breaking Japanese codes) that an overseas attack on Port Moresby was being prepared, under the protection of three Japanese aircraft carriers. So from Pearl Harbor two US aircraft carriers were dispatched to the Coral Sea to engage the enemy. During that battle the losses between the contending fleets were about the same. Both fleets lost one carrier and each of them had a damaged carrier to cope with. So the material losses were equal, though the personnel losses to the Japanese were greater due to the fact that a considerable number of their pilots, insufficiently trained in night landings, crashed into the sea. Anyhow, the Port Moresby attack was aborted, this being the first time since 7 December 1941 that the Japanese had to cancel a carefully prepared expedition (Willmott 1982:460; De Jong 1969-91, XIb:20-2).

As for the expedition to Midway, this led to the turning point of the entire war in the Pacific. In spite of the great naval preponderance of the Japanese – six carriers to three, 11 battleships to none; 22 cruisers to eight; 65 destroyers to 15; 21 submarines to 19 – the US carriers in the four-day battle of 3 to 6 June 1942, supported by US army bombers stationed in Midway, created sheer havoc among their opponents. Helped by the fact that US radar facilities were superior and that in one instance some of the Japanese carriers had insufficient air cover, the result was one US carrier lost and four Japanese carriers. As to aircraft, the US lost some 150 planes against some 300 lost by the Japanese. As to lives, the Americans lost about 300 men as against about 3,500 lost by the Japanese, the greater part of whom had belonged to the cream of the best-schooled airborne personnel of the Japanese navy. As to carriers, now seen as the most important vessels in future sea engagements, the Japanese had four against the US with six. Yamamoto thus concluded that the US would build new carriers at a speed his own country would be unable to match. As to Japanese aspirations in the southwest Pacific, the planned forays to New Caledonia, Fiji and Samoa were aborted. However, the Japanese were startled by new forays by the Americans in the Solomons, where a series of battles was fought for the strategic initiative between May and December 1942, with the Japanese Imperial Headquarters on 31 December 1942 breaking off the battle for Guadalcanal. Also, the Japanese overland attack on Port Moresby – Japanese forces of some 4,000 men had captured Buna on the north coast of Australian New Guinea by mid-July 1942 and attempted to reach Port Moresby by scaling the Owen Stanley Range – was finally thrust back at the Kokoda trail by elements of the Sixth and Seventh Australian divisions. Reinforced by US army units, this combined Allied force recaptured Buna by the end of January 1943. The military balance had thus swung in favour of the US-British-Australian alliance, and Japan, having definitely lost the strategic initiative, was now facing the prospect of a *kyusen*, the Japanese term for protracted war, a spectre that had haunted Admiral Yamamoto and his fellow strategists. Yamamoto got a foretaste of the growing power of the Allied air forces in the southwest Pacific when, while on an orientation tour to that area, his Mitsubishi bomber plane was intercepted on 18 April 1943 by a squadron of US P-39 fighters, who killed him as well. On 31 May 1943 the Imperial Conference in Tokyo discussed the political strategies that this new situation demanded. The decision was made to erect massive defence networks throughout the theatre of war and at the same time to enlist stronger cooperation from all the nations of Southeast Asia. So, to intensify the defence build-up, the Japanese decided upon an even larger mobilization of indigenous labourers (*romusha*) and of indigenous *heiho* (auxiliary soldiers) (Willmott 1983:513-4; Sato 1994:60; Zwaan 1981:88), while in

Java on 3 October 1943 Lieutenant General Harada announced the formation of the first Indonesian volunteer corps, the Soekarela Tentara Pembela Tanah Air (mentioned above). As to the *heiho*, the first recruitment drives began in Java in May 1943. These men served with Japanese units, initially performing such services as driving lorries and guarding military establishments, Allied prisoners-of-war camps, and civilian internment camps in Java. Only during 1944-1945 were they trained for combat, with considerable numbers of them being dispatched as far as New Guinea and Burma.[87]

All these events were to have repercussions in Indonesia, and particularly in densely populated Java and Madoera, where the indigenous population was pressed by the Japanese to mobilize all forces for the war effort. Admiral Yamamoto's death was disclosed in Java much later, with *Pewarta Perniagaän* on 22 May 1943 announcing that 'Laksamana Isoroku Yamamoto tiwas sebagi pendekar' (Admiral Isokuru Yamamoto perished in action as a hero). On 5 June 1943 Soekarno paid homage to the lost leader as well, during a brief ceremony at Poetera headquarters. On the night of 21 to 22 July 1943, Port Darwin-based Allied bombers executed the first air raid bombardment on Soerabaja, forcing the Japanese high command to realize that the overall safety of Indonesia could no longer be guaranteed.[88]

Soekarno divorces Inggit and marries Fatmawati

While political fortune in Soekarno's case seems to have favoured the bold, his domestic circumstances at Pegangsaan Timoer 56 turned from bad to worse. Longing for Fatmawati, whom he had left in Bencoolen with promises not to forget his affection for her, he sent her (through a Bencoolen-based dealer in golden trinkets) a chain with a little toy showing cucumber seeds and a red stone.[89] With these tokens, Soekarno perhaps wanted to convey the symbolic message of wishing to be chained to her for good. Soekarno went further, mainly through correspondence with his former Bencoolen Chinese associate Hien, and urged Hien to approach Fatmawati's parents in his name with an official marriage proposal and ask whether they would agree to be his stand-in during the wedding ceremony by proxy. Hien reports in his own recollections that Fatmawati initially showed disappointment at this proposal, since

---

[87]   Sihombing (himself having been a *heiho*) 1962:137-40; *Asia Raya*, 29 April 2603(1943):2.
[88]   For *Pewarta Perniagaän*'s announcement see Zwaan 1981:138. For Soekarno's homage to Yamomoto, see Hatta 1971:77. For the Soerabaja air raid see Brugmans et al. 1960:48, 330-1; De Bruin 1982a:86.
[89]   Fatmawati Soekarno 1978:41-2. Giebels 1999:296 refers to Soekarno sending postcards to Fatmawati adorned with drawings showing bees and flowers citing Fatmawati Soekarno 1978: 4. We found no reference to this bee and flower story on that page nor in the entire book.

she had hoped that Soekarno would show up in person to propose to her. Also, since she was a *seorang perawan* (a virgin), she wanted Soekarno to be at her side during the wedding ceremony. However, later on, persuaded by her parents and soothed by the news that Soekarno, due to his important activities, would not be allowed by the Gunsei to travel to Bencoolen, she agreed to have his stand-in at the ceremony by proxy soon to come. But she was adamant about Soekarno divorcing Inggit first. As for Hien, he refused to be Soekarno's stand-in in order not to upset Inggit, of whom he was quite fond, and therefore proposed to ask a public works overseer named Sardjono to do the job (Abdul Karim 1982:90-1, 94-5; Fatmawati Soekarno 1978:42).

Naturally, Inggit at Pegangsaan Timoer 56 had got wind of something being afoot, and several verbal clashes with Soekarno followed. Soekarno no longer shared the bedroom with Inggit but sought refuge in the small house attached to their home where Omi and her family were housed. The world outside the household soon got to know of Soekarno's domestic troubles as well. Said, an announcer for the Djakarta radio, who had befriended Dr Leo Jansen of the Djakarta Overseas Broadcasting Service, had it that 'Inggit was to divorce Soekarno' and that Soekarno had 'a relation with three young women' (Jansen 1988:133). Another important outsider, however, came to be directly involved in Soekarno's marital troubles, namely Poetera's vice-chairman and a close associate of Soekarno, Mohammad Hatta. Hatta readily came to the conclusion that a split between Inggit and Soekarno was inevitable, partly because, as Hatta believed, Inggit could not bear Soekarno any children. Together with Empat Serangkai members Mas Mansoer and Ki Hadjar Dewantoro, Hatta drew up a rather handsome financial separation agreement, including a home to be built in Bandoeng for Inggit, and the conditions were accepted by both parties (Hatta 1979b:418; Ramadhan 1981:446). Both Soekarno's adopted daughters, Omi and Kartika, suffered from the divorce because they had always been quite fond of their foster father. Omi and her family left the annex at Pegangsaan Timoer 56, but Omi's husband Asmara Hadi continued to remain politically tied to Soekarno. He begged the family to leave Soekarno alone and not to trouble him, since he was indisputably the leader the nation wanted and needed the most. Kartika, though severely torn by the split, chose to remain with Inggit whenever it was established where they were to stay in Bandoeng. Another person quite torn by the separation was Riwoe, Soekarno's faithful servant since the Endeh years. With eyes still red from the tears he shed, Riwoe, always quite fond of Inggit, decided to stay with Soekarno. Some two years later, when he was one of the few to witness Soekarno proclaiming Indonesia's independence from the front steps of Pegangsaan Timoer 56, Riwoe suddenly mused that it would have been right if Inggit, hailed by Soekarno in earlier times as an indefatigable Srikandi, had stood there instead of Iboe Fatmawati. Alas, Clio the Muse of History decided otherwise, and perhaps rightly so, since it was Iboe Fatmawati who bore Soekarno five children, one of whom was Indonesia's fifth president. However, let us return to the break between Inggit and Soekarno.

The moment the separation agreement was arranged, the divorce was finalized, with Soekarno personally escorting Inggit and Kartika to Bandoeng together with Mas Mansoer, who had the task of signing the divorce papers in front of such people as Sanoesi, the former husband of Inggit. Perhaps he had in mind that Sanoesi might take her back again. However, that did not occur since Sanoesi had remarried. So Inggit and Kartika would stay for the time being with Hadji Anda and his family, old friends and owners of a thriving woodwork business called Lentjana (Cockade), at Djalan Lengkong Besar, close to Tjiateul, where Inggit and Soekarno in the late 1920s had lived together so blissfully. Inggit at Hadji Anda's house now bid Soekarno a final farewell, vividly realizing that they would no longer stand hand-in-hand at the portal of a new era.[90] Yet whenever Soekarno was in Bandoeng, he would visit Inggit, leaving her all the money he had in his pocket at such times. However, the home to be built for her according to the arrangements made up by the Empat Serangkai was only erected in 1951, with the Bandoeng municipality bearing the costs.[91]

As to Fatmawati, now married by proxy to Soekarno, she arrived in Dja-karta after several delays, this time taking a route the reverse of Soekarno's in 1938 toward Bencoolen. She left Bencoolen by car, accompanied by her parents and by Ahmad Kantjil and Semaoen Bakri, went by way of Loeboek Linggau, and from there by train to Teloek Betoeng, where they all stayed for ten days with her mother's brother. Then they went by ship to Merak and left Merak by car to stay at Rangkasbitoeng with the local village chief (*camat*). It was there that local people learned that she was Soekarno's new wife, while Fatmawati herself learned from local papers that her husband was in East Java, probably in Blitar, to inform his family about his new wife's coming to Java. Fatmawati reached Djakarta at the end of June 1943, where she was met at the Tanah Abang railway station by Mr Sartono and Ir Sakirman. They took her to Mas Mansoer at Djalan Waringin, where she was to stay until Soekarno came back from East Java. A week later Soekarno, now back in Djakarta, took her to Pegangsaan Timoer 56, a house she admired due to the many paintings and antique things she saw displayed there. At her new home her marriage to Soekarno was solemnized on 22 August 1943. Somewhat later in the year she met Soekarno's Blitar family, while her own parents came to see her as

---

[90]   Ramadhan 1981:449, 452-4. As to Riwoe musing about Inggit on 17 August 1945, see Gie-bels 1999:359.
[91]   Interview with Marcel Koch in Bandoeng, 8 January 1952. Koch informed us that Soekarno, on various trips to Bandoeng, would often visit Inggit first to pay his respects.

well, staying in the annex. Just afterwards, she was found to be pregnant, after which Soekarno's parents also joined them. The child, a boy, was born on 3 November 1944, and named Goentoer Osamu Soekarno-poetera. The name Osamu was apparently added in order to honour the former Saiko Shikikan, Imamura, now left useless in Rabaul surrounded by Allied forces (Abdul Karim 1982:96; Fatmawati Soekarno 1978:42-5, 49-50).

The Tokyo visit: medals for Soekarno, Hatta, and Bagoes Hadikoesoemo, yet no promises

From 5 to 6 November 1943, Premier Tojo convoked in Tokyo the Greater East Asia Conference, which José Laurel of the Philippines, Ba Maw of Burma and the Tokyo-based Chandra Bose of India attended, along with representatives of the Japanese puppet states of Henry Pu'i's Manchukuo, Wang Ching Wei's China and Pibul Songram's Thailand. The conference decided, by way of a so-called East Asia Charter, to work toward an even tighter cooperation between Dai Nippon and those states officially represented at the conference.[92] The fact that there had been no representation, official or unofficial, of Java – let alone Indonesia – prompted the Gunsei of Java to seek a middle way, mainly in order to keep the Indonesian top nationalist foremen on the Japanese side now that the Choo Sangiin so clearly served to meet Japanese interests and the Poetera leadership was usually kept at bay. For some time, small Indonesian delegations had visited Japan, mostly as a token gesture to promote deeper understanding between the two countries, and now the Gunsei entertained the idea of having Soekarno, Hatta and Bagoes Hadikoesoemo come to Tokyo as well, as a token of gratitude for the Seiji Sanyo (Political Participation) granted to the Poetera intellectuals. Earlier visits, for example the one referred to above, when both Dr Boentaran and Soetardjo Kartohadi-koesoemo were promoting an Indonesian indigenous militia, were followed by visits of journalists such as Parada Harahap, Soemanang Soerjowinoto, Manai Sophiaan and Adinegoro, who had also attended the Greater East Asia Conference. The Java Gunsei anticipated in return that such encounters would result in favourable impressions being aired in Java-based newspapers and other outlets.[93] Why Bagoes Hadikoesoemo had been picked for the proposed visit to Tokyo and not Empat Serangkai member Mas Mansoer

---

[92]   Bharadwaj 1997:181-2; Aziz 1955:217; Dahm 1969:257. Pakpahan 1948:40, sees the Tokyo conference as the Asian answer to the Atlantic Charter of Churchill and Roosevelt.
[93]   See Soebagio 1980:103, 114, 116; *Pandji Poestaka*, 1 November 2603(1943); *Djawa Baroe* 1-16, 15 August 2603(1943) and *Djawa Baroe* 1-22, 15 November 2603(1943); Parada Harahap 1944; Kanahele 1967:294, note 59 and 60 but placing the Greater East Asia Conference on 16 November instead of 5 to 6 November 1943.

had to do with the fact that the latter was seen as too close to Hatta. Hatta, due to all kinds of Kenpeitai intrigues, was really picked with the intention of keeping him in Tokyo as a temporary exile. The Japanese hoped he would immerse himself in both the *nippon seishin* (the Japanese spirit) and the *koodo seishin* (spirit of the imperial way), as suggested earlier by Captain Murase, an operation which neatly exemplifies the Japanese Kenpeitai concept of *tor-ishimari* (control) and *dan'atsu* (suppression).

Finally the Gunsei announced the composition of the delegation: Soekarno heading it and Hatta and Hadikoesoemo being members, with Miyoshi and Kuchi Terada attached to it as well. It was further revealed that the visit would last two weeks and that its main purpose was to express wholeheartedly and in the name of all the people of Java their gratitude for being allowed to participate in the government. Another more important motive for the visit, however, was to impress the Indonesian visitors with Dai Nippon's industrial strength and advancement.[94] However, no mention was made at all of the hidden agenda: for the two Japanese members to indirectly enquire while in Tokyo about the Kenpeitai's disposition of Hatta's case. On 10 November 1943, the delegation flew to Tokyo by way of Makassar, Manila and Formosa. In Manila, with a display of flags still on show due to the celebrations connected with the recently proclaimed Philippine independence, Soekarno on two occasions was seen close to tears and quite enraged at the same time – first at the statute of José Rizal and then at a Manila Hotel dinner. During the stopover at Formosa, Soekarno was again startled and annoyed to see locomotives from Java in use there.[95] The delegation arrived in Tokyo on 13 November with Soekarno entertaining Japanese journalists at the Teikokoe Hotel that evening, on which occasion he thanked the Japanese armed forces who had made it possible for his people in Java to revive their hopes for the freedom they had so long cherished.[96] The next day Soekarno, Hatta and Hadikoesoemo had a one-hour audience with Premier Tojo, during which the three Indonesian leaders thanked the Japanese leader for the participation they had been granted in the administration of Java. Later the three leaders visited the Yasukuni shrine, where they rendered thanks to the Japanese for having freed Indonesia from the Dutch.[97]

On 15 November the three leaders were decorated with the order of

[94] *Asia Raya*, 15 November 2603(1943):1 with the headline 'Oetoesan-oetoesan Tjoeo Sangi-in mengoendjoengi Tokio' (Delegates of the Choo Sangiin visiting Tokyo) with Miyoshi being labelled as the one in charge of the escort (*pemimpin-pengantar*) and Terada as his assistant (*pem-bantu*). For the other motive of the visit see Hatta 1971:91, note 14.

[95] Friend 1988:107, citing an interview with Hatta on 6 March 1968 and Kanahele 1967:294, note 62, citing Miyoshi.

[96] 'Telah tiba di Tokio' (Having arrived in Tokyo), *Asia Raya*, 15 September 2603(1943):1.

[97] *Tjahaja*, 15 September 2603(1943):1.

the Holy Treasury (Bintang Ratna Suci), with Soekarno getting the seldom-
bestowed award of the second class and Hatta and Hadikoesoemo receiving the award of the third class. The next day the three Indonesian leaders
were personally received by Emperor Hirohito, with the Tenno shaking only
Soekarno's hand.[98] As to Hatta staying in Japan due to Kenpeitai wishes to
have him exiled to Japan or even arrested, none of that was known to army
headquarters officials when they were probed by Miyoshi and Terada about
the so-called Hatta case. In fact, Miyoshi was informed that Hatta would be
returned to Djakarta, since it was not possible 'to provide proper supervision
or service in Tokyo for a person of such prominence'.[99] Hatta confided in his
memoirs that shortly before his return to Djakarta, Count Kodama (Imamura's top political adviser during the early months of the Japanese occupation),
handed him several English-language works dealing with the 'Japanese spirit'. Hatta further confided that the Japanese Gunsei in Djakarta 'had decided
that it was not necessary now for me to stay behind [in Japan]' (Hatta 1981:
220). During the remainder of their visit, the three leaders were given a tour
of the country, mainly to impress on them Japan's potential as a great industrial nation and the sacrifices it was making for realizing the Greater East
Asia Co-Prosperity Sphere. Soekarno recalls in his autobiography (Adams
1965:189) that he marvelled to Hatta:

> Their industry is overwhelming. If the aim was to impress me they've succeeded.
> [Hatta responded:] This is your first time outside Indonesia. When viewed in that
> relation the difference is monumental. And they know it. That's why you're invited
> here. But I spent eleven years in Europe, where I have seen even bigger factories.

Nevertheless, Soekarno did not allow himself to be distracted from what he
viewed as the primary purpose of his journey. So, before the departure for
Java on 3 December 1943, Soekarno had four interviews with the Japanese
premier Tojo on 14, 16, 17 and 21 November 1943. On these occasions Soekarno reiterated the demands for a promise of future independence, for
using the Indonesian red and white banner, and for allowing the anthem
'Indonesia Raja' to be sung. Tojo merely responded that he would soon touch
in writing upon these issues. After Soekarno had returned to Djakarta, he
received a noncommittal answer from Tojo on all these questions. The only
gesture Tojo was prepared to make at this time was to ship 100 kilograms
of salvarsan (synthetic arsenic) for the people in Java to benefit from.[100]

---

[98]   Pakpahan 1948:41. Pakpahan comments that the handshake indicated 'Betoel ini soeatoe
kedjadian ketjil sadja toch sangat mendjolok dalam perasaän djoega' (Though it was only a small
matter it still remained a sign of good manners).
[99]   Kanahele 1967:107, citing Miyoshi's *Djawa Senryo Gensei Kaikoroku* (privately circulated).
[100]   Aziz 1955:219; Bharadwaj 1997:182; Dahm 1969:258. For the gift of salvarsan see *Asia Raya*,
4 December 2603(1943):1.

Soekarno and Hatta were told shortly after their return that Mr Amir Sjarifoeddin had been imprisoned in Malang, East Java. He had been accused of leading an anti-Japanese underground movement and was sentenced to be executed. Timely intervention by Soekarno – he approached the Gunseikan pleading that the culprit was a national leader and that an execution would enrage the Indonesian people – resulted in the sentence being commuted to life imprisonment (Hatta 1981:220-1; Sutamto Dirdjosuparto 1998:64).

Poetera is absorbed by the Jawa Hokokai

Even before his trip to Japan, Soekarno was given notice by Miyoshi, Saito and Shimizu of the Poetera Guidance Board (Minshu Shidobu, the group of Japanese advisers attached to Poetera) of their plans to dissolve Poetera in order to integrate it into a new mass organization and asked for his support for this new venture. Soekarno's first reaction was to reject any support out of hand, since he felt it was a betrayal to his nationalist comrades. The meeting was held just before Soekarno was to solemnize his wedding with Fatmawati on 22 August 1943; this may have added to Soekarno's annoyance at the Japanese proposal. Why, just at the time that he, the chairman of the Choo Sangiin, wanted to impress his new bride with all he had achieved so far, did they bother him with a new organization of the masses by which his own position could well be challenged? Thus, to the Japanese involved, it came as a surprise that, a few days after the blissful ceremony with Fatmawati, Soekarno approached Saito and quite cheerfully assented to the scheme. And so, it was decided between the schemers to keep the plans secret for a while.

So Poetera continued to function as usual, but it seems that Hatta was aware of the fact that Poetera was committed more strictly by the Minshu Shidobu to propaganda matters, such as emphasis on rural agricultural production increases, an intensifying anti-Allied campaign, and the mass volunteering of labourers, paramilitary units, youth groups, neighbourhood and women's associations (Tonarigumi and Fujinkai respectively[101]), and the like.

---

[101] Fujinkai, set up in August 1943 in Java (see *Kan Po*, no. 26, 10 September 2603(1943):34), had some pre-war feminist and nationalist women leading it, such as Raden Nganten Siti Soekaptinah Soenarjo Mangoenpoespito (Fujinkai chairwoman), Raden Ajoe Abdoerachman (Fujinkai chairwoman of the Djakarta branch); Njai Raden Boerdah Joesoepadi Danoehadinigrat, Maria Ulfah Santoso, Njonja Soenarjati Soedorowerti Soekemi and Rasoena Said, see Maria Ulfah Santoso, 'Pergerakan wanita Indonesia dalem tahoen 2602-2605', *Pradjoerit* no. 11(1 March 2605 (1945)):31-2 and Gunseikanbu 1944a:475, 473, 474, 478. For the Tonarigumi in Java and Madoera starting just prior to the year 1944 and then taking a rapid network development all around, see Sato 1994:72.

All in order to support Japanese-inspired mobilization programmes to create a 'total war structure' on the home front. Hatta (1971:65-6), in his second Poetera report, stressed that the focus upon all these activities threatened to cause Poetera's other activities to dwindle sharply:

> The people hoped for leadership from those who promote Poetera, but they were not able to give it. Aside from propaganda, the people see no concrete results. [...] Within Poetera the question often arises what more there is for Poetera to do. The youth have been taken over by Seinendan. Women have been organized into the Fujinkai. Sports are regulated by the Jawa Tai Ibu Kai. For culture there is the Cultural Centre or Keimin Bunka Shidosho. Effective leadership in the field of education and economics is not permitted. (Hatta 1971:61.)

And yet he was surprised, even annoyed, by the Saiko Shikikan's announcement on 8 January 1944 that a new people's organization would be established to succeed Poetera. In his 9 March 1943-29 February 1944 report he stated:

> But lo and behold came the Saiko Shikikan's decree ordering the Gunseikan to develop a new organization by combining all existing bodies and movements into one! According to His Excellency's order, Putera was to be absorbed into this new organization. So all Putera's preparations came to a halt. (Hatta 1971:75.)

The Empat Serangkai waited four days before they issued a somewhat sour statement of support for the new organization.[102] But Soekarno went further during the Choo Sangiin's second session of 30 January to 3 February 1944. There the Saiko Shikikan, Lieutenant General Harada, arranged to mobilize the population even further by forming two committees in which the interests of the government and of the people were kept carefully separate. Strengthening of defence preparations was handled in the first committee, while in the second there were suggestions for food production to be increased. Soekarno in his closing address somewhat ironically suggested that the Gunsei was naturally specially interested in the results of the first committee. He noted that 'We trust the Gunsei and the Gunsei trusts us, but bear in mind that there is nothing more shameful than a breach of trust.'[103] The following day, this time in a radio speech entitled 'Menenoen nasib dengan tenaga sendiri' (Weaving destiny by our own efforts), he again elabor-

---

[102]   Pakpahan 1948:47; Jansen 1988:257-8. Soekardjo Wirjopranoto and the Sultan of Djokjakarta were the first Indonesian leaders to welcome it. The former commented that Poetera never did develop strongly and that only now would Indonesian leaders be able to show their skills. Poetera was never an expression of Asian solidarity since it was too Indonesian-centred, Jansen 1988:258.

[103]   *Asia Raya*, 4 February 2604(1944):1.

ated on trust and the breach of it, providing a message clear to all:

> Why is it that true partnerships fail to materialize with powers that colonize or
> are imperialist? Why do they miscarry or fail to get results? Well, that is because
> colonizers fail to trust the people. In our case the moment the Dutch withheld
> their trust toward our people their power collapsed. And it is this mutual feeling
> of trust that will bring about a new reconstruction in our own country. [...] We are
> now engaged in a war, and with the peoples of Asia we are together weaving our
> common destinies, so it is necessary that all forces be mobilized under the leader-
> ship of Dai Nippon. Our own entire enthusiasm in this vast struggle needs to be
> directed by ourselves to that one primary goal, that of assuring and weaving a
> happy future for ourselves.[104]

These remarks were hailed by Bernhard Dahm as one of Soekarno's most
glorious speeches. It was a synthesis 'such as had never been experienced
in a long colonial history'. Although the Gunsei was not mentioned in the
context of trust and distrust (Soekarno only referred to distrust of the Allies
and of the Dutch), Dahm felt it should nevertheless be interpreted as 'the
feeling of distrust will bring down the Japanese in our land'. Soekarno, here
taking recourse to past colonial regimes and their distrust toward the common people under their yoke, left it to his listeners to decide whether the
current Gunsei was showing distrust as well. On the other hand, Soekarno's
emphasis 'upon weaving a glorious future for ourselves', indicating that such
a prospect should be handled by the Indonesians themselves, according to
Dahm (1969:267-8) should be interpreted as saying 'that the hour had now
also arrived for Indonesia'. In that context, even the Japanese collaborator
Dr Leo Jansen considered that the Japanese/Indonesian fraternity issue was
some kind of a fable.[105]

As to the first and second sessions of the Choo Sangiin, they were both
exclusively geared to the Japanese programme of 'defence and construction', with freedom of speech being quite restricted. In both these sessions,
the oath at the start of the gatherings 'stipulated the delegates' obligation to
discuss the Gunsei's wish of coordinating all forces in order to reach final victory'.[106] Yet as we have seen above in the case of Soekarno, the Choo Sangiin
nationalist members were not altogether stifled. Also, their enthusiasm, often
led by Soekarno as chairman, about the defence of their homeland and the
measures they proposed were often beyond Japanese willingness to imple-
ment. However, later, when the fortunes of war disfavoured the Japanese,
Choo Sangiin nationalist members increasingly made demands for a proper
defence of their fatherland. In the third session of 8 to 11 May 1944, they first

104   Soekarno's radio address was serialized in *Asia Raya*, 4-8 February 2604(1944).
105   Jansen 1988:270, also referred to by Houben 1996:131.
106   *Asia Raya*, 30 January 2604(1944):1.

eliminated the opening oath phrase about their responsibilities until final victory was reached, and then proposed that real weapons instead of bamboo sticks be provided to the general public,[107] while in the sixth and seventh sessions of 11 to 17 November 1944, and of 21 to 26 February 1945, proposals were made about elite corps such as the Muslim Hizboellah and the nationalist Barisan Pelopor being properly trained and equipped with modern weapons. In that latter session veteran nationalist Woerjaningrat predicted that Java would soon be invaded by the Allies and that armed struggle against them would ensue. So he moved to adopt the slogan 'Merdeka atau mati' (Independence or death).[108]

The impact of the Jawa Hokokai and the Tonarigumi

As to the new mass organization, it was named Jawa Hokokai or Himpoenan Kebaktian Rakjat (People's Loyalty Association), but it was mostly referred to by its Japanese name. The leader of it was not an Indonesian politician but the Gunseikan, Major General Kokubu, who assumed the presidency of the Jawa Hokokai, and the Somubucho, Major General Yamamoto, the vice-presidency, with below these two Japanese dignitaries a Choo honbu (central headquarters) manned by Poetera executives. Another prominent Japanese civilian, also serving as an adviser to Lieutenant General Harada, was Hayashi, a former ambassador to Brazil, who chaired the advisory council, with Hatta as vice-chairman. Soekarno was made Choo honbucho, head of the central headquarters, with the following serving below him: Abikoesno, Soedjono, Soemanang Soerjowinoto, Samsoedin, Oto Iskandardinata, Soekardjo Wirjopranoto, Soerjo, Sofwan, Sartono, Anwar Tjokroaminoto, Soenarjo, Soewandi and Datoek Djamin. But the truth is that Jawa Hokokai was merely a replica of the Japanese Taisei Yokusan Kai, the Imperial Rule Assistance Organization, founded in 1940 in order to get rid of political parties. An ominous sign indeed. Soekarno as Choo honbucho was in fact crushed in the middle between the Gunsei at the capital city level and the *pangrèh praja*, the latter now in sole charge of the rural organization of the Jawa

---

[107] *Asia Raya*, 8 May 2604(1944):1; the Japanese at once responded that delegates should feel responsible for aiding the population in their own way, *Asia Raya*, 8 May 2604(1944):4; *Jawa Shinbun*, 11 May 2604(1944).
[108] For the sixth session see *Kan Po*, no. 55:13-5; *Asia Raya*,17 November 2604(1944):2. For the seventh session *Jawa Shinbun*, 25 February 2605(1945); *Kan Po*, no. 62:45; *Asia Raya*, 27 February 2605(1945). Dahm 1969:285-6 concludes that between the Muslim Hizboellah and the nationalist Barisan Pelopor no genuine rivalry existed; he cites Soekarno in his 'Erat-seerat-eratnja' (As close as possible), printed in *Asia Raya*, 21 October 2604 (1944):2, who held that 'unity between Muslim and nationalist leaders is firm as a rock'.

Hokokai. Dahm attests that 'Sukarno was thus only an organ for the execution of orders, shackled from above as well as below'. As Hatta somewhat cynically has it, 'the *pangrèh praja* were very pleased with the Jawa Hokokai since under it, from the *kabupaten* [regency] level on down, they would be in charge', and they felt 'that their desire to become the leaders of the popular movement had finally been fulfilled'.[109] No wonder that Soekarno and Hatta, fearing that they were losing an organ for expressing the Indonesian national identity, tried their utmost to persuade the Japanese to maintain Poetera as a subservient association to the Jawa Hokokai in order to at least save some semblance of that identity. In this quest, which was unsuccessful, they further worried about the fact that the Japanese had made no real attempt to turn Jawa Hokokai into a spontaneous people's movement or organization. Worse, in their eyes, was that it was polluted, since Chinese, Arabs and even Eurasians were allowed to join it. It was exactly this multi-racial character that deprived the nationalist elite, despite the many nominally prominent positions assigned to it in the Jawa Hokokai's leading organs, of an exclusively nationalist forum. In addition, the Jawa Hokokai comprised all other organizations and associations previously created by the Gunsei, particularly the women's and youth groups, in which nationalist control and influence were as yet rather weak.[110] Particularly Japanization – Japanese was taught at all school levels together with doses of the Japanese spirit – and militarization were to leave deep imprints on the younger Indonesian generation. Indonesia's Java-based youth, whom the Gunsei had eagerly wooed and then made to be quite comfortable in a number of organizational associations, all designed to break down the seclusion of the Javanese *desa*, was to provide the Gunsei with an army of young and keen cooperators. Consequently, the younger generation was a vital group that was to experience the tidings of a new era with continuing relish. So, in the various youth associations and in the far more important paramilitary and military units, new youthful leaders were gradually coming to the fore. This nucleus was to be quite indispensable in the post-war struggle for Indonesian independence.

As to the Gunsei's disenchantment with Poetera, that stemmed mainly from the growing belief it cherished of Poetera's so-called self-serving nationalism clashing more and more with the notions of the *pangrèh praja* and those

---

[109] Sato 1994:71-2; Sluimers 1998:353; Friend 1988:96; for Hatta's remarks see Hatta 1971: 63-4, and for Dahm's Dahm 1969:269. For Kokubu and Yamamoto elaborating on the Jawa Hokokai see Brugmans et al. 1960:562-3; the latter source also refers to Taisei Yokusan Kai, and an unnamed Indonesian who posited that with the central and local advisory councils being established and the Seinendan and Keibodan never put under Poetera control, and with the rural economy and administration being managed by the *pangrèh praja*, Poetera was doomed to be absorbed by Jawa Hokokai.

[110] Benda 1958:153; *Asia Raya*, 30 January 2604(1944):1.

of the racial minority groups. Even Hatta realized that ultimately Poetera was more burdened by its failures than by its achievements. All that, according to the Gunsei, had turned Poetera into a divisive rather than a unifying force. Therefore, the Gunsei considered it not quite capable any longer of achieving the desired joint coordination of the entire Javanese community. Hence, it was decided that a novel mass movement for patriotic service should emerge, in which all the Javanese inhabitants together with other racial minority groups would duly participate in mobilizing all resources in order to construct a Djawa Baroe, while at the same time achieving ultimate victory. As Major General Yamamoto later recalled:

> Poetera had several flaws. It was a movement of Indonesians exclusively. Other ethnic minorities did not join it. Moreover, it opposed the indigenous administrative officials [the *pangrèh praja*], which resulted in the common people alienating themselves from these administrators, which in turn made it extremely difficult for the masses to be impregnated with Japanese political thought patterns. [...] Therefore, I felt keenly the need for forming an organization rooted in the masses, and so after negotiations with representatives of all races and classes the Jawa Hokokai was organized.[111]

Unlike the Gerakan Tiga A and Poetera, which the Japanese were now fond of labelling somewhat disparagingly 'native movements', the Jawa Hokokai was plainly an organization headed by Gunsei dignitaries. Here, nationalists of Soekarno's and Hatta's ilk were side-tracked and merely used as the necessary window dressing for the Gunsei-inspired motives of the Jawa Hokokai. At that time the Gunsei's greatest worry was the fear of Java being drawn still closer into the orbit of an Allied counter-offensive. So the major purpose of the Gunsei-led Jawa Hokokai was not merely to jointly coordinate the entire Javanese community, but to gear it up speedily into a structure of total war to ward off Allied forces when they came. Structurally, the Jawa Hokokai, therefore, was closely patterned after the pyramidal line-up of the government bureaucracy, with Jawa Hokokai branches established at all administrative levels from the centre down to the village. To strengthen this huge administrative machinery, the already established Tonarigumi (neighbourhood association, *rukun tetangga* in Indonesian) was turned into the lowest substructure of both the Jawa Hokokai and the government bureaucracy, but this time on a far more massive scale. As Shigeru Sato (1994:72) attests, 123,000 associations consisting of 1,600,000 households and 8,200,000 inhabitants had been established by the end of February 1944, while by June 1944 the network was near completion in all parts of Java except the cities of Djakarta and Cheribon, comprising 554,033 associations and 9,338,212 house-

---

111   Brugmans et al. 1960:561; also cited in Sato 1994:56.

holds. He concludes 'that Jawa Hokokai was now equipped with the structural foundation through which to reach every household in Java'. Benda
(1958:154) asserts that:

> The Tonari Gumi doubtless constituted the most ambitious Japanese endeavor at
> penetrating to the Indonesian village, and of mobilizing the *tani* for the war effort.
> Hitherto only the *kiyayi*, the spiritual village leaders, had been drawn into the orbit
> of Japanese propaganda; now the military administration went one step further
> in organizing the population itself in small groups within the villages and town-
> ships, which were to become the lowest units in the governmental pyramid.

Concurrently with these efforts, the Gunsei, through the Jawa Hokokai, tried
to win support on another home front as well, that of religion. Attention was
given here to the rural *kiyayi* and *ulama* (Muslim teachers and law experts)
already organized in Masjoemi, a body which was now closely cooperating
with the Jawa Hokokai but, unlike Poetera, retained organizational control
of its chapters. Many of the Muslim teachers and law experts headed rural
Tonarigumi as *kumichoo* (leader of some ten to twenty households) at the
village level. These *kumichoo* in the *desa* were responsible in turn to the *desa*
head, the *lurah* (*ko-cho* in Japanese).

Both Harry Benda and Leo Jansen have analysed the Gunsei's motives
for winning Muslim support. Jansen believes that, whereas Dutch colonial
policy vis-à-vis the Muslims was one of keeping matters as peaceful as possible so as not to stir them up politically, the Japanese followed Hoesein Djajadiningrat's dictum of 'one cannot stir up the people without Islam'. Whereas
the Dutch in their time respected freedom of religion and demanded that
ulama and *kiyayi* not meddle in politics, the Japanese policy, while predominantly negative, at least gave the rural people some semblance of religious
freedom. For Jansen as well, Japanese meddling in the Muslim religious
schools was two-sided. A policy of arresting *kiyayi* for the seditious language
they used was alternated with recruiting *kiyayi* and *ulama* for three-month
saturation courses about Asia Raya and Djawa Baroe concepts before sending them back to their rural areas (Jansen 1988:261-2).

Benda, on the other hand, posits that as long as the Allied enemy remained
distant, the identification of Greater East Asia and Islam had been difficult
to achieve. However, by the onset of 1944 matters had drastically changed.
Not only had Japan lost the strategic initiative in the southwest Pacific, but at
home Poetera had been absorbed by the Jawa Hokokai, while Masjoemi was
attached to the Jawa Hokokai without losing its organizational independence.
For Masjoemi, always far better represented in Java's rural areas than Poetera
ever was, new exciting perspectives loomed. With the reordering instituted
in early 1944 and with the Gunsei having embarked on a more direct control
of Javanese life, the Gunsei sought and obtained explicit Islamic support for

both the Jawa Hokokai and the rurally based branches of the Tonarigumi. In Djakarta, after the Gunsei on 1 March 1944 had appointed Masjoemi chairman Hasjim Asj'ari as *komon* (adviser) to the Gunseikan Major General Kokubu, on 17 May 1944 the president of the Court for Islamic Affairs ruled that the Jawa Hokokai and the Tonarigumi were both in complete agreement with the teachings of Islam.[112]

In achieving explicit approval for its new measures from the capital-based Islamic central leadership, the Gunsei, as Jansen notes, did not ignore the rurally based *ulama* and *kyayi*. The Gunsei's ambition was to mobilize the *tani* (farmers) even more intensively for the war effort. According to Benda, therefore, the *lurah* (*ku-cho*, in Japanese), 'the lowest grade officials on Java, found themselves drawn into the era of the *latihan'* (exercise or drill), a drill where incessant demands for increased food production and a ruthlessly enforced requisitioning of rice combined with accelerated inflation due to the harsh Gunsei-inspired monetary policies. Benda (1958:155) concludes that all that rendered 'the *tani*'s lot – in the villages or as forced laborer (*romusha*) – ever harder'. All these drills, together with the strict measures as well as the ongoing centralization among the Muslim community, did not prevent a serious Nahdatoel Oelama-inspired popular rebellion breaking out in Tasikmalaja/ Singaparna on 18 February 1944.

Socio-political developments prior to the 7 September 1944 Koiso declaration

In the rebellion, the people of Singaparna village, near Tasikmalaja in the southeast region of the Priangan residency, took up arms against the Japanese. Led by a Nahdatoel Oelama orthodox *kiyayi* and head of a local *pesantren* named Zainal Moestafa, the decision to rebel was arrived at during a mass meeting of some 4,000 led by Moestafa, now also acknowledged as a *wali Allah* (representative of Allah). In fact, it was a prime example of grassroots power confronting infidel rulers. Historian Muhammad Dimyati has compared the Singaparna rebellion to the so-called Afdeeling B Sarekat Islam revolt of 1917 where, just as with Moestafa, violent outbursts of peasant protest crystallized around local Islamic leadership. The spearing to death of a Japanese Kenpeitai army officer on a pole in Singaparna caused the Kenpeitai to take violent action and to arrest the *wali Allah* and some 400 of his followers, with local crowds then engaging in an attempt to free Moestafa and his supporters. During these fights, some Japanese were killed and there were huge casualties among the local peasants who failed to free Moestafa

---

[112]   *Asia Raya*, 1 March and 18 May 2604(1944) for these events.

and his followers.[113] Having thus taken dreadful local vengeance, the Gunsei, duly startled by the events, issued an official statement three weeks after the rebellion. This official release, though filled with righteous indignation and ample warning to the people, avoided putting any general blame on Muslim prominents.[114] Masjoemi emissaries were sent by the Gunsei to Singaparna after release of the official statement to pacify Muslim feelings locally. It was to serve as well as a sign that the Gunsei still trusted Islamic leaders and the *ulama* as a whole. Yet the Gunsei could not resist a divide-and-rule ploy by blaming local district *pangrèh praja* for the grassroots disorders of early 1944. The *guncho* (or *wedono*) of Singaparna was punished and dismissed, while the *kencho* (regent, or *bupati*) of Tasikmalaja, Raden Toemenggoeng Aria Wiradipoetra, and three *guncho* were allowed to resign at their own request with forfeiture of income and pension.[115]

As to other *pangrèh praja* still in office, they were ordered to assist Muslim leaders in the drive for greater production in the war effort, while the Gunsei on 5 March 1944 decreed regional sections for religious (Islamic) affairs (*shomuka*) to be erected. They were to be established in all the residencies, the Djakarta municipality and the Central Javanese sultanates. These regional religious sections were to establish closer contact with the Muslim community and to foster the idea that the Gunsei policy was still one of honouring Islam. In fact, the Gunsei, along with the new *shomuka* sections, granted some considerable degree of home rule to Muslims at the expense of *pangrèh praja* administrative control.

Soekarno himself also saw this as an opportunity to question the ability of the *pangrèh praja* to lead the common people.[116] He and Hatta had viewed the *pangrèh praja* with scepticism from the outset. So the losers in this reordering of religious affairs were the *pangrèh praja*. The *kencho* (regents) and all other members of the *pangrèh praja* were made aware that all Gunsei orders related to the Islamic faith and customs needed to be smoothly carried out. As to Moestafa, he was officially declared insane and considered to have committed acts at variance with the true tenets of the Islamic faith. It saved him from being executed, a Gunsei gesture to spare the feelings of the Muslim community. However, of the close to 400 Moestafa followers detained, 82

---

[113] Benda 1958:160; Dimyati 1951:16; Zwaan 1981:180; De Bruin 1982:80-1; De Jong 1969-91, XIb:556; Jansen 1988:274.

[114] For the official release see Brugmans et al. 1960:449-50; *Kan Po*, no. 39, March 2604(1944): 28-30.

[115] *Kan Po*, no. 42, 10 May 2604(1944) and *Kan Po*, no. 43, 25 May 2604(1944); for Tasikmalaja's *kencho* see also Gunseikanbu 1944a:110.

[116] Soekarno's comments in *Asia Raya*, 1 March 2604(1944):2. His criticism was also evident in a radio address titled 'Melatih diri' (Exercise yourselves), urging the *pangrèh praja* to seek closer union with the common *rakyat*, serialized in *Asia Raya*, 20-22 April 2604(1944).

were sentenced to death by the Djakarta military court.[117] Soekarno, however, in a speech on 9 March 1944, may well have had Singaparna in mind
when he told his audience that 'before the curtain falls on the Greater East
Asia War, we as well will have proved to the whole world that we can fight
like a tiger to defend our homeland and our people'. Bernhard Dahm saw the
connection, commenting that Soekarno's audiences, always alert for hidden
meanings, were thus left to decide who was really the opponent, the Allies
or the Japanese. Dahm concluded that the Japanese on 9 March might well
have recalled 'an event that had occurred scarcely three weeks earlier – the
first sizeable rebellion, Muslim-engineered, by the rural population against
the Japanese occupation'.[118]

Yet this was not all. During the main harvesting season of 1944 an even
larger rural rebellion on a far wider scale took place in the Indramajoe *ken*
(regency), one of the major rice-producing areas on the north coast of West
Java, starting in April 1944 and continuing to August. Both Aiko Kurasawa
and Shigeru Sato – the most recent chroniclers of Java's wartime plight in a
socio-economic sense – attest that the Indramajoe uprisings not only lasted
for several months but spread from the east at Kaplongan village, to the
extreme west of the *ken* at Bugis village and its environs. They both also feel
that these rural uprisings had very much to do with the strict local official
demands to requisition rice from the farmers. *Desa* officials such as the *jaga-
baja* (security officers) and policemen were killed by the angry farmers in the
requisition process, which somewhat ironically was called *padi sukarela* (vol-
untary paddy). The Gunsei reacted quickly, dispatching troops and policemen to the eastern part of the *ken*. They finally suppressed the Kaplongan
uprising, but only after two *kiyayi* from neighbouring villages had mediated
and calmed down the farmers. Still the Indramajoe *ken* was far from being
peaceful: rural unrest was followed by outright resistance, and violence
moved like a chain reaction westward to reach Bugis village and other
nearby *desa*. The process here, as in Kaplongan, was that households had to
surrender all their paddy rice except for 10 kilograms. Again some district
heads and their bodyguards were killed, and again the Japanese attempted
to combine placation with outright repression. Only by August 1944 were
the rebellions finally over, after a large-scale bloody repression and a heavy

---

[117]   Benda 1958:160-2; Pakpahan 1948:55; De Bruin 1982:82; De Jong 1969-91 XIb:556.
[118]   *Asia Raya*, 10 March 2604(1944):2. For Dahm's comment see Dahm 1969:270-1, though
we remain puzzled that he does not refer at all to the far greater rebellion occurring in the
Indramajoe *ken*. Neither does Benda 1958, apart from some obscure references to it on p. 268,
note 46, pp. 270-1, note 62 and 63, while he also overlooks that Dr Hoesein Djajadiningrat on 1
August 1944 was sacked as Shomubu-cho, being 'the innocent victim' of both the Singaparna
and Indramajoe debacles, Kanahele 1967:303, note 17. De Jong 1969-91, XIb:940 also refers to a
sacking.

toll of hundreds of farmer deaths had been extracted by Japanese forces and Indonesian police in the Bugis area. Still farmers' anger against local Chinese rice dealers – whom they suspected of hoarding rice – continued. So Chinese shops were looted and Chinese women raped, even long after the rebellion had been crushed (Sato 1994:144-5, 148; Kurasawa 1988a:646-71, 1988b:95-7, 100-3, 1983:52-72). Kurasawa concludes that the widespread shortage of food due to the Japanese military's rice requisitioning may well have contributed to these violent uprisings. But she also reveals that it was not the poor peasants who initiated the rebellions but rather wealthy farmers who owned between 20 and 100 hectares of land. Some small farmers who were dependent on wealthy farmers joined the rebellion in the wake of the *pangrèh praja* attempting to requisition rice from these large landowners. Shigeru Sato concludes that while some of the poor farmers joined the rebellions, the riots were essentially a struggle between the *pangrèh praja* and exceptionally rich farmers, a view which is partly shared by yet another source.[119]

This source is Raden Prawoto Soemodilogo, an adviser (*sanyo*) attached to the Jawa Hokokai who was charged by the Gunsei to write a report as to how Islamic fanaticism or other factors were to blame for the Indramajoe upheavals. That Raden Prawoto Soemodilogo was selected had to do with the considerable experience he had gained in the past. First, as a Volksraad delegate charged with *pangrèh praja* affairs during the Dutch colonial era, he had at that time also served as *patih* of Indramajoe for one and a half years and therefore had first-hand knowledge of the area. Though an aristocrat himself and a former member of the *pangrèh praja*, in his report handed in to the Gunsei in October 1944 he clearly put the blame on the *pangrèh praja*. Raden Prawoto Soemodilogo labelled them as arrogant, arbitrary and ignorant of the living conditions of the poor farmers. He also accused them of receiving bribes from Chinese rice-millers, and assisting the millers to buy huge amounts of rice at low prices. Like Kurasawa, Prawoto Soemodilogo also observed that Indramajoe farmers were well aware of the huge rice levies, and of the fact that these were much lighter in neighbouring regencies. And so Indramajoe farmers came to hate their *pangrèh praja* and did their utmost to get their paddy rice out of the *ken* before the rural officials could collect it. Due to the heavy levies and the large-scale exporting of paddy rice out of the *ken*, many people, mainly children and old people, were dying of malnutrition. And so, while the rebellion had been brutally suppressed, the widespread shortage of food not only in the Indramajoe *ken* but also increasingly beyond it, caused growing concern in nationalist circles. In the wake of the Koiso declaration, the Council of Advisers – chaired by Soekarno, and

---

[119]   Kurasawa 1983:68; see also her *kesimpulan* (conclusion) in Kurasawa 1988b:105-7; Sato 1994: 148.

with Prawoto Soemodilogo as a member – would again investigate the rice requisition issue, in view of the poor harvest and the growing famine.[120] But before we discuss these developments we need to look at some other events taking place in Djakarta.

In the capital city during the third session of the Choo Sangiin from 8 to 11 May 1944, nationalist members – through senior delegate Soekardjo Wirjopranoto – recommended the establishment of a special youth corps, the Barisan Pelopor (Vanguard Corps, Suishintai in Japanese), which was to be placed under Jawa Hokokai control. The motives for the nationalist delegates were clear: from the outset of the session they wanted to regain the ground they had lost ever since the establishment of the Jawa Hokokai. Naturally they used the need for the defence of the fatherland, aware as they were of the fact that the Java-based Sixteenth Army at this time was quite short of adequate manpower. Also, in spite of the sensational war-zone successes being claimed in local newspapers, they must have noticed that the war-zone perimeter was gradually shifting to Dai Nippon's disadvantage. The Japanese had surrendered positions in New Guinea, American forces landed in Hollandia on 22 April 1944, and on 2 May the Dutch tricolour was hoisted and the Netherlands Indies Civil Administration located there. Also the Solomons, the Marshalls, and then on 9 July 1944 Saipan, the most vital point in Dai Nippon's outer defence perimeter, came into American hands. In the wake of all the military defeats suffered in New Guinea, with Biak falling to the Allies on 20 June 1944, Choo Sangiin delegates Mr Raden Soenarko, Raden Pandji Soeroso, Raden Roeslan Wongsokoesoemo and Hadikoesoemo proposed that military training with real weapons should be provided to the general public as widely as possible. As to the Barisan Peloper, in the usual reply to the Saiko Shikikan, Lieutenant General Kumakichi Harada, it was recommended 'to form at once a Vanguard Corps under the auspices of the Jawa Hokokai with mature young men who are fully aware of the duty of achieving final victory and are further prepared to sacrifice themselves in that struggle'.[121] In spite of this recommendation, it took over three months

---

[120] Prawoto Soemodilogo, 'Menindjau keadaan di Indramajoe dari djoeroesan ekonomi, bagian kesatoe', pp. 4, 6-7, and 'Menindjau keadaan di Indramajoe-ken, politiek pemerintah, bagian kedoea', pp. 1-3, 5-7, in ARA, Algemene Secretarie, Eerste Zending 25, also cited by De Jong 1969-91, XIb:557 and by Sato 1994:149-53. As to further developments on the paddy rice deliveries and the accompanying mishaps, these were discussed for the first time by a new Dewan Sanyo chaired by Soekarno on 16 December 1944 and again on 27 December, with no Japanese attending, De Jong 1969-91, XIb:558-9 and Kanahele 1967:168.

[121] For Soekardjo Wirjopranoto's recommendation see *Kan Po*, no. 43, 25 May 2604(1944):29; Soekardjo Wirjopranoto also elaborated his views on the Barisan Pelopor in 'Barisan Pelopor dan persahabatan' (The Vanguard Corps and friendship), *Asia Raya*, 19 May 2604(1944):1. On Soenarko and his followers see *Jawa Shinbun*, 11 May 2604(1944); as to the reply to Lieutenant General Harada about the Barisan Pelopor, see *Asia Raya*, 19 May 2604(1944):1.

before the Japanese finally approved the establishment of the paramilitary Barisan Pelopor, a decision probably arrived at because with Saipan in American hands communications with the Nanyo (the Southern Regions) were severely disrupted.

The immediate socio-political impact of Koiso succeeding Tojo as premier of Japan

In Japan itself, repercussions in the wake of the Saipan debacle had been even more severe, with General Tojo resigning as premier on 17 July 1944 and General Kuniaki Koiso, the governor-general of Korea, succeeding Tojo as premier. It seems that Japanese policy-making elements at that dramatic juncture went so far as to urge peace negotiations to be opened. Premier Koiso, though personally believing that the war was lost, still committed his government to continuing the war. In the wake of this decision, Indonesian policy matters were reappraised on the top level, with elements of the army, the navy and government officials debating the Indonesian independence issue. The army delegates for the first time were in favour of Indonesian independence, with the navy delegates finding it premature. Navy delegates insisted that if the army and the Koiso government remained determined to grant independence, Java and Sumatra, under the jurisdiction of the Sixteenth and Twenty-Fifth Armies respectively, should be dealt with separately from the territory of the Kaigun (Navy). In this case the eastern outer islands of Indonesia – Borneo, Celebes, the Moluccas, and the Lesser Soenda Islands – would resort under the Southwest Area Fleet (Nansei Homen Kantai), with headquarters in Makassar. In spite of the navy's rather adamant position, the Supreme Council meeting on 4 to 5 September 1944 ratified a new policy granting independence to the East Indies in the near future (Kanahele 1967: 161-2).

Meanwhile, in Java, on 15 August 1944, the installation of the Barisan Pelopor was at last officially announced, though only on 1 November 1944 was it finally established. After that date other paramilitary organizations were established, such as the Barisan Mati (Suicide Corps, Jibakutai in Japanese) on 8 December 1944, obviously inspired by the last-ditch stand of Japanese *kamikaze* suicide pilots at that time, and the Masjoemi's Hizboellah (Allah's Army, Kaikyo Seinen Teishintai in Japanese) on 15 December 1944. With the nationalist-inspired Barisan Pelopor – led by nationalist leaders under the guidance of Soekarno, with Soekarno having worked out the details for the structure of it – the nationalists had achieved their first real success since the establishment of the Jawa Hokokai, although the creation of the Hizboellah was still a sign that the Gunsei was attempting to counterbalance increased nationalist strength. Soekarno, seeing through this ploy, maintained in an essay called 'Erat-seerat-eratnja' that 'the eternal unity between the leaders of the Muslims and the leaders of the nationalists is firm as a rock'. Also, in the seventh session of the Choo Sangiin, both Muslim and nationalist delegates claimed that the unity between the two new organizations was as solid as Soekarno had suggested. As to the central leadership of the Barisan Pelopor, there was only one Japanese adviser, which was totally different from the situation for the central leadership of the Seinendan, for instance, which was almost completely in Japanese hands.[122]

However, before these paramilitary units were consolidated, the Indonesian leadership, whether nationalist, aristocratic, or Muslim, was quite surprised, even taken aback, when on 7 September 1944 Prime Minister General Koiso of Japan made the following rather vague statement about a future independent status:

> As to the East Indies, Japan has allowed the East Indies inhabitants to participate in politics according to their wishes. The inhabitants throughout the East Indies have continuously endeavoured to carry out the Greater East Asia War, recognizing the real intention of Japan. They have also been cooperating remarkably well with the military government there. In view of these facts we declare here that we intend to recognize their independence in the future in order to ensure the eternal happiness of the East Indies race.[123]

And yet, as Kanahele saw it, the promise 'remained conspicuously vague in one important respect – no deadline was set other than the definite future' (Kanahele 1967:163). De Jong (1969-91, XIb:981) states that

> it could hardly be vaguer, and yet Soekarno and his following may have assessed it as a step forward since Japan did acknowledge that it was the final target of his [Soekarno's] policy all along. Moreover (and that was made public as well on September 7) the song 'Indonesia Raja' and the red and white banner were permitted, and these were certainly not the symbols of an independent East Indies, let alone an independent Java, but the symbols of an independent Indonesia!

It seems that the basis for Koiso's concept had been laid by Hayashi as early as 20 March 1944, when he sent a rather lengthy memorandum to the Gaimusho (Japanese Ministry of Foreign Affairs). Noting that the war was in its third year and acknowledging the urgency of fully utilizing the resources of the southern occupied territories, he warned that peace and order in the occu-

---

[122]   Nugroho Notosusanto 1979:46-7; as to Soekarno's 'Erat-seerat-eratnja' (As close as possible) see *Asia Raya*, 21 October 2604(1944):2; and for the Muslims and nationalists vouching unity in the Choo Sangiin see *Asia Raya*, 27 February 2605(1945):2.
[123]   Brugmans et al. 1960:580; an Indonesian version of the promise appeared in *Asia Raya*, 8 September 2604(1944):1.

pied areas needed to be secured and the hearts of the local inhabitants won. He reviewed the dire circumstances especially in crowded Java, Madoera and Bali. 'There is no mistaking the fact that with the passing of time and confronted with the hardships of daily life arising from shortages of food and clothing, an increasing number of natives have become disillusioned.' As to the prospects for 1944, he considered these 'becoming progressively worse', with 'shortages of daily necessities having increasingly worsened'. Familiar as he was with Indonesian socio-political aspirations – he had chaired the so-called Adat Committee since late 1942 and served as an adviser (*sanyo*) – he was in far more intimate contact with Indonesian leaders than other highly placed Java-based Japanese authorities thought proper. Even before chairing the Adat Committee, Hayashi praised Soekarno to Saiko Shikikan Imamura as having an 'admirable genius for eloquence with a knack for moving his audiences to deeply felt passions'.[124] Also, Hayashi shared, together with the Djakarta-based Kaigun representative Rear Admiral Maeda, ideas which were far more progressive than those held by most members of the Japan-based and Java-based Japanese establishments. He and Maeda for some time believed that Japan was hurting its own interests by not offering independence to Indonesia, or at least Java, as it had done with Wang Ching Wei's China, Henri Pu'i's Manchukuo, José Laurel's Philippines and Ba Maw's Burma. He posited that 'Japan differentiated in her treatment of Burma, the Philippines and Java' and that moreover there was 'increased suspicion that Japan [was to] assume direct control of Java together with the Malay Peninsula'. He argued that such a prospect of the 'increased deprivation in livelihood being more and more aggravated' needed to be avoided at all costs. He concluded that Java, having a 'geographic and historic cultural homogeneity' and therefore holding 'a unique position in the South Seas', should, after some proper training, be granted independence sooner rather then later, 'for delay would only bring regrets'. In an attached supplement, Hayashi listed the following proposed measures to be taken by the Gunsei: increased efforts in secondary and tertiary education; the diffusion of Japanese language and culture; increase of Indonesian political participation in the Choo Sangiin and residency assemblies; lifting the ban on the song 'Indonesia Raja' and the red and white banner, and an increase in the number of higher-echelon indigenous officials.[125]

---

[124] For Hayashi's praise of Soekarno see Brugmans et al. 1960:480.
[125] For the Hayashi memorandum see Benda, Irikura and Kishi 1965:244-8, document 65. For comments on the memorandum, calling the author 'the Sixteenth Army's top adviser', see De Bruin 1982a:164-5, also De Jong 1969-91, XIb:979-80. See *Kan Po*, no. 51, 8 September 2604 (1944):11 for Harada's announcement about 'Indonesia Raja' and the red and white banner. The chief of staff of the Seventh Army Group in Shonanto (Singapore), showing his disdain for the promise, proclaimed on 7 September that it was prohibited to refer in any way to the time of

Domestic events in the wake of Koiso's promise

One can easily conclude that in Java and Madoera from 7 September 1944 onwards socio-political developments gained a remarkable momentum, with Soekarno and his followers playing an increasingly dominant role. At first, Soekarno was completely taken by surprise when he was informed by Major General Yamamoto of Koiso's promise, but he may also have been disappointed by its vagueness. And yet he was surprised that the proclamation referred to independence for all of Indonesia, after years of total Japanese rejection of that territorial concept. Soekarno must have mused about the many times he had spoken of Indonesia, while Prime Minister Tojo in July 1943 and November of that same year had only spoken of Java. So Soekarno must have sensed that it was largely due to his own dogged efforts that the wider territorial concept was finally adopted by Tokyo as well. On the other hand, and this was soon borne out by the Java Gunsei reactions, Soekarno was quite aware that the promise was not entirely altruistically inspired. He sensed that it was far more aimed at extracting even more efforts from the Indonesian people in the common struggle still to come. This soon became clear, with the Gunsei accelerating quotas for military auxiliaries, labourers, rice and other foodstuffs, as well as defensive construction works. In return, Soekarno used these as leverage for extracting even more concrete concessions for his own side. He adopted the initial stance of hailing the Koiso promise as one of path-breaking importance. On 8 September 1944, he led a thank-you manifestation with representatives of all sectors of the population at the palace of the Saiko Shikikan, Lieutenant General Harada. To the latter's warning that 'the East Indies would never reach independence in the case of a Japanese defeat in war and that therefore the Indonesian people needed to double their efforts to support Japan to make victory possible', Soekarno responded that 'together with Dai Nippon we will live or die until ultimately victory is reached'.[126] In the evening, using the Djakarta radio broadcasting facilities, he addressed first the Japanese and then his own people. To the former he promised, as he had to Harada that morning, 'that since Dai Nippon has promised the entire Indonesian people that they will be independent in the near future, he and his people will fight to the death to make final victory possible'. To his own people Soekarno said 'that the dawn

---

granting independence, to the size of the area, or to the future political status of the East Indies. Also, no great changes in the political and economic structures were to be expected. However, the national consciousness needed to be upgraded as well as defence and the cooperation with the Japanese authorities in order to mould Japan and Java into an indivisible unity. The red and white banner, the 'Indonesia Raja' anthem, and the use of the term 'the Indonesian people' were all allowed, Brugmans et al. 1960:582.

[126]   *Asia Raya*, 8 September 2604(1944):1.

has arrived and that in the near future all of Indonesia will be independent, but that in order to reach that goal, victory needs to be secured and America, England, and the Dutch defeated, since if not, the latter will return and suppression will then surely recur'. So he urged his people 'to be together with Dai Nippon in life and death until we are independent, and with Dai Nippon in life and death after we are independent'.[127] He was to repeat this pledge at a special 12 September 1944 session of the Choo Sangiin, while on a subsequent session of the Choo Sangiin of 12 to 17 November 1944 he issued a Pantja Dharma (Five Obligations for Indonesians) resolution:

1. In this life-and-death struggle together with the other peoples of Greater East Asia, we stand firmly united with Dai Nippon and are firmly prepared for sacrifice, since this is indeed a struggle in defence of right and truth;
2. We are laying the foundations of an Indonesian nation that will be independent, united, sovereign, just and prosperous, a state that will give credit to Dai Nippon and that moreover will live as a faithful member within the orbit of the Greater East Asian community;
3. We strive with unfeigned ardour for fame and splendour, as we guard and exalt our own civilization and culture, while promoting Asian culture in order to bring its impact to bear on the other cultures of the world;
4. We therefore serve – in close fraternity with the other peoples of Greater East Asia – our own nation and people with undeterred loyalty, and in continuous accountability before our own Almighty God;
5. We will also struggle with ardent longing toward a lasting peace throughout the world, a peace based upon the brotherhood of all humanity and one that conforms to the ideal of Hakko Ichiu [Hakko Ichiu literally means 'Eight corners of the world under one roof', referring to Japanese leadership over Greater East Asia].[128]

Soekarno must have perceived this opportunity as an avenue of escape from the humiliations he had endured over the past two years. He was keenly aware that the promise of independence, the prospect of creating an independent Indonesia, and the use of the red and white banner and the national anthem, while undeniably quite important, were still only partial gains on the road for his nationalists to ultimately secure genuine authority. Only such a stance would allow him in the not-too-distant future to seriously prepare the conditions for genuine Indonesian independence. And so he began to chart the way toward that lofty goal with a greater degree of personal confidence. The Japanese must have sensed this as well, and so with further losses

---

[127]   For Soekarno's radio addresses, *Asia Raya*, 8 September 2604(1944):2. Both these texts were released by the Gunsei under the title *Perdjalanan kearah Indonesia Merdeka* (The road toward Indonesia's freedom) and spread as pamphlets from the air; *Asia Raya*, 12 September 2604(1944): 2 for Soekarno's statement to the Choo Sangiin special session, also Brugmans et al. 1960:581-2.
[128]   *Kan Po*, no. 55, 25 November 2604(1944); *Asia Raya*, 25 November 2604(1944):2.

all along their battle fronts and the Gunsei not knowing where the Allied foe would strike next, they consolidated the youth paramilitary units, erected a Dewan Sanyo, an all-Indonesian Council of Advisers, and enlarged the proportion of Indonesian members in the Choo Sangiin. The recommendations of veteran adviser Hayashi were thus followed almost to the letter. So in the wake of the Koiso declaration, the total number of advisers (*sanyo*) was boosted to 19, with all but one being prominent nationalists, and the Choo Sangiin to a total of 62, with some 12 prominent nationalists being among the 22 newly added. As L. de Jong has it, the new Dewan Sanyo seemed to be the forerunner of a Soekarno-led cabinet, while the enlarged Choo Sangiin could be seen as the forerunner of an Indonesian parliament.[129]

Forerunners or not, these establishments were to increasingly set their stamp upon socio-political issues. On 16 December 1944 the Dewan Sanyo met, without any Japanese attending, to discuss the quite dismal situation surrounding the distribution of rice. Noting that the Gunsei demanded 23% of the rice harvest, which was considered to be modest, the Dewan Sanyo was disturbed by reports of shortages everywhere, with some rural districts bordering on famine. Six members led by Oto Iskandardinata and seconded by Raden Prawoto Soemodilogo were charged with personally investigating the situation in a number of key residencies. Their report was presented at the fourth session of the Dewan Sanyo on 8 January 1945, and revealed a rather dismal story of serious misconduct among rich farmers and other influential persons handling the rice harvests. Also, the distribution of rice was not conducted properly, with no control at all at the rice-milling factories, run by Chinese owners or other well-connected merchants. Hatta proposed that all *desa* needed to be properly assessed and the remainder allocated to the administration without utilizing the rice-milling factories or rice merchants, since they were only out to serve their own interests and were not to be trusted. In the end, the Dewan Sanyo decided to urge the Gunsei to nationalize all milling factories and to raise the price of paddy rice. Only the latter request was honoured, and the price of paddy rice was raised from 4 cents per kilogram to 15. The Gunsei rejected nationalization, probably since the current situation suited its own interests. And so the Gunsei-imposed economic policy of strict autarchy within each residency created ever more hardships for the people. Most of these factors were revealed by the Iskandardinata investigation as Raden Prawoto Soemodilogo had earlier described in his Indramajoe reports, together with the analyses referred to above made by Kurasawa and Sato. Sato suggested that the Gunsei carry out the production increase campaign relentlessly, despite its obvious adverse effects, until the

---

[129]   De Jong 1969-91, XIb:558; also Benda 1970:203 posits that the nationalists, at the expense of the Muslim leaders, 'even formed a "shadow cabinet"'.

Japanese surrender (De Jong 1969-91, XIb:559-63; Sato 1994:179).

Meanwhile, on 1 March 1945, Lieutenant General Harada announced the formation of a Badan Oentoek Menjelidiki Oesaha-Oesaha Persiapan Kemerdekaan (Committee to Investigate Preparations for Independence), a commission which angered Soekarno and his following as yet another ploy by the Japanese to set their own slowly paced agenda. Tokyo had seen fit on 9 and 18 March, respectively, to proclaim Annamese and Cambodian independence.[130] In a radio address of 2 March 1945 Soekarno declared that he, like everybody else, had looked forward impatiently to the day of independence only to find himself fobbed off by yet another committee investigating the merits of independence. At the end of his address he cautioned the Japanese that Indonesian independence was not merely a question of a piece of paper but instead a serious matter of the survival of the fittest. He cited an old 1913 nationalist slogan utilized by his own erstwhile political mentors Tjipto Mangoenkoesoemo, Ernest Douwes Dekker and Soewardi Soerjaningrat: 'Rawé-rawé rantas, malang-malang poetoeng' (Along your road let nothing hamper you, and master every obstruction).[131]

Harada's commission, however, seems to have been prompted by yet another Indonesian-inspired open rebellion, this time caused by some Blitar-based PETA units sparked by a twenty-year-old platoon commander (*shodancho* in Japanese) named Soeprijadi. This youngster was remembered by his tutor captain Yanagawa as one of his best pupils at the PETA cadet school in Bogor (the so-called Bo-ei Giyogun Kanbu Kyoikutai). In an area where for some time the Blitar battalion (*daidan* in Japanese) had closely worked with *romusha* on a rather broad network of erecting fortifications, the battalion soldiers got increasingly upset about the wretched suffering experienced by the *romusha*. The male *romusha* were so decimated that female *romusha* were recruited to take their place. And so platoon leaders of the Blitar battalion, together with *shodancho* of nearby battalions in East Java, resolved that all these humiliations should stop, and they took part in efforts to end them. After several meetings led by Soeprijadi, rumours circulated that the battalion's ammunition would be sent to Soerabaja, save for a few rounds for training purposes. Soeprijadi and his followers were afraid that the Kenpeitai would get wind of the plot, and not awaiting the support of other platoons, Soeprijadi ordered his followers on 14 February 1945 to open fire on the Blitar-based Kenpeitai detachment and on the residence of the local *shidokan* (guidance officer of the Blitar battalion). After these brief encounters, Soeprijadi then moved his supporters to the Mount Keloed area, killing some Japanese along the way. In suppressing

---

[130] Kanahele 1967:192; *Asia Raya*, 12 and 19 March 2605(1945).
[131] Serialized in *Asia Raya*, 3, 5 and 6 March 2605(1945); Dahm 1969:290-1.

the revolt the Japanese used the classic KNIL colonial tactic of employing indigenous troops to confront their own compatriots, with for instance the Blitar battalion commander and his immediate assistant commander both being actively engaged to defeat Soeprijadi's short-lived rebellion. After some failed negotiations, the rebels were all captured and moved to Blitar and the ringleaders brought to Djakarta, where 55 men were brought to trial – six of them sentenced to death, three sentenced for life and six sentenced to 15 years of imprisonment. Soeprijadi was not among them; most likely he was captured by the Japanese in the vicinity of Blitar and tortured to death during interrogations.[132]

That the nationalists of Soekarno's and Hatta's ilk were emboldened by these events was aptly shown during the seventh Choo Sangiin session of 21 to 26 February 1945. Hatta demanded that recruitment of *romusha* be stopped and measures taken immediately to improve their miserable condition. As Soekarno was to stress somewhat later, in his 2 March 1945 radio address, the nationalist delegates during the session grumbled openly about the lingering reluctance on the part of the Gunsei to take meaningful steps toward the achievement of Indonesian independence. Attention was drawn to the economic hardships experienced by the rural masses and the urban workers. Other demands made by the nationalist delegates related to the need of extending proper universal military training to the indigenous masses. However, coming a few days after the events in Blitar, this issue of universal training of the masses found no response at all, the Gunsei understandably being afraid of the risks involved. The Gunsei allowed only an increase in PETA volunteers, as well as an increase in the membership of paramilitary organizations such as the nationalist Barisan Pelopor and Barisan Mati and the Masjoemi's Hizboellah. That the nationalist delegates thought of universal training at all probably had to do with their wish to prepare the people for the future struggle for independence in the sense of 'Merdeka atau mati' (Freedom or death). This prospect loomed ahead, now that American forces on 19 February 1945 had invaded Iwojima, the last strategic bastion in Japan's inner defence perimeter, and Manila had fallen into American hands on 23 February 1945. Also, within Indonesia's air space, Allied bombers had for some time been raiding cities in Java and Sumatra almost daily and at

---

[132] Nugroho Notosusanto 1979:120-3, 125. Kanahele 1967:185-8 is less sober in his analysis than the former and suggests that PETA grievances were caused by Japanese fraternizing with women belonging to PETA members. However, Sato 1994:196-7 maintains that Japanese oppression of the Indonesian work force caused the Blitar PETA to rebel. He adds some intimate detail about Soeprijadi's father, a Kertosono district head so mentally and physically exhausted after undergoing some harsh training at a Jakarta-based *pangrèh praja* camp, causing his son to lose his temper about the oppressive nature of the Japanese administration. Also, Soeprijadi's mother believes that all this was one of the causes for the Blitar PETA rebellion, led by her son.

will, while Allied mastery of the sea and the air had completely cut off shipping to and from Java.[133]

The Badan Oentoek Menjelidiki Oesaha-Oesaha Persiapan Kemerdekaan

This committee, Badan Oentoek Menjelidiki Oesaha-Oesaha Persiapan
Kemerdekaan, which finally came into being after some protracted consulta-
tions with Indonesian leaders, was officially announced by the new Sixteenth
Army supreme commander, Lieutenant General Yoichiro Nagano, on Tencho
Setsu (Emperor's Birthday), 29 April 1945. In the wake of the change of
premiers in Japan proper, with Koiso being replaced by the octogenarian
Admiral Kantaro Suzuki on 7 April 1945, Nagano replaced Harada on 26
April 1945.[134] Nagano appointed the 62 Indonesian-born members to the
committee, together with eight Japanese special members. An unexpected
choice as chairman of the Badan was the appointment of the 65-year-old
veteran and former Boedi Oetomo prominent Dr Radjiman Wediodiningrat
instead of Soekarno, although the latter seems to have agreed to this since
he wanted to engage himself more actively in the deliberations of the new
Badan.[135] Two vice-chairmen were also appointed, the Japanese *shochokan*
(*resident*) of Tjirebon Ichibangase Yoshio as first vice-chairman and Raden
Pandji Soeroso, the *shochokan* of Kedoe, as second vice-chairman. According
to Kanahele, the non-Japanese members represented the very core of the elite
of Java: the main leaders in the Jawa Hokokai and its auxiliaries, such as the
Barisan Pelopor, the Fujinkai (women's associations), the Badan Pembantoe
Pradjoerit; nearly all of the advisers (*sanyo*) and all of the Indonesian *residenten*, several *vice-residenten*, some prominent *regenten*, as well as major figures representing the Eurasian, Chinese and Arab organizations. Kanahele
also refers to some notable omissions, such as R.A.A. Koesoemo Oetojo,
Mr Raden Soedjono, Mr Raden Mas Soemanang, Prawoto Soemidilogo and
Gatot Mangkoepradja, all of these holding leading positions at that time as
well as seats in the Choo Sangiin. Of the Choo Sangiin members, less than
half were appointed to the Badan. The Badan represented a rather broad
spectrum of groups and interests by including members from the Central
Javanese principalities; two women representing the women's associations,
Njonja Maria Ulfah Santosa and Njonja R.S.S. Soenarjo Mangoenpoespito; a

---

[133]   See *Kan Po*, no. 62, 10 March 2605(1945); *Jawa Shinbun*, 25 February 2605(1945); Sato 1994:
67; Kanahele 1967:185, 189-90.
[134]   *Tjahaja*, 27 April 2605, also reprinted in Zwaan 1981:211.
[135]   *Asia Raya*, 29 April 2605(1945):1; for the mention of Radjiman and Soeroso and the names
of the other sixty members, Subardjo 1978:276-8; Kanahele 1967:192-3.

member of Maeda's Bukanfu (Naval Liaison Office), Mr Achmad Soebardjo; and a PETA *daidancho* (battalion commandant), Lieutenant Colonel Abdoel Kadir. Finally, and not unexpectedly, the nationalists dominated the Badan, not only in numbers but also politically and psychologically, for after all, as Kanahele (1967:194-5) points out, the Badan 'in a real sense epitomized their [the nationalists] cause', with '*prijaji* officials and the much smaller Islamic representation following, in that order'. However, the Badan, now set up, was still not ready to be convened, since its members, including the entire group of Japanese special delegates, were fanned out across Java and Madoera to inform the people of the Badan's purposes. This excursion lasted until the Badan's first formal convention, which took place on 28 May 1945. This development stood in marked contrast to the establishment of the so-called Kenkoku Gakuin (State Foundation Institute), an institution to train top leaders for the forthcoming independent state of Indonesia. Announced on 1 March 1945, a 40-member committee was formed on 2 March, including Soekarno, Hatta, Soepomo and Sartono among the 20 Indonesian members appointed to organize the new institution; by mid-March its operational plans were posted and by the end of April the Kenkoku Gakuin opened its doors to the first group of students.[136]

Meanwhile, on 25 June 1945, eight Indonesians were added to the Badan Oentoek Menjelidiki Oesaha-Oesaha Persiapan Kemerdekaan, among whom were two youth (*pemuda*) leaders, Soekarni and Chaeroel Saleh, who were also in charge of the Asrama Angkatan Baroe Indonesia (Student Dormitory of the New Indonesian Generation) at Menteng 31 in Djakarta, where before the Dutch capitulation the Dutch Schomper family had managed a hotel. This army-sponsored *asrama*, conceived by Shimizu of the Sendenbu in early 1943 mainly for indoctrination purposes as well as for creating a core of *pemuda* activists, included lectures by Soekarno, Hatta, Soebardjo, Soenarjo and Mohamad Yamin. With the reopening of the law and medical faculties in the capital city, a number of politicized *asrama* were established in addition to the one created by the Sendenbu. The medical faculty catered to an *asrama* located at Parapatan 10, near the Senen district in Djakarta, while students of the law faculty were drawn to the Menteng 31 *asrama*. Older *pemuda*, such as the assistant editor of *Asia Raya* Anwar Tjokroaminoto, the assistant editor of *Asia Raya* Boerhanoedin Moehammad Diah, as well as Adam Malik and Harsono Tjokroaminoto, who were affiliated with the Japanese news agency (Domei), were also in regular communication with the Menteng 31 *asrama*,

---

[136]   *Asia Raya*, 14 April 2605(1945):1, with the title 'Gedoeng Kenkoku Gakuin segera selesai' (The Kenkoku Gakuin building will soon be erected) and *Asia Raya*, 30 April 2605(1945):1, head-lined 'Toelang poenggoeng tenaga Indonesia Merdeka; Pemboekaan Kenkoku Gakuin' (Backing up the energy of Free Indonesia; The opening of the Kenkoku Gakuin).

making that group larger than its official membership (Sidik Kertapati 1961:48). However, the most well known of these *asrama* was the Asrama Indonesia Merdeka, located at Kebon Sirih 80, which was established soon after the Koiso declaration under the patronage of Rear Admiral Maeda but supervised by Maeda's capable assistants Nishijima and Yoshizumi and the former Gerindo youth leader Wikana. Maeda declares that: 'I felt very strongly that Indonesia would need capable leaders of the younger generation. I invited almost all the top Indonesian leaders to lecture there on whatever they liked. Even Sjahrir appeared – though of course not collaborating with us!' (Anderson 1972:44.)

So the lecturers at Maeda's *asrama* were virtually identical with the teachers at the Asrama Angkatan Baroe Indonesia, thus including Soekarno, Hatta, Singgih, Soebardjo, Soenarjo and Mohamad Yamin, with the most striking addition being Soetan Sjahrir. Soekarno lectured on politics, Hatta on economics, Soebardjo on international law and Sjahrir on socialism in Asia and on the youth movement (Mrázek 1994:249; Subardjo 1978:256).

From 16 to 18 May 1945, some of these young or somewhat older *pemuda* would attend an All-Java Youth Congress at Villa Isola just north of Bandoeng, the first ever to take place during the Japanese occupation. This congress did indeed signal the emergence of the *pemuda*, a composite of impetuous and rather undisciplined but still dynamic and militant segments of the Java-based younger generation. Not only were they quite wary of the Gunsei's not granting immediate independence, but they also chastised the nationalist leadership for being too cautious and too humble. However, this latter reproach immediately led to a Djakarta-based rival body being organized in the wake of the Isola congress. In the capital city, a group led by Soekarni, Chaerul Saleh, Asmara Hadi, B.M. Diah, Wikana and Harsono Tjokroaminoto established the Gerakan Angkatan Baroe Indonesia (Movement of a New Indonesian Generation), which was also immediately endorsed by Soekarno and Hatta. These developments prompted the final session of the Choo Sangiin to herald this youth group as being fighters in the vanguard of freedom. These *pemuda* would leave an indelible stamp on the developments leading to the ultimate proclamation of Indonesian independence.[137] Another event on the road toward that proclamation took place during the first convention of the Badan Oentoek Menjelidiki Oesaha-Oesaha Persiapan Kemerdekaan, when Soekarno, in an hour-long address, revealed his Pantja Sila concept as the foundation of the new state soon to emerge.

[137] *Asia Raya*, 24 May 2605(1945):1, 25 May 2605(1945):2, 26 May 2605(1945):2, 31 May 2605(1945):1; Jassin 1956:33-5; Subardjo 1978:281-2.

CHAPTER VIII

Soekarno paving the way for the Republic of Indonesia
1 June – 17 August 1945

Soekarno expounding on the Pantja Sila, the five basic tenets for the new nation to adopt

Under further deteriorating circumstances – Nazi Germany had capitulated on 8 May 1945 and Tarakan on Borneo's east coast had been invaded by Allied forces on 1 May 1945[1] – the first convention of the Badan Oentoek Menjelidiki Oesaha-Oesaha Persiapan Kemerdekaan (Investigating Committee for the Preparation of Independence) finally took place from 28 May to 1 June 1945. According to the Gunseikan Major-General Yamamoto's inaugural address, this convention needed to devote attention not merely to Java and Madoera but to the larger problem of founding an independent Indonesia.[2] This statement diverged remarkably from the initial statement made by Lieutenant General Harada, who in March spoke of Java specifically in order not to upset the Sumatran Twenty-Fifth Army Gunsei or the Kaigun (Navy) authorities in Makassar. As to the latter, a new naval commander, Vice-Admiral Yaichiro Shibata, had been instrumental, perhaps acting on the advice of his Djakarta-based liaison officer Rear-Admiral Maeda, in arranging visits of prominent Indonesian leaders to the Kaigun area under his jurisdiction.[3] So from 25 to 30 April 1945 Soekarno, Soebardjo, Soemanang, Ratulangi and Tadjoeddin Noor, accompanied by Rear Admiral

---

[1]   On 13 May 1945, in a rather pathetic display, the Gunseikanbu's Head of General Affairs (Sombucho), Major General Otoshi Nishimura, during a special meeting with some Djakarta-based committee members, had assured his audience that the Nazi surrender would not deter Japan from continuing the war until ultimate victory was reached; see *Djawa Baroe* no. 10, 15 May 2605(1945):4-5. Nishimura's audience, having access to clandestine radio outlets, Allied leaflets and even the current dailies, knew better about the predicament Japan was facing at that time, Kanahele 1967:195-6 citing *Asia Raya*, 7 May 2605 on the Tarakan invasion.
[2]   *Kan Po*, no. 68, 10 June 2605(1945):10.
[3]   For these Kaigun-inspired visits, Anderson 1961:12; *Asia Raya*, 7 May 2605(1945):2.

Maeda, Nishijima and Yoshizumi, were hosted by Vice-Admiral Shibata first at Soerabaja, where some of his fleet units were now sheltering, and then at Makassar, still his headquarters at that time. The vice-admiral informed Tokyo that the red-and-white banner and the 'Indonesia Raja' anthem were now permitted in the entire Kaigun area as well. On 11 May 1945 Vice-Admiral Shibata flew together with Mohammad Hatta and Pangeran Mohammad Noor to Bandjarmasin in Borneo, a somewhat hazardous trip due to the presence of Allied fighter planes operating from the oil-producing island of Tarakan now under Allied control.[4] As to Soekarno, after his trip to Makassar he did not seek the limelight because his father had passed away on 8 May 1945. After his father's burial, Soekarno also kept to himself, perhaps in order to prepare for the forthcoming convention of the Badan Oentoek Menjelidiki Oesaha-Oesaha Persiapan Kemerdekaan.

Just prior to that convention the chairman, Dr Radjiman Wediodiningrat, had circulated a letter to the members urging them to specifically address state issues and work them out to the smallest detail. And so during the first three days a number of learned and less-learned addresses devoted to formal speechmaking followed, rather than substantive deliberations on specific questions, while it was also clear that speakers remained divided on many issues, even as to the prospect of *kemerdekaan* (independence). Much later in his autobiography, Soekarno refers to these first three days as 'a great twisting and turning and lack of cohesion [and] solid disagreement concerning the basic principles of Indonesia Merdeka [with] many ifs and conjectural problems'. He concludes that 'at this rate none of us would know Merdeka until we were in our graves. If the Japanese had liberated us that day we'd have had to say, "Wait a while... hold it a minute. We're not ready yet."' (Adams 1965:197.) The Japanese members did not take part in the deliberations, although Ichibangase, the first vice-chairman of the Investigating Committee, in his recollections, perhaps anticipating Soekarno's approach of achieving independence sooner rather than later, seemed to be rather wary of a *kemerdekaan* based upon 'an immediate independence even if it was deficient'.[5] As to Soekarno, his turn came on 1 June 1945, when he expressed some bewilderment about Dr Radjiman's request and the deliberations following it. Soekarno specifically chided his audience that if it had 'to make plans to the smallest detail, he himself as well as all the members present here today would never see the day of a Free Indonesia'. Consequently,

[4]   Adams 1965:195-6; Reid and Oki 1986:280-3. On 25 July 1945 Shibata flew to Bali with Maeda, Soekarno and Soebardjo for a two-day visit to that island. Soekarno's visit to Bali was his second and last trip to the islands under Kaigun jurisdiction prior to the Japanese capitulation (Reid and Oki 1986:284).
[5]   Brugmans et al. 1960:590, with J.H.A. Logemann 1959:210 calling Ichibangase and his followers a bunch of *dwarskijkers* (snoopers).

Soekarno urged the members of the Investigating Committee 'to together seek a unified philosophical basis, a world view, on which we all would agree, I repeat: agree'.[6]

Having established that, Soekarno turned to what he considered the concept of freedom, drawing attention to a 1933 booklet he had written called *Mentjapai Indonesia Merdeka* (To achieve Indonesia Merdeka). In that booklet he had stated 'that freedom, political freedom was nothing more than a bridge, a golden bridge, and that on the far side of that bridge we would rebuild our own society'. Drawing from this 1933 treatise, Soekarno proposed as the first *sila* (pillar) of the state the concept of nationalism – an Indonesian nationalism or *Kebangsaan Indonesia,* which meant not 'nationalism in a narrow sense' but one vested in a state 'where all would dwell who had earned the right of having a homeland in Indonesia'. This concept is somewhat reminiscent of his 1927 PPPKI, where the requirement of *mufakat* established that minorities would also have a say. As we will see below, *mufakat* or unanimous consensus was the third *sila* Soekarno proposed.

Returning to the first *sila,* Soekarno further perceived it as a unity struck between men and territory, with 'men' referring to the people of Indonesia whether Javanese, Sundanese, Sumatrans, or other ethnic groups, and 'territory' being the Indonesian archipelago stretching from Sabang to Merauke. Soekarno stated that 'even a small child looking at a map will see that the Indonesian archipelago forms a unit'. Soekarno then mentioned other island states such as Japan, Greece and the British Isles, which were all 'created by God as unities'. He urged the delegates 'to aim for a national state throughout the myriad Indonesian islands', saying that 'the seventy million inhabitants have the feeling of *le désir d'être ensemble* [a desire to be together, as defined by Ernest Renan and Otto Bauer] as well as a *Schicksalgemeinschaft* [a common solidarity, also defined by Renan and Bauer] already well established'. As to the Chinese minority living in Indonesia, Soekarno was quick to remind the Chinese delegates – the Muslim delegates were still somewhat wary of nationalism – that 'Sun Yat-sen through his *San Min Chu I* (Three Democratic Principles) had been instrumental in getting [Soekarno] back to nationalism from erstwhile cosmopolitan ideas he had cherished as a 16-year-old youngster for a while'. So, the three principles of nationalism (*Min-tsu*), socialism (*Min-sheng*) and democracy (*Min-chuan*) 'flourished in his heart' and he 'feels forever grateful to Dr Sun Yat-sen' (clapping from the Chinese delegates). Soekarno, however, warned his audience that there was 'a danger inherent

[6]   All these extemporaneous references made by Soekarno are derived from four sources: *The birth of Pantjasila* 1958; *Lahirnja Pantja Sila* 1960; Yamin 1959; Feith and Castles 1970:40-9, while Logemann 1962 sketches the major constitutional issues before and after the Committee's first convention. Hatta 1979a:95-8 also touches briefly upon these issues, as well as Bocquet-Siek and Cribb 1991.

to the principle of nationalism due to a narrowing nationalism open to chauvinism and to the creed of an Indonesia *über Alles*'. Here, Soekarno hailed Gandhi, who said, 'I am a nationalist but my nationalism is one of humanity'. Soekarno cautioned the Committee delegates 'not to advocate a nationalism of isolation nor to cater to a chauvinism adhered to by supermen and blue-eyed Aryans who considered their nation as the greatest while other nations were deemed to be worthless'. This was apparently a dig at a racist nation once strong but now occupied by foreign powers.

Soekarno's appeal was: 'let us not abide by such bold formulas but rather proceed toward the unity of the world, the brotherhood of the world, since not only must we establish the state of Indonesia Merdeka but we also have to proceed toward the familyhood of nations'. He then stated that this ideal formed the foundation of his second *sila*, which he termed *internasional-isme atau kemanusiaan* (internationalism as well as humanitarianism). Here, Soekarno, again borrowing from Gandhi, stressed that *kebangsaan* (nationalism) was in fact quite inseparable from internationalism or humanitarianism: 'we should not only strive to establish the state of an Indonesia Merdeka but we should also aim to become part of a family of nations'. He added that 'internationalism will not flourish at all if it is not rooted in the soil of nationalism [and] nationalism will not flourish if it does not grow in the flower garden of internationalism. [T]hese two principles which I propose first of all to you all, are indeed closely linked one with the other.'

As to the third *sila*, Soekarno intertwined the principle of *mufakat* (unanimity) with the principle of *perwakilan* (representation) as well as with the principle of *permusyawaratan* (deliberation among representatives). Here again, he demonstrated his trust in well-established Indonesian traditions that in the past so often formed the heart of his own intellectual and ideological treatises. Using this third *sila* he challenged those in his audience who were in favour of a Muslim state:

> If we are indeed a Muslim people, we should labour feverishly to get many Muslim delegates in our people's representative bodies. Then the laws in these bodies will naturally be Muslim laws. Also, we assert that 90% of our people are Muslim in religion, but look around here in this assembly and watch the slender percentage giving their vote to Islam. Forgive me for raising this question. For me this demonstrates that Islam as yet is not truly alive among the people. Therefore, I ask you all, both those who are not Muslim and those who are, please do accept this third *sila*, the principle of *mufakat-permusyawaratan-perwakilan*, unanimity arising out of deliberation among representatives.

In advocating his fourth *sila*, Soekarno expounded the principle of *kesejahteraan sosial bagi seluruh rakyat* Indonesia (social justice for the entire Indonesian people). Taking a leaf from Jean Jaurès, a French leader he was fond of citing,

Soekarno said:

> I remember Jean Jaurès stating that in parliamentary democracy every man has
> equal rights, equal political rights; every man can vote, every man may enter
> parliament. But is there social justice, is there evidence of well-being among the
> masses? Since as Jaurès also held, in parliament a worker's delegate can cause a
> minister to fall [...] but in his place of work, in the factory, even though today he
> can bring about the fall of a minister, tomorrow he can be thrown into the street,
> made unemployed, with nothing at all to eat. Do we want conditions like that?

I think not, and I would like to suggest that if we are looking for democracy
and social justice, we should reject Western democracy and embrace the concept of *permusyawaratan*, which brings life to politico-economic democracy
and is capable of bringing social prosperity. And what is meant by Ratoe
Adil is that Ratoe Adil is social justice. [Here Soekarno, like his father-in-law
Tjokroaminoto before him, elevated the idea of a just king to a social phenomenon.] Let us accept this principle of social justice. It is not just political
equality, for we must create equality in the economic sense. The *permusyawaratan* body we shall establish must therefore not be a deliberative body for
political democracy alone, but a body which, together with the community,
will be able to put into effect the two principles: political justice and social
justice. We shall discuss these matters together in the *permusyawaratan* body.

In his fifth *sila* Soekarno proposed the Almighty God as the fifth and integ-
rating principle, considering it not so much a plea for theism as a call for
freedom of worship:

> A principle to build Indonesia Merdeka in awe of the One Supreme God. Not only
> should Indonesian people believe in God, but every Indonesian should believe in
> his own God. Christians should worship God according to the teachings of Jesus
> Christ, Muslims according to the teachings of the Prophet Mohammed; Buddhists
> should perform their religious ceremonies in accordance with the books they
> have. But let us all believe in God. [...] Let us, within the Indonesia Merdeka which
> we are going to build, declare in keeping with that: the fifth principle of our state
> is belief in God in a cultured way [...] belief in God with mutual respect for one
> another. [...] Do remember the third principle of *mufakat*, of representation, where
> there is a place for each of us to propagate our ideals in a manner that is tolerant,
> that is, in a cultural way.

In concluding his long address, Soekarno appealed to the need for *gotong
royong*, or mutual cooperation:

> The state of Indonesia which we are to establish must be a *gotong royong* state.
> *Gotong royong* is a dynamic concept, more dynamic than the family principle, since
> the latter is somewhat static while *gotong royong* portrays one endeavour, one act
> of service, one task, what was called by delegate Soekardjo one *karyo* one *gawé*.
> Let us complete this *karyo*, this *gawé*, this task, this act of service, together. *Gotong*

royong means toiling hard together, sweating hard together, a joint struggle to help one another. Acts of service by all for the interests of all. *Ho-lopis-kuntul-baris* – One, two, three, heave! for the common interest. That is *gotong royong*.

Finally Soekarno warned his audience to prepare for the struggle that still lay ahead to realize Indonesia Merdeka:

> In this time of war, have faith and cultivate the conviction that an Indonesia Merdeka cannot be realized if the people of Indonesia do not take risks [...] if the people of Indonesia fail to be united and are not determined to live or die for free-dom. [...] Freedom can only be attained or owned by a people whose soul is filled with the urge of reaching Merdeka whatever the cost.

It has been claimed that Soekarno's Pantja Sila oration was greeted by a deaf-ening ovation from the enthusiastic delegates who endorsed the Pantja Sila by acclamation as the proper philosophical source for an Indonesia Merdeka soon to come, but that the eight Japanese delegates were fuming. Soekarno's autobiography (Adams 1965:199) specifically states that:

> The applause was deafening. The representatives jumped out of their seats and accepted my State philosophy by acclamation. One area of the room was not jump-ing with joy. The Japanese. [A]ngry Japanese now fumed. Not once did I advocate devotion to their 'God', the Emperor. Not once did my words praise Dai Nippon. [...] No, the Japanese definitely weren't happy about Pantja Sila. But I did not care. [...] The time had come to assure the world I was not a Japanese puppet.

The reality may well have been otherwise. Yet as Kanahele (1967:199-200) posits:

> Doubtless Soekarno won the plaudits of the nationalists, for his speech was un-questionably the most decisive and clearest exposition of the ideals of Indonesian nationalism before or during the Occupation. [...] Indeed, the speech was void of any sycophantic allusions to Dai Nippon. [Instead] Soekarno showed that even after three years of intimate contact with Japanese officials and almost total immersion in Japanese propaganda, he remained ideologically untouched by it all.

Events leading to the Piagam Djakarta, the Gerakan Rakjat Baroe and the Panitia Persiapan Kemerdekaan Indonesia

In the wake of Soekarno's Pantja Sila address, a subcommittee of nine del-egates was immediately formed to study the Pantja Sila as conceived by Soekarno as well as to design a preamble for a future Indonesian constitu-tion. Chaired by Soekarno, the committee of nine consisted of Soekarno, Mohammad Hatta, Achmad Soebardjo, Hadji Agoes Salim, Mohamad

Yamin, Abikoesno Tjokrosoejoso, Wahid Hasjim, Alex Andries Maramis and Kiaji Abdoel Kahar Moezakkir. As to the preamble, which was in fact a declaration of independence, Soekarno had requested Mohamad Yamin to draft it. On 22 June 1945, as the first action of the subcommittee, this preamble was introduced under the name Piagam Djakarta (Djakarta Charter). Inspired by the American Declaration of Independence, Yamin's draft started with the establishment of the right of freedom for all the people. This was followed by a long-winded accusation against former dominating alien oppressors, excluding, however, the Japanese, who were portrayed as freeing the Asian peoples from the colonial yoke. This was linked with the obligation to partake in the Japanese struggle for freedom and to act as true members of the Greater Asian Community (Yamin 1959-60, I:153-5, 273-6; Logemann 1962: 5-6, 13, 1959:210-1; Subardjo 1978:280). From the start, Soekarno's committee of nine worked toward realizing a compromise between nationalist – *pihak kebangsaan* – and Muslim – *pihak Islam* – interests. The Piagam Djakarta, which in fact became the preamble to the Indonesian constitution, therefore promoted Soekarno's fifth *sila* – that of *Ketuhanan*, the Almighty God – to the first position. Another concession to the *pihak Islam* was that the *Ketuhanan* 'was based upon belief in God with the duty for adherents of Islam to observe the religious laws'. In spite of this regulation, the *pihak kebangsaan* accepted that the state to be was in fact a secular one and not a theocracy, since 'the Pantja Sila was proclaimed as forming the moral foundations for the republic' (Logemann 1962:9; Bocquet-Siek and Cribb 1991:53).

During the second convention of the Investigating Committee held from 10 to 17 July 1945, Soekarno was therefore pleased to report on 10 July about these compromises being inserted in the Piagam Djakarta. The next day an editorial committee (Panitia Perantjang) of 19 delegates was installed, again with Soekarno as chairman. It was charged with establishing a draft constitution, and therefore a working group of seven delegates chaired by Professor Soepomo was formed. The draft prepared by Soepomo's group was ready on 12 July. It apparently did not show undue influence from the Piagam Djakarta. As to religion, it specifically stated in article 29: 'The state guarantees the freedom of each citizen to embrace whatever religion one desires in order to fulfil the religious duties in accordance to one's own beliefs'. On 14 July Soekarno's editorial committee presented Soepomo's draft to the Investigating Committee. Bernhard Dahm (1969:299) claims that Soepomo had here 'translated the decades-old political ideas of Soekarno into legal terminology'. On that same day the Investigating Committee was nonetheless faced with a verbal row between Muslim and nationalist delegates. The Muslim delegates suggested that a non-Islamic president could not suitably enforce the duty to observe the religious laws and the nationalist delegates claimed that the Piagam Djakarta as well as Soepomo's draft had proclaimed the equality of all citizens before the law. Muslim delegate Abdoel Kahar Moezakkir became so upset about this that he thumped his fist on the table and proposed to scrap all references to God and Islam from the Piagam Djakarta. Until deep into the night no compromise was reached. Neither did the whole committee reach a consensus the next day. However, on 16 July the nationalists were beseeched by Soekarno in a compassionate and tearful address to make an offer: so a prescription for a president to be a Muslim was inserted into the constitution (Yamin 1959-60, I: 253, 259, 264-5; Logemann 1962:6-7, 10-1; Brugmans et al. 1960:589-90). The hard-fought victory by the *pihak Islam* had been achieved; whether it would stay that way we will see presently.

Before his Piagam Djakarta report to the Investigating Committee, in his inaugural speech on 10 July 1945 Soekarno sounded the rallying cry 'Indonesia Merdeka sekarang', an obvious dig at the Japanese delegates present. Soekarno was quick to stress that Burma, Thailand, the Philippines, Manchukuo, Cambodia and Annam were now all independent, while Indonesia was not. He then drew attention to the fact that 'Indonesians in Tarakan and Balikpapan are now dying by the hundreds without a country'.[7] Another issue was debated as well during this second convention: whether the new state should be a monarchy or a republic. It seems that proponents of a monarchy had aired the possibility before the session of the Sultan of Djokjakarta Hamengkoe Boewono IX becoming the monarch of the new state. Kanahele cited Miyoshi, suggesting that some Japanese were in favour of a monarchy since it seemed to be the closest parallel to the imperial system of Dai Nippon. Miyoshi, however, was quick to observe that these Japanese did not realize that Indonesian nationalist leaders had far more exposure to Western political ideas and institutions than they had. Miyoshi proved to be right, since when the vote was cast on the issue of a monarchy versus a republic, there were only six who voted for a monarchy while 55 favoured a republic (Kanahele 1967:209-10; Yamin 1959-60, I:184).

The convention, finally, touched upon the issue of the extent of the territory of the new Indonesian state. Some delegates, with Mohamad Yamin the most vocal proponent, desired a Greater Indonesia consisting of the former Netherlands East Indies and adding Malaya, British North Borneo, Portuguese Timor and the whole of New Guinea. Some backing for a Greater Indonesia, but only including the former Netherlands East Indies and Malaya, came from Soekarno. Like Yamin, Soekarno based his claim on the *tanah tumpah darah* (native soil, a kind of *Blut und Boden*), the habitat of the people belonging to the Indonesian stock, as well as on the fact that the language of the two countries was very similar. Also, Soekarno had recently

---

[7]   Yamin 1959-60, I:155-6. Kanahele 1967:318-9, note 56, however, reports that Soekarno's figures seem to be inflated, since only a few *heiho* were used in the fighting.

heard some Malayans – including the nationalist Malayan leader Ibrahim Ya'acob – expressing a similar desire. Hatta was in favour of such a state as long as Malayans were so inclined. Other delegates were in favour of just the former Netherlands East Indies, thus including West New Guinea, with another minority vote going to the former Netherlands East Indies without West New Guinea. In the end the tally was as follows: for the former Netherlands East Indies including West New Guinea 19 votes were cast, for the former Indies excluding West New Guinea 6 votes, and for Yamin's Greater Indonesia 39 votes.[8]

Meanwhile, a large *pemuda* preparatory committee had been formed to realize a Gerakan Rakjat Baroe (New People's Movement). The committee included the following *pemuda*: Chaerul Saleh, Soekarni Kartodiwirjo, B.M. Diah, Asmara Hadi, Harsono Tjokroaminoto, Wikana, Soediro, Soepeno, Adam Malik, Iboe Soerastri Karma Trimoerti (the wife of Soekarno's private secretary Sajoeti Melik), Soetomo and Pandoe Kartawigoena. The Gunsei, through Major-General Nishimura, was quick to assert that a Gerakan Rakjat Baroe, like any other youth organization, would be subject to the Gunsei's control.[9] The official announcement of the formation of the Gerakan Rakjat Baroe was issued on 2 July 1945. In line with what appear to have been the expectations of these *pemuda*, the leadership was entrusted to a reborn Empat Serangkai, with Soekarno and Hatta, erstwhile members of the earlier Empat Serangkai, and two new members: R.A.A. Wiranatakoesoema, an aristocratic Soendanese *priyayi* and former Volksraad delegate, and Kiaji Wahid Hasjim, son of the founder of the pre-war Nahdatoel Oelama K.H. Hasjim Asjari. These four leaders selected an organizational committee of eighty, with the *pemuda* delegates including B.M. Diah, Moewardi, Soepeno, Soekarni Kartodiwirjo, Asmara Hadi, Adam Malik, Soediro, Harsono Tjokroaminoto, Wikana, Chalid Rasjidi (a prominent member of the 31 Menteng *asrama*), Pandoe Kartawigoena, Soetomo (later known as Boeng Tomo) and Iboe Trimoerti. This gave the *pemuda* for the first time a large and powerful representation in a national network. The importance of the *pemuda* was further enhanced by the appointment of B.M. Diah as secretary of the Gerakan Rakjat Baroe's working committee, while the *pemuda* were also proud to be hailed by *Asia Raya* as 'a force not wanting to build their aims upon filthy ground but prepared to get rid of filth before any new structure would arise'.[10]

---

[8]   For Ibrahim Ya'acob, a former leader of the Malayan Pembela Tanah Air (PETA), and his contacts with both Soekarno and Hatta prior to the Japanese capitulation, see Poulgrain 1998: 314. For the *tanah tumpah darah* see Logemann 1962:14. For the votes cast on Indonesia's territory, see Yamin 1959:187.

[9]   *Asia Raya*, 4 July 2605(1945):2.

[10]   Subardjo 1978:281-2; Anderson 1961:39-41. For *Asia Raya*'s appraisal of the *pemuda* see *Asia Raya*, 3 July 2605(1945):2. Mrs Trimoerti referred to it as well during our interview with her in

On 6 July, just before the first session of this working committee, the Angkatan Baroe leaders (on the Angkatan Baroe see Chapter VII) met in order to prepare their strategy for the first session, though without taking any concrete decisions. Yet, at the working committee session the *pemuda* insisted that the term 'Republic of Indonesia' be used. This issue, however, was deemed unacceptable by the Japanese authorities present, claiming that constitutional questions belonged to the realm of the Investigating Committee, which had not yet met. So Soekarno was faced with a Japanese demand that the question of republican status was one that only the Japanese emperor could bestow. The older nationalist leaders such as Soekarno, Hatta, Soebardjo, Yamin and Abikoesno therefore proposed a compromise whereby the term republic would remain in parentheses, thus indicating a state of affairs still to be realized. This compromise was put to a vote with 70 to 7 being in favour of the compromise and only the most 'brave' of the *pemuda* voting against it (Subardjo 1978:282-3; Anderson 1967:59-61, 148, note 113; Lucas 1986:154). For Soekarno this was a sign that the Gerakan Rakjat Baroe was different from all previous movements, since it would be devoted exclusively to the interests of the common people.[11] Finally, on 28 July 1945, a council of Gerakan Rakjat Baroe leaders, in which all previously existing associations and paramilitary organizations were represented, was installed. But by that time most of the Angkatan Baroe pemoeda, still smarting over their defeat during the 6 July working committee session, had left the Gerakan Rakjat Baroe.[12] And so only two rather obscure *pemuda* were assigned to the council of Gerakan Rakjat Baroe leaders. As to some of the militant *pemuda*, who had turned their backs on the Gerakan Rakjat Baroe, such as Soekarni Kartodiwirjo and Chaerul Saleh, they were removed from their posts in the Sendenbu. Their patron Shimizu was in Shonanto (Singapore) at that time from 20 July to 13 August, together with Hayashi, the top political adviser of Saiko Shikikan Lieutenant General Nagano, in order to discuss the Indonesian independence issue as well as the defence strategy to be adopted in the case of Allied landings in the western part of the Southern Regions.[13]

It seems that both Hatta and Soekarno at that time felt relieved to be

---

Jakarta, 12 June 1983. Mrs Trimoerti's biography, prepared by Bob Hering, will soon go to the printer. A manuscript of it is available at the KITLV.

[11]   *Asia Raya*, 2 July 2605(1945):1.

[12]   *Asia Raya*, 28 July 2605(1945):2. On the exodus of the *pemuda* and their estrangement from the established leadership see Subardjo 1978:284; Anderson 1972:58-60; Brugmans et al. 1960: 567.

[13]   NEFIS (Netherlands Forces Intelligence Service), AI2/21242/G interrogation of Shimizu, 27 November 1945, p. 2, no. 6, signed by Colonel S.H. Spoor, see Verbaal Q 16 of 31 December 1945, ARA, The Hague. Brugmans et al. 1960:195-6 refers to Shimizu being in Singapore for talks with Lieutenant General Seishiro Itagaki, since he had been dismissed from the Sendenbu. Shimizu flew back to Java through the auspices of an unnamed Japanese pilot just prior to the Japanese capitulation. Also, Anderson 1972:59 maintains that the Java Gunsei wanted to get rid of him.

released from the rather sharp criticism so often voiced by impatient or even impertinent *pemuda*. Soekarno maintained that the Gerakan Rakjat Baroe was a unique phenomenon and therefore a blessing to the unnamed and patient *wong marhaen*. Hatta, on 3 August 1945, during the first meeting of the Gerakan Rakjat Baroe council of leaders at Soekarno's home, told his host, who had just been elected to head the new movement, 'that Ir Soekarno was now called to truly fulfil the Mandate of History'. Hatta then urged him 'to lead the people from their present misery into a happy and glorious future'.[14] At that first meeting of the Gerakan Rakjat Baroe leadership it was decided to still assemble the youth organizations by mid-August for a mass meeting in the capital city in order to arrive at a mutual understanding and so restore a united front.[15] This was not to be, since the 'mandate of history' Hatta spoke of was closer than anybody could have imagined. As to the *pemuda* feeling deserted by their elders, they decided to wait and see how events would evolve and then await opportunities for turning Djakarta into a tinderbox. Benedict Anderson, who sees himself, perhaps with some justification, as the prominent chronicler of the *pemuda* movement, opines that with the *pemuda* having abandoned the Gerakan Rakjat Baroe in droves, that organization in fact collapsed.[16] In stating this, he ignores the events taking place at Soekarno's residence on 3 August 1945, as well as the elaborate reporting of it in the 4 August issue of *Asia Raya*.

In the meantime, with Dai Nippon diplomatically increasingly outwitted, constitutional developments in Indonesia engaging the top nationalist leadership accelerated. On 30 July 1945 Lieutenant General Itagaki of the Shonanto-based Seventh Area Army Command summoned all the General Affairs Department Heads (in Japanese the *somubucho*) of Java, Sumatra, Malaya and the Navy area to Shonanto (Singapore) together with their staff aides to apprise them of general constitutional instructions which had reached him from Tokyo as well as from Field Marshal Terauchi's Saigon headquarters. In Tokyo the Saiko Senso Shido Kaigi (Supreme War Guidance

---

[14]   *Asia Raya*, 10 August 2605(1965):2 with the heading on the first column 'Dewan Pimpinan' (Council of leaders). *Asia Raya*, 4 August 2605(1945):1 includes a photograph with the caption 'Sidang Dewan Pimpinan Poesat Gerakan Rakjat Baroe' (Session of the Gerakan Rakjat Baroe Central Council of Leaders), as well as a call signed by Soekarno and Hatta for a 'Pertemoean Besar Pemoeda Indonesia Seloeroeh Djawa dan Madoera' (Grand Meeting of the Java and Madoera-based Indonesian Youth) on p. 1, column 5. Finally, at the bottom of the paper, in columns 5 to 7, an article appears titled 'Djangan Ngawoer' (Do not waste your time in empty talk). This article stresses the importance of the Gerakan Rakjat Baroe, while it also seems to be a hidden dig at the *pemuda*.

[15]   See for that appeal *Asia Raya*, 4 August 2605(1945):1, column 5.

[16]   Anderson 1972:61. As to Soekarno, Hatta and the *pemuda*, a corrective analysis is given by Han Bing Siong, erstwhile professor at the law faculty of Universitas Indonesia, in Han Bing Siong 2000:233-73, 2001:799-830.

Council) had met on 17 July 1945, with foreign minister Shigenori Togo having persuaded his colleagues that immediate puppet independence should
be granted to the former Netherlands East Indies (Benda, Irikura and Kishi
1965:274). On 21 July this Togo proposal was ratified by the Japanese War
Cabinet and then transmitted to Java's Saiko Shikikan, Lieutenant General
Nagano, while on 29 July Field Marshal Terauchi was instructed by Tokyo to
go ahead with these independence preparations but not to make them public
until the Soviet Union's entry into the war had become imminent (Anderson
1972:61-2).

Accordingly the Shonanto conference was held hurriedly. Java was
marked as being the initial recipient of independence, to be informed of it
in early September. The other areas were to follow later. Also, the Panitia
Persiapan Kemerdekaan Indonesia (PPKI, Committee for the Preparation of
Indonesian Independence, in Japanese Dokuritsu Junbi Iinkai), would soon
be established (Benda, Irikura and Kishi 1965:275; Brugmans et al. 1960:592-
3). However, this scenario was disrupted on 7 August 1945 – one day after
the atomic holocaust at Hiroshima[17] – with Marshal Terauchi's Saigon command, upon instructions from Tokyo, now announcing the establishment of
the PPKI.[18] Domei on that date revealed that Sadao Iguti, the spokesman
of the Japanese Information Agency, had labelled the PPKI a speedy link
toward Indonesian independence. On the Indonesian side, Soekarno hailed
the new committee as 'the final step toward Indonesian independence'. He
added that whereas the soon to be defunct Investigating Committee had
been 'an organ of the Gunsei, the PPKI was indeed an instrument of the
Indonesian people themselves'.[19] Soekarno further expressed his gratitude
to the Saiko Shikikan Lieutenant General Nagano, raising his hands thrice
for a Banzai yell. Also, Hatta, Soebardjo, Wahid Hasjim and Dr Radjiman
expressed their gratitude in quite lengthy articles on the PPKI.[20] *Asia Raya's*
editor, R. Soekardjo Wirjopranoto, in a radio address of 9 August 1945, was
quick to link the PPKI with the attempts of Van Mook to re-establish Dutch
colonial rule in Indonesia, with Soekardjo ruling it out since Indonesia was
to be free soon.[21]

On the morning that address was aired, Soekarno, Hatta, Radjiman
Wediodiningrat, Dr Soeharto (Soekarno's private physician), Lieutenant

---

[17]   *Asia Raya*, 9 August 2605(1945):1, citing Domei of 7 August, with the heading 'Moesoeh
menggoenakan bom baroe' (The enemy using a new bomb). This issue also announced, citing
Domei again, the installation of the PPKI.
[18]   *Kan Po*, no. 72, 7 August 2605(1945); Brugmans et al. 1960:593-4.
[19]   *Asia Raya*, 7 August 2605(1945):1.
[20]   *Asia Raya*, 7 August 2605(1945):1.
[21]   See for that radio address *Asia Raya*, 13 August 2605(1945), the three bottom columns of
p. 1.

Colonel Nomura and Miyoshi (as interpreter) left by military plane first to Shonanto (Singapore), with Nomura reporting to Lieutenant General Itagaki and Major General Funio Shimura, deputy chief of staff to Itagaki, and then to Saigon for a day of rest. On 11 August they went to Dalat, 250 kilometres northeast of Saigon, where they were hosted by Field Marshal Terauchi and informed by him about the PPKI, with 21 members: 13 representing Java, 3 Sumatra and 5 the Kaigun area (1 for Borneo, 2 for Celebes, 1 for the Lesser Soenda islands, 1 for the Moluccan islands). As to the area to be independent soon, Terauchi listed the former Netherlands Indies. According to Miyoshi, Soekarno wanted Malaya as well as North Borneo included, with Hatta declining.[22] On 12 August, as the nationalist leaders were about to leave for home, they received a final official word from Terauchi that an Indonesian independence proclamation was to come in a matter of days. Hatta (1979b: 437) recalls in his memoirs that: 'I was especially glad since 12 August 1945 happened to be my birthday'.

On 14 August 1945 the three nationalist leaders arrived back in Djakarta at noon. Soekarno, Hatta and Radjiman were hailed by an enthusiastic crowd of several thousand. After that, Gunseikan Yamamoto, Somubucho Nishimura and Rear Admiral Maeda of the Bukanfu congratulated the nationalist leaders, followed by a host of other authorities. R.M.A.A. Koesoemo Oetoyo, as representative of the Indonesian people, welcomed the leaders, hoping that what they had learned in Dalat would please the Indonesian people. In reply Soekarno thanked all the people for their enthusiasm shown during the arrival ceremony, and then he recalled his 7 August radio speech, where he had stated 'that Indonesia would be free before the maize plant would bear fruit'. Now, however, he was sure 'that Indonesia would be free before the maize plant would bloom' (*Sebeloem djagoeng berboenga, Indonesia pasti Merdeka*).[23] At the same time, *Asia Raya* announced the names of the 21 members of the PPKI: representing Java the chairman Ir Soekarno, the vice-chairman Drs Moh. Hatta, Radjiman, Oto Iskandardinata, Hadikoesoemo, Wahid Hasjim, Soerjohamidjojo, Poeroebojo, Soetardjo, Soeroso, Dr Soepomo, Abdoel Kadir and Yap Tjwan Bing. Representing Sumatra Mohd. Amir, Teukoe Md. Hasan and Abd. Abbas. Representing the Kaigun area Ratulangi, Andi Pangeran, A.A. Hamidhan, I Goesti Ketoet Poetje and J. Latuharhary. In addition Soebardjo was appointed special adviser (*zimukyoku sanyo*) to the committee.[24] The membership was dominated by non-Muslim politicians of the older generation, with no *pemuda* at all.

The day after the enthusiastic reception of the three returning leaders,

---

[22]   Miyoshi's report given in Brugmans et al. 1960:594-5.
[23]   Brugmans et al. 1960:595-6; *Asia Raya*, 14 August 2605(1945):1, left upper columns 1 and 2.
[24]   *Asia Raya*, 14 August 2605(1945):1, middle columns 1 and 2 on the left side of the page.

the prospect of the Mandate of History (Sidang Mahkamah Sedjarah) Hatta had so candidly referred to only 12 days previously was about to reveal itself. Some Japanese were to adorn the Mandate of History as well. In a secret yet historic occasion, Soekarno was presented, by a Japanese member of noble birth, Count Genkichi Yamaguchi, then a major attached to the Gunseikanbu, with a ceremonial sword once made by a famous swordsmith named Kanenori Miyamoto, who had also forged swords for Taisho Tenno (Hirohito's father) and for several Japanese field marshals and fleet admirals. It seems that a more open and formal presentation had been scheduled, but did not materialize due to the Japanese surrender. As a matter of fact, such an open ceremony would only have led to Soekarno again being labelled a mere puppet of the Japanese. This also explains why R.M. Abdul Gaffar Pringgodigdo, who was to serve Soekarno as presidential state secretary, and knew about the presentation made by Count Yamaguchi, kept the sword in his custody.[25]

The Indonesian proclamation of independence and its immediate aftermath: myth and reality entwined

It was left to Soetan Sjahrir, someone to stay out of the limelight whenever he deemed it opportune and fitting, to unlock the Sidang Mahkamah Sedjarah with a chain of rather dramatic events on the fringes of Indonesian politics, soon to be characterized by Sjahrir himself as activities having a *gelisah* (restless or feverish) nature. On 10 August Sjahrir informed Chairil Anwar of the atomic bomb dropped at Nagasaki and that Japan had received an ultimatum to surrender. This led to the message being spread in Djakarta among Sjahrir's youthful supporters, with Sjahrir later recalling that Japan would soon surrender.[26] Seeing Hatta after his return from Dalat on 14 August, Sjahrir was enraged about the Dalat proceedings, terming them 'a Japanese swindle, because their surrender would be announced at any moment' (Sjahrir 1949:253). Sjahrir prodded Hatta to proclaim Indonesian independence immediately, while perhaps also recalling that even before the trip to Dalat he had reiterated that 'all was over for the Japanese' and that the time had arrived for a 'situation to be made as revolutionary as possible in order that there would be no division in the nationalist camp between those of the resistance and those who had col-

---

[25]   Han Bing Siong 1997:22-3, 25-6. The sword seems to have been given by Soekarno to his state secretary, who in 1970 took it to Holland, where it then became the property of Han Bing Siong.
[26]   Subadio Sastrosatomo 1987:11, 13; Kahin's interview with Sjahrir of 15 February 1949. As to *gelisah* meaning upset, restless, trembling, see Mrázek 1994:259, stating 'no better word could be found now for Sjahrir in action'.

laborated' (Sjahrir 1949:253-4). Rather bold words for someone whose resistance had so far been confined to listening to foreign radio broadcasts.

Yet, aware that the *pemuda* activists had been side-tracked by the older nationalists, Sjahrir saw a golden opportunity to revolutionize the *pemuda*. But in this, Sjahrir would soon clash with both Hatta and Soekarno. Hatta, always more sober in outlook, promised to approach Soekarno right away about Sjahrir's ideas. Sjahrir then admonished his *pemuda* following to gear themselves up 'in the city to prepare for demonstrations and perhaps fighting if the Japanese try to use force'. He also informed them that 'the sign for demonstrations was to be the proclamation' and that he 'had already drawn up the draft [of the proclamation] and sent it throughout Java to be printed and distributed' (Sjahrir 1949:254). However, Hatta, talking to Soekarno about Sjahrir's blueprint for immediate and unilateral action, was cautioned by Soekarno that he had 'no right to proclaim independence alone, since that right belonged to the PPKI', adding 'how curious it would look if I just bypassed this committee'. Hatta recalled in his memoirs that 'this put an end to Sjahrir's ideas of changing the procedure for proclaiming Indonesian independence' (Hatta 1952:333, 1981:227). Here Hatta seems to have been a bit too optimistic, since Sjahrir's *pemuda* following was not to cave in that easily.

As to Soekarno and Hatta, having heard persistent rumours that Japan was about to surrender or had already, they decided to approach Gunsei authorities on 15 August for an official confirmation. The two leaders, accompanied by Soebardjo, went around noon that day to the Gunseikanbu (Military Administration Headquarters) located on the northeast corner of Gambir Square (formerly Koningsplein and currently Medan Merdeka). However, there they found nobody to confirm the news they were so eagerly anticipating. Unknown to Soekarno, Hatta and Soebardjo, all top Gunsei authorities had been summoned to the Gunshireibu (Army Headquarters) in the NKPM building on the opposite (southwest) corner of Gambir Square to listen to the Emperor's noon radio broadcast about the surrender. Somewhat later that afternoon, at 14.30, and upon Soebardjo's suggestion, it was decided to go to Rear Admiral Maeda's Bukanfu office, referred to by Indonesians as the Kantor Penghoeboeng Angkatan Laoet, to get some information there. Meeting Maeda there, he congratulated both Soekarno and Hatta on what had happened at Dalat. However, in return Soekarno asked somewhat bluntly whether it was true that the Japanese had asked the Allies for a cessation of hostilities. After some considerable silence and with his head bowed, Maeda managed to confirm it more or less. He added, however, that no official confirmation had reached him and that therefore, before imparting more solid information to his visitors, he had to await instructions from Tokyo. Dahm concludes that 'Maeda, the only friend of the Indonesian nationalists during the years of humiliation under the Japanese, promised to inform Sukarno as soon as he knew more details'.[27] After leaving Maeda, Soekarno and Hatta immediately made preparations to have the PPKI assemble at ten o'clock on 16 August at the Pedjambon 2 office of the Sanyo committee in order to discuss all constitutional issues pertaining to a forthcoming Indonesian independence. Hatta was to work out a constitution in the evening hours of the 15th, for the PPKI to consider the next day. Still, on 15 August some growing pressure for an immediate solely Indonesian takeover was to be mounted by quite a considerable number of Sjahrir's followers. First, in the late afternoon at Hatta's home, and then around ten o'clock at night at Soekarno's place, a *pemuda* delegation gathered to propose their own scenario, or rather that of Sjahrir. At Hatta's place, some 15 *pemuda* led by Soebantio Djojohadikoesoemo – the son of Margono Djojohadikoesoemo who had once been a member of Hatta's *kikan* – and Soebadio Sastrosatomo, a law student, demanded that Soekarno immediately proclaim independence over the radio network, to be followed by an immediate takeover of authority. Hatta retorted that 'he was for a revolution but not for a putsch'. Upon 'hearing this, they [the *pemuda*] became even angrier', and when leaving they told him, 'you cannot be counted upon when the revolution comes' (Hatta 1981:228-9, 1952:334).

At Soekarno's home that night, with Soebardjo having alerted Hatta about a swarming crowd of *pemuda* being there, Hatta and Soebardjo went there as well. A delegation of *pemuda* led by Wikana, Chaerul Saleh, Soekarni and Adam Malik were rather loudly challenging Soekarno to follow the scenario earlier suggested by Soebantio and Soebadio. They also rejected the plan for the PPKI to proclaim independence on 16 August, as well as drafting a constitution and forming a government, arguing that all that was not needed. As Hatta later recalled, the *pemuda* 'did not think all this was necessary [since] this whole procedure gave the impression that Indonesian independence was made in Japan; they wanted an independent Indonesia made by Indonesians themselves'. So they wanted Soekarno to proclaim independence that night over the radio 'out of the clutches of the Japanese'. Hatta recalled that Soekarno rejected this demand out of hand 'with all the logic and evidence he could muster; and where necessary I supported him'. Soekarno maintained that 'what the youth were demanding was irresponsible. It was clear that the two views could not be reconciled.' Wikana – once an *anak buah* of Soekarno during Soekarno's 1930s Bandoeng years – retorted that if Soekarno did not proclaim independence that night, 'tomorrow there will be killing and spilling of blood'. Hearing this threat, Soekarno angrily rushed across to Wikana, and while pointing to his own throat he yelled: '[Here is] my throat, take me over to that corner and do away with me here and now, and don't wait until tomorrow'. Wikana, quite taken aback by Soekarno's fierce outburst, said that

<hr>

[27]   Hatta 1981:227-8; Subardjo 1978:299-301; for Dahm's comments see Dahm 1969:311.

he had no intention at all of killing Soekarno, but that he only wanted to remind him that if independence was not proclaimed tonight our people will act and kill anyone they suspect of being pro-Dutch, such as Ambonese and others. Hatta later dryly commented on Wikana's reply that all of it 'was sheer bluff' (*gertak tidak lain daripada gertak*). Han Bing Siong, formerly an associate professor of law at the Universitas Indonesia, in a long-overdue and well-documented analysis of the *pemuda* confronting Soekarno and Hatta about the *proklamasi*, asserts that 'on the 15th Sukarno and Hatta did not yield an inch, however, and resisted all pressure'.[28] Sjahrir became enraged by Soekarno's adamant stand and, according to Soebadio's testimony, called Soekarno a *banci* (transvestite). Here, Sjahrir was suggesting that Soekarno was a lackey of the Japanese. Dahm, however, concludes: 'This Sukarno had never been. He had at no time subordinated his goal, Indonesian independence, to Japanese interests. [He had remained] one who was decisive in setting the course of negotiations for future independence, but had also remained for the masses the symbol of freedom and a hope for a better future, even when he preached total war and made struggle at the side of the hated oppressor into a duty.'[29]

As for the PPKI meeting scheduled for ten o'clock on 16 August, that did not take place at all since Soekarno and Hatta did not turn up. Still unknown to the assembled delegates, something had occurred earlier that morning which henceforth would enter the annals of history as the Insiden Rengas-dengklok (Rengasdengklok Incident), which Hatta would later describe as an event where legend and reality were entwined. In the early hours of the 16th both Soekarno – accompanied by his wife and nine-month-old son – and Hatta, just after finishing their *sahur* (final meal before daybreak during the *puasa*, the fast during Ramadan), were in fact kidnapped and driven from their respective Djakarta homes. Apparently all this had been planned immediately after the Wikana and Chaerul Saleh groups left Soekarno's home close to midnight on the 15th. The embittered and humiliated *pemuda* had assembled at the nearby Hawaii café and decided to take the two leaders to some place 'free of Japanese interference and the filth of Japanese politics'. According to Dahm, the prank truly 'demonstrates the Pemoedas' immaturity [making it] easy to guess what a catastrophe would have ensued if they had actually launched their planned revolt against the Japanese Army'.[30]

---

[28] Hatta 1981:229-30, 1979b:446; Subardjo 1978:308-9; Han Bing Siong 2000:234: Adam Malik 1956:35-7. Adam Malik, throughout this book, and in Malik 1980:184-9 and 1988:109-10, is prone to exaggerate the role of the *pemuda* as well as his own; see for this also Dahm 1969:312, note 126 and Hatta 1952:332, note 1.

[29] Subadio Sastrosatomo 1987:13. For Dahm's analysis see Dahm 1969:315.

[30] Malik 1978:217. Subadio Satrosatomo 1987:20 reveals that Sjahrir was informed by him about the Hawaii café plans but 'did not agree with the kidnapping plan'. For Dahm's comment see Dahm 1969:313.

So, escorted by *pemuda*, the two nationalist leaders were driven first in two motorcars to just outside Krawang and then in a pickup truck to the PETA barracks at Rengasdengklok, some 80 kilometres by road east of Djakarta. Apparently the aim was to have the two leaders 'carry on the leadership of the republican government from there', since, as Soekarni told Hatta the morning he picked him up from his home, 'at midday fifteen thousand people would descend on the capital city to, together with the university students and members of the PETA, disarm the Japanese'. Hatta retorted that 'what they were planning was sheer fantasy and something inconsistent with reality', and that it all would end 'not in a revolution but in a putsch' (Hatta 1979:446, 1952:334-5). Yet Sjahrir in the capital city seemed to be in high spirits about the plans Soekarni had revealed to Hatta. He confided to his diary that 'we are ready for the great performance [and] we simply had to ensure that the proclamation would be made rapidly'. When he was informed that both Soekarno and Hatta were being held prisoner in a garrison thirty miles outside the city, he stressed that 'the proclamation had to be made that day'; we will issue it 'ourselves and begin our direct action [since] retreat is no longer possible' (Sjahrir 1949:256-7). Sjahrir must have been pleased as well about the agreement made by Chaerul Saleh and Captain Latief Hendraningrat, second in command at Djakarta's PETA militia garrison, for coordinating actions within the capital city the moment he set the proclamation in motion. As his most recent biographer has it, 'Sjahrir had decided to go with the stream of events, and not to distance himself any more'.[31] However, events were soon to rob this highly intelligent man, who remained a loner at heart, of the prominent place he thought was about to be bestowed on him on 16 August.

That day was in fact to feature some unforeseen events, first at Rengasdengklok and then in the private home in Djakarta of a Japanese rear admiral. In Rengasdengklok, Soekarno, his wife and son, and Hatta had now been moved from the barracks to more comfortable surroundings. A house some 300 metres from the barracks belonging to a Chinese landowner named Djiauw Kie Siong had been vacated for them (Setiadi Kartohadikusumo 1995: 11). In spite of some sources' explicit claims, no discussions whatever took place in Djiauw Kie Siong's home between *pemuda* and nationalist leaders.[32] As Hatta (1952:335) recalled, 'not a single discussion took place. [W]e were

---

[31] For the Latief Hendraningrat/Chaerul Saleh agreement see Subadio Sastrosatomo 1987:21. For the biographer's recent comments on Sjahrir, Mrázek 1994:265.

[32] Such as Dimyati 1951, a source inspired by Adam Malik, sources cited by Mohammad Hatta but rejected as being mere mythologies in Hatta 1952:311-2. The fact that no discussions took place is corroborated by the local PETA acting commander Oemar Bahsan 1955:52-3. Han Bing Siong 2000:234 too blames authors such as De Graaf and Giebels for far too glibly accepting Malik's and Sidik Kertapati's (1957) accounts, while rejecting Hatta's and Soekarno's.

doomed to do nothing at all, and were condemned to witness from afar the failure of an idea which was not based upon reality at all.' Most likely no discussion took place because the *pemuda* were eagerly awaiting news of the upheavals they hoped would occur in Djakarta. Around noon, Hatta somewhat mischievously prodded Soekarni to phone Djakarta to find out. After some considerable delay, Soekarni told the leaders he could not reach Djakarta at all. Hatta retorted that most likely 'your revolution has failed'. This was further confirmed when at six o'clock in the evening Soebardjo suddenly entered the landowner's home together with Soekarni, with Soebardjo stating that he had been ordered by the Gunseikan to bring them all back to Djakarta. He also confirmed that conditions in Djakarta were normal and nothing dramatic had happened.[33] Nishijima, after Soebardjo had alerted him and Rear Admiral Maeda to Soekarno's rather strange absence, played a crucial role in ascertaining Soekarno's and Hatta's whereabouts. Through his close contacts with *pemuda* such as Wikana and Joesoef Koento – the latter was to escort Soebardjo to Rengasdengklok – Nishijima, after some intense prodding, was finally told by these *pemuda* where Soekarno and Hatta were.[34] So in the end Iboe Fatmawati and her son Goentoer travelled in Soetardjo's motorcar – Soetardjo as *residen* (*shochokan* in Japanese) of Djakarta had been in Rengasdengklok to inspect some rice deliveries – while the nationalist leaders and Soekarni travelled in Soebardjo's motorcar back to their respective homes in the capital city. They arrived there about eight o'clock in the evening, with Hatta dryly concluding that 'this evening the leadership of the nearby revolution remains again firmly in the hands of Soekarno and Hatta'.[35] Adam Malik, however, claims that Soekarno's and Hatta's return to Djakarta was in fact due to a so-called 'Persetoejoean Rengasdengklok' (Rengasdengklok Agreement), with both leaders at last having succumbed to *pemuda* pressure.[36]

During the remaining night and the early hours of 17 August, final preparations for an immediate Indonesian independence fell neatly into place. But here again legend and reality, as we have seen above in Adam Malik's case and will see below in Soekarni's and Sajoeti Melik's case, seem to blur together. Some participants adamantly claim an important niche in the his-

---

[33]   Hatta 1981:233; for Soebardjo showing up and being alerted about Soekarno and Hatta's whereabouts see Subardjo 1978:319-21.
[34]   See for Nishijima's account Reid and Oki 1986:316-7 and Nishijima's testimony in Wild and Carey 1988:95. Anderson 1972:76 states that Wikana, by revealing the two leaders' location, could then count on Maeda and Nishijima's full cooperation in getting Indonesian independence declared.
[35]   Hatta 1981:234, and for his concluding remark Hatta 1952:335.
[36]   Malik 1975:56-7. Hatta dubs Malik's version (first published in 1948) a legend pure and simple, Hatta 1952:332, note 1.

torical process that was now about to evolve.[37] As to Soekarno and Hatta, now determined to set that process into motion, they first urged Soebardjo to get the PPKI delegates promptly assembled in the Hotel des Indes, only to find out after a while that this could not be arranged at this late hour. So the three of them then decided to see Rear Admiral Maeda at his home. Here they were told that their PPKI assembly could be held at the Admiral's home at Myakodoori 1 (the pre-war British Consulate at what was then Nassau Boulevard 1 and is presently Jalan Imam Bonjol – not Jalan Diponegoro (formerly the Oranje Boulevard), as Anderson states[38]). As to Maeda, he tried to reach the Gunseikan, Major General Yamamoto, since he did not want the Kaigun to be seen as the sole instrument handling the Indonesian independence issue. This was to no avail, however, since the Gunseikan, well aware of Maeda's sympathy for the nationalist cause as established for instance in the Bukanfu-inspired Asrama Indonesia Merdeka at Kebon Sirih 80, declined to see him. The Gunseikan's refusal also had to do with him receiving word from Tokyo via General Itagaki in Shonanto (Singapore) that Japan was bound by the surrender terms to maintain the status quo in all territories still under Japanese control. Yamamoto was ordered to freeze all political activities and programmes in the area under his jurisdiction (Nishijima and Kishi 1963:502; Reid and Oki 1986:320; Anderson 1972:79).

Maeda then decided to phone the Somubucho, Major General Nishimura, in order to arrange a meeting at the latter's home with him, together with Soekarno and Hatta. It seems that the Somubucho only consented to this meeting after the rear admiral had stressed the dangers of widespread rioting occurring in the capital city. So Soekarno and Hatta followed Maeda to Major General Nishimura's home, a five-minute ride from Maeda's. There they found the Somubucho assembled with his top political advisers, Lieutenant Colonel Nomura, Captain Nakamura, Saito, Miyoshi and Dr Nakatani. The two nationalist leaders wished to discuss with Nishimura as Somubucho the PPKI independence deliberations to commence later that night. After being informed of their plans, Nishimura insisted that matters

---

[37]   Hatta claims a Soekarni text was circulated first, with the message: 'The Indonesian people declare themselves independent and will therefore capture all existing bodies still maintained by foreigners', and when this was not approved, Sajoeti Melik then produced one: 'We, the Indonesian People, hereby declare Indonesian Independence. Matters concerning the transfer of power and other matters will be executed in an orderly manner and in the shortest possible time.' Hatta retorts that 'this new legend pushes Sajuti Melik as the one responsible for the ultimate content of the proclamation. The original document shows that the proclamation was personally written by Bung Karno, while the sentence structure and style absolutely do not tally with that of Sajuti Melik.' (Hatta 1952:332.)

[38]   For Anderson referring to Jalan Diponegoro, see Anderson 1972:75. He is clearly not familiar with Djakarta's street map at the time, as he also refers to Prapatan instead of Parapatan, Anderson 1972:39, 54, 76, 81-2.

had changed dramatically; the Gunsei was now under Allied orders not to tamper with the status quo at all. The Somubucho was quite sorry not to have carried out the promises made earlier about Indonesian independence, but as of now the Gunsei no longer had freedom of action, reduced as it was to being a mere tool of the Allies. He was therefore forced to explicitly forbid the holding of the politically inspired PPKI assembly scheduled by Soekarno and Hatta that evening. The two leaders attempted to persuade Nishimura to change his mind, but to no avail. Hatta went so far as to remind the Somu-bucho of the samurai code of not breaking promises. A frustrated and tired Soekarno is said to have suggested that the Somubucho would be wise to commit *hari kiri*.[39] The Somubucho, according to many sources, then prom-ised not to interfere if the PPKI meeting was just a private gathering, with a Captain Nakamura, another Japanese present, stating that the Somubucho in fact meant a private tea party. All this seems, as Han Bing Siong has recently claimed, to have been yet another myth.[40] In the end – Maeda had already left, probably frustrated by Nishimura's stubborn refusal to cooperate polit-ically – Soekarno and Hatta returned to Maeda's home, with Miyoshi turn-ing up there somewhat later. According to Nishijima, who was also present, Maeda wanted the presence of somebody from the army and so the choice fell on Miyoshi, a trusted confidant of the Somubucho but also of both Soekarno and Hatta, and he was requested by phone to be present. Miyoshi, perhaps in view of the solemn occasion soon to evolve, was a bit tipsy; this, however, did not prevent him from giving advice about the proclamation to be conceived soon in the small hours of the 17th.[41]

The two nationalist leaders were now, as Hatta had earlier stated upon his return from Rengasdengklok, determined to take matters solely into their own hands regardless of the consequences. Still, they seemed pleased to have Japanese like Maeda be part of the process as well. They not only felt pro-tected from possible armed Japanese intervention, but they also sensed they had finally taught the unruly *pemuda* a lesson in diplomatic brinkmanship. At Myakodoori 1 the PPKI delegates and a group of *pemuda* were assembled

---

[39]   Hatta 1981:235-6; Subardjo 1978:331-2; Anderson 1972:79. As to the samurai code, Roem 1970:51 praises Hatta as being more of a samurai than the samurai. See also Han Bing Siong, 2000:241, note 14. As to the *hari kiri* suggestion, see Friend 1988:119 citing a 5 July 1968 interview with Hatta.

[40]   Han Bing Siong 2000:240, but also alleging that in several interviews Nishimura 'most vehemently denied having dropped any hint that tea parties and the like would be tolerated'. Han Bing Siong cites a large number of authors, including Lambert Giebels, Ben Anderson, John Legge, Anthony Reid, L. de Jong (in spite of the presence of documents at his Institute for War Documentation) and Joop de Jong, who all insist that Soekarno and Hatta were given the green light as long as it was done without Nishimura knowing about it. Han Bing Siong (2000:241) wonders whether Nishimura was indeed so accommodating.

[41]   Nishijima's recollections in Reid and Oki 1986:321.

around 2 a.m. on the first floor in a reception room and a waiting room, where Hatta says some fifty to sixty of Indonesia's most prominent people were eagerly awaiting the unfolding of a historic event. Soekarno, Hatta, Soebardjo, Maeda, Miyoshi, Yoshizumi and Nishijima had in the meantime retired to the admiral's study.[42]

It seems that there the text of the independence proclamation was carefully worked out by Soekarno, Hatta and Soebardjo, in consultation with Maeda, Nishijima and Miyoshi. Because none of the Indonesians had bothered to bring along the Piagam Djakarta, Soekarno requested Hatta to draft a text, since he had by far the best literary skills. Hatta had memorized the end of the third line of the Piagam Djakarta and dictated it as an opening phrase: 'We, the people of Indonesia, hereby declare Indonesia's Independence', while Soekarno wrote down what Hatta dictated. The formulation of the next phrase caused some discussion, however, since it concerned the transfer of power. Hatta had dictated it as 'Matters concerning the transfer of power and other matters will be executed in an orderly manner and in the shortest possible time'. This prompted the *pemuda* led by Soekarni to make another attempt to influence the course of events, with Soekarni objecting to the caution of Hatta's second phrase and demanding its replacement as follows: 'All existing government organs must be seized by the people from the foreigners who still occupy them'. However, this phrase was not included in the text since it was rejected by the PPKI majority. And so the text was finally approved to read as Hatta had dictated it to Soekarno: 'We, the people of Indonesia, hereby declare Indonesia's Independence. Matters concerning the transfer of power and other matters will be executed in an orderly manner and in the shortest possible time.' The *pemuda* then demanded that six of them together with Soekarno and Hatta rather than the PPKI delegates should sign the proclamation, since they represented the people while the PPKI represented the Japanese. As a compromise, Soekarno and Hatta ultimately signed as follows: 'In the name of the Indonesian People, Soekarno-Hatta, 17 August 2605'.[43]

It was now five o'clock in the morning, and the assembly at Myakodoori 1 began to disperse, with the understanding that a public announcement of the *proklamasi* would occur later that day. Initial plans had been to call a mass meeting at Gambir Square, but since the Gunsei had ordered troops to intensively patrol the square and its surroundings the proclamation announcement was scheduled to take place at Soekarno's home at Pegangsaan Timoer

---

[42]   Hatta 1981:237; Reid and Oki 1986:321; Nishijima's testimony is in Wild and Carey 1988:96; Subardjo 1978:331.
[43]   Hatta 1981:237; Subardjo 1978:334; Reid and Oki 1986:322-3; Reid 1974:28; Anderson 1972: 82-3 and his testimony in Wild and Carey 1988:90; Han Bing Siong 2000:244.

56. So exactly at ten o'clock Soekarno, flanked by Hatta, read out the proclamation to a crowd of some one hundred people, with PETA captain Latief
Hendraningrat then hoisting on a bamboo pole the *dwi warna* (red and white)
banner which Fatmawati had diligently sewn together in the early hours of
the night. After the singing of 'Indonesia Raja', the crowd started to disperse
from this rather unnatural and sobering occasion – this, the grand moment
for which Soekarno – along with Hatta and Sjahrir but also the *pemuda*, who
had only recently entered centre stage – had striven so tirelessly, in faithful readiness for sacrifice. In its immediate wake there were several hurried
attempts to announce the independence of Indonesia to the outside world.
Maeda and Nishijima both had a hand in this, utilizing the Bukanfu's press
office to get copies of the proclamation printed and distributed in Djakarta,
and using internal telephone and telegraph outlets to spread the news across
Java and Madoera. Adam Malik states that the Japanese News Agency
Domei's Morse code was used by *pemuda* working there to carry the story
throughout the country as well as overseas. The Gunsei, upon realizing what
was going on, first tried to retract it and then denied the authenticity of the
Domei message, all to no avail.[44] Also, the Gunsei had taken steps to disarm
and disband the PETA and *heiho*, while putting their own army units on alert
at positions near the PETA and *heiho* garrisons, not only in the capital city but
all over the country. According to one source, this justified Soekarno's and
Hatta's efforts to avoid antagonizing the Japanese, only to be faced again by
pemuda criticizing the two leaders for this (Han Bing Siong 2000:245).

All this showed that both Soekarno and Hatta needed to exercise extreme
caution vis-à-vis the Japanese authorities, as well as to keep the anti-Japanese
pemuda in check. The first step toward Indonesian statehood was taken on
18 August by the PPKI. Both Soekarno and Hatta assembled the PPKI, adding eight new members to it, including the *pemuda* leaders Chaerul Saleh,
Soekarni and Wikana. Wikana, by way of Chaerul Saleh, launched an attack
on the PPKI's legitimacy as it was now constituted, since it still stank of the
Japanese, therefore insisting the PPKI change its name to Komite Nasional
Indonesia (Indonesian National Committee). Both Hatta and Soekarno
countered that it was difficult to separate their responsibility to the Japanese
from their responsibility to the Indonesian people. They proposed informing the Japanese that it was still a PPKI assembly while guaranteeing to the
Indonesian people that it was in fact the first meeting of the Komite Nasional
Indonesia. This did not appease the *pemuda* delegation, and so they left the
meeting harbouring yet another grudge against their elders. Before the
meeting broke up, Soekarno and Hatta were officially acclaimed *presiden* and

---

[44]   Anderson 1972:83; Malik 1980:190; Colin Wild's contribution in Wild and Carey 1988:163.

wakil presiden (president and vice-president), respectively, of the Indonesian Republic, while in the popular jargon they were often referred to as the *dwi-tunggal* (unity in two).[45]

The *dwitunggal* nationalist leadership, now left to themselves, made some crucial decisions. The next day a start was made in drafting a constitution more in accordance with the new situation. In order to guarantee unity throughout the new republic, the hard-won victory of the *pihak Islam* just two months ago for the president to be Muslim was annulled. Hatta asserted this was in order not to offend the Christians living in the eastern parts of Indonesia or the Hindus living in Bali (Logemann 1962:11-2; Anderson 1972: 87-8). On 19 August the PPKI, now named Komite Nasional Indonesia (KNI) in order to rid itself of the odium of being a made-in-Tokyo organization, met again, mainly to decide on the administrative divisions (provinces, residencies and villages) to be used in the new republic. There was a subcommittee led by Soebardjo to debate how the functions of government should be divided among the twelve ministries soon to be established (Raliby 1953:15). At the end of the session Soekarno initiated the idea of a Staatspartij (State Party) as a possible medium for mobilizing the population behind the new republican government. In the next session of 21 August, a subcommittee was appointed to discuss the structure and goals of the Staatspartij, now called Partai Nasional Indonesia, a deliberate evocation of Soekarno's pre-war Bandoeng-based party. It was founded on 23 August 1945, and was an extension of Soekarno's pre-war ideas that had re-emerged in the Poetera of the Japanese period. Yet it soon petered out and was dissolved, since it was considered unrepresentative due to the small number of Muslim leaders involved. Meeting again the next day, the KNI ruled to establish a formal Komite Nasional Indonesia Poesat (KNIP, Central Indonesian National Committee) as the provisional representative advisory medium supporting the president in his daily work, and thus acting more or less as a provisional parliament. Negotiations were started to determine its membership (Raliby 1953:16-7). On 27 August a full list of 137 representatives was formally announced by Soekarno, while on the same day the KNI was absorbed by the KNIP. Somewhat earlier, on 23 August 1945, it was decided to form a body called the Badan Penolong Keluarga Korban Perang (BPKKP, Body to Aid Families of War Victims), soon to be reformed into the Badan Keamanan Rakjat (BKR, Body Preserving the Safety of the People). This was a national armed force to replace the disbanded PETA, Giyogun and *heiho* units. In order not to unduly provoke Japanese retaliation, it would assume the character of a lightly armed home guard aiding war victims and the like.[46] As to

---

[45] Malik 1956:61, 63, 1980:190; Sidik Kertapati 1964:100-1; Subardjo 1978:346; Raliby 1953:14.
[46] Raliby 1953:17, 20; Nugroho Notosusanto 1979:142. Already on 5 October 1945, no longer

the KNIP, at its first session on 29 August 1945 it became clear what powers the KNIP was to have, with its main task being to advise the president in running the country. The former PETA commander Kasman Singodimedjo, as first chairman of the KNIP, declared his willingness to carry out the orders of the central government.[47]

On 5 September 1945, already bereft of his PNI, Soekarno formed his first cabinet, usually referred to as the *bucho* cabinet. As a presidential and not a parliamentary cabinet, it was responsible solely to him. However, as we will see below, these presidential powers would soon cause some consternation because of the danger of absolute power in a president responsible to no one. On 10 September, Soekarno issued a decree that in future the orders of the Republican government were the only ones to be obeyed. This was contrary to Allied orders for maintaining the status quo. But Soekarno insisted that he and Hatta, through person-to-person contacts, had reached a gentlemen's agreement, most likely since most of the members of that first cabinet (as its name suggests: *bucho* means departmental supervisor) were still employed in Japanese offices and thus had a dual role. Hatta dryly refers to the many *bucho* and *sanyo* (adviser) sitting in Soekarno's first cabinet.[48] That some of the Japanese seemed to cope with it is supported by Yamamoto's statement a fortnight later on the occasion of yet another mass demonstration whipped up by Soekarno and showing his astonishing power over the people. Yama-moto cautioned the small Allied advance party then dwelling in the Hotel des Indes led by British major A.G. Greenhalgh not to underestimate Indo-nesian nationalism and above all not to view Soekarno and Hatta as ordinary war criminals. According to Major General Yamamoto, these two nationalist leaders had cooperated with the Japanese merely in order to protect their people and to faithfully secure the cause of Indonesian independence.[49]

---

fearing Japanese reprisals, Soekarno decreed the formation of the Tentara Keamanan Rakjat (TKR, People's Security Army) as the first regular army of the Indonesian Republic, Nugroho Notosusanto 1979:143.

[47] Raliby 1953:22-3; Dahm 1969:321; Kasman Singodimedjo 1979:20. The three KNIP vice-chairmen were Soetardjo Kartohadikoesoemo, Johannes Latuharhary and Adam Malik (Raliby 1953:23).

[48] Anderson 1972:111-3. For its 17-member composition Raliby 1953:33: Soekarno, Prime Minister; Wiranatakoesoema, Internal Affairs; Achmad Soebardjo, Foreign Affairs; A.A. Maramis, Finance; Soepomo, Justice; Soerachman Tjokroadisoerjo, Welfare; Soeprijadi, Defence (to honour the Blitar PETA revolt by his absence, he never turned up); Boentaran Martoatmodjo, Health; Ki Hadjar Dewantoro, Education; Amir Sjarifoeddin, Information; Iwa Koesoema Soemantri, Social Affairs; Abikoesno Tjokrosoejoso, Public Works; Abikoesno Tjokrosoejoso, Communications (thus holding two ministerial posts); Wahid Hasjim, Minister of State; M. Amir, Minister of State; Sartono, Minister of State; Oto Iskandardinata, Minister of State. With the exception of Soeprijadi, this list is remarkably close to the list of ministerial posts forwarded to the Japanese in mid-March 1942. The cabinet list is also in Finch and Lev 1965:2 and in *Internationale Spectator*, 22 October 1954:517.

[49] Dahm 1969:323 citing Anderson 1961:120-1.

The occasion the Gunseikan was referring to was on 19 September 1945, at Ikada Square, where Soekarno briefly addressed a crowd of 200,000, yet another occasion where myth and reality were intertwined. According to one source it was the *pemuda* who, frustrated by their repeated failure to wrest power from the Japanese, had been instrumental in assembling the mass rally in yet another attempt to force a showdown with Japanese authority. That the Japanese seemed prepared was demonstrated by the presence of army units all around Ikada Square with their machine guns trained at the crowd. As our source Han Bing Siong puts it, 'the stage seemed set for a massive confrontation [...] likely to end in hundreds, if not thousands of casualties and sweeping away the republic in the process'. Tan Malaka (now lodging incognito at Soebardjo's home) and Adam Malik (at that time third vice-chairman of the KNIP) remained basically hostile to the *dwitunggal* (Soekarno-Hatta). In their accounts of the 19 September rally this is aptly demonstrated. Tan Malaka states that the *dwitunggal* were no fighters, let alone true revolutionaries. He says that Soekarno at first wanted to cancel the demonstration in view of a Japanese order forbidding such rallies, but that Adam Malik and the *pemuda* wanted it to go ahead. Adam Malik, in his own account, confirms Soekarno's initial plans to cancel the rally. Soekarno, however, boasted to Cindy Adams years later that he alone had convened the mass rally.[50] And so reality and legend seemed to be entwined once more.

Soekarno in the end seems to have tried to get Japanese permission for the meeting, going so far as to threaten the Japanese that otherwise he and Hatta would resign. This ploy by Soekarno was in vain. So there was nothing left but for Soekarno to appear at the rally and address the assembled crowd. Before he approached the hastily improvised dais, he was met by a Japanese staff officer, a lieutenant colonel named Shizuo Miyamoto, who cautioned him not to unduly incite the huge crowd. In his short speech, which according to Han Bing Siong he was fond of calling his 'state of the union address', Soekarno 'ordered the crowd to disperse, after explaining that he had given orders for the meeting to be cancelled and that he had only come because he had no alternative'. Han Bing Siong adds: 'The *pemuda* thus provided Sukarno with the opportunity, though unintentionally, to give a convincing show of his authority'.[51] Thus, at a critical moment fraught with danger, Soekarno once again demonstrated his astonishing power over his people. Both

---

[50]   Han Bing Siong 2000:246. For the *pemuda* forcing a confrontation with the Japanese see Tan Malaka 1991, III:100 and for his remarks on the *dwitunggal*: Tan Malaka 1991, III:99-100; for Malik see Malik 1975:94. For Soekarno's boast: Adams 1965:224-5.

[51]   Han Bing Siong 2000:246; Reid 1974:33 concludes that 'violence was avoided' and that Soekarno had 'demonstrated in compelling terms his indispensability to the Japanese or anyone to take their place in Java'. Ominous signs to be heeded by the British and Dutch forces soon to land in Java.

Tan Malaka's and Adam Malik's confrontational efforts disappeared in the face of an address lasting a mere five minutes. As Raliby reports, Soekarno implored the huge crowd to return home peacefully and be aware that His Government would defend the Republic of Indonesia at all costs (*Pemerintah kami tetap akan mempertahankan Negara Republik Indonesia*).[52]

Ten days after the Ikada Square rally, the bulk of the British forces landed in Djakarta without meeting any Indonesian resistance. It seems that Soekarno's address had given his people sufficient self-confidence to patiently await the circumstances now created by the presence of British forces in the main cities of Java's north coast. In Djakarta, meanwhile, other significant developments had taken place. Sjahrir, who earlier had set out on a fact-finding trip throughout Java, had come to some startling conclusions. He first found out that many Indonesian civil servants, administrators, police and paramilitary organizations were faithfully serving the new Indonesian Republic. Sjahrir also noted that national strength and unity had reached greater heights than anything he had experienced before. He also observed that Soekarno's close ties with the people had in no way been disrupted. And that Soekarno, regardless of all he demanded of the people, had been quite able to establish an accord which affirmed him as their true leader (Sjahrir 1949:259; Dahm 1969:325). These revelations may have caused Sjahrir to abandon his earlier rather noncommittal stance. He could well have been moved in that direction by the 7 October petition signed by some 40 KNIP members (not some 75 as Giebels (1999:395) states). In that petition Soekarno was urged to change the existing *pembantu* status of the council into a true legislature, with cabinet ministers being responsible to the council instead of to the president. A month after the 19 September rally at Ikada Square, Sjahrir joined a KNIP Dewan Pekerdjaan (working committee), of which on 20 October 1945 he was elected chairman. This committee soon became the initial curb on Soekarno's presidential powers (Sjahrir 1949:263). Sjahrir and Hatta were far more prone to Western-inspired constitutional modes and thus addressed themselves to some of the anxieties that had arisen in the wake of Soekarno's presidential *bucho* cabinet. Vice-President Hatta, after Soekarno and he had accepted the 7 October petition, issued the following presidential decision no. X on 16 October, on behalf of Soekarno who was in Central Java:

---

[52]   Raliby 1953:35. Even Giebels, in an account fraught with myths and inaccuracies, admits that Soekarno prevented a bloodbath, Giebels 1999:381. Malik 1975:95 and Sidik Kertapati 1964:139 curiously omit noting that the rally was planned by the *pemuda* as a final confrontation against the Japanese, and so do not mention that it was in fact a failure of *pemuda* intentions. Instead they both claim the rally was crucial for unifying the many different groups in society who, with independence, were more self-confident and determined than ever, also Han Bing Siong 2000:246.

> The KNIP shall, pending the formation of the MPR [People's Consultative Assembly] and the DPR [People's Representative Council], have legislative powers and share in establishing the broad outlines of the aims of the state [*haluan negara*] and agrees that the day-to-day work of the KNIP, in view of the critical situation, will be carried out by a working committee [Badan Pekerdja] to be chosen from among its members and responsible to the KNIP as a whole.

And so Hatta, with Sjahrir and Sjarifoeddin as chairman and vice-chairman respectively of the Badan Pekerdja, started a quite open four-week procedure which finally reduced Soekarno from an absolute ruler to a mere figurehead. A process which by some was turned into a mix of reality and legend.

Anderson, in his account of Java's revolution, devotes a well-documented chapter to it, calling it 'a silent coup', mainly in the sense of diligent, quiet and peaceful work being done. The process resulted in Hatta's 1 November 1945 manifesto[53] and ended a fortnight later in the *bucho* cabinet being replaced by Sjahrir's more democratically based ministry. This achievement, moreover, was hailed by all Indonesian leaders and prominents at that time as presenting some semblance of parliamentary democracy. Curiously enough, Giebels, parroting Anderson, calls it Sjahrir's coup instead of Hatta's coup. This Dutch historian – who is a lawyer to boot – chooses to adopt a coup scenario while at the same time turning it into yet another blatant myth. He places Soekarno, the Dutch *onderdaan* (citizen),[54] far away from Djakarta on 1 November, seeking solace in the south of Banten at Pelaboehan Ratoe (formerly the Wijnkoopsbaai) consorting with Njai Loro Kidoel (the mythological queen of the South Seas). In order to affirm their *wahyu* (divine inspiration) or their *kesaktian* (cosmic energy), the Central Javanese monarchs would indeed take a dip once a year in the Indian Ocean, the realm of Njai Loro Kidoel, at the beach resort Parangtritis just south of Djokjakarta. Their example has sometimes been followed by presidents inspired by *kejawen* (Javanese cultural tradition), such as Soekarno and Soeharto. As a matter of fact, it was not a silent coup in Giebels' sense, but an act inspired by both Hatta and Sjahrir for bringing parliamentary democracy to life in the young Indonesian Republic. This scenario immediately won Soekarno's blessing when he returned from Ambarawa and Magelang (and thus not from Pelaboehan Ratoe, as Giebels insists, citing a former Eurasian parliamentarian named Rudi Koot, an expert on Njai Loro Kidoel).[55] And as Y.B. Mangunwijaya stresses, it was not a silent coup at all but a move Soekarno

---

53   For Hatta's manifesto see Raliby 1953:73, 525-8 (*lampiran* (supplement) xiv).

54   The Dutch *onderdaan* status is just one of Giebels's convoluted arguments; at that time NICA officials and the British considered Soekarno an Indonesian republican pure and simple. See for instance Jan Blokker, 'Als de dag van gisteren', *De Volkskrant*, 29 June 2001 and *Tempo*, 24 June 2001:106 stating: 'Only Dutch reactionaries such as Giebels consider Sukarno until the year 1950 to be a Dutch subject'.

55   Giebels thus ignores Anderson, who specifically states that Soekarno was in 'Central Java

approved of the moment he returned from Central Java. Years later he recalled that it was indeed

> a peaceful revolution and an act of open democracy wrought on 14 November 1945 under the inspiration of Sutan Syahrir and Mohammad Hatta. This act brought parliamentary democracy to life in Indonesia. It was not 'a silent coup' as is often claimed, but a change that won the blessing of the Republican President and Vice-President of the day.[56]

So when Hatta issued his manifesto, Soekarno had in fact been in Central Java, where he was instrumental in achieving a ceasefire between British and Indonesian forces in that area. Shortly before that success, this time together with Hatta, Soekarno had been working at a similar ceasefire agreement in Soerabaja, a city where *pemuda* led by Boeng Tomo had been successful in disarming the Japanese and where hostilities between British forces and Indonesians had erupted in the wake of the British landing, causing some observers to state that 'here the *pemuda* experienced their finest hour', and 'the fact that the British needed Soekarno's help against the Indonesian insurgents was quite striking'. A British reporter wrote that the 'heroic resistance of the British 49th Brigade was bound to end in extermination unless someone was able to quell the passions [of the Boeng Tomo-led *pemuda*;] all hopes rested on Sukarno's influence' (Han Bing Siong 2000:255-6). Initially, and due to Soekarno's fearless conduct, a ceasefire was achieved in an Indonesian-British agreement, the very first international accord between a foreign power and the Indonesian Republic.[57] However, it fell apart due to the assassination of the local British commander, Brigadier General Mallaby, the day after Soekarno and Hatta had returned to Djakarta. The *pemuda* in Soerabaja now reduced the 49th Brigade and came close to wiping it out altogether, thus scoring an impressive military victory. The feat, however, was diminished by brutalities against (mostly Dutch) women and children initiated by uncontrollable urban mobs. The British reaction was fierce, starting with an all-out attack involving naval and air forces as well as engaging the entire Fifth Indian Division, a battle memorialized as the second battle of

---

trying to halt the fighting in Ambarawa and Magelang', see Anderson 1972:181, note 29. As to Rudi Koot, a long-time friend of Bob Hering, during a 15 December 1999 phone conversation, Koot dismissed Giebels' concoction as yet another of his *isep jempol* (spin a yarn) stories.

[56]   Y.B. Mangunwijaya's 17 October 1998 'Open letter to the University of Indonesia alumni association', *Inside Indonesia*, no. 58(April-June 1999):10; as to Giebels see Giebels 1999:394-5.

[57]   Here Giebels, citing Hatta's *Memoir*, concocts yet another story claiming that Soekarno and Hatta upon their landing in a British aircraft were shot at by Indonesians and Soekarno had to be persuaded by others to get off the aircraft. Han Bing Siong states that he did not find any reference to this in Hatta's *Memoir*, Han Bing Siong 2000:258, note 48. Han Bing Siong 2000:258, citing Christison's unpublished memoirs, p. 184, states that 'Sukarno was quite fearless'.

Soerabaja. Soekarno and Hatta objected to the ruthless shooting and bombing of helpless Soerabajan citizens. Soekarno doubted the British justification for it and tried to draw the attention of the world to the punitive measures taken by the British as being out of all proportion.[58] In doing that, with the eyes of the world briefly focused on him, Soekarno may well have scored some points diplomatically. Even with Soerabaja now firmly in the hands of British forces and some Dutch units and officials entering the city as well, on the diplomatic front it began to seem that a negotiated settlement could not be postponed any longer. At that time, Soekarno did not mean the British at all – the British had been aware that Soekarno and his followers could not be ignored – but here Soekarno was pondering possibilities of an Indonesian-Dutch negotiated settlement. Such a scenario also started to dawn in the minds of prominent Dutch officials based in Djakarta.[59]

In that context the Catholic parish priest Y.B. Mangunwijaya, often referred to as Romo Mangun, who until his recent death lived among Yogyakarta's poor along the Tjode River, once remarked to Bob Hering that the 1945 revolution was indeed the golden age of Indonesian nationalism. He considered the battle of Soerabaja comparable to the opening shots fired in an event that inaugurated the American revolution. He also remarked that Soekarno's first national party was founded on 4 July way back in Bandoeng. Romo Mangun admitted that his favourite heroes were Soekarno and Soetan Sjahrir; he viewed the setting up of Sjahrir's first parliamentary-oriented cabinet as a highlight in the careers of both leaders. He was fond of comparing these leaders to the Javanese shadow puppets Bima and Yudisthira. Soekarno resembled Bima because of his tenacity of purpose and his audacity, as well as his rather rough style of expressing himself in Low Javanese (*ngoko*). As to Sjahrir, he resembled the more refined Yudisthira, since in solving national problems he preferred to use intellectual knowledge and diplomacy rather than brute force. Romo Mangun showed me part of a piece he once wrote: 'However different they may be, Soekarno and Soetan Sjahrir represent two poles of the same world of fighters. They were the soul of bravery and faced exile for the sake of their comrades' freedom.'[60]

---

58   See for Soekarno's press release, Raliby 1953:89-90.
59   Hering 1985:1, 8, note 2; also our neighbour at Oranje Boulevard 2 (now Jalan Diponegoro 2 and the *istana* of Indonesia's vice-president). Walter Foote, former US consul and then a US political adviser, told my mother and me that Soerabaja should be compared to the opening phase of his own country's revolution. Van der Plas and Lieutenant Colonel Laurens Van der Post, frequent visitors to our home, concurred, and concluded that negotiations should now go ahead with Indonesian officials. Another frequent visitor, the *ritmeester* Claas Kooij, a KNIL liaison officer to the British Twenty-Third Division, informed us that British staff officers had been impressed in Soerabaja by Soekarno's pluck and courage displayed there several times during his brief visit. For Laurens Van der Post's recollections see Van der Post 1996:226-7.

With this evaluation made by our late friend Romo Mangun, our biography sketching Soekarno from his early youth to the presidency in the wake of the Indonesian proclamation now nears its conclusion. What remains is to highlight some of the crucial events occurring during the closing months of 1945.

With Sjahrir in charge of a more democratically inspired cabinet, the prospects of more meaningful Indonesian-Dutch negotiations had come into sharper focus. As a matter of fact, a meeting between Soekarno, Hatta and Van Mook did indeed occur on 23 October 1945, although Van Mook was later severely reprimanded for this by the Dutch home government. But now, with the presence of men like Soetan Sjahrir and Amir Sjarifoeddin, anti-fascists to the core, at the helm of the new cabinet, *diplomasi* with the Dutch began to hold a brighter promise. And as the Dutch minister of overseas territories Dr J.H.A. Logemann intimated to Laurens Van der Post: 'I do not know them all, but I know some of them personally and most by reputation, and I think they are all good and decent men.' The South African lieutenant colonel then mused: 'For the first time it seemed that between the Logemann and Sjahrir elements there could be a productive two-way traffic' (Van der Post 1996:126). On the other hand, and specifically in the wake of the armed struggle of the Soerabajan *pemuda* against the British, the situation in the capital city became quite tense, finally erupting into a number of serious clashes between NEI and Republican forces. These events then led to some dramatic moves involving the Soekarno-Hatta *dwitunggal*. Again, elements of legend and reality merged.

Armed NICA elements – with a core of Ambonese, Menadonese and Timorese war veterans of the recent Tarakan-Balikpapan campaign – then based at the former KNIL Tenth Battalion Complex at the Hospitaalweg, started acting on their own. They forced civilian truck drivers of the NICA motor transport service to move them into the Parapatan, Kwitang, Senen and Kramat areas, where upon arrival they went on a rampage killing Indonesians. First the Seventh Indonesian Republic Police barracks at Parapatan was targeted and the entire police force including their families was completely wiped out. At the Kwitang thoroughfare across from the Indonesian police barracks Mohammad Roem, a prominent nationalist, was shot in front of his home; he survived due to an AMACAB officer taking him to a nearby

---

[60] Mangunwijaya 1977:24-42; Priyanahadi 1999; Catherine Mills, 'Romo Mangun Tribute to a multi-talented, national figure' *Inside Indonesia*, no. 68(2001):10-1; Interview Bob Hering with Romo Mangun, Yogyakarta, 12 September 1974. On 30 August 1974 Romo and Bob Hering attended a seminar at the Sixth Congress of the International Association of Historians of Asia (IAHA) together with Bernhard Dahm, Nugroho Notosusanto, Mohammad Hatta, Soedjatmoko and Dr Sartono, where the November 1945 silent coup story by the latter three and by Romo was specifically dismissed as not true to the historical facts.

hospital. Next the entire Senen and Kramat areas were searched house to house by these NEI units and all Indonesian males killed. The outraged NEI soldiers informed surviving members of these households that all this was being done to avenge the onslaught in Soerabaja. The rampage was finally stopped by Indian elements of the Twenty-Third Division. The British top command was furious about these events and considered the Dutch armed-forces command totally incapable of disciplining their Indonesian units. So the British consigned the NEI forces to their barracks for some time.[61]

Somewhat later, when tempers had cooled among the Allies, most of the Dutch forces – at the time three battalions strong – were permitted to man several posts on the outskirts of the capital city. However, tension in the city did not easily yield to calmness. Several incidents occurred, such as Sjahrir's motor car being shot at, while there were shooting incidents near Soekarno's home. Such events led to Republican moves to get the *dwitunggal* out of harm's way, or at least to secure its survival if something went astray. As early as late August, when Soebardjo discovered Tan Malaka's whereabouts in Djakarta, Soekarno (through Soebardjo) contacted the veteran national-ist on 9 September 1945. At subsequent meetings, Soekarno was advised by Tan Malaka to locate his government in Java's interior, since a growing British and NICA presence in Djakarta would surely turn the capital city into a messy battleground. Soekarno, in return, while pointing at Tan Malaka, mused about the possibility of the latter taking over the leadership of the revolution if he himself lost the ability to act or *tidak berjaya lagi* (became pow-erless). All that, with Hatta now participating as well, led to a *surat warisan* (bequest), with some referring to it as a *surat wasiat* (testament or will), being drawn up on 1 October 1945.[62] This version, perhaps duly influenced by the more sober-minded Hatta, appointed four successors instead of a single heir in the case of the *dwitunggal* losing their ability to act. The four heirs named were Tan Malaka, Iwa Koesoema Soemantri, Sjahrir and Wongsonegoro – though the latter two were not even consulted. As to Tan Malaka, he left Djakarta on 1 October, never to return. While touring Java's interior he seems to have circulated yet another testament, this time with him being named as the single heir. Most likely this version was part of legend construed by our veteran nationalist himself during his travels far beyond the capital city. As to the Djakarta-based *dwitunggal*, perhaps mindful of Tan Malaka's predic-tion of Djakarta turning into a messy battleground, they decided to follow the advice to move to the safer interior. So on 4 January 1946, Soekarno and

---

[61]   Van der Wal 1971-73, III:118, 142-3, 147-8, 153; Bob Hering's recollections in *Limburgs Dag-blad*, 19 August 1995:27; Van der Post 1996:150-1.
[62]   Yamin 1951:32-3; Subardjo 1978:362-4; Poeze 1998, a superb analysis revealing the myths about the *surat wasiat*.

his family and Hatta boarded a blinded train on the rail tracks just behind the Pegangsaan Timoer thoroughfare. They managed to slip out of Djakarta through Manggarai station toward Djokjakarta, a city soon to be named *kota perjuangan* (city of struggle).

One politically inspired odyssey had thus come to an end; another was about to begin. According to one of Soekarno's biographers, the Australian John Legge, Soekarno, though a mere figurehead president, turned out to be the true 'chairman of the revolution', who in spite of Djokjakarta's recent heroic nickname remained 'clearly, even if reluctantly, on the side of *diplomasi* rather than *perjuangan*' (Legge 1984:217).

Glossary

abangan[*]
a person nominally Muslim, strongly adhering to Hindu-Buddhist and animist religious notions

adat
customary law or traditions

adil
honest, fair

adviseur (Dutch)
advisor

agama
religion

Algeme(e)ne Recherche Dienst (ARD)
General Investigation Branch

Algeme(e)ne Studieclub
General Study Club

Algeme(e)ne Zaken
(Ministry of) General Affairs

aliran
Indonesia's socio-cultural community

Angkatan Baroe Indonesia
New Indonesian Generation

Asahi Akari no Asai (Japanese)
Japan, Light of Asia

Asahi Amijiban no Asai (Japanese)
Japan, Protector of Asia

Asahi Aniki no Asai (Japanese)
Japan, Elder Brother of Asia

asrama
student dormitory

badan
body

Badan Pembantoe Pradjoerit
Body to Aid the Fighters

Badan Pembantoe Pradjoerit Pekerdja
Aid Organ for Labour Combatants

Badan Persiapan Organisasi Ra'jat
People's Organization Preparatory Board

Badan Oentoek Menjelidiki Oesaha-Oesaha Persiapan Kemerdekaan
Committee Investigating Preparations for Independence

bagian politiek
political column

bahasa
language

bangsa
people

banteng
wild buffalo

Barisan Pelopor
Vanguard Corps

bedane Mekka koro Digoel (Javanese)
the difference between Mecca and Digoel

Bei Giyogun Kanbu Kyoikutai (Japanese)
PETA cadet school

Beikoku Kai (Japanese)
Rice Corporation

Beikoku Oroshisho Kumai (Japanese)
Central Association of Rice Traders

Beppan (Japanese acronym for Tokubetsu Han)
intelligence unit of the Sixteenth Army

---

[*]   For many of the Indonesian and Dutch words listed below, the orthography of the colonial period has been used.

Betawi — Batavia
bestuur — administration, party executive
Binnenlandsch Bestuur (BB) — Colonial Administration
bid'ah — innovation or practice deviating from the true teachings of Islam

bintang — star
Bintang Ratna Soetji — Order of the Holy Treasury
blijver (Dutch) — permanently settled expatriate
Boeah Pikiran Politik — On the Subject of Political Thought
Boedi Oetomo (BO) — Noble Endeavour, party of high priyayi
bu (Japanese) — department, bureau
bucho (Japanese) — head of department
bumiputera — native son

cahaya — radiant light or glow
camat — head of small village (desa)
candung — indigenous sword
Centrale Sarekat Islam (CSI) — Sarekat Islam's central executive body
chokan (Japanese) — director, administrator
Chung Hwa Hui (CHH) — Chinese Association, conservative party of Western-educated peranakan Chinese

Choo honbu (Japanese) — Central Headquarters
Choo honbucho (Japanese) — Head of Central Headquarters
Choo Sangiin (Japanese) — Central Advisory Council
Choo seinen kunrenjo (Japanese) — Central Youth Training Institute
College van Gedelegeerden — Volksraad Committee of Delegates
Comintern — Communist International
Comité Persatoean Indonesia — Indonesian Unity Committee
Comité Persiapan Nationale Consentrasi — National Concentration Preparatory Committee
Communistische Partij Holland (CPH) — Dutch Communist Party

daidan (Japanese) — PETA battalion
Daitoasho (Japanese) — Greater East Asia Ministry
dan'atsu (Japanese) — suppression
desa — village
desascholen (Dutch) — village schools
Djawa — Java, Javanese
Djawa Baroe — New Java
Dienst der Oost-Aziatische Zaken (DOAZ) — Office of East Asian Affairs
do'a qoenoet — special Muslim prayer
Doctorandus (Drs) — Dutch master's degree in the humanities
dokter jawa — Java-trained physician

Empat Serangkai — Four Leaf Clover
ethici (Dutch) — progressives, aiming to lift up the indigenous of the Indies

ethisch (Dutch) — progressive, emancipated
Europeesche Lagere School (ELS) — European primary school
externeeren (Dutch) — banish or expel

fajar — dawn
fatwa — authoritative interpretation
fikh — Islamic jurisprudence
fonds nasional — national fund
fractie or fraksi — faction
Fraksi Nasional — National Volksraad faction
Fujinkai (Japanese) — women's association

Gaboengan Partai Indonesia (GAPI) — Indonesian Party Federation
Gaimusho (Japanese) — Ministry of Foreign Affairs
Gedo(e)ng Permoefakatan — House of Consensus
gemeenteraad (Dutch) — municipal council
genjomin (Japanese) — native
genjomin gunta (Japanese) — indigenous troops
Gerakan Angkatan Baroe Indonesia — Movement of a New Indonesian Generation
Gerakan Rakjat Indonesia (Gerindo) — Indonesian People's Movement
gezagsapparaten (Dutch) — institutions of power
gicho (Japanese) — chairman
giyogun (Japanese) — volunteer corps
golongan merdeka — independent groupings
gotong royong — mutual self-help
Gouverneur-Generaal (GG) — Governor-General
gun (Japanese) — district
guncho (Japanese) — district head
Gunsei (Japanese) — Military Administration
Gunseikan (Japanese) — Chief of the Military Administration
Gunseikanbu (Japanese) — Staff of the Gunseikan

Hadith — codified statements/actions of the Prophet
Hakko Ichi-u (Japanese) — literally 'eight cords under one roof'
Handelingen Volksraad — Record of the People's Council
heerendiensten (Dutch) — labour and corvée services
heiho (Japanese) — auxiliary soldier
Herzieningscommissie — Revision Commission
Hidjrah — non-cooperative withdrawal policy
Himpoenan Kebaktian Rakjat — People's Loyalty Association; the Indonesian name for the Jawa Hokokai
Hindia — British India, also used for the (Dutch) Indies
Hindia Belanda — the (Dutch) Indies
Hinomaru (Japanese) — Rising Sun banner
Hizboellah — Allah's Army
Hollandsch-Chineesche School (HCS) — Dutch elementary school for Chinese

Hoofd Parket	prosecutor's department of the Indies attorney general
hoofdbestuur (Dutch)	chief executive of parties or associations
Hoogere Burger School (HBS)	Dutch secondary school
Ibu Indonesia	Mother Indonesia
ijtihad	right of individual interpretation
Ikatan Atletik Djakarta (Ikada)	Djakarta-based Athletic Union
Ikatan Sport Indonesia	Indonesian Sports Federation
Indië Weerbaar	'the Indies able to defend itself' (slogan)
Indisch Staatsblad	Indies Gazette
Indische Bond	Indies League
Indische Katholieke Partij (IKP)	Indies Catholic Party
Indische Partij (IP)	Indies Party
Indische Sociaal-Democratische Partij (ISDP)	Indies Social Democratic Party
Indische Sociaal-Democratische Vereeniging (ISDV)	Indies Social Democratic Association
Indische Staatsregeling	Indies Constitution
Indo-Europeesch Verbond (IEV)	Indo-European Union
Indonesia Berparlemen	call for a full-fledged Indonesian parliament
Indonesia Merdeka	call for an independent Indonesia
Indonesia Moeda	Indonesian youth association
Indonesische Nationalistische Volkspartij	Indonesian Nationalist People's Party
Indonesische Studie Club	Indonesian Study Club
Indonesische Vereeniging (IV)	Indonesian Association, based in Leiden
Ingenieur (Ir)	holder of a master's engineering degree
inheemsche fractie	indigenous municipal (or Volksraad) faction
inheemsche militie	indigenous militia
inlander (Dutch)	Indonesian indigenous
inlandsch or inheemsch (Dutch)	indigenous, native
Inlandsch Bestuur	indigenous branch of the Colonial Administration
inlandsche meerderheid	indigenous majority in the Volksraad
Inlandsche Zaken	(Ministry of) Indigenous Affairs
Instellingsordonnantie	Act of Incorporation
Insulinde	from insula (Latin for island) and Inde (India); the name Insulinde (for Indonesia) was adopted in 1913 by the Indische Partij
istana	mansion or palace
jagabaya	security officer
jambatan emas	golden bridge envisaged by Soekarno
Jawa Hokokai (Japanese)	People's Loyalty Association

jempolan	number one, champion or crack
Jimukyoku (Japanese)	general secretariat
Jong Indonesia	Young Indonesia
Jong Java	Young Java
kabupaten	regency
kaigi (Japanese)	council
Kaigun (Japanese)	Japanese navy
Kaigun Bukanfu (Japanese)	Navy Liaison Office
Kaikyo Seinen Teishintai (Japanese)	Allah's Army, Hizboellah in Indonesian
kampung	indigenous quarter, area or administrative unit
kantoor (Dutch)	office
Kaoem Betawi (KB)	Batavian indigenous association
karsa (Javanese)	wish fulfilment
kaum	people, group, community
kaum kekuasaan	the ones holding power
kaum kolot	conservatives often linked to devout Muslims
kaum mardika	the free independent community
kaum muda	youth, the new generation
kaum terpelajar	learned people
kawula-gusti	subject-to-ruler relationship
kebangunan	awakening
Keibodan (Japanese)	auxiliary police corps
kejawen	the Javanese cultural tradition
ken (Japanese)	regency
Kenpeitai (Japanese)	military police corps
kepala banteng	head of the wild buffalo
keterangan azas	statement of principles
kikakuka (Japanese)	planning section
kieskring (Dutch)	constituency
klenteng	Chinese temple
koeliekwestie	the issue of the coolies
koelieordonnantie	coolies ordinance
Koloniale Raad	Colonial Council
kolot	old-fashioned, conservative
Komintern	Communist International
Kominterncongres	Communist International congress
komon (Japanese)	advisor
Kongres Rakjat Indonesia (KRI)	Indonesian People's Congress
Koninklijk Besluit (KB)	Royal Decree
Koninklijk Nederlandsch-Indisch Leger (KNIL)	Royal Netherlands Indies Army
Koodo Seishin (Japanese)	Spirit of the Imperial Way
kraton	royal compound
kromo	commoner without rank or status
ksatria	knights of Javano-Balinese legends

ku (Japanese) — village (desa)
kumichoo (Japanese) — leader of ten to twenty households
Kyukan Seido Chosa Iinkai (Japanese) — Studying Traditional Customs Committee

Landraad — court for indigenous Indonesians
lencana — decoration
lidi — palm-leaf rib
Liga gegen Kolonialgreuel und Unter-druckung (Liga) — League against Colonial Oppression

maandverslag (Dutch) — monthly report
Madjelis Pertimbangan (MP) — Advisory Council
Madjelis Rakjat Indonesia — Indonesian People's Council
Madjlisoel Islamil A'laa Indonesia (MIAI) — Supreme Islamic Council of Indonesia
magang — apprentice
maju — progressive
maklumat — manifesto, announcement
Marhaen — poor commoners, a name coined by Soekarno
Mas — a title below Raden for Javanese nobles
medan — forum, front
Meester (Mr) — Dutch master's degree in law
merdeka — free, independent
mesjid wakaf — Muslim house of prayer and service
Minshu Shidobu (Japanese) — Guidance Board
moderen — modern
Moehammadijah — cultural/modernist Muslim association
muballigh — Muslim propagandist
mufakat — consensus
mulia — exalted, glorious
mundur mapan — retreat in order to gain strength

Moetamar al-Alam al-Islami far'al Hind asj-Sharqyah (MAIHS) — Islam World Congress East Indies Section
Moetamar al-Alam al-Islami 1334 H — First International Islamic Congress of 1926

Nahdatoel Oelama (NO) — literally 'revival of religious scholars', an Islamic fundamentalist association
Naimubucho (Japanese) — Head of the Military Internal Affairs Section
Nansei Homen Kantai (Japanese) — Southwest Area Fleet
Nationaal Indonesische Volkspartij — Indonesian National People's Party
Nationaal-Socialistische Beweging (NSB) — Dutch National Socialist Movement
Nederlandsch Verbond van Vak-vereenigingen (NVV) — Dutch Trade Unions Association
nenek — grandmother

nggendong ngindit (Javanese)   literally 'equalizing matters', well-off members supporting poorer family members

Nippon Seishin (Japanese)   Japanese spirit
ningrat   aristocrat
nota (Dutch)   account, memorandum
notulen (Dutch)   minutes
nyai   concubine

Ondernemersbond   Employers' Union
Opleidings School voor Inlandsche Ambtenaren (OSVIA)   Training School for Native Officials
Orde der Dienaren van Indië   Order of Servants of the Indies
organisatie plan (Dutch)   organization plan
Osamu (Japanese)   Sixteenth Army

Pakempalan Kawoelo Ngajogjakarta (PKN)   Yogyakarta People's Party
Pakempalan Kawoelo Soerokarto (PKS)   Surakarta People's Party
pancaran   ray, transmission, source
Pangeran   prince
Pangreh Praja   literally 'rulers of the realm'; colonial indigenous tier of the Colonial Administration

Panitia Sebelas   Eleven Members Board
Pantja Dharma   five obligations for Indonesians to adopt
Pantja Sila   five basic principles in Soekarno's blueprint for a future Indonesian state

Parlemen Indonesia   Indonesian Parliament
Partai Indonesia (Partindo)   Indonesia Party
Partai Indonesia Raja (Parindra)   Greater Indonesia Party
Partai Nasional Indonesia (PNI)   Indonesian Nationalist Party
Partai Sarekat Islam (PSI)   Party of the Islamic Association
Partai Sarekat Islam Indonesia (PSII)   Party of the Indonesian Islamic Association

pasek   Balinese commoners clan
pasisir   sandy littoral
pasar   bazaar, market
pasar-Maleisch   bazaar Malay (pidgin Malay)
Pasoendan   name commonly used for the Sundanese party Pagoejoeban Pasoendan

Passen- en Wijkenstelsel   pass and ward system
pecinan   Chinese quarter
pelita   lamp, light
pemerasan   exploitation
Pendidikan Nasional Indonesia (PNI or PNI Baroe)   Indonesian National Education Party

peranakan	a person who was born in the Indies with at least one expatriate parent
pergerakan	movement
Perhimpoenan Indonesia (PI)	Indonesian Association, based in Leiden
Perhimpoenan Peladjar-Peladjar Indonesia (PPPI)	Indonesian Students Association
perjuangan	struggle
Permoefakatan Perhimpoenan-Perhimpoenan Politik Kebangsaan Indonesia (PPPKI)	Consensus of Indonesian Political Associations
permusyawaratan	discussion to resolve opposing views
persatean	broiled meat-pieces on a stick suggesting superficial unity
Persatoean Bangsa Indonesia (PBI)	Indonesian People's Association
Persatoean Minahasa (PM)	Minahasa Association
Persatoean Moeslimin Indonesia (Permi)	Indonesian Muslim Association
persatuan	union, association, unity
Perserikatan Nasional Indonesia (PNI)	Indonesian National Association
pesantren	traditional rural Muslim school led by a kiyayi
pewarta	bulletin, messenger
Poesat Tenaga Rakjat (Poetera)	Concentration of the People's Energy
Politiek Economische Bond (PEB)	Political Economic Association
Politieke Inlichtingen Dienst (PID)	Political Intelligence Branch
priyayi	traditional bureaucratic aristocracy of Java
Procureur-Generaal (PG)	attorney general
putri	daughter
Raad van Nederlandsch-Indië	highest advisory council of the Indies
Raden (R)	Javanese title for man of high standing
Raden Ajoe (R.A.)	Javanese title for woman of high standing
Raden Toemenggoeng (R.T.)	usual title for a regent (bupati)
Radicale Concentratie	Radical Concentration
raja	indigenous king
raja (raya)	great, glorious
Rechts Hooge School (RHS)	Indies Law Faculty
referaat (Dutch)	report
Regeerings Reglement (RR)	Government Regulation
Regeeringsgemachtigde voor Algemeene Zaken (RGAZ)	Government's Envoy for General Affairs
regent	indigenous official in charge of a regency
Regentenbond	Regents' Union
regentschapsraden	regency councils
resident	Dutch official in charge of a residency
Roekoen Tani	farmers' cooperative
Roekoen Tetangga	Neighbourhood Association; the Indonesian name for Tonarigumi

romusha (Japanese) — requisitioned labourer
rukun — literally 'harmony', cooperative
rust en orde — law and order
Rijkseenheid — 'Unity of Empire'

sahabat karib — great friend
Saiko Shikikan (Japanese) — Supreme Commander
San A Seinen Korensho (Japanese) — Triple-A Movement Youth Training Facility
San A Undo (Japanese) — Triple-A Movement
sana — the other side, their side
santri — literally 'pesantren student', devout Muslim
sanyo (Japanese) — advisor
sarekat or sarikat — union, association
Sarekat Ambon (SA) — Ambonese Association
Sarekat Hindia/Nationaal Indische Partij (SH/NIP) — Indies' Association/National Indies Party
Sarekat Islam (SI) — Islamic Association
Sarekat Kaoem Boeroeh Indonesia (SKBI) — Indonesian Labour Union
Sarekat Prijaji (SP) — Priyayi Association
Sarekat Rajat Sama Rata Hindia Bergerak — People's League for the Common Struggle in the Indies
Sarekat Rakjat Nasional Indonesia (SRNI) — Nationalist Indonesian People's Party
Sarikat Dagang Islamiah (SDI) — Islamic Commercial Association
School tot Opleiding van Inlandsche Artsen (STOVIA) — Native Physicians Training School
Seiji Sanyo (Japanese) — political participation
Seinendan (Japanese) — Youth Corps
Seinin Dojo (Japanese) — drill hall for young men
Sekolah Tjina — Chinese schools
sembada — whole
Sendenbu (Japanese) — Propaganda Department
Senjinku (Japanese) — Code of Conduct
seorang perawan — virgin
Serikat Soematera (SS) — Sumatran Association
Shari'ah — the law of Islam
shi (Japanese) — city, municipality
Shi i-in (Japanese) — Big Four, referring to the Empat Serangkai
sho (Japanese) — residency
Sho Sangikai (Japanese) — Residency Advisory Council
shochokan (Japanese) — resident
shodancho (Japanese) — PETA platoon commander
Shomubu (Japanese) — Religious Affairs Office
Shomuka (Japanese) — Religious Affairs Section
Siang Hwee — Chinese chamber of commerce
sinar — ray, light, glitter

singkeh	person of Chinese descent
sinjo	nickname for Eurasian male
sini	this side, our side
Sociaal-Democratische Arbeiders Partij (SDAP)	Social Democratic Labour Party
Soekarela Tentara Pembela Tanah Air	army to defend the fatherland
Soempah Pemoeda	Oath of Indonesian Youth Congress
Soesoehoenan	title of Solo's Javanese monarch
Somubucho (Japanese)	Head of Military General Affairs Department
soncho (Japanese)	village head
Stuw, De	literally 'The Push', organ of the Stuw group which promoted an Indies commonwealth
Suishintai (Japanese)	Vanguard Corps (Barisan Peloper in Indonesian)
Sultan	title of Yogyakarta's Javanese monarch
suluh	torch
taisho (Japanese)	self-defence drill
Taman Siswa	literally 'garden of pupils', Dewantoro's private school system
tani	peasant, farmer
taqlid	adoption of established fatwa and practices as authoritatively binding
Technische Hooge School (THS)	Technical Faculty
tempo doeloe	the past seen as 'good old times'
Tencho Setsu (Japanese)	Japanese Emperor's birthday
timur	east
Tjahja Volksuniversiteit	Radiance People's University
Tokubetsu Koto Keisato (Japanese)	Thought Control Police
tolong menolong	mutual self-support
Tonarigumi (Japanese)	neighbourhood association
torishimari (Japanese)	control
totok belanda	Dutch settlers
trekker (Dutch)	temporary, mainly European settler of the Indies
ulama	Muslim scholar
utusan	messenger, delegate
Vaderlandsche Club (VC)	Fatherland Club, an ultra-conservative association
Vereeniging van Spoor- en Tramweg Personeel (VSTP)	Association of Rail and Tramway Personnel
verhoor op vraagpunten (Dutch)	interrogation following pre-set questionnaire

verslag (Dutch)	report or survey
Volksraad	People's Council of the Indies
vorst (Dutch)	prince, ruler
Vorstenlanden	Principalities of Surakarta and Yogyakarta
Vreemde Oosterlingen	Foreign Orientals
wakil	representative
wakil penduduk	representative of the people
wali Allah	representative of Allah
warta	news
wedana	indigenous district officer
Wilde Scholen Ordonnantie	private schools supervision ordinance
windu	cycle of eight years
wong cilik	literally 'little people', commoners
zaman	era
zegepraal (Dutch)	triumph
ziarat	pilgrimage to Mecca

Bibliography

Archives

Algemeen Rijksarchief (ARA, Dutch State Archives), The Hague: Ministerie van Koloniën (Ministry of Colonies); Correspondence, reports and minutes organized as Verbaal (a collection of various items on a given subject considered important), Mail-rapport (Mr., a single report often with supporting bijlagen (appendices); Memorie van Overgave (MvO, end of assignment report), for the years 1900-1942; Londens Archief, as above for the years May 1940-March 1942; Archieven Procureur-Generaal bij het Hooggerechtshof van Nederlandsch-Indië; Archieven Algemene Secretarie te Batavia. Private collections: A.C.D. de Graeff; B.C. de Jonge; P.A. Kerstens; P.J. Koets; H.J. Lovink; J.W. Meijer Ranneft; W.G. Peekema; Ch.O. van der Plas; A.W.L Tjarda van Starkenborgh Stachouwer.

Internationaal Instituut voor Sociale Geschiedenis (IISG, International Institute of Social History), Amsterdam: Private collections: Ch.G. Cramer; J. van Gelderen; B.B. Hering; H.J. Kiewiet de Jonge; D.M.G. Koch; W. Middendorp; L.N. Palar; H. Sneevliet; J.E. Stokvis; W. Wertheim.

Koninklijke Bibliotheek (Royal Library), The Hague: Reels of pre-war Dutch and Indonesian periodicals.

Koninklijk Instituut voor Taal-, Land- en Volkenkunde (Royal Institute of Linguistics and Anthropology), Leiden: Pre-war Indonesian periodicals, Private collections: G.A.J. Hazeu; E. Gobée.

Ministerie van Buitenlandse Zaken (Ministry of Foreign Affairs) WOB section, The Hague: Reports on the nationalist movement.

Vrije Universiteit van Amsterdam (Free University of Amsterdam), Amsterdam: Private collections: A.W.F. Idenburg; G.F. Pijper.

Perpustakaan Nasional (National Library), Jakarta: Notulen Gemeenteraad Batavia (Minutes of Batavia's Municipal Council), 1917-1941; Reels of pre-war Indonesian newspapers and other periodicals; Pre-war Indonesian newspapers and other periodicals from the erstwhile Lembaga Kebudajaan Indonesia (Cultural Institute of Indonesia).

Arsip Nasional (Indonesian National Archives), Jakarta: Documentation about Soekarno.

USA National Archives, Washington: USA consulate correspondence about Soekarno, Thamrin, Soetardjo and Ratulangi.

Interviews

During the periods 1945-1952, 1976-1983 and 1987-1999 interviews and talks were held with:
Roeslan Abdulgani, Basoeki Abdullah, Affandi, Soetan Takdir Alisjahbana, Tito Zaini Armen, Doel Arnowo, Harjono Sigit Bachrunsalam, Utari Sigit Bachrunsalam, Ali Boediardjo, Mohamad Bondan and Molly Bondan née Warner, R. Bonnet, Muhamad Ali Chanafia and Salmiah Chanafia, Ratna Djoeami, Soewarsih and Soegondo Djojo-poespito, Mahbub Djunaidi, Ernest Douwes Dekker and Harumi Wanasita Douwes Dekker, H.J. de Dreu, Maria Duchâteau-Sjahrir, Dullah and Riby Fatimah Dullah, Francisca Fanggidaej, W. Foote, A.K. Gani, Pauline Gobée, Go Gien Tjwan, Kenichi Goto, Andrew Gunawan (formerly Goei Hok Gie), Basuki Gunawan, Hendra Guna-wan, Han Bing Siong, A.M. Hanafi, Abu Hanifah, Ganis and Diati Harsono, Moham-mad and Rahmi Hatta, Hoegeng Iman Santoso, I Ketut Loka, Inggit Garnasih, Jusuf Isak, Junus Jahja, L.G.M. Jaquet, J. de Kadt, Hermen Kartowisastro, Taunus Kema-sang, G.P. Kiès, P.F. Kiewiet de Jonge, Marcel Koch, J.P. Koets, R. Koot, U. Koot, Klaas Kooy, Kwee Hin Goan, Lee Man Fong, J. Leimena, Mochtar Lubis, Tadashi Maeda, Isak Mahdi, Marzoeki Mahdi, Waruno Mahdi, Adam Malik, Y.B. Mangunwijaya (also known as Romo Mangun), Maskoen, Tjipto Munandar, M.P.M. Muskens, Abdul Haris Nasution and Jo Nasution-Gondokoesoemo, Mohammad Natsir, Deliar Noer, Nugro-ho Notosusanto, Oei Tjoe Tat, Oey Hong Lee, W. Oltmans, Onghokham, L.N. Palar, Cisca Pattipilohy, Ch.O. van der Plas, A.G. Pringgodigdo, G.F. Pijper, Ramadhan K.H., Zus Ratulangi, Basuki Resobowo, J.H. Ritman, Mohammad Roem, Ali Sadikin, Solichin Salam, Maria Ulfah Santoso, Shigeru Sato, Soekartini Saroyo, R. Sastromoel-jono, Sri Sastromoeljono, Soebadio Sastrosatomo, Frans Seda, Sabam Siagian, Siauw Giok Tjhan, Sie Hok Tjwan, T.B. Simatupang, Sitor Situmorang, Soetan Mohammad Sjah, Poppy Sjahrir, Soebagijo I.N., Soedjatmoko, Ir. Soekarno, Fatmawati Soekarno, Hartini Soekarno, Ratna Sari Dewi Soekarno née Nemoto Naoko, Guntur Soekar-noputra, Guruh Soekarnoputra, Megawati Soekarnoputri, Rachmawati Soekarnopu-tri, Soekmawati Soekarnoputri, Soemanang, Soemarsono, Soenarjo, Soeriadarma, Soetardjo Kartohadikoesoemo, Manai Sophiaan, Ahmad Subarjo Dyoyoadisuryo, Sumitro Djojohadikusomo, Suparna Sastradiredja, Supeno, Jos Suprapto, Abdur-rachman Surjomihardjo, Mohamad Tabrani, Ed and Els Tahsin, Mély Tan, Roesdi Thamrin, Thung Sin Nio, Anwar Tjokroaminoto, Harsono Tjokroaminoto, Soekanto Tjokrodiatmodjo, Pramoedya Ananta Toer, Maimoenah Toer-Thamrin, S.K. Trimurti, B. van Tijn, Kartika Uteh, Eileen and Ernst Utrecht, Laurens Van der Post, Jusuf and Sofjan Wanandi, Soekarmini Wardojo (formerly Soekarmini Poegoeh), Hetty and Wim Wertheim.

Published sources

45 Tahun Sumpah Pemuda
1974   *45 Tahun Sumpah Pemuda.* Jakarta: Yayasan Gedung-Gedung Berse-
            jarah Jakarta.
Abeyasekere, Susan
1987   *Jakarta; A history.* Oxford: Oxford University Press.
Abdul Karim (Oey Tjeng Hien)
1982   *Mengabdi agama, nusa dan bangsa; Sahabat karib Bung Karno.* Jakarta:
            Gunung Agung.
Abdulgani, Roeslan
n.d.   *Propaganda Djepang.* Djakarta: Kempen.
Adam, Ahmat B.
1984   *The vernacular press and the emergence of modern Indonesian consciousness
            1855-1913.* [PhD thesis, University of London.]
Adams, Cindy
1965   *Sukarno; An autobiograpy, as told to Cindy Adams.* Indianapolis: Bobbs-
            Merrill.
1980   *Sukarno my friend.* Second revised edition. Singapore: Gunung Agung.
            [First edition 1971.]
1982   *Bung Karno penyambung lidah rakyat Indonesia.* Jakarta: Gunung
            Agung.
Alers, Henri J.H.
1956   *Om een rode of groene Merdeka; 10 jaren binnenlandse politiek Indonesië
            1943-1953.* Eindhoven: Vulkaan.
Alfian
1969   *Islamic modernism in Indonesian politics; The Muhammadijah movement
            during the Dutch colonial period (1912-1942).* [PhD thesis, University of
            Wisconsin, Madison.]
Algemeen verslag Inlandsch onderwijs
1907-15   *Algemeen verslag van het Inlandsch onderwijs in Nederlandsch-Indië 1900-
            1914.* Batavia: Landsdrukkerij.
Algemeen verslag onderwijs
1917   *Algemeen verslag van het onderwijs in Nederlandsch-Indië 1915.* Batavia:
            De Verwachting.
Amelz
1952   *H.O.S. Tjokroaminoto hidup dan perdjuangannja.* Djakarta: Bulan Bin-
            tang. Two vols.
Anderson, Benedict R. O'G
1961   *Some aspects of Indonesian politics under the Japanese occupation 1944-
            1945.* Ithaca, NY: Cornell University Press. [Cornell Modern Indonesia
            Project Publications, Interim Report Series.]
1965   *Mythology and the tolerance of the Javanese.* Ithaca, NY: Modern Indone-
            sia Project.
1966a   (ed.) 'The problem of rice; [Stenographic notes on the fourth session of
            the Sanyo Kaigi, Januari 8, 2605, 10:00 A.M.]', *Indonesia* 2:77-123.

1966b   'Japan; "The light of Asia"', in: Josef Silverstein (ed.), *Southeast Asia in*
             World War II; Four essays, pp. 13-50. New Haven, Conn.: Yale Univer-
             sity, Southeast Asia Studies. [Monograph Series 7.]
1967   *The pemuda revolution; Indonesian politics 1945-1946.* [PhD thesis, Cor-
             nell University, Ithaca, NY.]
1972   *Java in a time of revolution; Occupation and resistance, 1944-1946.* Ithaca,
             NY: Cornell University Press.
1973   Notes on contemporary Indonesian political communication', *Indone-*
             sia 16:39-80.

Any, Andjar
1978   *Bung Karno siapa yang punya.* Solo: Sasongko.

Aziz, M.A.
1955   *Japan's colonialism and Indonesia.* 's-Gravenhage: Nijhoff.

Baars, A. en H. Sneevliet
1991   *Het proces Sneevliet.* Ingeleid en bewerkt door Emile Schwidder en Frit-
             jof Tichelman. Leiden: KITLV Uitgeverij. [Socialisme in Indonesië 2.]

Babad Pasek Gelgel
n.d.   *Babad Pasek Gelgel.* N.p.: n.n.

Bahsan, Oemar
1955   *PETA (Pembela Tanah Air) dan peristiwa Rengasdengklok.* Bandung:
             Melati.

Benda, H.J.
1955   'Indonesian Islam under the Japanese occupation, 1942-45', *Pacific*
             Affairs 28:350-62.
1958   *The crescent and the rising sun; Indonesian Islam under the Japanese occupa-*
             tion 1942-1945. The Hague/Bandung: Van Hoeve.
1966   'The pattern of administrative reforms in the closing years of Dutch
             rule in Indonesia', *Journal of Asian Studies* 25:589-605.
1970   'South-East Asian Islam in the twentieth century', in: P.M. Holt, Ann
             K.S. Lambton and Bernard Lewis, *The Cambridge history of Islam*, vol-
             ume 2, pp. 182-207. Cambridge: Cambridge University Press.
1972   *Continuity and change in Southeast Asia; Collected journal articles of Harry*
             J. Benda. New Haven, Conn.: Yale University, Southeast Asia Studies.
             [Monograph Series 18.]

Benda, H.J., James K. Irikura and Kïichi Kishi (eds)
1965   *Japanese military administration in Indonesia; Selected documents.* New
             Haven, Conn.: Southeast Asia Studies, Yale University. [Translation
             Series 6.]

Bescheiden Indische partij
1913   *Bescheiden betreffende de vereeniging 'De Indische Partij'.* Batavia: Lands-
             drukkerij.

Bescheiden Sarekat Islam
1913   *Bescheiden betreffende de vereeniging 'Sarekat Islam'.* Batavia: Lands-
             drukkerij.

Bharadwaj, Ram Dev
1997   *Sukarno and Indonesian nationalism.* Delhi: Rahul.

Birth of Pantjasila
1958   *The birth of Pantjasila*. Djakarta: Ministry of Information.

Blom, J.C.H.
1983   *De muiterij op de 'Zeven Provinciën'; Reacties en gevolgen in Nederland.* Second edition. Utrecht: HES. [HES Historische Herdrukken 19; First edition 1975.]

Bloys van Treslong Prins, P.C.
1934-39   *Genealogische en heraldische gedenkwaardigheden betreffende Europeanen op Java.* Batavia: Albrecht. Four vols.

Bocquet-Siek, Margaret and Robert Cribb (eds)
1991   *Islam and the Panca Sila.* Townsville: Centre for Southeast Asian Studies, James Cook University of North Queensland. [Monograph 28.]

Boeke, J.H.
1923   'De begrippen dualisme, unificatie en associatie in de koloniale politiek', *Koloniale Studiën* 2:153-69.

Bolitho, Hector
1954   *Jinnah; Creator of Pakistan.* London: Murray.

Bondan, Molly
1992   *Spanning a revolution; The story of Mohamad Bondan and the Indonesian nationalist movement.* Jakarta: Sinar Harapan.

Broeshart, André C.
1988   *Soerabaja; Beeld van een stad.* Purmerend: Asia Maior.

Brugmans, I.J. et al.
1960   *Nederlandsch-Indië onder Japanse bezetting; Gegevens en documenten over de jaren 1942-1945.* Franeker: Wever.

Bruin, Rodney de
1967   'Sense and non-sense in the Three-A-Movement', Paper, XXVII International Congress of Orientalists, Ann Arbor, 13-19 August.
1968   De Seinendan in Indonesië 1942-1945. [MA thesis, Universiteit van Amsterdam.]
1982a   *Indonesië; De laatste etappe naar de vrijheid 1942-1945.* [PhD thesis, Universiteit van Amsterdam.]
1982b   *Islam en nationalisme in door Japan bezet Indonesië 1942-1945.* 's-Gravenhage: Staatsuitgeverij. [Cahiers over Nederland en de Tweede Wereldoorlog 3.]

Bung Karno
1988   *Bung Karno, sebuah bibliografi; Memuat daftar karya oleh dan tentang Bung Karno.* Edisi ke-4. Jakarta: Haji Masagung.

Bijllaardt Gzn., A.C. van den
1933   *Ontstaan en ontwikkeling der staatkundige partijen in Nederlandsch-Indië.* Batavia: Kolff.

Chailley-Bert, J.
1900   *Java et ses habitants.* Paris: Colin.

Chauvel, Richard
1990   *Nationalists, soldiers and separatists; The Ambonese islands from colonialism to revolt 1880-1950.* Leiden: KITLV Press. [Verhandelingen 143.]

Cobban, James L.
1970   *The city of Java; An essay in historical geography.* [PhD thesis, University
              of California, Berkeley.]
Cohen Stuart, A.B.
1938   'De Volksraad en de regeeringsverklaring van 18 November 1918',
              Koloniale Studiën 22:285-99.
1946   *De politieke partijen in Nederlandsch Indië.* N.p: n.n.
Colijn, H.
1928   *Koloniale vraagstukken van heden en morgen.* Amsterdam: De Standaard.
Cribb, Robert
1991   *Gangsters and revolutionaries; The Jakarta People's Militia and the Indone-
              sian revolution 1945-1949.* Sydney: Allen and Unwin. [Southeast Asia
              Publications Series 20.]
Dachlan, E.M.
1954   *Bung Karno dihukum 4 tahun.* Bandung: Dachlan.
Dahm, Bernhard
1969   *Sukarno and the struggle for Indonesian independence.* Ithaca, NY: Cornell
              University Press.
Dimyati, Muhammad
1951   *Sedjarah perdjuangan Indonesia.* Djakarta: Widjaya.
Dirdjosuparto, Sutamto
1998   *Sukarno membangun bangsa dalam kemelut perang dingin sampai Trikora.*
              Jakarta: Badan Kerja Sama Yayasan Pembina dan Universitas 17 Agus-
              tus 1945 se-Indonesia.
Djajadiningrat, Achmad
1936   *Herinneringen van Pangeran Aria Achmad Djajadiningrat.* Amsterdam/
              Batavia: Kolff.
Djojopoespito, Soewarsih
1947   *Buiten het gareel.* Third edition. Utrecht: De Haan. [First edition 1940.]
Doel, H.W. van den
1994   *De stille macht; Het Europese binnenlands bestuur op Java en Madoera,
              1808-1942.* Amsterdam: Bert Bakker.
1996   *Het rijk van insulinde; Opkomst en ondergang van een Nederlandse kolonie.*
              Amsterdam: Prometheus.
Douwes Dekker, E.F.E.
1908   *Het boek van Siman den Javaan; Een roman van rijst, dividend en mensche-
              lijkheid.* Amersfoort: Wink.
1912a   *Een natie in de maak; Rede uitgesproken 17 September 1911.* Batavia:
              Kolff.
1912b   *De Indische Partij; Verslag van de openbare vergadering gehouden te Sema-
              rang op 19 October, 1912.* Semarang: Misset.
Douwes Dekker, E.F.E. and Harumi Wanasita
1949   *Zeventig jaar konsekwent.* Bandung: Nix.
Eerste Al-Indië-Congres
1922   *Eerste Al-Indië-Congres te Bandoeng 3, 4 en 5 Juni 1922.* Weltevreden:
              Visser.

ENI
1917-39   *Encyclopaedie van Nederlandsch-Indië.* 's-Gravenhage: Nijhoff. Eight
           vols.

Erka
1978a   *Bung Karno; Kepada bangsaku.* Semarang: Aneka.
1978b   *Bung Karno!; Perginya seorang kekasih, suamiku dan kebanggaanku.* Sema-
           rang: Aneka.

Faber, G.H. von
1931   *Oud Soerabaia; De geschiedenis van Indië's eerste koopstad van de oudste
           tijden tot de instelling van den Gemeenteraad (1906).* Soerabaia: Kolff.

Federspiel, Howard M.
1966   *Persatuan Islam.* [PhD thesis, McGill University, Montreal.]

Feith, Herbert and Lance Castles (eds)
1970   *Indonesian political thinking 1945-1965.* Ithaca, NY: Cornell University
           Press.

Finch, Susan and Daniel S. Lev
1965   *Republic of Indonesia cabinets, 1945-1965.* Ithaca, NY: Modern Indonesia
           Project, Southeast Asia Program, Department of Asian Studies, Cor-
           nell University. [Interim Reports Series.]

Fischer, Louis
1959   *The story of Indonesia.* New York: Harper.

Flores
1935   'Flores', in: *ENI* VII:148-53.

Florida, Nancy
1995   *Writing the past, inscribing the future; History as prophecy in colonial Java.*
           Durham/London: Duke University Press.

Frederick, William H.
1989   *Visions and heat; The making of the Indonesian revolution.* Athens, OH:
           Ohio University Press.

Friend, Theodore
1988   *The blue-eyed enemy; Japan against the West in Java and Luzon, 1942-1945.*
           Princeton: Princeton University Press.

Fromberg, P.H.
1926   *Verspreide geschriften.* Leiden: Nijhoff.

Gedenkboek Jong-Java
1930   *Gedenkboek Jong-Java; 7 Maart 1915-1930 = Kitab-peringatan Jong-Java; 7
           Maart 1915-1930.* Jakatera: Pedoman Besar Jong-Java.

Geertz, Clifford
1960   *The religion of Java.* Glencoe: Free Press.
1965   *The social history of an Indonesian town.* Cambridge, Mass.: MIT Press.
1968   *Islam observed; Religious development in Morocco and Indonesia.* New
           Haven, Conn.: Yale University Press.
1970   *Peddlers and princes; Social change and economic modernization in two
           Indonesian towns.* Chicago/London: University of Chicago Press. [Pub-
           lications on various aspects of social, political, economic, and cultural
           change in the new states of Asia and Africa 1.]

404   Bibliography

1972   'Religious change and social order in Soeharto's Indonesia', *Asia* 27:
                62-4.
Geertz, Hildred
1961   *The Javanese family; A study of kinship and socialization.* New York: The
                Free Press of Glencoe.
Gibb, H.A.R. and J.H. Kramers (eds)
1953   *Shorter encyclopaedia of Islam.* Leiden: Brill.
Giebels, Lambert J.
1995   *Beel, van vazal tot onderkoning; Biografie 1902-1977.* Den Haag: Sdu.
1999   *Soekarno; Nederlandsch onderdaan; Biografie 1901-1950.* Amsterdam: Bert
                Bakker.
Glissenaar, Frans
1999   *D.D.; Het leven van E.F.E. Douwes Dekker.* Hilversum: Verloren.
Gobée, E. and C. Adriaanse (eds)
1957-65   *Ambtelijke adviezen van C. Snouck Hurgronje 1889-1936.* Vol. 3. 's-Graven-
                hage: Nijhoff. [Rijks Geschiedkundige Publicatiën, Kleine Serie 33, 34,
                35.]
Goldenberg, B.
1933   *Beiträge zur Soziologie der deutschen Vorkriegs-sozialdemokratie.* [PhD
                thesis, Universität Heidelberg.]
Gonggrijp, G.F.E.
1949   *Schets ener economische geschiedenis van Nederlands-Indië.* Third editon.
                Haarlem: Bohn. [Volksuniversiteitsbibliotheek, 2e Reeks 23.]
1991   *Geïllustreerde encyclopaedie van Nederlandsch-Indië.* Wijk en Aalburg:
                Pictures Publishers.
Gonggrijp, G.L.
1944   *Brieven van opheffer.* Maastricht: Leiter-Nypels.
Gouda, F.
1995   *Dutch culture overseas; Colonial practice in the Netherlands Indies 1900-
                1942.* Amsterdam: Amsterdam University Press.
Groen, Petra and Elly Touwen-Bouwsma (eds)
1992   *Nederlands-Indië 1942; Illusie en ontgoocheling.* 's-Gravenhage: Sdu.
Gunawan, Basuki and O.D. van den Muijzenberg
1967   'Verzuilingstendenties en sociale stratificatie in Indonesia', *Sociolo-
                gische Gids* 14:146-58.
Gunseikanbu
1944a   *Orang Indonesia jang terkemoeka di Djawa.* Djakarta: Gunseikanbu.
1944b   *Boekoe pengoempoelan oendang-oendang.* Djakarta: Gunseikanbu.
Hadi, Syamsu
1978   *Tragedi Bung Karno; Perjalanan terakhir seorang proklamator.* Jakarta: Pus-
                taka Simponi.
Ham, J.G. van
1913   *Eerste boekjaar der Indische Partij: 1912.* Bandoeng: Nix.

Han Bing Siong
1997   'An exceptional katana in an exceptional army mounting of equally
            exceptional provenance', *Newsletter Japanese Sword Society of the United
            States, Inc.* 29-4:22-31.
2000   'Sukarno-Hatta versus the pemuda in the first months after the surren-
            der of Japan (August-November 1945)', *Bijdragen tot de Taal-, Land- en
            Volkenkunde* 156:233-73.
2001   'The Indonesian need of arms after the Proclamation of Independence',
            Bijdragen tot de Taal-, Land- en Volkenkunde 157:799-830.
Hanafi, A.M.
1998   *A.M. Hanafi menggugat; Kudeta Jend. Suharto dari Gestapu ke Supersemar;
            Catatan pengalaman seorang eksponen Angkatan 45.* Lille: Édition Mont-
            blanc.
Handelingen Volksraad
1918-42   *Handelingen van den Volksraad 1918-1941/42.* Batavia: Volksraad van
            Nederlandsch-Indië.
Hanifah, Abu
1972   *Tales of a revolution; A leader of the Indonesian revolution looks back.* Syd-
            ney: Angus and Robertson. [Sources of Modern Indonesian History
            and Politics 1.]
Harahap, Parada
1939   *Riwajat Dr. A. Rivai.* Medan: Indische Drukkerij.
Hardjono, Joan and Charles Warner (eds)
1995   *In love with a nation; Molly Bondan and Indonesia.* Picton, NSW: South-
            wood Press.
Harsono, Ganis, C.L.M. Penders and B. Hering (eds)
1977   *Recollections of an Indonesian diplomat in the Sukarno era.* St. Lucia: Uni-
            versity of Queensland Press.
Haslach, Robert D.
1985   *Nishi no kaza, hare; Nederlands-Indische inlichtingendienst contra agressor
            Japan.* Weesp: Van Kampen.
Hatta, Mohammad
1952   'Legende en realiteit rondom de proclamatie van 17 augustus', in: M.
            Hatta, *Verspreide geschriften*, pp. 330-40. Djakarta/Amsterdam: Van der
            Peet.
1953   *Kumpulan karangan.* Jakarta: Balai Buku Indonesia.
1971   *The Putera reports; Problems in Indonesian-Japanese wartime cooperation.*
            Ithaca, NY: Cornell University.
1972   *Portrait of a patriot; Selected writings.* The Hague: Mouton.
1979a   *Bung Hatta antwoordt; Een vraaggesprek met dr. Z. Yasni opgenomen in
            1978 ten huize van dr. Moh. Hatta.* Djakarta: Gunung Agung.
1979b   *Mohammad Hatta; Memoir.* Jakarta: Tintamas.
1981   *Mohammad Hatta; Indonesian patriot; Memoirs.* Singapore: Gunung
            Agung.

Hering, B.
1982   *The Van der Most Report; A P.I.D. view of Soekarno's P.N.I.* Townsville:
            South East Asian Studies Committee, James Cook University. [Occa-
            sional Paper 18.]
1985   *Ch.O. van der Plas and the P.N.I. leadership; An analysis and source book.*
            Townsville: Centre of Southeast Asian Studies, James Cook University.
            [South East Asian Monograph Series 20.]
1986   'Aliran and Golongan; Indonesian conflict management under Sukar-
            no', *Kabar Seberang* 17:5-19.
1987   'Indonesian nationalism revisited', *Journal of Southeast Asian History*
            18-3:294-302.
1988   'The Rhemrev Report', *Kabar Seberang* 19/20:201-5.
1991a   *Soekarno's Mentjapai Indonesia merdeka.* Townsville: Centre of Southeast
            Asian Studies, James Cook University.
1991b   *From Soekamiskin to Endeh.* Townsville: Centre of Southeast Asian Stud-
            ies, James Cook University.
1991c   'Mohammed Hoesni Thamrin; Marginal or crucial figure of interbel-
            lum Indonesian nationalism?', *Kabar Seberang* 22:87-98.
1991d   *Mr. Ir. H.J. Kiewiet de Jonge and the Indonesian nationalist movements of the
            1920s and early 1930s.* Townsville: Centre of Southeast Asian Studies,
            James Cook University.
1992   'Het afscheidswoord van het dagelijks bestuur van de Parindra', *Kabar
            Seberang* 23:59-61.
1996   *M.H.Thamrin and his quest for Indonesian nationhood 1917-1941.* Stein:
            Yayasan Kabar Seberang.
1997   'Politiek', in: M.E. de Vletter et al., *Batavia/Djakarta/Jakarta beeld van een
            metamorfose*, pp. 17-21. Purmerend: Asia Maior. [Indische Stedenreeks
            1.]
1998   'De nationale bewegingen in Solo en Djokja', in: M.P. van Bruggen et al.,
            Djokja Solo beeld van de vorstensteden, pp. 45-9. Purmerend: Asia Maior.
Herkusumo, Arniati Prasedyawati
1984   *Chuo Sangi-in; Dewan Pertimbangan Pusat pada masa pendudukan Jepang.*
            Jakarta: Rosda Jayaputra.
Hinloopen Labberton, D. van
1916-17   'De invoering van eene militie in Indië, welke rekening houdt met het
            karakter van den Inlander en de stroomingen in de Inlandsche maat-
            schappij', *Orgaan der Vereeniging ter Beoefening van de Krijgswetenschap*
            1916-17:577-622.
Hinloopen Labberton, D. van and H.J. van Brink
1904   'Rapport over den stand van de bemoeiingen van de Afdeeling Buiten-
            zorg van den Indischen Bond inzake de stichting van een landbouw-
            dorp', *Het Bondsblad* 5(31 December 1904).
Hodgson, Marshall G.S.
1974   *The venture of Islam; Conscience and history in a world civilization. Vol. 2:
            Expansion of Islam in the middle periods.* Chicago: University of Chicago
            Press.

Hoëvell, W.R. van
1849   'De demonstratie der ingezetenen van Batavia op den 22 Mei 1848',
            Tijdschrift van Nederlandsch-Indië 11, I:84-93, 159-62, 220-4, 290-5, 440-1,
            II:79-80, 297-8, 335-6.
Hoogendoorn, C.W.
1900   'Het pauperisme onder Indo-Europeanen', *De Indische Gids* 22:666-78.
Hoop, L. de
1984   'Ethicus in een koloniaal conflict.' [MA thesis, Rijksuniversity Gronin-
            gen.]
Houben, Vincent
1996   *Van kolonie tot eenheidstaat; Indonesië in de negentiende en de twintigste*
            eeuw. Leiden: Vakgroep Talen en Culturen van Zuidoost-Azië en Oce-
            anië, Rijksuniversiteit Leiden. [Semaian 16.]
Ike, Nobutaka
1967   *Japan's decision for war; Records of the 1941 policy conferences.* Stanford:
            Stanford University Press.
Im Yang Tjoe
1933   *Soekarno sebagai manusia.* Solo: Ravena.
Indisch Verslag
1930-41   *Indisch verslag.* 's-Gravenhage: Rijksuitgeverij.
Ingleson, John
1979   *Road to exile; The Indonesian nationalist movement 1927-1934.* Singapore:
            Heinemann. [Southeast Asia Publications Series 1.]
1986   *In search of justice; Workers and unions in colonial Java 1908-1926.* Singa-
            pore: Oxford University Press. [Southeast Asia Publications Series 12.]
Jaarboek Mijnwezen
1907   *Jaarboek van het Mijnwezen in Nederlandsch Oost-Indië.* Jaargang 36.
            Amsterdam: Stemler, Batavia: Landsdrukkerij.
Jansen, L.F.
1988   *In deze halve gevangenis; Dagboek van mr dr L.F. Jansen, Batavia/Djakarta*
            1942-1945. Franeker: Van Wijnen.
Jaquet, L.G.M.
1978   *Aflossing van de wacht; Bestuurlijke en politieke ervaringen in de nadagen*
            van Nederlandsch-Indië. Rotterdam: Donker.
Jassin, H.B.
1956   *Chairil Anwar, pelopor Angkatan 45; Satu pembitjaraan.* Djakarta: Gunung
            Agung.
Jay, Robert R.
1963   *Religion and politics in rural Central Java.* New Haven, Conn.: Yale Uni-
            versity, Southeast Asia Studies. [Cultural Report Series 12.]
Jedamski, D.
1998   'Mabuk modern and gila barat; Progress, modernity and imagination;
            Literary images of city life in colonial Indonesia; in: Harry A. Poeze
            and Antoinette Liem (eds), *Lasting fascinations; Essays on Indonesia and*
            the Southwest Pacific to honour Bob Hering, pp. 176-85. Stein: Yayasan
            Kabar Seberang.

Jones, Howard Palfrey
1971   *Indonesia; The possible dream*. New York: Harcourt Brace Jovanovich. [Hoover Institution Publications 102.]

Jong, L. de
1969-91   *Het Koninkrijk der Nederlanden in de Tweede Wereldoorlog*. 's-Gravenhage: Staatsuitgeverij. 28 Vols.

Jong-Java's jaarboekje
1923   *Jong-Java's jaarboekje*. Weltevreden: Kolff.

Jonge, B.C. de
1968   *Herinneringen van Jhr. Mr. B.C. de Jonge; Met brieven uit zijn nalatenschap*. Edited by S.L. van der Wal. Groningen: Wolters-Noordhoff.

Jonkers, J.E.
1940   *Het vooronderzoek en de telastelegging in het Landraad-strafproces*. Groningen/Batavia: Wolters.

Kahin, George McTurnan
1952   *Nationalism and revolution in Indonesia; The secret Eisenhower and Dulles debacle in Indonesia*. Ithaca, NY: Cornell University Press.

Kanahele, George S.
1967   *The Japanese occupation; Prelude to independence*. [PhD thesis, Cornell University, Ithaca, NY.]

Kartodirdjo, Sartono et al.
1975   *Sarekat Islam Lokal*. Jakarta: Arsip Nasional.
1976   *Sejarah nasional Indonesia*. Vol. V. Jakarta: Departemen Pendidikan dan Kebudayaan.

Kartowisastro, Hermen
1978   'Masa muda', in: Syamsu Hadi (ed.), *Tragedi Bung Karno; Perjalanan terakhir seorang proklamator*, pp. 61-74. Jakarta: Pustaka Simponi.

Kasman Singodimedjo (ed.)
1979   *Negara Republik Indonesia*. Second edition. Jakarta: Mutiara. [First edition 1945.]

Kenpeitai
1986   *The Kenpeitai in Java and Sumatra; Selections from 'The authentic history of the Kenpeitai (Nihon Kenpei Hishi)*. Translated by Barbara Gifford Shimer and Guy Hobbs. Ithaca, NY: Cornell Modern Indonesia Project, Southeast Asia Program, Cornell University.

Kertapati, Sidik
1964   *Sekitar Proklamasi 17 Agustus 1945*. Third edition. Djakarta: Pembaruan. [First edition 1957.]

Kiewiet de Jonge, H.J.
1919   'De tweede Volksraadzitting', *De Gids* 81:360-1.

Koch, D.M.G.
1919   *Indisch-koloniale vraagstukken*. Weltevreden: Javasche Boekhandel.
1922   *Herleving; Oorsprong, streven en geschiedenis der nationalistische beweging in Britsch-Indië*. Weltevreden: Kollf.
1950   *Om de vrijheid; De nationalistische beweging in Indonesië*. Jakarta: Pembangunan.

1956   *Verantwoording; Een halve eeuw in Indonesië*. 's-Gravenhage/Bandung:
               Van Hoeve.

Koentjaraningrat
1957   *A preliminary description of the Javanese kinship system*. N.p.: Yale Univer-
               sity, Southeast Asian Studies. [Cultural Report Series 4.]

Koloniaal Verslag
1911-30   *Koloniaal verslag; Verslag van bestuur en staat van Nederlandsch-Indië,
               Suriname en Curaçao*, 's-Gravenhage: Staatsdrukkerij (1911-1921),
               Buitenzorg: Landsdrukkerij (1922-1930).

Kruijt, J.P. and W. Goddijn
1962   'Verzuiling en ontzuiling als sociologisch proces', in: A.N.J. den Hol-
               lander (ed.), *Drift en koers; Een halve eeuw sociale verandering in Neder-
               land*, pp. 232-49. Assen: Van Gorcum.

Kuiper, R.J. en H.G. Surie
1967   *De Indo en Tong Tong; Een onderzoek naar de Indo-Europeaan vroeger en nu*.
               Amsterdam: n.n.

Kurasawa, Aiko
1983   'Forced delivery of paddy and peasant uprising in Indramayu; Japan-
               ese occupation and social change', *Developing Economies* 21-1:52-72.

1988a   *Mobilization and control; A study of social change in rural Java, 1942-1945*.
               [PhD thesis, Cornell University, Ithaca, NY.]

1988b   'Pendudukan Jepang dan perubahan sosial; Penyerahan padi secara
               paksa dan pemberontakan petani di Indramayn', in: Akira Nagazumi
               (ed.), *Pemberontakan Indonesia di masa pendudukan Jepang*, pp. 83-113.
               Jakarta: Yayasan Obor Indonesia.

1990   'Marilah kita bersatu! - Japanese propaganda in Java - 1942-1945', in:
               K.M. de Silva et al. (eds), *Asian panorama; Essays in Asian history, past
               and present*, pp. 486-97. New Delhi: Vikas.

1993   *Mobilisasi dan kontrol; Studi tentang perubahan sosial di pedesaan Jawa,
               1942-1945*. Jakarta: Grasindo. [Seri Pengkajian Kebudayaan Jepang.]

1996   'Rice shortage and transportation', *Bijdragen tot de Taal-, Land- en
               Volkenkunde* 152:633-55.

Kuijk, Otto and Bart van Veen
1967   *Soekarno tabeh; Een documentaire in samenwerking met De Telegraaf en De
               Courant Nieuws van de Dag*. Amsterdam: Becht.

Kwantes, R.C.
1975-82   *De ontwikkeling van de nationalistische beweging in Nederlandsch-Indië*.
               Groningen: Tjeenk Willink (1975), Wolters/Noordhoff, (1978, 1981,
               1982). Four vols.

Kwee Kek Beng
1948   *Doea poeloe lima tahoen sebagai wartawan 1922-1947*. Batavia: Kuo.

Labrousse, Pierre
1983   'La deuxième vie de Bung Karno; Analyse du myth (1978-1981)', *Archi-
               pel* 25:187-214.

1986   'La culture urbaine de Surabaya; Aspects de la modernité (1928)', in:
                     C.D. Grijns and S.O. Robson (eds), *Cultural contact and textual interpre-*
                     tation; Papers from the fourth European Colloquium on Malay and Indone-
                     sian Studies, held in Leiden in 1983, pp. 45-53. Dordrecht/Cinnaminson:
                     Foris. [KITLV, Verhandelingen 115.]

Lahirnja Pantja Sila
1960   *Lahirnja Pantja Sila.* Djakarta: Ministry of Information.

Larson, George D.
1987   *Prelude to revolution; Palaces and politics in Surakarta. 1912-1942.*
                     Dordrecht/Cinnaminson: Foris. [KITLV, Verhandelingen 124.]

Leclerc, Jacques
1986   'Underground activities and their legal double (in the context of Amir
                     Sjarifuddin's relationship with communism in Indonesia)', *Kabar*
                     Seberang 17:72-98.

Leerdam, Ben F. van
1995   *Architect Henri Maclaine Point; Een speurtocht naar het wezenlijke van de*
                     Javaanse architectuur. Delft: Eburon.

Legge, J.D.
1984   *Sukarno; A political biography.* Second edition. Sydney: Allen and
                     Unwin. [First edition 1972.]

Lev, Daniel S.
1966   *The transition to guided democracy; Indonesian politics, 1957-1959.* Ithaca,
                     NY: Modern Indonesia Project. [Monograph Series.]

Lind, Elisabet
1983   'The rhetoric of Sukarno', in: Thommy Svensson and Per Sørensen
                     (eds), *Indonesia and Malaysia; Scandinavian studies in contemporary*
                     society, pp. 19-46. London/Malmø: Curzon. [Studies on Asian Topics,
                     Scandinavian Institute of Asian Studies 5.]

Locher-Scholten, E.B.
1981   *Ethiek in fragmenten; Vijf studies over koloniaal denken en doen van Neder-*
                     landers in de Indonesische archipel 1877-1942. Utrecht: HES.

Logemann, J.H.A.
1959   'Indonesië's terugkeer tot de grondwet van 1945', *Bijdragen tot de Taal-,*
                     Land- en Volkenkunde 115:209-31.
1962   *Nieuwe gegevens over het ontstaan van de Indonesische grondwet van 1945.*
                     Amsterdam: Noord-Hollandsche Uitgevers Maatschappij. [Mededeel-
                     lingen der Koninklijke Nederlandsche Akademie van Wetenschappen,
                     Afdeeling Letterkunde, Nieuwe Reeks 25-14.]

Low, D.A.
1986   'Counterpart experiences; Indian and Indonesian nationalisms 1920s-
                     1950s', *Itinerario* 10-1:117-43.

Lubis, Muhammad Ridwan
1987   *Pemikiran Sukarno tentang Islam dan unsur-unsur pembaharuannya.* [PhD
                     thesis, Institut Agama Islam Negeri Syarif Hidayatullah, Jakarta.]
1986   *Local opposition and underground resistance to the Japanese in Java 1942-*
                     1945. Clayton: Centre of Southeast Asian Studies, Monash University.
                     [Monash Papers on Southeast Asia 13.]

Lucas, Anton (ed.)
1986   *Local opposition and underground resistance to the Japanese in Java 1942-*
            1945. Clayton: Centre of Southeast Asian Studies, Monash University.
            [Monash Papers on Southeast Asia 13.]

Lustrumuitgave jaarboek
1935   *Jaarboek Technische Hoogeschool Bandoeng lustrum I.* Bandoeng: Tech-
            nische Hoogeschool.

Lijphart, Arend
1968   *The politics of accomodation; Pluralism and democracy in the Netherlands.*
            Berkeley: University of California Press.

Malaka, Tan
1991   *From jail to jail.* Translated, edited and introduced by Helen Jarvis.
            Athens, OH: Ohio University Center for International Studies. Three
            vols.

Malik, Adam
1956   *Riwayat dan perdjuangan sekitar proklamasi kemerdekaan Indonesia, 17*
            Agustus 1945. Third edition. Jakarta: Widjaya. [First edition 1948.]
1975   *Riwayat dan perjuangan sekitar proklamasi kemerdekaan Indonesia 17 Agus-*
            tus 1945. Sixth edition. Jakarta: Widaya. [First edition 1948.]
1978-79   *Mengabdi Republik.* Jakarta: Gunung Agung. Three vols.
1980   *In the service of the Republic.* Singapore: Gunung Agung.

Mangkupradja, Gatot
1968   'The Peta and my relationship with the Japanese', *Indonesia* 5:105-34.

Mangoenkoesomo, Tjipto
1917   'Insulinde's politiek programma', *Koloniale Studiën* 1-3:43-6.
[1927]   *Het communisme in Indonesië; Naar aanleiding van de relletjes.* Bandoeng:
            Indonesia Moeda.

Mangunwijaya, Y.B.
1994   'The Indonesian raya dream and its impact on the concept of demo-
            cracy', in: David Bourchier and John Legge (eds), *Democracy in Indone-*
            sia 1950s and 1990s, pp. 79-87. Clayton: Monash University, Centre of
            Southeast Asian Studies. [Monash Papers on Southeast Asia 31.]
1999   'Open letter to the University of Indonesia alumni association', *Inside*
            Indonesia 58:10.

Marco Kartodikromo
1916   *Boekoe sebaran jang pertama.* The Hague: n.n.
1917   'Boekan persdelict, tetapi klachtdelict', *Indische Gids* 7:1079-82.
1918   'R. M. Tirto Adhi Soerjo', *Sinar Hindia,* 12 December.

Masuda
1971   *Indoneshia Gendaishi.* Tokyo: Chuo Koronsha.

May, Brian
1978   *The Indonesian tragedy.* London: Routledge and Kegan Paul.

McIntyre, Angus (ed.)
1993   *Foreign biographical studies of Indonesian subjects; Obstacles and shortcom-*
            ings. Clayton: Monash University, Centre of Southeast Asian Studies.

McVey, Ruth T.
1965   *The rise of Indonesian communism.* Ithaca, NY: Cornell University
            Press.
Mededeelingen
1917-28   *Mededeelingen der Regeering omtrent enkele onderwerpen van algemeen
            belang.* Weltevreden: Landsdrukkerij.
Miert, H. van
1991   *Bevlogenheid en onvermogen; Mr. J.H. Abendanon en de ethische richting
            in het Nederlandse kolonialisme.* Leiden: KITLV Uitgeverij. [Working
            Papers 6.]
1995   *Een koel hoofd en een warm hart; Nationalisme, javanisme en jeugdbeweging
            in Nederlands-Indië, 1918-1930.* Amsterdam: De Bataafsche Leeuw.
Mills, Catherine
2001   'Romo Mangun; Tribute to a multi-talented, national figure', *Inside
            Indonesia* no. 68:10-1.
Mook, H.J. van
1945   *Nederlandsch-Indië en Japan; Hun betrekkingen in 1940-1941.* London:
            The Netherland Publishing Company.
Mrázek, Rudolf
1994   *Sjahrir; Politics and exile in Indonesia.* Ithaca, NY: Southeast Asia Pro-
            gram, Cornell University. [Studies on Southeast Asia 14.]
Mul, Alice
1988   'Ir. Baars (1892-1944), een linkse activist in Nederlandsch-Indië'. [MA
            thesis, Universiteit van Amsterdam.]
Mulder, Niels
1992   *Inside Southeast Asia; Thai, Javanese and Filipino interpretations of everyday
            life.* Bangkok: Duang Kamol.
Muskens, M.P.M.
1969   *Indonesië; Een strijd om nationale identiteit; Nationalisten, Islamieten,
            Katholieken.* Bussum: Brand. [De Grote Oecumene, 1e Reeks, Interreli-
            gieuze Ontwikkelingen.]
Nagazumi, Akira
1972   *The dawn of Indonesian nationalism; The early years of the Budi Utomo
            1908-1919.* Tokyo: Institute of Developing Economies. [Occasional
            Papers Series 10.]
1988   (ed.) *Pemberontakan Indonesia di masa pendudukan Jepang.* Jakarta: Yaya-
            san Obor Indonesia.
Nakamura, Mitsuo
1970   'General Imamura and the early period of Japanse occupation', *Indo-
            nesia* 10:1-26.
Nalenan, Ruben
1982   *Iskaq Tjokrohadisurjo; Alumni desa bersemangat banteng.* Jakarta: Gunung
            Agung.
Nasution, M. Yunan
1951   *Riwajat ringkas perdjuangan dan penghidupan Ir. Sukarno.* Seventh edi-
            tion. Djakarta: Aida. [First edition 1945.]

Natsir, Mohammad
1973   *Capita selecta.* Third edition. Djakarta: Bulan Bintang. [First edition 1955.]
Nehru, Jawaharlal
1941   *Toward freedom; The autobiography of Jawaharlal Nehru.* N.p.: n.n.
Neys, Karel
1945   *Westerse acculturisatie en Oosters volksonderwijs.* Leiden: Luctor et
              Emergo. [PhD thesis, Universiteit van Utrecht.]
Nieuwenhuys, Rob
1978   *Oost-Indische spiegel; Wat Nederlandse schrijvers en dichters over Indonesië*
              hebben geschreven vanaf de eerste jaren der Compagnie tot op heden. Third
              edition. Amsterdam: Querido. [First edition 1972.]
1988   *Tussen twee vaderlanden.* Third edition. Amsterdam: Van Oorschot.
              [First edition 1959.]
Nieuwenhuijze, C.A.O. van
1958   *Aspects of Islam in post-colonial Indonesia; Five essays.* The Hague: Van
              Hoeve.
Nio Joe Lan
1940   *Riwajat 40 taon dari Tiong Hoa Hwe Koan-Batavia (1900-1939).* Batavia:
              Tiong Hoa Hwe Koan.
Nishijima, Shigetada
1986   'The independence proclamation in Jakarta', in: Anthony Reid and
              Oki Akira (eds), *The Japanese experience in Indonesia; Selected memoirs of*
              1942-1945, pp. 299-324. Athens, OH: Ohio University, Center for Inter-
              national Studies. [Monographs in International Studies, Southeast
              Asia Series 72.]
1988   'The writing of the proclamation', in: Colin Wild and Peter Carey (eds),
              Born in fire; The Indonesian struggle for independence; An anthology, pp.
              95-7. Athens, OH: Ohio University Press.
Noer, Deliar
1973   *The modernist Muslim movement in Indonesia 1900-1942.* Singapore:
              Oxford University Press. [East Asian Historical Monographs.]
Nomes, Jan
1978   'De Indische Partij; Poging tot het verkrijgen van onafhankelijkheid
              op multi-raciale grondslag; Nederlandsch-Indië–Indonesië 1912-1913'.
              [MA thesis, Vrije Universiteit Amsterdam.]
Nortier, J.J., P. Kuijt and P.M.H. Groen
1994   *De Japanse aanval op Java; Maart 1942.* Amsterdam: Bataafsche Leeuw.
Notosusanto, Nugroho
1964   'Instansi jang melaksanakan pembentukan tentara Peta', *Madjalah Ilmu*
              Sastra Indonesia 2:285:90.
1979   *Tentara Peta pada jaman pendudukan Jepang di Indonesia.* Jakarta: Grame-
              dia.
Onghokham
1987   *Runtuhnya Hindia Belanda.* Jakarta: Gramedia.
Ontwerp eenheidsprogram
1921   *Ontwerp voor een Indisch nationaal eenheidsprogram.* Weltevreden: Een-
              heids-Comité.

Onze verbanning
1913   *Onze verbanning; Publicatie der officieele bescheiden, toegelicht met versla-*
            gen en commentaren, betrekking hebbende op de Gouvernements-Besluiten
            van den 18en Augustus 1913, nos. 1a en 2a, regelende de toepassing van
            artikel 47 R.R. (interneering) op E.F.E. Douwes Dekker, Tjipto Mangoenkoe-
            soemo en R.M. Soewardi Soerjaningrat. Schiedam: De Indiër.

Oostingh, Roelof van Zeeveld
1970   *The pegawai negeri of Bandung; Structure and process in Indonesia.* [PhD
            thesis, University of Virginia, Charlottesville.]

Oshikawa, Noriaki
1990   'Patjar Merah Indonesia and Tan Malaka; A popular novel and a revo-
            lutionary legend', in: Audrey Kahin (ed.), *Reading Southeast Asia,* pp.
            9-39. Ithaca, NY: Southeast Asia Program, Cornell University. [Transla-
            tion Series 1.]

Overzicht CSI
1922   *Overzicht van de gestie der Centraal Sarikat-Islam in het jaar 1921.*
            Weltevreden: Landsdrukkerij.

Overzicht Inlandsche pers
1921-40   *Overzicht van de Inlandsche en Maleisch-Chineesche; Samengesteld door het*
            Bureau voor Volkslectuur en Aanverwante Aangelegenheden. Weltevreden:
            Volkslectuur.

Pacific
[1937]   *De Pacific; Verzameling opstellen van Dr. G.S.S.J. Ratu Langie, Moh. H.*
            Thamrin, M. Soetardjo Kartohadikoesoemo. N.p.: n.n.

Paget, Roger K.
1975   *Indonesia accuses! Soekarno's defence oration in the political trial of 1930.*
            Kuala Lumpur: Oxford University Press. [Oxford in Asia Historical
            Memoirs.]

Pakpahan, G.
1948   *1261 hari dibawah sinar matahari terbit 6 Mar. 2602-17 Ag. 2605.* Jakarta:
            n.n.

Palar, L.N.
1939   'De Indonesische beweging en Japan', *Socialisme en Democratie* 1:793-
            805.

Palm, C.H.M.
1965   'Inleiding', in: *Bali, kringloop van het leven; Tentoonstelling gehouden naar*
            aanleiding van het tweede lustrum van de Delftse Ethnografische Vereniging,
            Ethnografisch Museum, Delft, 17 december 1965-31 mei 1966, pp. 10-22.
            Delft: Ethnografisch Museum.

Pauperisme
1901-02   *Het pauperisme onder de Europeanen in Nederlandsch-Indië.* Batavia:
            Landsdrukkerij. Five vols.

Pemberton, John
1994   *On the subject of 'Java'.* Ithaca, NY: Cornell University Press.

Pemeriksaan Soekarno
n.d.   *Pemeriksaan perkara Ir Soekarno oleh Landraad Bandung.* N.p.: n.n.

Penbrook, J. (ps. Jan Kippenbroek)
1972   'Soekarno and Marcel Koch; A personal account', *Kabar Seberang* 23: 69-77.

Penders, C.L.M.
1974   *The life and times of Sukarno*. London: Sidgwick and Jackson.

Perron, E. du
1946   *Indies memorandum*. Amsterdam: De Bezige Bij. [Het Zwarte Schaap 2.]

Perthus, Max
1976   *Henk Sneevliet; Revolutionair-socialist in Europa en Azië*. Nijmegen: Socialistiese Uitgeverij Nijmegen. [Sunschrift 105.]

Peters-Hesselink, E.Q.
1971   'Vereeniging van Spoor- en Tramwegpersoneel in Nederlandsch-Indië'. [MA thesis, Universiteit van Amsterdam.]

Petrus Blumberger, J.Th.
1920   'Stemmingen en stromingen in de Sarekat Islam', *Moederland en Koloniën* 19:25-8.
1931   *De nationalistische beweging in Nederlandsch-Indië*. Haarlem: Tjeenk Willink.

Pluvier, J.M.
1953   *Overzicht van de ontwikkeling der nationalistische beweging in Indonesië in de jaren 1930 tot 1942*. 's-Gravenhage: Van Hoeve.

Poerwadarminta, W.J.S.
1982   *Kamus umum bahasa Indonesia*. Sixth edition. Jakarta: Balai Pustaka. [First edition 1953.]

Poeze, Harry A.
1982   *Politiek-Politioneele Overzichten van Nederlandsch-Indië. Deel I 1927-1928*. 's-Gravenhage: Nijhoff.
1983   *Politiek-Politioneele Overzichten van Nederlandsch-Indië. Deel II 1929-1930*. Dordrecht: Foris.
1986   *In het land van de overheerser; I. Indonesiërs in Nederland 1600-1950*. Dordrecht: Foris. [KITLV, Verhandelingen 100.]
1988   *Politiek-Politioneele Overzichten van Nederlandsch-Indië. Deel III 1931-1934*. Dordrecht: Foris.
1994a   'Political intelligence in the Netherlands Indies', in: Robert Cribb (ed.), *The late colonial state in Indonesia; Political and economic foundations of the Netherlands Indies 1880-1942*, pp. 229-45. Leiden: KITLV Press. [Verhandelingen 163.]
1994b   *Politiek-Politioneele Overzichten van Nederlandsch-Indië. Deel IV 1935-1941*. Leiden: KITLV Uitgeverij.
1998   'Soekarno's political testament', in: Harry A. Poeze and Antoinette Liem (eds), *Lasting fascinations; Essays on Indonesia and the Southwest Pacific to honour Bob Hering*, pp. 291-305. Stein: Kabar Seberang.
1999   *Tan Malaka, 1925-1945; Pergulatan menuju republik*. Jakara: Grafiti.

Poser, F.H.
1927   *Het Inlandsch Reglement of het reglement op de uitoefening van de politie, de burgerlijke rechtspleging en de strafvordering onder de Inlanders en de*

Vreemde Oosterlingen op Java (Stb. 1848 no. 16) en de revisiebepalingen van het reglement op de Strafvordering ten dienste van de politie. Weltevreden: Regnier.

Poulgrain, Greg
1993 'The Loveday exchange, Australia, 1942; The Japanese naval spies return to Java', *Indonesia* 55:140-9.

PPPKI Congres
1928 *PPPKI Congres 30 Aug.-2 Sept.; Boekoe tekst programma pertoendjoekan seni kebangsaän Indonesia di Gedong Stadstuin-Theater Soerabaja.* Soerabaja: PPPKI.

Prawiroatmodjo, Soehoed
1953 *Perlawanan bersendjata terhadap fasisme Djepang.* Jakarta: Merdeka Press.

Pringgodigdo, A.K.
1950 *Sedjarah pergerakan rakjat Indonesia.* Third edition. Djakarta: Pustaka Rakjat. [First edition 1949.]
1955 *Perubahan kabinet presidensiil mendjadi kabinet parlementer.* Jogjakarta: Jajasan Fonds Universitas Negeri Gadjah Mada.
1956 *Kedudukan presiden menurut tiga undang-undang dalam teori dan praktek.* Djakarta: Pembangunan.

Priyanahadi, Y.B. (ed.)
1999 *Romo Mangun di mata para sahabat.* Yogyakarta: Kanisius.

Pijper, G.F.
1950 'De Aḥmadīyah in Indonesia', in: *Bingkisan budi; Een bundel opstellen aan Dr. Philippus Samuel van Ronkel door vrienden en leerlingen aangeboden op zijn tachtigste verjaardag 1 Augustus 1950*, pp. 247-54. Leiden: Sijthoff. [Uitgave van het Koninklijk Bataviaasch Genootschap van Kunsten en Wetenschappen.]

Rahim, S. Saiful
1978 *Bung Karno masa muda.* Jakarta: Yayasan Antar Kota. [Seri Apa & Siapa 1.]

Raliby, Osman
1953 *Documenta historica; Sedjarah dokumenter dari pertumbuhan dan perdjuangan negara republik Indonesia.* Djakarta: Bulan Bintang.

Ramadhan, K.H.
1981 *Kuantar ke gerbang; Kisah cinta Ibu Inggit dengan Bung Karno.* Jakarta: Sinar Harapan.

Rassers, W.H.
1959 *Panji, the culture hero; A structural study of religion in Java.* The Hague: Nijhoff. [KITLV, Translation Series 3.]

Reid, Anthony
1974 *The Indonesian national revolution 1945-1950.* Hawthorn: Longman. [Studies in Contemporary Southeast Asia.]

Reid, Anthony and Akira Oki (eds)
1986 *The Japanese experience in Indonesia; Selected memoires of 1942-1945.* Athens, OH: Ohio University Center for Southeast Asian Studies. [Monographs in International Studies, Southeast Asia Series 72.]

Ricklefs, M.C.
1981   *History of modern Indonesia, c. 1300 to the present.* London: Macmillan.
            [Asian Histories Series.]

Roem, Mohamad
1970   *Pentjulikan, proklamasi dan penilaian sedjarah.* Djakarta: Hudaya, Sema-
            rang: Ramadhani.

Romein-Verschoor, Annie
1978   *Omzien in verwondering; Herinneringen van Annie Romein-Verschoor.* Vol.
            1. Amsterdam: Arbeiderspers. [Privé-domein 17.]

Rose, Mavis
1987   *Indonesia free; A political biography of Mohammad Hatta.* Ithaca, NY: Cor-
            nell University. [Cornell Modern Indonesia Project, Monograph Series
            67.]

Roth, Günther
1963   *The social democrats in imperial Germany; A study in working-class isola-
            tion and national integration.* Totowa, NJ: Bedminster.

Rush, James
1977   *Opium farms in nineteenth-century Java; Institutional continuity and
            change in a colonial society, 1860-1910.* [PhD thesis, Yale University, New
            Haven, Conn.]

Said, Edward W.
1978   *Orientalism.* London/New York: Routledge and Kegan Paul.

Salam, Solichin
1966   *Bung Karno putera fadjar.* Djakarta: Gunung Agung.
1974   *Sekitar Wali Sanga.* Kudus: Gunung Agung.

Salim, Agoes
1929   'De Perhimpoenan Indonesia en de Indonesisch-Nationalistische
            Beweging', *De Socialist* 19 October 1929:2-4.

Sarekat Islam Congres
1916   *Sarekat Islam Congres: (1e nationaal congres), 17-24 Juni 1916.* Batavia:
            Landsdrukkerij.
1919a   *Sarekat Islam congres: (2e nationaal congres), 20-27 Oct. 1917.* Batavia:
            Landsdrukkerij.
1919b   *Sarekat Islam congres: (3e nationaal congres), 29 Sept.-6 Okt. 1918 te Soera-
            baja.* Batavia: Landsdrukkerij.

Sastrosatomo, Soebadio
1987   *Perjuangan revolusi.* Jakarta: Sinar Harapan.

Sato, Shigeru
1994   *War, nationalism and peasants; Java under the Japanese occupation 1942-
            1945.* New York/London: Sharpe.

Schepper, J.M.J.
1931   *Het vonnis in de P.N.I. zaak.* Batavia: De Unie.

Scherer, Savitri Prastiti
1975   *Harmony and dissonance; Early nationalist thought in Java.* [PhD thesis,
            Cornell University, Ithaca, NY.]

Schrieke, J.J.
1918   *Ontstaan en groei der stads- en landgemeenten in Nederlandsch-Indië.*
            Amsterdam: De Bussy.
Schulte Nordholt, Henk
1996   *The spell of power; A history of Balinese politics, 1650-1940.* Leiden: KITLV
            Press. [Verhandelingen 170.]
Seda, Frans
1981   'Bung Karno, mikul duwur, mendem jero', in: Solichin Salam (ed.),
            Bung Karno dalam kenangan, pp. 66-79. Jakarta: Pusaka.
Seegers, W.A.I.M.
1987   *Changing economy in Indonesia; A selection of statistical source material
            from the early 19th century to 1940. Volume 8: Manufacturing industry,
            1870-1942.* The Hague: Nijhoff.
Setiadi Kartohadikusomo, H.M.
1995   *Rengasdengklok.* Jakarta: Cindy Press.
Shadily, Hassan
1973   *Ensiklopedi umum.* Djakarta: n.n.
Shiraishi, Takashi
1990   *An age in motion; Popular radicalism in Java, 1912-1926.* Ithaca, NY: Cor-
            nell University Press. [Asia East by South.]
Siauw Giok Tjhan
1982   *Siauw Giok Tjhan remembers; A peranakan-Chinese and the quest for Indo-
            nesian nation-hood.* Edited by Bob Hering. Townsville: James Cook
            University of North Queensland.
Sihombing, O.D.P.
1962   *Pemuda Indonesia menantang fasisme Djepang.* Jakarta: Sinar Djaya.
Sjahrazad (ps. Soetan Sjahrir)
1945   *Indonesische overpeinzingen.* Amsterdam: De Bezige Bij.
Sjahrir, Soetan
1933   *Pergerakan sekerdja.* Batavia: Daulat Ra'jat
1949   *Out of exile.* New York: John Day.
1968   *Our struggle.* Ithaca, NY: Modern Indonesia Project, Southeast Asia
            Program, Department of Asian Studies, Cornell University.
Skinner, G. William
1963   'The Chinese minority', in: Ruth T. McVey (ed.), *Indonesia,* pp. 97-117.
            New Haven, Conn.: HRAF Press. [Survey of World Cultures.]
Sluimers, L.E.L.
1968   '"Nieuwe Orde" op Java; De Japanse bezettingspolitiek en de Indone-
            sische elites 1942-1943', *Bijdragen tot de Taal-, Land- en Volkenkunde* 124:
            336-67.
1978   *A method in the madness? Aanzetten tot een vergelijkende politicologische
            studie van de Japanse periode in Zuidoost-Azië, 1942-1945.* Amsterdam:
            Antropologisch-Sociologisch Centrum, Amsterdam University.
1996   'The Japanese military and Indonesian independence', *Journal of South-
            east Asian Studies* 27:19-36.
1998   'De Japanse nieuwe orde en de Grote Bung', in: Harry A. Poeze and
            Antoinette Liem (eds), *Lasting fascinations; Essays on Indonesia and*

the Southwest Pacific to honour Bob Hering, pp. 343-61. Stein: Kabar Seberang.

Snoek, Kees
1990   *De Indische jaren van E. du Perron.* Amsterdam: Nijgh and Van Ditmar.
1995   'E.F.E. Douwes Dekker; Beeldenbreker en opvoeder op de grens van twee tijden', *Bzzlletin* 25-228:22-32.

Snijtsheuvel, Karel C.
[1958]   *Onthullingen van achter het bamboegordijn.* Breda: Neerlandia.

Soe Hok Gie
1990   *Di bawah lentera merah; Riwayat Sarekat Islam Semarang 1917-1920.* Jakarta: Frantz Fanon Foundation.

Soebagijo, I.N.
1978   *Bung Karno, anakku.* Jakarta: Pustaka Antar Kota. [Seri Apa & Siapa 2.]
1980   *Sumanang; Sebuah biografi.* Jakarta: Gunung Agung.
1985   *Harsono Tjokroaminoto; Mengikuti jejak perjuangan sang ayah.* Jakarta: Gunung Agung.

Soebandi , Jro Mangku Gde Ktut
1991   *Babad Pasek.* Jilid ii. Denpasar: Adhi Sapta Kerthi.

Soekarno [Sukarno]
1931   *Indonesië klaagt aan!; Pleitrede voor den landraad te Bandoeng op 2 December 1930 gehouden.* Amsterdam: Arbeiderspers.
1959   *Dibawah bendera revolusi. Djilid I.* Djakarta: Panitya Penerbit Dibawah Bendera Revolusi.
1966   *Under the banner of revolution.* Vol. 1. Djakarta: Publication Committee.
1970   *Nationalism, Islam and Marxism.* Translated by Karel H. Warouw and Peter D. Weldon, with an introduction by Ruth T. McVey. Ithaca, NY: Modern Indonesia Project, Southeast Asia Program, Department of Asian Studies, Cornell University. [Translation Series 9.]
1978   *Indonesia menggugat; Pidato pembelaan Bung Karno di depan pengadilan kolonial Bandung, 1930.* Solo: Sasongko.
1986a   *Sarinah; Kewajiban wanita dalam perjuangan Republik Indonesia.* Jakarta: n.n.
1986b   *Pancasila sebagai dasar negara.* Jakarta: n.n.

Soekarno, Fatmawati
1978   *Catatan kecil bersama Bung Karno.* Jakarta: Dela-Rohita.

Soekarno, Rachmawati
1984   *Bapakku, ibuku.* Jakarta: Garuda Metropolitan Press.

Soerat kiriman
1900   *Soerat kiriman kapada sekalian bangsa Tjina, terkirim oleh lid-lid pengoeroes dari Pakempalan 'Tiong Hoa Hwe Koan' di Batavia.* Batavia: n.n.

Stange, Paul
1984   'The logic of rasa in Indonesia', *Indonesia* 38:113-34.

Stokvis, J.E.
1931a   *Soekarno gestraft; Zijn rechters veroordeeld.* Amsterdam: Arbeiderspers.
1931b   'Een landvoogdij', *Socialistische Gids* 16:824-31.

Subardjo Djojoadisuryo, Ahmad
1978   *Kesadaran nasional; Otobiografi.* Jakarta: Gunung Agung.
Sudiro
1974   *Pengalaman saya sekitar 17 Agustus '45; Ceramah yang diucapkan didepan Lembaga Pembina Jiwa 45, Jakarta, awal September 1972.* Second edition. Jakarta: Idayu. [First edition 1972.]
Sugriwa, I Gusti Bagus
1957   *Babad Pasek.* Denpasar: Balimas.
Suminto, H. Aqib
1985   *Politik Islam Hindia Belanda; Het kantoor voor Inlandsche Zaken.* Jakarta: Lembaga Penelitian Pendidikan dan Penerangan Ekonomi dan Sosial (LP3ES).
Suprijatna, F.A.
1981   *Bung Karno milik rakyat semua.* N.p.: n.n.
Surjohudojo, Supomo
n.d.   *Traditional Yogya in the changing world.* Melbourne: Monash University, Centre of Southeast Asian Studies. [Working Paper 7.]
Suryadinata, Leo
1971   *Pre-World War II Peranakan Chinese press in Java; A preliminary survey.* Athens, OH: Southeast Asia Series, Ohio University.
1972   *Prominent Indonesian Chinese in the twentieth century; A preliminary survey.* Athens, OH: Southeast Asia Series, Ohio University.
1979   (ed.) *Political thinking of the Indonesian Chinese 1900-1977; A sourcebook.* Singapore: University Press.
1981   *Peranakan Chinese; Politics in Java, 1917-1742* Revised edition. Singapore: Singapore University Press. [First edition 1976.]
Sutherland, Heather
1979   *The making of a bureaucratic elite; The colonial transformation of the Javanese priyayi.* Singapore: Heinemann. [Southeast Asia Publications Series 2.]
Swift, Ann
1989   *The road to Madiun; The communist uprising of 1948.* Ithaca, NY: Southeast Asia Program, Cornell University. [Monograph Series Cornell Modern Indonesia Project 69.]
Tan Malaka
1991   *From jail to jail.* Athens, OH: Ohio University Center for International Studies. Three vols. [Monographs in International Studies, Southeast Asia Series 83.]
Tas, S.
1969   'Souvenirs of Sjahrir', *Indonesia* 8:135-54.
Taselaar, Arjen
1998   *De Nederlandse koloniale lobby; Ondernemers en de Indische politiek 1914-1940.* Leiden: Research School CNWS, School for Asian, African, and Amerindian Studies. [CNWS Publications 62.]

Teitler, G.
1981   *The Dutch colonial army in transition; The militia debate, 1900-1921.*
            Townsville: Southeast Asian Studies Committee, James Cook University. [Occasional Paper 12.]
Tichelman, Fritjof
1985   *Socialisme in Indonesië; De Indische Sociaal-Democratische Vereeniging,*
            1897-1917. Dordrecht: Foris.
1990   'Indonesians and Chinese on Java during the emergence of Chinese
            nationalism and revolutionary movements'. Paper, Conference on
            New Perspectives of the Chinese Communist Revolution, Amsterdam,
            8-12 January.
Tien jaar Volksraad arbeid 1918-1928
[1928]   *Tien jaar Volksraad arbeid, 1918-1928.* Weltevreden: Landsdrukkerij.
Tien jaar Volksraad arbeid 1928-1938
1938   *Tien jaar Volksraad arbeid, 1928-1938.* Batavia: Landsdrukkerij.
Tjokroaminoto, Harsono
1983   *Menelusuri jejak ayahku.* Jakarta: Arsip Nasional. [Penerbitan Sejarah
            Lisan 2.]
Tjokroaminoto, H.O.S. and H. Agoes Salim
1927   *The restoration of Islamic unity.* Weltevreden: n.n.
Toer, Pramoedya Ananta
1985a   *Jejak langkah.* Amsterdam: Manus Amici.
1985b   *Sang pemula dan karya-karya non-fiksi (jurnalistik), fiksi (cerpen/novel)*
            R.M. Tirto Adhi Soerjo. Jakarta: Hasta Mitra.
1988a   *De pionier; Biografie van Tirto Adhisoerjo.* Amsterdam: Manus Amici/
            Novib.
1988b   *Het glazen huis.* Amsterdam: Manus Amici.
Tollenaere, Herman Arij Oscar de
1996   *The politics of divine wisdom; Theosophy and labour, national, and women's*
            movements in Indonesia and South Asia, 1875-1947. Nijmegen: Katholieke
            Universiteit Nijmegen. [PhD thesis, Katholieke Universiteit Nijmegen.]
Treub, M.W.F.
1927   *Het gist in Indië; Een analyse der hedendaagsche Inlandsche beweging.*
            Haarlem: Tjeenk Willink.
Tsuchiya, Kenji
1987   *Democracy and leadership; The rise of the Taman Siswa Movement in Indone-*
            sia. Honolulu: University of Hawaii Press. [Monographs of the Center
            for Southeast Asia Studies, Kyoto University, English Language Series
            18.]
Utrecht, Ernst
[1969]   *Soekarno-Soeharto; Indonesië's dekolonisatie dreigt te mislukken.* Odijk:
            Sjaloom. [Kosmo-story 11-12.]
1974   *De onderbroken revolutie in het Indonesisch dorp.* Amsterdam: Universiteit
            van Amsterdam. [Voorpublikatie/Afdeling Zuid- en Zuidoost-Azië,
            Antropologisch-Sociologisch Centrum, Universiteit van Amsterdam
            9.]

Van der Post, Laurens
1996   The admiral's baby. London: Murray.
Van Niel, Robert
1984   The emergence of the modern Indonesian elite. Dordrecht/Cinnaminson:
              Foris. [KITLV, Reprints on Indonesia.]
Verslag BOW
1912   Verslag over de Burgerlijke Openbare Werken in Nederlandsch-Indië 1911.
              Batavia: Landsdrukkerij.
Verslag Commissie herziening staatsinrichting
1920   Verslag van de Commissie tot herziening van staatsinrichting van Neder-
              landsch-Indië. Weltevreden: Landsdrukkerij.
Vervoort, Hans
1975   Jubileumboek HBS-Soerabaia 1875-1975. N.p.: n.n.
Veth, P.J.
1899-1907   Java, geografisch, ethnologisch, historisch. Second edition. Haarlem:
              Bohm. Four vols. [First edition 1875-1884.]
Veur, P.W.J. van der
1955   Introduction to a socio-political study of the Eurasians of Indonesia. [PhD
              thesis, Cornell University, Ithaca, NY.]
1958   'E.F.E. Douwes Dekker; Evangelist for Indonesian political national-
              ism', Journal of Asian Studies 17-4:551-66.
1968   'The Eurasians of Indonesia; A problem and challenge in colonial his-
              tory', Journal of Southeast Asian History 9-2:191-207.
1969   'Race and color in colonial society; Biographical sketches by a Eurasian
              woman concerning pre-World War II Indonesia', Indonesia 8:69-79.
Vickers, Adrian (ed.)
1996   Being modern in Bali; Image and change. New Haven, Conn.: Yale South-
              east Asian Studies. [Monograph 43.].
Visker, D.A.
1988   Indische familienamen. Deel II. Den Haag: Moesson.
Visman, F.H. (ed.)
1941   Verslag van de Commissie tot bestudering van staatsrechtelijke hervormin-
              gen. Batavia: Landsdrukkerij. Two vols.
Volksraad
1922-28   Jaarboekje zittingjaar 1922-1923, 1923-1924, 1924-1925, 1925-1926, 1926-
              1927, 1927-1928. Weltevreden: Kolff.
1927-42   Handelingen en bijlagen 1927/1928-1941/1942. Batavia: Landsdrukkerij.
1931-42   Handelingen Gedelegeerden 1930/1931-1941/1942. Batavia: Landsdruk-
              kerij.
Vos van Zalingen, P.J.A.F.
1973   'Douwes Dekker en de Indische Partij; Een onderzoek naar de achter-
              gronden van de 'onafhankelijkheidsbeweging' van 1912'. [MA thesis,
              Universiteit van Amsterdam.]
Vreede, A.G.
1926   Rapport van het Hoofd van het Kantoor van Arbeid over de arbeidstoestanden
              in de metaalindustrie te Ssoerabaja. Weltevreden: Landsdrukkerij.

Vries, S. de
1919   'Necrologie Tirto Adi Soerja', *Maandblad van den Nederlandschen Jour-*
                nalistenkring 268:88.
Vugt, R.T.J. van
1987   'Het belang van de Liga tegen Imperialisme, tegen koloniale over-
                heersing en voor de nationale onafhankelijkheid in de strijd voor
                de onafhankelijkheid van Indonesië'. [MA thesis, Universiteit van
                Amsterdam.]
Wal, S.L. van der
1965   *De Volksraad en de staatkundige ontwikkeling van Nederlands-Indië. Tweede*
                Stuk 1927-1942. Groningen: Wolters. [Uitgaven van de Commissie voor
                Bronnenpublicatie betreffende de Geschiedenis van Nederlands-Indië
                1900-1942 van het Historisch Genootschap 3.]
1967   *De opkomst van de nationalische beweging in Nederlandsch-Indië*. Gron-
                ingen: Wolters. [Uitgaven van de Commissie voor Bronnenpublicatie
                betreffende de Geschiedenis van Nederlands-Indië 1900-1942 van het
                Historisch Genootschap 4.]
1971-73   *Officiële bescheiden betreffende de Nederlands-Indonesische betrekkingen*
                1945-1950. Vol. 1-3. 's-Gravenhage: Nijhoff. [Rijks Geschiedkundige
                Publicatiën, Kleine Serie.]
Wehl, David
1948   *The birth of Indonesia*. London: Allen and Unwin.
Werkman, P.R.
1976   'Het ontstaan en de beginperiode van de Indische Bond'. [MA thesis,
                Vrije Universiteit, Amsterdam.]
Wertheim, W.F.
1946   *Nederland op den tweesprong; Tragedie van den aan traditie gebonden*
                mensch. Arnhem: Van Loghum Slaterus.
1986   'Een vergeten pionier van het Indisch ontwaken', *Bijdragen tot de*
                Taal-, Land- en Volkenkunde 142:454-5.
Wild, Colin and Peter Carey (eds)
1988   *Born in fire; The Indonesian struggle for independance; An anthology.*,
                Athens, OH: Ohio University Press.
Willmott, H.P.
1982   *Empires in the balance; Japanese and Allied Pacific strategies to April 1942*.
                London: Oris
1983   *The barrier and the javelin; Japanese and Allied Pacific strategies, February*
                to June 1942. Annapolis, Md.: Naval Institute Press.
Willner, Ann R.
1968   *Charismatic leadership political leadership; A theory*. Princeton: Princeton
                University, Center of International Studies.
Wiselius, J.A.B.
1872   'Djaja Baja, zijn leven en profetieën', *Bijdragen tot de Taal-, Land- en*
                Volkenkunde 19:172-217.
Woesthoff, P.F.
1915   *De Indische decentralistiewetgeving*. Leiden: Brill.

Wolf, Charles
1948   *The Indonesian story; The birth, growth and structure of the Indonesian Republic.* New York: Day.
Yamin, Muhammad
1951   *Proklamasi dan konstitusi Republik Indonesia.* Djakarta: Djambatan.
1959-60   *Naskah persiapan Undang-Undang Dasar 1945.* Djakarta: Prapantja. Three vols.
Zee, D. van der
1928   *Het Indische gemeentewezen.* 's-Gravenhage: Nijhoff.
Zwaan, Jacob
1980   *Nederlands-Indië 1940-1946; Gouvernementeel intermezzo 1940-1942.* Den Haag: Omniboek.
1981   *Nederlands-Indië 1940-1946; Japans intermezzo 9 maart 1942-15 augustus 1945.* Den Haag: Omniboek.
Zwitzer, H.L.
1995   *Mannen van 10 jaar en ouder; De jongenskampen van Bangkong en Kedoengdjati, 1944-1945.* Franeker: Van Wijnen.

Contemporary periodicals and newspapers

Only newspapers and other serials consulted in depth are cited with the period indicated

Adil	1939-1941
Algemeen Indisch Dagblad; De Prangerbode	1927-1941
Asia Raya	2602-2605(1942-1945)
Bangoen	1939-1940
Bataviaasch Nieuwsblad	1927-1941
Berita Oemoem	1938-1942
Bintang Betawi	1900-1906
Djawa Baroe	2602-2605(1942-1945)
De Expres	1921-1922
De Fakkel	1940-1941
Hong Po	1939-1941
Indië Hou Zee	1935-1938
De Indische Gids	1920-1940
Het Indisch Volk	1920-1940
Indonesia Merdeka	1930-1935
Indonesia Merdeka	2605(1945)-1946
Indonesia	1936-1939
De Java Bode	1927-1941
Jawa Shinbun	2602-2605(1942-1945)
Kan Po	2602-2605(1942-1945)
Kebangoenan	1936-1941
Keng Po	1927-1941.
Koloniale Studiën	1916-1941

Koloniaal Tijdschrift	1912-1940
Kritiek en Opbouw	1938-1941
De Locomotief	1927-1941
Medan Prijaji	1910-1912
Midden Java Post	1938-1939
Nationale Commentaren	1937-1941
Nederlandsch-Indië	1935-1941
De Nieuwe Rotterdamsche Courant	1930-1940
De Nieuwe Tijd	1933-1941
Het Nieuws van den Dag	1927-1941
Panggoegah	1919-1925
Pemandangan	1933-1941
Pemberita Betawi	1901-1916
Pemimpim	1937-1941
Persatoean Indonesia	1930-1933
Pertja Selatan	1927-1941
Pewarta Deli	1927-1941
Pewarta Oemoem	1939-1940
Pewarta Perniagaän	2602-2605(1942-1945)
Plopor Gerindo	1937-1941
Pradjoerit	2605 (1945)
De Rijkseenheid	1929-1939
Sedya Tama	1927-1941
Siang Po	1930-1941
Sinar Baroe	2602-2605(1942-1945)
Sinar Matahari	2602-2605(1942-1945)
Sinar Pasoendan	1933-1941
Sin Jit Po	1927-1941
Sin Po	1927-1941
Sin Tit Po	1929-1941
Sipatahoenan	1927-1941
Soeara Asia	2602-2605(1942-1945)
Soeara Parindra	1936-1941
Soerabajaasch Handelsblad	1927-1941
De Stuw	1930-1933
Tempo	1936-1941
Timboel	1926-1933
Tjahaja	2602-2605(1942-1945)
Tjaja Timoer	1935-1941
Tohindo Nippo	1937-1941

Index